Passion to Dance

THE NATIONAL BALLET OF CANADA

JAMES NEUFELD

Foreword by Karen Kain

DUNDURN
TORONTO

Project Editor: Michael Carroll
Editor: Cheryl Hawley
Design: Jennifer Scott
Printer: Friesens

Library and Archives Canada Cataloguing in Publication

Neufeld, James E., 1944-
   Passion to dance : the National Ballet of Canada / by James Neufeld ; foreword by Karen Kain.

Includes bibliographical references and index.
Issued also in electronic formats.
ISBN 978-1-4597-0121-2

1. National Ballet of Canada--History. I. Title.

GV1786.N3N485 2011   792.8'0971   C2011-903833-1

1   2   3   4   5   15   14   13   12   11

We acknowledge the support of the **Canada Council for the Arts** and the **Ontario Arts Council** for our publishing program. We also acknowledge the financial support of the **Government of Canada** through the **Canada Book Fund** and **Livres Canada Books**, and the **Government of Ontario** through the **Ontario Book Publishing Tax Credit** and the **Ontario Media Development Corporation**.

Care has been taken to trace the ownership of copyright material used in this book. The author and the publisher welcome any information enabling them to rectify any references or credits in subsequent editions.

J. Kirk Howard, President

Printed and bound in Canada.
www.dundurn.com

Dundurn
3 Church Street, Suite 500
Toronto, Ontario, Canada
M5E 1M2

Gazelle Book Services Limited
White Cross Mills
High Town, Lancaster, England
LA1 4XS

Dundurn
2250 Military Road
Tonawanda, NY
U.S.A. 14150

For Lynn
— now as always

Contents

Acknowledgements

It was Julia Drake, the director of communications for the National Ballet of Canada, who suggested to me several years ago that I write this book. I had published a history of the company in 1996 (*Power to Rise: The Story of the National Ballet of Canada*), but in the intervening years the National Ballet had changed significantly. James Kudelka, who led the company for nine years from 1996 to 2005, was acknowledged in the earlier book as an important choreographer, but made only a fleeting appearance at the end as artistic director designate. Karen Kain, the company's artistic director since 2005, was an important presence, but only as a dancer. As artistic directors, these two individuals have transformed the company, so that the National Ballet of 2011 is a fundamentally different company from the one of 1996. Julia thought that the company's sixtieth anniversary season would be a good time to tell the complete story.

Without the active cooperation of the company's senior administration this book could not have been written. I want to thank Karen Kain for her gracious foreword and for the role she played personally in encouraging this project and setting the standard for helpfulness that the rest of her colleagues have followed. Among them, I am especially grateful to Julia Drake, Kevin Garland, and Diana Reitberger for answering my questions and encouraging my work.

I also owe a huge debt of gratitude to James Kudelka, who agreed to be interviewed in the midst of a hectic schedule. He gave his time generously, both in the interview and in reviewing an early draft of portions of the manuscript.

What started out to be simply a revised and updated second edition turned into much more. All of the original material was, of course, carefully edited, corrected, and brought up to date, but the final product also contains two substantial new chapters, an extensive new opening, and new illustrations, many of them now in colour. The appendices, listing the company's itinerary and personnel, have been corrected and updated to

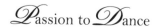

the end of the 2010–11 season, a mammoth task in itself. One chapter (on board affairs and finances) has been omitted. So *Passion to Dance* builds on previous work, but stands on its own as a comprehensive history of the mature company, a full decade into the twenty-first century.

Many people helped in the creation of *Power to Rise*, some fifteen years ago. Though I have not repeated the earlier acknowledgements here, my debt to all of those individuals remains enormous. All who agreed to be interviewed, both for the 1996 volume and for the present one, are acknowledged, with thanks, at the beginning of the "Notes" section of this book.

In the past two years, while preparing *Passion to Dance*, I received invaluable help from Sharon Vanderlinde, the company's senior manager — education and archives, and from Adrienne Nevile, its archives coordinator. Adrienne guided me through the National Ballet's rich archival resources and answered my many questions and requests for information cheerfully and with good grace. Pamela Ouzounian, the board secretary, responded to countless questions relating to board activities. At the company, Laurie Nemetz, Bridget Benn, and Brianne Price helped to collect and verify the information that makes up the various appendices to this volume. At Canada's National Ballet School, Katharine Harris supplied information about graduates of the school who went on to dance with the company. Setareh Sarmadi did the scans of all the photographs supplied by the National Ballet of Canada. Both Julia Drake and Catherine Chang arranged my interview schedules at the company. Ernest Abugov and Jeff Morris allowed me to watch a performance from the wings and gave me a new admiration for the technical and professional skills that keep a show running smoothly. My thanks to all of them.

I am grateful to Jocelyn Allen for permission to use a photograph from her personal collection, and to Amy Bowring, director of research at Dance Collection Danse, for locating and giving me permission to use the photo of Celia Franca and Erik Bruhn in *The Lovers' Gallery*. Carol Bishop Gwyn answered many questions and allowed me to read her new work, *The Pursuit of Perfection: A Life of Celia Franca*, in manuscript.

With *Passion to Dance*, Dundurn Press continues its strong commitment to producing books about the arts in Canada. My thanks to the Press and to Kirk Howard, its president and publisher, for this ongoing support. At Dundurn, my special thanks to Michael Carroll, associate publisher and editorial director, to Marta Warner, publicity assistant, and to Cheryl Hawley, for her careful final editing of a long and complex manuscript.

My greatest debt of gratitude is to my friend, Ramsay Derry, and my wife, Lynn Neufeld. Ramsay acted as editor and mentor for this project, as he has done for my other books. His eagle eye and alert editorial sense have improved the text in countless ways, and saved me from embarrassing errors and questionable turns of phrase. Lynn's superhuman work and devotion to accuracy in bringing the appendices up to date are acknowledged in the note at the beginning of those appendices. Her patience and unflagging support have made this, and all my work, possible.

Acknowledgements

In preparing this book, Lynn and I spent many hours at the Walter Carsen Centre for the National Ballet of Canada, where the archives are housed and the company leads its offstage professional life. As I observed the dancers, they seemed like perfectly ordinary young people, dressed in dancers' motley, preoccupied, busy, hurrying from class to rehearsal, getting coffee, chatting during their breaks. However, as I spoke with them, and with non-dancing members of the company in preparation for this book, I found them to be quite extraordinary — thoughtful, intelligent, articulate, generous — in a word, gracious toward the curious stranger disrupting their routines with questions and interviews. The gracefulness of their profession seemed to condition the rest of their behaviour as well. For all their grace, then, I thank them. It reaffirms ballet's past, and assures its future.

Foreword

BY KAREN KAIN

When all is said and done, a ballet company, like any performing arts organization, will be remembered primarily for what it accomplishes on the stage. How well it brings to life the works it mounts and articulates a particular choreographic vision, how powerfully and memorably it connects with its audiences, and how deeply it enriches the artistic tradition of which it is a part, will always be the principal criteria by which it is defined and valued.

But at the same time, a ballet company is an institution that exists in history, the product of a particular time and place and range of forces. It is a living, workaday operation made up of many individuals, all with different talents, backgrounds, and personalities, and all intricately enmeshed not just with the art of ballet, but with the broader processes of the larger culture. Marked by ups and downs, elation and struggle, and the ongoing effort and sheer determined labour of making the whole endeavour function year in and year out, it is a story of sweat, ingenuity, love, high purpose, courage, and belief.

When James Neufeld's *Power to Rise: The Story of The National Ballet of Canada* was published in 1996, many people were aware of our work on stage. In the forty-five years since our founding, we had established ourselves as one of the best classical companies on the international scene and had long been embraced within Canada as one of the country's brightest cultural jewels. Many of our dancers were widely recognized for their talent both at home and abroad.

Fewer people, though, were aware of the extraordinary story of the company's beginnings, of its amazing and redoubtable founders, of the people both on the stage and behind the scenes who had shaped and nurtured a fragile and fledgling dance troupe into one of the glories of modern classical ballet. James's book told that story. And it told it with both a scholar's diligence and a ballet-lover's passion. As insightful about the financial, structural, and administrative realities of running the company as it was about the artistic and production decisions, repertoire, casting, and choreography, the book brought the National Ballet's astonishing narrative to thrilling life, capturing a good part of the tenor of the times in Canadian culture along the way. Above all, the book captured the personalities of the extraordinary number of people involved in the story, in so many different capacities, with real understanding. For anyone wanting to know how the wonderful company they saw on stage had come into being and grown, they had only to read James's book.

Karen Kain, artistic director, the National Ballet of Canada.

Power to Rise was published at a crucial moment in the National Ballet's history. James Kudelka had just been appointed artistic director, after occupying the role of artist in residence for three years. His appointment was the first time a practising choreographer had assumed the position, but he was also a graduate of the National Ballet School and a former dancer with the National Ballet itself. This was a vote of confidence, not just in James and his choreographic talent, but in the whole homegrown system of artistic development of which he was a shining example.

Both as choreographer and as artistic director, James went on to oversee a wonderfully fertile period in the company's history, creating such extraordinary works for us as *The Four Seasons* and new versions of *Cinderella*, *Swan Lake*, and *The Nutcracker*. Some of the chief results of this period have been a company that now more eagerly embraces the new and challenging, that has acquired a greater spirit of adventurousness in its expanded repertoire and aesthetic range, and that has attracted a fresh generation of ballet lovers to its audience.

Passion to Dance: The National Ballet of Canada is James Neufeld's updating of *Power to Rise*, taking us from 1995 to the present. Like his earlier work, this continuation of our story is marked by James's sure grasp of technical detail as well as his vivid evocations of the people involved in the company's ongoing evolution. At sixty, The National Ballet of Canada is as strong — both creatively and institutionally — as ever. When you know where you've been, it's said, it's easier to know where you're going. Looking back, through the lens of my own experience and through the pages of this rich and heartfelt book, I can see what an extraordinary journey it has been thus far. Looking forward, with the knowledge and historical understanding James has given us, the future seems that much brighter, the way before us more clearly marked than it otherwise ever would have been.

Chapter One

THEY WERE GOING TO HAVE A COMPANY

Curtain Up

On a dull November Saturday, in the year 2010, the streets of downtown Toronto are relatively quiet. At the corner of University and Queen, however, the Four Seasons Centre for the Performing Arts shows signs of activity. Since mid-morning, dancers, dressers, and crew have been filtering in through the stage door around the corner, off Richmond Street, to begin their rituals and routines in preparation for the matinee performance by the National Ballet of Canada. Once through the stage door, dancers head for one of the theatre's two studios, one on the second floor, overlooking Queen Street, the other a windowless room on stage level, where, in the daily regimen of company class, they will limber up their muscles in preparation for the demands of the performance. Dressers make for the dressing rooms to fuss with costumes, inspect them for damage, stains, or wrinkles, and move one or two to makeshift changing areas erected in the wings, ready for the quick changes that will take place there. Crew members wander the stage, making sure set pieces and props are in their appointed places, where they were left the night before, ready for the opening curtain. Their work day has begun.

An hour before curtain, the main doors of the theatre open and the early birds stream into the foyer. Most of them head immediately up the stairs to the Richard Bradshaw Amphitheatre at the front of the house, overlooking University Avenue. The first hundred or so grab places in the tiered seating area, while the rest crowd the overhanging balconies for a bird's-eye view. Today, the pre-performance talk is by Rex Harrington. Though he retired from dancing several years back, he still has star power. A young admirer, who may never even have seen him dance, has left a carefully wrapped gift on the stool by the microphone. Harrington enters and, without missing a beat, flashes a winning smile at the crowd. "Is this for me? Should I open it now?" The audience is in his hands.

Bruce Zinger

A ballet talk at the company's first performances in the Four Seasons Centre for the Performing Arts in 2006. Karen Kain and ballet critic William Littler discuss The Sleeping Beauty *before the opening curtain.*

Fifteen minutes to curtain and the crowd in the foyer buzzes with anticipation. Since it's a matinee, the audience contains more than the usual number of children and young people, including a few pint-sized ballerinas, five-year-olds in pink organza, one with a rhinestone tiara, cheeks flushed with anticipation. Adults with children in tow, or in mind, make a beeline for the ballet boutique, tucked under the grand stairs of the main foyer, intent on souvenirs or trinkets, books or CDs. The bar is busy, but at this performance it's selling more ice-cream bars and chocolate chip cookies than flutes of champagne. Elsewhere in the foyer, dressed in their uniforms of green blazers and plaid skirts or grey flannels, shoals of youngsters from the National Ballet School dart through the crowd, chattering excitedly and dreaming of their futures. They keep their eyes peeled for a glimpse of one of their idols. Maybe, if they're really lucky, they'll even see Karen Kain.

"Five minutes to curtain," comes the announcement, and gradually the foyer empties as audience members head for their seats. Settling down, they consult their programs, study the cast list, look for the notes and synopsis that will help them to understand today's ballet. Since it's *Cinderella*, in the version choreographed by James Kudelka, the story is well-known. The buzz of conversation diminishes. Orchestra members complete their last-minute tuning and fall silent. The audience waits expectantly for the house lights to go down and the follow-spot to pick out the conductor entering the orchestra pit. Once he gives the downbeat, Prokofiev's slightly astringent music will carry them through the familiar narrative of *Cinderella*, her cruel stepmother, ugly stepsisters, fairy godmother, and Prince Charming.

Backstage, however, the ballet unfolds according to a completely different narrative, its rhythms dictated by the unyielding technical demands of lighting cue and set change, not by Cinderella's adventures. Every detail is carefully scripted and controlled by the two stage managers. Jeff Morris is seated at his console in the downstage left wing, glued to three television monitors and a heavily marked musical score. From his perch he calls every event over headsets to those responsible for the smooth running of the show. Ernest Abugov, Morris's eyes, ears, and hands, roams the backstage area constantly, relaying Jeff's cues where necessary, alerting him to any unforeseen problems, troubleshooting, checking, nudging people into place. At another ballet, the two will reverse roles.

In the murky half-light of the wings, the dancers assembling for the first entrance look nothing like the beautiful creatures we admire from the audience. At close quarters, their makeup is grotesque, exaggerated, and, even before the intense stage lights go on, already unbearably hot. They have spent the better part of an hour warming up, and now pull a motley of leg warmers and cover-ups over their costumes to retain their body heat. Some favour voluminous full-length bloomers of heavy, dung-coloured vinyl that make a delicate ballerina look, from the waist down, like a marine in combat fatigues. Cinderella, all warmed up and made up, sucks ice-water thirstily through a long straw, with an exaggerated, Marilyn Monroe pucker to prevent her scarlet lipstick from smudging. Nervously they fight the dancer's two great enemies — cold muscles and dehydration.

The conductor, in matinee concert dress, pauses for a few words with some of the dancers, waiting for the stage manager's cue to descend to the orchestra pit. As he moves away, dancers shed leg warmers and tatty sweaters like butterflies emerging from the drab cocoon of the high-performance athlete. The show has begun.

"Lighting: warning on cue number one. Curtain: up — *now*. Lighting: cue number one — *now*. Spot one: be ready to pick up Cinderella, downstage right, and follow her upstage — *now*." Morris has begun calling the show. From here on, no matter what happens, no pause is possible until the first intermission, at least thirty minutes away.

Today, despite the tricky dream sequence that opens the ballet, everything goes as planned through Cinderella's reverie, her persecution by the stepsisters, and her rescue by the fairy godmother. But suddenly, toward the end of Act One, the male corps of pumpkin heads runs into a problem. In the few seconds available for a quick turnaround, one of the men can't find his pumpkin headdress where he left it in the wings, races to the prop table, grabs a pumpkin at random, and barely makes his entrance on time. "That's wrong," mutters Abugov nervously. "That's a prop pumpkin, not a headdress pumpkin. There's no harness inside. It'll fall off his head when he moves." Luckily, it doesn't, but at intermission an announcement still has to be made over the backstage intercom, as the dancers change for the next act. "Men, someone went out with the wrong pumpkin head today. Please make sure that you pre-set your own pumpkin head before your entrance, and don't grab the wrong one by mistake. Everything was OK, but we could have had a catastrophe onstage."

Act Two, and backstage nerves are high as the crew prepares for Cinderella's entrance at the ball, flown down at the rear of the stage from high above the proscenium arch in her magic pumpkin coach. This show is bedevilled by pumpkins.

"Paging Cinderella for her entrance. Please come backstage *now*," Morris calls insistently to the dressing rooms over his headset. But this Cinderella, one of the five National Ballet ballerinas dancing the role this season, is nervous about heights and doesn't like to spend any more time than absolutely necessary suspended in the flies in an open coach with no barrier between her and the stage far below.

"This call is getting earlier and earlier," she grumbles as she scoots into the upstage left wing at the last possible minute.

"I know," Abugov reassures her, "it's because of the music. We have to get you up there while there's enough sound from the pit to cover the noise of the pumpkin going up." Cinderella's dresser gets her into her glamorous evening wrap, tying it securely round her waist.

"We need to get Cinderella up — *now*," murmurs Morris over the headset.

After a slight pause, "I'm aware of that," responds Abugov in measured tones, as he detaches Cinderella firmly from her dresser and moves her into her seat in the pumpkin. Very carefully, he buckles her into the industrial-grade seatbelt, covered in white satin that will be hidden by the drapery of her white satin coat. The pumpkin is already moving upwards, Cinderella frowning nervously and leaning forward to fuss with her costume as she ascends. "We made it — just," mutters Abugov, as the music fades to delicate strings and Morris cues the pumpkin's magical descent from the flies. And just as the pumpkin clears the proscenium on its diagonal descent ("Spot two: pick up Cinderella in the pumpkin — *now*") and comes into full view of the entranced audience, Cinderella leans back confidently and smiles radiantly out from the heavens, all signs of nervousness banished. Regally poised, she steps delicately onstage onto one pointe, to be received by the waiting gentlemen at the ball.

Cinderella (Sonia Rodriguez) arrives at the Prince's ball in James Kudelka's popular production of Cinderella.

In the wings though, there is no time for self-congratulation. The four fairies who guide the long streamers attached to the pumpkin as it clears swiftly upwards, collide with each other in the narrow offstage wing and scamper out of the way as quickly as possible, leaving Abugov to catch the yards of fabric and keep them from drifting back into view. "It's not as though they've never done this before," he grumbles as he passes the fabric to one of the crew and moves on to his next duty, preparing a bucket of ice in the stage-right wing so Prince Charming can ice a troublesome ankle when he comes offstage.

Front of house, the next intermission drags on for spectators eager to re-enter Cinderella's fairy-tale world. They fidget in their seats, waiting to be entertained. Backstage, it's barely long enough for the costume changes, set preparation, and last-minute instructions needed to keep the show going. His back to the curtain, a ballet master talks to one of the young apprentices, already positioned for the opening tableau, asks him how his sore leg is holding up. With a professional's sixth sense, the coach completes his conversation and clears out of sight just before the curtain rises.

Act Three, and the round-the-world panorama of Prince Charming searching for the woman who will fit the slipper calls all the backstage resources into play. Dancers are in constant movement in the crowded wings, often with almost no time to run from their downstage exit to the upstage position for their next entrance. Morris mutters lighting cues over the headset in a non-stop, insistent stream. Dressers, props people, and crew hand off a never-ending succession of props to the dancers — riding crops, umbrellas, ski-poles, a prop rifle — and collect them seconds later to return them to their places on the props table. "Gangway!" whispers a dancer on roller skates, as a friend pushes her toward her entrance, generating momentum for her headlong traversal of the stage, wobbling and waving gaily to the audience. Morris and Abugov spot a potential crisis. One of the dancers has knocked over the armchair that is supposed to remain onstage throughout. "Warn the aviatrix that her chair has fallen over. She'll have to set it up for herself when she enters." The lighting cue is adjusted by a split second to allow her the time she needs and the act proceeds smoothly to its conclusion. Prince Charming finds his Cinderella, marries her in a simple, flower-strewn ceremony, and turns his back on the splendours of his court for the bucolic charm of her kitchen garden. This is, after all, a modern retelling of the fairy tale, one that rejects the grasping materialism of the stepsisters, and refuses to compromise Cinderella's simple ideals with a concluding display of wealth and ostentation.

The ballet is over, but not the theatrical experience. Audience members applaud and cheer, anxious to play their appointed part in the curtain calls, that quaint ritual in which the spectators send back over the footlights, as their gift to the dancers, some of the pent-up energies generated by the performance. Abugov huddles behind the hanging black, downstage left, to chivvy the dancers through these calls. "You've just danced for two and a half hours and it's as though you don't want to take your bows," he complains.

"We don't need to learn the call," quips one of the dancers in reply. "You're going to tell us what to do anyway."

"Keep it moving, keep it moving," Abugov calls to the dancers, one ear cocked to the level of applause from the house. It would embarrass both parties in this little post-performance drama if the curtain rose once too often, to find the audience intent on departure, gathering coats rather than applauding the dancers. The *Cinderella* bows are done in character, and the stepmother hams up her drunkenness outrageously. "What about that?" Abugov asks Morris over the headset.

"I don't know. I'll think about it," comes the quiet reply. Suddenly, the bows are over and the dancers melt away, anxious to get into the lineup for the single elevator that takes them to their dressing rooms on the upper floors of the theatre. The crew are already preparing the set for the evening performance, ensuring that everything is ready once again for the beginning of Act One. Abugov notes the total running time of the show and enters it into the performance sheet that logs the details of every performance. Then he heads out of the theatre. People scurry to get on their way as quickly as possible, long before the audience out front has cleared. Most of the company members have less than two hours to get out of costume, grab some dinner, and return for the evening performance, when the onstage drama will unfold once again, minutely choreographed by the offstage drama no audience member should be aware of.

As the parents and grandparents, children and students, ballet fans of all ages, head for the subway or the carpark, they chat at leisure about the performance they have just seen. All will have opinions, some will have criticisms, but very few will be aware just how remarkable their Saturday afternoon experience has really been. Seated in a theatre built specifically to house ballet and opera, they have just watched an elaborate, full-length ballet created by a Canadian choreographer. That choreographer was trained at a school devoted to ballet, the National Ballet School, located just a few blocks to the east of the theatre where this performance has taken place. He came up through the ranks of the ballet company that calls this theatre home. The company's dancers, a newer, younger generation of Rex Harringtons and Karen Kains, are well-known, beloved by the regulars in the audience. The National Ballet of Canada has been a fixture on the Toronto scene, and in Canada itself, longer than most of today's audience members have been alive. They take it for granted.

How can they be expected to know that just sixty years ago, none of this existed? There were very few trained dancers in the country. There was no school, no company, no theatre capable of housing the spectacle they have just witnessed. They can't be expected to remember a time when the dream of creating such a company struck many as absurd, not only unnecessary, but completely unachievable. Nor would most of them know that this ridiculous dream originated with three Toronto women, none of them dancers, who simply thought that Canada ought to have a national ballet company.

Some might remember that the driving force behind the National Ballet of Canada was a woman from England named Celia Franca, a dancer with a striking profile and quite a reputation for getting her own way, but they would find it difficult to imagine the cultural landscape into which that determined young woman was parachuted. And how on earth did she come to be here? Sixty years after it all started, few members of the ballet public know the names of Aileen Woods, Sydney Mulqueen, and Pearl Whitehead, the three dreamers who issued an invitation to Celia Franca. And yet, even they were responding to the work of others and to historical circumstances that combined to make their initiative possible, perhaps inevitable. The founding of the National Ballet of Canada was no isolated event, independent of the currents of the time. To discover why, and how, Mrs. Mulqueen, Mrs. Whitehead, and Mrs. Woods issued their invitation to Miss Franca in the first place, we need to take a few steps back in time, before the events of 1950 and 1951 that brought her to Canada. We need to consider briefly the state of ballet as a popular art form after the Second World War as well as the climate for dance in pre–Canada-Council Canada.

This photo of an unidentified entertainment committee includes the three women who would go on to agitate for the creation of the National Ballet of Canada: Pearl Whitehead (standing, top right), Sydney Mulqueen (seated, bottom right), and Aileen Woods (seated, bottom left).

BALLET IN CANADA BEFORE THE NATIONAL BALLET OF CANADA

In the twentieth century, the popularization of ballet outside of Russia began with Serge Diaghilev, the Russian impresario who introduced the performers and repertoire of imperial St. Petersburg to Paris, London, and then the rest of the world. Once permanently exiled from Russia, he turned his company into the cradle of the avant-garde, nurturing the talents of choreographers, dancers, painters, and musicians in an outburst of creative energy that defined the artistic identity of the century. Stravinsky and Picasso were his collaborators. George Balanchine choreographed for him. And to him were drawn the aspiring dancers who, touched by his influence, would go out to embody their conceptions of the art he represented for them.

The Polish Marie Rambert (born Cyvia Rambam) and the Irish Ninette de Valois (born Edris Stannus) were two such pioneers. After working with Diaghilev in Paris, they settled in London and introduced ballet, as their experience with Diaghilev had revealed it to them, to the British public. Ballet in England had none of the tradition of royal patronage or public subsidy that had given the art a long life in Russia, France, and Scandinavia. Rambert, through her work at the Ballet Club in London's tiny Mercury Theatre, and through the formation of Ballet Rambert, de Valois, through her founding at the Sadler's Wells Theatre of the company that eventually became the Royal Ballet, established the art form in England. Through the 1930s and 1940s, these two women built, almost from scratch, a British version of ballet tradition that, for much of the mid-twentieth century, would dominate the world's vision of ballet. The 1948 release of the movie *The Red Shoes*, starring the Sadler's Wells ballerina Moira Shearer, prepared the way for the Sadler's Wells's triumphant appearances at the Metropolitan Opera in New York in 1949. Ballet became redefined as one of Britain's cultural treasures, despite its arrival there a mere twenty years earlier.

Not everyone thought so highly of the British product. George Balanchine made only a brief detour to England, where he worked in its popular musical theatre, the Cochran Revues and Sir Oswald Stoll's variety entertainments at the Coliseum. After moving to the United States, he founded first a school and then a company, the New York City Ballet, which also traced its roots to the Russian heritage exemplified by Diaghilev. Balanchine, however, developed out of that common source a tradition of neoclassical, abstract ballet antithetically opposed to the ideals of British ballet. These large historical differences later became the source of conflicting views about the proper direction for the young National Ballet of Canada; the differences between de Valois and Balanchine touched even the Canadians' fate.

Diaghilev's dancers also taught. Enrico Cecchetti, an Italian expatriate, had made a brilliant dancing career in St. Petersburg and then became the ballet master for Diaghilev's company, the Ballets Russes. Cecchetti then settled in London, where he coached virtually every prominent dancer of the era. Through his teaching, and through the teaching of such pupils as Stanislas Idzikowski, the Cecchetti conception of style and the Cecchetti syllabus of movement for ballet became a living force in the creation of the British performance tradition. Established artists, like Marie Rambert, and developing ones, like the young choreographer Antony Tudor, found in the Cecchetti tradition a strong basis for their art and communicated their respect for Cecchetti to younger colleagues, aspiring youngsters like Celia Franca and Betty Oliphant. Far-flung as the world of professional ballet eventually became, one of the main branches of its tradition led inevitably back to London and the handful of dancers and choreographers who had come into direct contact with Diaghilev.

Prior to 1950, however, that tradition had virtually no foothold in Canada. Even the conception of dance as a profession seemed alien and exotic, frustratingly out of reach of the few who might have dreamed of it. Indeed, the desire to dance and the need to earn a living were mutually exclusive goals in the Canada of the late 1940s. The resultant conflict inevitably drove the talented and the ambitious away from their own country.[1]

David Adams left Winnipeg for study in England, where he eventually wound up as a dancer with the Metropolitan Ballet.[2] Lois Smith, on the west coast, had to supplement summer employment at Theatre Under the Stars with work in San Francisco and Los Angeles, as well as with American touring companies of Broadway musicals.[3] Mildred Herman, a student of Boris Volkoff in Toronto, made a career in New York with the Rockettes at Radio City Music Hall and with Ballet Theatre. Under her stage name of Melissa Hayden, she enjoyed a long and distinguished career as a prominent member of the New York City Ballet and one of Balanchine's most popular ballerinas. She returned to Canada in 1963 as an international celebrity, the first guest artist to be invited to dance with the National Ballet.[4]

Hayden's experience provided the most conspicuous illustration of the problem that plagued dance teachers in Canada: the complete absence of professional opportunities within the country that would stimulate and retain their most promising students. Without such opportunity, without a tangible, professional goal for the serious student of dance, their teaching would forever be restricted to the beginners and the mediocre. As in so many areas of Canadian cultural life during this period, real promise in an individual conferred on her the dubious distinction of exile. To stay at home was to admit either cowardice or defeat. In commenting on the Third Annual Canadian Ballet Festival of 1950, Guy Glover, a National Film Board producer and prominent Canadian balletomane, lamented the fate of Jury Gotshalks and Irene Apiné, recently arrived in Canada and facing the dilemma head-on:

> Here are two young dancers, with a formidable technical grounding, who attempt material which is technically beyond almost any other Canadian dancer, yet the relative isolation of their home-base [Halifax], the lack of frequent opportunity to dance before audiences, the lack of contact with a first-rate *maître de ballet*, are rapidly ruining them as dancers of top quality.[5]

Such a climate could do little to sustain dancing or teaching at an advanced level.

But teachers there were, and not only of the small-town, ballet-tap-baton-twirling variety. In the 1930s, June Roper of Vancouver had placed ten of her students in Ballet Theatre and the two Ballet Russe international touring companies.[6] These companies, distant cousins of the earlier Diaghilev Ballets Russes, were among the chief popularizers of ballet for international audiences through this period. Few people realized that their "Russian" ballerinas were often British, American, or Canadian dancers, recruited on the road and rechristened for their new profession. One of them, Roper's pupil Rosemary Deveson (who had danced as Natasha Sobinova), later gave the young Lois Smith her first ballet instruction in studios on top of the Georgia Hotel in Vancouver.[7]

Jury Gotshalks and Irene Apiné in one of their showstoppers, the pas de deux from Don Quixote, *1952–53.*

Meanwhile, a small invasion of expatriates was assembling the forces that would become prominent in the development of Canadian dance. In 1929, Boris Volkoff arrived in Toronto from Russia, by way of Shanghai and Chicago, and by 1930 he had established the dance studio that was to function until his death in 1974.[8] The British emigrants Gweneth Lloyd and Betty Farrally planted their flag in Winnipeg in 1938.[9] Out of their pioneering efforts sprang, in remarkably short order, the Winnipeg Ballet Club and then the Royal Winnipeg Ballet. The daring, resilience, and determination of its founders still characterize the company, whose demonstrated ability to adapt to changing circumstances has kept it a vital force in Canadian ballet and a significant rival to the National for the affections of the Canadian public. Betty Oliphant, a former student of Marie Rambert, destined to become the moving force behind the National Ballet School and an acknowledged authority on dance education in Canada, arrived in Toronto in 1947 and quickly established her leading role in dance-teaching circles. She assisted at the birth of the Canadian Dance Teachers Association, which emerged, with Toronto teacher Mildred Wickson as its first president, at the Second Annual Canadian Ballet Festival in Toronto in 1949.[10] Jury Gotshalks and Irene Apiné, after enduring the privations of enforced labour in Latvia, had fled to Halifax where, in 1947, they began teaching ballet through the Conservatory of Music, for want of any other established outlet.[11] By the late 1940s, the major players had arrived, anxious to do something to create continuing opportunities for professional dance in Canada.

Some efforts had already been made. The Winnipeg Ballet, successor to the Winnipeg Ballet Club founded in 1938, offered sporadic performance opportunities to its dancers. But none of them was paid for dancing until 1949, and by 1951 the maximum honorarium for a dancer was a scant one hundred dollars a month for a nine-month season.[12] Boris Volkoff, in response to a request from Mr. P.J. Mulqueen of the Sports Committee for Canada, had taken a group of dancers to compete in the *Tanzwettspiele* of the 1936 Berlin Olympics, "Hitler's Olympics," which the American modern-dance pioneer Martha Graham had staunchly boycotted. Here, Volkoff's essentially amateur troupe of students had been well received in predominantly professional surroundings.[13] From that point on, the indefatigable Volkoff lost no opportunity to promote his dancers whenever an occasion presented itself. His flamboyant Russian personality and vigorously athletic approach to style made him openly contemptuous of the emerging British school of dancing, which he considered anaemic and prissy. From his Toronto teaching studios he took on any and all choreographic assignments, from promenade concerts to figure-skating shows, and during the 1940s he established himself as a dominant force in Toronto ballet circles. However, despite efforts to raise funds for professional operation, the Volkoff Canadian Ballet remained a non-professional enterprise, its dancers making their livings in other careers.[14]

But if the goal of full-time professional operation for their troupes eluded both Gweneth Lloyd and Boris Volkoff during this period, they did succeed in bringing together some of the far-flung amateur performing groups in the nation at the annual

Canadian Ballet Festivals. These festivals, the brainchild of Lloyd's Winnipeg associate David Yeddeau, created performance opportunities, public awareness, and a heightened sense of anticipation for the development of dance in Canada.[15] Between the first festival, of 1948, in Winnipeg, and the Montreal edition of 1950, a number of dreams had begun to form themselves into more or less concrete plans. As a result, Celia Franca, former dramatic ballerina of the Sadler's Wells Ballet and aspiring freelance choreographer, was a guest at the 1950 festival, invited to assess the possibilities for forming a professional dance company on a national scale in Canada.

How exactly did she come to be there? Many people, over the years, have claimed at least partial credit for setting in motion the train of events that brought her. One of them, by Max Wyman's account, was Gweneth Lloyd herself, who had left Winnipeg for Toronto in early October 1950, and quickly became deeply involved in the dance scene there.[16] (The program for the Fourth Canadian Ballet Festival in 1952 lists Gweneth Lloyd, Celia Franca, and Betty Oliphant, all of Toronto, among the executive committee members of the Canadian Dance Teachers Association.)[17] Another was Boris Volkoff, who counted himself among the individuals consulted by Mrs. Mulqueen, Mrs. Whitehead, and Mrs. Woods about the feasibility of forming a professional ballet company in Canada.[18] Stewart James, who eventually made the first direct contact with Franca on behalf of the Canadian group, was another agitator for the cause. He had been trying to advance the Volkoff Canadian Ballet in the Far East as early as 1948 and 1949. In a letter commenting on his efforts, Volkoff stated that "in order to be recognized and accepted as an essential part of our own National culture, we must be accepted elsewhere first."[19] However, the same letter urged that a decision to tour be held off until the spring of 1950, so that there would be "ample time to discuss every angle and to perfect our plans." Those plans had included a survey that James had done, on Volkoff's behalf, of the performance opportunities on the Ontario touring circuit.[20] Volkoff and James clearly had great hopes for the development of professional dance in Canada. James, in his turn, stressed the importance of Kay Ransom's contribution, as secretary of the Canadian Ballet Festival Association, to the dreams and plans. At the time of her death in 1977, he wrote in a letter to the *Globe and Mail*:

> As the catalyst that brought together all the parts to make the National Ballet a reality, I, probably more than any one other person, know how it all actually came about. This last week saw the passing of one of the true heroes — though truly unsung — of the formation of the National Ballet and the development of dance in this country.[21]

Janet Baldwin, a daughter of Toronto's upper middle class who studied dance with Volkoff and then married him and became his business associate in the studio, was also a key player in the plans for the formation of a national company.[22]

With a common goal, but with conflicting ideals and personal ambitions, these were the principal individuals whose active concern for the cause of dance in Canada eventually involved Mrs. Mulqueen, Mrs. Whitehead, and Mrs. Woods in the project. Much later, Dame Ninette de Valois recalled the general climate of opinion in Canada at the time that her advice was solicited: "I remember about the same time I made a lecture tour of Canada, and I got up against this proposition, that they were going to have a company, everywhere."[23] Franca herself agreed that the three founders acted not as initial catalysts, but in response to a genuinely felt need and to specific pressures from the Canadian dance community.[24] The officially recognized founders of the National Ballet did not operate in isolation.

Franca, in costume for Offenbach in the Underworld, *in her dressing room with the company's own Lois Smith (left) and Svetlana Beriosova (right), rising young star of Britain's Royal Ballet.*

Nor was Franca's initial role entirely clear-cut. At the earliest stages of negotiations, she was apparently approached to be ballet mistress, not artistic director, of the fledgling enterprise. A handwritten sheet of paper, unsigned and undated but identified in a separate hand as "from Stewart James," exists in the National Ballet Archives. Addressed to Mrs. Whitehead, it summarizes the state of negotiations with Franca at the time of writing. Two of its paragraphs are worth quoting in full.

Aprox Sept 20th I wrote to Miss Franca confirming my talks in London: —
$60.00 per week per session of 1 year plus an option of 2nd & 3rd
seasons. return fare London/Toronto/London to be Ballet Mistress and
assistant to Artistic Director Position —
She would like to know exact relation to Director and to dancers.[25]

THE TERMS OF FRANCA'S INVITATION CLARIFIED

According to this evidence, then, Franca was originally asked, by Volkoff's associate
Stewart James, to be ballet mistress for an artistic director whose identity is unspecified
in the surviving documents. But on October 19, 1950, Aileen Woods wrote to Franca
as follows:

> We feel very strongly that this Professional Ballet Company would ben-
> efit greatly by having someone with your reputation and qualifications
> as its Producer and Director as well as being its Ballet Mistress. Can you
> possibly accept this further responsibility?[26]

The invitation to Franca to serve as artistic director was thus clearly stated as early
as October 1950, *before* her visit to the Third Canadian Ballet Festival in Montreal. It
appears, however, to have been a revision of an earlier approach to her along somewhat
different lines.

The background and precise sequence of events matter, because the date and contents
of Aileen Woods's letter argue against an interpretation of early events that gained some
currency in the 1960s. This version of the founding would have it that Franca accepted
the offer to become ballet mistress for Volkoff's proposed company and then manoeu-
vred him out of the key position of artistic director after her arrival in Canada. Brian
Macdonald implied as much in an address delivered in England and published in the
British dance periodical the *Dancing Times* in April 1963.

> Volkoff sent his company manager to England to study the adminis-
> tration of the Sadler's Wells Ballet, and while here the English dancer
> Celia Franca was recommended to him. She came out to see a ballet fes-
> tival, decided to accept a job as ballet mistress for Volkoff, and settled
> in Canada in the spring of 1951. She met with Volkoff and his board of
> directors and, in the strange ways of ballet companies, emerged as artis-
> tic director of the National Ballet of Canada.[27]

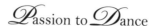

Macdonald, although a charter member of the company, would seem to be mistaken about the sequence of events. Whether or not Volkoff saw himself at this point as artistic director of a national company, Franca had in hand a clear offer of the position before her first trip to Canada. None of the documents surviving in the company's archives or in the Volkoff papers refers to the infant board of directors as Volkoff's board or to Volkoff as artistic director of the proposed company.

VOLKOFF AND LLOYD INEVITABLY FELT PASSED OVER

Today, long after the events in question, the motives and expectations of the key individuals are difficult to reconstruct. However, one hypothesis presents itself with considerable force. Both Boris Volkoff and Gweneth Lloyd had national aspirations that had received a degree of gratification through the medium of the first two Ballet Festivals. By late 1950, Gweneth Lloyd and David Yeddeau had left Winnipeg and relocated in Toronto, which was clearly mobilizing to provide the impetus for a national ballet. (Lloyd had left Winnipeg for Toronto a scant two weeks before Aileen Woods's October 19 letter of invitation to Franca.) Was Lloyd hoping to become the founding artistic director of a new, national company? Despite Lloyd's statements to the contrary, it seems a reasonable enough assumption, and one to which Max Wyman lends some support in his history of the Royal Winnipeg Ballet.[28] But Boris Volkoff, with the help of Stewart James, had been moving in the same direction, as Macdonald suggested in his speech and as the initial invitation to Franca to serve as ballet mistress would argue. Franca herself acknowledged that James probably had Volkoff in mind as artistic director when he made the first overtures to her.[29]

In this version of events, Volkoff and Lloyd, the two most prominent figures in the very small field of Canadian ballet in the 1940s, were on a collision course just at the time when some real progress toward a national company was finally being made; compromise, whether voluntary or imposed, was an absolute necessity. That compromise might take the form of a company structure that accommodated all the principal players. An undated, and clearly hypothetical, masthead for the proposed company, now in the National Ballet archives, lists the following personnel:

Artistic Director	Celia Franca
Resident Choreographer	Boris Volkoff
Artistic Consultant and Choreographer	Gweneth Lloyd
Stage Director and Company Manager	David Yeddeau
Business Manager	Stewart James
Wardrobe Mistress	Janet Volkoff[30]

The parity accorded to Gweneth Lloyd and Boris Volkoff under this scheme suggests a careful desire to offend neither party, with Franca handed the herculean task of mediating between the two — an uneasy triumvirate at best. Volkoff's own notes of 1964 hint at some such motive for this kind of compromise: "Neutrality was important and so my manager at that time was asked to go to London, England and search for such a person."[31]

Two other factors must have tempered the ambitions of Lloyd and Volkoff. One, of course, was Franca's own unwillingness to act as ballet mistress for Volkoff, a person she had never met and for whom she had little respect.[32] The second was the nature of de Valois's advice to the Toronto group, advice that stressed the desirability of heading the proposed company with a person of undisputed authority and an objective distance from the existing circumstances. As notes in the Aileen Woods papers state: "Miss de V. heartily agreed that to bring in someone whose artistic ability was beyond question was a good idea."[33] This advice is clearly echoed in a piece of correspondence with the Canadian Dance Teachers Association, dated November 5, 1950:

> We were strongly advised in the field of ballet to bring someone from outside Canada, a person with the highest recommendations, fullest qualifications and with undisputed professional knowledge and experience. This in the opinion of the Board will provide the stimulus that will make it possible to achieve the highest artistic standards.[34]

Once de Valois had been consulted, the die was cast: a national company for Canada would not be headed by any of the teachers or coaches already working in the country. This decision may well have represented an implicit judgment by de Valois on existing standards. Given the politics of the situation, it also represented for the founders the least contentious solution to a delicate diplomatic problem.

In 1963, Sydney Mulqueen recorded her recollections of the sequence of events leading to the founding of the company. Her general account provides verification of some important points.

> The founding of the National Ballet Company of Canada was first considered in 1950. At that time, numerous dance studios viewed with increasing alarm the rate at which their most promising pupils were leaving the country for professional employment elsewhere. Certain studios sent representatives to a group of Toronto women to learn whether some constructive move could be made to change this trend.
>
> A number of meetings were held and Miss Ninette de Valois, Director of the Sadler's Wells Ballet, was consulted in England. Fortunately at the time Miss de Valois had under consideration a tour of Canada and

promised to meet those interested in the problem during her visit. Before leaving England she stated that in her view Miss Celia Franca was the person best qualified to organize the Canadian project as its Artistic Director.

Meanwhile the Toronto group had reached a basic decision in that the proposed organization should be founded and operated on a national basis and that it should draw its dancers from all sections of the country.

During her visit to Toronto, Miss de Valois had a long and interesting meeting with the Toronto group, during which she gave them much valuable advice and confirmed her previous recommendation regarding Miss Franca.[35]

This account suggests that de Valois's advice to the founding group was extensive and taken seriously. In retrospect, the emphasis on "a national basis" speaks volumes. A genuinely national company could not be a simple extension of the Volkoff Canadian Ballet or the Winnipeg Ballet. A genuinely national organization would have to try to overcome regional prejudices and preconceptions. An outsider might be better able to look beyond those regional allegiances than someone closely allied with the existing structures. Only by bringing in an outsider could the organizers hope to strike a balance between the aspirations of Volkoff and Lloyd, the two established figures of Canadian ballet.

The coalition of forces interested in promoting ballet in Canada managed to suppress its internal rivalries and operate harmoniously at the time of the Third Canadian Ballet Festival, to try to convince Celia Franca to come to Canada and take up the role of artistic director that had been offered to her. Years later, Bernadette Carpenter, another early supporter of the cause, recalled some of the lobbying which took place in Montreal at that festival.

> After the opening night performance, our room was a hive of activity; each and every "drop in" came with the hope we could interest Celia enough to stay to form a National Company. Into the early morning, a few diehards lingered on, Anatole Chujoy, Mildred Wickson, Gweneth Lloyd, Janet Baldwin, and my husband, Don — each one of us hoping we were on the brink of a better future for young Canadian dancers.[36]

Given the acrimony that was soon to develop, the degree of friendly cooperation suggested by this account is touching. The picture of a small, determined band of Canadian ballet enthusiasts (Anatole Chujoy, the visiting American critic, the only outsider present), united in their efforts to woo Franca and keep her in their midst, lingers in the memory as the unofficial counterpoise to the official account of formal invitation and response.

Anthony Crickmay

Twenty-one years after recommending her protegée to the Canadian committee, Dame Ninette de Valois met Celia Franca again at the first European performance of the National Ballet of Canada, London, 1972.

There was at least one other lobbying effort as well. David Adams had worked with Franca at both Sadler's Wells and the Metropolitan Ballet. By the fall of 1950, he had returned to Canada and was active at the Third Canadian Ballet Festival. He recalled a luncheon conversation with Franca during which he tried to convince her of the potential of young Canadian dancers, if they could only be given proper direction and professional performance opportunities. Adams's perspective on the situation was by then international. Franca herself retained a dim recollection of Adams's writing to her from Canada, while she was still in England, urging her to consider the move.[37] She was thus being appealed to not only by complete strangers in a foreign land, but also by a recent professional associate. The small, interconnected world of postwar ballet had its representative, even in the far-flung outposts of the Commonwealth. Franca's decision to accept the Canadian offer (she had had similar ones, earlier in her career, from Australia and South Africa)[38] would extend that world and draw Canada decisively into its sphere of influence. The direction in which ballet in Canada was to develop hinged on one woman's response to a challenging invitation and a concerted effort to persuade her to accept it.

What made the matter so decisive, more so than the original issuers of the invitation can have realized, was the particular set of associations that Franca brought with her. If the original plan called for her simply to preside over a company in which the creative impetus would come from Volkoff and Lloyd, the proponents of that plan had not reckoned with the breadth of experience, strength of professional commitment, and sheer force of personality that supported Franca's skills as a teacher and producer of ballets. Despite her youth, she was a seasoned professional with fully formed artistic views, a daunting list of contacts in the world of ballet, and formidable reserves of willpower and artistic ambition. In choosing her, the original organizers of the company chose the militant champion of an entire tradition.

De Valois and her unqualified recommendation of Franca symbolized an important element of that tradition. To the end of her life, she remained unequivocal in her evaluation of the young Franca's particular gifts.

> She was an extremely fine artist, very good in dramatic roles. I also saw her do an exceedingly interesting piece of choreography at Sadler's Wells when she was in the company. She had very strong artistic views and great integrity of purpose in all her work.[39]

The National would trade on this recommendation for years, repeatedly quoting de Valois as saying that Franca was "the finest dramatic dancer the Wells has ever had."[40] Accurate though the quotation was, the emphasis on it did Franca a disservice. As the National's publicity kept recycling this endorsement, de Valois was becoming identified in the North American consciousness with the establishment Royal Ballet. Memories of the barnstorming Sadler's Wells days faded quickly. By implication, Franca became associated with the Royal. But Franca had never danced with the Royal. She had left for Canada a full five years before the Sadler's Wells became the Royal Ballet. Her experience with British ballet's groundbreaking early years distanced her from the stodgy reputation the Royal gradually acquired, and gave her invaluable qualifications for the kind of pioneering that lay ahead of her. But the repeated use of de Valois's accolade obscured these facts.

Celia Franca had received her early professional experience with Ballet Rambert, which she joined while still a teenager. It was there that she encountered the work and personality of Antony Tudor, both as teacher and as choreographer.[41] There, she served as one of the models on whom Tudor built *Dark Elegies*, in the first performance of which she danced at the Duchess Theatre, London, on February 19, 1937.[42] Other roles she danced with Ballet Rambert included the Woman in His Past (*Lilac Garden*) and the Chief Nymph in *L'Après-midi d'un Faune*, two works that would be significant in her Canadian career. At Ballet Rambert as well, she gained her first experience of the core works of the classical repertoire, adapted to the small stage of the Mercury Theatre.[43] After leaving Ballet Rambert, Franca danced very briefly with Mona Inglesby's International Ballet, where she learned Fokine's *Le Carnaval* from her teacher, Stanislas Idzikowski, who had taken over the role of Harlequin from its originator, the legendary Vaslav Nijinsky. In late 1941, she joined the Sadler's Wells Ballet, where she remained until 1946. As a principal with Sadler's Wells, she solidified her reputation as a dramatic dancer in roles like the Queen of the Wilis in *Giselle*, the Queen in *Hamlet*, and the Prostitute in *Miracle in the Gorbals*. The latter two were created for her by Robert Helpmann, the Australian dancer whose versatility gave him such varied careers as choreographer, dancer (as one of Margot Fonteyn's great partners), actor, and, eventually, artistic director of the Australian Ballet.

In 1946 and 1947, Franca choreographed two original works, *Khadra* and *Bailemos*, for the Sadler's Wells Theatre Ballet, as the smaller touring company was called after the main company had made the move to Covent Garden. Alexander Grant, who would later succeed Franca as artistic director of the National, danced in *Khadra*,[44] with David Adams and John Cranko alternating in the role of the father;[45] Cranko and Kenneth MacMillan, both of whom were to develop into major choreographers of distinctly different styles, performed in *Bailemos*.[46] In 1947, Franca served briefly as a teacher with Ballet Jooss, the German modern dance company that had made its home in England since before the war. In the same year, she joined the Metropolitan Ballet as a leading dancer and ballet mistress.

The title fails to do justice to the variety of functions Franca performed in that fascinating company. In addition to dancing, teaching class, coaching, and taking rehearsals, she gained practical experience in such matters as casting, making up programs, checking the proofs, preparing for tours, and, as she later put it, "just doing everything, really."[47] During its brief lifespan, the Metropolitan Ballet Company fostered an extraordinary array of international talent.[48] There, Franca worked closely with Nicholas Beriosoff, the custodian in the second half of the century of much of the Fokine repertoire, whose daughter, the fifteen-year-old Svetlana Beriosova, was one of the stars of the Metropolitan. Her haunting stage presence and luminous face later made her one of the Royal Ballet's greatest dancers. With Beriosoff, the Metropolitan learned Fokine's Polovetsian Dances from *Prince Igor*, which Franca would reproduce in the National's first season at Eaton Auditorium. [49] John Lanchbery, later to become the principal conductor of the Royal Ballet, was the Metropolitan's conductor. Here Franca's path once again crossed that of David Adams. And here she first encountered the nineteen-year-old Erik Bruhn, who had broken with the rigid hierarchy of the Danish Ballet to gain some international experience. With him, she danced a pas de deux in Frank Staff's *The Lovers' Gallery*.[50] By 1950, when she was just twenty-nine years old, Celia Franca had a range of experience that extended well beyond the confines of the Sadler's Wells Ballet.[51] She knew the rough-and-tumble of professional dance from the ground up.

The significance of this background can scarcely be overemphasized. The major contacts on whom Franca would rely for repertoire included the likes of Tudor, Cranko, and Bruhn, individuals whose creative lives functioned largely outside the Sadler's Wells–Royal Ballet sphere of influence. Through Idzikowski, Rambert, and Tudor, Franca felt a clear connection with the Diaghilev tradition and with the stylistic principles of Diaghilev's

Celia Franca and Erik Bruhn in The Lovers' Gallery, *the Metropolitan Ballet, circa 1947.*

ballet master, Enrico Cecchetti. Cecchetti had assembled his teaching practices into a movement syllabus that particularly emphasized the fluid, graceful coordination of the upper body. Its proponents believed that it prepared dancers to adapt easily to any style of choreography. Examinations organized by the Cecchetti Society eventually became one of the two standards of examination, along with the Royal Academy of Dancing examinations, for ballet instruction in England.

Franca's experience of the professional theatre, both in London and on tour, had formed in her, from a very early age, an uncompromising sense of professional standards and the behaviour appropriate to them. Her work as a choreographer, especially two original commissions for BBC-TV, then still in its infancy, had extended her range beyond the central classical repertoire and given her a glimpse of the possibilities of dance in a new medium. She was, in fact, a rarity: an experienced dancer with the skills and the ambition to look beyond her own performances to the entire artistic enterprise. Her range was not universal, but it was wide, and she had a well-defined conception of her own standards and goals.

Small wonder, then, that Franca, once she had arrived in Canada to set about the business of founding a company, chose to make her own alliances rather than fall in with Volkoff or Lloyd, with whom she had very little in common professionally. Lloyd had had no professional performing career. From her youthful interest in Greek dancing, a British technique based on revived forms of Greek dance, she moved to teaching and then straight into the operation of the Winnipeg company, for which she choreographed, immediately, extensively, and enthusiastically.[52] In a thirteen-year choreographic career, she produced thirty-five works ranging from prairie subjects (*Grain* and *Kilowatt Magic*) to abstract works and even a dance version of *Pride and Prejudice*. By sheer facility and versatility, she established herself as a major Canadian choreographer before Canadian choreography was recognized as a serious artistic possibility. To Franca, who had worked with the likes of Antony Tudor, Lloyd's choreographic efforts seemed provincial and amateurish.

Lloyd had come relatively late to ballet training and, except for studies with Margaret Craske, a pupil of Cecchetti's, had had little direct contact with the formative influences in Franca's career. Volkoff, with considerable professional experience, came from an entirely different tradition. He had trained in Moscow, not St. Petersburg, the home of Diaghilev and his dancers, and had danced his way around the world (including a stint in a Shanghai night club and a period with the Adolph Bolm Ballet in Chicago) before settling in Toronto.[53] To Franca, his teaching techniques represented the "old-fashioned Russian training" that was antithetical to her canons of taste, athletic and energetic rather than refined. When asked her opinion, de Valois had said, "Oh he's just a Russian drunk, my dear."[54] Volkoff, for his part, thought that Franca's standards represented "the very tidy English-governess school of dance."[55] In addition to having these differences of taste, experience, and tradition, both Volkoff and Lloyd were a full generation older than Franca. There was little, on the face of it, to suggest a mutually rewarding partnership.

Some attempts at cooperation did take place. Betty Oliphant remembered discussing with Franca ways to make "both Gweneth and Volkoff feel important parts of this early company."[56] Franca recalled that she and the board tried to remain on good terms with both of them.[57] According to the minutes of the Ballet Guild's board of directors' meeting for May 21, 1952:

> Miss Franca had asked Miss Gweneth Lloyd to choreograph a ballet for the National Ballet Guild and Mr. Homburger [Walter Homburger, the first General Manager of the company] had followed up this request with a letter. The General Manager then read a letter received from Miss Lloyd thanking the Guild for the invitation, but saying that she found she would be too busy at this time to undertake this work.[58]

The contentious question of whether or not to invite Lloyd to participate in this way had been vigorously debated. The perfunctory nature of her refusal, as reported in the minutes, suggests that she saw the invitation as too little, too late. From this point on, even though she remained resident in Toronto, Lloyd redoubled her support of the Winnipeg Ballet. The rift between the two companies would eventually reach melodramatic proportions.

Volkoff had a slightly longer, though largely unofficial, association with the company. He agreed to take some of the male classes for the company, prior to its opening performances at Eaton Auditorium in 1951.[59] For the next decade or more, some of the company's principals, Lois Smith, David Adams, Lawrence Adams, and Galina Samsova among them, found it useful to take private classes at his studio.[60] In July 1952, after the National's first year of operation, relations were still cordial enough to allow Volkoff and David Adams to form Toronto Theatre Ballet. Volkoff and Adams acted as artistic directors of this summer operation, which included among its dancers Natalia Butko, Angela Leigh, and Colleen Kenney, all charter members of the National. Stewart James, who had served very briefly as the National's company manager, played the same role for Toronto Theatre Ballet. Kay Ambrose, close friend of Franca and a stalwart of the National's production team, did some of the costumes.[61] Whereas Lloyd seems to have severed relations with the company decisively, Volkoff lingered a little while longer on the periphery. His disillusionment and bitterness, however, finally became as public as Lloyd's. After the initial years of agitation for a national company, neither Volkoff nor Lloyd played a role in its development.

BETTY OLIPHANT, FRANCA, AND THE FIRST SUMMER SCHOOL

This shifting pattern of aspiration, rivalry, and suppressed hostility provides the background to the earliest events in Franca's Canadian experience. The experience itself began in November 1950, when, in response to the invitation from the provisional Toronto group, Franca visited the Third Canadian Ballet Festival in Montreal to observe the standards of ballet in Canada. "I think you need me here," was her diplomatic comment,[62] and in February 1951, after completing commitments in London, she returned to Toronto, nominally as an employee of the T. Eaton Company but actually to conduct a feasibility study for the proponents of a national ballet for Canada. Gossip among dancers and dance teachers was rife, and Franca was seen as the mysterious outsider whose purposes were not entirely clear. At this point, Betty Oliphant made her entrance onto the scene. As Oliphant later told the story, the members of the Canadian Dance Teachers Association were apprehensive that no real change would take place. They feared the much-vaunted national company would simply become an extension of the Volkoff enterprise, which they considered to have a virtual monopoly on dance activity in the city. Volkoff was not a member of the CDTA. When Franca announced her first classes, to be taught in his studio, she received a call from Betty Oliphant, sent by the CDTA to find out just how open the newcomer was to the full range of talent and experience in the country.

Basil Zarov

Betty Oliphant, as ballet mistress, giving notes to the young company.

"Why don't they trust me, Miss Oliphant?" Franca asked.

"Well, why should they? They don't even know you; they don't have any reason to trust you," Oliphant responded, and the two women began discussing the new enterprise in earnest.[63]

From this initial conversation sprang an alliance that shaped the development of the National Ballet of Canada. Franca was absolutely clear in her own mind as to the range and scope of the project she had in hand.

> Ninette de Valois had given advice to the ladies, saying that you should have a national company, that auditions should be held nationally to make sure you get the best possible talent, that your governing body should be national. It was de Valois who really advised them of the set-up; and of course, before I came over I talked to de Valois. I knew all this.[64]

But she needed as an ally someone sympathetic to her own background and standards *and* someone able to help her navigate the tricky waters of the Canadian dance teaching establishment. Whatever their standards or level of accomplishment might be, it was from among the students of these teachers that the dancers of the future company must be drawn. Without the teachers' cooperation, the politics of Franca's immediate task would be treacherous in the extreme. She needed help to overcome the suspicions and hostilities of the teachers who wanted to consider themselves her professional colleagues, yet were unsure of her motives and intimidated by her international qualifications and theatrical experience. Above all, she needed to remain impartial, to avoid identifying her own search for talent with any one studio or teacher.

In Betty Oliphant, a woman of her own generation, Celia Franca found the natural ally that Volkoff and Lloyd could never be. Although they had not met before coming to Canada, the two women had a great deal in common. Both counted Antony Tudor as their first teacher in the Cecchetti syllabus,[65] both had had experience in London's commercial theatre, and both had studied with Marie Rambert. Betty Oliphant recalled their student days:

> We weren't in the same class, but we were at Marie Rambert's at the same time. Franca wasn't allowed in the professional ballet class because she was in a musical comedy. I did a lot of musical comedy but Rambert didn't know about it, so I was in the professional class; but we were there at the same time.[66]

Though Oliphant's subsequent career had taken her into teaching rather than performance, she drew her inspiration from essentially the same source as Franca: the Diaghilev tradition in its British manifestation and as expounded through the teachings of Cecchetti. With such a background, she was certainly not one to be intimidated by Franca; Oliphant thoroughly understood the standards and ideals Franca stood for. But most valuable of all, Oliphant already had a position of some respect among teachers of dance in Canada. As a founding member of the CDTA, she had been animated by a desire to break down hostilities and get dance teachers talking to one another.[67] As emissary from this group to Franca, she came as close as anyone would to representing a group of teachers speaking with a common voice rather than an individual teacher with a vested interest. And that common voice already had a Canadian organizational structure. Through this organization, the impartiality and inclusiveness essential to the founding of the company might actually be realized. If Betty Oliphant and the CDTA had not already existed in 1951, it might have been necessary to invent them.

The crisis that had prompted Oliphant's initial visit to Franca was resolved by having the CDTA take over sponsorship of the classes in question in order to avoid the appearance of bias on Franca's part. The classes, advertised by the CDTA, were open to pupils of any teacher, whether a member of the CDTA or not, as long as the students had the requisite amount of training.[68] The opportunity these preliminary classes offered to aspiring dancers to be seen by the artistic director of the future national company needed no emphasis. It was a logical development, then, for the CDTA to co-sponsor Franca's cross-country audition tour, as it did in August 1951.[69] If Franca needed the CDTA to smooth over the rivalries among the local Toronto teachers, how much more did she require the sponsorship of a national organization in dealing with the country's regional sensitivities?

But before the audition tour, a school — or, at any rate, a summer school — was needed to begin the long-term process of raising the standards of instruction to meet the professional requirements of a national company. Existing standards, in Franca's opinion, were not high, despite the enthusiasm and visionary zeal that had fuelled the national project in the first place.[70] Even though she bruised some feelings with this assessment of the situation, Franca's analysis was crucial to the success of her venture.[71] If money and opportunity alone were enough to give professional ballet a start in Canada, why import someone to do the job? Franca was more than an administrator; she was a teacher of professionals and saw with a teacher's eye that the raw material before her had to be shaped and trained if it was to fulfill anyone's dreams of its future potential and if it was to bear her distinctive stamp. Many fine dancers had already left the country to perform; they had also left for the advanced training that turned promising students into distinctive, professional artists. Teaching would be the key to the company's success and the real justification for Franca's entrance onto the Canadian scene.

Accordingly, she set about organizing the first summer school, to be conducted under the sponsorship of the National Ballet Guild but entirely at her personal financial risk.[72] The five-week session, running from July 2 to August 4, 1951, attracted both teachers and advanced students of dance.[73] Through the summer schools, which continued annually until they were taken over by the National Ballet School in the early 1960s,[74] Franca "preached the gospel"[75] of high standards and demanding pedagogic practices. She also preached the gospel of the Cecchetti method of teaching basic technique. Although that first summer school at the St. Lawrence Hall included both the Cecchetti and the Royal Academy of Dance methods of instruction, the balance was clearly inclining in favour of Cecchetti, with decisive implications for the development of the company and eventually the National Ballet School.

Franca's emphasis on Cecchetti could be seen as an astute tactical move. She and Oliphant were the only Cecchetti advocates on the scene at the time; by emphasizing this method, Franca ensured that no other teachers, representing other methods, would pose any real threat to her authority. The choice of this method offered a graceful way, if one was needed, of avoiding undue entanglement with either Volkoff or Lloyd.

But the real basis for the choice, one on which Franca and Oliphant agreed long after they had stopped agreeing on most other things, was stylistic. As Franca saw it: "It was important for us to have a system that we believed in as a basic training, which had good scientific reasons behind it about the placement of the body, the use of the arms, and the carriage of the neck." The Cecchetti system met those requirements, "because the Cecchetti system is very pure. And it's very Petipa."[76] A company that aspired to dance the works of Petipa, the pre-eminent Russian classical choreographer of the canonical works like *Nutcracker*, *Swan Lake*, and *Sleeping Beauty*, laid the foundation for that repertoire with this choice of basic schooling.

Sally Brayley and Earl Kraul as Princess Mother and Prince Siegfried with artists of the ballet in Celia Franca's Swan Lake.

Oliphant had come to essentially the same conclusions in her own evaluations of teaching methods. For her, Cecchetti was "probably the best method in the whole world for the use of the head, the use of the arms, the use of *épaulement*, nuances, and subtleties." One reason, in her view, for the strength of the system was the emphasis it placed on basic technique; "It lays a base which is better than any other method that I've seen, including Vaganova [the technique of the legendary Kirov Ballet and School]. It's death on affectations and mannerisms. It has very, very good lines."[77] This fundamental agreement on the merits of the Cecchetti system formed the basis of the strong partnership that was to exist between Franca and Oliphant for years to come. It also dictated the stylistic direction in which the new company would develop and, to a large extent, the speed at which that development would take place. The dancers would be taught Cecchetti's pure, unaffected line, however long the process took. They would not be allowed to settle for easier solutions, more theatrical effects, in their pursuit of the ideal. The goal that Franca and Oliphant set was a lofty one; there could be no shortcuts. (Like any technique, the Cecchetti method was only as good as the teachers espousing it; with the passage of time, the original standards of the Cecchetti syllabus became eroded, in Oliphant's view.[78] Today, the National Ballet School, arguably founded on the Cecchetti method, has absorbed a wide spectrum of pedagogical influences, and no longer bases its curriculum exclusively on it.)

With the 1951 summer school, Franca and her colleagues took the first, small step toward their goal. Whereas logic might have argued that *all* her efforts should be directed toward education for at least a few years, until she had dancers ready for professional exposure, circumstances dictated otherwise. When Lincoln Kirstein was courting George Balanchine to come to America and start a company, Balanchine uttered his famous dictum, "But first a school."[79] Franca, though fully committed to the same ideal, could acknowledge it in the first instance only by these summer sessions. The reason was purely practical.

> It didn't take me five minutes to find out that in Canada you had to use the word "sell," and I knew damn well I couldn't get anybody to support a school. I had to show why we needed a school. From my own background in England I knew that a school was essential, the type of school that we finally did found, the National Ballet School. But in 1951 there was no way.[80]

Franca was joined in that first summer session by a number of other teachers, among them Betty Oliphant. Oliphant had scheduled her own summer session that year; on hearing of the National Ballet Guild's plans, she telephoned Franca in panic, frightened that the conflict would reduce her student numbers. When Franca suggested they join

Celia Franca as Swanilda and Sydney Vousden as Dr. Coppélius in Coppélia, *Act II, at Varsity Arena in 1951.*

forces, Oliphant was happy to agree.[81] The National Ballet of Canada, though not yet officially constituted, had moved out of the planning stages, into the studio.

Students came to that first summer session with varying expectations and varying degrees of experience. Judie Colpman arrived, fresh from high school graduation and from Bettina Byers's Toronto studio, attracted by the luxury of taking class every day of the week for the first time in her life; at first, she had no thought of auditioning for the company.[82] Howard Meadows, a student of Gerald Crevier in Montreal and deeply involved in amateur performances there, attended in the hope that he might be noticed and offered a chance.[83] David Adams already had the promise of a summer performance and a prominent place in the company, if it materialized; he helped to sweep out the St. Lawrence Hall so that it could be used for class.[84] With him, from Winnipeg, came his wife, Lois Smith, with extensive experience in musical comedy and no clearly formulated ambitions to become a ballerina; she had been taken more or less sight unseen, on the basis of a photograph and the recommendation of her husband.[85] The 1951 summer school functioned as both a training ground for the committed and a means of attracting potential talent to Toronto, thereby heightening interest in the possibility of a national company.

Almost simultaneously with the organization of the summer school, Franca presented a performance, on June 14, 1951, of *Coppélia* Act II at the annual Promenade Concerts in Varsity Arena.[86] Ballet performances, usually organized by Boris Volkoff,[87] had been a feature of the Prom Concerts for some years. This performance offered another opportunity for Franca to signal her presence and her intentions in Canada, and to do so in a manner that would appeal to the tastes of a family audience looking for light summer fare. *Coppélia*, originally choreographed for the Paris Opera by Arthur Saint-Léon in 1870, has one of the most beautiful scores in all of ballet, by Léo Delibes. The ballet retold the fantastical E.T.A. Hoffmann tale of the deranged toymaker who attempts to give life to one of his marvellous dolls by stealing the life force from an unsuspecting village lad who has blundered into his workshop. The catastrophe is averted, but not before the villager and his sweetheart, in Act II, discover a host of marvellous automatons in the famous toyshop scene. Franca's *Coppélia* met with enough success to be repeated in Montreal on August 8, and again in Toronto on September 13, with the addition of a sprightly duet from the first act of *Giselle*, known as the peasant pas de deux, for Lois Smith and David Adams. None of these could be considered the first performance of the National; they were simply guest spots on a musical program. At the time of the June and August performances, the national audition tour had not yet taken place and no company was formally constituted. Furthermore, these independent performance ventures broke even without any financial support from the Guild; they were crucial precursors to the company's activities, an official preview rather than a formal debut.

THE NATIONAL AUDITION TOUR IGNITED
EXCITEMENT AND CONTROVERSY IN EQUAL MEASURE

The summer school had turned a profit of one thousand dollars.[88] Under the terms of the start-up loan that the Guild had advanced to her for the school, Franca was obliged to use that profit "to travel to West Coast and intervening cities for the purpose of auditioning dancers for the Canadian National Ballet Company, if and when formed."[89] In late August 1951, the tour took place, but not without its share of controversy. The idea of creating a national company using the most talented dancers in the country had seemed a splendid one in the formative, theoretical stages of discussion; now that a flesh-and-blood artistic director, and a British one at that, was travelling from Toronto to the west coast to have a look at that talent, two contradictory fears arose. One was that the stranger entrusted with this task would overlook the homegrown talent available; the other was that she would find it and steal it away, thus robbing the regions of their principal contact with the art form, which was struggling to establish itself regionally as well as nationally. It was a diplomatic tightrope that Franca walked as adroitly as any human could. But despite tact and diplomacy, reaction was sometimes negative. Halifax, not even a stop on the tour, was "much annoyed." The Halifax Ballet should have been approached before the husband-and-wife team of Jury Gotshalks and Irene Apiné was lured away by Franca's offer to join the new company.[90] Winnipeg was irate and complained formally to the Guild, asking the meaning of the word "National" in the name "National Ballet Guild of Canada," and pointing out that the Winnipeg Ballet was already committed to a season of its own.[91] The implication, clearly, was that the National should stick to its own territory and stop stealing dancers from the relatively limited pool of experienced talent available. But what precisely was that territory? National dreams seemed suddenly less potent when confronted with the realities of regional rivalry.

While the Guild tried to mend fences from its base in Toronto, Franca did her best on the road. In Winnipeg, she gave an interview to the *Winnipeg Free Press*.

> "The decision of the [National Ballet Guild] board to go ahead with the national company came simultaneously with the decision of the Winnipeg board of directors to continue the Winnipeg Ballet for another year," Miss Franca explained.
>
> "When I heard this, I didn't approach any Winnipeg dancers afterward because of an unwritten code of ethics by which the director of one company does not solicit dancers from another company.
>
> "Naturally, unless any Winnipeg dancers came to me of their own free will I wouldn't approach them." She said she had already signed dancer David Adams and his wife Lois under these circumstances before the Winnipeg Board's decision came out.[92]

After the fact, Franca expressed herself more forthrightly on the subject. "By this time the Winnipeg Ballet had decided to open up again and also turn professional, so I was preceded in every town by Arnold Spohr, at that time the Winnipeg's ballet master, who cleaned up the best dancers."[93] Spohr was eventually to direct the company for thirty years, during which time the rivalry between the Winnipeg Ballet and the National would never entirely vanish. Perhaps because of this initial competition, Franca found fewer qualified dancers than she might have hoped for.[94]

The Winnipeg issue was far more complicated than it appeared on the surface. From October 1950, the Winnipeg (after 1953, the Royal Winnipeg) Ballet operated under long-distance artistic direction. Gweneth Lloyd did not give up the title of artistic director until June 1955. Throughout this period, however, she remained in Toronto; it was a sign of the distance between them that, when her company performed in Winnipeg in March 1951, it did so, for the first time, without an original Lloyd work on the program.[95] Lloyd and David Yeddeau, in Toronto, had told Franca that "the Winnipeg Ballet was finished."[96] In approaching Betty Farrally in Winnipeg, regarding studio space for the audition tour, Franca believed that she was dealing with a ballet school, not with another professional performing company. But she underestimated Lloyd's determination and Winnipeg civic pride. In June 1951, the Winnipeg board announced honoraria for its dancers, thereby reasserting the company's claim to professional status, and in October of the same year it staged a full-blown media event: a command performance before Princess Elizabeth and the Duke of Edinburgh during their Canadian tour.[97] The National was not going to be allowed to claim centre stage unchallenged. If, as Franca had been told, the Winnipeg Ballet was on the verge of collapse early in 1951, her national audition tour goaded a second Canadian company back into being.

Amid such controversy, the whirlwind audition tour rolled on, its methods of selection not always orthodox. Grant Strate, with no ballet training at all, did not audition for the company, but met Franca at a reception in Edmonton.

> She came to the studio and she saw a couple of things I had choreographed, after which she looked at me and said, "Would you join the National Ballet of Canada?" and I said, "Sure." And we both wandered away wondering what we'd done. So that was how I joined the National Ballet, an interesting process, something that I think would never happen again and maybe shouldn't even have happened then.[98]

When Oliphant questioned another choice, Franca explained: "I wanted someone who looked good stripped to the waist for 'Danse Arabe' in *Nutcracker*."[99] Earl Kraul, who would become the company's leading male dancer after David Adams's departure, auditioned unsuccessfully. "I finally did the audition, and at first Celia was not going to take

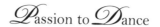

me; but there was supposed to be a boy coming from Vancouver and he had had an accident, and at the last minute she decided to take me."[100] Judie Colpman, after her participation in the summer school, was invited to audition to fill another unexpected vacancy and was accepted.[101] Natalia Butko didn't go through a formal audition. She had danced extensively with Volkoff's group and appeared in the first Prom Concert performance of *Coppélia* Act II. Perhaps Franca valued her comic and dramatic gifts and saw a place for them in her projected repertoire.[102]

David Adams, as an observer of the audition process, could not discern the rationale for all of Franca's choices.

> Some people were not able to do very much at all, and people who were able were told that they weren't good enough. I didn't see, I don't see to this day, the reason why that group were there. We did, eventually, fit. As a matter of fact we fit like a glove; it was fantastic. But those are the personalities, and in an audition system you don't find out personalities. She was lucky.[103]

Luck surely played its part in the process, but so did Franca's skill and intuition. She was not simply auditioning talent; she was beating the bushes, looking for personalities who were willing to pioneer with her and body types that would be able to take her instruction; if experience and training came with the package, so much the better. Franca had seen enough of the country and its attitudes toward culture to realize just how much depended on her choices. The company she assembled had to make a splash with its very first performance. There wasn't enough experienced, trained talent in the nation to carry the project off on skill alone. She was, in many cases, assessing raw material in order to judge what she might be able to make of it, not what it already was. The cohesiveness of the group of people she finally brought together proved to be one of its strongest initial assets. Natalia Butko assessed the situation astutely: "We were all equals and we really worked our hearts out."[104] Given the turbulent climate in that summer of 1951 when the company was formed, this sense of equality and devotion to the cause was the company's strongest suit.

Chapter Two

IT WAS AN OKAY BEGINNING

FRANCA'S CHALLENGE: TO TAILOR THE REPERTOIRE TO THE DANCERS' ABILITIES

With that hectic summer of preparatory activity behind her — the preview performances at Varsity Arena and in Montreal, the first summer school, the audition tour — Franca could concentrate all her professional and artistic energies on grooming her dancers for their opening performance as a company. In the disparate group of professionals and aspiring professionals assembled about her, she found malleable material, eager to accept all the direction she had to offer. The principles of taste and style that she applied at this early stage would remain her standards for the duration of her career with the National. Throughout the varying fortunes of the company, its artistic successes and its failures, Franca insisted on the ideals that guided this first performance. Such assumption of authority on her part was no mere display of ego; it was the logical consequence of her uncompromising artistic idealism. Only through firm artistic direction could her artistic vision for the company be realized. And despite the glowing public rhetoric that greeted the company in its early years, she remained its severest critic; she knew all too well the discrepancies between her vision and its realization, just as she recognized the moments of fulfillment.

Franca's fifteen years of professional experience in England had given her an invaluable set of resources for the task at hand. In this period, before the widespread use of standardized dance notation systems and before the advent of videography, choreography was transmitted by the individuals who had danced it, relying on notes, diaries, documentation like photographs and design sketches, and, overwhelmingly, personal recollection. It was a generational process, and many stagers of ballets could claim a dance genealogy leading back to the choreographer him or herself. Based on her experience at

Sadler's Wells, Franca knew, by memory, much of the standard classical repertoire. Her extensive work with contemporary British choreographers in the process of creation had also given her a strong sense of the nuances of style appropriate to a given work or period. Like many other professionals, then, she could teach her dancers the steps they had to know; but more than that, she could demand from them the refinements of style and of phrasing that raise a performance out of the realm of the ordinary. She was knowledgeable; she had a discriminating sense of style; and she had the confidence to impose her sense of style on dancers who would have been lost without her guidance.

Without hesitation, participants in that first series of performances at Eaton Auditorium gave Franca the credit for producing the coherent sense of style that distinguishes a company from a pick-up group. It was no mean feat, given the disparity in background, training, and experience that met her in the rehearsal hall. Franca's response to this challenge showed her mettle immediately. With characteristic practicality, she settled on a choice of works that were choreographically within the range of possibility for her dancers at their present level of experience, the mastery of which would nevertheless begin the painstaking process of discipline and training necessary to achieve her long-term goal — creating a major classical ballet company.

One of these was *Les Sylphides*, choreographed to orchestrations of Chopin's piano music by the early twentieth-century Russian choreographer Michel Fokine. In this abstract ballet, Fokine presented the Romantic figure of the poet (in white tights, loose shirt, and black doublet) surrounded by a female corps and soloists in long white dresses, all framed in a moonlit woodland setting. The ballet emphasized mood and atmosphere over bravura dancing and featured as a central part of the repertoire for Diaghilev's Ballets Russes and the companies of the same name that came after him. Through Fokine's association with Diaghilev, *Les Sylphides* found its way into the repertoires of almost all Western ballet companies. By the mid-fifties, it had come to symbolize ballet itself in the minds of many spectators.[1]

Franca recalled the central place which Fokine's *Les Sylphides* occupied in the company's early repertoire: "If you have a classical ballet company you have to have a well-trained corps de ballet. *Les Sylphides* was the very first thing we did which was the beginning of training a corps and getting a feeling for uniform style."[2] Judie Colpman remembered rehearsals as a struggle "to get the turnout, to get the form for a professional company." But, like many others, she remembered also the sense of shared commitment among the dancers that fuelled the endeavour and made the hours of work worthwhile. In pursuit of a coherent, authentic style, Franca worked her inexperienced company long and hard. Her attention to detail, especially in the ensemble, was relentless. Colpman also recalled "particularly in *Les Sylphides*, the hours we used to spend just doing the arms and the hands."[3] Franca was after a sense of poetically inspired unison that went beyond mere precision. To achieve this end, she drilled her dancers repeatedly, then urged them to contemplate some image, whether of dreams or of moonlight, as she put it, "to get their

Angela Leigh, one of the early stars of the company, in costume for Les Sylphides.

imaginations working, so they would all move in unison without looking like a bunch of soldiers."[4] Every dancer was expected to be dramatically present — not simply filling up a place in the line, but rather contributing actively to the overall effect. According to Natalia Butko, the company's major objective at this stage was "to think of the dance as a whole picture, not just as bits and pieces."[5] Once that picture had been set, Franca maintained it with scrupulous care and attention. The frequent critical notes for the dancers were, by her own admission, "very tough on them. If I didn't give them a correction after a performance they would feel I was ignoring them."[6] Such an atmosphere could have been discouraging, but in the young company it bred a "rivalry in detail" (in Colpman's phrase) in which all the dancers participated, to try to maintain the ensemble playing at the highest possible level.

Behind Franca's emphasis on the detail and coherence of the ensemble lay an innate awareness of musical values. If dance takes its inspiration from music, then choreographic effects can be successful only insofar as they build upon and relate to the music sustaining them. Franca's conception of phrasing in dance, of the linking of movements into a continuous, expressive sequence that "speaks" to an audience, derived from her sensitivity to phrasing in music. Her criticism of the unmusical dancer was timeless: "You're thinking in short phrases. You are thinking one step at a time. There is no big phrase-line that you'd see on the score, that lovely beautiful semicircle that goes from this bar to that bar."[7] The respect for musical values inherent in such criticism is by no means universal in the world of ballet. A yawning chasm separates the dancer for whom music is accompaniment, to be manipulated as may be convenient, from the dancer for whom music is the soul of dance, the muse whose dictates must be obeyed. Franca was the latter kind of dancer. Betty Oliphant described musicality in a dancer as "the ability to play with the music, to phrase the music, to know when you can steal this extra moment and make it up," and recognized musicality as one of Franca's significant attributes.[8] As a teacher and coach, Franca tried to impart to the young company some of her own sensitivity to musical values. Earl Kraul acknowledged the debt. As his basic technique began to develop, he needed something more to turn him into a dancer, "And Celia was the one who showed me how to handle technique, how to treat it musically and how to place it."[9] Franca's determination never to compromise the music placed a stylistic stamp on the emerging company as surely as her attention to the detail of the ensemble had done. She had chosen to stake her reputation, and the reputation of the company, on detailed authenticity of mood and style and on refined musical sensibility rather than on pyrotechnics and dazzling theatrical effects.

She had little real choice in the matter. With only one or two exceptions, Franca's dancers simply didn't have the technical ability to sustain flamboyant displays and virtuoso tricks. In reporting on the choreography at the Third Canadian Ballet Festival in Montreal for the *Royal Academy of Dancing Gazette* she had written: "Choreographers must avoid the dangerous tendency to tax dancers beyond their technical ability."[10] Her

conception of professionalism thus involved a scaling down of aspirations to meet existing abilities on some reasonable middle ground. Franca would, if necessary, make modi-
fications in standard choreography to enable her dancers to realize the spirit of the choreographer's intentions, when the letter might have defeated them. Betty Oliphant admired
Franca's skill in this regard.

> Celia was absolutely brilliant at never giving away the limitations of the
> dancers. She managed to produce a homogeneous, artistically presented,
> very well lit company. But always, and this frustrated the dancers very
> much — "If you can't do two *clean* pirouettes, only do one. If you can't
> lift your leg in the air and balance, then don't lift your leg." The very, very
> first performance I ever saw of the company (I wasn't the ballet mistress
> then), I couldn't believe that out of what I knew were very different styles
> and, by and large, not very well-trained dancers (although some were
> good), she managed to produce this effect.[11]

As late as 1956, in her report to the Guild's fifth annual meeting, Franca admitted
candidly to the occasional need for this kind of protective camouflage. "As far as possible,
I have tried to insulate the public from any inadequacies by occasionally changing the
choreography to fit the dancers' capabilities."[12] Reflecting on that period, she later said:
"My job was to make dancers who had not had an ideal training look professional. It was
a very, very difficult process, because there was an awful lot wrong with their basic technique."[13] Lois Smith concurred:

> Franca was a very good teacher, but what she taught us as a whole com-
> pany was how to dance together, how to be professional about what we
> were doing, how to really produce, how to move properly. So in that way,
> we were quite professional looking, even though we didn't have all the
> technique in the world.[14]

Theatrical professionalism: that was the value Franca sought to instill and for which
the company's charter members always admired her. Those first steps toward its achievement must have looked like a cramped and shrunken version of the grandiose ambitions
that had led to the founding of a national company. The dawn of professional activity cast
a cold light on the dreams that had preceded it. The dancers who had been proclaimed
ready for national exposure were being taken back to the first principles of their art, like
neophytes rather than professionals. But Franca recognized the necessity for this humble
beginning if the long-term goal of a classical ballet company for Canada was to be placed
on a firm footing from the very start.

Lois Smith, Yves Cousineau, Glenn Gilmour, Kenneth Melville, and David Scott in the Rose Adagio from Princess Aurora.

It Was an Okay Beginning

Opening Night: The Critical Response

On November 12, 1951, after just two months of rehearsal as a full company, the Canadian National Ballet (the company's name was changed to the National Ballet of Canada in January 1952)[15] opened a three-night run at Eaton Auditorium in Toronto. The full program consisted of *Les Sylphides*, Franca's own *Dance of Salomé*, the peasant pas de deux from Act I of *Giselle* (for David Adams and Lois Smith), Kay Armstrong's *Étude*, and, as a closing number, the Polovetsian Dances from Borodin's opera *Prince Igor*, another Fokine-choreographed staple from the Diaghilev era. With the exception of *Étude*, which Franca had admired as one of Vancouver's contributions to the 1950 Ballet Festival in Montreal, the program came entirely out of the storehouse of her own memory.[16] She had choreographed the *Dance of Salomé* for BBC-TV a few years earlier; the rest of the repertoire she had acquired during her years with Ballet Rambert, Sadler's Wells, and the Metropolitan Ballet. As was to be the case throughout the early years, Franca's prodigious memory saved the impoverished company a bundle in choreographic fees.

Her choice of program was both judicious and practical. It leaned a little heavily on Fokine, but with good cause: *Les Sylphides* exemplified the stylistic virtues Franca had decided to emphasize, and the Polovetsian Dances provided an opportunity to display the men, as well as the vitality of the whole company. If they couldn't be virtuosos, they could at least kindle some sparks of energetic excitement. The excerpt from *Giselle* gave the audience a hint of the romantic repertoire, and of the dance partnership that was to develop between Smith and Adams to sustain the company through its early years; the Franca and Armstrong pieces stood for contemporary and Canadian choreography. The only glaring omission, for the debut program of a classical company, was any piece of genuinely classical choreography. There was nothing by Petipa, the pre-eminent classical choreographer, whose work displays the purity of form and technique that ballet attained by the close of the nineteenth century. (Franca added to the repertoire his *Don Quixote* pas de deux, for Jury Gotshalks and Irene Apiné, in less than a month's time.) There was little that would startle Toronto dance audiences. The Polovetsian Dances and *Les Sylphides* had been staple pieces in the de Basil Ballets Russes touring repertoire, and had been seen in Toronto during that company's 1941 engagement at the Royal Alexandra Theatre. Volkoff had mounted versions of both in Toronto, and in the 1938–39 season had retired from dancing with a final virtuoso performance in the starring role of the Warrior Chief.[17] But the program served its purpose: it introduced the company to Toronto audiences in such a way as to appeal to their own previous knowledge of ballet, assert Franca's arrival on the scene, emphasize the company's strengths, and discreetly mask its weaknesses.

The significance of this conservative beginning lay not in any tumultuous, overnight success, but in the fact that it happened at all. For the company's organizers and supporters, the evening represented a culmination of years of hope and aspiration and the beginning, whether they knew it or not, of the real, the herculean efforts to keep the company

Gene Draper

Lois Smith as Salome, Grant Strate as John the Baptist, and artists of the ballet in Dance of Salomé. *Earl Kraul is on the platform, second from the right.*

afloat. For Franca, the performance was simply the first step on the road toward the creation of the kind of company few of her Canadian associates envisioned at the time. For many of those first performers, like Howard Meadows, the euphoria came from the declaration of purpose and sense of professional status that the occasion symbolized. "We were now part of a professional, full-scale company. How big, how bad, how good, that didn't matter; you had finally stepped over that threshold. You were not an amateur anymore, you were a professional."[18]

But Earl Kraul's memories testified to the realistic response to the performance itself which Franca and her dancers preserved in the face of all the excitement.

> I mostly remember standing, holding the spear in *Salomé* beside Brian Macdonald, while everyone else was doing the dancing and I was wishing I was doing it. I think that I recall hearing from Celia that it was okay. Not that it was sensational or anything, but we were okay. We pulled it together; it was an okay beginning.[19]

On the critical front, the opening night demonstrated, not surprisingly, that Toronto had little by way of professional critical experience to evaluate what was being offered. Like its audience, critics of the company would have to be developed. The reviewer for the *Telegram* waxed ecstatic, but his only yardstick for the performance seemed to be the legendary Pavlova, dead for some twenty years. The comparison was too absurd, and too outdated, to be flattering.

> Enthusiasm of the large audience was inspiring, but not at all surprising. Music was in perfect register with what was happening on the stage. Scenery and costumes were in perfect alignment, too. Dancing of Celia Franca throughout the evening had all the enchantment of Pavlowa's faultless dance technique. Last evening she touched the whole art of ballet as it used to be and can never be again.[20]

Whether intentionally or not, the nostalgic note of the final sentence lent an air of doomed, if noble, futility to the long-term hopes of the company.

The *Globe and Mail* took things more seriously. It sent its drama critic, Herbert Whittaker, who would become one of the company's most faithful observers and critics, as well as its first official historian. He provided a much fuller, more optimistic account of the proceedings. Although critical of the "turgid theatricality" of the *Dance of Salomé*, he admired Franca's highly dramatic performance in the ballet and provided a valuable description of some of its choreographic features.

> After a somewhat cluttered beginning — mock Schéhérazade, not helped by the bulky costuming — the figure of Salomé begins to dominate the action and a genuine tension was achieved. The Dance of the Seven Veils, a pitfall if ever there was one, proved exciting although perhaps it outlasted its excitement a bit.
>
> A pas de deux by Salomé and the Young Syrian, danced by David Adams, and another with the Jokanaan, Grant Strate, built to the moment in which Salomé performs her dance for the head of the Prophet. But it was after this that Miss Franca's gift for groupings of fluidity and sustained invention. [Here the *Globe*'s typesetter cut short Whittaker's intended praise.]
>
> There is an ingenious passage in which Salomé tries to escape and is blocked by the other dancers, with Herodias [Natalia Butko] attempting to aid her daughter. A similarly effective moment came with the death of Salomé behind the soldiers' shields, her hands describing a last tortuous measure.[21]

With Polovetsian Dances concluding the program, the opening night audience must have gone reeling into the night under the onslaught of so much unabashed exoticism. Whittaker saved his unstinting praise, however, for the chaster *Étude*.

> Miss Armstrong's ballet opens with a beautifully sculptured grouping and then proceeds from it through a series of designs which flow rhythmically and interestingly until the first grouping is resumed. The lack of strain and cleanness of this work was worthy of Balanchine.

Whittaker concluded optimistically, looking to the future, rather than the nostalgic past as the *Telegram* had done: "Miss Franca's training has obviously built the foundation for a successful future." Clearly, Franca's basic values were visible to an audience from the very first company performance.

But these early strengths also implied some of the weaknesses with which the company would have to deal in years to come. Careful, correct schooling, an unquestioned necessity in the early years, could lead to careful, correct dancing, even when a more mature level of technical accomplishment might have allowed for greater freedom. Franca's limitations as a choreographer ruled out the possibility of her becoming the company's chief

Earl Kraul, Oldyna Dynowska, Katherine Stewart, and Natalia Butko in Kay Armstrong's Étude.

source of original works. That elusive creature, the Canadian choreographer, might be welcomed in effusive terms, as Whittaker had welcomed Kay Armstrong, but, in the early years, was to make furtive, isolated appearances at best, overawed, perhaps, by the daunting genius of Balanchine south of the border. Not until much later in its life would the company produce choreographers with a consistent record of creation and a reputation that went beyond the company itself.

Whittaker's comparison of Armstrong's work to Balanchine, doubtless intended as a compliment, foretold as early as 1951 the powerful influence of Balanchine in North America: to be good was to be derivative of him; to be outside his frame of reference was dangerous. And Franca stood outside. Her taste and experience allied her with the British school of choreography. With the rising of Balanchine's star in the United States, critical opinion turned against the British canons of taste. As the company developed, an impatient and sometimes ungrateful public came to interpret Franca's loyalty to the British tradition as inflexibility. She saw it as the consistent adherence to standards needed to create a well-trained, well-disciplined classical company, one sufficiently free of stylistic eccentricities to be able to dance convincingly the works of a wide variety of choreographers.

FRANCA BUILT THE ADMINISTRATIVE TEAM THAT WOULD SHAPE THE COMPANY

While busily whipping her dancers into shape and performing with them, both in Toronto and on tour, Franca also had to turn her attention to the task of assembling an artistic support staff. The company began operations with a healthy representation of the old Volkoff team in its employ. James Pape and Suzanne Mess, two former Volkoff students, designed some of the opening productions. Margaret Clemens, Volkoff's long-time studio pianist and associate, became the first company pianist. Stewart James, after initiating the original negotiations with Franca and managing the first summer school,[22] took on the job of company manager.[23] But James resigned abruptly in March 1952,[24] and by the end of that first season the last connections to the Volkoff organization were severed. Franca quickly began to build her own artistic support structure, one that would see the company through her period as artistic director and beyond.

De Valois had advised the founding committee that the new company ought to have a music director, presumably in preference to hiring a succession of visiting conductors as occasion demanded.[25] The fact that Franca and the first board immediately attended to this matter provides some indication of the importance that would be attached to the musical side of the company's activities. By October 1951, Pearl Whitehead, heedful of de Valois's instructions, had introduced George Crum, a young family friend, to Franca. His musical career to that point had been primarily in opera, and for a time he managed to balance commitments to the National Ballet with operatic conducting for the

CBC and the precursors of the Canadian Opera Company. Eventually, however, ballet won out. Crum conducted the company's opening performances at Eaton Auditorium, became its first musical director, and guided its musical fortunes until 1984. On his retirement from the company, he was named music director emeritus. He died in 2007.[26] Throughout his career, he fought for the strengthening and development of the orchestra, which, because of budget constraint, was often far too small to produce the fullness of sound required by the ballet scores of the standard repertoire. And even if adequate personnel were there, budget and union regulations limited the number of rehearsals available in which to coordinate the ensemble and integrate it with the stage action. Ironically, Crum often bore the brunt of harsh criticism of the company's musical standards, which were imperilled as much by these externally imposed limitations as by any inherent musical deficiencies.

After the musical director, the rehearsal pianist, though rarely seen by the public, provides crucial musical support for the company. Several individuals followed Margaret Clemens in this role until, in 1958,[27] George Crum engaged Mary McDonald,

Adrienne Nevile

Mary McDonald (far left) remained a friend of the company long after her retirement from the music staff. At the celebration for Celia Franca in 2007, she reminisced with other company stalwarts from the administrative and artistic staff, (from left to right) Seta Nigoghossian, Jenny Mah, and Lorna Geddes.

who was to be its principal pianist for the next thirty-one years. McDonald became a close personal friend of Franca's and a staunch supporter of the company and its dancers, a mother-figure whose level-headed sense of humour and passionate devotion to dance provided stability and support through good times and bad. She locked horns on questions of musical integrity with dancers, from temperamental stars like Rudolf Nureyev to the most junior member of the corps, she played for their weddings as well as their rehearsals, and she supported them backstage through the terrors and insecurities of performance. On the way, she developed into a rehearsal pianist of international renown, who worked with virtually all the greats of the ballet world. But it was the irrepressible McDonald personality that made her the stuff of company legend. Her Catholicism was never far beneath the surface. On a tour of eastern Canada, she prayed non-stop through one of the worst blizzards on record, and firmly believed that her prayers had brought the company bus to a safe arrival in Amherst, Nova Scotia.[28] In Lafayette, Louisiana, she commandeered a police cruiser (taxis were expensive) to get from the company hotel to the theatre in time to play for warm-up. She had thought the hotel a little on the seedy side, but was horrified to discover, from the local staff hired to look after costumes, that she was billeted in the local "whore house." As soon as rehearsal was over, she rushed back and moved her things to a respectable hotel across town, heedless of the additional six-dollar-a-night expense. Franca couldn't understand what the fuss was about. She simply barricaded her door with an armchair overnight and saved the six dollars.[29]

Two English dancers, who joined the company in 1959, were encouraged by Franca to develop careers as coaches when injuries compelled them to give up dancing with the National.[30] Joanne Nisbet and her husband, David Scott, formed the nucleus of the company's coaching staff through its middle years. Before the days of archival video, they became one of the company's chief repositories of knowledge of the repertoire. Scott retired from the position of principal ballet master in 1984, amid critical controversy about the company's artistic standards. Nisbet remained as senior ballet mistress until her retirement in 2002, after the company's fiftieth anniversary season.

Among the administrative support staff, too, Franca's loyalty to colleagues from the company's early days was instrumental in building the National Ballet team. David (Kerval) Walker and James Ronaldson made the transition from early performing careers with the company to long-term service in its administration. David Haber joined the company as stage director in the spring of 1952. He resigned from that position in 1956 to join the William Morris Concert Agency in the United States, which booked the company's tours throughout its early years.[31] He would make a controversial reappearance in later years as Franca's right-hand man. Franca valued dependability and personal loyalty. From this nucleus of associates and supporters, she created a stability and continuity for the company that would last well beyond the years of her own direct control.

Lilian Jarvis in costume for Winter Night, *examining the score with the company's longtime director of music, George Crum.*

On the senior management side, matters were different. Walter Homburger, who went on to a distinguished career as managing director of the Toronto Symphony and who was already established as an impresario with his International Artists Concert Agency, served as the National's first tour manager and, until 1955, as its general manager.[32] Homburger's was, incredibly, a part-time appointment, but on his departure the position became full-time and was filled by a succession of individuals. During Franca's term as artistic director, the company had six different general managers. This statistical fact reflected Franca's firm belief in the authority of the artistic director to direct the company, and her unwillingness to see that authority eroded. During her time, continuity came not from the administrative but from the artistic side of the organization, where her own contacts and control were strongest. The change to a corporate structure in which the administrative head of the company bore equal responsibilities and authority with the artistic head could not be implemented fully until after her departure.

Betty Oliphant, Ballet Mistress and Friend

There was, unquestionably, an inner circle, and one of its key members was Betty Oliphant. Aside from her early involvement through the Canadian Dance Teachers Association and her participation in the company's first summer school, Oliphant's formal association with the company began one full year after its founding, in September 1952, when she joined the staff as ballet mistress.[33] When Franca approached Oliphant during the company's first season to try to recruit her, Oliphant was intensely interested, but there were problems. As a single mother, she depended on regular revenue from her own school to support herself and her young family and she could hardly abandon two small children to follow the company on its frequent tours. But Franca was determined, and suggested a compromise whereby Oliphant became ballet mistress to the company while it was in rehearsal and performing in Toronto, and Shirley Kash, a young and talented pupil of Oliphant's, came on as assistant for the tours. Oliphant's was another ostensibly "part-time" appointment; she worked for the company from 9:00 until 3:30, then went on to teach at her own school until 9:00 at night, somehow squeezing her children in along the way. The press announced that Miss Oliphant had been "appointed mistress to Walter Homburger."[34]

Oliphant devoted her full energies to the company until she took on responsibility for the National Ballet School, and she continued to play a central role in the company even after the school's founding in 1959. After Franca, she exercised the single most decisive influence on the schooling of its dancers, both as ballet mistress and as teacher and mentor of the children who aspired to join the company. Franca had worked to achieve, in her own words, a "veneer of professionalism"[35] for the company's opening season; as ballet mistress, Oliphant examined basic technique and began rebuilding it from the ground up. After the exhilaration of the first season's performances, the dancers, understandably, found this approach unpalatable. Eventually, Franca and Oliphant worked out an alternating system, whereby Oliphant concentrated on the minutiae of the dancers' technique and Franca provided some relief with classes that offered an opportunity for broader movement and expression.[36] But some of the dancers still went surreptitiously to Volkoff for classes that would stretch them out and give them a sense of dancing, not just doing exercises.

Oliphant's early involvement gave her a proprietary interest in the company's development that she never lost. Her basic function as trainer of its dancers extended logically and influentially into her role as principal and then artistic director of the National Ballet School. When she left the company and moved to the school in 1959, she retained her seat on the company's board of directors. Through turbulent times in the late sixties and early seventies, she used that *ex officio* position to maintain her vigilance over the state of the company. Her position as a director gave her legitimate grounds to criticize the company's development without implying any personal responsibility to answer for its

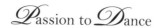

shortcomings. As the company matured, she aligned herself increasingly as Franca's critic rather than her ally. In either role, she was formidable. A woman of infinite charm, iron will, and consummate political skill, she could manoeuvre with the best of them when it came to politics and intrigue. Her indisputable authority, however, stemmed from the classroom, from her knowledge of dance basics, and her ability to communicate them to students. By the mid-seventies, most of the company's dancers looked to her as the person who had formed their dance technique and given them their start in their chosen profession. Furthermore, her reputation as a dance educator had become international in scope. She had been invited to reorganize the school of the Royal Swedish Ballet and had developed close ties with the school of the Bolshoi Ballet. Oliphant's voice counted, both at home and abroad. Eventually, her differences with Franca spilled out into the open, and she lost her position in the inner circle. But she never lost her voice. Even after her retirement from the school, and almost until her death in 2004, she remained the gadfly whose sporadic comments in the press always guaranteed a public reaction.

DESIGNER KAY AMBROSE HAD A HAND IN VIRTUALLY EVERY ASPECT OF THE COMPANY'S OPERATIONS

The other early member of the inner circle was Kay Ambrose. Deeply loved and deeply hated by various individuals inside and outside the company, Kay Ambrose was long remembered with a mixture of veneration and exasperation by those who worked with her. Like Franca and Oliphant, she was English, but unlike them, she was not a professional dancer. As an author and illustrator, she published a number of short works in England on the technical aspects of ballet, including *The Ballet-Lover's Pocket-Book* and *The Ballet-Lover's Companion*. It was in this connection that she met and became close friends with Franca, who posed for her sketches and helped her with advice on technical matters. The two were collaborating on *Beginners, Please!* (published in North America as *The Ballet-Student's Primer*) when Franca moved to Canada to take up her new position. Desperate to meet her publisher's deadlines, Ambrose followed in order to complete the collaboration. She arrived before the opening performance at Eaton Auditorium, saw the impossible array of practical problems confronting her friend, and stayed on to help.[37] Above all, her talents were practical, and she had no hesitation in turning those talents to use, whatever the needs of the occasion might be.

Her readiness to act, coupled with the formidable range of her knowledge and experience, made her a daunting force. She designed costumes and sets; she sewed costumes and quickly discovered the cheapest sources in Toronto for materials and supplies; she did publicity and public relations for the company. On tour, her efforts to advance the company and its interests knew no bounds: in Lethbridge and many other centres, she sketched dancers in the local department store windows as a promotional stunt,[38] while

Ken Bell

Celia Franca (left) and Kay Ambrose, in the 1950s.

in Victoria she successfully argued before a committee of the legislature for a reduction in the amusement tax as it applied to National Ballet ticket sales.[39] She taught dancers how to apply theatrical makeup[40] and, in the name of promoting the ballet, demonstrated cosmetics in the local Hudson's Bay Company store.[41] Before the days of resident physiotherapists, she treated dancers' injuries with her own nostrums and traditional remedies;[42] a superb cook, she fed countless meals to dancers and company hangers-on. Before coming to Canada, she had collaborated with Ram Gopal, one of the great exponents of Indian classical dance in the West, on a book about Indian dancing and costume and had even performed briefly with his company on tour in India.[43] Small wonder, then, that charter members of the company spoke of her years later as witch, sorcerer, or shaman,[44] or that some found her quick intelligence and almost compulsive energy intimidating.[45]

Franca relied heavily on that intelligence and dedicated support. In purely practical terms, Ambrose's willingness to turn her hand, for very little pay, to any number of tasks,

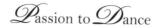

particularly the designs for early productions, helped to ease the company's perennial insolvency. With characteristic practicality, Franca acknowledged her indebtedness to Ambrose's versatile talents: "Kay did all that stuff, and whether people liked those sets or not, we had sets; whether they liked the costumes or not, we had costumes; besides which, she knew how to *sew* them."[46] Furthermore, Ambrose was an accommodating designer, always ready to adjust or find a compromise to solve a practical or financial problem.[47] But many did not like her sets and costumes, nor did they like the increasing power that they saw her gaining in the company and its affairs, as much through her personal relationship with Franca as through her official position. [48]

Kay Ambrose joined the company officially, after almost a year of unofficial association with it, in September 1952, as public relations officer. Jack-of-all-trades would have been a more accurate title; after a further year, "Artistic Adviser" emerged as the reasonable compromise. "It is understood," said the minute recording her appointment as public relations officer, "that in her position she will assist in the designing of sets and costumes."[49] She became, in effect, the company's resident designer through its first decade of operation. (This function created union difficulties with IATSE, the International Alliance of Stage and Theatrical Employees, until Ambrose went to New York and qualified for membership in the alliance.)[50] But she was also the company's moving force, a sympathetic partner on whom Franca could rely for decisive action. Judie Colpman described Ambrose's tendency to act while others debated alternatives: "If there was a problem with someone making a decision or taking responsibility to do something, Kay would have done it already."[51]

She was clearly a useful ally, but also a headstrong force whose energy could be difficult to live with. And Franca did live with it, both at the company and, for a period when the two women shared an apartment, at home. As the opposition to Ambrose's influence and the criticism of her designs became harsher, Franca found herself trapped between her roles as Ambrose's boss and Ambrose's friend. If she bowed to external pressure, she betrayed a deep personal loyalty; if she defended Ambrose professionally, she appeared to allow personal ties to influence professional judgment. Criticism in the press became intense; as late as 1974, twelve years after Ambrose's departure and three years after her death, an innuendo-laden article in *Chatelaine*[52] pilloried her, and by association, Franca, for her undue influence on the company. Franca always recognized the criticisms to which her friendship with Ambrose left her vulnerable, but she knew as well that she needed Ambrose and that her skills were real. As a reproducer of designs she was without peer, and her original designs for the company's Bavarian-flavoured *Coppélia* were admired by many. Moreover, the company, in its early days, simply couldn't afford anyone else.

On the personal level, the demands finally became too intense. Exhausted by the relationship which, paradoxically, gave her strength, Franca could not hold out indefinitely.

There wasn't anything she couldn't do. She was so kind to me — I mean *really* kind. But you see I had to be kind to her too, and that was energizing. It was also exhausting, because when people were complaining about her, I had to protect her from all that. I suppose mainly I needed her. Also, I loved her. But she did in the end get too difficult. You see by that time she was having terrible headaches which turned out in the end to be a tumour which killed her. I didn't know what was wrong with her — she didn't know — she was taking aspirins and vitamins and painkillers and smoking and not getting enough sleep because of the headaches, living on nerves, and it really just became too much, in the end, for all of us.[53]

At the conclusion of the 1961–62 season, Ambrose took a sabbatical from the company, from which she never returned. On her departure, two people had to be hired to fill her shoes.[54] When Kay Ambrose died of cancer in London in 1971, Franca cabled to her surviving relatives: "Ballet world has lost one of its most talented and best loved artists."[55] The formal tribute concealed the personal grief which Franca felt at the loss of one of her closest friends.

GRANT STRATE'S LONG APPRENTICESHIP IN THE ART OF CHOREOGRAPHY

The new company was slow to designate a resident choreographer. Franca herself, although she turned her hand to choreography as the need arose, did not aspire to the role. Barring Gweneth Lloyd, whose prolific choreography was more significant as pioneering work than for its inherent artistic value, experienced choreographers simply did not exist in a nation with no professional ballet activity to produce them; and Franca held to the firm belief that a choreographer had to be nurtured with a thorough education in the principles and vocabulary of classical ballet before being turned loose to choreograph.

Grant Strate joined the company as a charter member largely on the strength of his promise as a choreographer. While still a student in the University of Alberta's law program, he began, without formal training, to dance in student shows. This interest introduced him to an Estonian post-war refugee, Laine Mets, who, after several years of struggle in Canada, was setting up a dance studio in Edmonton. Mets had been a student of Mary Wigman, one of the pioneers of the modern dance movement in pre-war Germany. Strate helped Mets to set up her studio, and began to study dance seriously, but it was modern dance, not ballet. He also undertook some choreographic experiments in the modern dance idiom, and Franca, on her cross-Canada audition tour, came to the studio to see his work. On the strength of his choreographic potential she issued her invitation to him to join the company. As far as Strate knew at the time, he hated ballet.

From left to right: Grant Strate, the choreographer John Cranko, and ballet mistress Joanne Nisbet during a rehearsal. Mary McDonald is at the piano.

As soon as he joined the company, however, she required him to learn ballet, and to dance, principally in character roles like Dr. Coppélius, as the necessary prerequisite to undertaking choreography. Strate chafed under the classical discipline Franca imposed.

> She thought I could develop into a choreographer. And then when I joined the company, rather to my surprise, I learned that you really would never get the opportunity to choreograph till you had spent about five years learning the vocabulary. There was a very strong belief at that time in classical ballet that choreography is something you do at the end of the spectrum, whereas, in fact, creativity doesn't work that way. You must start at earlier stages. So I was somewhat frustrated the first five years.[56]

Eventually, in 1963, Strate was named the company's first resident choreographer,[57] and he choreographed seventeen works for it before his departure in 1970 to found the dance department at York University.[58] From his earliest years with the company his organizational and administrative skills were also put to use. "I was always, right from the beginning, involved in organizational matters, and eventually became Celia's assistant."[59] In this capacity, Strate gradually assumed a role of greater and greater importance in the inner counsels of the company. He negotiated directly with choreographers like Balanchine and Cranko for the acquisition of new works and served as Erik Bruhn's assistant throughout the creation of Bruhn's *Swan Lake* in 1967. He travelled frequently in order to absorb new trends and influences and to scout out talent. Above all, he became the champion of the avant-garde, associating himself with young and adventurous company members in choreographic workshops[60] and arguing that the company must look to American rather than European developments if it was to join the mainstream of twentieth-century dance. During a 1963 visit to England, he articulated this position forcefully in a letter home, arguing that New York, not London, was now the Mecca for dance, that "British ballet can sink into the ocean for all of me."[61]

Such opinions flew in the face of the tradition Franca herself held dear. Strate was, for many years, her trusted and valuable colleague, but he differed fundamentally from her in his views on the nature of movement and the possibilities of dance. He was interested, not in the deployment of the classical dance vocabulary, but in "the manipulation of movement, or the invention of movement."[62]

So Franca and Strate eventually had to part ways. Strate was a modernist, an admirer of Balanchine, a seeker of new concepts; Franca was a traditionalist, an admirer of Petipa and Tudor, a custodian of the classics. Inevitably, when he could no longer hope to exercise a decisive influence on the direction the company was taking, when its interests diverged from his own, he drifted away. But through its first nineteen years, he counted as an active force in its development, urging it on to experiments it might not otherwise have attempted.

FRANCA DEMANDED UNSWERVING LOYALTY TO THE CAUSE

In Oliphant, Ambrose, Crum, Strate, Nisbet, Scott, and many others, Franca assembled with amazing speed a group of extremely strong, highly motivated individuals, all committed to the task of bringing into being the National Ballet of Canada. Their professional roles subjected their personal relationships to severe strains. In the common cause of creating the company, friendships grew and were broken. But among them, Franca's was unquestionably the dominant personality. Her vision for the company took precedence; her image represented it, visually, to its growing public. Through radical swings in popularity and critical acceptance, she remained its symbol and its guiding genius, by turns its whipping boy and patron saint.

The team that she had assembled had no choice but to adjust to the extraordinary force of her personality and vision. Those who could do so thrived; those who could not eventually went their separate ways. This position of pre-eminence exacted its toll from Franca

Ken Bell

Celia Franca in 1951, the first in a long series of portraits to capitalize on her striking features.

herself in the exhausting demands it placed on her. (She was, for the first years, one of the company's two principal ballerinas as well as its artistic director.) Few individuals could have had the strength to take on such a role, and fewer still could have sustained it for as long as she did. The conflicts and bitterness that inevitably arose were eloquent testimony to the level of emotional investment which the early company demanded of its creators. For Franca, and for those who threw in their lots with her, the game had to be played for keeps.

Chapter Three

I WON IN THE FIRST FEW YEARS

ADMINISTERING ON A SHOESTRING: THE LIMITS TO ARTISTIC FREEDOM

If Franca ruled like an autocrat, she ruled over an extraordinarily meagre empire. Rich in aspirations and ambitions, the early company endured financial and material hardships that can, in retrospect, hardly be credited. The rehearsal space at the St. Lawrence Hall, which would eventually become the company's first permanent home, could initially be used only during the summer months; in the winter it served as a hostel for Toronto's street people.[1] The company found makeshift rehearsal locations to fill in the gaps — a restaurant, the Orange Lodge, St. Margaret's Church near Eglinton and Avenue Road[2] — until, in 1967, a centennial project by the City of Toronto renovated the St. Lawrence Hall premises and turned them over for the company's use on a year-round basis.[3] Eventually, the company outgrew even these facilities, ample by the standards of 1967, and spilled out of the hall into rehearsal and office space in nearby buildings. When plans for a combined Ballet Opera House with complete production facilities at Bay and Wellesley fell victim to government austerity in the early 1990s, the company temporarily abandoned the quest for a theatre of its own. Instead, in the summer of 1996, it acquired a new home for its behind-the-scenes operations, with the move to excellent administrative, production, and rehearsal facilities on Queen's Quay West. Named after philanthropist Walter Carsen, the Carsen Centre amalgamated most of the company's scattered facilities into one spacious, up-to-date complex. In 2010, with generous help from board members Gretchen Ross and Jerry Lozinski, the company acquired its own production centre, a 59,000 square foot construction and storage facility located on Nantucket Boulevard in Scarborough that replaced previous rental accommodation.

But at the beginning, ambitions were far more modest. It took a full year before Franca could be provided with a telephone,[4] fifteen before she got an office for her exclusive use.[5]

Ken Bell

Celia Franca and James Ronaldson in Antony Tudor's Lilac Garden, *"nearly a perfect production."*

Production and storage facilities were scattered around the city, and in the resulting confusion the company could, and did, depart on a tour missing crucial drops and set pieces.[6] The dancers, ill paid at best, on one occasion took up a collection among themselves to try to keep the beleaguered company afloat.[7] The adventure of touring took on added suspense when no one knew for sure whether or not the tour would have to be cancelled for lack of funds. It was 1959 before the company could afford even a cursory dress rehearsal prior to setting out on tour,[8] 1963 before it could manage a complete dress and technical rehearsal in Toronto.[9]

With the cumulative deficit mounting annually, Franca poured every penny into the new productions she so desperately needed in order to attract and hold an audience. But even here there was not enough to go around. Mounting new productions and maintaining old ones involved the company in never-ending rounds of robbing Peter to pay Paul, with the inevitable consequences to the onstage picture. "It is frustrating," wrote Franca in 1953, "how every ballet we possess is just not quite right because we have been forced to economise on something. *Lilac Garden* is nearly a perfect production but because we only have two sets of flats instead of three and because they are flats instead of wings it just falls short."[10] Against this background of enforced penny-pinching, the resourcefulness of an accommodating designer like Kay Ambrose assumed its full value, as did the patience of an Antony Tudor, whose royalty payments from the company, like those of many another choreographer, were frequently in arrears.[11]

Freedom to determine the artistic policy of the company was one thing; the ability to implement that artistic policy effectively, in the face of financial pressures that threatened to terminate the venture at almost every point, was quite another matter. Franca's mandate required a certain basic level of funding in order to make artistic development possible. But in the period before government funding and corporate sponsorship were accepted realities, no such level of funding could be assumed. Franca had to live with the vagaries of inadequate financing from the company's inception, and when the board blew the financial whistle, Franca regarded its actions as interference in artistic matters, her proper sphere within the company. Factions on the board would, in their turn, accuse her of financial irresponsibility.

Celia Franca's twenty-four years as artistic director of the National Ballet of Canada were to be characterized by a "hands-on" approach to artistic management. In her initial advice to the founding committee, de Valois had "begged them not to tie her hands artistically,"[12] and Franca's first contract, according to the board's minutes, gave her "the sole and entire artistic direction of the Company."[13] No copy of that contract survives, but in her 1963 notes for a projected history, Sydney Mulqueen recorded that Franca "accepted the position of Artistic Director of the proposed National Ballet Company of Canada with the proviso that she would always be given a completely free hand in the artistic direction of the company."[14] The challenges to Franca's leadership that surfaced during her tenure as artistic director reflected broad questions about the scope of artistic control

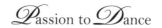

within an arts organization, and about artistic direction itself — the extent of its authority and the nature of its relationship to non-artistic company activities, particularly financial ones. In Franca's own mind, however, the issue was clear. The direct, personal control she exercised over the company's dancing extended logically into all its other facets. Her responsibility for the artistic product put her in charge of the entire company, with artistic achievement the overriding goal. The board existed in order to serve the same ideals. In an artistic enterprise, what authority could be higher than the artistic director's?

The concept of artistic director as autocrat was not new. Precedents in the world of twentieth-century ballet included the likes of Diaghilev, Rambert, Balanchine, and, above all, de Valois, all of whom had provided the "sole and entire artistic direction" for their companies. But the de Valois model had a fatal structural flaw: it expected the artistic director to exercise a nineteenth-century, autocratic authority, but without the political and economic mechanisms, the direct government financial support, that had made such authority workable. In de Valois's "begging" of the organizers not to tie Franca's hands, it is just possible to hear the frustrations of an experienced artistic director attempting to come to terms with the paradoxes inherent in this state of affairs, where personal magnetism and tenacity had to fill the gap created by inadequate support.

Much later, Franca herself, in an address to new members of the board of directors, would summarize de Valois's advice as stating that the new artistic director should "be given complete freedom to set and fulfill artistic policy with no interference from the board."[15] But society's attitudes toward the arts were changing, as was its willingness to provide finances for them. These changes conspired, even by the mid-point of the century, to invalidate the model of unquestioned authority under which Franca was invited, and chose, to operate. As business responded to the challenge of becoming a partner in artistic enterprise, business principles inevitably asked to be heard alongside artistic ones. Franca thus entered into a peculiarly hazardous position in twentieth-century ballet management, asked to organize a company on one model and then required to guide it into the relatively new and unknown territory of corporate cooperation and fiscal responsibility. By the end of the century, the board would find a structural solution to this intractable problem. With the appointments of James Kudelka and then Karen Kain to lead the company, the artistic director and executive director were formally acknowledged as its joint chief executive officers. This equality of artistic and executive directors, at least as far as the organizational chart was concerned, made each of the two leaders keenly aware of the responsibilities and priorities of the other.

Franca herself was all too familiar with the overriding power of the budget. She had, after all, seen through rehearsal *Deidre*, her own choreographic work for the Metropolitan Ballet, only to have it cancelled for lack of funds prior to its London opening by the company's patron, Cecilia Blatch.[16] Nor was she opposed to the idea of working with a board of directors. She herself had made an "eloquent appeal" that a corporate structure be drafted to strengthen her position, even before a formal commitment to launch the company had been made.[17] She was a shrewd judge of character, with the essential requisite for genuine pioneering work, the ability to adapt old ways to new circumstances. The ways that she knew, through the examples of Rambert and de Valois, represented a method of operation that could not be maintained indefinitely. But before altering them she would first have to be convinced that they required alteration, and she would never be able to forget the initial, broad-ranging terms of her appointment. Thus, though she was promised sole and entire authority in the running of the company, force of circumstances clipped her wings. As artistic director, however, she never gave up trying to soar.

Photo courtesy of Jocelyn Terelle

Jocelyn Terelle, another dancer of the company's early years, demonstrates the beauty of her line in Andrée Howard's Death and the Maiden.

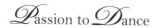

Franca's intensely practical nature led her quickly to actions designed to make the general public aware of the company's precarious financial position. In 1954, the company undertook an extensive, financially perilous tour of Quebec, Ontario, the United States, and western Canada. With debts spiralling, the board, at home in Toronto, gave serious consideration to the possibility of cancelling the tour, while Franca, on the road, took to including in performances a personal appeal from the stage for fifty thousand dollars to help the National through this crisis period. From Montreal, in late January, she wrote: "Our 'appeal-from-the-stage' each night has brought in about $350 so far: not much compared to $50,000, but better than nothing. At least it is worth the trouble of making a little speech!"[18]

Had she known the full effect these little speeches would have, she might have revised her opinion. When the company reached Toronto, Gweneth Lloyd, now completely alienated from the Toronto enterprise and committed more than ever to Winnipeg, got wind of the appeal and took out an advertisement in the Toronto newspapers, on the same page with the National's daily show ads. In it, she reassured the general public that opportunities for professional dance would continue to exist, notably with the Royal Winnipeg Ballet, even if the National were to fold. "While it is regrettable," the advertisement concluded, "that one company finds itself unable to remain solvent despite generous public support, it would be more regrettable that the hard-working young dancers should be misled and disillusioned regarding their opportunities in the future."[19] The notice was signed "Gweneth Lloyd, Director, The Royal Winnipeg Ballet."

Lloyd was throwing down the gauntlet. With this gesture, she brought to a public climax the rivalry and animosity that had long been smouldering and had flared up sporadically ever since Winnipeg's reaction to Franca's audition tour and recruitment tactics. If Lloyd's words betrayed the bitterness of frustrated personal hopes, they also bore eloquent testimony to the desperate level of competition for audience support to which she felt her company had been reduced. The advertisement occasioned a flurry of press interest in "the battle of the ballets," but Franca's public response was muted. In the eyes of at least one columnist, she emerged from the scuffle smelling a little more sweetly than did Lloyd. "Miss Franca's retort, ostensibly a 'no comment,' was as devastating as a long rebuttal. 'It isn't in my nature to reply to statements like that,' she said."[20] Nevertheless, the National's board prudently decided that no appeal from the stage would be made when the company played Winnipeg in April, and took steps to reduce the dancers' salaries for a period of three weeks; the decision had already been taken that there would be no appeals on the American portion of the tour. Decades later, in 1995, when the Ontario Arts Council severely cut its grant to the company during mid-season, dancers once again resorted to the desperate measure of an appeal from the stage, this time for political action rather than financial assistance. The tactic drew a few written complaints from audience members, but more than ten thousand ballet fans signed letters of protest to Premier Mike Harris, as requested.[21]

As the company tottered from one financial crisis to another, Franca applied herself with optimistic vigour to the immediate challenge of building a repertoire. Through the first ten years of the company's life, repertoire had to be acquired as cheaply as possible; there was no money for new commissions from established international choreographers. Even if there had been, the eminent ones would have been unlikely to offer their services, at any price, to a new and untried company without an international reputation. As Franca learned, even the influence of personal friendship had its limits. "If I could have got the Ashtons," she was to comment later with some asperity, "I would have."[22] This complete lack of a bargaining position was a point frequently lost on the public and the critics, who seemed to think that new works from major choreographers could be had simply for the asking. Few realized that neither love nor money would pry great choreographers loose from the companies that provided their creative home, in order to mount a new work on unknown dancers.

In order to establish a new, classically based company, it made sense to start with the classics of the standard repertoire. Accordingly, Franca undertook what turned out to be a three-stage process in the early acquisition of repertoire, drawing on her own capital before investing tentatively in the volatile and unpredictable market of original choreography. First, she mounted the classics, from her own memory of them; second, she turned to the friends of her past for works from the recent British repertoire; third, she began to commission original Canadian works.

THE CENTRALITY OF THE FULL-LENGTH CLASSICS

Franca's astonishing memory, her "little brain-box," as she called it,[23] produced a wealth of works for the National in its early years. That retentive memory never received the full credit it deserved. In more recent times, when the remounting of a single classic involves copious historical research and requires the assistance of an entire community of artists, there has been a tendency to undervalue the precise, efficient mind that stored away countless details of movement and groupings, then recreated them on demand for Canadian audiences of *Coppélia*, *Swan Lake*, *Giselle*, and *The Nutcracker*. There were few memories equal to the task, fewer still whose source was as impeccable as Franca's. She had learned the classics by dancing in them and by watching from the wings, in de Valois's Sadler's Wells Ballet. They had been staged for de Valois by Nicholas Sergeyev, the former director general of the Mariinsky Theatre (home of the great Petipa tradition), who fled Russia in 1918, bringing with him an invaluable set of notebooks that recorded the Russian classics.[24] For the first half of the twentieth century, Sergeyev became the lifeline for the transmission of the Russian tradition in the West, the authoritative source for the classics throughout the period when, for political reasons, direct contact with Russian ballet and its artists was impossible. Franca never worked with Sergeyev directly, but she danced in his productions while they were still fresh in the Sadler's Wells collective memory.[25] In the art form that depends absolutely on personal transmission of the tradition from generation to generation, Franca stood in the direct line of that tradition as it was then known in western Europe, and passed it on as she knew it to the artists and audiences of Canada.[26]

Her productions came thick and fast in those early years, often in bits and pieces, as circumstances allowed. *Coppélia* first, and first of all, the toy shop scene, "a very tiny little version of it in Varsity Arena before we had a company." A complete Act II entered the repertoire during the company's first tour (the Eaton Auditorium stage being too small to house the set) in 1951–52; the two-act version had its premiere in Calgary, during the company's first western tour (October 27, 1952); the third act had to wait until the 1958–59 season, when Franca "had dancers who I thought could cope with the technical demands of the difficult pas de deux."[27]

Irene Apiné as Swanilda with artists of the ballet in Franca's early production of Coppélia, *Act I.*

Next, *Giselle*, the second act only (Giselle and a repentant Albrecht in the graveyard, dancing among the spectral shades of the Wilis), in the company's first season, to be rounded out with the first act (the simple peasant girl, Giselle, betrayed by the callous nobleman, Albrecht) in 1952–53. Calgary audiences, once again, saw the premiere of the company's first complete *Giselle* on the evening of October 28, 1952. With the mounting of *Giselle*, Franca introduced into the repertoire one of its most durable pieces, as well as the role with which she would become most closely identified as a performer in the minds of North American audiences. Although she had made her reputation in England as a dramatic dancer with the cold and forbidding Myrtha, Queen of the Wilis, she would make her Toronto farewell appearance in 1959, deluged with flowers and affectionate good wishes, as the fragile Giselle. In this 1952 production and the 1956–57 remounting of the complete ballet, Franca, Lois Smith, and David Adams would appear repeatedly, with Smith and Franca alternating the roles of Giselle and Myrtha to Adams's Albrecht.

The Kay Ambrose designs for these productions attracted their share of critical scorn, especially the large, mothlike wings for Myrtha's first entrance. Wrote one critic: "Lois Smith's costume, unfortunately, was in such bad taste that each of her entrances provoked laughter."[28] But the designs had the desired effect on one little girl, who went with her family to the Odeon Palace Theatre in Hamilton to see *Giselle* on December 6, 1958.

> All I remember is Celia Franca. I thought the second act was boring, but I remember the mad scene. She was very dramatic in it. And the costumes. I wanted to wear those costumes. I was enraptured. I actually got to return to the Palace Theatre and dance Giselle myself before they tore it down. I thought that was a lovely completed circle.[29]

Without Franca to start it, Karen Kain, the child in that Hamilton audience in 1958, could never have completed the circle to become one of the National's authentic home-grown stars, one of the major figures in Canadian professional dance, and ultimately the artistic director of the company Franca founded.

Barnstorming performances of the classics in the movie theatres and hockey arenas of the nation had their grotesque moments, like the night in Kitchener, Ontario, when local stagehands forgot to lock the elevating device that raised a wraith-like Giselle from behind her tombstone. Instead of casting himself tragically on top of the grave, Earl Kraul, as a despairing Albrecht in the ballet's final moments, threw himself, quite unexpectedly, into it, his head unfortunately still visible to the audience above the tombstone.[30] But without such performances, the dreams that led to major careers for Canadian dancers like Karen Kain, Veronica Tennant, and Frank Augustyn might never have been born. Franca and her colleagues were dealing in magic, the magic that could build theatrical ambition in a public for whom professional theatre was almost unknown.

Hard on *Giselle*'s heels in the acquisition of basic repertoire, and once again in instalments, came *The Nutcracker*. "We are now busy rehearsing Casse Noisette," wrote Franca to a supporter of the National in November 1951, "although I haven't as yet dared to mention this to our Directors, as I can't think how we are going to pay for its production."[31] But somehow they did pay for it, and *Casse-Noisette* Act II entered the repertoire during the company's second Eaton Auditorium engagement in January 1952. Under its English title, the complete *Nutcracker* premiered before Quebec City audiences on November 19, 1955.

Swan Lake completed the company's early sampling of the classics. It might not have found a place in the repertoire at this point, had it not been for the chance that brought Lois Smith into the company along with her husband, David Adams. Smith was, at the time, a dancer with reliable basic training, a long-legged, classically proportioned body, latent powers of dramatic projection, and largely unformed ambitions as far as ballet itself was concerned. Her early experience had been confined almost entirely to musical comedy. In seventeen seasons with the National, she developed into one of its most reliable ballerinas and its first star. Her partnership with Adams was one of the great drawing cards for the company, both in Toronto and on tour. After the breakup of their marriage, and Adams's departure from the company, she developed a new partnership with Earl Kraul and continued her development, discovering new maturity and expressive powers to her very last season with the company.

In the young Lois Smith, Franca recognized a dancer willing to be trained for *Swan Lake*. "She was a very willing learner. I could coach her. She wanted to do duets and partnering work." Franca decided to build this element of her repertoire on the opportunity represented by Smith, the potential classical ballerina. "I think one has to be an opportunist. If I hadn't had Lois I would have done something else, I expect, at that time."[32] Fortunately, she did have Lois, and so *Swan Lake* Act II premiered at St. Peter's High School auditorium in Peterborough on November 17, 1953, to be followed by the complete *Swan Lake* in Hamilton on January 19, 1955. A program called *Dances from the Classics* had introduced some of the *Swan Lake* divertissements to the stage piecemeal, as the company learned them.[33]

One obvious gap waited to be filled. The National had no full-length *Sleeping Beauty*, the crowning achievement of Marius Petipa's career as choreographer at the Imperial (or Mariinsky) Theatre in St. Petersburg and of his collaboration with nineteenth-century ballet's seminal composer, Peter Ilyich Tchaikovsky. It was *Sleeping Beauty* with which Diaghilev had sought to dazzle London in his landmark production of 1921, *Sleeping Beauty* with which de Valois's Sadler's Wells had reopened Covent Garden in 1946, after the war, and the same Oliver Messel-designed *Sleeping Beauty* with which Sadler's Wells and a radiant Margot Fonteyn had conquered New York in 1949. The best the National could muster at this early stage of its development was excerpts, modelled on those of the Ballets Russes, under titles like *Dances from the Sleeping Beauty* and *Princess Aurora*. The company's first full-length production of this touchstone of the classical repertoire would be long in coming, but when it finally arrived, it would herald a significant new phase in the National's development.

The fact that almost all these major premieres took place in communities outside Toronto indicates the importance of touring in the company's early life. Despite frequent criticisms, at this early stage of its development the company was not an exclusively Toronto phenomenon. The typical pattern for the National's introduction of a new production into the repertoire was preparation and rehearsal in Toronto, opening night (which was actually the first full dress rehearsal the ballet would receive) on the first stop on the tour, and

Ken Bell

The Bluebird pas de deux, seen here with Hans Meister and Judie Colpman, was included in the selections from The Sleeping Beauty *that appeared under the title* Princess Aurora.

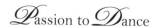

performances in Toronto after extensive exposure across the country and in the United States. Toronto audiences were thus denied the prestige of a company premiere, and the previous exposure on tour didn't even guarantee them the most polished performance possible. The tour's value as road-show tryout before the Toronto opening was negligible. Theatrical conditions on the road in Canada and in many of the American towns the company toured were primitive, more often than not high school auditoriums, gymnasiums, community halls, or arenas without proper lighting facilities and with cramped, inadequate stages. There was no network of established, professionally equipped theatres across the country that could allow a tour to iron out technical difficulties in preparation for a grand opening at the Royal Alexandra Theatre, which became the company's Toronto performance home in January 1953. On tour, every theatre and high school auditorium presented a different challenge in technical improvisation; a new production arrived at the relative splendours of the Royal Alex with many of its technical difficulties intact, waiting to be resolved in the first few performances before the Toronto audience.

Despite these obstacles, the company persevered in its pioneering work of bringing the standard repertoire to audiences in small and often remote centres throughout Canada and the United States. And in doing so, it filled a pressing need. It could not, it is true, claim the first North American production of any of these works. Willam Christensen, a student of Fokine's and one of three Danish-American brothers who helped to establish dance in the western United States, produced America's first full-length *Coppélia* in San Francisco in 1939, its first complete *Swan Lake* in 1940,[34] and its first full-length *Nutcracker* in 1944.[35] Under the direction of Willam Christensen, and later of his brother, Lew, the San Francisco Ballet became one of the major ballet companies on the continent. *Coppélia* had been in American Ballet Theatre's repertoire since 1942, *Giselle* since 1940.[36] In 1946, the British-Canadian dancer and teacher, Nesta Toumine, who had danced in Britain and North America with various of the Ballets Russes companies, returned to Ottawa to teach ballet. In its inaugural performances in 1947, her Ottawa Ballet Company presented a full-length *Nutcracker* featuring the fifteen-year-old Svetlana Beriosova as guest artist, well before her rise to fame at the Royal Ballet. George Balanchine's famous and influential complete *Nutcracker* appeared in New York in 1954.[37]

Christensen, however, had never seen a complete *Swan Lake* before producing it, and had had to piece the choreography together at second hand; his complete production was not performed after 1942.[38] Balanchine never mounted the entire *Swan Lake*, his 1951 production being essentially Act II (the lakeside scene) of the original four-act version.[39] So in the early 1950s, when the National toured its complete *Swan Lake* based on Franca's recollections of the Sergeyev Sadler's Wells production, no other authoritative, professional version of the work was on display anywhere in North America.[40] In bringing *Swan Lake* and other works from the classical repertoire to its far-flung audience, the National not only defined its own identity; it formed its audience, by showing it, often for the first time, what classical ballet could be.

Despite the inevitable compromises forced upon these early productions by lack of funds, the results were good. Knowledgeable critics, at home and in the United States, noticed Franca's care for ensemble style in her mountings of the classics, and commented on the considerable promise of the company and some of its individual dancers. Franca's strategy of careful schooling and attention to detail paid off with an artistic product that was recognized as modest in its pretensions but of undeniable quality and integrity within those self-imposed limits. Of the company's first full-length production of *Giselle*, Sydney Johnson in the *Montreal Star*, who had in his day seen the immortal Alicia Markova and Anton Dolin in the principal roles, wrote that he had "never seen a *Giselle* in which the drama was expressed with such consistent clarity and with every tiny detail of panto-mime so carefully integrated into the whole pattern of the dance." "This was not the most exciting *Giselle* I have ever seen," he went on to say, "but it may have been the best-balanced production ever danced on Her Majesty's stage."[41] John Martin, reviewing the new four-act *Swan Lake* when it played the Brooklyn Academy of Music in 1955, expressed his admiration in similarly measured terms.

> If the *Swan Lake* was perhaps over-ambitious for so inexperienced a company to attempt, nevertheless it was in the famous second act of this work that the best results were obtained. The corps de ballet danced, indeed, better than many a more experienced corps de ballet has danced in this same act. It was precise, unified, and in good style throughout. Furthermore, the very capable young conductor, George Crum, held them strictly to tempo, even in the pas de quatre.[42]

Martin also concurred with Franca's judgment about Lois Smith as a dancer worth the gamble of a full production of the ballet. He saw in her already the lyric, expressive qualities that were the hallmark of her dancing; he awaited hopefully the development of the technical skills of speed, agility, and attack that would enable her to command the contrasting aspects of the dual role on which the ballet is built.

> Her Odette, considerably better than her Odile, has a definite lyric charm and is frequently touching. If the variation was not impeccably achieved, the pas de deux was beautifully danced, and technically it would seem to be only a matter of time and training before we have a swan queen of real distinction.

Musicality, attention to stylistic detail, and the careful nurturing of individual potential could thus be seen in the company's earliest attempts at the classical repertoire; these qualities became the cornerstone of its early North American reputation.

Lois Smith and James Ronaldson as Odile, the black swan, and Von Rothbart, the evil sorcerer, in the company's first production of Swan Lake.

That early reputation, however, is hard to document today. One of the drawbacks of the pioneering mode was the fact that very little genuinely informed newspaper and magazine coverage was granted the company. Local critics assigned to the company's visit to town were frequently simply writers taken off other beats, with no knowledge of or sympathy for ballet as a performing art. But regional ballet had not yet established itself as a significant force on the continent, and so experienced critics in major centres, with exceptions like Martin, tended to ignore the company's barnstorming appearances or pass them off with little consideration. Most of the company's early press consists of news stories and public interest items generated by Ambrose, Franca, and the hard-working publicity staff, rather than knowledgeable evaluations of its ambitions and achievements.

FRANCA SUPPLEMENTED WITH CHOREOGRAPHIC BORROWINGS FROM OLD FRIENDS

In the second stage of Franca's acquisition of early repertoire, she called upon her British contacts for any existing works they would allow her to have. The international world of professional choreography operated on a far more casual basis in the 1950s than it does today. Friends passed their works on to other friends without formal contracts, and without requiring the direct personal control of the final production that now accompanies the transfer of a work from one company to another. Thus Antony Tudor, far and away Franca's most significant source of twentieth-century repertoire during her first decade of operation, trusted her to mount *Lilac Garden* (in 1953) from her own memory of the work, with just one visit by Franca to Tudor in New York in order to set a few details.[43] *Dark Elegies* entered the repertoire in Kingston on November 15, 1955, in the same fashion. But the company also had significant direct contact with Tudor. He coached *Lilac Garden* when the National visited Jacob's Pillow, the important summer home for dance in the Berkshire Hills of Massachusetts founded by American dance pioneer Ted Shawn, in the summer of 1953, and he set his *Gala Performance* on them in person. For the 1954–55 season, he also set *Offenbach in the Underworld*. (Franca would, at the time of her retirement in 1975, revive it for the National and for the Joffrey Ballet in New York.) Franca and Joanne Nisbet, the company's principal ballet mistress, travelled to New York together prior to the 1962–63 season to learn *Judgment of Paris* from Tudor so that they could teach it to the company. Tudor then came to Toronto in Franca's absence for final rehearsals of the ballet.[44]

Thus by the 1962–63 season, the National had as the core of its twentieth-century repertoire five Tudor ballets, including the two monuments of his early career, *Lilac Garden*, his foray into the delineation of romantic and psychological relationships through dance, and *Dark Elegies*, his heart-wrenching depiction of grief and mourning, set to Gustav Mahler's song cycle, *Kindertotenlieder* (Songs on the Death of Children). The National shared with American Ballet Theatre, which had been Tudor's home since he left England in 1939, the distinction of keeping the Tudor repertoire alive in North America. With *Offenbach in the Underworld*, a version of which Tudor had originally created for the Philadelphia Ballet Guild, the National actually got the jump on Ballet Theatre, by bringing it into the repertoire a full year before ABT and even performing it in New York before

Ballet Theatre premiered its own production of the work there.[45] *Offenbach* was a plotless romp, to selections from the composer's operetta scores, set in a fashionable European café, complete with casual flirtations, romantic trysts, and even a naughty cancan. The National Ballet's music director, George Crum, arranged and orchestrated the music. But with the exception of *Offenbach*, the National did not participate in the American phase of Tudor's choreographic development. It was the early Tudor, of Franca's London acquaintance, not the contemporary Tudor of American Ballet Theatre, to whom Canadian audiences were introduced. Given the slump in his own creativity during this period, the Tudor repertoire may have looked slightly passé. But it called to mind a younger Tudor of variety, complexity, and psychological subtlety, whose example and personality were to affect company members deeply. Grant Strate, who valued Tudor for both his strict Cecchetti training and his eclectic openness to other forms of dance, acknowledged him as the first major influence on his own development as a choreographer.[46] From Franca's point of view, the exposure to Tudor represented a vital part, the "contemporary classical" part, of her young company's education.[47]

Anthony Crickmay

Tudor's Judgment of Paris *enjoyed a long life in the repertoire. A 1972 cast featured Karen Bowes as Venus, Jacques Gorrissen as the Waiter, and David Scott as the Customer.*

Continuing to draw on her old Ballet Rambert connections, Franca also turned to Andrée Howard and Walter Gore, not remembered as well as Tudor today, but key members of the group who created British choreography in the 1930s. Gore's ballet, *Winter Night*, set to the Rachmaninoff Piano Concerto in C minor, was a romantic work on the theme of the eternal triangle, with passionate parts for the three principals. It had been a popular, if not a critical, success in London since its first performance in 1950.[48] Howard's 1937 work, *Death and the Maiden*, to the slow movement of the Schubert quartet of the same name, was a brief but intense exploration of the theme of death, remarkable for the concentration of its effects in pure dance terms. Dame Marie Rambert wrote of it that "everything in it is expressed through sheer movement without the help (or hindrance) of realistic gesture or mime. The deep emotion felt is the result of a moving idea expressed by perfect choreography."[49]

Negotiations for the acquisition of Howard's *The Mermaid* proceeded with almost comic informality. After several unanswered letters to Howard and some prompting by a mutual friend in London,[50] Franca finally received the following response to a letter with technical questions about the decor:

> Well, I think in general the Mermaid costumes and décor should be a bit more glorified than the old production. With the wonderful things in the way of plastics and the like that are made now the Mermaid and undersea corps could look much more *wet*! than in the original production and I'm not at all averse to a bit of sparkle discreetly touching up their headdresses and part of costume. (A bit shiny on one side of their tails and little on the body.) The weeds for the underwater could be mixed with plastic and do have a rock or two if you like![51]

A far cry from the rigid control that ensures the faithful reproduction of every detail of the original, as frequently stipulated in agreements regarding the company's current acquisitions of repertoire. On the choreographic side, Howard exercised a more watchful eye. Franca, who had danced in the original, travelled to London with Grant Strate to relearn and record the work in descriptive, longhand notes (which survive among her papers in Library and Archives Canada), the method preferred for many years by the company to any of the established systems of notation.[52] Earl Kraul, who was in England studying during that summer of 1959, served there as guinea pig and model for them[53] and then demonstrated the steps when Franca and Strate later taught the ballet to the company in Canada. Howard herself never worked directly with the company. It was a mark of Howard's respect for Franca that this method of acquisition was permitted. As Franca later put it: "I had the trust of Antony Tudor, I had the trust of Andrée Howard, so I could bring these things back."[54]

The same trip to London netted the company another staple of its early repertoire, *Pineapple Poll*, a nautical romance to a potpourri of the music of Sir Arthur Sullivan, with a libretto of love triangles and mistaken identity based on a ballad by W.S. Gilbert called *The Bumboat Woman's Story*. *Pineapple Poll* established a connection with the choreographer John Cranko, that exercised a decisive influence on the National's character for the next fifty years. Cranko was another of Franca's personal contacts, this time from her Sadler's Wells days.[55] Grant Strate recalled that he was to meet Cranko for the first time at the intermission of a Cranko premiere at Covent Garden in 1959. While Strate, Franca, and Andrée Howard awaited Cranko in the Royal Box, a message was whispered to Howard. Cranko had been arrested. The Canadian contingent had stumbled inadvertently into one of the more sordid encounters between British public morality and the British artistic community.

In 1959, Cranko's fame went far beyond the elite artistic world of the Royal Ballet. He was also the toast of London's popular theatre, the creator of an immensely successful musical review called *Cranks*, which had transferred to New York after its London run. So it made national headlines when Cranko was fined £10 and released after he admitted to "persistently importuning men for an immoral purpose" on a street in Chelsea. *The Daily Express* took this relatively minor incident and blew it up into a moralistic vendetta against homosexuals, the "unpleasant freemasonry" and "secret brotherhood" that, the newspaper insinuated, controlled London's West End theatre. Cranko suffered greatly under the attack. The publicity surrounding the incident contributed in the long term to his disillusionment with England and his departure for Stuttgart,[56] where he gained international recognition for his work until his untimely death in 1973, on a flight home to Stuttgart from his company's appearance in New York.

On that night in 1959, when Cranko was to have met Franca and Strate, the arrest so demoralized and frightened him that he remained locked in his home for the next few days, refusing to answer his phone. Strate and Franca finally made contact with him, and he agreed to teach them *Pineapple Poll*, as previously arranged, but insisted on doing so in the security of his home, the bachelor flat which had been described in the press as "almost as weird as the birdcage and chicken-wire scenery of *Cranks*."[57] "So," Strate remembered, "we spent over a week learning *Pineapple Poll* in his living room."[58] The friendship that Strate established with Cranko in these unusual circumstances was instrumental in the negotiations for *Romeo and Juliet*, which he undertook four years later.

But two of Franca's major contacts were not to be so easily exploited — Sir Frederick Ashton and Dame Ninette de Valois. Franca's concerted efforts to acquire two of Ashton's major works, *Symphonic Variations*[59] and *La Fille mal gardée*[60] met with polite evasions, every bit as effective as outright refusal. The only Ashton work produced during Franca's tenure as artistic director was *Les Rendez-vous*, which Dame Peggy van Praagh mounted for the company in 1956.[61] *Les Patineurs* was apparently offered, but only in 1963, after it had already been acquired by the Royal Winnipeg Ballet.[62] Franca thought it best not

Jack Blake

Grant Strate (seated) and Celia Franca learn the choreography for Pineapple Poll *from its creator, John Cranko, in London.*

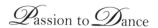

to step on their toes, or to appear to follow their lead. After protracted negotiation, de Valois's *The Rake's Progress* finally entered the repertoire in 1965. De Valois herself never saw the production, despite Franca's invitations to her to participate in its staging.[63] Franca, who was accused by her detractors of turning the National into a mini Royal Ballet, had little success in gaining the cooperation of Ashton and de Valois, its two leading lights. By force of circumstance, she relied far more heavily on Cranko and Tudor, both renegades as far as the Royal Ballet was concerned, than she did on the mainstream Royal Ballet tradition.

DAVID ADAMS, CANADIAN CHOREOGRAPHER AND THE COMPANY'S FIRST PREMIER DANSEUR

Having restaged the classics and called on old friends from England for twentieth-century works, Franca grasped the thorny problem of developing original Canadian choreography. Box office, of course, constituted a major risk. Everyone, especially the press and, eventually, the granting agencies, expected a national ballet to produce national works, but few customers were ready to back up this expectation by buying a ticket to a new work by an untried choreographer. In the national and theatrical conditions under which Franca operated two other factors complicated the straight financial problem and gave it delicate political overtones.

The first was the international perspective that Franca applied to her artistic judgments. For her, ballet was an international art form; she strove to recognize a choreographer's talent, not nationality. Gweneth Lloyd, a choreographer for whom Franca had little respect, had carved out for herself a name as Canada's choreographer. But Lloyd had worked, through the thirties and forties, in relative isolation, unfettered by fears of comparison with the larger world of ballet; some might call her work provincial. The National, because of its high public profile, could not risk being called provincial. And Franca thought of herself as the standard-bearer, bringing an international vision of dance and choreography to Canada. Even if a reconciliation with Lloyd had been possible, Franca was not about to assign her work a place of any importance in the National's repertoire.

The second complicating factor was Franca's firm belief that a classical ballet company should present a modern repertoire consistent with its classical heritage, not antithetical to it. If classical training, to which she was devoting so much of her energy, stood for anything, it mustn't be contradicted every time the company ventured into contemporary work. With a company as new to the classical tradition as this one, she had a point. The pressure to develop contemporary Canadian choreography could not be allowed to sabotage the fundamental purpose for which Franca had committed herself to Canada. She thus had to look for, or develop, a special choreographer, one who would conceive of dance in terms of the vocabulary and traditions of classical ballet, not in reaction to them, and one who might eventually pass the acid test of comparison to international choreographic standards.

Franca paid for her adherence to international artistic standards by appearing to be insufficiently Canadian, and for her loyalty to the classical tradition by seeming to be a hidebound conservative. In the period when chauvinistic fervour and radical artistic experimentation set the dominant tone, she remained her own woman and took the consequences. That her refusal to compromise the principles of her classical heritage came

Ken Bell

Lois Smith and David Adams in Pas de Deux Romantique, *which Adams created for his wife.*

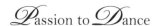

to be interpreted as resistance to modern trends never concerned her unduly. Under constantly mounting pressure to innovate, she stood steadfastly for the tradition she knew best. Her deep personal commitment to her own values gave the company a clear sense of definition, but also created a stumbling block for those who dreamt of moving it into a different choreographic world.

Only two Canadian choreographers, David Adams and Grant Strate, contributed with any regularity to the National's early repertoire. Adams had already had some choreographic experience when he joined the company, having created *Ballet Composite* for the Winnipeg Ballet in 1949 and two further works for the same group in 1951.[64] Franca called upon that experience immediately. *Ballet Composite* entered the repertoire in the 1951–52 season, unchanged from the earlier, Winnipeg version of the work. In all, Adams mounted a total of seven ballets for the company before his departure in 1964 — enough to be noticed, but not enough to make a real mark as a choreographer. They ranged from divertissements like *Pas de Six* (to the music of the pas de trois from *Swan Lake*, but otherwise unrelated to it)[65] or *Pas de Deux Romantique* (a gift to his wife, Lois Smith, that capitalized on the remarkable freedom of movement which entered her dancing after her studies with Audrey de Vos in England),[66] to short narrative works like *Barbara Allen*, *Pas de Chance*, and *The Littlest One*. Following Tudor's lead, Adams felt compelled to explore the possibilities of narrative in contemporary ballet. Given the company's emphasis on classical story ballet, this inclination toward narrative fit in well with the National's emerging character.

With *The Littlest One*, Adams ventured into the realm of child psychology. "The littlest one was the small child in the family, the youngest. She had problems communicating with the rest of the family, and the ballet was done part of it through her eyes and the rest through the eyes of her parents and her sisters and brothers."[67] In *Barbara Allen* he reworked the sensational American folk narrative of Barbara Allen, object of a fundamentalist preacher's desire, whose love for a mysterious Witch Boy turns her mountain community into a lynch mob. In this ballet, Adams used an original Louis Applebaum score that had been commissioned by the company for *Dark of the Moon* seven years earlier. *Dark of the Moon*, first choreographed in 1953 by another Canadian, Joey Harris, on the same story material, had had to be retitled *Barbara Allen* by 1955, to avoid violation of copyright. An early publicity release describing the piece as "a dance-drama based on the play by Richardson and Berney" evidently overstepped the bounds.[68] But Harris's version, under either title, was short-lived in the repertoire in any case. Adams thus gave extended life to a score and an idea that might otherwise have faded prematurely. Even the Kay Ambrose sets for the original, which Adams had admired,[69] were reused, including a backdrop that Franca remembered as being "quite revolutionary at the time,"[70] with slits in it to allow for entrances and exits.

Despite this exposure as a choreographer, Adams felt finally that he and Strate represented a modern trend within the company that was losing out to Franca's more traditional view of choreography. Adams later remarked: "Supposing Grant and I had won and said, 'Well, we're going to do contemporary works,' it would change the whole direction of the company."[71] His choreographic ambitions frustrated, he maintained his career as the company's premier danseur until his departure, in 1964,[72] to dance with the London Festival Ballet (for whom he also did some choreography) and the Royal Ballet, and then to direct Ballet for All, the Royal Ballet's educational arm that took pocket-sized précis of the repertoire to schools and community centres too small for the full-dress versions.

GRANT STRATE'S INVENTIVENESS CHALLENGES THE TRADITIONS

The other major contender for the role of Canadian choreographer was Grant Strate, whose enforced apprenticeship in the vocabulary and craft of classical dance delayed his choreographic debut with the company until 1956, when the National presented his *Jeune Pas de Deux* (in August) and *The Fisherman and His Soul* (in November). After these initial efforts, Strate quickly declared his creative independence by declining, thereafter, to accept Kay Ambrose as his designer, a move that had symbolic as well as practical significance in that it asserted the choreographer's artistic control over the individual choreographic project.[73] He introduced Mark Negin into the company as a designer and, on the single, spectacular occasion of *The House of Atreus*, collaborated with Harold Town, the bad boy of Canadian art at the time. Strate was attracted to him because of a scathing public denunciation Town had made of theatrical design at the Stratford Festival.[74] *The House of Atreus*, a version of the Agamemnon legend of Greek mythology, put the dancers in form-fitting body suits, on which Town painted his stark geometric designs, in effect using the dancers' bodies as his canvas. But with the single exception of *The House of Atreus*, Strate, by his own admission, had little interest in stage spectacle. In 1964, the National transferred to the large stage of the O'Keefe Centre at Front and Yonge Streets (now the Sony Centre), and moved more decisively into spectacular stagings of the classical repertoire. As it did so, Strate felt increasingly alienated from the company's primary goals.[75]

More and more, Strate wanted to choreograph in a way that Franca did not admire. After eighteen years in the company, he was quoted as saying: "Miss Franca and I have almost always been on opposite sides as far as ideas of choreography go. I suppose, though, that's one of the reasons we've worked so well together."[76] This fundamental difference of opinion, inherent in Strate's early training and interests, declared itself fully after his exposure to contemporary developments in American ballet, most notably the work of George Balanchine. After visits to New York in the early 1960s had introduced him to the work of Paul Taylor, Merce Cunningham, and Anna Sokolow, as well as Balanchine, Strate dared to articulate an aesthetic in which dance was not subservient to music, in which movement was supreme. Balanchine set the standard. "He could work with Bach, but he worked with him as an equal partner, if not a superior partner. It was never a kind of obeisance."[77] Strate's predilection for contemporary scores (he three times commissioned

Harry Somers to provide original scores for his work) may well have reflected this desire to work with the composer as an equal creative partner. When he was preparing *The House of Atreus*, which had an electronic score by Somers that baffled Strate and the dancers, Strate sometimes set the choreography for a passage before receiving the corresponding instalment of music from the composer.[78] Such iconoclasm, especially in the area of the relationship between music and dance, put him at odds with Franca, who must have been perplexed by the creative chaos she had unleashed.

Curtain call for Grant Strate's Électre *at the Stratford Festival. Arthur Mitchell, guest artist from New York City Ballet partnered Lois Smith (front row). Grant Strate and Jürgen Rose, the designer, are in the second row.*

A significant portion of Strate's output for the National originated outside the confines of the main company. *Électre*, *Sequel*, and *Time Cycle*, while full company productions, were commissioned by the Stratford Festival, where they received their only performances. *The Arena* and *Cyclus* were created in Belgium in 1966–67, a year Strate spent on sabbatical from the company, teaching and choreographing for the Royal Flemish Ballet.[79] *Cyclus*, with an original score by a Flemish composer, Peter Welffens, had an elaborate design that had worked well on the opera house stage in Antwerp, but caused problems at the O'Keefe Centre and had to be modified beyond recognition on tour. Consequently, a central visual effect of the piece, when large cloth sails flew up, transforming what had appeared to be a peaceful arena into a cage, could never be fully realized. As Strate pointed out, the ballet made an overt, anti-war, political statement: "It was not at a time when that kind of political statement was favourably looked on by the National Ballet. I don't know that it ever has been looked on favourably."[80]

The House of Atreus first saw the light of day in New York, at the Juilliard School of Music. Strate went to New York in 1962–63, on a Canada Council Senior Arts Fellowship, and while there he was invited to teach at Juilliard by Antony Tudor. The invitation to choreograph a work for the school followed quickly.[81] The young choreographer was suddenly keeping heady company. He wrote home in great excitement: "On same programme 2 ballets by Tudor — ballets by José Limón, Doris Humphrey, Anna Sokolow. Some competition."[82] He chose to do a version of the ancient Greek story of Electra, "preliminary to my more epic work for the National Ballet of Canada,"[83] and set it to the String Quartet No. 2 by Alberto Ginastera. The larger-scale work, with the Somers score and Town designs, entered the National's repertoire the following season. Despite advance publicity touting the work as the National's first genuine encounter with the avant-garde, it had a mixed critical reception. Allen Hughes, of *The New York Times*, was one of the few critics to have seen the work in both its forms. When the company brought the full-scale *House of Atreus* to the Brooklyn Academy of Music in 1964, he opened his review of it with a reference to the Juilliard version.

> At that time, the ballet seemed remarkably strong, and it made a telling dramatic impact despite interruptions in the narrative by the multi-movement form of the Ginastera string quartet to which it was set.
>
> But the *House of Atreus* shown by the Canadians is not the same thing. The drama, if it is still there, has been concealed completely by Harold Town's rash costumes, masks, headdresses, wigs and whatnot. There is a riot of presumably symbolic drawing on the costumes and much color, all of which adds up to nothing in regard to Electra, Orestes, Clytemnestra, Agamemnon and company.
>
> Harry Somers's new score for the ballet has few organic tensions of its own, but its sound effects might have supported *House of Atreus* in last year's genuinely dramatic version. As things stand now, they seem pointless, especially when they accompany the balletic clichés that have crept into what was terse, expressive dancing.
>
> In any case, what appeared once to be a forceful depiction of credible human beings caught in tragic conflicts seems to have been killed by chichi. *House of Atreus* deserved a better fate.[84]

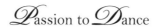

In retrospect, Strate's opinion of the ballet differed from Hughes's because of the position he saw the work as occupying in his own development as a choreographer.

> Looking back, I think that of the three elements — the choreography, the design, and the music — the choreography was the most lacking, because it was the beginning of the transition into movement discovery as opposed to movement assimilation.[85]

Strate was breaking with the dependence on classical forms of movement that Franca had attempted to impose on him. His growing interest in teaching and in the discovery of radically different forms of movement led finally to his departure from the company in 1970 to found Canada's first university department of dance at Toronto's York University. He then went on to direct the School for the Contemporary Arts at Simon Fraser University in Burnaby, British Columbia. The company's resident choreographer, always something of a maverick on his home turf, had to seek residence elsewhere.

ORIGINAL CANADIAN WORKS TO ROUND OUT THE REPERTOIRE

Aside from Adams and Strate, Franca looked to a succession of isolated contracts to bring Canadian choreography into the company's early repertoire. Canadians Kay Armstrong, Joey Harris, Elizabeth Leese, company member Ray Moller, Brian Macdonald (after his departure as a dancer), and Don Gillies were all represented by single works. Franca never concentratedly developed the career in choreography she had begun in England, but she discovered some of the pitfalls of choreographing in the Canadian cultural climate when she created *Le Pommier* for the company's second season. Responding to the need to represent French Canada in the company's offerings, Franca and Ambrose researched French-Canadian folk songs and arts and crafts, commissioned a score, on George Crum's recommendation, from Hector Gratton, and put together what was intended as a light and amusing ballet on folk themes. It was well received outside Quebec, but met strong opposition in Montreal, where it was seen as the worst kind of tokenism as well as a slight to the true nature of Quebec culture.[86] Paul Roussel, reviewing for *Le Canada*, called into question the validity of its inspiration. He suggested that, suitably revised, it might make an amusing trifle, but in its present form it could not lay claim to any Quebecois cultural authenticity. "Quelques variations animées, quelques bons solis et le reniement de son inspiration folklorique, convertiraient *Le Pommier* en un joli divertissement."[87]

Despite this well-intentioned miscalculation, there was enough Canadian content in those early years for Franca to defend herself against her nationalist critics, but clearly

Ken Bell

Sylvia Mason and Robert Ito in Post Script, *choreographed by Brian Macdonald for the 1956–57 season.*

nothing that could be looked upon as the careful, concerted development of Canadian choreographic talent. In David Adams's estimation, there was too much "chopping and changing." "We would try something for a short time. Ditch it. All kinds of people were tried, all kinds of people were brought in, and all kinds of things went on, but you don't establish a foundation this way." But Franca was laying a different kind of foundation. Both Adams and Strate thought that she may initially have come hoping to create a contemporary dance company and then radically changed her direction.[88] It is true that Franca had arrived in Canada with a reputation as an emerging avant-garde choreographer. Indeed, her departure from Sadler's Wells had been occasioned, ironically, by a surfeit of *Sleeping Beauties*. "I went to the first rehearsal to the Royal Opera House and looked at the notice board, and it said they were going to be dancing *Sleeping Beauty* for two months. I thought, 'That's it.' That's when I left."[89] But in the new country her firebrand energies burned with a zeal to establish classical ballet, to create the very environment that she, as a dancer, had forsaken. She established those priorities early, in accordance with the terms set out for her at the time of her appointment. In the ongoing debate about the overall direction that the company should take, she never wavered

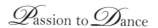

from this determination to create a major classical ballet company for Canada; if that meant that the development of choreographers had to come at a later stage, as Franca herself believed, so be it.

THE VARIETY AND STIMULUS OF THE EARLY PROGRAMMING

For some, including even Franca herself, this first phase of the company's development, the phase before the full-length classics came to dominate the repertoire and the public's expectations, provided its greatest artistic satisfaction. Franca thrived on challenge, the challenge of advancing her artists and their audience, step by step, from the world of the possible to the realm of the ideal. As she acknowledged the challenge, she also acknowledged its elusiveness. "I didn't win," she said in summing up her twenty-four-year struggle, and then immediately revised that judgment: "I won in the first few years."[90] Only in those first few years, perhaps, did the company remain small enough in size, ambitious enough in temperament, flexible enough in organization, and varied enough in repertoire, for Franca's hands-on, authoritative leadership to produce the results she aimed for. As the company itself grew and its dancers gained the experience necessary to present the classics convincingly, it acquired also a complexity of structure and an independence of spirit that inevitably diluted the effect her own personality could have in determining the artistic character of the enterprise.

The first ten years of operation represented a honeymoon period between the company and the public, even between the company and the press. In part, it was based on the euphoria of new beginnings, in part on the integrity of purpose that Franca was able to transmit to every aspect of the relatively small organization. By 1961, despite a variable performance standard, the company was riding high. Nathan Cohen, the *Toronto Star's* acerbic drama critic, had by then developed into a knowledgeable, if cantankerous and eccentric, commentator on the company. His frequent scathing attacks could be balanced by positive assessments too.

> It is a company which deserves to be taken with the utmost seriousness, and which is evolving its own character, its own spirit of interpretation, through its dancers, choreographers, composers, designers, and its program balance of full-length classics, important works in the modern repertoire, and original vehicles tailored to the talents and temperaments of the members of the company.
>
> For all these reasons the quality of most of the ballet presentations is greater in sum than their faults, however glaring they may be. There is never an impurity in the essential feeling.[91]

Strong praise from anyone, and especially from Cohen. It spoke of a company build-ing its character slowly and surely, a company whose artistic vision outstripped its techni-cal accomplishments in a way that exposed its weakness, but that also encouraged it to progress to greater achievement.

Even slightly discounted to allow for nostalgic bias, the dancers also recalled the distinctive achievements of the early company. The major Tudor repertoire, though it was carried over into the O'Keefe Centre, had its greatest success at the Royal Alexandra Theatre. Lois Smith remembered:

> The best time of *Dark Elegies* was in the Royal Alex. O'Keefe's too big. At the O'Keefe you're not close enough to it, you're not part of it. And we did have a very good cast. But all of those works were better at the Royal Alex. *Lilac Garden* was better there too.[92]

The variety of the repertoire, and particularly the performance opportunities pro-vided by the high proportion of shorter works, made the early company particularly attractive to dancers. Two ballerinas who became international stars after their associa-tion with the National paid tribute to the attractiveness of its early repertoire. Galina Samsova, the company's first Russian ballerina, joined the company in 1961, just when the Tudor repertoire was giving way to a sprinkling of Balanchine. "I did a lot of wonder-ful things, a lot of Balanchine ballets that were there, *Serenade* and *Barocco*, which I really enjoyed very much, Tudor ballets, *Lilac Garden*, *Offenbach in the Underworld*."[93] Martine van Hamel, who trained at the National Ballet School and went on from the company to become a star of American Ballet Theatre, echoed these sentiments, and drew particular attention to the advantages that a repertoire of short works held for the dancer beginning her career, hungry for experience and public exposure.

> The first year I was in the company was absolutely, totally exciting. I did so many things and so many roles that I think I was spoiled forever. When I joined, the repertoire was wonderful. It had a lot of short ballets by Tudor and by Balanchine. You got so much opportunity for versatility.[94]

Those early years, in retrospect, seemed like halcyon days of exploration and devel-opment for a group of like-minded individuals sharing a common goal and submitting themselves willingly to dedicated, single-minded leadership. But artistic fulfillment alone could not guarantee financial and political stability, nor could the National rest indefi-nitely in a niche so similar to the one the Royal Winnipeg already occupied. The National Ballet of the first ten years had not reached artistic equilibrium. The growing pains as it entered the next phase of its development were difficult and protracted.

Chapter Four

NOT WITHOUT HONOUR

The Demands for a More Diverse Repertoire

By the beginning of the company's eleventh season, Celia Franca was feeling beleaguered. The annual general meeting was usually a time for praise and self-congratulation, but in the fall of 1961 she was in no mood to mince words. "The general feeling is that our 10th season was a ghastly one but nobody wants to admit it publicly. Those of us 'in the know' are horribly aware that the future prospects do not look bright — short of miracles." The constant scramble for funds in the preceding ten years had diverted too much of Franca's attention from artistic concerns, and the inevitable inadequacy of the funds she could procure had forced cutbacks in the artistic product and made a shambles of long-range planning. Since the result was immediately visible on stage, Franca took the criticism for it. As she told the AGM, "Anyone who wanted to take a verbal pot-shot at Churchill picked the times of crisis to do so." [1] And in true Churchillian vein, she used her crisis to dream of victory, going on to enumerate the things the company would be able to do if it had "a bit to spare right now."

Her budgetary wish list included: adequate rehearsals; technical rehearsals in a theatre with proper lighting, in order to evaluate sets and costumes before putting them onstage; an orchestra rehearsal for each new work, and for each cast in it; a dancing-shoe factory; a physiotherapist on tour; a large enough orchestra to allow choreographers to use full symphonic scores; design budgets that could run to imported materials where necessary; adequate workshop space for scenery and paint frames; an enlarged wardrobe; funds to invite major choreographers to set pieces on the company. "If the above list sounds greedy and luxurious," she concluded, "let me assure you that it barely includes the necessities with which our artists and technicians would be given a fair chance to execute their work competently."

Lorna Geddes in the Walter Carsen Centre Pointe Shoe Room.

Far from sounding greedy or luxurious, this list, by present-day standards, simply covers the bare minima for a genuinely professional level of performance. Only the shoe factory has not been realized, and even in this area, company staff and services have greatly improved the dancers' lot. Whereas in the company's earliest days Natalia Butko had to prevail on Ruth Carse's brothers, players with the Chicago Black Hawks, to smuggle ballet slippers into Canada for her and her friends in the company, today Lorna Geddes, the company's pointe shoe manager, coordinates orders from British manufacturers and maintains an extensive stock of shoes fitted to individual dancers' specifications. There has been only one concession to changing technologies in footwear manufacture. American-made pointe shoes constructed out of polymer, rather than the paste and canvas of traditional shoes, and lasting three to five times longer, have gained a significant portion of the market, and are used by a number of the company's dancers.[2]

But in the early 1960s, no one would have predicted with confidence the facilities and relative security enjoyed by the National today. The Canada Council, finally created in 1957, six years after the Massey Commission had recommended it, could not supply money to the company fast enough to meet its growing demands, and refused on principle to advance funds to cover its mounting cumulative deficit.[3] Nor could it find a rational basis for allocating funds among the country's three competing, and highly competitive, dance companies.

For by the early sixties, another contender for the country's dance loyalties had established itself on the scene — Les Grands Ballets Canadiens. Ludmilla Chiriaeff, a wartime refugee of Polish and Russian parentage, had emigrated to Montreal in 1952. With her Russian dance training, extensive European professional experience, and personal acquaintance with the choreographer Michel Fokine, she quickly became a dominant force on Quebec's cultural scene. Her company, Les Ballets Chiriaeff, was formed in 1953 to provide dance programming, much of which she choreographed herself, for Société Radio-Canada, the French-language television service. Chiriaeff quickly developed a reputation for innovative choreography in the new medium. In 1955, Les Ballets Chiriaeff began performing in Montreal theatres, and in 1957 her troupe, rechristened Les Grands Ballets Canadiens, made its debut at the Montreal Festival.[4] By the early 1960s, Les Grands Ballets Canadiens had become a strong regional company, competing with the Royal Winnipeg and the National not only for the attentions of the Canada Council, but for the financial support of public and patrons as well. The two smaller companies could claim a clearly defined regional base and regional identity; the National, aspiring to national significance, got backed into the corner of the Toronto establishment. But while the Toronto establishment had been generous to a degree, it could not support a national enterprise single-handedly.

The National's early fundraising campaigns consistently fell short of their stated goals. This lack of success was enough to prompt the Canada Council, in 1959, to ask E.P. Taylor, one of Canada's richest and most successful businessmen, to provide discreet advice to the company on its fundraising strategies.[5] Every shortfall in fundraising cut with a double edge, forcing reductions in the current production budgets while driving the accumulated deficit still higher.

An inexorable downward spiral had begun. The close scrutiny of the Council placed a greater emphasis than ever before on the company's deficit; efforts to reduce it led to economies in the operating budget that adversely affected the artistic product, just when the public was becoming increasingly demanding; fundraising from the public sector became the only way of closing the gap, yet every shortfall in fundraising widened that gap, reduced the company's credibility, and damaged further the artistic product, thus making the public even less inclined to contribute to its cause; and with every increase in the deficit, the Council increased its scrutiny of the company's operations. There seemed no way out of the dilemma, and Franca, who wanted to concern herself with artistic policy, found herself constrained more and more to concentrate on financial crises.

The effects of the squeeze could most readily be seen in the acquisition of repertoire. The 1961–62 season introduced only two new works. The 1962–63 season looked a little better on paper, with six new works on the official list, but of those, two were Grant Strate's commissions for the Stratford Festival, which were never performed in the company's regular seasons, and two were simply divertissements, the *Corsaire* pas de deux and the pas de six from *Laurencia*, a full-length Russian ballet of the soviet era. The latter work enjoyed the briefest of lives in the repertoire; it played eleven times, only on tour and never in Toronto.

There could not have been a worse time in the company's development for the stream of new repertoire to dry up. Franca's productions of the full-length classics, all with Ambrose designs, had begun to look shopworn and to come under heavy critical fire; meanwhile, the repertoire of short works by Tudor, Fokine, and the British had lost much of its original savour; after the 1960–61 season, David Adams choreographed no more; and Grant Strate's work, finally coming onstream during this period, turned out to be too experimental for good box office. To sell Strate's ballets to a conservative public, the National needed the drawing power of short works with popular appeal by proven choreographers. Franca had played virtually all the cards she held in her own hand during the formative years; she could do little more through her old formula of low-cost personal contacts to replenish the repertoire. Just when the company had to move more aggressively onto the international scene, the deficit decreed a fallow period of consolidation and retrenchment. But by the mercurial measures of box office and public response, consolidation looked ominously like backsliding; to try to stand still was really to fall behind.

Even in these trying times, Franca's resourcefulness and luck did not entirely forsake her. In the spring of 1961, she asked Strate, then in New York, to call on George Balanchine. Although, according to Strate, Franca never liked Balanchine's work, she could not neglect the opportunity to acquire an example of it. And the opportunity, briefly, incredibly, was there.

> Celia had said to me, "Try to get an appointment with Balanchine and see if he'll let us have a work." So I set up an appointment. He said, "Sure, what would you like?" Just at that time, there was an open window. Balanchine was very anxious to give his works for a very short period, including those things he was most fond of. Shortly after that, it all changed.[6]

Balanchine suggested one of two relatively early works, *Serenade* or *Concerto Barocco*, for the National. Franca, who had seen neither, weighed the merits of each as described to her by Una Kai, the associate ballet mistress of the New York City Ballet, who would mount the work on the company, and chose *Concerto Barocco*. Aside from Miss Kai's very modest fee and expenses, no other financial charges would be involved.[7] The National had acquired its first work by Balanchine, virtually as a gift.

Concerto Barocco is Balanchine's choreographic realization of the contrapuntal intricacies of Bach's Double Violin Concerto in D Minor. A demanding work requiring precision in the execution of steps, a command of syncopated rhythms, and, in its middle movement, a smooth, seamless, legato delivery of line, it challenged the female corps of the company and provided exciting opportunities for soloists like Jocelyn Terelle, Martine van Hamel, and Galina Samsova. It also brought Melissa Hayden, by then a star of the New York City Ballet, back to Canada as one of the company's first guest artists in

Ken Bell

Martine van Hamel and Hazaros Surmeyan with artists of the ballet in George Balanchine's Concerto Barocco.

1963. Franca later complained of Hayden's lack of discipline, which manifested itself not only in last-minute alterations to the Balanchine choreography, but also in her chewing caramels throughout rehearsals. Franca, who strictly forbade gum-chewing among her own dancers, had to hold her tongue out of deference to the visiting celebrity.[8] *Concerto Barocco*, like Balanchine's *Serenade*, enjoyed a double life in the company's repertoire. After numerous performances in the 1960s, both works dropped out of sight, and then in the 1980s returned to become essential elements in the company's homage to Balanchine. *Concerto Barocco* was last seen in 1991, but *Serenade* played as recently as 2010.

Serenade arrived in the 1962–63 season, with the help of direct intervention by Balanchine's staff with the Canada Council. When the National returned to Balanchine to negotiate for *Serenade*, they found Strate's "open window" closed. Balanchine had come to realize that he could no longer afford the altruistic practice of giving ballets away. In

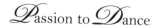

acute embarrassment at having to discuss finances at all, he requested the modest initial fee of one thousand dollars, for which he threw in forty royalty-free performances of the work. (The company's standard contracts with choreographers generally stipulate a fee for acquisition and separate royalties for every performance, usually with a specified date at which performance rights lapse and must be renegotiated.) To help matters along further, Balanchine's general manager, Betty Cage, interceded with the Canada Council on behalf of the cash-strapped National Ballet. She wrote to Carman Guild, her counterpart at the National: "Mr. Peter Dwyer of the Canada Council telephoned me today and I explained the situation to him. He thought it possible that the Council could help if you apply."[9] The company did so, and in January 1963 the Canada Council, despite a drastic reduction in its overall operating grant to the National, approved an extraordinary grant of one thousand dollars to cover the costs of acquiring *Serenade*.[10]

For the supplier of the new work to have direct conversations with the funding agency was somewhat unusual. For the arm's-length funding agency, which supported Canadian arts organizations without intervening directly in their daily operation, such involvement in the acquisition of a specific work was genuinely remarkable. It had directed its financial support with the clear intention of influencing a specific choice of repertoire and so had crossed over into the area of artistic judgment theoretically reserved for the company, and for its artistic director, alone.

In this instance, given the end result, no one complained. *Serenade*, less challenging technically than *Concerto Barocco*, nevertheless displayed the corps as few other works have done. The impersonality central to Balanchine's conception was warmed, ever so slightly, by the loving, vulnerable characterization which the National's dancers imparted to it. They responded as much to the lush, romantic strains of the Tchaikovsky score (his Serenade in C for String Orchestra) as to the abstract demands of Balanchine's choreography. Homespun Balanchine, perhaps, rather than the cool sophistication of a big city approach, but a Balanchine the dancers and their audiences welcomed. Of the many fine performances the work has received, none was more moving than Veronica Tennant's last, in 1988. Borne aloft by the men and bathed in light from offstage, she was carried slowly one last time into the wings at the ballet's conclusion. In its understated simplicity, it was a farewell to her art as touching as the final Juliets or the nostalgia-laden gala in 1989 that rounded out her career.

The excursion into Balanchine in the early 1960s was an invigorating departure for the company, a real change from the essentially conservative, predominantly British character that Franca's personal vision had imparted to it. At about the same time, Russian energy and temperament invaded the artistic ranks in the person of Galina Samsova. In 1961, the same year in which Rudolf Nureyev's sensational defection started the process of change, which redefined ballet in Europe and North America and cast it in a Russian mould, Samsova, a soloist with the Kiev Ballet, entered Canada quietly, and legally, as the wife of a Canadian citizen, Alexander Ursuliak, whom she had met and married in

Ukraine. At a time when artistic contact with Russia was virtually impossible, her arrival generated excitement and artistic ferment within the company. Samsova was an electrifying performer, in full command of the Russian strength and athleticism Canadian dancers and audiences had only heard about. Some attributed that strength to her early training as a gymnast. But she was more than a mere technician. Samsova, who became the artistic director of Scottish Ballet after her retirement from dancing in England, had direct contact with a Russian performance tradition and repertoire, which she could transmit in the West. After an initial fallow period in Canada, during which she sold books in a Ukrainian bookshop and took class with Boris Volkoff,[11] Samsova joined the company in 1961, technically at the rank of corps but, in fact, taking on principal roles from the outset.

Franca drew almost immediately on Samsova's past experience for stagings of two rarities of the Russian repertoire, the pas de six from Chabukiani's *Laurencia* and the pas de deux from Leonid Lavrovsky's *Walpurgis Night*. These two offerings had a limited lifespan in the repertoire, but a third, the pas de deux from *Le Corsaire*, established itself firmly with the National just before the work took centre stage internationally as one of Nureyev's bravura showstoppers. Samsova's version, attributed to Robert Klavin, differed from Nureyev's (based on the Petipa choreography). It had its premiere, on tour in Nacogdoches, Texas, ten days before Nureyev and Fonteyn introduced their version at the Royal Ballet.[12]

Ken Bell

Galina Samsova, Earl Kraul, and artists of the ballet in the Laurencia *pas de six, which Samsova staged for the company after her arrival from Russia.*

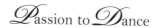

For the 1963–64 season, Svetlana Beriosova, another one of Franca's contacts from her Metropolitan Ballet days, now a star at the Royal Ballet, staged the pas de deux from Petipa's *Don Quixote*, which had been absent from the National's repertoire since its first two seasons, when it served as a vehicle for Jury Gotshalks and Irene Apiné. With the advent of Balanchine, Samsova, and these bravura pieces from the Russian repertoire, the character of the company in the early 1960s began to take on a distinctly Russian flavour.

In December 1962, mere months after the Cuban missile crisis had brought American-Soviet relations to the brink of catastrophe, the Bolshoi Ballet performed in Toronto for the second time in its history. (It had also played Toronto in 1959, during the company's first North American tour.[13]) The appearance of any company as large and prestigious as the Bolshoi was a major artistic event; the appearance of a Soviet company at this period in East-West relations added a political dimension to the visit that escalated the level of excitement immeasurably. In Montreal, demonstrators carrying anti-Communist placards had picketed its performances at the Forum.[14] The sense of occasion that accompanied the Bolshoi's tour is difficult to recreate today, when the Cold War has eased and the barriers between East and West have largely disappeared, when a Russian ballet star like Diana Vishneva is a principal dancer simultaneously with American Ballet Theatre in New York and the Kirov Ballet in St. Petersburg. In 1962, the Bolshoi was exotic, mysterious, and glamorous. It brought with it coaches and teachers of note, like Leonid Lavrovsky and Asaf Messerer, but above all it brought its former prima ballerina assoluta, Galina Ulanova, now a coach, but still a personality whose international reputation and influence approached the legendary Pavlova's, even though her career had been confined for the most part to Russia.

During the Toronto engagement, Lavrovsky, the director of the company, accepted an invitation to teach at the National Ballet School. The senior women's class at that time included Vanessa Harwood, Veronica Tennant, and Martine van Hamel, all on the verge of major professional careers. Betty Oliphant recalled Lavrovsky's arrival.

> Lavrovsky took one look at the class and said, "You know, I'm a company director, and I can't teach for nuts. And it never matters because when I give these classes the dancers aren't any good. But now it really matters. Do you mind if I ask Madam Ulanova to come and teach?"

Ulanova taught at the school the next day. She and Asaf Messerer taught class at the company as well, and the entire Bolshoi Company came to watch the National in rehearsal.[15] "The dancers' arms in America are very bad," Ulanova was quoted as saying. "That is not true here. Here they are very good. This school is serious and knows what it is about."[16] International recognition for Betty Oliphant as a dance educator and for the National Ballet School as a professional training ground stemmed from this contact with the Russians. But the Russian connection was crucial for the company as well, in its influence on repertoire and its opening up of the dancers to a new range of influences.

As a result of this contact with Moscow, Eugen Valukin, a young teacher with the Bolshoi, began a series of extended visits to Canada, teaching at the school and mounting several short works for the company. His association with them culminated in his staging of *Bayaderka* Act IV in the 1966–67 season. The company was moving well beyond the familiar territory that Franca had initially staked out for it.

ROMEO AND JULIET REJUVENATES THE COMPANY

Franca was skilful at exploiting any and all opportunities that came her way during this period, but such expediency resulted in stop-gap programming at best. Longer-range planning took her company to a much more ambitious level of operation and required proportionately more risk. As with so many things in the company's history, it required its share of luck, too. In 1960, the O'Keefe Centre had opened in Toronto to immense fanfare and publicity. The building at Front and Yonge Streets would undergo two name changes in subsequent years, becoming the Hummingbird Centre in 1996 and then, in 2010, the Sony Centre. With twice the seating capacity of the Royal Alexandra Theatre (3,200 seats as opposed to 1,497)[17] and with a much larger and better-equipped stage, the O'Keefe could accommodate stage spectacle like the Broadway-bound musical *Camelot*, which had inaugurated the new theatre in 1960. It could also give spectacular ballet productions the facilities they demanded, but the company decided initially not to move there because the larger capacity of the auditorium would have meant fewer performances and therefore a shorter working year for dancers.[18] It pinned its hopes instead on negotiations with Ed Mirvish, the owner of the Royal Alex, to remodel its stage and dressing-room facilities. In 1963, when these negotiations fell through because of the company's inability to commit to an extended contract with the theatre, the board decided to present the National at the O'Keefe, beginning in April 1964.[19]

The new theatre meant a new kind of dancing and a new standard of production values. The larger stage and auditorium challenged the dancers to extend their powers of dramatic projection and increase their physical stamina. The O'Keefe's improved lighting and cavernous dimensions exposed every limitation of the company's stock of sets and backdrops. The recently acquired Balanchine repertoire alone could not meet the challenge. A large, dramatic gesture was called for.

Franca believed she had one ready. She had prevailed upon Dame Ninette de Valois to mount her production of *The Rake's Progress* for the National. Moreover, she intended to invite Lynn Seymour, the native of Wainwright, Alberta, who had left Canada as a teenager and become a renowned artist and international celebrity with the Royal Ballet, to open the show in Montreal and Toronto.[20] *The Rake's Progress* is a highly dramatic work,

Jeremy Blanton as The Rake with artists of the ballet in The Rake's Progress.

with music by Gavin Gordon, and had become established as a classic of the British repertoire since its first performance in 1935. Its sets and costumes by Rex Whistler (eventually adapted for the Canadian production by Lawrence Schafer) were closely modelled on Hogarth's famous series of engravings depicting the gradual corruption and sad demise of an eighteenth-century man of fashion. They would show well in the new theatre. The dramatic challenge it represented would help the dancers find their way to the broader style required by the theatre's size and sightlines. The prestige of de Valois's and Seymour's names would divert public attention from the fact that this newest addition to the repertoire was nearly thirty years old, another one of Franca's calls on colleagues from her past. An eminently sensible choice, entirely consistent with Franca's goals for the company and her previous track record, it had a pleasing historical appropriateness as well. The move to the new theatre would be sealed by the presence of her early mentor, the woman who had recommended Franca for her job.

But the choice had political pitfalls. Mounting *The Rake's Progress* at this stage in the National's development was bound to raise the spectre of Royal Ballet influence once again. Criticisms that Franca was too bound by British models, that she was not abreast of current developments in choreography, might gain even more strength. Whatever virtues *The Rake's Progress* possessed, no one would claim that it was up to the minute. In fairness, the National's Balanchine repertoire was hardly any more recent. But in 1964 Balanchine represented the dominant contemporary force in North American ballet; de Valois had effectively ceased choreographing in 1950.[21]

Then, in the summer of 1963, with the company's opening at the O'Keefe Centre less than a year away, de Valois abruptly pulled out. She notified Franca that illness prevented her from mounting the ballet for the National and that it was impossible for her to send a *répétiteur* to teach it in her place.[22] The company was desperate, and it was also broke. With the stakes high and pressure mounting, Franca gambled and won. The terrifying void created by the withdrawal of *The Rake's Progress* was filled, on amazingly short notice, by a brand-new ballet from an old, old friend. John Cranko's *Romeo and Juliet* found its second home at the National Ballet of Canada.

The credit for acting fast enough to accomplish this coup must be shared. Franca paid tribute to the decisive risk taking of Carman Guild, the company's general manager, who authorized her to proceed with the project on the basis of a purely speculative budget at a time of dire financial necessity.[23] Franca herself made an impressive leap of faith, backing the work on the strength of others' recommendations rather than personal knowledge, and with scanty information as to its technical requirements. But the lion's share of the credit went to Grant Strate, who saw the ballet soon after its premiere in Stuttgart, recognized its significance and its suitability to the National, alerted Franca to the possibility of staging it, and extracted from Cranko the permission to mount it in Canada.

Romeo and Juliet was the first of Cranko's full-length story ballets, to be followed shortly by *Onegin* and *The Taming of the Shrew*. These three works gave the genre of story ballet new life in the twentieth century and brought the Stuttgart Ballet to international attention. The Stuttgart opening of *Romeo and Juliet* in 1962, however, was just a local entry on the German dance calendar, not a major event on the international ballet scene. Strate was present at just the right time to recognize an impending sensation and cash in on it for the National. Despite strong resistance from the Stuttgart management, Strate prevailed on the ties of friendship that had been established when he worked with Cranko learning *Pineapple Poll*. According to Strate, Cranko "was anxious at that time to do some work somewhere else. It took some talking, but he agreed to do it."[24] The National became the first, and for many years the only, North American company to carry a full-length Cranko ballet in its repertoire. It was the first company anywhere in the world to acquire *Romeo and Juliet* and the only company, outside Stuttgart, to have the ballet produced by Cranko personally.

The theatricality of the piece was sensational. In Act One, the guests at the Capulet ball arrived in shadowy semi-darkness, huddled in voluminous cloaks of pale pink silk; then the stage leapt into brilliant light and the cloaks were discarded to reveal, at a stroke, the dazzling black and gold display of the ballroom scene. The opulence and extroverted

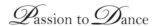

swagger of the gesture proclaimed both the new theatre and the company's intent to occupy it with style. Cranko's realization of the drama provided the company with a canvas large enough to support the lavish colour of the Jürgen Rose designs. (Kay Ambrose, already on prolonged sabbatical from the company, was not present to experience any unflattering comparisons.) It was all supported musically by the romantic grandeur of the Prokofiev score, already familiar to audiences worldwide as part of the standard symphonic repertoire. Here was a work that called forth from its dancers precisely the kind of projection needed to communicate to the nether reaches of the large auditorium. The love duets for the central characters seduced audiences with their passion and romance, but they were far from being the ballet's only attractions. It had an abundance of mime and dancing roles for the entire company, from the vivid action in the crowd scenes to the virtuosity of Mercutio and Benvolio and the high drama of Lady Capulet and Tybalt. Franca herself came out of retirement to play the role of the grief-stricken Lady Capulet. When she let down her long black hair and prostrated herself on the body of the slain Tybalt as bearers carried it at shoulder height into the wings, she left an indelible impression on all who saw her that sealed her reputation as one of the great dramatic dancers of the century.

Romeo and Juliet could not have come into the National's repertoire more opportunely. It ushered the company not only into a new theatre, but into a new phase in its development. Peter Dwyer, the assistant director of the Canada Council, sensed the significance of the acquisition. Even before opening night, he wrote privately to Guy Glover of the National Film Board, whose opinions on ballet were frequently consulted by the Council:

> It seems to us that a wind of change is blowing through the National Ballet. Grant Strate's recent period of study in New York and Europe on a Canada Council scholarship appears to have had a profound effect on him, and I gather that it was largely at his urging that the National Ballet decided to put on the Cranko ballet which was done originally last year at Stuttgart.[25]

In *Romeo and Juliet*, Franca and the National got exactly what they needed: a spectacular ballet to meet the opportunities and challenges of the O'Keefe and the other large new theatres springing up across the country, a popular success, and a significant work with which to win some leverage with the Canada Council. The enormous gamble paid off. The company, by no means out of the woods, had nevertheless turned a decisive corner. The future lay with works of *Romeo and Juliet*'s scope, not with a steady diet of *Lilac Gardens*. *Romeo and Juliet* became one of the company's major box-office attractions for the next forty-six years, eventually to be joined by the other major Cranko works, *Onegin* and *The Taming of the Shrew*.

Barry Gray

This close-up of Deborah Todd in the ballroom scene from Romeo and Juliet *reveals some of the detail of Jürgen Rose's opulent designs.*

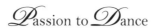

On April 14, 1964, the National opened *Romeo and Juliet* in Montreal, playing for the first time in that city's newly constructed Place des Arts. On April 21, it brought the production to the O'Keefe. Thus, in the space of one week, the company made its entrance on two of the country's major new, modern stages. *Romeo and Juliet* was genuinely new. The significance of Cranko's Stuttgart success was just beginning to be felt around the world, and the National had become a part of it.

Yet, because of the circumstances surrounding its acquisition, the full extent of *Romeo and Juliet*'s significance to the National Ballet was a family affair, little known to observers outside Canada. The first of the company's "hot" international properties, it was the last to be acquired informally, by verbal arrangement with its creator. As a result of the dispute that subsequently arose regarding the extent of the company's performance rights to it, this ballet, so closely identified with the company, could not be played on tour when the company first set about establishing an international profile. In its two hundred and forty-two complete performances, the National's production of Cranko's *Romeo and Juliet* never played in New York, London, Paris, or Stuttgart.

This curious state of affairs hinged on a legal ambiguity. Was *Romeo and Juliet* Cranko's to give to another company, or did it belong, as a property, to the Stuttgart Ballet, of which Cranko was technically an employee? In their initial negotiations, Franca and Strate sidestepped this question by going directly to the choreographer, an old friend, and dealing with him, as had been their practice with most of the acquisitions of repertoire in the first fifteen years of the company's existence. But the Stuttgart administration, then headed by Dieter Gräfe, recognized the potential value of the Cranko repertoire. With canny foresight, it saw that the Stuttgart Ballet's international reputation would rest on its exclusive performances of the Cranko full-length ballets, and that its impact on the world stage would be lessened if these works found their way into the repertoires of other companies. Cranko may not have guessed the extent of Stuttgart's international possibilities when he seized the opportunity for immediate international exposure represented by Strate's request to stage the work for the National. As Strate recalled the negotiations, Cranko's agreement did not delight the Stuttgart administration, but they could not prevent the production from being mounted. "I think Dieter will never forgive me for getting it, because they thought of it as their property. There was a condition on it that we were not to perform it in any major centre outside of Toronto. They were quite angry with me in Stuttgart."[26] The informal nature of the arrangements, and the speed required to mount the ballet once it had been decided to go ahead, meant that the company's formal agreement with Cranko took the form of a letter from the company to Cranko (not to the Stuttgart administration), dated April 21, 1964, *after* the Montreal opening of *Romeo and Juliet*. The letter covered Cranko's fees and royalties, but left the question of performance rights vague. The copy of this document in the National Ballet Archives bears Cranko's signature and that of Carman Guild, for the company. A handwritten addendum to this letter, initialled by Guild but not by Cranko, gives the National the right to perform *Romeo and Juliet* anywhere *except* in "the New York area and Europe, including the United Kingdom."[27] The addendum was evidently an attempt to placate Stuttgart's concerns about international exclusivity, while still allowing the National to get some international mileage out of its highly successful acquisition. In the long run, the addendum did more to obscure than to clarify the situation.

In 1965, the National Ballet performed *Romeo and Juliet* during its summer engagement at the Carter Barron Amphitheatre in Rock Creek Park, outside Washington, D.C., a large outdoor summer venue that specialized in musicals and popular fare. The company regarded these performances as allowable within the terms of its agreement with Cranko and did not seek his explicit approval.[28] In June 1967, Grant Strate, who was on leave from the company and working in Belgium at the time, arranged to meet Cranko to try to reach a clear, satisfactory agreement about performance rights.

> I had called ahead and made an appointment to see John in Kiel, about eight hundred kilometres up the coast. I got there to find that John was in Morocco, and Dieter met me and said, "Oh, so sorry." I was angry. They had sent John to Morocco so that he wouldn't give me the rights to do it. It was a very bizarre story.[29]

In August 1967, still on the authority of the original agreement, the National again performed *Romeo and Juliet* at the Carter Barron.

The Stuttgart Ballet enjoyed a tumultuous success when it toured North America with its full repertoire of Cranko ballets in 1969. In New York, Strate saw Cranko, for the last time in his life as it turned out, flushed with his company's triumph. In the euphoria of the moment, Cranko gave Strate his permission for the National to perform *Romeo and Juliet* anywhere it wanted to, but that permission, being verbal, only confused matters further.[30] In 1970, the National Ballet appeared at Expo in Osaka, Japan, in the first high-profile international engagement in its history. On the strength of Strate's report of Cranko's permission, Franca programmed *Romeo and Juliet*. This action finally brought the accumulated grievances of the Stuttgart administration to a head, and Gräfe wrote to forbid the Osaka performances on the grounds that Cranko had never given anyone permission to perform *Romeo and Juliet* outside Canada.[31] With the success of the engagement and the future of the company in the balance, Franca cabled frantically to Cranko himself:

> Have read devastating correspondence regarding *Romeo* in Japan Stop
> Tried to reach you by phone Stop
> Hopeless to try to unravel situation without meeting you but time running
>   out Stop

> Osaka engagement very important for dancers' morale as it is first oppor-
> tunity to represent Canada abroad Stop
> Cannot take different production now as it takes 3 months for shipping
> effects Stop
> Cancellation of engagement impossible as could mean end of National
> Ballet resulting from heavy financial loss and loss of future govern-
> ment subsidies to say nothing of dancers' spirits Stop
> I implore you as friend and colleague to bestow your blessing.[32]

Cranko relented, but only partially.

> Contract invalidated by performance in Washington Stop
> Under circumstances agree to Osaka performances but not television Stop
> Condition that ballet dropped from repertoire after Japan Stop
> Require written confirmation from you.[33]

The Osaka performances went on as scheduled, and the ballet, except for the hiatus caused by the destruction of its costumes in the fire of 1973, was not dropped from the repertoire. After Cranko's death, once the ballet had lost some of its novelty as an international sensation and money-maker, the two administrations were finally able to come to terms on the question of performance rights. By then, however, *Romeo and Juliet* had established itself firmly as a domestic feature of the National's character. It could never serve to give the company a distinctive international identity. Dieter Gräfe inherited the rights to Cranko's ballets and today, when the National performs one of them, the program credits read: "Copyright: Dieter Gräfe."

Fortunately, the administrative bickering did nothing to diminish the good spirits of the production itself, which bubbled out in the vibrant crowd scenes, filled with individual touches of characterization that gave the company members new-found scope. One of the reasons for its success undoubtedly lay in the happy atmosphere in which Cranko, Jürgen Rose, the designer, and the members of the National worked. A letter that Rose wrote to Franca, in German, the year following their initial collaboration, reflected the extraordinary sense of camaraderie he experienced in Toronto.

> Has much changed in your company? — Somehow I'm attached to all
> the kids. They're a good bunch. You get aggravation everywhere, once in
> a while, but in your group you get over it quickly, because everyone is so
> enthusiastic about the work. They all give it their best, and that's a really
> great feeling![34]

Earl Kraul learned Romeo from Cranko himself, with Galina Samsova as his Juliet. He remembered the spirit of cooperation that prevailed throughout the rehearsal period. Cranko even modified a few details of the production to suit the characteristics of the National's dancers.

Alex Gray

During rehearsals for Romeo and Juliet *in 1964, John Cranko demonstrates a lift with Galina Samsova on his shoulders, while Celia Franca and Earl Kraul look on.*

Basically the steps are all the same, but some of the sword fights, some of the things in the ballroom scene are a little different. I think it had a lot to do with how he was working with Galina and me at that time, how we reacted toward each other, and how I reacted to Tybalt. After Mercutio had been killed, he said, "Your best friend is dead. What do you feel like doing?" And it was the reaction between Mercutio, Lawrence Adams at that time, how we reacted to each other.[35]

But Cranko could make mistakes, too. At one of the last rehearsals, Samsova, attempting to execute a difficult sequence exactly according to Cranko's instructions, sprained her foot.

And I always said to John it was in a way his fault, because he told me to pirouette in arabesque and the boy catches me at the back. I said, "That's impossible. It's so difficult." And he said, "Well, Marcia Haydée does it." And when Marcia came, she didn't do it, she did plain pirouette, finish in arabesque. So I always told him that, and he said, "Well it seemed to me that it looked right."[36]

Romeo and Juliet represented a watershed for the dancers individually as well as for the company as a whole. The expansion that followed in its wake spelled the end of the close family feeling that had characterized the company during its earliest years. It also accelerated the inevitable process of turnover among artistic personnel. With the 1961–62 season, David Adams had begun an arrangement whereby he remained with the National as his home company, but guested for as many as six months of the year with London's Festival Ballet (now the English National Ballet). He attributed his subsequent decision to leave the National completely to the loss of individuality in the bigger, more highly structured company called into existence by *Romeo and Juliet*.[37] His departure was also influenced by the Festival Ballet management's unwillingness to adjust his schedule with them for the spring of 1964, in order to allow him to appear as Romeo with the National.[38] When forced to make a choice, Adams decided to sever his thirteen-year association with the company in favour of a return to England, where he had spent some time early in his career. Guest stars Ray Barra and Marcia Haydée, the Romeo and Juliet of the original Stuttgart production, opened the ballet as planned; but Earl Kraul, not David Adams, became the National's first Romeo and thereby solidified his position as dependable company lead, often eclipsed by the imported superstars but always there to support and partner the dancers who needed him.

This ballet about youthful love was a cruel reminder of the passage of the years and the tyranny of youth in the professional life of the dancer. *Romeo and Juliet* was the first major addition to the repertoire in which Lois Smith, by now the company's senior

Ken Bell

Karen Bowes rehearsing the role of Juliet in 1968.

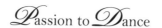

ballerina, did not dance the leading role. Even though she requested it (the only time she ever asked for a specific role with the company), she was never given the part of Juliet, which went initially to Samsova. Watching from the sidelines during Cranko's rehearsals with the younger ballerina, Smith absorbed the role she would never dance. "I learned it all, and I did it on the side for my own benefit."[39] Despite the significant achievements that still lay ahead of her in *La Sylphide*, *The Rake's Progress*, and Erik Bruhn's *Swan Lake*, not dancing Juliet was the signal to her and to the company's first generation of dancers that their time was drawing to a close. In the days before Equity contracts, formal discussions with the artistic director, or written notices of intent, dancers had to rely on signs such as these to assess the progress of their careers.

The public did not have long to wait for the next generation to declare itself. Martine van Hamel, who went on to become one of the great stars of American Ballet Theatre, danced one of the gypsies on opening night. And Lois Smith was not the only dancer learning Juliet on the side. Incapacitated by a back injury, the young Veronica Tennant, who would enter the company from the National Ballet School later in 1964 at the rank of principal, observed every rehearsal John Cranko conducted with Galina Samsova.[40] Tennant interpreted this privilege as a sign that she had been chosen from the beginning for the role of Juliet; Franca acknowledged that she must have had her eye on Tennant even then.[41] Franca was never one to choose repertoire simply as a vehicle for a single dancer; *Romeo and Juliet* was not, in that sense, Tennant's ballet. But as she had done with Lois Smith in *Swan Lake* almost fifteen years earlier, Franca recognized Tennant's unique characteristics and potential for a given role. On January 7, 1965,[42] just one week shy of her nineteenth birthday, Tennant made her debut as Juliet, and made the role her own for twenty-four years, until her retirement in 1989. Her blend of classical training and dramatic intensity set a standard that influenced the company's image decisively. Other dancers from the early days also had personal triumphs in this ballet. Franca's Lady Capulet, Tomas Schramek's Mercutio, and Yves Cousineau's Tybalt lived on in the memories of those who saw them as ideal examples of the powerful expression of drama through dance. *Romeo and Juliet*, the last-minute substitution, moved the company out of its early stages and established the direction in which its future lay.

GALINA SAMSOVA, MARTINE VAN HAMEL, AND THE INTERNATIONAL WORLD OF DANCE

The company could not afford to pause long, even at such a milestone. With the public's appetite whetted by the success of *Romeo and Juliet*, Franca made it her top priority over the next five years to acquire big productions adequate to the new surroundings of the O'Keefe Centre and the new theatres being planned across Canada as national centennial projects: a new *Nutcracker*, with designs by Jürgen Rose, and *La Sylphide*, both in 1964–65; *The Rake's Progress* in 1965–66; *Bayaderka* Act IV and *Swan Lake* in 1966–67; the ill-fated *Cinderella* in 1967–68. An impressive list — all of these ballets, except for *The Rake's Progress*, survived in the company's repertoire for decades, albeit in different productions. And of these acquisitions of the sixties, only two, *Nutcracker* and *Cinderella*, were mounted by Franca herself. As the National grew beyond the intimate company of the early years, Franca's control gradually shifted away from the detailed supervision of individual productions into planning and administration, a shift that eventually placed severe strains on her relationship with the company.

But those strains did not manifest themselves immediately. After the relatively fallow period of 1960–63, a golden age was dawning. Finances continued perilous, but onstage the company flourished. A marked improvement in the technical accomplishments of its dancers, particularly of its women, accounted for the change. Galina Samsova's brilliant, extroverted technique and romantic grandeur of style appealed directly to the public. The dancers in the company felt its influence as well. Joanne Nisbet, by this time its ballet mistress, could see the difference Samsova's example made in the training of the others:

> Sometimes we would say to the dancers that a particular dancer was wonderful technically, doing such and such a step, and they'd never quite be able to believe us. But when Galina came, they *saw* it, and that already brought the company up another notch.[43]

In 1963, while still a member of the National, Samsova created a European sensation dancing a new production of *Cinderella* in Paris. The guest engagement cut into her rehearsals for *Romeo and Juliet*[44] (another monkey wrench in the works, as far as Franca was concerned), but the attendant international acclaim opened the company's eyes, if only vicariously, to a wider world. Lilian Jarvis, one of the National's most charming Coppélias since the early days, accompanied her friend Galina to Paris and sent a proud account of the opening back to the troops at home.

> At the end Galina got a fantastic standing ovation like I've never seen before. The whole stage was filled with flowers. She could hardly walk out for her call — after call — after call. Then people flocked onto the stage. There were literally hundreds of photographers as well. The choreographer — Russian — gave me his flowers, along with numerous hugs and kisses. Thanking me for Galina. You'd think I bore her and made her dance.[45]

Decades later, with a distinguished international career to her credit, Samsova, still kept her *Cinderella* scrapbooks handy in her London home as a reminder of "the glamour that doesn't exist any more" in today's theatrical world. Overnight, she was the toast of Paris. She recalled the post-performance party vividly:

> By the time I arrived at Régine's, doors were opening, people are screaming, "Cinderella is coming!" and I had never heard anything like it, being brought up in Soviet Union. And then being in Canada where one was treated as if you were lucky you have a job. It was complete triumph.[46]

Martine van Hamel added to the lustre of this period by winning the gold medal, counter to her own expectations, in the Junior Women's category at the 1966 International Ballet Competition in Varna. She danced the repertoire she knew from the National — excerpts from *Bayaderka*, *Solitaire*, even Tudor's *Dark Elegies*[47] — but she dazzled the jury with her performance of the pas de deux from *Le Corsaire*, as taught to her by Samsova in the version originally created for Samsova's graduation performance in Russia.[48] In Samsova and van Hamel, whose careers with the company overlapped for the 1963–64 season only, Franca had distinctive, confident, even flamboyant ballerinas, stronger and more muscular than the restrained and technically less accomplished dancers typical of the early years. Their stage-presence and powers of projection opened the eyes of dancers and audience alike to a new standard of performance.

Van Hamel's success had a special significance. She won at Varna both as a member of the company and as a recent graduate of the National Ballet School. Though she studied at the school for only a few years, her entry into the company signalled the school's emergence as a training ground for company members. Founded in 1959,[49] after years of agitation by Franca and Oliphant, the school was able to graduate female dancers into the company in remarkably short order because Oliphant closed her own studio and absorbed its most serious students into the National Ballet School. Strong male dancers were slower in coming, simply because of the general prejudice of the time against encouraging boys to undertake dance studies. As early as the 1960s, dancers trained for performance careers by the National Ballet School began to enter the ranks. Following hard on van Hamel's heels, Veronica Tennant, Victoria Bertram, Vanessa Harwood, and Nadia Potts graduated into the company, with Karen Kain making the transition a little later. Kain, Potts, Tennant, and Harwood, all products of the school, developed into the ballerinas who defined the company's identity through the sixties and seventies. A few decades later, in the seventies and eighties, the male roster of the company was enriched with graduates of the school like Raymond Smith, Peter Ottmann, Owen Montague, Jeremy Ransom, Rex Harrington, Serge Lavoie, Kevin Pugh, John Alleyne, and Pierre Quinn. In the company of 2010, however, only four of ten Principal Dancers credit the National Ballet School as source of some or all of their training. In anticipation of the school's opening, Franca had said: "The day our permanent school opens will be the most important in the Guild's history to date."[50] That school, in the twenty-first century, enjoys an international reputation, with splendid new facilities to match. But the company has entered the international world of dance as well, and opened its doors to international recruitment more widely than before.

Martine van Hamel with Earl Kraul in a special performance of Le Corsaire *in the ballroom of the company's old home at the St. Lawrence Hall.*

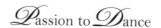

INTRODUCING ERIK BRUHN AND RUDOLF NUREYEV

During the expansion of the early 1960s, Franca established two immensely significant contacts, one the result of her own previous experience and perseverance, the other, once again, pure luck. For the 1964–65 season, she had to capitalize on the interest and expectations that *Romeo and Juliet* had aroused. In her new *Nutcracker*, which premiered in December 1964, she had a visually spectacular crowd-pleaser that developed into an annual Christmas ritual, delighting generations of dance lovers and their children. Franca's version of *The Nutcracker* survived in the National's repertoire for thirty years, as Christmas staple in the Toronto seasons but also out of season on tours throughout the United States, in Mexico, and even the Far East. In 1995, however, the Franca version, with designs by Jürgen Rose, was replaced by James Kudelka's production, set in czarist Russia and sumptuously designed by Santo Loquasto. But despite being a reliable revenue generator, *Nutcracker*, in whatever guise, could never sustain an entire season. In 1964, to follow the success of the previous season's *Romeo and Juliet*, something more was called for.

Franca's choice was inspired. With daring and imagination, she hit upon *La Sylphide*, the first ballet to be included in the National's repertoire by August Bournonville, the nineteenth-century Danish master. *La Sylphide* would be something old *and* something new. The seemingly effortless, ethereal Bournonville style relied on controlled technique and quick precision instead of Russian-style pyrotechnics and bravura leaps. It would contrast effectively with the company's existing repertoire, but could also build on the careful English training which Franca and Oliphant had given the dancers. A classic of the Danish school of ballet, *La Sylphide* had no connections with the Royal Ballet or Sadler's Wells. Nor had it been staged in North America. In going back to the Danish tradition, Franca was actually breaking new ground.

Franca had initially approached Niels Bjørn Larsen, ballet master of the Royal Danish Ballet, for permission to mount *La Sylphide* in the 1963–64 season,[51] but hesitations on the part of the Danes delayed plans by a year and led her back to one of her old friends, then the world's greatest exponent of Bournonville style. Erik Bruhn, whom Franca had known as a youngster in his Metropolitan Ballet days, received the invitation to mount *La Sylphide* and thus entered the orbit of the National Ballet, never to leave it entirely until his death in 1986. By chance, he introduced to the company the other blazing talent of the time, Rudolf Nureyev. These two great friends and rivals, sometime lovers, and constant competitors for the spotlight on the world's principal stages, revitalized male dance in the latter part of the twentieth century. Through *La Sylphide*, they first encountered the National Ballet; for the next twenty years, they became the two most formative influences on its growth.

La Sylphide: No Ordinary Premiere

La Sylphide opened at the O'Keefe Centre on December 31, 1964, with Erik Bruhn danc-ing the lead role of James, the bewitched young Scot who spurns mortal happiness with his fiancée for the delusory enchantment of the Sylph. Opposite him on opening night and on the New Year's Day performance on January 1, 1965, was Lynn Seymour in the role of the Sylph. The presence of these two international stars made the opening a major event, but much greater excitement was in store. Rudolf Nureyev, the mere whisper of whose name was by that time enough to attract the press in droves, paid an unscheduled visit to Toronto to see Bruhn and his new production. When Bruhn, suf-fering under the physical strain of preparing the production and dancing in it, had to withdraw from some of his scheduled appearances, he prevailed on Nureyev, who had never danced the role in his life, to replace him for one performance as James. Nureyev was injured himself, and undertook this remarkable test of skill while dancing on two badly twisted, bandaged ankles.[52] The sensational turn of events electrified the press and brought an unprecedented level of publicity and critical attention to the opening run of a ballet that might otherwise have been overlooked as merely a charming and delicate nineteenth-century evocation of romanticism. Bruhn returned for a final performance with an added passion that many attributed to rivalry between Bruhn the established star and Nureyev the brash newcomer.[53] But not all the excitement was generated by the imported stars. Two of the National's stalwarts gave some of the most memorable performances of their careers in *La Sylphide*.

Earl Kraul had been scheduled to dance James, but not until the company took the work on tour later in January. All the O'Keefe Centre performances were to be by Bruhn. When Bruhn first decided that he was unable to appear as scheduled, Kraul agreed to step in for him, even though he had yet to learn large portions of mime and the scarf dance with the Sylph. Shortly after asking him to help, Bruhn phoned to say that Kraul was off the hook. Nureyev had agreed to dance. Since Kraul was already scheduled to dance the demanding pas de deux from *Le Corsaire* on the program in question, in a repeat of the gala format used on New Year's Eve, he felt considerably relieved. Relief evaporated later the same night when he received a call from Celia Franca, asking him to replace Bruhn as originally suggested, since the company wanted some lead time to publicize the windfall of the upcoming Nureyev performance. For the good of the company, Kraul agreed, but with the stipulation that he get a great deal of help from Bruhn with the sections he had yet to learn. Kraul vividly recalled the events that followed.

> Erik said he would help, and Lynn Seymour came in. She was marvellous.
> Erik taught me these sections, but while he was teaching them to me,
> Rudi was behind me learning them as well. Rudi would say things like,

Erik Bruhn rehearsing Rudolf Nureyev for his unscheduled appearance in La Sylphide *in 1965.*

"Well, no, no, I change that. I do that this way," and Erik was saying, "No
you don't change. It's Bournonville. You don't change." All this was going
on while I was trying desperately to get ready.

That evening, after this frustrating day in the studio, Kraul danced *Le Corsaire*,
removed his body makeup, and got into James's kilt, conscious that he would make his
debut in the role with minimal preparation, under the watchful eyes of the two greatest
male dancers in the world.

La Sylphide opens with a tableau, James dozing in the armchair by the fire, the Sylph
kneeling at his side. Kraul and Seymour took their places and waited for the curtain. But
before it went up, they heard an announcement over the theatre's public address system
that Kraul never forgot: "That I would be replacing Erik, and that if they wanted to get
their money back they could go to the box office. Lynn, who was already kneeling beside
me, put her head up and looked at me, and said, 'They didn't say that, did they?'" Kraul
took strength from the members of the company, who had emerged silently from the

wings to wish him luck, and launched into his performance. "After the first scene, I was looking out at the audience, and I knew it was one of those performances where I felt I couldn't put a foot in the wrong place. Through the whole performance, I was five feet off the floor."[54] Kraul's sense of achievement remained undiminished, even after Nureyev's blaze of glory three days later.

And there were those who thought Nureyev's appearance rode more on its sensation than on the strength of its dancing. In his own account of the evening, Nureyev later stressed the integrity of his performance against the enormous odds of his injuries, not its inherent merits.

> Very foolishly, I took one of the bandages away, so I let the blood spread even further inside of my ankle. However, I rebandaged again and waited for the second act. I danced. I did all the steps. I didn't change or cut anything. Everything was as was rehearsed. The next day of course my legs were both very enormous, and Erik miraculously suddenly recovered and he danced to glorious acclaim.[55]

The "glorious acclaim" of that final performance was not reserved for Bruhn alone. Lois Smith danced her first Sylph that night and remembered it as yet another magic evening in the theatre.

> It was one of those performances where everything was right. Now there are very few times that this kind of thing really happens. It was like a dream. Everything was working together, it was a wonderful performance, and the audience got up and clapped and cheered at the end, and I thought, "Great, that's what it's all about, that's wonderful."[56]

The Nureyev appearance made most of the headlines, and Bruhn's return took whatever space was left, but Kraul and Smith, buoyed up by the excitement of the superstars' presence, captured their own places in the hearts of the audience that knew them well.

The company as a whole stood up well under the intense glare of the publicity. Both Ralph Hicklin and Nathan Cohen singled out Lois Smith for special praise. (Cohen found her to be generally more persuasive than Seymour.)[57] Cohen, who would savage the company's dancing in *Romeo and Juliet* the very next day, summed up the closing night of *La Sylphide* with carefully chosen words of praise: "Altogether it was a moving performance. It reached the heights of grandeur when Mr. Bruhn was the centre of the action, and it never lied or deteriorated into the chic or trivial."[58]

Offstage as well as on, it was a heady holiday season. The company premiered three new productions (*Nutcracker*, *Sylphide*, and Grant Strate's *Triptych*) within the space of

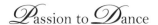
ten days. Celebrating this extraordinary achievement, and the New Year, with them were Erik Bruhn, Lynn Seymour, Rudolf Nureyev, Frank Schaufuss (Martine van Hamel's partner for *Nutcracker*), and his son, Peter, both from the Royal Danish Ballet. Peter Schaufuss later returned to dance with the National for two separate periods, once as a promising beginner in 1967–69, and again as an established star from 1977 to 1984. For the younger Schaufuss, it was quite a New Year's Eve.

> I had just started smoking, very young, and Rudolf and Erik were trying to convince me that you shouldn't smoke, you should drink whisky instead. On the New Year's Eve they showed me how to drink whisky, and I was sick for three days afterward. Ever since I have never smoked, and I haven't really been drinking either.[59]

In all this hullabaloo, no one cared very much that the National narrowly missed out on the distinction of mounting North America's first *La Sylphide*. American Ballet Theatre stole the march on them with the premiere of their production, staged by Harald Lander, in San Antonio, Texas, on November 11, 1964, just a month and a half before the National began its eventful first run of the work.[60]

ERIK BRUHN'S RADICAL *SWAN LAKE*

The need for a new *Swan Lake* to replace the worn-out Franca-Ambrose production had been decisively demonstrated by a brief run at the O'Keefe Centre in 1964. In the new theatre, the old warhorse had shown its age; it should no longer be trotted out. Furthermore, the fairy-tale drama of the brooding young prince, the enchanted princess transformed into a swan, and the evil sorcerer who controls their fate was by this time well-known to Toronto audiences in versions other than the National's. In recent years, they had had ample opportunity to see *Swan Lake* danced by three major visiting companies — the Bolshoi in 1959 and 1962, the Royal Ballet in 1961, 1963, and 1965, and the Kirov Ballet in 1961 and 1964.[61] These international comparisons increased the need for a production of large scale and ambitious scope.

By returning to Bruhn with the commission, Franca hoped, as with *La Sylphide*, to gain a fresh, new perspective on an old classic. Bruhn's long-standing desire to give more prominence to the role of Prince Siegfried,[62] as well as his success with *La Sylphide*, augured well for the project. Desmond Heeley's rising reputation at the Stratford Festival made him an obvious choice to provide the opulent designs. Even the Tchaikovsky score would be reconsidered and revised to fit Bruhn's conception of the work. The new *Swan Lake* became the company's major new production for Canada's centennial year and the

Erik Bruhn as Prince Siegfried in CBC Filming of Swan Lake.

National's appearances at Expo 67. The world premiere in Toronto, on March 27, 1967, was one of the most eagerly awaited in the company's history. With this production, Bruhn gave the National an intensely personal statement, a revisionist *Swan Lake* that created controversy from the very beginning.

One of the ways in which Bruhn sought to strengthen the figure of the Prince was by giving him a lyrical and murderously difficult new solo in Act I to establish his introspective character. Once again, Earl Kraul had the unenviable task of following in Bruhn's footsteps.

> It was really difficult to do. Erik designed it on himself. He looked posi-
> tively magnificent doing it, and I didn't have that kind of line. Partnering

was my forte. I could jump. I had a lot of strength and energy. But I had to work really hard to get a good line on my body all the time, and I found that type of solo very difficult to pull off.[63]

According to Rudolf Nureyev, that solo had an interesting genesis. In 1964, Bruhn had been present in Vienna when Nureyev staged a complete *Swan Lake*. Even earlier, however, in 1963, Bruhn had seen the controversial solo for Prince Siegfried that Nureyev choreographed for the Royal Ballet.[64] Bruhn had originally sided with the critical opinion of the time that dismissed this interpolation into the Petipa original, but later, according to Nureyev, changed his mind.

> Suddenly he got excited, after he'd seen it two or three years. He saw that it worked and it did portray the mood of prince — brooding, melancholy — that essentially prepares for the event of white swans by the lake and makes him unique. So he used the same solo again, with his own modifications.[65]

In the Act I solo, then, Kraul and the Siegfrieds who came after him wrestled with choreography born of the formidable combination of Bruhn line and Nureyev virtuosity. In later casts, Jeremy Ransom came closer than any of them to recapturing the spirit of the original. It was only one of many places where the highly individual nature of Bruhn's choreography made the production resistant to the personalities of dancers other than the original cast.

The Nureyev influence went deep. At the beginning of the project, Bruhn considered, briefly, doing a collaborative production with his friend. Before any contracts were signed, however, he changed his mind. In October 1965, Grant Strate reported to Celia Franca on a meeting he had had about the project with Bruhn in Montreal: "Bruhn would now rather stage *Swan Lake* alone without Nureyev. He thinks this collaboration could work artistically, but in practice the physical difficulties of getting together are too great."[66] But though the idea of collaboration came to nothing, the fact of Nureyev's earlier version of the ballet, and Bruhn's familiarity with it, remained. According to Nureyev, Bruhn adopted the musical cuts and revisions to the score that he himself had used in Vienna.[67] When Nureyev, in later years, came to dance the Prince, he obtained Bruhn's permission to revert to some of the traditional choreography. In 1977, on tour in Los Angeles, Nureyev was quoted on the subject.

> We have made some modifications, with Bruhn's permission. I asked to dance the original pas de deux, and he didn't object. And in the last act, I use my own choreography. Erik had modelled his on mine anyway, so I said, "Why not go whole hog?"[68]

PHOTO: MIRA

Vanessa Harwood and Sergiu Stefanschi in the Black Swan pas de deux from Erik Bruhn's production of Swan Lake.

Going "whole hog" meant that many audiences saw the Bruhn original with a Nureyev facelift. Over its lifespan, the Bruhn *Swan Lake* probably sustained more of this kind of tinkering than any other production in the National's repertoire.

Two important aspects of the production, however, were Bruhn's and Bruhn's alone. One was the conflation of the original four-act action into two acts of two scenes each. The swift, smooth transition in each act from court to lakeside, without the interruption of a curtain, gave the production dramatic momentum and focused attention on the emotional conflict of the Prince, caught between the forces these two worlds represent. Bruhn had to insist in order to make this radical innovation in the staging of the ballet. The arguments against it were purely practical. Could the elaborate scene change and the necessary costume changes be accomplished in the brief space of time allowed by the music that would be used for the transition? The Black Swan had to change back into the Swan Queen's white tutu, and virtually all the court ladies had to transform themselves into swans once again. Would the second act, without intermission, prove too gruelling a test of the lead dancers' stamina? Even if these problems could be solved, would the two

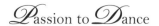

large acts prove too long for the audience's attention span?[69] Bruhn's insistence, and the technical ingenuity of the production staff, carried the day. Audiences did not notice that the court ladies, one by one, slipped discreetly out of the ballroom scene in order to undo the hooks on the backs of their costumes, careful not to turn their backs on the spectators after their return. Only with this preparation could they manage the quick change necessary for the last lakeside scene. The two-act presentation of *Swan Lake*, which seemed impossible until Bruhn insisted on it, proved one of the most attractive features of the production, and has been widely imitated by others, among them Rudolf Nureyev in his production for the Ballet of the Paris Opéra.[70] When James Kudelka mounted his version of *Swan Lake* for the National in 1999, the printed program acknowledged the ballet's four-act structure, but the single intermission between Acts II and III essentially retained Bruhn's two-part format.

The other distinguishing Bruhn trademark in this production was the transformation of von Rothbart, the evil genius in control of the swans, into a woman. Precedent for the change existed in Myrtha and Carabosse, the other arch-villains of classical ballet, both of them women, but those closely associated with the production believed the change had been motivated by something deep within Bruhn's own personality, not by any desire for conformity with the rest of the canon. Grant Strate worked with Bruhn as the artistic coordinator of the project and watched the idea of a female von Rothbart grow from its inception. "That had a lot to do with his own psychology, his own background, his own Danish attitude toward life."[71] Celia Franca concurred. The entire conception of the character "was very, very psychological and something deep inside him that I think probably Freud couldn't analyse."[72] However complicated the origins of the idea, it never worked in performance. Strate, who worked through the scenario in detail with Bruhn, had great difficulty in making him develop the Black Queen (as von Rothbart was rechristened) as a character and as a choreographic entity beyond his initial idea. At a planning session in Rome, where Bruhn was mounting *La Sylphide*, Strate tried to make Bruhn come to terms with the conception.

> I spent four days talking to Erik, and we still hadn't gotten to the essential thing. He wanted von Rothbart to be a woman, but he didn't know what that woman should do. And when he choreographed the ballet, he still didn't know. I was trying to force him to materialize that concept. It was the weak point of the ballet, a female doing a male role.

Franca, the first of the Black Queens, was given the role and then left largely to her own devices to work it out.[73] The part rode on the strength of her own considerable dramatic presence, rather than on Bruhn's choreography or detailed elaboration of the character.

It was only strength of personality that got anything across, just sheer physical and emotional personality. I used to be worn out at the end of it, trying to make it look convincing, but I couldn't get the character in my own mind. I couldn't understand what Erik was getting at.[74]

After Franca left the role, Bruhn took to tinkering with it in an attempt to make it work. He had Desmond Heeley design a new costume and, when Ann Ditchburn took the part, put her on pointe,[75] but nothing seemed to work.

Bruhn's Black Queen baffled many of those who took her on. Lois Smith danced her only once, on the occasion of "Lois Smith Night," her farewell appearance with the National on November 24, 1969. "I didn't have very much rehearsal on it. In that fourth act you were in and out and around, running here and running there, and up and down lines, and it was always, 'Where the hell do I go next?'"[76] Probably no dancer, other than Franca, had more experience in the role than Victoria Bertram, who, during a career spanning forty-seven years, from 1963 to her retirement in 2010, worked her way through the ranks to that of principal character artist, specializing in the character roles that so frequently provide crucial dramatic motivation and continuity in the story ballets. The Black Queen presented her with one of the enduring challenges of her career. "I tried to make it work. I really tried to connect the thing to get a thread of the Black Queen through it. I wanted to make it a little bit more interesting and I wanted to dig down a little bit and see if I could find a whole other side." Even though Bruhn complimented Bertram warmly on her conception of the role, she herself remained dissatisfied. "He was quite pleased with that. I don't feel happy about it, but I feel that there's something there and if I keep hammering at it, maybe — ."[77] Bruhn relied too heavily on the force of Franca's own personality in creating the original to give it the choreographic substance it required. A challenge for Franca, the Black Queen remained an enigma to those who came after her, a graphic reminder of the importance of character roles in classical ballet. But despite its shortcomings, Bruhn's *Swan Lake* flourished in the repertoire. When it was replaced with Kudelka's startling new production in 1999, some diehard fans lamented the loss of the Bruhn version, which for them had taken on the status of an old standard.

THE HIGH COSTS OF MOUNTING *CINDERELLA*

A crueller fate awaited *Cinderella*, which entered the repertoire one year after *Swan Lake*, in 1968. The Prokofiev score for this full-length ballet, not nearly as well-known or popular as his *Romeo and Juliet*, had inspired major Soviet productions in Moscow and Leningrad (with choreography by Konstantin Sergeyev) and Sir Frederick Ashton's famous version for the Sadler's Wells Theatre Ballet (1948), revived at the Royal Ballet

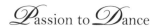

in 1965 with Ashton and Sir Robert Helpmann dancing the roles of the ugly stepsisters. Franca undertook the choreography of the National's *Cinderella* herself, with an acute awareness of the company's straitened circumstances. "I probably wouldn't be choreographing *Cinderella* at all except that it's cheaper if I do it. You can't ask Sir Frederick Ashton when you don't know until the last minute if the money will be available."[78] Such awareness could not work to her advantage. Since the National had become a larger organization, her role as artistic director placed her in an invidious position as a creative artist. Administrative responsibility prevented her from allowing artistic ego a free rein. As artistic director, Franca had been able to act as a buffer between the board, with its responsibility for financial prudence, and Cranko or Bruhn, whose primary concern was for the artistic product. As choreographer, she had no one to run similar interference for her. And as artistic director, she did not receive the payment for her choreography that any outsider demanded as a matter of course. The question of performance royalties for *The Nutcracker*, for example, the National's perennial money-maker, was not even raised until after she had left the company.[79] She was the available house choreographer, and her services were more or less taken for granted.

From the outset, financial difficulties bedevilled Franca's *Cinderella*. At a hundred thousand dollars, its budget was uncomfortably high. Then illness prevented Jürgen Rose from meeting some of the design deadlines, and expenses rose by another ten thousand. When Franca requested a further nine thousand, the board's Executive Committee declined her request, unless equivalent savings could be realized elsewhere.[80] The board had just moved away from its practice of amortizing the cost of a new production over a three-year period; thus all the production costs for *Cinderella* had to be charged within a single, disastrous, financial year.[81] At precisely that time, the Canada Council's scrutiny of the rising cumulative deficit placed the board under intense pressure. Once again, talk of retrenchment filled the air.[82]

Under these clouds of mounting tension, Franca's *Cinderella* opened at the O'Keefe Centre on April 15, 1968. There was some cause for rejoicing. No less a critic than Clive Barnes wrote in the pages of *The New York Times*:

> Lavishness, spectacle or simple extravagance are not always associated with our neighbor Canada. Yet within the last few years the National Ballet of Canada has, almost unobtrusively, become the most elaborately mounted ballet company in North America. This *Cinderella* is the most sumptuous looking ballet ever produced in North America.[83]

Writing in the *Telegram*, Ralph Hicklin maintained: "Franca has come much closer to the spirit of the music, and to the unique *féerie* implicit in the mythic world of Cinderella, than Frederick Ashton or Konstantin Sergeyev, creators of the only other versions I have seen of this ballet."[84] But there the praise stopped. Barnes's review went on to castigate Franca's choreography:

> The choreography rarely enchanted or amazed. It had, of course, class-room competence, but little theatrical magic. I have certain reservations about Frederick Ashton's version for the Royal Ballet, but compared with this Franca version it is outstanding. There are errors of judgment in the Ashton (it was his first full-evening work), but there are also many moments of genius entirely lacking in this Canadian production.[85]

Significant critical response to this, Franca's first original, full-length work and the first production of *Cinderella* by a North American company, was lukewarm at best. At worst, it amounted to a backlash against the very lavishness and spectacle that had won

Nadia Potts and Hazaros Surmeyan in a tableau from Celia Franca's 1968 production of Cinderella, *with sets and costumes by Jürgen Rose.*

Barnes's honest admiration. Wendy Michener, writing in the *Globe and Mail*, gave voice to a point of view that would make itself increasingly heard:

> Just what purpose it serves for the National or the Canadian public at this time I can't see, unless the directors have concluded from the successes of *Swan Lake* and *Romeo and Juliet* that traditional spectacles are all their public really wants from them.[86]

She, too, went on to lament the absence of choreography sufficiently inspired to justify the spectacle.

Cinderella received only thirteen complete performances (the Act II pas de deux appeared by itself on a few mixed programs) before being retired from the active repertoire. Most of its costumes were destroyed in the fire of 1973.[87] But *Cinderella*'s story did not end in ignominy. The production was taped for television, its choreography appropriately modified by Franca for the demands of a different medium.[88] In this version, it won an Emmy in 1970, in the category of Best Classical Musical Production. The irony of the award, given the production's reception just two years previously, must have cut deep. A rental production of *Cinderella*, by Ben Stevenson, the artistic director of the Houston Ballet, entered the repertoire briefly in 1995, long after the memories of Franca's version had faded. For the National, the ballet seemed jinxed until James Kudelka took it on in 2004, near the end of his tenure as artistic director of the company.

ORIGINAL CHOREOGRAPHY FAILED TO EXCITE THE PUBLIC

Franca's heavy personal involvement in *Cinderella* undercut her overall reputation as artistic director during this crucial period. The contempt for "traditional spectacles," evident in critical comment like Michener's, attached itself, perhaps unfairly, to Franca's artistic policies. She was thought of as the conservative opponent of radical, new choreography, choreography that relied less heavily on production values for its effects. While the bulk of her energy in the 1960s had undeniably gone into the development of the spectacular, "O'Keefe Centred" repertoire, her record was not entirely one-sided. The company produced original works during this period too.

It had its greatest investment, in creative terms, in Grant Strate. His period as apprentice in the vocabulary of classical ballet long since over, he produced the bulk of his output during the sixties. But despite considerable time and energy spent in mounting these works, Strate's ballets failed to find a large public. As his ideas about movement took him further and further away from the methods and assumptions of classical ballet, Strate's work became peripheral to the company's main interests. In 1969, he was in Stockholm, at Erik Bruhn's invitation, working with the Royal Swedish Ballet, of which Bruhn was then the artistic director. In a letter to Franca, Bruhn reported on the work in progress:

> I saw his ballets today for the first time. Though it is hard to judge from a first orchestra rehearsal I still feel he has not developed choreographically as much as I had hoped. Though my company is not the greatest they have on other occasions responded better, however it all might pull itself more together before the premiere.[89]

Strate had great difficulty discovering a genuinely distinctive style of movement. Of only one section of his *Triptych*, for example, could Ralph Hicklin say, "We can think of their dance as Strate movement, not just dance movement."[90] The demands of the large theatre and its conservative audience were also a problem. Strate took greater pleasure in experiment, working with the radical, younger members of the company to challenge accepted ideas of movement, than in conventional choreography. The smaller-scale surroundings of the Stratford Festival or Ballet Concert, the company's small touring group, provided a more suitable creative environment for him. He did not become the major source of original choreography that the full company needed.

With hopes for Strate's development on the wane, and no other potential resident choreographer in the wings, Franca looked to guest choreographers to supply original repertoire that could succeed at the box office. The search was scattered and, by and large, unsuccessful. Commissioned works by Zachary Solov, Heinz Poll, Daniel Seillier (then ballet master with the company), and Heino Heiden filled up programs but took the company in no single, distinctive direction. Guest choreographers could not know the company members well enough to choreograph to their particular talents and capabilities. Their work could not spring from a close, continuing relationship with the dancers. Heino Heiden's *La Prima Ballerina*, an elaborate dramatization of events from the life of the nineteenth-century dancer Marie Taglioni, played like a send-up rather than the serious drama it was intended to be.[91] Its utter failure, in the same season with *Cinderella*, cast a gloomy pall over the company's reputation for encouraging original work. The issuing of another stern warning from the Canada Council about "the necessity of beginning an effective debt retirement plan"[92] sounded an ominously familiar note. The decade would apparently close, as it had opened, gloomily.

1968: Franca Precipitates a Crisis

The 1960s ended, as far as the National Ballet of Canada was concerned, on November 15, 1968, precisely seven months after the opening of *Cinderella*. On that day, the Guild

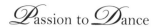

held its seventeenth Annual General Meeting, the public gathering for its members at the St. Lawrence Hall, at which the Guild, its board of directors, and the company's senior staff, with the press routinely in attendance, reported on the year's activities and the ballet's general state of health. The event was usually as carefully choreographed as any of the company's best productions, with nothing left to chance or improvisation. On this occasion, however, Franca astounded the assembled audience by delivering the following carefully worded statement in place of the expected report of the artistic director.

> I and my policies are currently receiving overwhelming criticism from very many quarters. I am used to criticism, and have weathered much of it, but I have always had enough support to carry on.
>
> However, there is reason to believe that the majority of our directors, guild members, staff members, company members, governmental grant-giving bodies and the news media have lost confidence in me. There is no accurate method of assessing the opinions of the general public, but even if there were, and even if those opinions were in my favour, I can't run the company's artistic affairs in an atmosphere of dissension, nor compromise my ideals beyond the point of honesty and self-respect.
>
> Of course, I will finish out this season; but in due course our president will receive my official letter of resignation. I am conscious of the wishes of the board for the remainder of this season, and will carry them out. However, as from today I renounce responsibility for any actions I may be pressured to take against my better judgment.
>
> Ladies and gentlemen, if I go into details on this occasion, the event will become nauseatingly dramatic and theatrical. I hope you will receive this brief report calmly, so that I may retire gracefully.[93]

She had her wish. As the audience of the ballet faithful watched in disbelieving silence, Franca made the most dramatic exit of her career, first to her office and then to seclusion at her home.

Chapter Five

A VOICE CRYING IN THE WILDERNESS

THE DELICATE NEGOTIATIONS TO RESOLVE THE CRISIS

Franca's dramatic statement made the reason for her resignation perfectly clear. She felt that her authority in artistic matters, which was to have been undisputed, had been undermined to the point where she was forced into artistic compromises against her better judgment. With her statement, she intended to shift the blame for those artistic compromises away from herself and place it where it belonged, squarely at the feet of those who controlled the purse strings. John Godfrey was chairing the Annual General Meeting, as president of its board of directors, when Franca dropped her bombshell. Completely unaware of Franca's intentions, he spoke to the meeting before she did. He too addressed head-on the issue of fiscal as opposed to artistic responsibility, but from the opposite point of view. "Although the last thing I, as President, or the Board of Directors, should do is interfere, if the artistic side is not prepared to make recommendations for retrenchment, then in my opinion it is the duty of the General Manager to do so."[1] The conflict between the board's financial priorities and the director's artistic ones had finally come out into the open. The 1968 crisis played itself out in precisely these dualistic terms, as a conflict between financial responsibility and artistic freedom. Godfrey's statement, however, drew attention to a third factor, the role of the general manager, whose alignment, whether with the board or with the artistic director, thus became a crucial factor in the governance of the company.

Franca's surprise announcement elicited strong reactions among the dancers, the board, and the company's supporters. For some, the National without Franca was unthinkable. From Edmonton, a long-time supporter of the ballet telephoned to say that out west, the National Ballet *was* Celia Franca, and to warn of the serious damage her resignation would cause.[2] Within the company itself, reaction ranged from panic and denial at one extreme to acceptance and planning for the future at the other. Lawrence Adams, David Adams's brother and a member of the recently formed Dancers' Council, was in the vanguard of those for whom the world had not come to an end with Franca's announcement. "Within the Dancers' Council we took the attitude, 'Well, she's gone, so now we just have to get on with the business here.'"[3] For Adams, who welcomed the idea of change, Franca's resignation offered a real opportunity to rethink the company along more contemporary, less elaborate (and hence less expensive) lines. The five-member Dancers' Council raised this issue in a cable to John Godfrey:

> The company has grown to a proportion which imposes on its mobility and versatility, and with no future prospect of a reduction in operational costs. Then a serious reconsideration of the proportions of the company must be made. There has been no precedent set that size and expenditure of a company affect its artistic calibre.[4]

The same cable spoke of the need to develop a significant body of contemporary repertoire for the company.

Erik Bruhn and Lynn Seymour as James and the Sylph in La Sylphide.

The issues had been debated before: financial responsibility, artistic authority, the company's overall character. But this time, the debate was conducted in an atmosphere of tension, consternation, and crisis. The dancers, on tour in the Maritimes when Franca announced her resignation in Toronto, had had no prior warning from her. She flew out a few days later to speak with them in person, but their sense of isolation could not be so easily overcome. With nine of their number away from the tour, performing for the Prologue to the Performing Arts program in the schools, the majority of dancers felt that no genuinely collective opinion could be expressed; the Dancers' Council, though duly elected, spoke as a separate entity, not for the entire company.[5] As events played themselves out, the Council found itself more and more isolated from the dancers it sought to represent, identified as an anti-Franca faction rather than a planning group trying to cope with a crisis.[6] Meanwhile, in Toronto, communication between Franca and Godfrey deteriorated even further. The key players in the affair were becoming dangerously isolated from one another.

Staff at the Canada Council kept a careful watch on the situation. Lawrence Adams, in Halifax, consulted at least twice with Peter Dwyer, who, along with Jean Roberts of the Council staff, spoke directly with Franca as well.[7] Hamilton Cassels, Jr., who had chaired the board before Godfrey and who was the son-in-law of Aileen Woods, conducted diplomatic talks with Franca, Godfrey, Betty Oliphant, and Christopher Knobbs, a dancer who called him from the tour in an attempt to gain a clearer understanding of the situation.[8] Confusion was rife. At all levels, there existed a fundamental difference of opinion as to the best way of handling the resignation. The forces pressing for change saw it as an opportunity to reshape the company completely, under a new artistic director; but a significant faction considered Franca indispensable to the company's well-being and wanted to use the occasion simply as a way of urging on her the values of fiscal restraint and choreographic innovation. The crisis had already registered at the box office; subscription sales for the Toronto season, which had been initiated only a year earlier, fell off dramatically immediately following Franca's announcement.[9]

After a two-week cooling-off period, during which the Dancers' Council attempted, unsuccessfully, to reach consensus among the dancers and Cassels pursued his diplomatic course with the company's officers, the board met to consider Franca's resignation. It in turn referred the matter to a special three-person committee, made up of Lyman Henderson, James Fleck, and Helen Balfour, which was asked to report back to the full board within a month's time.[10] On December 20, 1968, the board met to receive this committee's recommendations. Immediately following the meeting, the company issued a press release stating that the board had refused to accept Franca's resignation and that she had been prevailed upon to remain as artistic director of the company. In the press release, John Godfrey was quoted as saying:

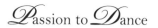

The pressures which led to the current difficulties were basically financial, and all have agreed management procedures will be altered so Miss
Franca will not have to take sole responsibility for almost every decision
in the company.

Better financial disciplines have already been introduced to ensure
that Miss Franca has the time she needs to devote to the artistic direction
of the company.[11]

The same meeting that reinstated her invited Betty Oliphant to become the company's associate artistic director and also reaffirmed its confidence in the general manager, Wallace A. Russell. Russell had been doing lighting design for the company since
its 1961–62 season and had joined the staff, as production manager, the following year.
He remained on the production side, working with both the ballet and the Canadian
Opera Company,[12] for some years, before going full time with the ballet. In 1967, following the departure of John H. Wilson from the post of general manager, he made the
shift to administration as the company's business administrator. After a year in that position, he became general manager in 1968–69, just before the crisis of Franca's resignation.
Though new as general manager, he had a long-standing association with the company
and knew its productions and production staff intimately. He also had the confidence of
the board. In Oliphant and Russell, Franca was now flanked by two powerful figures, each
with considerable influence within the company. This volatile combination of personalities determined the company's internal politics for four tempestuous years.

Though the board invited Franca to take the helm once again, it asked her to steer a
different course. The invitation was coupled with the express wish that greater emphasis
be laid on contemporary works in the future.[13] Confrontation had, apparently, been negotiated into compromise, but the real issues, financial and artistic, had not been laid to rest.

A gesture as dramatic as Franca's resignation could hardly have been genuine, or so
some people thought, particularly when the resolution to the crisis left her in control of
the company, nominally at least. But if Franca's resignation was a ploy, it failed in its central purpose, since it returned her to only a conditional leadership, not to the unqualified
control she presumably sought. And if her actions looked to some to be contrived or tactical, the evidence nevertheless indicates that there was much heartfelt agony in Franca's
decision. Three days after the event, she wrote to Aileen Woods, her friend and supporter
from the beginning:

I know you must be feeling awful at the turn of events. Please believe
me — I thought over my horrible decision very carefully before I made
it. I thought particularly of you and the many friends who supported me
in building our beloved National Ballet. The truth is, dear, that life with

Ken Bell

Lynn Seymour and Rudolf Nureyev as the Sylph and James in La Sylphide.

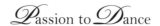

the ballet has become intolerable for me and I feel I cannot continue the
struggle. Feeling this way I would let the ballet down if I continued with
it. I hope so very much that my successor will be treated with sympathy
and understanding for he (or she) will have a monstrous task.[14]

In the public eye, the Franca of this period was the iron lady, clinging grimly to personal power for her own purposes. Because her dreams of a ballet company dedicated to
the full-length classics were becoming critically unfashionable, as well as expensive, the
public failed to recognize her unswerving purpose as dedication to the art form itself, as
she conceived of it. But Franca's intense personal identification with the art that had been
her entire life meant that her fight was for the ballet, and only incidentally for herself as
its champion. Public opinion could not recognize such selflessness, especially when it was
coupled with such unwavering strength. And public opinion of the time was not inclined
to admire this combination of selflessness and strength in an artist, especially a woman.
Her resignation could be one of two things only: foolhardy idealism or Machiavellian
manipulation. The cynical interpretation of her motives became the easier, though not
necessarily the fairer, one to accept. The public eye never saw the vulnerable, discouraged
human being revealed in Franca's letter to Woods.

Either as idealistic stand or as tactical manoeuvre, however, Franca's gesture did little
to increase her real power base within the company or to resolve the underlying tensions.
In withdrawing her resignation, she accepted significant limitations on her authority as
artistic director. She who had initially been given "the sole and entire artistic direction of
the company" now had to function within a structure that included an associate artistic
director, with strong ideas of her own, and an Artistic Management Council, soon to be
renamed the Artistic Management Committee. This committee had been set up in the
fall of 1968 to improve liaison between the board and the artistic and management arms
of the company.[15] Its membership included Franca, Oliphant, Strate, and, later, George
Crum. This emerging company structure contributed to the increasing power of the role
of general manager.

In the fall of 1967, the board received the Townsend Report, which subjected the
management side of operations to formal scrutiny. A year later, the board accepted this
report's affirmation of the importance of the position of general manager in management's working with the board to exercise budgetary control of the company's affairs.[16]
The board evidently hoped that the general manager would function as its instrument
for ensuring financial responsibility, with the artistic director virtually removed from
the financial sphere and given complete autonomy in the artistic. But as long as finances
remained tight, the distinction between financial and artistic authority was illusory at
best. Thus the "better financial disciplines" that the board instituted at the time of Franca's
reinstatement came eventually to cramp her style as surely as they were intended to free

her to concentrate on artistic matters. Franca herself, though she worked hard to adapt to the new organizational structure, was temperamentally ill suited to function within it. The rival claims of business and artistic principles would have one more day in court.

In the longer term, Celia did eventually receive the vindication she craved for her strong-willed leadership of the company during the 1968 crisis, and from the man who had been her principal opponent at the time. On November 16, 1976, Senator John Godfrey rose in Canada's Senate Chamber to pay tribute to Franca on the occasion of the company's twenty-fifth anniversary, which had just been celebrated with a gala performance of *Romeo and Juliet*, in which Franca came out of retirement to reprise her role as Lady Capulet. Without entirely abandoning the principles of fiscal prudence he had championed as president of the board of the National, Godfrey nevertheless acknowledged the justice of what he now described as Franca's complete victory.

> It is easy now to see with 20-20 hindsight that Celia was right in plunging ahead to maintain and improve the high standards of the company, in the complete faith that somehow the financial difficulties would be taken care of. It is the Celia Francas of this world who accomplish great things, not the cautious, pragmatic, timid types like myself.[17]

On the choreographic side, matters moved more swiftly. For a period of three years following this resolution to the administrative crisis, the company's concerted efforts to build the classical side of its repertoire gave way to a pursuit of the avant-garde. Partly a response to the pressures exerted by critics, board members, Canada Council staff, the Dancers' Council, and individuals like Grant Strate, this emphasis on the contemporary also came about as the result of a unique combination of circumstances and opportunities. The opening of the National Arts Centre in Ottawa made possible a large-scale investment in op-art chic, while, on the home front, the presence of an extraordinary group of young people led the company into a period of radical creative experimentation that prepared the way for some of the important choreography of the seventies and beyond. Franca, once a fledgling choreographer herself, was ready to let the members of the next generation test their wings, even if she was not the one who could teach them how to fly.

THE *KRAANERG* EXPERIENCE

The opening engagement at the new National Arts Centre in Ottawa, Canada's most lavish and superbly equipped theatre to date, was unquestionably the theatrical plum of 1969. At the National Arts Centre, the National Ballet had influential friends. Hamilton Southam, the director general, had wide-ranging tastes in the arts and the confidence to act upon them; David Haber, formerly the National Ballet's stage manager, was the Arts Centre's director of programming, and retained strong loyalties to Franca and the company. Between the two of them, they managed to ride out the inevitable controversies attendant upon the decision to offer to the National Ballet the distinction of opening the new house. The National responded to the invitation with the suggestion of a major, commissioned work by Roland Petit, the French choreographer of high fashion who had one foot in Hollywood and the other in the Champs Elysées. Originally planned as a revolutionary ballet about Maiakovsky, then as a modern version of Mary Shelley's *Frankenstein*, the commission eventually became *Kraanerg*, an abstract ballet in two acts. Attempts to interest Petit in working with the internationally acclaimed Quebec artist Jean-Paul Riopelle as his designer came to naught, as did efforts to prevail upon the Royal Opera House, Covent Garden, to release Rudolf Nureyev to star in the production.[18] But even so, *Kraanerg* as it eventually appeared on the stage of the Opera at the National Arts Centre, on June 2, 1969, had international glamour to spare. With a commissioned electronic score by the Greek Iannis Xenakis, stunning op-art designs by the Hungarian-born

Ken Bell

Artists of the ballet in Roland Petit's Kraanerg, *with which the company opened Ottawa's National Arts Centre in 1969.*

French artist Victor Vasarely and his son Yvaral, the American composer Lukas Foss as guest conductor, and the French Georges Piletta and expatriate Canadian Lynn Seymour as guest stars, *Kraanerg* represented the last word in contemporary ballet. Petit's and Piletta's names may have been intended to satisfy the need for significant francophone representation on the important occasion of the opening of a national facility. (Les Grands Ballets Canadiens had been strong contenders for the honour at one point.)[19] Seymour's presence provided international stature as well as Canadian content.

Kraanerg represented a landmark in the company's development. In Haber's view, it proclaimed to the world that the National Ballet, as a Canadian company, was capable of international collaboration on the highest level.[20] The production of *Kraanerg* thus crystallized the debate between the nationalist and the internationalist points of view in the performing arts. To the nationalist, it represented failure because none of its creators was Canadian; to the internationalist, it represented success precisely because its international creators had validated the company by mounting an original work for it. The Arts Centre, which had invested substantial funds in the production, got what it paid for: a glittering event to celebrate the opening of its theatre. The company, in the longer term, got a more mixed return on its investment.

Kraanerg lasted four seasons in the repertoire and played a total of twenty-one performances to generally cool critical response but warm, sometimes heated audience reaction. It served as the occasion for the company's first major experiment in audience research, when its Toronto dress-rehearsal was thrown open to a predominantly young and lower-income audience, whose reactions were surveyed.[21] It unquestionably altered the company's approach to programming and audience building, and probably helped to attract a younger, less conservative element into the theatre. In all these respects, the gamble paid off. Many original creations have shorter lives and less effect on a company than this. And *Kraanerg* did not remain an isolated phenomenon. Balanchine's *The Four Temperaments* entered the repertoire in the same year, to be followed in 1969–70 by Petit's *Le Loup* and Flemming Flindt's *The Lesson* and in 1970–71 by Peter Wright's *The Mirror Walkers*. After *Kraanerg*, continental European and contemporary ballet finally gained a real foothold in the National's repertoire.

But in other important ways, the National lost the *Kraanerg* gamble. As so frequently happens, the aggressively up-to-date quickly became dated. Despite rumours of European productions, Petit never mounted the work on any other company. It thus failed to gain a place in the international repertoire and died when the National stopped performing it. Even the National was denied the kind of mileage it might have hoped for from the work. *Kraanerg* went along on the company's first European tour in 1972, but, at Petit's request, it did not play Paris. The press at the time reported that he had withheld it because of a planned production in Marseilles. In fact, just three years after its premiere, Petit was afraid it might look *passé* in the capital of France.[22] Divorced from its occasion, *Kraanerg* soon betrayed the limitations of its occasional origin.

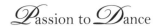

However, the National opened the Arts Centre with much more than just *Kraanerg*. On opening night, June 2, 1969, *Kraanerg* was preceded by an eight-minute curtain raiser, choreographed by Grant Strate in a neo-baroque style, to original music by Louis Applebaum.[23] The company played a full week of performances that included, along with *Kraanerg*, Sir Kenneth MacMillan's *Solitaire* and the company's full-length productions of *Romeo and Juliet* and *Swan Lake*. For David Haber, watching from the rear of the theatre, it was *Swan Lake*, danced on the Arts Centre stage on June 8, that really opened the theatre and put the seal on the company's success.[24] What other Canadian arts organization could have brought such variety, such spectacle, such professionalism, and such artistry to the opening of the nation's showcase theatre? It was a far cry from *Les Sylphides* on the Eaton Auditorium stage.

EXPERIMENTAL WORKSHOPS FOR A GENERATION OF YOUNG REBELS

Ironically, Strate's curtain raiser for the National Arts Centre rang down the curtain on his own career as the National's resident choreographer. It was his last work for the company. But his contribution was not to be measured by his choreographic record alone. Before he left the company, he participated in the development of the choreographic workshops that were to provide an invaluable training ground for the volatile talents of a new generation of choreographers.

> There was so much I wanted to explore in new territory, and I think this was probably more effective with a certain group of young dancers who came up, like Tim Spain and Ann Ditchburn, David Gordon, David Hatch Walker, Ross McKim. A number of them were coming through the school with a creative fervour, and I fed into that because I found it very interesting. I helped them as much as I could.[25]

In April 1969, less than a month before the opening of *Kraanerg*, the company had mounted a week-long season of contemporary ballet at the Edward Johnson Building of the University of Toronto. The program was made up of Strate's Stratford Festival commission, *Électre*, and original works by company members Ann Ditchburn, Charles Kirby, and Ross McKim. Now that the main company was entering more enthusiastically into the acquisition of modern repertoire, the time was right for workshops. With Franca's and Oliphant's blessing, a committee made up of Strate, Karen Bowes, an elegant young dancer who joined the faculty of York University after her career with the company, and Victoria Bertram[26] set about organizing workshops on a frequent, though not quite annual, basis. The low budgets and the informal surroundings of the smaller theatres they used placed

Ann Ditchburn and Tomas Schramek in Pilgrimage, *created for the 1973 choreographic workshop.*

the emphasis on experiment and innovation, without the pressures and risks involved in choreographing for the full company. It was no coincidence that the goals of the workshops bore a close resemblance to the goals defined by the Dancers' Council in its attempt to suggest a restructuring of the company in 1968. Bowes, Bertram, and Spain had been three of that Council's five members.

The 1970 workshop, at the Ryerson Theatre, had two different programs with works by ten company members. It received informal adjudication from four distinguished guests: Monique Michaud of the Canada Council; Peter Brinson, director of the Royal Ballet's Ballet for All; Norman Campbell, the CBC television producer who made a specialty of

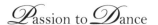

televising the company; and Selma Jeanne Cohen, the American dance critic and scholar and the editor of *Dance Perspectives*.[27]

If Franca had been slow to encourage original choreography from company members up to this point, she now moved a little hastily to incorporate the results of the workshops into the regular repertoire. She acknowledged her eagerness in her own report to the Annual General Meeting of 1971.

> Encouraged by the highly promising ballets presented by Timothy Spain and Ann Ditchburn for the Workshop, and in my somewhat over-anxious desire to push Canadian choreographers in the hope that we could show their works in Europe next May and June, I programmed Tim's *For Internal Use Only* and Ann's *Brown Earth* on opening night. For several reasons, these ballets were not entirely successful. Nevertheless these young choreographers, while temporarily disillusioned, have regained their spirit, and are at present rehearsing new works for the next workshop performances.[28]

The process, once begun, could not be hurried. The transition from promising workshop piece to a finished work for the full company required careful judgment and nurturing. But given the extraordinary talents coming from the school into the company at the time, Franca could be forgiven a little haste. Victoria Bertram thought Franca's willingness to promote these young artists was based on deeply felt personal sympathy. "They were a very talented, very interesting bunch, and I think she was really taken with their energy and their youth. It probably reminded her of her own youth, because she was terribly rebellious, I believe, and very talented."[29] Much of the rebellion and talent in the group burned itself out, unfortunately, but not without producing some results. The workshops, over the years, offered young choreographers the congenial environment for experimentation that no longer existed in the large dance organization the National had by then become. They thus provided a starting-point for the work of Ann Ditchburn, James Kudelka, Constantin Patsalas, and David Allan, all of whom choreographed major works for the full company later in their careers. Though the company did not place its highest priority on the development of choreographic talent, it had, through the institution of the workshops, at least allowed Canadian choreography to establish a beachhead.

A New *Giselle* Recalled the Company to its Central Emphasis

By her encouragement of the workshops, Franca bowed to the long-standing pressures to modernize the repertoire; she did not, however, change her fundamental strategy for the company's development. While the winds of fashion blew in a contemporary direction, she maintained her long-term goal of creating a major classical ballet company, a goal that had not yet been reached, despite the company's expansion following *Romeo and Juliet*. The debate at this time regarding the acquisition of a new production of *Giselle* demonstrated just how strongly the winds of fashion did blow.

Since the move to the O'Keefe Centre in 1964, there had been only two renewals of existing classical works, *Swan Lake* and *Nutcracker*. The complete *Giselle*, once a staple in the National's repertoire, had last been danced in Hamilton on January 17, 1964; Toronto had not seen it since March 7, 1963. Franca planned a new production for the 1969–70 season.

Andrew Oxenham

Keiichi Hirano, Jillian Vanstone, Piotr Stanczyk, and Je-an Salas, in the peasant pas de quatre in a 2004 performance of Peter Wright's production of Giselle.

Although it is, strictly speaking, the prime example of romantic ballet and thus a precursor of the more formal classical tradition represented by the works of Petipa, *Giselle*, originally choreographed for the Paris Opera in 1841 by Jean Coralli and Jules Perrot, holds a central place in any classical ballet company's repertoire. Its heroine dominates our conception of ballet itself, gripping audiences with her pathos and ethereal serenity and challenging ballerinas to refine their lyric and dramatic gifts. The Ambrose-designed production of *Giselle*, now in mothballs, had been a cornerstone of the early company's repertoire. For historical, artistic, and sentimental reasons, then, a really first-rate new *Giselle* seemed a self-evident, long overdue addition to the repertoire. But Franca, speaking on behalf of the Artistic Management Council, had to argue forcefully at the board level in order to secure the necessary commitment of funds. She could have spoken very personally, from her experience as the pre-eminent interpreter of the role in the company's earliest years. Instead, her argument touched on the fundamental objectives of the company, the recent trend toward contemporary work, and the underlying significance of the classics to any ballet company, whatever its specific emphasis.

> Why present *Giselle* today?
>
> So long as it is decided to maintain our original policy and strive toward our aims, we must continue to mount the classics. So long as we are training and producing classical dancers of quality in our school and employing them in our company we must continue to mount the classics. While the world's *best* classical dancers, actors and musicians enjoy performing contemporary works, none of these artists have the incentive to develop without the challenges the classics present. Many of you must have heard of dancers who switch from "ballet" to "modern" because they can "express" themselves better in modern. This is true — they can — but simply because they lack the talent and ability to meet the technical and artistic challenges the classics present.
>
> But, when a company possesses dancers who at the least can come close to meeting those classical challenges, they deserve the opportunity to try. If the opportunities are not present here, they will seek employment elsewhere.[30]

Franca's presentation pulled no punches. The classics, and here she included the repertoire of both the Classical and the Romantic periods, were and always would be the true test of a dancer's capabilities and hence the pinnacle of a company's achievement. To profess a preference for contemporary work was to evade the ultimate challenge presented by the repertoire of the classics, and Franca had never been one to balk at a challenge. The impassioned tone of her presentation, however, indicated that Franca had to argue, and argue strongly, for an acquisition that would have required no justification at all fifteen years earlier. Though Franca's goals had remained the same, the climate in which she worked had changed considerably during those fifteen years. She must have felt like a voice crying in the wilderness.

Despite some grumbling from among the dancers,[31] *Giselle* entered the repertoire on April 16, 1970, with Lynn Seymour and the Stuttgart Ballet's Egon Madsen as guest artists, but otherwise without the fanfare that later came to be associated with a major premiere. Designed by Desmond Heeley and mounted by Peter Wright, yet another alumnus of the Metropolitan Ballet, it has endured for forty years as one of the most satisfying productions of the standard, full-length works in the National's repertoire. Like many ballerinas before her, Chan Hon Goh chose it in May 2009 for her farewell performance with the company. Traditional and tasteful, rather than idiosyncratic, Wright's production displayed from the outset the company's virtues of impeccable production values and well-schooled execution. His expansion of the first-act peasant pas de deux into a pas de quatre was not universally admired, but on the whole, critical response recognized the integrity of the production. During the company's 1975 London engagement, the prominent British critic John Percival, writing in *The London Times*, welcomed it with enthusiasm.

> To bring Peter Wright's production of *Giselle* to London, where we already have two slightly different editions of it in the Royal Ballet's repertory, might seem risky, but the Canadian National Ballet knew what it was about. For one thing, their version is in some important respects an improvement on ours; for another, the ballet shows several of their principals and soloists to excellent advantage. Another advantage of the Canadian production is the marked superiority of its decor.[32]

Richard Buckle, not always a friend of the company, said simply, "The National Ballet of Canada's production of *Giselle*, which they have presented at the Coliseum, is much the most intelligent I have seen."[33] Its strength has always lain in its simplicity. Wright's production does not compete with the dancers for the audience's attention and consequently allows their individual abilities and personalities to shine forth from within the central roles with freshness and vitality. Thirteen years after its premiere, it proved the ideal ballet for Evelyn Hart's historic debut with the National.

Evelyn Hart had defied the odds to become one of the foremost ballerinas in Canada. Asked to leave the National Ballet School as a young student, she trained at the Royal Winnipeg Ballet School instead, and then made her career in Winnipeg. But any thought that she was languishing off the radar of the ballet world was dispelled when, in 1980, she won the gold medal at the Varna International Ballet Competition. With her signature piece from that competition, the sensuous modern pas de deux "Belong," from Norbert Vesak's ballet, *What to do Till the Messiah Comes*, she instantly became the hottest property in the Canadian dance world.[34] Sensational as she was in this modern repertoire, however, Hart was by temperament a classical ballerina in the dramatic mould. In the minds of many, she became a dancer in search of a repertoire, looking for opportunities to perform the full-length dramatic ballets that the Royal Winnipeg could not then command. On February 26, 1983, her first Giselle held the sold-out audience at O'Keefe

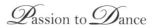

Centre spellbound and proclaimed Hart's homecoming, not to the company but to the Romantic repertoire she was born to dance. She came on her own terms, as the star of the Royal Winnipeg, not as aspirant to membership in the National. Yet the National's *Giselle* offered her the artistic fulfillment she most needed at that time. In its hospitable setting, and with the strong, tactful partnering of Frank Augustyn, her interpretation of the character of Giselle, fragile, idealistic, consumed as much by her passion for dance as by her love for Albrecht, glowed with intensity and conviction. She went on to perform the role to acclaim around the world.

In 1970, however, there was no time to linger over the entry of Wright's *Giselle* into the repertoire. One month after its opening, the company flew to Japan to perform *Swan Lake* and *Romeo and Juliet* at Osaka's Expo '70. Mixed programs of *The Four Temperaments*, *Concerto Barocco*, *The Lesson*, *Le Loup*, *Solitaire*, and Grant Strate's *Phases* reflected the company's excursions into contemporary repertoire. Osaka, however, was but a prelude to even greater things.

THE LONG-AWAITED EUROPEAN DEBUT

Talk of a European tour for the company went back at least as far as 1955.[35] In 1972, the dream was finally to become a reality, and the elaborate preparations for the National's European debut had to begin almost immediately upon its return from Japan. Given the origins of the company and Franca's own background, the opening engagement of the tour in London, at the Coliseum, was charged with emotional significance.

But the pragmatic reasons for the venture far outweighed the sentimental. Franca knew that without the experience of performing in the world's major ballet centres, the company would never be more than a good provincial troupe. And without international exposure for the company, she would never be able to entice major international choreographers, unless they were old friends, to work with the National. Her attitude toward European touring was hard-headed rather than sentimental. "It is not particularly vital that we achieve a resounding success in London and Paris. It is important that our company experiences international competition."[36] The National had come tantalizingly close to realizing its European dream in 1965, when Ian Hunter, the director general of the Commonwealth Arts Festival in England, expressed strong interest in having the National and the Orchestre Symphonique de Montréal appear at the Festival with a repertoire that would include *Romeo and Juliet* and *The House of Atreus*.[37] Collaboration with the OSM had contributed greatly to the success of *Romeo and Juliet* at its Montreal opening the previous year. But the federal government gave the nod to the Royal Winnipeg Ballet instead, and when, the following year, the company tried to exploit the politically attractive Montreal connection to participate in a government-sponsored tour of French-speaking European countries, Ottawa chose to send the OSM alone.[38]

Backstage after the London opening of La Sylphide *on May 17, 1972, Celia Franca, still in costume as Madge, the witch, presents David Scott, Nadia Potts, and Joanne Nisbet to HRH the Princess Anne.*

By 1969, however, David Haber had returned to Canada following a period of work with the William Morris Concert Agency in the United States. He returned, initially, as producer of theatrical attractions at Expo '67 in Montreal, then served as a consultant to the World Festival for Osaka's Expo '70, and eventually became involved in setting up the Canada Council's Touring Office, in addition to carrying out his duties at the National Arts Centre. Through these international connections and his contacts in the Department of External Affairs, he was well placed to assist the National's strenuous lobbying efforts for government support in travelling to Europe. (He had, indeed, worked to bring about the 1970 Osaka engagement.)[39] In the late fall of 1969, Haber, as government representative for cultural trips abroad, was able to announce to the company that the Department of External Affairs had decided to send the National to Europe in the summer of 1972.[40]

The major challenge in planning for the tour, aside from the logistical problems of transporting a company of fifty-five dancers plus artistic and technical staff, sets, and costumes to seven different European cities, lay in the selection of repertoire. In its European debut, the company had to show as a competent exponent of the classical repertoire, yet it had to appear distinctive as well, not simply a country cousin of the major European classical companies. To that end, the company selected Bruhn's *La Sylphide* and *Swan Lake* as its two full-length programs. Outside Denmark, the complete *La Sylphide* was still something of a novelty, and Bruhn's radical reworking of *Swan Lake* guaranteed the National a degree of critical attention that a more traditionally mounted classic would not have commanded. On the contemporary side, apart from a few performances of *Kraanerg*, the National presented several mixed programs of short works that included Wright's *The Mirror Walkers*, Eliot Feld's *Intermezzo*, and, in a graceful acknowledgement of Antony Tudor's importance to the young company, *Fandango* and *The Judgment of Paris*. *Romeo and Juliet* could not be shown because of the company's agreement with Cranko forbidding its production in major European centres. The only original Canadian choreography presented was *Session*, a short piece by Robert Iscove premiered in Windsor in the February preceding the tour and not performed again after the tour concluded.

The tour's main purpose was unquestionably to introduce the company to a knowledgeable European audience and to expose it to European critical opinion. But despite a generally hospitable climate, the company was not a hot item on the European circuit; box office had to be taken into consideration along with artistic goals. A guest star would assure good box office, but at the risk of obscuring the company itself. Erik Bruhn's name presented itself as the obvious solution. With two of his works as major elements of the tour repertoire, and with his eight-year association with the company as choreographer, coach, and teacher at the school, Bruhn already had a special status with the National. A guest yet not a guest, by his presence he would build box office without throwing too large a shadow over the company. Accordingly, Bruhn was engaged to appear as guest artist with the company in *La Sylphide* and perhaps a new pas de deux in London and Paris, the two major stops on the tour.[41]

But Bruhn did not fulfill the engagement. In late December 1971, the undiagnosed chronic pain that he had suffered for some years reached such agonizing proportions that he abruptly announced his retirement from dancing, after a final performance as James in Harald Lander's production of *La Sylphide* with American Ballet Theatre.[42] The National received formal notification in early January 1972 that Bruhn would not appear with them five months hence on the European tour.[43] Bruhn's withdrawal placed Franca in an impossible quandary. Despite her desire to showcase the company itself, despite her long-standing reluctance to rely on guest artists, the company had to turn to guest stars to create some publicity hype for the tour. At Bruhn's suggestion, Niels

Kehlet of the Royal Danish Ballet appeared in *La Sylphide* in London and Paris, while Georges Piletta repeated his role in *Kraanerg* in London, Brussels, and Glasgow. Plans for an original pas de deux for Bruhn and Veronica Tennant were scrapped; Stuttgart's Marcia Haydée and Richard Cragun appeared instead at the gala opening in a performance of Cranko's *Legende*. On May 17, 1972, the curtain rose on the National Ballet's all-important London debut.

London was home to an influential international ballet press and to a remarkable concentration of ballet professionals whose opinions on matters of dance were authoritative. But for all Franca's hard-headed realism about this tour, playing London was like making a pilgrimage to a holy shrine. In London, all the important people from her past, her mentors and teachers, Rambert, de Valois, and above all Stanislas Idzikowski, would see what she had managed to achieve on her own. The company appeared at the Coliseum, a notch below the Royal Opera House, Covent Garden, whose exclusive portals opened by invitation only, and certainly not to a newcomer like the National, but a distinct notch above Sadler's Wells Theatre, where new touring companies traditionally made their London debuts.[44] (To Ann Ditchburn, the Coliseum was "a more honest place than Covent Garden for foreign people to play in London."[45]) For company members old enough to remember the Royal Alexandra Theatre, the ornate decor of the Coliseum had a familiar, welcoming air, but to the post-O'Keefe generation, the excitement of the London opening was heightened by the experience of performing in such faded but authentic Edwardian elegance. Those with a sense of history knew that the Coliseum, despite its music hall origins, had presented the greatest dancers of the past, including the Diaghilev Ballets Russes in their triumphant return to London after the First World War. Stanislas Idzikowski, seated in the Coliseum's auditorium in 1972, had danced Harlequin in *Le Carnaval* on its stage in 1918. A circle, of which many of the young artists on the stage were unaware, had been completed.

Despite his inability to perform, Bruhn did accompany the dancers to lend moral support to their important venture. Veronica Tennant, although deprived of her chance to dance with him, felt his presence in London, as so often in her career. "Even though he didn't dance with me in London, he was there. Erik was very much there, before the performance, after the performance. Erik has been there, I realize, all my life, from the time I started."[46] Tentatively but forcefully, the Bruhn influence was asserting itself, preparing the way for his much fuller commitment to the company in years to come.

The London press coverage was positive, but not ecstatic. *Dance and Dancers* gave it three separate articles, and commented favourably on Bruhn's interpolated pas de deux for Effy and James in the first act of *La Sylphide*. Two of its reviewers especially liked his innovative staging of *Swan Lake* in two acts instead of the traditional four.[47] Reporting on the company's visit for the *Dancing Times*, James Monahan commented on both its reception and its characteristics.

Everyone, the critics included, wanted to like them and everyone did like them — but … Not all the critics, of course, put equal stress on that "but"; nearly all of them, however, made at least as much of what had still to be achieved as of what had been achieved already. London's good-will was tinged with avuncular condescension. Before the event I shared, I must confess, in that attitude. But the company taught me to see it differently.

We had been told to expect a company which had no star-ballerina and no choreography, or at least no choreographer, of its own; to expect also to find that it was well-schooled. This description turned out to be dead accurate, and yet misleading; it had not led me to expect that the one plus would so well compensate for the two minuses.[48]

Though the company could not be said to have taken London by storm, it established its international credentials with this visit. Following the Coliseum engagement, the company made stops in Stuttgart, Paris, Brussels, Glasgow, Lausanne, and Monte Carlo. The Paris press was less enthusiastic than the London, but overall the company's competence in presenting the classical repertoire, its flair for attractive productions and tasteful innovation, its concern for stylistic ensemble, and its reservoir of young, developing talent were seen and duly noted. It had yet to impress the international community, however, as an ensemble of genuinely distinctive style and authority, and, aside from London, Stuttgart, and Paris, the tour had not played cities known as major ballet centres. The National had made its presence felt, but had not yet asserted its own identity.

THE SLEEPING BEAUTY FORCED UNPRECEDENTED GROWTH

The effort and accomplishments of the European tour were immediately eclipsed, in that event-filled year of 1972, by the realization of yet another long-standing company dream. Franca knew from the outset that any company claiming to specialize in the classical repertoire had to perform the ultimate test piece of the canon, the full-length Petipa *Sleeping Beauty*. In the fall of 1972, only two months after the company's last performance on the European tour, the complete *Sleeping Beauty* was to enter the repertoire at last. But not just any *Sleeping Beauty*; this lavish production, the largest and most complex undertaking in the company's history, was to be the cornerstone of a major North American tour, culminating in the National's debut at the Metropolitan Opera House in New York, under the auspices of the Hurok organization.

Sol Hurok, the foremost artistic and theatrical promoter in the world, had introduced the Royal Ballet to North America and kept its international profile high for many years. He held the key to all the major theatres of the continent; his sponsorship of a theatrical

Anthony Crickmay

Veronica Tennant as Princess Aurora in the rose adagio from The Sleeping Beauty.

attraction guaranteed access to all the number-one houses on the circuit. Moreover, he represented the superstars. Re-enter Rudolf Nureyev, the star on whose drawing power Hurok had predicated this particular scheme. Nureyev was to choreograph the entire production and dance in almost every performance of *Sleeping Beauty* and the other standard repertoire of the National throughout the gruelling, continent-wide tour. This combination of the European debut and the Nureyev North American tour gave the National more international exposure in 1972 than ever before, but at the price of a superhuman expenditure of effort from each of its members that stretched the company's organizational structure to the breaking point.

The National had grown gradually from a troupe of twenty-nine dancers in 1951 to a company that hovered around the forty mark through the late 1950s and early 1960s. The acquisition of *Romeo and Juliet* and the move to the O'Keefe raised that number into the fifties; gradual expansion resulted in an all-time high of fifty-five dancers on the roster for the seasons of 1967–68 and 1968–69. The 1968 financial crisis took its toll on company size, however, reducing the company drastically to its earlier level of forty-one dancers by 1970–71. Reduced numbers limited the choice of repertoire and left the company dangerously understaffed to provide understudies or replacements for injured dancers, a critical problem on tour. In 1971–72, company size jumped from forty-one to fifty-two dancers, to accommodate the needs of the European tour; for *Sleeping Beauty* in 1972–73, the

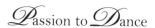

company added thirteen more dancers, for a total of sixty-five. It stayed above the sixty mark for some time, but in recent years has contracted once again. In 2010, the company roster stood at fifty-eight dancers, plus ten apprentices.[49]

These numbers speak of more than mere size. A larger company is a more complex, less informal organization, as David Adams had anticipated at the time of the first major expansion for *Romeo and Juliet*. It can handle a wider range of repertoire, but it also has to cope with a greater range of competing interests among dancers, more of whom are of a calibre to hope for major roles. By the time of the European tour and *Sleeping Beauty*, Lois Smith and Earl Kraul had retired; David Adams was long gone; and Galina Samsova and Martine van Hamel had flashed across the horizon and moved on to major international careers. But the company for the 1970s boasted talent, some of it new and some of it already established, that set a new standard of proficiency and a new character for the ensemble. Five ballerinas vied for attention: Veronica Tennant, Karen Kain, Vanessa Harwood, Mary Jago, and Nadia Potts. Frank Augustyn emerged as the first internationally acclaimed male dancer the National had produced, but the older men — Tomas Schramek, Sergiu Stefanschi, and Hazaros Surmeyan — gave strength and depth to the male roster. *Sleeping Beauty* was a challenge, but it was a challenge the developing company longed for.

The gorgeous spectacle of the final act of The Sleeping Beauty. *Charles Kirby as King Florestan.*

Cylla von Tiedemann

Preparations for *Sleeping Beauty* could not wait for the completion of the European tour. Although rehearsals were scheduled for August, after the company's return, a September opening in Ottawa meant that production of sets and costumes coincided exactly with preparations for the tour and, indeed, with the tour itself. Dieter Penzhorn, at that time the company's production manager, had the job of coordinating the production aspects of this mammoth undertaking. There were, he remembered, "so many costumes to be done, and there just wasn't the time when the company was here to do it all, so we brought some of the wardrobe staff to England to do a lot of the fittings while we were in London."[50] Even the National, which by then had had some experience with staging spectacles, had never encountered as opulent an imagination as that of Nicholas Georgiadis, the Greek-born designer of such Covent Garden spectacles as MacMillan's *Romeo and Juliet*, who was to provide the sumptuous visual setting for Nureyev's vision of the work. But once the Hurok contract was signed, there was no looking back, not even when it became apparent that Franca's preliminary budget for the show, an astronomical two hundred and fifty thousand dollars, was inadequate to the commitments that had been made. Franca recalled the frustrations of dealing with Nureyev and Georgiadis, who conceived of the show only as it would appear on the major stages of the continent, without any thought for the exigencies of touring.

> By this time we had already signed a contract with Hurok, so there was nothing we could do except try to persuade them to cut down. Poor Jimmy Ronaldson, our wardrobe supervisor, was going crazy in London with Georgiadis, who was picking out the most expensive silks and brocades he could find. Nureyev and Georgiadis were under the impression that they could build the production for the National Arts Centre–size stage. And of course we don't have anything like that anywhere else in Canada.[51]

The board, which had seen financial crisis in its day, blanched at the cost overruns. Bankruptcy loomed, and the year of the company's greatest achievements to date teetered on the verge of catastrophe.

A MAJOR CHALLENGE TO FRANCA'S AUTHORITY

Worse was in store. In the midst of all the anticipation, preparation, and confusion caused by the European tour and *Sleeping Beauty*, the administrative tensions that had simmered within the company since 1968 finally came to a rolling boil. The rival interests of artistic and administrative control, which had defined the 1968 crisis, declared themselves decisively in 1972, in a series of events which Lyman Henderson, then president of the board,

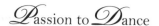

came to refer to as the Palace Revolution. Within the board and the staff, the company was split between rival factions, one backing Wallace Russell, the National's general manager, the other loyal to Franca and fighting to maintain her position and authority.

On the personal level, the stakes were high and the in-fighting fierce. Franca saw the struggle as a personal attack, an attempt to remove her from the artistic direction of the company. "The board and Wally Russell were very close, and there were certain members of the board who really wanted to get me out. And so they became in league."[52] Nor was she alone in this interpretation of events. Lyman Henderson remembered it as a time "when a dissident section of the board, largely spearheaded by the general manager, decided it was time to get rid of Celia Franca."[53] Veronica Tennant told a similar story. In her position as the dancers' representative on the board, she interpreted events as

> a plot to terminate Miss Franca's directorship. Basically we rallied to stop it because we felt it to be very, very wrong, especially at that particular time. And to be done for reasons that didn't particularly take into account what the dancers might feel. But it didn't seem to originate from within the dancer core of the company; it was more a machination within the board at that time.[54]

Rumour had it that the dissident group intended to approach Erik Bruhn and offer him the position of artistic director.[55] Just when the company needed to present itself in the best possible light on the international stage, it was rent by internal dissension.

Betty Oliphant, who had been associate artistic director of the company since 1968, had achieved a greater independence from Franca than she had had earlier, when she was ballet mistress. She certainly had as fierce a dedication as anyone to the company into which she had poured her energies and whose dancers she groomed at the National Ballet School. Indeed, by 1972 the company was substantially made up of graduates of the school, like Tennant herself, Kain, Potts, and Augustyn, many of whom Oliphant had known and worked with since their childhoods. A more astute political survivor than Franca, she assessed the situation and responded to it, not out of personal loyalty, but out of concern for the future of the company. She recognized that compromise between the opposing forces was no longer a possibility, as it had seemed to be in 1968; however difficult the terms, a choice had finally to be made. And if the choice forced upon the company had to be between an artistic director and a general manager, the issue was clear.

> It reached the point where the board was willing to get rid of Celia and keep Wally Russell. And that's where everybody rallied around to support Celia. Not because we really believed in her that much, but because we certainly did not believe in Wally Russell and we found the whole exercise

a really rotten stunt. I organized a meeting, and every single department of the company was represented: the wardrobe, the musical, the artists, every area. And each person presented their point of view, which was that Celia certainly had faults, but there was no way that anybody in the company was prepared to stay if Wally took over and Celia was fired.[56]

This concerted demonstration of support for Franca forced Russell's hand, and he resigned just two months before the National's departure for London. The company had little warning. He had first tendered his resignation in January 1972, to take effect after the European tour, and then, in March, after the events described by Oliphant, he abruptly walked out.[57] The company was left, on the eve of its first European engagement and in the midst of preparations for *Sleeping Beauty*, without a general manager.

Seen in organizational rather than personal terms, the 1972 crisis simply continued the conflicts that had been deferred, but not resolved, in 1968. At that point, faced with Franca's resignation, the board had tried to assert both the autonomy of the artistic director and the authority of the general manager. But that tenuous balance had not held for long. During the intervening period, the general manager's position, particularly in

Cylla von Tiedemann

Margaret Illmann and Robert Tewsley in 1994 as Princess Aurora and Prince Florimund in Nureyev's production of The Sleeping Beauty.

relation to the board, had strengthened significantly. In the effort to bring sound business principles to bear on an artistic organization, the general manager and the board naturally became allies in a common cause. As Franca put it, the board "didn't want the headaches of deficits. They just wanted to be sure that the budget was clean, and the general manager's position became very, very important."[58] But in the last analysis, however important it may have been to rein in artistic temperament and break it to the bit of financial prudence, artistic vision still had to take the lead. The reassertion, on this occasion, of the centrality of Franca's position within the company amounted to a public declaration that the cart would not be put before the horse. If a working balance could not be achieved between the artistic and the management sides of the company, then the artistic must win out. From a situation she had not precipitated, Franca thus emerged in a much stronger position than the one her 1968 resignation had created for her. But even so, the spectre of artistic versus managerial authority had not been laid to rest. Nor would it be, until well after Franca's departure from the company.

Because Russell's successor, Gerry Eldred, could not take over the position in time for the European tour, interim help had to be found. In such circumstances, the fact that the tour could take place as planned testified to the soundness of Russell's preliminary arrangements and the competence and efficiency of the company's staff. The interim help came in the person of David Haber, seconded from his duties at the National Arts Centre and the Canada Council Touring Office to guide the company through the administrative details of a tour in whose planning he had already been involved.[59] Haber retained a strong affection for Franca from his days as the company's first stage manager. His reappearance just at the time of Russell's departure rescued Franca from potential disaster; overnight, a serious rival to her authority had been replaced by a staunch ally. Haber's presence provided welcome support for someone who valued personal loyalty as much as Franca did. As events unfolded, he turned out to be more than just an interim replacement.

SUCCESSION PLANNING

In all the tumult of the events of 1972, Franca had other important matters to consider. Despite the reassertion of confidence in her leadership following the Palace Revolution, she was ready to lighten her own load. After twenty years of living the National Ballet of Canada night and day, she wanted some relief.

Ever since her arrival in Canada, Franca's personal life had taken a back seat to the concerns of the ballet. Her 1951 marriage to Bert Anderson, whom she had met shortly after coming to Canada, ended in divorce, and in 1960 she married James Morton, the principal clarinet with the National Ballet Orchestra. In the early 1970s, when Morton moved to Ottawa to join the National Arts Centre Orchestra, Franca added the stresses of commuting between Ottawa and Toronto to her already impossible schedule. By 1972, she was ready to think of a successor, and of diminishing her daily involvement with the company so that she could devote more time to herself and her husband.

She discussed possible successors frankly with Betty Oliphant, and, inevitably, Erik Bruhn's name came up in their conversations. But the two women did not see eye to eye on the question of his suitability. His recent retirement from dancing and presence with the company in London served as catalyst for a reconsideration. One night, after the curtain had come down at the Coliseum, Franca and Oliphant returned with Bruhn to Rudolf Nureyev's home for a late-night supper. Their recollections of the evening illustrated their opposing points of view.

Franca:

Betty and I had a dinner with Erik one night after one of our performances at the Coliseum, and I fell asleep after it. It was in Rudi's house; Rudi wasn't there, but Erik was staying in Rudi's house. And I knew immediately then, although Betty and I had discussed Erik, that Erik was not right for the job, not at that time. His health had not been good, he was very nervous, and I just didn't think that he would be the right person for the company — at that time. But his association with the company and with the school continued, so that when it was the right time he was ready.[60]

Oliphant:

I told her that Erik would be a wonderful director for the company, and she was so scornful. We went out after the show at the Coliseum to Nureyev's place; he wasn't there, and Erik was staying there. We went there about two in the morning, and at six in the morning Erik was still talking in this very neurotic way he has. He used to be very paranoid about people being out to get him. I listened to Erik all that time; she fell asleep. And as we left she said, "Now you see why he can't be the director of the company." But anyway, when he was, he was superb.[61]

Bruhn was not ready for such responsibility at that time. And in 1972, Franca was not in a position to recognize his suitability for the job. The characteristic that she described as "nervous," Oliphant as "neurotic" and "paranoid," constituted a real obstacle for her, when the issue at stake was something as close to her as the National Ballet. Franca had to be able to trust those with whom she worked, and it can be difficult to trust someone who veils his essential character as Bruhn evidently did. Oliphant recognized that inaccessibility herself, but refused to be put off by it. "He had built his own defences, and you couldn't have reached him in a million years. In fact you might have destroyed him if you'd tried

Ken Bell

Celia Franca, David Haber, and Betty Oliphant at the St. Lawrence Hall in 1953, with Lois Smith in the background. By 1972, Haber had returned to the administrative team, though it was no longer as harmonious as it had been in the early years.

to reach him in the psychological sense."[62] Franca's reluctance to hand over the company of her creation to someone who could not be reached was hardly surprising. Even though it was an academic argument at this point, it illustrated the significant change that had come into the relationship between Oliphant and Franca. The two women who had so long and so successfully shared a common vision now moved and worked independently.

Franca had an important conversation with David Haber while she was in Monte Carlo, the last stop on the European tour.[63] She broached the idea of his joining the company permanently as her close associate, someone who could relieve her of significant portions of her professional duties and give her the personal freedom she sought. There was no explicit understanding at the time that such a relationship would eventually develop into Haber's taking over the company, but anything might happen. As Haber put it: "Celia, consciously and unconsciously, was always keeping options open."[64] Franca, for her part, recognized in Haber "an old theatrical friend" who had bailed the company out of a difficult situation after Russell's sudden departure. "He was always crazy about ballet, and he had worked with me in the early years, and he had a broad theatrical experience that was fantastic."[65] Haber had proved his worth and won Franca's trust. An old friendship had been re-established and a new alliance formed.

Chapter Six

I DON'T BELIEVE IN A FLIMSY
SLEEPING BEAUTY

The Pros and Cons of the Nureyev Connection

On the company's return from Europe, the juggernaut that was *Sleeping Beauty* was already gaining momentum. In choosing to accept the conditions of the association with Nureyev and the Hurok organization, the company had taken a carefully calculated risk. The disadvantages, clearly recognized from the outset, lay in the arbitrary control that Hurok exercised over the venture. Hurok had responsibility for the tour; the company had responsibility for mounting the production; and Nureyev had artistic control over the entire project. The company was left with a huge financial risk and very little ability to control its own destiny.

Hurok had Nureyev under contract and needed a company to show him off in North America in the proper setting of a full-length Petipa classic. The National, with its North American reputation for lavish staging and its considerable touring experience, would do. But Nureyev's drawing power at the box office unquestionably provided the motivating force for the enterprise and consequently gave him what amounted to despotic control. As choreographer and star of the production, slated to appear in virtually every performance, Nureyev had to be kept happy. And the terms of the contract were such that Hurok's financial responsibility applied only to the tour itself; the cost of mounting the production to Nureyev's satisfaction fell to the National alone. Franca summed up the situation succinctly in some private notes she made regarding the "cons" of accepting the Hurok offer. "1) No Nureyev, no job. 2) No new productions for Nureyev, no job. 3) Nureyev has final artistic say because our contract with Hurok dictates that if Nureyev doesn't dance the N.B. doesn't get paid."[1]

The advantages lay in the enormously increased number of performance opportunities for the company (except for its leading male dancers, who toured under the shadow of the omnipresent superstar), the entry to the Metropolitan Opera House in New York, which Hurok's connections guaranteed, and the chance for the company to work on a daily basis with an artist of Nureyev's experience and stature. And the National would finally acquire a production of *Sleeping Beauty*, the one major Petipa work missing from its repertoire as a classical company. On balance, these factors were judged to outweigh the real risks and frustrations the collaboration entailed. With her eyes wide open, Franca had decided to take the plunge; now, in late 1972, in the midst of the chaos of preparation, it was all the company could do to keep the project going. Reflection and evaluation were luxuries reserved for some later date.

The difficulties the company experienced in trying to keep the production costs under some semblance of control paled beside the experience of coping with Nureyev's

Rudolf Nureyev as Prince Florimund in The Sleeping Beauty.

demands in the rehearsal room. Nureyev had already staged a complete *Sleeping Beauty*, with designs by Georgiadis, for La Scala in Milan and thought of the National's production as a "second reading" of the work.[2] As is frequently the case in such circumstances, the ballet's steps themselves were taught to the company by one of Nureyev's collaborators from the earlier production. The National had closed its European tour in Monte Carlo on July 3, 1972, and, as Franca later reported:

> In mid-July, 1972, Gilda Majocchi, a ballet mistress from La Scala, Milan, sent by Nureyev, arrived in Toronto to teach our dancers Nureyev's version of the Petipa choreography. She was pleasant and efficient. However, when Nureyev arrived, on August 3rd, he proceeded to change much of what Mme Majocchi had set — and not always necessarily for the better. Further, Nureyev insisted on having the whole company present during his rehearsals, whether they were needed or not, which meant that the other ballets in the repertoire were insufficiently rehearsed — with the exception of *The Moor's Pavane* [another vehicle for Nureyev]. We had difficulty in getting Nureyev's co-operation during our photo calls at Ottawa's National Arts Centre, and the staging and dress rehearsals were nightmarish.[3]

Not all Nureyev's choreographic changes were whimsical. He had had much larger forces at his disposal at La Scala; for the National (as large as it had ever been at sixty-five dancers), he had to trim numbers and hence modify the choreography. And to cope with the demands of touring (virtually unheard of at La Scala), he had to allow changes in design and construction as well. For all that he seemed intransigent to his Canadian collaborators, Nureyev thought of himself as making concessions.

> First of all, from this enormous, mammoth production of La Scala, I have to draw out of Georgiadis a production which would be able to tour, that stagehands could move, and still the story had to be told and the production had to look awesome, because I don't believe in a flimsy *Sleeping Beauty*.

Nureyev choreographed *Sleeping Beauty* in homage to his idealized memories of the Kirov Ballet in St. Petersburg,[4] the company of his youth and a state-supported organization with hundreds of dancers in its employ. With La Scala and the Kirov as his models, small wonder that he deployed dancers as lavishly as Georgiadis did fabrics and materials. Yet he did nothing simply for the sake of extravagance, everything in obedience to the dictates of his imagination. His imagination, however, functioned on a scale the National had never before encountered.

Even the demands on company rehearsal time, so inefficient from an administrative point of view, had their purpose. Nureyev wanted the whole company immersed in the entire ballet, so that it could give a coherent, convincing account of the work. And he wanted to push all the dancers to go beyond anything they had done before. Mary Jago remembered the gruelling rehearsal period.

> He made us do run-throughs of *Sleeping Beauty* twice a day. And it's a hard, hard ballet; technically, it's hard, hard, hard. He had all his Auroras running it every single day full out. You never marked anything. He pushed us — he worked us hard — but he also was very giving. He pushed you hard because he knew you were capable of more. His reasons and his intentions were so productive.[5]

Though Franca, who had other repertoire besides *Sleeping Beauty* to consider, chafed under the difficulties created by Nureyev's all-consuming passion for detail, the dancers thrived on it. For this generation of performers, Nureyev's coaching in *Sleeping Beauty* provided the same zeal for professionalism and authentic classical style that Franca had instilled in another, technically less proficient group twenty years earlier. For Karen Kain, whose rising career was propelled into the international arena by her association with Nureyev, the fabled tantrums and displays of temper told little of the artist underneath. Before his untimely death, she spoke of the nature of their partnership.

> He bullied me, but underneath it he always made sure that I knew that he really cared about me. He really believed in me. He was never cruel to me. He did have his tempers sometimes, and I would know when to stay away from him, but he never really took things out on me, and he was very generous. I think that's the key word. Not all artists of his calibre are generous people, but he is a very generous person. I think that's what makes you forgive any of the other little things in his character that are difficult. He was special to me. But he took time with everybody, every member of the corps de ballet, and he made them dance better.[6]

Not only did they dance better, but, according to Veronica Tennant, the company discovered essential performance values under his teaching and goading.

> He'd say, "You must eat up the stage and so audience will go wild." He gave great lessons in theatricality. I think probably we weren't that theatrical a company before Rudolf, and it was after working with him that you realized that this was very much a reciprocal occasion with the

audience. And that it was a communicative art. And that, yes, there were ways of getting response, not only in an adulatory sense, but in a sense of the audience being a participatory force in the performance.[7]

Though Nureyev's presence gave the male dancers less opportunity to shine, it nevertheless opened other kinds of experience to them. Frank Augustyn, at the time a young and relatively inexperienced principal dancer, got considerable exposure in the bravura role of the Bluebird and did, on the rare occasions when Nureyev was not dancing, take on the role of the Prince. Tomas Schramek had come to the National from a background in folk dancing in his native Slovakia. At the time of Nureyev's arrival, he was not yet a principal and did not aspire to the Prince roles that were Nureyev's special domain. He shared the stage with him frequently, however, in supporting male roles like Catalinon in *Don Juan* and Gurn in *La Sylphide*. Schramek remembered a more complex, less directly generous mentor than did the women.

> He has helped me quite a bit. I don't mean actually physically, because he is not very generous in teaching and giving you correction — he wouldn't tell *you* — he would tell somebody else, and then it was up to that person to go to you and say, "I heard him say that if you do this it will help you." Hardly ever would he come and say it directly, unless he would do that to his partners.[8]

The *Sleeping Beauty* rehearsal period did far more than simply teach the dancers a new and important piece of repertoire. It opened their eyes to the Russian ballet heritage (albeit interpreted through the Westernized experience of the most celebrated defector of the day) and to the imperious demands of a difficult, uncompromising, meticulous, and inspiring imagination. The Nureyev phenomenon unleashed itself unchecked upon the company and moved the dancers to a new level of professionalism, a new conception of their art, and a new set of demands upon their own performances.

The rehearsal hall wasn't big enough for two large egos. Franca, whose real love was working in the studio with the dancers, and who was herself cast as the wicked fairy, Carabosse, the major dramatic character role in the ballet, removed herself to the administrative offices and allowed Nureyev a free rein with the company members. Victoria Bertram, as the second-cast Carabosse, wound up running interference between them.

> When we were doing Carabosse together, she'd never show up for any of the rehearsals, because she and Rudolf were not getting on very well. She couldn't stand another master in the studio — one had to give in, and she just would not show up. I had to do all the rehearsals and then write

Lise-Marie Jourdain, as the Lilac Fairy (right), confronts Victoria Bertram as Carabosse in The Sleeping Beauty.

> it down and take it upstairs and talk to her about the role because she'd
> have to do the full rehearsals.[9]

Franca, for her part, was willing to give Nureyev the latitude he required. With the administrative responsibilities involved in the production and the tour, she had not wanted to perform at all.

> In rehearsal, he was actually quite good to me because he admired me
> as a performer, ever since 1964, when he saw me do Madge the witch in
> Erik's production of *La Sylphide*. That was why he insisted that I do the
> Carabosse role, which I didn't want to do because I knew I was going to
> have my hands full. There I was with a million things on my mind, trying
> to remember his choreography for this Carabosse.

Among her many administrative headaches, she had to deal with Nureyev's cavalier attitude toward union rehearsal regulations, which he had a tendency to ignore if the required break interrupted his creative process.[10] Whether he was aware of causing any difficulties or not, Nureyev appreciated the welcome and the freedom he received. "Celia Franca greeted me with nice open arms, of course now and then imposing her ideas, remembering Covent Garden version, or Sadler's Wells. But she was tactful and she kept away and didn't get into my soup."[11] His comment revealed the fundamental stylistic difference between the two. *The Sleeping Beauty* had been the Sadler's Wells's (and later the Royal Ballet's) signature piece, the vehicle with which it created a North American sensation and established its international reputation. Like all the de Valois generation, Franca, who had herself danced the Bluebird pas de deux at Sadler's Wells,[12] could lay a special claim to the ballet. But Nureyev, who had by this time had ample experience of the later Royal Ballet versions staged by Ashton and MacMillan and had often partnered its legendary Aurora, Margot Fonteyn, nevertheless considered himself the pipeline to the authentic, the Russian, tradition of the ballet, as preserved at the Kirov, the theatre where *Sleeping Beauty* had had its premiere. Though the fact received little public recognition, the National's production of this crown jewel of the Royal Ballet's repertoire represented a break from the English tradition, not a perpetuation of it. The production, which Franca had long regarded as an absolute necessity for a classical company,[13] and in which she must have had a certain proprietary interest, owed little to the English tradition or to her personal storehouse of knowledge.

On the Road with *The Sleeping Beauty*

The Sleeping Beauty opened at Ottawa's National Arts Centre, one of the largest and best-equipped stages on the continent, on September 1, 1972. Both Georgiadis and David Hersey, the lighting designer, had worked to the specifications of the NAC, thus assuming conditions that could not be duplicated anywhere else on the tour. Even at the superbly equipped National Arts Centre, the huge, cumbersome set pieces, like the grand staircase and the three-dimensional chandelier the size of a small room, created problems onstage and impossibilities for storage in the wings or the flies when not required. The chandelier alone took two stagehands several hours to assemble and could not be flown out of sight because the spacing of the overhead lines and pipes would not allow free clearance for an object of its depth. (The three-dimensional model was soon replaced with a two-dimensional one that could be flown.) Set pieces designed to take advantage of the maximum NAC stage height snagged on the lines whenever they were moved. Drunk with the technical riches the Arts Centre afforded, Hersey used some three hundred lamps in his lighting plot, many more than the company could travel with.[14] Having survived the chaos of a week's production time at the NAC, the technical crews then had to endure a baptism of fire on the road. After playing the NAC and the Place des Arts in Montreal, the show went on to Philadelphia, the first of the significantly smaller stages into which Hurok had booked the company on its cross-continent tour. Larry Beevers, who, after a serious injury, had just made the transition from dancer to assistant stage manager, recalled the experience vividly.

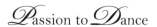

I remember someone saying to Georgiadis, "What do we do in these small theatres?" "Well, that's up to you." Now we were stuck with a huge set going into smaller theatres. And our intermissions became so long, and our shows became so long. Three and a half hours in those days was nothing for *Sleeping Beauty*.[15]

The wear and tear of awkward scene changes caused damage to the set. Attempts to follow the original lighting plot without the resources of the NAC left parts of the show in semi-darkness. Road crew kept on quitting, unwilling to take the strain of the long hours and the physical demands of assembling and striking the huge set within the unyielding, impossible deadlines of the touring schedule.[16]

Somehow, *Sleeping Beauty* staggered through the autumn portion of the tour, into the O'Keefe Centre and a Toronto opening night as exciting as any in the company's history. Thanks to the resourcefulness of the technical crew, the dedication of the dancers, and the unflagging energy of everyone involved, the curtain rose to reveal not the difficulties and shortcomings of a technically complicated production, but the ornate splendour of Nureyev's vision of *Sleeping Beauty*. It was, as Nureyev had intended, a substantial, even a weighty production, and the dancers, in some cases, had not yet gained the full authority necessary to carry it off. But in Veronica Tennant, the company had an Aurora who could subdue the technical demands of the role to an affecting impersonation of character, and in the Bluebird pas de deux it rejoiced in the electrifying performances of Karen Kain and Frank Augustyn, giving audiences a foretaste of the partnership that was to develop between them. Nureyev may have been the star, but he was far from being the evening's only attraction. This *Sleeping Beauty* was a major achievement in itself, as well as a harbinger of things to come. The most extravagant production in the company's history had justified itself as the most vivid realization the National had ever achieved of the fairy-tale world that constituted ballet's central fantasy.

Following the Toronto run and the television taping in the O'Keefe Centre, *The Sleeping Beauty* was given a brief rest. The dancers embarked on the Christmas round of *Nutcracker*s in Windsor, Ottawa, Toronto, and London (with a few *Swan Lake*s thrown in for good measure), while production regrouped its forces for an assault on *Beauty*'s unsolved problems. After set maintenance and repairs had been effected in the Toronto workshops, the production department, en route to Vancouver for the opening of the 1973 portion of the Hurok tour, took a detour to Regina, where a large enough stage was available for the week of production work essential to the success of the remainder of the tour. At the Hurok organization's expense, the show was set up and properly "trimmed," all the pieces positioned so that lighting pipes were masked and wing space would not show from anywhere in the audience. Then measurements and markings were made, so that the desired effect could be duplicated in any theatre on the tour. David Hersey returned

Rudolf Nureyev (right) and Winthrop Corey as The Moor and His Friend in José Limón's The Moor's Pavane.

from England to relight the entire production to the specifications of the touring electrical equipment.[17] With somewhat lighter minds, the company resumed the *Sleeping Beauty* tour; its demands were now merely unmanageable, not completely impossible.

The Hurok itinerary was daunting, exhausting. Carrying as repertoire *Beauty*, *Swan Lake*, and a mixed program of *La Sylphide*, *The Moor's Pavane*, and *Fandango* (with occasional additions of the pas de deux from *The Nutcracker* or *Le Loup*), the National worked its way across the continent for four uninterrupted months, routinely doing a minimum of seven performances in six days with never more than one day off in seven. While *Swan Lake* concluded the run in one city, an advance crew would proceed to the next to begin the set-up for *Sleeping Beauty*. For the dancers, the tour became an endurance test. As Veronica Tennant, who shared the role of Aurora with Nadia Potts and Vanessa Harwood, recalled: "Absolutely everybody was stretched to their limit. All the ballerinas were on stage all the time. If they were on in Aurora one night, they were doing Fairies the next." A short break of eight days preceded the final engagement of the tour at the Metropolitan Opera House, but the company was still exhausted when it opened the New York performances.

Nothing in their previous experience had prepared the dancers for the audience response. New York provided the grand climax of the tour for the company and for Nureyev himself, as Veronica Tennant's account of the evening testified.

> I was utterly dazed by the whole thing, it was so exciting. And it meant so much to Rudolf too, which was interesting. I think probably the biggest surprise was the roar of the audience. He had already started to tune my ears to an audience response, but nobody roars like a New York audience. That opening night in New York in *Sleeping Beauty* was thrilling.[18]

Critical response, sensitive to the stature implied by playing the Met, considered Nureyev first, the company second. Clive Barnes, by this time no stranger to the National, summed the matter up in a review article midway through the company's New York stay.

> The company has style and taste, but little originality. It dances like the Royal Ballet — which is a very good way to dance — but with slightly less conviction. So what is a nice company like this doing at the Metropolitan Opera House when its previous New York engagement was a one-night stand in Brooklyn? The answer can be given in two words: Rudolf Nureyev.[19]

Barnes, clearly anxious not to accord the National the status of a genuinely front-ranking company, nevertheless struck a generally cordial note in the rest of his reviews. Referring to the La Scala precursor of the National's production, he went on to say: "This is one of the best productions of *The Sleeping Beauty* around. I thought so when I first saw it — with Fonteyn and Nureyev — at La Scala, and I think so now. But the Canadians dance it better." The reporter for *Variety*, after the obligatory references to Nureyev, was even more positive. "But with every acknowledgement of the spectacularity Nureyev brings to this *Beauty*, the ensemble still must and does bear the main responsibility. The evening rests on general merit."[20] For all that Nureyev garnered the lion's share of the attention, the company itself developed a following among the New York public, with the regulars in the audience returning to watch their favourite dancers and give them the adulation of loyal fans.[21] Nureyev and his *Sleeping Beauty* had triumphed in New York, as Hurok had so profitably foreseen. The National's thoroughly respectable, if less frenzied reception by the New York public and press had not been such a foregone conclusion; its significance would endure long after the Nureyev hoopla had died down.

It took years for the company and its public to assess the full impact of the Nureyev experience. The financial accounting was the easiest to perform. At $412,565, *The Sleeping Beauty* had cost almost double its initial projected budget and broken all former records for production costs. (By the end of the century, production budgets of a million dollars or more would be commonplace. James Kudelka's 1995 version of *Nutcracker* came in at a staggering $2.5 million, almost nine hundred thousand dollars over budget.)[22] Attempts to secure corporate sponsorship for *Sleeping Beauty* having proved largely unsuccessful, the company once again faced a staggering deficit and bleak short-term financial prospects. In the long term, however, the financial investment in *Sleeping Beauty* proved to be a sound one. Its immense and continuing popularity soon helped to recover those enormous costs, and by the time of its 1975 submission to the Canada Council, the company's management could point to the *Beauty* experience as evidence of its ability to emerge if not triumphant, then at least unscathed from the brink of financial catastrophe.[23] One other statistical assessment was easy, and revealing. The Hurok connection had increased the National's number of annual performances from one hundred and seven in 1971–72 (to the end of the European tour in July) to one hundred and ninety-eight, a record that has yet to be exceeded. The company estimated that its dancers would reach an audience of four hundred thousand people, compared with one hundred and ninety-three thousand the year before.[24] Never before had the company been so large, danced so continuously, or brought the pleasures of a full-scale production of the classical repertoire to so many.

Herein lay one of the principal intangible values of the experience. In associating itself with Nureyev in such a marathon of travel and performance, the National had, like Pavlova in her day, become one of the major popularizers of ballet on the North American continent. From this perspective, it mattered less that the company had been seen in New York than that smaller centres like Champaign, Iowa City, and Seattle had had the riches of Nureyev's production spread before them. (The tyranny of Hurok economics eliminated all but the major Canadian cities from this first tour.) And in this enterprise, the company members had been full partners with Nureyev; they had the satisfaction

Karen Kain and Frank Augustyn as Princess Aurora and Prince Florimund in The
Sleeping Beauty.

Andrew Oxenham

of equal participation in an artistic venture that might well inspire individuals and thus perpetuate the art form through successive generations.

But the full appreciation of Nureyev's significance to the company and its development could come only from another professional, and only, perhaps, with the perspective gained from the passage of time. Nureyev, one of the great performers of his or any generation, paid the dancers of the National a compliment by demanding of them no less than he demanded of himself. In retrospect, Franca recognized the value of his unyielding concern for accurate Petipa style. "In order to present his ballet — his Petipa as he had got it into his head and into his muscles and into his bones from his background — he was a stickler for academic accuracy with the dancers." His insistence that each position be carefully defined and clearly marked resulted at times in a certain staccato academicism, at the expense of lyrical style. As Franca recalled it, the dream vision scene of the second act could have been more mysterious. "My memory goes back to Fonteyn, and she was very ethereal. Our ballerinas were not ethereal in that particular scene." But for Franca the resultant accuracy of style far outweighed any disadvantages. "It was really because of his insistence on that kind of accuracy that Karen and Frank won the silver medal in Moscow in 1973." And she acknowledged that Nureyev's uncompromising stylistic example inspired the company members as much as his demands challenged them.

> He was a stickler with himself. He prided himself on that solo at the end, in the wedding scene of *Sleeping Beauty*. He prided himself on the *tours en l'air* finished in absolute clean fifth position; he'd grit his teeth, and there was no way he wasn't going to finish that whole solo, spinning away and getting as dizzy as hell and then standing up in a clean fifth position, saying, "I did it." Well that was a very good example for the dancers.[25]

Both example and precept worked forcefully on virtually every dancer. In the final analysis, one factor outweighed all the others: the company danced differently, and danced better, as a result of its association with Nureyev.

Like *Romeo and Juliet* in 1964, *The Sleeping Beauty* in 1972 propelled the company as a whole onto a different level of activity, from which there could be no retreat. As Dieter Penzhorn, of the company's production department, put it: "If you have a circle, you can't make a bubble in it on one side — the whole circle will expand. And that's what *Beauty* did to the company."[26] Expanded production facilities and skills broadened the company's horizons and raised its public's expectations; the larger company of dancers had to be supplied with appropriate material. The energies and resources that had been required to sustain *Sleeping Beauty* thus became the norm and called into being a more elaborate repertoire and an even higher standard of production values. And like *Romeo and Juliet* before it, *The Sleeping Beauty* put the seal on Franca's vision of the National as a large-scale classical company, at a time when debate about the appropriate direction for it to take had once again opened up genuine alternatives in the minds of some of its critics. *Beauty* stood as a spectacular vindication of Franca's long-standing goals, a gorgeous roadblock in the way of anyone who sought to streamline and modernize at the expense of the standard repertoire.

THE NATIONAL'S BLUEBIRDS, KAIN AND AUGUSTYN, AT THE MOSCOW BALLET COMPETITION

An important by-product of the *Sleeping Beauty* experience, with intrinsic, long-lasting significance for the life of the company, was the success of Karen Kain and Frank Augustyn at the Second International Ballet Competition in Moscow in the summer of 1973. The invitation to send competitors to the event was in itself a signal honour to the two women without whom there would have been no competitors to send. Betty Oliphant had strengthened the Bolshoi connections she had established in 1962 with a visit in 1969, during which, as she recalled, she "was given the run of the school for six weeks,"[27] a clear acknowledgment of her international reputation as a teacher of professional dancers. Franca's international

Bruce Zinger

Two of the company's more recent Bluebirds, Stacey Shiori Minagawa and Keiichi Hirano, await their entrance in the wings during The Sleeping Beauty.

eminence was recognized with an invitation to sit on the competition's jury, which included the likes of the British critic Arnold Haskell, the famed Kirov ballerina Irina Kolpakova, and the American choreographer Jerome Robbins. The participation of Kain and Augustyn in Moscow thus paid tribute to the two formative influences in their careers: the National Ballet School and the National Ballet Company.

The competition itself was a harrowing experience. The dancers had just completed the marathon *Sleeping Beauty* tour. The Bluebird pas de deux, at least, was well rehearsed, but little time remained to rest or to prepare any other repertoire. The difficulties of understanding the intricacies of competition protocol and dealing with a foreign language and culture hit the Canadians hard. As a result, they used their strongest piece, the Bluebird pas de deux, for the first elimination round, unaware that in that round it would not be marked, and that it could not then be repeated later in the competition. The European-style raked stage, sloped from the rear down to the footlights to improve sightlines for the audience, and wooden, rather than linoleum, floor were unfamiliar to them. Not knowing exactly when they would be called on to dance, they warmed up countless times, in a constant state of nervous tension, and found themselves rehearsing at one in the morning, the only time they could get the stage.[28] Against these odds, and competing against older and more experienced artists at a time before the competition was sectioned into junior and senior categories, Kain won the silver medal; as a pair, Kain and Augustyn, nominated by Kolpakova,[29] won a special prize for the best pas de deux in the competition. Kain attributed part of their success with the Russians to the Nureyev experience of the year preceding.

> They loved the way we did Bluebird because of the schooling, and that was from him so much. It was our schooling too, but the *port de bras* and the style were directly from him. They didn't know that, but they were very impressed by what we were doing.[30]

Whatever finish Nureyev had put on the dancers, it was the school and the company that had produced them. Their Moscow victory finally awoke the Canadian public to the extraordinary achievement of these two institutions.

It was not the first time that company members had placed well in international competition. At Varna, Martine van Hamel had won a gold medal in 1966, Nadia Potts and Clinton Rothwell a prize for the best pas de deux (from *Le Loup*) in 1970.[31] But the enormous prestige of the Bolshoi, where the competition was held, contributed to a higher public awareness of Kain and Augustyn's success. It was as much a personal as an official triumph. Kain, one of the official winners, remembered the reception the final night audience gave to Augustyn, who had not placed. "Some of the people who won gold medals got booed and hissed by the audience, and when Frank got up they wouldn't let him go, because they liked him so much."[32] And this competition received prominent

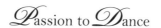

coverage in Canada from the outset. John Fraser, then writing regular dance criticism for the *Globe and Mail*, gave the venture the attention it deserved with regular feature stories covering the dancers' progress through the competition.

COPPÉLIA AND ERIK BRUHN'S RETURN TO PERFORMING

Even the trials and successes of *The Sleeping Beauty* could not entirely distract Franca from her intention to lighten her own load and step back somewhat from the active artistic leadership of the company. Her conversation with David Haber in Monte Carlo at the end of the European tour had led to further negotiations and resulted finally in the announcement, on November 30, 1972, of his appointment as co-artistic director of the company.[33] There was no indication at the time that this appointment would one day translate itself into the artistic directorship, a point that gave rise to enormous controversy when the translation eventually took place. Franca, indeed, remained open to any possibilities, and as late as the following July put out highly tentative feelers to John Neumeier, the American-born, German-based choreographer whose work with the Royal Winnipeg Ballet was attracting favourable attention and whose *Don Juan* was about to enter the National's repertoire.[34] Nureyev, meanwhile, strengthened his already close ties to the company through annual return visits for Hurok-sponsored tours that continued until 1977. Nor was Erik Bruhn ever very far away. His appointment as resident producer of the company, beginning with the 1974–75 season, formalized his long-standing association with the National and guaranteed his presence in Toronto for three months of the year.[35] The aura of three such plausible candidates hovering about the company at this crucial time provided ample material for gossip and speculation.

In the meantime, however, the public's hungry maw had to be fed with new ballets, and Franca and Haber applied themselves to the never-ending task of building repertoire with two additions that had an appropriately valedictory air about them. *Les Sylphides* and *Coppélia*, Franca's very first choices for the company's repertoire, would see out her final years with the National. Both were to be Bruhn productions, but the recurring illness that had caused his retirement from dancing plagued him during the rehearsal period for *Les Sylphides* and resulted in Franca's stepping into the breach.[36] Fittingly enough, the new *Les Sylphides* became a Bruhn-Franca co-production.

Coppélia, the staple of the National's early repertoire, had played in every season from the opening one to 1962–63, the last before the move to the O'Keefe Centre. There then followed a hiatus of nearly twelve years before it rejoined the repertoire, although there had been talk of a new production at least as early as 1972.[37] Rehearsals for *Coppélia* were delayed by Bruhn's surgery, in December 1973 and January 1974, which finally treated the perforated ulcer from which he had suffered, undiagnosed, for eleven years.[38] But rather than turn to someone else to keep to their original timetable, Franca and Haber accommodated their plans to Bruhn's revised schedule,[39] with the result that *Coppélia* premiered on February 8, 1975, seven months after Franca had stepped down as artistic director of the company.

At the suggestion of Robert A. Laidlaw, long-time benefactor of the National, the company dedicated this new *Coppélia* to its founding triumvirate, Sydney Mulqueen, Pearl Whitehead, and Aileen Woods.[40] The dedication highlighted the striking contrast between the company's tentative beginnings in 1951 and its confident professionalism in

Beverley Gallegos

Erik Bruhn and Rudolf Nureyev as Dr. Coppélius and Franz in Coppélia *in 1975.*

1975. Three casts alternated in the roles of the young lovers: Veronica Tennant and Tomas Schramek, Mary Jago and Hazaros Surmeyan, and Vanessa Harwood and the Australian-born Gary Norman. Among the dancers portraying Dr. Coppélius was none other than Erik Bruhn. Maurice Strike's evocative designs transformed the O'Keefe stage into a cheerful idealization of a European village, then a sinister, claustrophobic realization of Coppélius's workshop. Nostalgia and remembrance for days gone by complemented the youthful self-assurance of the new generation of dancers that now made up the National.

As he had done with *Swan Lake*, Bruhn compressed the staging of *Coppélia* in the interests of dramatic continuity, so that the traditional three acts became two. His first act, in two closely linked scenes, told the entire E.T.A. Hoffmann story of the toymaker who thinks he has brought his doll to life, while his second became simply the wedding celebration for Franz and Swanilda, with divertissements. This structure placed great emphasis, in the first act, on the grotesque pathos of Dr. Coppélius as a species of diabolical Pygmalion to Coppélia's Galatea, only to have the role descend to its more traditional level of buffoonery and compromise in the second act. Bruhn's *Coppélia* made Franz and Swanilda a pair of callous, middle-class opportunists, Dr. Coppélius a crazed visionary. As characters, they inhabited separate worlds, not to be bridged as easily as the concluding festivities suggested. In the unthinking victory of vigorous youth over thoughtful age, one could see mirrored some of the frustrations Bruhn must have felt at having to surrender the *danseur noble* roles of his youth to younger, less finished artists. With the role of Dr. Coppélius, Bruhn created one of the major vehicles of his mature career as a character artist. The macabre events of the second scene, in which Dr. Coppélius attempted to steal Franz's soul in order to infuse life into Coppélia, spoke poignantly of the desire to preserve and manipulate youthful energy, the energy for which the mature dancer must envy his younger colleagues.

Bruhn had retired from the stage for good, or so he thought, in 1971. But as he recuperated and adjusted to his changed life, he was prevailed upon by the National to attempt the character role of Madge, the witch, in his own production of *La Sylphide*.[41] A greater departure from the prince roles he had reluctantly forsaken could not be imagined. His first character role, and an exercise in cross-dressing at that, made the transition easier for Bruhn, if not for his adoring public.[42] Bruhn the character artist made his debut on the stage of the Metropolitan Opera House in New York on August 9, 1974, dancing with the National Ballet of Canada. Rudolf Nureyev appeared onstage with Bruhn for the first time ever on that August night,[43] dancing the role of James. With the National, Bruhn would appear frequently thereafter as Madge and then as Dr. Coppélius, his personal identity concealed behind the makeup, wigs, and costumes that, paradoxically, gave his dramatic personality a freedom it had never before enjoyed.

In April 1975, during the company's second European tour, the two friends, rivals, and one-time lovers danced together in Bruhn's production of *Coppélia* on the stage of London's Coliseum, Bruhn as the decrepit toymaker and Nureyev as the vigorous young man. Bruhn spent a week in London prior to the performance, teaching his younger friend the ballet.[44] Just ten years earlier, the two had competed on equal terms in the New Year's performances of *La Sylphide* at the O'Keefe Centre. At the Coliseum in 1975, the plot of *Coppélia* told a different story, in which the great age gap between Dr. Coppélius and Franz acknowledged the ten-year difference in age between Bruhn and Nureyev. In the physically demanding world of ballet, that age difference favoured Nureyev for just a little while longer. In purely dramatic terms, however, Bruhn, by yielding the field to his junior, had laid claim to a new territory, that of the character artist, in which his gifts were unrivalled.

CELEBRITY BY ASSOCIATION: THE BARYSHNIKOV DEFECTION

In August 1974, at its opening performance at Ontario Place just five days after the New York *La Sylphide*, the company played host to yet another Soviet defector. Mikhail Baryshnikov would dazzle North America with the elegance and refinement of his classical style, and soon edge Nureyev out of his position as ballet's international superstar. The vehicle, once again, was *La Sylphide*, and Bruhn was in the audience. The cloak and dagger conspiracy of Baryshnikov's defection in Toronto had occupied the better part of a month and had involved some of the company's dancers in elaborate efforts to elude the press.[45] His television appearance with the National (in excerpts from *La Sylphide*) and his New York debut with American Ballet Theatre (dancing in *Giselle* opposite Natalia Makarova)[46] served to whet the Canadian audience's appetite further. On August 14, 1974, with public interest whipped into a frenzy by rumours of romance and the political intrigue of the event, and despite a public transit strike that paralysed Toronto traffic, the Forum, Ontario Place's outdoor amphitheatre, began filling in the early afternoon for the evening performance. The scheduled afternoon rehearsal of *La Sylphide*, without Baryshnikov himself, took place before the attentive, patient crowd. By late afternoon, with every inch of seating space taken, the hillside surrounding the forum began swarming with the overflow, anxious for at least a glimpse of Baryshnikov and for a sense of participation in the event. By performance time on that hot August night, an estimated ten thousand people were on hand to greet the new sensation.

He did not disappoint them, even though it was Baryshnikov's first attempt not only at the role, but at any Bournonville choreography, which offers few opportunities for the kind of athletic display many were expecting from a Russian star. His performance as James, a haunting amalgam of grace and passion, conferred artistic grandeur on an evening that might otherwise have been merely a celebrity event. Admission to the Forum was, as usual, free with the price of general admission to the park. The egalitarian atmosphere of this tradition of popular entertainment contributed to the ecstatic, cheering welcome Baryshnikov received.

Harold Whyte

Veronica Tennant and Mikhail Baryshnikov in La Sylphide, *shortly after his defection from the Soviet Union in 1974.*

THE SHORT REIGN OF DAVID HABER

In early January 1974, Celia Franca had announced her decision to resign the artistic directorship of the company.[47] She intended, however, to maintain a close working relationship with the company and asked the board to ratify her choice of David Haber as her successor, effective July 1, 1974. She thus planned an orderly transfer of power to the deputy whom she had selected and trained over the past fourteen months. Had things worked as planned, comparisons might have been drawn yet again between Franca and de Valois, who had handed over the running of the Royal Ballet to her chosen successor, Sir Frederick Ashton, in 1963, without the benefit of selection committees or advertised vacancies.[48] But although the board initially acquiesced in Franca's choice, it was clear from the very beginning that there was significant opposition within the board both to the choice and to the procedures that had put it in place. Haber himself openly acknowledged this opposition to his appointment in his report, as artistic director, to the Annual General Meeting of September 9, 1974. "I am of course aware that some members of the Board were against my appointment. I sincerely hope the continuing development of the company will allay their fears."[49] His hopes were ill founded.

As Franca remembered events, it was she who made the first approach to Haber and asked him whether he felt ready, after his work with the company, to take over the artistic directorship. After a few days' reflection, he decided he was, and the two put their plan to Ian H. McLeod, then the chairman of the board of directors, who agreed to it without bringing it before the full board.[50] This procedure in itself lay at the root of many of the troubles to come. Board members felt they had been slighted in the process, among them Betty Oliphant, who was, of course, much more than just an ordinary board member.[51] There were also fears that Haber, whose experience was in management rather than in the studio, might encroach uncomfortably upon the sphere of the general manager at the time, Gerry Eldred.[52] Haber could not escape criticism on the grounds that he had never been a dancer or a choreographer, even though there were illustrious precedents in the history of ballet companies for the non-dancing ballet administrator. (In fact, Haber had studied dance and had even appeared on the Quebec night-club circuit in his youth.)[53] Haber never claimed to be anything he wasn't. He went into the job hoping to show that his own blend of skills and experience could bring advantages to the company different from those that a dancer might offer. Haber's appointment, then, violated the sense of procedure of at least some of the board members, and it plunged the company into debate about appropriate qualifications for the position. But had there not been fundamental discontent with the choice itself, these debates of principle might never have surfaced.

For those still hoping for a radical transformation of the artistic direction of the company, Haber's appointment merely continued the old régime, and it thwarted their desire for change. As Haber himself put it: "Celia wanted a certain amount of freedom, but she didn't want to let go." To the degree that Haber's appointment was seen as merely Franca's strategy for not letting go, it never had a chance. His close personal identification with her, and with her ideals and goals for the company, branded him as her creature and stood in the way of any independent assessment of his achievements.

For the brief period during which he held it, Haber was uncomfortable with the title of artistic director. He hoped the position would evolve into that of director general, or *Intendant*, on the model of continental European opera houses, with artistic, musical, technical, and managerial staff reporting to him on an equal footing. On such a model, his experience in management would be an asset, and his lack of experience as a dancer no impediment to his effective functioning. Given the inherent tension between the artistic director and the general manager in the company structure as it then existed, his scheme might even have solved some of its long-standing problems of power sharing as well. But his essentially conservative approach did not allow these ideas a chance to emerge. "I moved too slowly, and I didn't create waves at the beginning, and say, 'Ah, here's a new presence.'"[54] Haber had very little time to establish any kind of presence at all.

Cynthia Lucas and David Roxander as Isabelle-Marie and Patrice in Ann Ditchburn's Mad Shadows.

He did manage, however, to initiate a number of projects that bore fruit after his departure. The major one of these was *Mad Shadows*, Ann Ditchburn's most ambitious work. Ironically, given the never-ending pressures on the company to mount Canadian work, Haber had to fight hard to persuade the board to take a risk on this thoroughly Canadian project, based on Marie-Claire Blais's novel *La Belle Bête*, with an original score by André

Gagnon and designs by Jack King. Originally conceived as a joint choreographic venture between Ditchburn and James Kudelka, then a rising young choreographer in the company's ranks, *Mad Shadows* became Ditchburn's exclusive property when the proposed collaboration proved too difficult to carry out. *Mad Shadows* played twenty-two performances over four seasons, but reached a much wider audience through a very successful telecast and enjoyed the distinction, as well, of playing the Royal Opera House, Covent Garden, and the Metropolitan Opera in New York during its lifespan. Ditchburn herself later described *Mad Shadows* as a naive work, at least in the international context, but saw its naïveté as appropriate to its subject matter and theme. David Haber considered it a good theatrical piece and an important opportunity for Ditchburn, even though, as things turned out, it proved to be her last work for the company. Attending the premiere, not as artistic director but as Ditchburn's guest, Haber commented, with a mixture of bitterness and satisfaction, "It was worth the fight, wasn't it?"[55]

Another of Haber's acquisitions, *Whispers of Darkness* by Norbert Vesak, the Canadian choreographer who had created the Royal Winnipeg Ballet's highly successful *The Ecstasy of Rita Joe*, gave less cause for satisfaction. By Haber's own admission, the ballet did not work out,[56] and it closed after only ten performances. Haber helped to sow the seeds of interest, at the board level, in the acquisition of Sir Frederick Ashton's *La Fille mal gardée*[57] and tried to bring John Neumeier back to choreograph an original work for the company,[58] but the project which was undoubtedly closest to his heart reached only partial fruition, as a production stored in the company's videotape files but never fully mounted or performed in public. *Le Coq d'Or*, the ballet that would not be, became the phantom monument to Haber's aspirations for the repertoire.

First produced in 1914, in Diaghilev's heyday, Fokine's *Le Coq d'Or* (a spectacular opera-ballet to a score by Rimsky-Korsakov) had been revived by de Basil in the thirties and had thereafter fallen out of sight, along with most of the Fokine repertoire. The opportunity to acquire the ballet arose through Franca's old contact, from her Metropolitan Ballet days, Nicholas Beriosoff. "Papa" Beriosoff, as he was universally known in the ballet world by the seventies, was the self-appointed champion of the out-of-favour Fokine repertoire. He offered to mount *Coq d'Or* for the National and suggested that the company could buy sets and costumes (by André Delfau, after the originals by Gontcharova) at a cut-rate price from the Ballet de Wallonie in Charleroi, which had revived the work in 1966.[59] Haber, backed by Franca, saw Beriosoff's offer as an opportunity to perform an important act of historical preservation. Restoring this gem of the Fokine era would not only add a novel piece of exotica to the repertoire, but also demonstrate the historical line of descent from Petipa through Fokine to the present day.[60] Beriosoff, then sixty-nine, would not live forever. The time was ripe to take advantage of his offer, and his memory, in order to preserve *Coq d'Or* and transmit it to future generations.

Haber pursued this acquisition vigorously, not only for its potential box-office value but for the general direction it represented for the company. There was talk of Fokine's

The National Ballet of Canada's last curtain call at the Hummingbird Centre, after a performance of Petrouchka *on May 14, 2006.*

Schéhérazade and *Petrouchka* as well, both of which Beriosoff offered to produce.[61] (*Petrouchka* would eventually come into the repertoire, under entirely different circumstances, and not until 2006.) But Haber encountered serious difficulty, within the board and within the company, in defending what he described as "one of those wonderful, wonderful antique pieces" against the doubts of those who had not seen, or even heard of, the work.[62] Since he was a non-dancer, his own judgment carried less weight in such matters than it might have, and Franca, having resigned the artistic directorship, could not defend the choice too vigorously for fear of appearing to call into question Haber's own ability to do so. As internal opposition to the production grew, Beriosoff entered negotiations with London's Festival Ballet to mount *Coq d'Or* for them in 1976.[63] If the company was to capitalize on the originality of the plan, it would have to act fast. Beriosoff was engaged to come and teach the work, even though funds for the production itself, in the post-*Beauty* era of economic restraint, had not been fully committed.

But before the issue could be resolved, other events complicated matters even further. In March 1975, midway through Haber's first year as artistic director, Betty Oliphant announced her resignation as associate artistic director of the company, the position she had held since the 1968 crisis. She explained the reasons for her resignation in a full statement to the press.

Although I think that David Haber has many good qualities, I do not believe they are all the ones needed to be an effective artistic director. I was informed last year that he was to succeed Celia only a few hours before the press was, and although I had strong reservations, I also felt there was some hope. He did have some artistic background to draw on and with proper consultation and a reasonable acceptance of his own limitations, I thought he might make it. So I kept quiet.

Since Celia's resignation, however, it has become increasingly clear that her time with the company has become more and more limited and that this situation will likely increase in the future. Since David's appointment, I have had to demand two meetings with the artistic staff to present important problems. Since the last of those, there has been virtually no communication between us on the future plans of the company.

At a recent board meeting, the problems surfaced because I brought them up. I hated doing this since I feel artistic decisions should be made by the artistic staff, but the situation had reached, in my opinion, a crucial point.

I am terribly concerned about the choice of repertoire that is being proposed right now. I am worried about how the dancers are being used — and not used — and I feel particularly terrible about the fact that I have to train kids who will be joining a company that has weak leadership and appears to be drifting toward real trouble artistically.

Since the artistic staff have made it abundantly clear over the past season that they did not want to discuss anything with me, I have decided to resign. When you stop being useful, you clear out.[64]

The enormous respect that Oliphant enjoyed in the international ballet community made this announcement far more than a mere intimation of discord. It was a motion of non-confidence in Franca's chosen successor and a challenge to the board to do something about his artistic policies. Oliphant's comments about lack of communication probably referred to the fact that the Artistic Management Committee had ceased to function and had resisted Haber's efforts to revive it.[65] The complaint about repertoire, deliberately non-specific, could have referred to any number of initiatives, including the ill-fated *Whispers of Darkness*, which had closed in February, but the proposed move to Fokine must have been one of them.

Oliphant's highly public gesture and the board's general discontent with Haber coalesced to bring matters to a head over the issue of *Coq d'Or*. Lyman Henderson, at the time still an active member of the board, recalled the pursuit of *Coq d'Or* as one of many aspects of Haber's direction to come under heavy criticism.

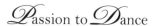

The board became extremely critical about his choice of resurrecting *Le Coq d'Or*, which he could do economically because he knew where the costumes were. It didn't strike the imagination of the board. It was just one of the heaps of criticism.[66]

The board instituted a review of senior artistic and management staff. It also declined, for financial reasons, to authorize funds for the full production of *Coq d'Or*. In May 1975, Haber wrote to Beriosoff, explaining that the board had authorized only that the company learn and videotape the work for future reference.[67] It was an unsatisfactory compromise between the company's prior commitments to Beriosoff and the board's desire to cancel the production outright. In October 1975, after efforts to secure corporate sponsorship for *Coq d'Or* had failed, the production, which had been fully cast, rehearsed, and videotaped, was finally shelved.[68] But before that, on June 3, 1975, the board asked Haber to leave.[69]

The company announced Haber's resignation on June 7, to take effect July 31, 1975. The press release, though not detailed, was extraordinarily candid.

> Mr. Haber said that his decision is the result of irreconcilable differences with the Board of Directors of the Ballet. These differences revolve around the choice of repertoire, cuts in productions and the procedure followed by a committee of the Board of Directors in their assessment of senior artistic and management staff.[70]

In the final analysis, Oliphant's public statement was less significant than the decision of the board to remove an artistic director in whom it no longer had full confidence. The authority to do so had always existed, but had never previously been exercised. Challenges to Franca's authority had resulted in the board's reaffirming its confidence in her and in her artistic policies, as it had done in 1972. In removing Haber, the board asserted its ultimate responsibility for the overall fate of the company. In effect, it resolved the tension between artistic authority and the authority of board and management, a tension that had existed from the very beginning of Franca's appointment. Such draconian resolution was possible only after her departure, and made inevitable by her attempt to establish her own successor. Perhaps any individual, or at any rate any non-dancer, she had tried to place in the position would have suffered Haber's fate. Implicitly at least, the removal of David Haber came out of a desire to allow a genuinely new broom the chance to sweep clean. Lyman Henderson recognized this possibility. "There may have been a feeling in the board that it really was time for a change in artistic direction and that pure succession might not achieve that. That certainly must have been in the minds of some, although it was not publicly expressed."[71] This direct board intervention and assertion of board interest in overall artistic policies would stand as precedent in the even more controversial case of Alexander Grant just a few years later.

David Haber served as artistic director of the company for just thirteen months, far too short a period to allow for any meaningful critical evaluation of his contribution or, indeed, for his direction to have assumed a distinctive character. However, in losing him the National lost his considerable range of international theatrical contacts, which might have brought about a higher international touring profile for the company in the seventies and eighties. And his attempt to resurrect the Fokine repertoire demands one further historical footnote. The London Festival Ballet did stage *Le Coq d'Or*, under Beriosoff's direction, in 1976. Although the production failed to set the world on fire, it earned the company a small place in the history books for its contribution to the preservation of an important piece of repertoire. In later years, the Joffrey Ballet enjoyed great success with its historical reconstructions of *Petrouchka* and Nijinsky's *Rite of Spring*. Les Grands Ballets Canadiens, seizing the opportunity which the National passed up, became the repository for important historical reconstructions of the Diaghilev repertoire, including Massine's *The Three-Cornered Hat* and Balanchine's early work *La Chatte*. As ballet companies became collaborators with dance scholars in the archival task of preserving significant repertoire, the pendulum swung, and the attempts to preserve little-known repertoire found critical respect as well as popular acceptance. When the National vetoed *Le Coq d'Or*, it effectively gave up the chance to be in the vanguard of these efforts at historical reconstruction.

The press release announcing Haber's resignation also stated that a search for his successor was being instituted immediately, "not only in Canada but throughout the rest of the world."[72] Such an extensive search took time, and in the interim the company required leadership. Given Franca's intense personal disappointment at the forced resignation of David Haber,[73] her willingness to act as artistic director through this difficult period indicated her deep loyalty to the institution which owed its existence to her but was outgrowing her. She resumed the office from Haber's departure on July 31 until September 30, 1975. On September 18, she wrote to Ian H. McLeod, chair of the board of directors, resigning thereafter from any position with the National Ballet. "As you may remember, I had originally asked for a year's leave of absence with the idea of returning to work with David Haber. However, it would not be fair to the incoming artistic director, should he or she be saddled with my presence."[74]

In attempting to secure the succession of her personal choice as artistic director of the company, Franca had gambled and lost. As a result, she had to forfeit the chance for a continuing direct relationship with the National. The demands of her personal life required that she live in Ottawa, at some remove from the activities of the company. Once she had no formal position within the National's structure, her ability to influence the direction of the company she had watched over for twenty-four years was abruptly cut off. At fifty-three, with her creative energy intact and her company just one year shy of

Anthony Crickmay

This portrait of Celia Franca and David Haber only strengthened opposition to his appointment as artistic director, which was seen by many as a bid by Franca to control the company after her retirement.

its silver anniversary, she found herself sidelined. At an age when many mature dancers were just beginning the transition to administration (Alexander Grant was fifty-one, Erik Bruhn fifty-five, when they took over the direction of the company), Franca's career with the National was over. She had taken on the role of artistic director at the remarkably early age of twenty-nine. Now, because she was the company's founder, with a strong reputation for hands-on management, and because there was no other dance company in Canada that could absorb the force of her personality and give scope to her talents and energy, Franca had no choice but to enter retirement. She involved herself in dance education, both in Canada and in the People's Republic of China, and served for a time as a member of the Canada Council, but she never again had the stature as a public figure she had enjoyed for most of her adult life. After a career that had repeatedly landed her in the headlines and at the centre of controversy, Celia Franca withdrew from public life with dignity and restraint. It took years before the press and public at large recognized the extraordinary nature of her contribution to dance in Canada, or the full magnitude of her achievement. She died in Ottawa in 2007.

Chapter Seven

A BALLET COMPANY IS NOT A SCHOOL

SPECULATION AND UNCERTAINTY IN THE WAKE OF HABER'S DEPARTURE

Erik Bruhn and Rudolf Nureyev had had an intimate, complicated personal relationship almost from the moment of Nureyev's defection to the West; they had also been professional rivals, the two greatest male dancers of their time, vying for public attention and lucrative engagements. Bruhn's genius was an inspiration and a source of plunder, from which Nureyev sought to learn and appropriate anything that he could use to fulfill his own artistic ambitions. Nureyev's youth and inexhaustible passion to perform reminded Bruhn of the limits that age and health imposed on his own career. Nor was he indifferent to the fact that Nureyev, the younger artist, commanded astronomical fees, far in excess of his own earning capacity. "I am sure you know what Margot and Rudi make, so what I am mentioning here for myself, is not only reasonable, but far below what I even get in Denmark," Bruhn wrote to Franca in 1964, during negotiations for his *La Sylphide*.[1] Nureyev and Bruhn had frequently been compared in their onstage roles; with Franca's departure from the National, public speculation had them competing once again, this time for the offstage role of artistic director of the company. Both had established strong ties with the National, Bruhn as resident producer and as choreographer of four of its major productions, Nureyev as presiding genius of *The Sleeping Beauty* and as regular guest artist for the Hurok tours. The only other high-profile contender for the position, John Neumeier, effectively took himself out of the running when he told David Haber privately that the National could not match the ideal conditions for creation that the opera houses of Frankfurt and Hamburg offered him.[2]

Both Nureyev and Bruhn were approached informally and sounded out about the artistic directorship. Betty Oliphant and Gerry Eldred, the company's general manager, discussed the selection of a new artistic director with Bruhn directly and asked him to

Jeannette Edissi-Collins

Erik Bruhn teaching the male class at the National Ballet School in the 1970s.

speak with Nureyev "regarding any thoughts he may have for a new director for the company."[3] Nureyev, who by this time felt a real rapport with the company,[4] had to fend off the dancers' pointed questions. According to Veronica Tennant, Nureyev was genuinely concerned about the fate of the company. "It mattered to him. I remember the dancers saying, 'Would you consider being our director?' But he just giggled. I was never quite sure what that meant. Rudolf would giggle a lot when he just didn't want to say anything."[5] Nureyev later acknowledged that talk of his directing the company was always "in the air. But it was never offered." In any case, "It really didn't attract me to be in one place,"[6] and the company needed a resident artistic director, not a glorified visitor.

Bruhn, who was already spending three months a year with the company and had received landed immigrant status in Canada by late 1974,[7] could not be lured into a fuller commitment to the National. His period as the artistic director of the Royal Swedish Ballet from 1967 to 1972 was one of self-doubt, overwork, and public criticism. It had done nothing to attract him to artistic administration. More important, just eight months before Franca's retirement, he had made a comeback to the full performing career he thought he had forsaken forever, savouring the sweetness of a triumphant return to the stage at American Ballet Theatre's thirty-fifth anniversary gala. He performed the villainous role of Jean, the valet, in a scene from Birgit Cullberg's ballet based on the August Strindberg play, *Miss Julie*, a role in which he had won great acclaim for his dramatic powers in 1958.[8] Bruhn had to come to terms with his own performing career as an international star before he could commit himself wholeheartedly to directing the development of other dancers.

As the issue of its artistic leadership came to a head, the company experienced another of the ructions brought about by press coverage and nationalist sentiments that materially altered its reputation and sense of self. In the summer of 1975, the company made its third summer appearance at the Metropolitan Opera House with Rudolf Nureyev as guest artist. On July 27, 1975, *The New York Times* published a lengthy and prominently displayed guest column by the *Globe and Mail*'s dance critic, John Fraser. "Nureyev, Leave Canadian Ballet Alone," trumpeted the headline; the article itself was hardly less incendiary. In it, Fraser mounted a concerted attack on the Nureyev presence and its effect, over the years, on the growth and development of the company. His brief analysis of the company itself was even-handed.

> It has often enough been observed that the Canadian company is as old as the Royal Ballet and the New York City Ballet, but has never come close to achieving the same stature. While that's true enough, it's a fairly specious argument. Toronto is not New York or London, and Canadian artistic and economic resources are correspondingly limited. The National started in a void, and a considerable part of its mandate

has been to educate Canadians in a tradition that never before existed. The building-up of the company was a slow process, hampered initially as much by public indifference as by an overly cautious and unexciting repertoire. This began to change when the school started providing dancers who could live up to demanding works which, in turn, aroused audiences and grant-giving institutions.

Things were moving ahead nicely, albeit slowly, when Nureyev arrived on the scene. The company was expanding while remaining true to the classical traditions under founder Celia Franca. Erik Bruhn had been enticed to help, and he fleshed out the repertoire with distinctive productions of the old warhorses that flattered the dancers rather than showed off their weaknesses. There was no distinctive new choreography, though. There never has been, and this, predictably, has always put the National on the defensive. With the mighty Russian, the company saw a chance of leaping to prominence through someone else's greatness — an old trap that many companies have fallen into.

The ensuing evaluation of Nureyev's direct influence tried to retain a similar sense of balance, but it stressed the debits of his extravagance and temperament far more than it did the credits of his encouragement to the company, and it frankly criticized the level of his recent performances.

If only his own technique and artistry remained at a consistently high level, perhaps his behaviour might be acceptable even inside Canada. But, of course, they haven't. Nureyev's stage presence is always awesome, but his dancing certainly isn't consistently so anymore.

The tone of the concluding paragraph, more in sorrow than in anger, did little to moderate the harshness of the previous comments.

In the end, Nureyev remains what he always has been since he left Russia — a stranger in strange lands. He is doomed to adoration and lack of appreciation, enthusiasm and resentment, to using and being used. Once again, in Canada this time, he will not find it surprising to hear that he must pack up and move somewhere else.[9]

The international prominence of the publication and the timing of the article, in the middle of the National's New York season and in the middle of the search for an artistic director, added immeasurably to its impact. If there *was* a serious courtship under way between the company and its guest star, Fraser's final words lent it no public encouragement. Nureyev was always sensitive to commentary in the press; the climate for negotiation suddenly became decidedly frosty.

Fraser's article provoked vigorous debate, including a condescending response from Clive Barnes calling attention to Fraser's relative inexperience as a dance critic and to the fact that Fraser, immediately after writing the piece in question, had forsaken dance criticism for drama at the *Globe and Mail*.[10] All ten of the company's principal dancers, the men included, sent a letter to the *Times*, dissociating themselves unequivocally from the sentiments expressed in Fraser's article. The chairman of the board, Ian H. McLeod, wrote to rebut Fraser's arguments, saying that the company, through its association with Nureyev, had achieved its two primary objectives, of increasing the number of performance opportunities for its dancers and of gaining access to the Metropolitan.

> The National does not share Mr. Fraser's eagerness to end an association
> which has been so helpful for our young company in its developing stage.
> Instead, we look forward to a continuing association with Mr. Nureyev
> as opportunities arise in the future.[11]

No amount of rebuttal, however, could undo the effect of the article's publication. By characterizing the National's continued appearances at the Metropolitan as a species of colonial exploitation, Fraser had both insulted the company's foreign guest star and undercut its own achievement. Though his intention had been to urge the company on to a vigorous pursuit of its own identity, his words encouraged introspection and self-doubt. No one had claimed that the company on its own had taken New York by storm; now its more modest achievement there had been called into question, and by a fellow Canadian in a major American newspaper at that. Whether the laundry was dirty or clean remained open to dispute, but it had certainly been hung out for all the neighbours to see.

The emphasis on Nureyev himself, both in Fraser's article and in the heated response it provoked, unfortunately clouded a real and important issue. The Hurok organization, not Nureyev personally, had exploited the company in the colonial manner Fraser described. Nureyev had treated the company members as fellow artists; Hurok saw them as back-up for his big star. Having contracted for *Sleeping Beauty* as the initial vehicle for Nureyev, Hurok did not scruple to specify other selections of repertoire for the company, always with an eye to box office and to displaying Nureyev to advantage. *The Moor's Pavane*, which Hurok bought from its choreographer, José Limón, as a birthday present for Nureyev,[12] was a welcome addition, but his strong pressure to add Roland Petit's *Carmen* to the repertoire met with resistance and even prompted a Canada Council staff member to ask, "Who's running the National Ballet, anyway?"[13] Such interference in artistic policy was old hat for Hurok. American Ballet Theatre had suffered a similar

When Hurok toured The Sleeping Beauty, *Simon Semenoff, one of Hurok's staff members (a former character dancer with the Ballet Russe de Monte Carlo and a trusted confidant), occasionally walked on in the mime role of the master of ceremonies, Catalabutte, seen here being humiliated by Celia Franca as Carabosse.*

fate at his hands during its association with him in the forties.[14] And in 1965, in order to build better box office for the Royal Ballet's upcoming North American tour, Hurok had decreed that Fonteyn and Nureyev dance the Covent Garden premiere of Kenneth MacMillan's *Romeo and Juliet*, not Lynn Seymour and Christopher Gable, on whom the roles had been created.[15]

The National's management also had to fight Hurok in order to get decent exposure on the tours for its own male principals. The Hurok organization, not the National, handled tour publicity. It promoted Nureyev heavily and gave short shrift to the infrequent non-Nureyev performances (usually the less-popular matinees).[16] The predictable results — sold-out houses for Nureyev and poor attendance for the company on its own — contributed further to the public perception of the company as mere stage dressing for the star. But even this state of affairs was part of the National's calculated risk in signing on with Hurok. Impressing the promoter was as important a part of the game as building an audience, and took just as long. Not until 1977, when Nureyev suddenly pulled out of a tour, did Hurok risk presenting the National in New York without him. And even then he felt the need to shore up box office by poaching the young Peter Schaufuss from New York City Ballet, where he was a rising star. Fraser, by couching his argument as a personal criticism of Nureyev, glossed over these complex issues of the economics and politics of promotion in the arts and shifted attention away from Hurok's pivotal role in the game. Furthermore, by publicly writing off one of the candidates with the inside track, he helped to throw the competition for the position of artistic director of the company wide open. With both Bruhn and Nureyev ruling themselves out, the committee now had to search in earnest. Their choice fell on Alexander Grant.

ALEXANDER GRANT, THE DARK-HORSE CANDIDATE

A New Zealander by birth, Alexander Grant had joined the Sadler's Wells Ballet at Covent Garden in 1946. He remained at Covent Garden, with Sadler's Wells and then the Royal Ballet, for thirty years, rising to the rank of principal and establishing himself not as a romantic lead, but in the subtle and demanding role of the character artist. Alexander Grant was the consummate actor-dancer, whose dramatic presence on stage projected the depth, humanity, pathos, and, at times, melodrama of the choreographer's vision. Short and stocky, with penetrating eyes and expressive features, he had the knack of appearing larger than life onstage without detracting from the main action. He was malevolent as Carabosse in *The Sleeping Beauty*, pathetic and vulnerable as Alain in *La Fille mal gardée*, a rustic contemplative as Bottom in *The Dream*, and, just a few months before his departure from Covent Garden, a haunting Yslaev, the neglected husband, in the premiere of Sir Frederick Ashton's late-career masterpiece, *A Month in the Country*. An internationally respected artist, Grant was a mainstay of the Royal Ballet. He would not suffer the disparaging criticisms of lack of stage experience that had plagued David Haber in his attempt to direct the company.

During his thirty-year association with Sadler's Wells and then the Royal Ballet, Grant worked closely with Sir Frederick Ashton in the creation of many of his most famous ballets, developing a special affinity for Ashton's style and for his method of operation as a choreographer. Grant particularly admired the independence that Ashton encouraged his dancers to exhibit as creative artists. Ashton invited them to improvise, then selected what was best from what he had seen and fashioned his own creation out of their contributions. As Grant, frequently Ashton's guinea pig in this process, put it: "You felt you could do anything in front of him and he would not let you be put in a bad light." Grant's professional collaboration with Ashton turned into a close personal friendship as well. In his will, Ashton left to Grant the performing rights to his enduringly popular ballet *La Fille mal gardée*.[17]

The other great influence in Grant's Covent Garden background was Dame Ninette de Valois. Like Franca, Grant held her in high esteem, but his perception of de Valois and her administrative style differed from Franca's. He had seen de Valois relinquish the strict control of her Sadler's Wells days and grow with the company into a director and coach who encouraged her dancers to exert their own artistic independence as their capabilities increased.[18] Grant represented the Royal Ballet tradition proper, as it had developed through the first thirty years of its existence, rather than the Sadler's Wells experience of its genesis, which was all that Franca had known directly. He also had some experience as an administrator, having directed the Royal Ballet's small educational ensemble, Ballet for All, from 1972 until his departure for Canada.[19] He had worked with Franca in 1946, when, in her *Khadra*, she had been the first choreographer to create a role on the young dancer,[20] but their paths had not crossed since then.

Grant's Royal Ballet background, with its emphasis on the classics as the basis for all the company's activities, his personal connections with Ashton, and his independence from Franca made him an attractive candidate for the job. Though a stranger to the National, he was nevertheless well acquainted with its founding traditions, someone who

Frederick Ashton and Michael Somes, of the Royal Ballet, with Alexander Grant and David Scott (standing, rear) during a rehearsal of the National Ballet of Canada.

could bring a fresh, independent approach to questions of repertoire and casting without radically altering the course that the company, under Franca, had charted for itself. As Grant later put it: "I had come from a company that had also looked after the classics, as well as doing its own works. This formula I was endeavouring to accomplish for the National Ballet."[21]

Not everyone welcomed his appointment. Lauretta Thistle, commenting in the *Ottawa Citizen*, said, "Dear God, they've done it again. By 'done it again' I mean they've gone to the Royal Ballet, and thereby refused to cut the umbilical cord which has tied the National to the Royal all these years."[22] The spectre of the Royal Ballet haunted Grant in his efforts to lead the company as surely, and almost as unjustly, as it had Franca.

He was haunted as well by the elusive but formidable spirit of Erik Bruhn. Grant recognized from the beginning that Bruhn was the obvious choice for the job, and said as much to Bruhn privately when he visited the company to consider its offer.[23] When Grant accepted the position of artistic director, Bruhn resigned his own as resident producer, not in protest, but in order to give the new artistic director complete freedom. As early as the transition period, however, Bruhn felt slighted by what he saw as Grant's lack of attention. In June 1976, he wrote privately to Gerry Eldred, the company's general manager:

> Perhaps I expected Alex to contact me about various things since he expressed he needed my support when we talked, but I also suppose that he has found the people he needs to work with by now and since I am not exactly in search of a job I consider my relation with the National has come to an end. It has been a good and happy ten years for me and I think it's time to make a change for all concerned.[24]

Having evaded the responsibilities of the artistic directorship, Bruhn nevertheless expected a role in the affairs of the company. It required infinite tact and diplomacy to negotiate such a minefield of unspoken assumptions and delicate feelings. Tact and diplomacy were not Grant's strong suits, but he did his best. He invited Bruhn back, to teach, to dance, and to add the pas de trois to his production of *Swan Lake*,[25] a variation that Bruhn had omitted when he originally staged the ballet because the company of 1967 lacked second soloists strong enough to cope with its technical demands. Grant used this expanded version of Bruhn's production to open the company's Covent Garden engagement in 1979. Grant even dedicated the fall season of 1977 to Bruhn, who appeared as guest artist in both *La Sylphide* and *Coppélia*. Even so, the two men remained on distant terms. For a period of about six months, from July 1976 to January 1977, Bruhn went so far as to have his name removed from the credits for *Swan Lake* and *La Sylphide*.[26]

REWORKING THE REPERTOIRE: ASHTON AND OTHERS

The search committee decided on Grant for the position of artistic director in the fall of 1975,[27] with the appointment to take effect July 1,1976. Grant thus had the better part of a year to work on the repertoire for his first season, which inevitably combined the advance planning of previous administrations with his own initiatives. The 1976–77 season, Grant's first as artistic director, also marked the company's twenty-fifth anniversary. The new repertoire planned for the season did justice to the special occasion.

After years of avoiding the company's advances, Jerome Robbins finally agreed to its acquisition of his *Afternoon of a Faun*.[28] It premiered during Grant's first season, as did Ditchburn's *Mad Shadows* (already in the planning stages prior to Grant's appointment) and Hans van Manen's *Four Schumann Pieces*, continuing the Dutch connection that had been initiated with *Monument for a Dead Boy* in 1975–76. To encourage the company's own burgeoning choreographic talent, Grant took James Kudelka's *A Party* and Constantin Patsalas's *Black Angels* into the 1976–77 repertoire directly from the company's April 1976 workshop, which he saw prior to his official arrival.[29] The centrepieces of Grant's first season, however, were a previously planned revival of *Romeo and Juliet*, which had not been performed since April 22, 1972, and whose costumes had been destroyed when fire ravaged the company's storage facility in 1973, and new productions of Sir Frederick Ashton's *Monotones II* and *La Fille mal gardée*, acquired by Grant after his appointment.

It was an exciting, well-balanced season, one that accurately foreshadowed Grant's influence on the company. Throughout his seven years with the National, he functioned as the custodian of the existing standard repertoire and the developer of short new works by company choreographers and outsiders, but also as the source of the Ashton repertoire that had so long eluded the company. Ashton's active career as a choreographer had enjoyed a late flowering with his production of *A Month in the Country* in 1976, in which Grant created his last Ashton role.[30] Ashton's reputation rested on his story ballets, lyrical narratives that revealed the humour, pathos, and irony of human interactions. His achievements in this form had made him the only twentieth-century choreographer whose name could be mentioned in the same breath with Balanchine, who still dominated the North American imagination with his vision of plotless, abstract ballet. Grant's personal friendship with Ashton gave him ready access to his works; he was well equipped to challenge the Balanchine monopoly on public taste and test the extent of Canada's appetite for the Ashton style.

Grant's first season as artistic director brought with it an unexpected public display of the tensions that had been simmering for years between its two *grandes dames*. Grant had chosen to mark the company's twenty-fifth anniversary during the fall run of the *Romeo and Juliet* revival. For opening night, on November 12, he brought Celia Franca back from Ottawa to dance Lady Capulet, with Karen Kain and Frank Augustyn in the lead roles. A special tribute to Franca followed. In her onstage speech, given without notes before the packed theatre, Franca thanked the many people who had helped make her achievement possible. Whether deliberately or by accident, no one was ever really sure, she omitted one important name. As she brought her remarks to a close, cries rang out through the auditorium and Betty Oliphant left in tears, supported on one side by Yves Cousineau and on the other by Erik Bruhn. Oliphant took the omission of her name as an intended slight. It brought to a head her long-standing resentments against Franca, which she detailed in a press story after the incident.[31] Any vestiges of friendship that might have remained between the two women shattered, and from that point on, they were bitter rivals in the public eye. Two days later, on November 14, beloved alumni of the company returned, some from retirement, to their original roles in the ballet — Lilian Jarvis and Hazaros Surmeyan as the star-crossed lovers, Yves Cousineau and Celia Franca as Tybalt and Lady Capulet. It was an inspired performance, with long-time fans delighted to see how well all four still commanded these roles. This nostalgia-laden performance of *Romeo and Juliet* salvaged something of the intended air of festivity. The company premiere of *La Fille mal gardée* followed just a few days later, on November 17.

In his first three years with the company, Grant mounted five Ashton ballets — *Fille*, *Monotones*, *The Dream*, *Les Patineurs*, and *The Two Pigeons*. *Monotones*, a miniature to a score by Erik Satie, showed Ashton in his purely abstract vein. *Fille* and *The Dream*, after inconspicuous starts, established themselves as staples of the National's repertoire for nearly twenty-five years, ballets whose popularity served to reveal the careful design

Barry Gray

Charles Kirby as Thomas, Karen Kain as Lise, and Jacques Gorrissen as Widow Simone, with pony, on their way to the harvest festivities in La Fille mal gardée.

and deft manipulation of narrative structure that become apparent on repeated viewings. With their economical exploitation of musical and dramatic values (Ashton story ballets are generally short, concentrated works), they proved particularly well suited to the talents of generations of the National's dancers. Key elements of Ashton style — an emphasis on fast footwork, inherent musicality, an abundance of effective character roles — challenged the company's abilities and forced it to develop in new directions. The role of Titania in *The Dream* was instrumental in bringing Veronica Tennant's dancing into its maturity, especially when she was partnered by the Royal Ballet's Anthony Dowell. *Fille* and *The Dream* justified the Ashton emphasis that Grant brought to the National.

However, his other Ashton imports failed to win over Canadian popular and critical tastes. The acquisition of Ashton's 1937 *Les Patineurs* was a mistake. It had already been reproduced all over the world — in Canada by the Royal Winnipeg Ballet in 1966, and by the National Ballet School for its 1978 school performance. (Grant himself gave the school permission to use the company's sets and costumes even before the company premiered the work.)[32] On the full company it looked dated, rather than quaint. *The Two Pigeons* was scarcely better received, even though it was a much more novel choice, never before produced in North America and regarded by connoisseurs as one of Ashton's "sleepers," a ballet that requires a second chance to reach its audience.[33] The lukewarm reception these two ballets received, coupled with Ashton's well-known aversion to trans-Atlantic travel, put an end to the promising connection Grant was establishing between the National and his friend and former mentor. The company enjoyed the enormous benefit of working directly with Ashton himself during the staging of *The Two Pigeons*, but missed out on a cherished dream — the opportunity to have him choreograph an original work on its dancers.

By the late seventies, Grant had developed a balanced artistic roster, with experienced principal dancers and character artists complemented by an energetic young generation of talent drawn largely from the National Ballet School. Karen Kain, Veronica Tennant, Mary Jago, Vanessa Harwood, Nadia Potts, Frank Augustyn, Tomas Schramek, and Peter Schaufuss (recruited into the company from New York by Grant) were coming into their own as principals; Charles Kirby, the company's most experienced character artist, was supported by the likes of Hazaros Surmeyan, Jacques Gorrissen, Constantin Patsalas, Victoria Bertram, and Lorna Geddes, all making the transition to character roles; younger dancers like Gizella Witkowsky, Karyn Tessmer, Peter Ottmann, and Linda Maybarduk, along with new recruits such as David Allan, Kimberly Glasco, and Kevin Pugh gave the company a variety and potential it had never known before. With such strength and depth, the National could have done justice to Ashton's *A Month in the Country*, perhaps even attempted his idiosyncratic, quintessentially British masterpiece, *Enigma Variations*. Both were ballets with which Grant had been closely associated. Had he been able, over time, to pry either of them loose from their creator and from the Royal Ballet, Ashton's significance to the National would have stood on an entirely different plane. As it was, the Ashton connection lay unexploited for almost twenty years, until the 1994–95 season,

when the National, by then a substantially different company as far as its artistic personnel was concerned, acquired *A Month in the Country* as a tribute to Karen Kain in the
twenty-fifth year of her professional career. Ashton's *Symphonic Variations*, his landmark
abstract ballet, followed in 1996, but for eight performances only.

Without a really significant core of Ashton works to define his direction, the rest of
Grant's acquisitions, though interesting, failed to focus the company. Neither MacMillan's
Élite Syncopations (a last-minute substitute for *Song of the Earth*, which had been promised
and then withdrawn),[34] nor Lander's *Études*, nor Béjart's *Song of a Wayfarer* established a
clear direction for the company's future development. Both *Études* and *Élite Syncopations*,
however, found lasting popularity in the repertoire, where they provided a valuable mea-
suring stick of the company's technical competence judged against other major companies that carried these works. In the "Calliope Rag" variation of *Élite Syncopations*,
Cynthia Lucas's witty, tongue-in-cheek performances as the bored vamp set standards for
this little cameo role that have never been surpassed. And *Song of the Earth*, MacMillan's
elegiac meditation on death set to Gustav Mahler's *Das Lied von der Erde*, finally did enter
the repertoire in 1988.

Only one of the new works, Glen Tetley's *Sphinx*, set the stage for a significant
future collaboration between an outside choreographer and the company. Ironically,
its arrival in Grant's final year with the National was almost completely overshadowed
by the controversy surrounding his departure. The nurturing of the Tetley connection
became one of Erik Bruhn's achievements, and few remembered that Grant had been
the one to establish it.

GRANT'S ENCOURAGEMENT OF CANADIAN CHOREOGRAPHERS

Within the company, focus was equally hard to achieve. The company had two aspiring young choreographers, James Kudelka and Constantin Patsalas, with a third, Ann
Ditchburn, just beginning to shift her interests to other endeavours. Grant tried to find
a way to develop their talents and give them the opportunity to create within the stric-
tures of low budgets and limited audience tolerance for new and experimental repertoire.
Kudelka, a brilliant and temperamental prodigy at the National Ballet School, had joined
the company at the age of sixteen and was soon choreographing for company workshops; the Greek-born, German-trained Patsalas was a protegé of Erik Bruhn's with a
flair for character roles and ambitions to choreograph works on a grand scale. Both came
to prominence under Grant, Kudelka with *A Party, Washington Square, Playhouse*, and
Hedda, Patsalas with *Black Angels, The Rite of Spring, Angali, Nataraja*, and *Canciones*.
Not since Grant Strate's most productive period had the National given such emphasis to
original choreography. The challenge was to find a distinctive, coherent direction for the
company in the midst of such choreographic variety.

Andrew Oxenham

Amalia Schelhorn, Gizella Witkowsky, David Nixon, and artists of the ballet in Constantin Patsalas's Nataraja, *with striking designs by Sunny Choi.*

New works continued to do poorly at the box office, relative to the standard reper-toire, but Grant persevered with the policy of introducing short new ballets on the same program with popular favourites like *The Dream* or *Élite Syncopations*.[35] He thus exposed audiences to original choreography along with the familiar, while increasing the number of performance opportunities, an important part of his strategy for making the dancers feel as comfortable onstage as in the rehearsal hall.

But despite this level of activity, throughout this period the National had trouble retaining and nurturing its own choreographers. After *Mad Shadows*, Ann Ditchburn, as part of a small group of the company's younger dancers, experimented with a touring program called Ballet Revue, performing short works from the standard and contem-porary repertoire integrated into a highly personal format. Ballet Revue's phenomenal popularity sealed its fate. In a cross-country tour of twenty-one performances, it sold out 108 percent. As future plans became more elaborate, the implicit competition with company activities forced the dancers and Grant to make hard choices. Tomas Schramek, one of the members of Ballet Revue, recounted the experience: "We wanted to do it again but met some resistance in the company, for obvious reasons. We were too successful." Originally, Ballet Revue had been active only during the dancers' vacation period. When its performance schedule began to conflict with the main company's rehearsal and tour-ing, however, it folded, with vague hopes for the future that never materialized.[36] The disappointment of Ballet Revue's short lifespan, coupled with changes in Ditchburn's per-sonal life and the possibility of a movie career, led her to resign from the company, an action that she accompanied with statements to the press regarding her disagreements with Grant's artistic policies.[37] These statements she later came to regret. "I was a pawn. I thought that I was doing something right for the company. I talked badly about Alex in the press and I'll never forgive myself for that." Ditchburn left the company after the 1978–79 season, halfway through Grant's term as artistic director. After his departure, she attempted to return, but without success,[38] and subsequently left the dance world to experiment with writing and film. Her resignation and the press coverage accompany-ing it contributed to a growing perception that the company under Grant was not doing enough to develop its own choreographers.

James Kudelka came to prominence just in time to fill the gap created by Ditchburn's going. His major works for the National during this early period of his prolific choreo-graphic career had a narrative component and a literary source appropriate to the com-pany's emphasis on story ballet. *Washington Square*, based on the Henry James novel, and *Hedda*, based on Ibsen's play, united an interest in psychological portraiture with a clearly recognizable narrative line. In both instances, Kudelka used Jack King as his designer, who had remained the designer for *Mad Shadows* after Kudelka's withdrawal from the proj-ect. King modelled his designs for *Hedda* on the sombre work of the Norwegian painter Edvard Munch and used back projections derived from his tortured images to enhance the feeling of psychological oppression in the ballet. Both ballets had commissioned scores by

Canadian composers, *Washington Square*'s by Michael Conway Baker (its original, work-shop version had been set to selections of chamber music by Brahms) and *Hedda*'s, a combination of orchestral score and sound collage, by Norma Beecroft. With their emphasis on psychological observation, both works also provided striking roles for the company's dramatic ballerinas. Veronica Tennant's Catherine Sloper and Gizella Witkowsky's Hedda were serious, substantial creations, challenging to the dancers and audience alike. Despite the difficulties of finding his way beyond gesture and mime to tell his stories in pure dance terms,[39] Kudelka had clearly established himself as one of the most promising choreographers ever to come through the company when he, too, resigned. He left after the 1980–81 season, a year and a half before the premiere of *Hedda*, to join Les Grands Ballets Canadiens. Despite the considerable choreographic opportunities he had enjoyed with the company, he later spoke of the frustrations with Alexander Grant's artistic policies that led to his departure. Kudelka's passion was for creation, not reproduction.

> Grant's whole career happened because people created roles for him. He should have brought choreographers in to set works on Mary Jago — or me, for that matter — instead of the Ashton repertoire. It's important to work with live people and not a notator from England with the score of *The Dream*! It's more important to be a creator than an interpreter.[40]

Colleen Cool as The Young Girl *and James Kudelka as* The Young Man, *with pigeons, in Frederick Ashton's* The Two Pigeons.

As a creator, Kudelka had had to share the choreographic limelight with Ditchburn and Constantin Patsalas, with whom he also shared the title of company choreographer.[41] Les Grands offered him the chance to dance a repertoire that he admired and gave him a clear field to choreograph his own works on a regular basis. His burgeoning choreographic career in Montreal and with companies in the United States all but eclipsed his beginnings with the National. Yet his complaints at the time of his departure hung in the air, an implicit reproach to Grant and to the company for its failure to meet his expectations. Rapprochement began nine years later, in the spring of 1990, with the premiere of an original Kudelka commission for the company. Kudelka undertook a daunting task, choreographing a ballet to the entire Symphony No.6 of Beethoven. In *Pastorale*, he created an enigmatic ballet depicting an eighteenth-century aristocratic ramble in the countryside, with charming designs by the American designer Santo Loquasto and, in what would become a Kudelka trademark, an appealing use of all the generations of the company, from children at the school to the most senior character artists. *Pastorale* began healing the rift between Kudelka and the company and opened the door to an exciting future. In September 1992, he was appointed artist in residence, a post that enabled him to resume a close and productive relationship with the National and that led, eventually, to his assuming the leadership of the company that had given him his start.

By 1981, however, Grant was left with only one of the three young choreographers he had inherited at the time of his arrival. Constantin Patsalas's *Angali*, *Nataraja*, *The Rite of Spring*, and *Canciones* made striking additions to the repertoire during his administration. The full flowering of Patsalas's brief and turbulent career, however, came later, under Erik Bruhn.

Grant's only other experiment with original Canadian choreography occurred in the 1980–81 season, with Brian Macdonald's *Newcomers*. After two seasons as a dancer with the National in its very first years, Macdonald had gone on to become Canada's best-known choreographer. He had worked extensively with both the Royal Winnipeg Ballet and Les Grands Ballets Canadiens, had preceded Erik Bruhn as artistic director of the Royal Swedish Ballet, and had directed the Harkness Ballet in New York and the Batsheva company in Israel.[42] With works like *Les Whoops-de-Doo* and *Rose Latulippe*, Macdonald had developed a domestic idiom in dance that modified classical ballet with popular elements. Early on he showed the willingness to draw on the full spectrum of dance traditions, from classical ballet to show-dancing, that later characterized his enormously successful Stratford Festival productions of Gilbert and Sullivan operettas and Broadway musicals, and established a reputation for working with Canadian music and Canadian themes. But for his past criticism of Franca, Oliphant, and Ambrose, he might have seemed a logical successor to Franca as artistic director of the company. Macdonald had contributed nothing to the National's repertoire since *Post Script* in 1956–57. Grant's commission of a Macdonald work was as much a political gesture of reconciliation as an artistic decision.

Newcomers had a distinctive business dimension as well, as a work sponsored by Imperial Oil in conjunction with its television series of the same name, to celebrate its one-hundredth anniversary in 1980. The National thus gained a new, original work for its repertoire, virtually gratis, but had to accept quite specific conditions from Imperial Oil regarding its commitment to give the new work a significant number of performances.[43] This was raising corporate sponsorship to the level of direct patronage.

The terms of the commission included the specific requirement that the ballet deal with Canadian themes. The end result was well meaning, sincere, and uninspiring. The score, in four separate sections by four different Canadian composers, contributed to a lack of continuity and coherence in the ballet, which depicted the waves of immigration from various points of origin that had settled the nation and transformed the country. The full ballet premiered in Toronto on November 19, 1980, although its first movement, "Fantasmes," was performed on tour in St. John's, Newfoundland, on October 17. Despite spirited and energetic performances by Mary Jago and Clinton Rothwell, the ballet, after its contracted number of performances, dropped out of sight. There were no further collaborations with Macdonald. As a self-conscious experiment in nationalism, *Newcomers* fractured the performance image of the company. Somewhere between the anglicized vocabulary of Ashton and the naive fervour of commissioned nationalism, the company had to assert an identity of its own.

THE NATIONAL'S NORTH AMERICAN REPUTATION AND THE RECRUITMENT OF PETER SCHAUFUSS

International touring highlighted this issue of the company's self-definition from a different perspective. In New York, which the National continued to visit annually until 1979, critical and public response began to take note of the company itself as distinct from its superstar guest artist Nureyev. In 1977, Walter Terry, writing in the *Saturday Review*, summed up the company's slow, steady progress toward establishing its own profile in the cutthroat New York dance scene.

> In recent years, the National had Rudolf Nureyev as guest artist to assure its box office solvency, and Nureyev did an unforgettable job in leading the National into the big time. This year the company made it comfortably on its own with its own excellent stars (Karen Kain and Frank Augustyn among them), a fine supporting group of soloists and corps, and the two young guests Fernando Bujones and Peter Schaufuss, who may well become superstars within a year or two.[44]

Earlier in the article, Terry had placed the National on an equal footing with the Stuttgart Ballet, saying that "each of them maintained the high level of performance the ABT had established" during the season they shared at the Met.

Schaufuss's presence, by a combination of lucky chance and conscious choice, opened the way for his future association with the company. Along with his mother, the character artist Mona Vangsaae, the young Schaufuss had been a member of the National briefly in the late sixties, shortly after his graduation from the school of the Royal Danish Ballet. By 1977, he had appeared with the London Festival Ballet and was a rising star with the New York City Ballet under Balanchine. The combination of his training and experience, his inborn muscular virtuosity, and his inherent star quality identified him early, as Terry had seen, as a major contender for public recognition. That recognition came, however, in the international arena, not primarily during the years of his association with the National.

David Street

Peter Schaufuss with Alexander Grant during the staging of Napoli.

Rudolf Nureyev had been scheduled for the 1977 Hurok tour as usual, but withdrew on short notice to mount *Romeo and Juliet* for the London Festival Ballet. To fill the gap, Alexander Grant invited New York City Ballet's Peter Martins, who received permission from George Balanchine to guest with the National, only to have that permission revoked when Balanchine learned he would be seen in the full-length *Swan Lake*. Balanchine, who did not present the full-length costumed classics in his company, did not want his dancers

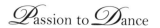

identified before their New York public in this repertoire.[45] Grant turned to Schaufuss, who was ready to broaden his horizons, and who realized that the National's invitation was incompatible with his own position under Balanchine, given Balanchine's stand on Martins's participation in the season.

> I knew by accepting that engagement that I had to leave New York City Ballet, and I took that risk, accepted the engagement, and danced with the Canadians in New York. Then, after the summer season, they invited me to join the company, and I took up the offer.[46]

The arrangement that he eventually worked out gave him prominent status within the National but also allowed him to accept the numerous other engagements he was offered worldwide. He became a full company member, but functioned as a resident guest artist, regularly, though not exclusively, associated with the National. Schaufuss later combined his superstardom as a performer with a major career in dance administration in England, Germany, and his native Denmark. As artistic director of the London Festival Ballet (rechristened the English National Ballet), he welcomed Alexander Grant back to a performing career after his stint with the National, brought Lynn Seymour out of retirement, and even cajoled Sir Frederick Ashton into reconstructing his *Romeo and Juliet*, which had long been considered irretrievably lost.

RITE OF PASSAGE: COVENT GARDEN, 1979

During Grant's administration, the National's emerging identity received a chastening setback in London, the other dance capital of the world after New York. The company had always wanted to win acceptance at the Royal Opera House, Covent Garden, home of the Royal Ballet. As early as 1973, the National had been advised by Peter Brinson, the British dance journalist and pioneer of Ballet for All, to hold out for Covent Garden for its next London engagement.[47] But in 1975, on its second visit to London, the company had again played the Coliseum, as it had done in 1972. Alexander Grant's long-standing connections with Covent Garden had undoubtedly helped him secure his appointment to the National. In 1978, those connections paid off with an invitation from the Royal Opera House to appear there for one week during the summer of 1979.[48] The preparation time for such a major engagement was short, and, as Grant knew, a week was not long enough to show the full range of the company's repertoire and artists,[49] yet the offer was irresistible. The company yielded to temptation, and the engagement that should have put the British dance establishment's seal of approval on its efforts became instead an arduous and painful rite of passage.

The opening, on August 6, 1979, was a gala occasion, starring the company's own Karen Kain and Frank Augustyn in *Swan Lake*, with Princess Margaret in attendance, a house liberally sprinkled with enthusiastic Canadian fans and the happy assurance of an entirely sold-out run. But the night, despite a gorgeously bedecked theatre and all the social trappings of a major debut, received lukewarm reviews; as the week progressed, the criticisms became harsher and eventually painted a picture of complete disaster. Galina Samsova, by 1979 a resident of London and a seasoned performer on its ballet stages, recalled that the company itself danced well. The problem, in her judgment, lay with the choice of repertoire. "It had nothing to do with their dancing. It was just — 'Don't bring us what we know better.'" [50]

As much as the week-long run allowed, Grant chose repertoire that would present the National as a classically based company of international stature, with both depth and versatility. In order to demonstrate its classical base, he scheduled Bruhn's 1967 *Swan Lake*, newly refurbished for the occasion and with the first-act pas de trois inserted in order to show off the capabilities of some of the younger dancers, along with the 1966 Valukin production of *Bayaderka*, which he had revived for the 1977 season. [51] *Mad Shadows* and Gerald Arpino's *Kettentanz* completed the mixed program (along with *Bayaderka*). The company's spanking-new *La Fille mal gardée* rounded out the week's offerings. There was very little security in these choices. Except for *Kettentanz* (which had been shown in London during the company's 1975 visit), each work represented a real gamble. *Mad Shadows* was a gamble of the right kind. However condescending the London audience might be, it was vital to show some of the company's original choreography on an occasion of such importance. And *Fille* was probably worth the risk as well. Though the ballet clearly belonged to the Royal, there might have been a cheeky kind of novelty in showing what it looked like, mounted on a different company. But *Swan Lake* and *Bayaderka* were harder to justify. Bruhn's *Swan Lake*, no longer a novelty, had been seen in London during the company's first visit in 1972. *Bayaderka* was bound to look upstart on the Royal Opera House stage. Nureyev's production for the Royal Ballet, based on the Kirov rather than the Bolshoi tradition, had come to be regarded as definitive by its fervent British admirers. For its first engagement on the foremost ballet stage in Europe, the National had, as the critics gleefully pointed out, brought coals to Newcastle.

Response to the company's classical repertoire ranged from indifference to outright scorn. *Bayaderka* suffered the most. Nigel Gosling and Maude Lloyd, the married couple who had befriended the young Rudolf Nureyev and offered him a London home, wrote ballet criticism under the ironically self-deprecating pseudonym "Alexander Bland." Writing in the *Observer*, and quite out of character with their nom de plume, Gosling and Lloyd led the charge. They characterized the inclusion of *Bayaderka* as "reckless," and the choice of the Bolshoi over the Kirov version as "foolhardy."

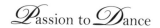

"Bayaderka," as the Canadians call it, was apparently mounted for them by
a Moscow choreographer in 1966 and restaged by him only two years ago.
The result is a travesty, with Minkus's simple, sweet tunes and Petipa's celes-
tially pure, romantic choreography souped up into a kind of circus display.[52]

Mary Clarke, commenting on the same ballet in the *Guardian*, was close behind.

Sadder than the production, however, was the way the company danced
it. It is, in this Kingdom of the Shades scene from the complete ballet, the
supreme test of a corps de ballet. And the Canadians gave it a staccato
style totally at odds with the flow of movement this masterpiece from St.
Petersburg demands.[53]

The opening night *Swan Lake* fared no better as a production, although the critics
restrained themselves slightly at the beginning of the engagement. Clement Crisp, of the
Financial Times, wrote:

The style of the ensemble is neat, well-mannered, but the staging is one
of those wilful exercises which perverts the accepted text of *Swan Lake*
in order to reassert Siegfried as the focal point of the ballet. Given the
dubious merits of the staging, the National Ballet do well, with sound
ensemble playing and promising soloists.[54]

The Canadian-born dancer and critic Fernau Hall deplored the Bruhn staging in his
review for the *Daily Telegraph*. "As it turned out, the decision to present *Swan Lake* was
unwise, for the defects of the production and the dancing stood out all too clearly. One of
the most disturbing features of the Canadian production was Erik Bruhn's choreography."[55]

Mad Shadows met with blank incomprehension, tempered by disdain. In Alexander
Bland's opinion the ballet sank to histrionics worthy of a silent film: "At moments gleams
of genuine talent shone out in the choreography and the performances were admirable.
But, with its undistinguished score and celluloid antics, the ballet trembled all the way on
the brink of farce."[56] Mary Clarke was nonplussed: "About Ann Ditchburn's *Mad Shadows*
I am at a loss to know what to say. I'd put it on my very short list of ballets never to be
endured again but I was told very firmly by a critic I respect that I was wrong."[57] Clement
Crisp was not: "The cast work their emotional fingers to the bone; there is a score that
should accompany a soap-opera, many set changes and copious use of gauzes. Oh."[58]

There were a few bright spots. Mary Jago received some of the best notices of her
career, and in the demanding classical test-piece of Nikiya in *Bayaderka* at that. Peter
Schaufuss was much admired, but at the expense of the rest of the company; "Danish

Andrew Oxenham

Mary Jago as Nikiya in Bayaderka. *Though the London critics hated the production, they praised her performance in it.*

Artist Saves Canadian Ballet," said the headline of one of Fernau Hall's reviews.[59] A succession of onstage accidents with sets and props,[60] which the company borrowed from the Royal Ballet to save shipping expenses, sabotaged *La Fille mal gardée*; even the National's own costumes misbehaved (the cockerel's splendid tail actually fell off during performance).[61] And here too, praise came mixed with condescension. As Nicholas Dromgoole, in the *Sunday Telegraph*, put it: "Their *La Fille Mal Gardée* was another matter, because this ballet is good enough to carry any average company home to success, but it showed up the rest of the repertory on view rather too sharply."[62]

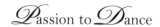

Summing up the entire season at a later date for the monthly *Dance and Dancers*,[63] John Percival gave a far more balanced and sympathetic account of the company. He suggested that the company should have brought more original choreography, one piece by each of Kudelka, Patsalas, and Ditchburn.

> If a work by each of them had been given, making clear (as the Stuttgart Ballet did last year) that they are newcomers to choreography, I believe the London audience would have watched them sympathetically and would have been more enthusiastic about the season as a whole.

He responded critically but with great sympathy to *Mad Shadows*.

> The first and most obvious thing to say about it is that the work is seriously flawed. But it was unfair that so many comments left it at that, without going on to the equally important facts that it was a courageous and ambitious endeavour by a young choreographer and that some aspects of it succeeded in an imaginative and individual way.

He then devoted a full column to an extended discussion of the piece's merits and flaws. But even Percival, though he tempered his overall comments, had to admit disappointment with the company's Covent Garden showing. Commenting on Mary Jago's development since the company's 1975 London appearance, he said:

> Unfortunately her progress draws attention by contrast to the absence of development in other leading dancers: good before, good now, but not progressing as they need to do for fulfillment. Could it be that the paucity of specially created work is a factor in this, stultifying talent and potential?

And Percival's comments, appearing in a monthly magazine for specialists, received far less circulation than did the harsh criticisms of the dailies, which had been quoted at length in Canadian press reports on the engagement. There was no softening the blow: Covent Garden had been a disaster.

The chastening effects of the experience could be seen in a number of ways. Silently, *Bayaderka* disappeared from the repertoire, never to be danced again until *La Bayadère: Act II* (the Kingdom of the Shades scene from the full-length work), in Natalia Makarova's Kirov-inspired staging, entered the repertoire in 1983–84. More publicly, the pages of the *Globe and Mail* became the forum for a debate about the responsibility for company technique and schooling. Grant had defended himself against some of the London criticisms about schooling by saying: "It is not our job to teach technique. I must take the very best that is available." Betty Oliphant's response became the subject of a news story in the *Globe*. "It is easy not to take responsibility for this, but a company, if it is not responsible for teaching technique, is definitely responsible for maintaining it."[64] The frustrated hopes of the Covent Garden debut thus became the focal point for public criticism of Grant's administration of the company and for the tension between Grant and Oliphant, which increased alarmingly over the next two years.

But criticism of the company's level of execution and technical competence paled in significance beside the fundamental questioning of its taste and artistic judgment. London critics had treated the National as provincial in the worst sense of the word, a company so far removed from the centre that it did not share, could not even recognize, the standards of taste that prevailed in the sophisticated world. For both the company and its home audience, the shock of this dismissal was hardest to bear but proved most salutary in the long run. It took some time for the company and its supporters to recover from the bludgeoning they had received, but when they did, they could look upon themselves and their mission with washed eyes.

In brutal fashion, the London critics had put paid to the secret hope that the National might one day conquer London just as decisively as the Sadler's Wells had conquered New York in 1949. The myth of the plucky little company, emerging from local obscurity to international acclaim, would no longer serve. Relinquishing that myth freed the company to pursue its own artistic course, indifferent to the approval or criticism of the Old Guard. There can be little doubt that the National deserved some of the harsh criticism it received; there can be equally little doubt that it had to learn to dance for itself and for its own audience, without undue regard for external approval, before it could develop a character of its own. Likewise the Canadian public, waiting eagerly for reports of praise and approbation, had to learn to look with its own eyes and make its own judgments. It had long since changed its allegiance from the imported to the domestic artistic product. London, 1979, taught it to forego the dubious luxury of imported critical opinion and to undertake the task of self-education that would allow it to evaluate the domestic product with confidence. Covent Garden forced the company and its audience into the mature, if rueful, realization that our centre was not elsewhere; our centre was here.

THE COMPLEX SERIES OF EVENTS LEADING TO THE DISMISSAL OF ALEXANDER GRANT

Troubled as Grant's career at the National became, it nonetheless brought a flowering of young talent into the company, comparable to the influx of women from the National Ballet School in the early sixties. Kimberly Glasco, Yoko Ichino, Kim Lightheart, Sabina

Allemann, and Amalia Schelhorn all entered the company during this period. All had distinguished careers with the company. (Glasco's lasted longer than any of the others', but spent itself in a parting of the ways as protracted, bitter, and acrimonious as any in the history of ballet.) Even more remarkable, however, was the deluge of male talent that descended on the National at this time. Grant had brought Stephen Jefferies from the Royal Ballet for his first season. (He later brought Anthony Dowell, the Royal's undisputed star, for extended visits, which inspired and educated the National's own principals, both male and female.) Jefferies's experience and vigour proved a welcome addition to a company that, like many, had decidedly more strength and depth among its women than its men. But when Jefferies left after only one season, to return to London and the Royal Ballet, his place was quickly filled, not by another visitor but by a succession of strong, distinctive male dancers drawn entirely from the National Ballet School. Kevin Pugh, David Nixon, William Stolar, Paul Chalmer, Jeremy Ransom, Serge Lavoie, Anthony Randazzo, and Owen Montague were all taken into the company by Grant. Ransom and Lavoie became principals, and mainstays of the company. Pugh, Nixon, and Montague made substantial impacts on the National before leaving, Nixon and Montague for careers in Europe, Pugh, following debilitating injuries and a courageous attempt to

The Royal Ballet's Anthony Dowell as Oberon partnering Veronica Tennant as Titania in The Dream.

resume his career, for other pursuits. Stolar, Randazzo, and Chalmer, after briefer associations with the National, made important dance careers with American Ballet Theatre, the San Francisco Ballet, and the English National Ballet. From the junior ranks of the National, the future stared Grant in the face and asked to be acknowledged.

As both the repertoire and the influx of new dancers indicated, Grant had charge of the company during a volatile and difficult period of transition. Years of stability and careful, incremental growth had suddenly given way to all the tensions, competition, and instability of an explosion of talent. That this explosion occurred during a period of economic recession, which, inevitably, cut into box-office receipts for all the performing arts,[65] didn't make the task of managing the company any easier. Grant came under increasing fire, from within the company and from without. One of the criticisms, which he still found illogical long after his departure, was that he gave too many dancers too many opportunities to dance,[66] in effect, that he refused to make the difficult choices among individual dancers that were necessary to a sound, carefully considered casting policy. In his defence, it must be said that if ever any artistic director suffered from an embarrassment of riches, it was Alexander Grant. Five senior ballerinas and two internationally experienced premiers danseurs constituted a sizeable block to the burgeoning talent in the lower ranks of the company. Casting was a major diplomatic, as well as artistic, challenge. The departures of Chalmer, Glasco (who returned to the National after two years in New York), and Stolar during this period hinted at some of the frustrations the younger generation felt. But Grant was not the man to tell experienced company members that their services would be in less demand, or not required at all, in order to give younger dancers their chance. That purge came later, at other hands.

Grant's contract had been renewed in the spring of 1979,[67] just prior to the company's Covent Garden appearance. In the period immediately following, the many pressures under which he had been operating came to a head. The press once again became the forum for a discussion of the state of the company and Grant's record as artistic director. Two of the credentials that had certainly helped him win the post, his access to the Ashton repertoire and his associations with Covent Garden, had lost their original lustre in the public eye. When company morale, always a volatile commodity, reached dangerously low levels, several of the dancers themselves entered the fray.

By the early eighties, Karen Kain and Frank Augustyn were two of the National's major stars and had the informal role of leadership within the company that their status and seniority conferred. Kain, who had been expressing her concerns privately to Grant and to various members of the board of directors, finally decided to speak out publicly on the issues that troubled her. Frank Augustyn acknowledged the same responsibility. As he later expressed their dilemma: "Whether we wanted it or not, we had a certain responsibility toward the National Ballet Company and so it was better to speak out. It was a necessary evil."[68] Their speaking out took the form of criticisms in the press of Grant's administrative policies. In an interview in the *Globe and Mail* in May 1982, they

commented specifically that Grant assigned too many alternate casts to works, and that he had not brought enough new, original ballets into the repertoire to stimulate the company creatively.[69] Public criticism from artists of this calibre could not be ignored.

But public criticism alone did not dislodge Grant from his position with the company. Opposition to his reappointment and concern about his artistic policies were expressed to the board privately, independent of the dancers' initiative. Betty Oliphant had written to the chairman of the board of directors at the time of the expiration of Grant's first contract, to say that, in her opinion, he ought not to be renewed. She saw him as the cause of the doldrums into which the company had fallen and, when his contract was renewed, wrote again to predict that only a radical slump in box office would bring the board round to her opinion. Erik Bruhn, who continued to perform as guest artist with the company, also became concerned about its condition. Aware of the influence Bruhn's opinion would have with the board, Oliphant undertook to mobilize his concern.

> I got a reputation, which I always feel was rather unfair, for being a stirrer up of trouble. But nobody else would fight for saving the company. I walked into Erik's dressing room one day when he was performing the witch in *La Sylphide*, and he said, "Betty, what are we going to do?" I said, "Well Erik, it's not really what *we're* going to do, because I have done all I can. But if you would also speak to people on the board — ." He said, "I'll speak to anyone. You just arrange it." And that was a big step for Erik. So I arranged for him to meet with the chairman of the board.[70]

The cumulative power of such opposition proved impossible to resist. In late June 1982, the board terminated Grant's appointment.[71]

When she spoke out about the company's problems, Karen Kain had not anticipated such drastic action and had, indeed, been unaware that the board was about to move. The board's announcement, coming as it did hard on the heels of her press statements of late May, looked like a direct response to her complaints, rather than the independent action it was. Kain, while she stood by the comments she had made, regretted the timing of events and the lack of full communication between board and dancers that made this interpretation of her actions possible. "I hurt Alexander's feelings terribly. It was not a very pleasant thing, and it was only because I wasn't informed. I reached a breaking-point and I said what I felt. I wasn't happy about the way that was handled."[72] The crisis over Grant's direction thus brought to light an important side issue, that of the dancers' right to express themselves, and to be heard, on matters of general company management. Dancers had had formal representation on the board since 1970,[73] but Kain's and Augustyn's actions really heralded the new era of self-awareness and independence. As Kain described the issue in 1988, well after the furor had died down:

We are not always as articulate as we would like to be because we are not used to using words. But we have very good instincts, and we know when things aren't right, and we know when the ship doesn't have a captain. It's part of our training to be quiet, to do what we are told. It's part of the discipline that you don't argue, you don't fight back. I think all of those things are changing. I think that we demand more of the people in front of the rehearsal room than we used to.[74]

Like the Covent Garden experience, the painful self-examination of the Grant crisis formed part of the company's necessary maturation process. For the dancers, rising on pointe had never been a problem; as individuals and as an organization, they now faced the greater challenge and responsibilities of standing on their own feet.

But analysis of the larger issues cannot gloss over the personal pain of the dismissal. Alexander Grant was in Jackson, Mississippi, serving on the jury of the International Ballet Competition, when André Galipeault, the chairman of the board, flew down to see him. His response, as quoted in the *Toronto Star*, came as something of a surprise. "I said I didn't want to resign. I wouldn't do it. It was the responsibility of the board to ask me if they felt I must, but I wouldn't offer it to them. I think you could say I'm more than a little hurt."[75] Rather than bow out quietly, Grant forced the board's hand. He commented on its decision publicly and furthermore chose to work out his year's notice of termination to the bitter end, in the full glare of the attendant publicity.[76] From July 1982 to June 1983, Grant worked without the confidence of the board that employed him.

PETER SCHAUFUSS'S *NAPOLI* RESTORED THE COMPANY'S SELF-CONFIDENCE

It would be an exaggeration to say of Grant's career with the National that nothing in his artistic directorship became him like leaving it. It is ironically true, however, that his final eighteen months in the job saw a distinct upswing in the company's fortunes, and that public opinion once again looked more favourably upon him. In November 1981, just as the storm clouds began to gather, the National opened Peter Schaufuss's landmark production of Bournonville's *Napoli*. Grant had suggested the project to Schaufuss, who was still a member of the company at this time, during the National's appearance at the Chicago Festival in 1979. He thereby beat out the Australian National Ballet, which was also negotiating with Schaufuss for his first *Napoli*. Schaufuss recalled the allegiance he felt to the National. "I really wanted to do it here, because I was a member of the company at that time and I felt that that was what I should accept, and then not do it in Australia."[77]

Napoli, the most popular of the Bournonville ballets in the Royal Danish Ballet's repertoire, was largely unknown outside its native Denmark. Received opinion held that the

Andrew Oxenham

All the strength of the senior ranks in Alexander Grant's company was on display in the Schaufuss production of August Bournonville's Napoli. *From left to right: David Roxander, Veronica Tennant, Raymond Smith, Nadia Potts, Karen Kain, Peter Schaufuss, Vanessa Harwood, David Nixon, Mary Jago, and Kevin Pugh.*

complete work, with its heavy emphasis on mime, Roman Catholicism, and the supernatural, would be unplayable outside the tradition that had nurtured it. The third-act divertissements enjoyed great popularity around the world, but the complete work remained a piece of relatively arcane ballet lore to all except the Danes and their followers. Schaufuss had not mounted *Napoli* before. He had, however, danced in a production of the complete work which Poul Gnatt, of the Royal Danish Ballet, staged for the Scottish Ballet in 1978,[78] and had received critical acclaim for his own production of Bournonville's *La Sylphide* for the Festival Ballet in 1979. The plan was daring and its scope was huge. Grant and Schaufuss proposed to give North America its first full-length production of a certified, if obscure, Danish masterpiece. If they succeeded, the National would gain new stature for its imaginative, independent approach to programming: no longer a provincial imitator of others; no longer a clone of the Royal Ballet; no riding on Nureyev's coattails.

But getting the production onstage took perseverance and determination. The obvious risks involved made many people nervous, from board members apprehensive about the production's cost (approximately $450,000),[79] to Canada Council officials skeptical about the "creative deficit" into which it forced the company,[80] to dancers less than enthusiastic about the ballet itself,[81] to members of the press doubtful that the first and second acts could be successfully staged outside Denmark.[82] Difficulties in scheduling adequate rehearsal time led to a postponement of the production from the spring to the fall of 1981.[83] Preparations were filled with equal portions of apprehension and excitement.

Napoli tells the story of a young Neapolitan fisherman's love for the beautiful Teresina, who is courted by old and inappropriate rival suitors. During a storm at sea, Teresina is washed away, and Gennaro, her youthful lover, survives only to be blamed by the townspeople for her loss. Aided by a medallion of the Madonna, Gennaro ventures forth to rescue his beloved from the Blue Grotto of Capri and the supernatural clutches of Golfo, the King of the Sea, who has transformed her into a naiad. As a concession to twentieth-century skepticism, Schaufuss played the entire Blue Grotto sequence as a tortured dream of Gennaro's. (No one pointed out that twentieth-century skepticism accepts, without a murmur, the supernatural transformations from woman to swan to evil seductress on which *Swan Lake* is built.) In deference, however, to the eternal appeal of stage spectacle, he retained the breakaway costumes that transform Teresina twice, in full view of the

The joyous final tableau of Napoli. *Veronica Tennant as Teresina and Peter Schaufuss as Gennaro.*

audience, from human to naiad and back to human form once again. Reunited, the lovers return to Naples, clear Gennaro of the false accusation that he is in league with the devil, and preside over the famous pas de six and tarantella that end the ballet. In a formula well-known to classical story ballet, two acts of complicated narrative are concluded with an act of pure celebration and dance.

Opening night, on November 10, 1981, proved that superlative dancing and strong production values could redeem even a contrived and creaky plot like *Napoli*'s. The O'Keefe Centre stage overflowed with vibrant colour and youthful, energetic dance. The company looked rejuvenated, free, and graceful, riding high on the spectacular production itself. The first-act mime sequences, for which Schaufuss had invited Denmark's Niels Bjørn Larsen as guest, communicated clearly and comically to the audience; the revised Blue Grotto scene of the second act continued to trouble some critics, but held audience attention with Teresina's breakaway costumes and a clever substitution trick for the male lead that enabled Gennaro to disappear at stage left and re-enter at stage right a split-second later; the procession and tarantella of the last act, in which the full company and scores of children from the National Ballet School crowded the stage, pulsated with unquenchable energy and radiated pure joy. The presence of the schoolchildren testified, as well, to the school's important role in turning out dancers able to do justice to the technical demands of Bournonville's elegant, buoyant choreography. If anything proved the wisdom of mounting the full work, it was the last act that, presented in context as the celebration of the peasant love-story that had gone before, created its proper effect as conclusion to the drama, not merely a string of unmotivated divertissements. The company's special way with Bournonville style, which Schaufuss described as slightly bigger and more powerful than the Danish,[84] showed off to great advantage. They had, after all, been dancing Bournonville since *La Sylphide* in 1964. It was as unqualified a success as was possible in the international dance world of the eighties. And it was a truly international event. Instead of going, cap in hand, to another world centre for inspection and approval, the National brought the international critical establishment to Toronto for the occasion. Special pre-performance talks on aspects of Bournonville style prepared the audience for what it was about to see. *Napoli* was a major acquisition for the company, and a major accomplishment for both Schaufuss and Grant. Though the impact of *Napoli* was insufficient to rescue Grant's own career with the company, it did much to wipe out memories of Covent Garden.

The ballet was not an instant success, but box office built satisfactorily over the forty-one complete performances it received to November 1989. After Grant left, with no one to champion it, the full-length *Napoli* fell out of the repertoire. Act III was performed on tour, but Act III alone could not give a full impression of the nature of the production and its achievement. In 2003, Nikolaj Hübbe staged excerpts from the ballet for the company, using the David Walker designs of the original production.

Just two days after *Napoli*'s opening, on November 12, 1981, the company celebrated its thirtieth anniversary with a dazzling special performance of *Napoli*. Schaufuss and

Veronica Tennant danced the leads, with Niels Bjørn Larsen, Alexander Grant, and Erik Bruhn in the principal character roles. Vanessa Harwood, Mary Jago, Karen Kain, and Nadia Potts appeared in the pas de six and tarantella, perhaps the first time since *Sleeping Beauty* that all five of the company's senior ballerinas had danced together in the same performance. Yves Cousineau, the redoubtable Tybalt of many a *Romeo and Juliet*, came out of retirement, as did Lois Smith, to take minor parts. And swanning about in the widow's weeds and black veil of one of the walk-on parts was none other than Celia Franca. Years later, Grant still looked back on the artistic and diplomatic triumph of that evening with pride.[85] It was a real celebration of the company's stature as well as a merciful hiatus in his personal tribulations.

ALEXANDER GRANT'S FINAL EXIT

The repertoire for 1982–83, Grant's final season with the company, was mixed but respectable. Nicholas Beriosoff, who was to have staged *Le Coq d'Or* for the company in 1975, produced *Don Quixote*, his version of that warhorse of the nineteenth-century Russian repertory created by Petipa and revised by Alexander Gorsky. Beriosoff produced it on a shoestring, because he could arrange for the purchase of the sets and costumes at a good rate from the London Festival Ballet. This *Don Quixote* met with only partial success, mainly because the sets and costumes proved, on arrival, to be garish and in disrepair. But Grant did give the company its first full-length *Don Quixote*. Redesigned by Desmond Heeley in 1985, it played consistently through the 1990s and, after a hiatus, returned to the repertoire in 2011. Grant's revival of John Neumeier's 1974 production of *Don Juan* was distinguished by guest performances by the Royal Ballet's Anthony Dowell, appearing for the first time, anywhere in the world, in the role of the Don. His elegantly restrained interpretation of the central role challenged the memory of Nureyev's more flamboyant approach to it, while his generous presence served as example and inspiration to the company's dancers. His discreet partnering highlighted Mary Jago's Lady in White, which had always been one of her most effective roles. The revival of Tudor's *Offenbach in the Underworld* (Grant had revived *Dark Elegies* just two seasons earlier) proved to have more sentimental than intrinsic value. But Glen Tetley's *Sphinx* held spectators spellbound and revealed a dark and mysteriously sensual side of the dancers that had seldom been seen before. The ballet, set to a powerful score by Bohuslav Martinů, focused on only one part of the familiar myth of Oedipus, his encounter in the desert with the sphinx and the god Anubis, just after unwittingly killing his father on the road to Thebes. Frank Augustyn and Karen Kain, whose partnership in the standard classical roles was waning, enjoyed an enormous success as Oedipus and the Sphinx, dramatizing a relationship in which romantic attachment is replaced by sexual tension and the struggle for power. Had Grant stayed one more year, he would have been able to leave to the glorious strains of

The Jürgen Rose-designed production of Onegin *stayed in the company's repertoire for many years. Here, a cast from 2003: Xiao Nan Yu as Tatiana, Rex Harrington as Onegin, and Sonia Rodriguez as Olga.*

Onegin, a ballet he programmed but did not see through production.[86] Its premiere on June 14, 1984, as the National's contribution to the Toronto International Festival, added the second Cranko story ballet to the National's repertoire, a dramatic vehicle for many of the company's ballerinas, and a perennial audience favourite. But even without the high point of *Onegin* to soften his departure, the coda of Grant's last months with the National reverted to a major key.

The bitterness and recrimination of the parting of the ways between Grant and the company had the unfortunate effect of obscuring his real achievements with the National. In repertoire and the hiring of dancers, he made choices for the company from which it benefited for years to come. And perhaps his failure rate in such areas was no worse than the average. But his managerial style, the antithesis of Franca's firm, direct control, was too liberal and accommodating for an organization in a state of transition. Company members complained of lack of direction; Grant, in his own defence, saw himself as trying to introduce them to the freedom and responsibility of the full professional. The responsibilities that accompanied such freedom could be frightening.

Under coaches like Franca and Nureyev, the dancers of the National had been drilled in the minutiae of performance. Lois Smith recalled, of the mad scene in Franca's *Giselle*, that every move, every reaction was carefully choreographed.[87] Very little was left to chance or the spontaneity of the moment. Such rigorous attention to detail gave the company the uniformity of style that had gained it its early distinction, but it also prompted the criticisms of hesitancy and lack of individuality that had later been applied to it. To achieve full creative expression, the dancers had to learn to take individual risks. For Grant, the difference was that between a company and a school. "A ballet company," he said, "is not a school. A ballet company are professional artists who have been trained in a school. And you don't run a ballet company like a school." What the dancers experienced as lack of direction, Grant thought of as adult, professional treatment. In Grant's view:

> Dancers never stop learning to polish their technique and develop their artistry. You give an artist a certain degree of independence. You don't tell an artist to raise an eyebrow here or an eyelash there unless that artist is raising that eyebrow in the wrong way. But he might raise it in a wonderful way that surprises even the person who is doing the coaching, and that's all to the good.

Grant had seen de Valois grow with her company from a strict teacher to a more liberal coach, willing to give her artists creative independence. As he recalled: "In the beginning, when she first had the company, she had to tell them, because it's a school in the beginning. De Valois, being the great woman that she was, grew, and as she grew, and the company grew, this whole attitude changed."[88] Undirected laissez-faire or room to grow? Grant's attitude of benign detachment came out of a combination of his own past experience and a genuine desire to move the company on to the next stage of its development. But the company was not ready to hear this message of increased artistic independence, or at any rate not willing to accept it from Alexander Grant. Erik Bruhn, his successor, was to deliver a strikingly similar message to the company, but with markedly greater success.

Chapter Eight

OUTSPOKEN IN OUR WORK
AND IN OUR DANCING

BRUHN TAKES THE PLUNGE

As early as 1952, Erik Bruhn had turned down a half-joking invitation from Celia Franca to join the National Ballet of Canada;[1] since 1964, he had circled on its periphery, almost always involved, never at its centre. With the announcement of Grant's departure, the stage was set, but for whose entrance? Bruhn had played the reluctant debutante for so long that his name was no longer the first to become the subject of speculation. One newspaper report of Grant's dismissal mentioned Veronica Tennant, Brian Macdonald, and Peter Schaufuss as possible successors,[2] but not Erik Bruhn. He was finally chosen only after a rigorous public search, carried out at his own insistence. Despite his disclaimers to the contrary, Bruhn had considerable skills as a politician. By playing up his genuine reluctance to be a candidate, he assured himself of an enthusiastic welcome when he did become artistic director. He needed such enthusiasm to support him through the difficult reorganization of artists and staff that constituted his first responsibility.

By discreetly intimating to a number of key people that he might, finally, be interested in the position, Bruhn encouraged the groundswell of support that made it his. As in 1975, in 1982 he was an obvious adviser to the search committee and to all those concerned about the National's future. The man who had so steadfastly resisted the company's previous blandishments became, in private, remarkably amenable to suggestion. Robert Johnston, who had replaced Gerry Eldred as the company's general manager in 1979, remembered his approach to Bruhn in the matter.

> I had arranged with Erik to have a drink with him. One of the things I
> wanted to find out was whether there was the remotest chance that he'd

be interested in this job. As we walked down to San Lorenzo's to have our glass of wine, he said, "You know, if you really can't find anybody else, I might be willing to take it on." Well, we knew the search was over the minute he said that. He literally volunteered, which, given how he felt in '75, was quite a transition.[3]

Lyman Henderson chaired the board's search committee for a new artistic director.[4] Following up a tip from Betty Oliphant, he too consulted Bruhn, again with an eye to interesting him in the position.

I asked his advice, and then I said, as we were coming to the close of the conversation, "Would you be interested yourself?" And he said something to this effect: "I swore I would never take on the artistic direction of any company again, but I love the National Ballet so much that maybe I might change my mind." We certainly went through the whole search process, but the target was obvious pretty early on.[5]

Valerie Wilder had, by 1982, left a career as a dancer with the National and become a dancers' agent. Among her clients was Erik Bruhn. She was also surprised by Bruhn's easy acquiescence to the idea of directing the company.

Valerie Wilder (left) and Lynn Wallis (right), Erik Bruhn's artistic associates, photographed at a media conference with choreographer Glen Tetley.

He was in town in the early summer of '82 when, in the course of our conversation, one of my topics was: "As you know, the National Ballet has started a search. It has been speculated that you will be asked to do it. How do you want to respond to this?" Much to my surprise he said, "Well, you know, I am getting sick and tired of travelling around. I think I might like to do it, but I don't really know if we will be able to reach an agreement. You can negotiate it for me." And off he went.[6]

Betty Oliphant summed up the informal part of the search procedure most succinctly: "Well, we all asked him to consult, and then he said, 'How about me?'"[7]

Bruhn's strategy in the matter was carefully thought out, as he indicated in an interview in *Dance and Dancers* shortly after his appointment.

> When the time came to decide for a new director, I was willing to be an advisor to the search committee, to help and recommend. I said "if you come to a point where you feel that there is no-one right for the moment, I wouldn't mind helping you out for a short time, 2 or 3 years." That gave a seed to all the committee and board people here. So I said "you have to go through all the Canadians and even all the foreigners who are interested. That will give me the chance to rethink whether or why I want to come back and help you out as a temporary director."[8]

It also protected him from any subsequent accusations of having stolen a march on other qualified candidates and unquestionably heightened the anticipation surrounding the final announcement. Instead of making a dramatic entrance, Bruhn sidled into the job that had long awaited him.

Bruhn's interest was kept strictly confidential, but even so, the search, though rigorously conducted, took on a certain *pro forma* air. David Adams, having returned to Canada from England, was among those interviewed for the position. "Although I made application, I had a sneaking suspicion that they had already chosen the person, and of course they had."[9]

The fact that Bruhn already held Canadian landed immigrant status smoothed the way for his appointment in one significant respect. During the search process, the committee received a delegation from the Department of Employment and Immigration, which stressed the importance of appointing a Canadian (broadly defined to include naturalized citizens and landed immigrants) to the job. With the target of the search already clearly in mind, Henderson was able to say, "If we depart from that, I'll let you know." Public opinion, as well as government regulations, made the nationalist issue a particularly sensitive one. Despite strong pressures to make citizenship status one of the

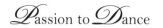

deciding criteria for the position, the search committee was looking for the best possible candidate anywhere in the world. In a profession as international in its orientation and methods of operation as ballet, the chances of finding the citizenship and artistic criteria embodied in a single individual were slim indeed. As a landed immigrant, Bruhn passed the citizenship test on a technicality. And, from Henderson's point of view, "that was purely a fortuitous circumstance."[10] The committee took seriously its responsibility to find the best possible artistic director for the company, regardless of nationality.

Bruhn's appointment brought an interesting perspective to bear on the ongoing debate about nationalism and the arts. As the following three years proved, he was undoubtedly the right choice for the position, the individual capable of restoring the company's self-confidence, and hence its identity, and the one to push it into a more active relationship with other parts of the Canadian dance scene. Had he not been appointed, it is impossible to predict with any certainty where the National would have stood in its own country or in the world during the next decade of its operations. Bruhn's landed immigrant status and his insistence on a full-scale search for qualified Canadians satisfied the technical requirements. Yet his citizenship status was the least of his qualifications for the job.

His long-standing association with the company gave him the insight he needed to function sympathetically and effectively as its artistic director. His international experience allowed him to consider its problems objectively. And his international reputation helped to restore the dancers' own sense of self-confidence and win the Canadian public's respect. Through a stroke of pure luck, Bruhn's appointment satisfied the political considerations inherent in the choice of an artistic director for a national cultural institution. But it also pointed up the fact that in this instance, the political considerations contributed nothing to the choice itself; had they been applied in such a way as to block it, they could have done real harm.

One factor did complicate Bruhn's appointment. Knowing his own limitations and his distaste for certain aspects of the administrative responsibilities he must face, Bruhn made his interest in the job contingent upon the appointment of two colleagues who would work with him to form a three-person administrative team. As Bruhn's negotiator, Valerie Wilder had the responsibility of winning the board over to this new concept of artistic administration. It was a hard sell, as she recalled. "It wasn't an easy concept to sell. The board wanted one star. They didn't really see the value of a team and couldn't see why that would be necessary." As negotiations proceeded, Bruhn agreed to begin his term with only one of the two colleagues in place, the other to be added after his first year in the job. At about the same time, he specified that he wanted Valerie Wilder to become the first member of the team.

She was joined after one year by Lynn Wallis, in the position of artistic coordinator. Wallis, whose background was with the Royal Ballet School in England, had initially worked with the National during Alexander Grant's administration, when she mounted Ashton's *Les Patineurs* and *Monotones* for the National Ballet School, and *The Two Pigeons*

Andrew Oxenham

By the time Bruhn became artistic director, his former students from the National Ballet School had joined the company. Rex Harrington, Serge Lavoie, and Owen Montague in Here We Come.

for the company. During one of her visits to the school, she had seen Bruhn's *Here We Come*, which he created as a special tribute to the school's extraordinary male students for its 1978 graduation program. It was an appealing suite of dances for twelve men, set to a selection of sprightly march tunes by the popular American composer Morton Gould. Bruhn had said, "I've always stood for strength in male dancing,"[11] and this work certainly bore him out in its demands for both bravura display and lyrical expressiveness on the part of the men. Wallis later invited Bruhn to mount *Here We Come* for the Royal Ballet School. It was, as she recalled, "his first time back with the Royal Ballet establishment after he had left as a dancer." In 1984, she accepted his invitation to work as guest ballet mistress with the National for three months. After that trial period, she became the third member of the administrative team.[12]

The concept of genuine teamwork was new in artistic administration and absolutely central to Bruhn's approach. He used it, not only as a way to lighten his own load — particularly of the duties to which he was ill suited — but also to bring the artistic side of the company back to a sense of real collaboration and cooperation. The early company had often been characterized as a kind of family. Under Bruhn, "team" replaced "family" as

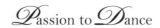

the metaphor for community. The difference was significant. The authority of the artistic director, as team leader, was less obtrusive, though no less real, than it had been as family head. More important, the responsibility for the success of the joint venture devolved in a more direct way onto each member of the team. Bruhn stressed administrative teamwork that went beyond a simple division of duties, teamwork in which each member could do parts of the other's job, in which real opportunity existed to contribute to artistic policy-making.[13] That sense of opportunity and responsibility worked its way through to all levels of the company, drawing individuals together in the common artistic enterprise. As Bruhn noted in a private memorandum in Copenhagen, following the European tour of 1985: "A strong team of a ballet staff must be based on mutual respect and artistic understanding before a fruitful collaboration can be expected to take place."[14] It was Bruhn's response to the problem that had defeated Alexander Grant. Neither family nor school — a company, in Bruhn's terms, should be a team.

But when Bruhn finally decided to take the company on, his only assurance was of the challenges involved, not the success he would enjoy. Those challenges were, if anything, greater in 1983 than they had been in 1975. What accounted for his change of heart? Veronica Tennant supplied part of the answer in highly personal terms.

> I believe that it took Erik many, many years to get over the fact that he was no longer a dancer. I think he suffered deeply and greatly from stopping dancing. It was the kind of suffering that was almost physical for him. I think that by the time '83 came along, he had resolved this within himself. He was a great artist, and so to cut off that part of his self-expression would take him longer than it would take somebody else. By the time '83 came along he was ready and resolved within himself. He had matured enough now to want to be challenged again, and he called us his ultimate challenge.[15]

Another part of the answer lay with the nature of the company itself, and of Bruhn's relationship with it, as he pointed out in the *Dance and Dancers* interview.

> I did 5 months of good thinking, and came to the conclusion that although I would not accept to be director of any other company in the world (I've refused Denmark twice, and La Scala, and the Paris Opera even, and at one time I was a candidate for ABT after Lucia Chase) I liked this company. The possibility was there, the organization as such, not just the dancers whom I knew very well, but the office people, the musicians, the wardrobe.[16]

But something else had changed in the years since Bruhn had last sidestepped the artistic directorship. Two very large and influential personalities had receded from the company's view. In 1975, he would inevitably have had to work in the shadows of Celia Franca and Rudolf Nureyev. By 1982, Bruhn could take over without appearing to supplant Franca, whose retirement to Ottawa and participation in other dance activities had removed her from direct involvement in the company's life. And with the Nureyev connection far less prominent than it had been in the years immediately following *Sleeping Beauty*, he could avoid even the appearance of rekindling those old rivalries. The timing was right and the coast was clear.

Because he so successfully mobilized his team, Bruhn's three years at the head of the company instituted a surprising number of different initiatives. Radical re-evaluation of the repertoire and the artistic complement of the company; an aggressive approach toward development and marketing; daring experiments with choreographers from at home and abroad; continued, direct contact with the dancers in the studio; effective long-range planning; a passion for youth and for developing international contacts — Bruhn and his colleagues touched on all of these areas in their planning for the development of the company. No single event characterized the tactical astuteness and artistic daring of Bruhn's approach more dramatically than his choice of programming for his first gala on February 18, 1984. A manifesto in the guise of a fundraiser, it served notice on the National's established audience that a new era was about to dawn.

A FEARLESS COMMITMENT TO NEW CHOREOGRAPHY

The gala made its obligatory bow toward superstardom with Mikhail Baryshnikov, partnering Elaine Kudo in Twyla Tharp's *Sinatra Suite*, but his presence was merely a hook to catch the patrons. The real program, light years away from standard gala fare, was carefully constructed to announce to the world the shape of the National Ballet's future, as Erik Bruhn conceived it. It opened with a company master class, conducted by Bruhn himself. The class presented the entire company to its public, not as stars and supporting dancers, but as equal participants in the rigorous demands of the preparation for dance. It demonstrated both the discipline of the art form and the concept of teamwork with which Bruhn intended to approach it. And it revealed Bruhn in relation to his dancers: personal, ironic, challenging, goading them on to new discoveries about their technique and about themselves, daring them to risk failure in pursuit of impossible ideals. Baryshnikov, the company outsider, resisted Bruhn's onstage, impromptu invitation to him to come on from the wings and join the class for a warm-up. Even though it was a staged event, the master class gave the public an authentic glimpse of Bruhn where he most loved to be — in the studio coaching his company, watching, perhaps, to see if there were any dancers who could challenge his own past accomplishments. It showed them,

Andrew Oxenham

Owen Montague, one of the dancers whose career blossomed under Bruhn's guidance, in Constantin Patsalas's Oiseaux Exotiques.

too, the extraordinary respect and admiration that his dancers had for him. Here, at the heart of the company's enterprise, the relationship between dancers and artistic director was healthy, edgy, and stimulating.

The bulk of the program consisted of modern works, all of them new to National Ballet audiences, only one of them danced by company members. It was the standard gala formula of guest artists coming in to do their star turns, but with a twist. The star turns, instead of being warhorses from the traditional repertoire, were radical examples of contemporary choreography; the guests, not the usual string of international celebrities, were mostly Canadian artists from outside the National Ballet. The landed immigrant had landed with his eyes wide open to the Canadian cultural scene.

Mary Jago and Veronica Tennant joined Tomm Ruud, of the San Francisco Ballet, in a performance of his *Mobile* (1969), which later entered the company's repertoire for six performances on the 1984–85 tour of eastern Canada. The company's resident choreographer, Constantin Patsalas, created a new pas de deux, *S'Agapo*, for the Royal Winnipeg Ballet's Evelyn Hart and John Alleyne, who was then dancing with the Stuttgart Ballet. Hart, under Grant's administration, had established a friendly guest-artist relationship with the National that Bruhn would foster and encourage. Alleyne, a graduate of the National Ballet School, would leave Stuttgart to join the National at the beginning of the 1984–85 season. James Kudelka and members of Les Grands Ballets Canadiens performed the first movement of Kudelka's *In Paradisum*. Bruhn's invitation to them could be seen as a preliminary gesture of reconciliation toward Kudelka, an indication that, in the company's view at least, past differences should be forgotten.

The program's centrepieces, however, were performances by three of Toronto's modern dance groups. Danny Grossman performed his *Curious Schools of Theatrical Dancing: Part I — 1977*; Toronto Dance Theatre brought the "Miserere" section from David Earle's *Exit, Nightfall*; and, to an onslaught of rock and electronic music unlike anything the National's audiences had ever experienced, the Desrosiers Dance Theatre initiated the gala patrons into the mysteries of Robert Desrosiers's *L'Hôtel Perdu*. Grossman's *Endangered Species* had entered the company's repertoire just three days earlier; all three choreographers had been invited to create original works for the company in the very near future. With the exception of Baryshnikov's appearance, every item on the program had a specific purpose closely related to Bruhn's plans for the National. The three major Canadian ballet companies had been included. Canadian modern dance had given the evening its central emphasis. Bruhn had converted the gala into a political gesture, a declaration of his own forthcoming agenda more potent than a thousand press releases. No more debates in the public press; the company would henceforth speak through its performances, with a voice that had not been heard before.

The gala concluded with a performance by the full company, led by Kain and Augustyn, of the last act of *The Sleeping Beauty*, an acknowledgement, perhaps, of the importance of the company's classical heritage. As a part of this gala, it looked curiously old-fashioned

Nadia Potts as Lise and Tomas Schramek as Colas with artists of the ballet in La Fille mal gardée, *the ballet Potts chose for her farewell performance.*

and over-dressed. Was the gesture ironic, a silent demonstration that the classical repertoire could not remain central to the kind of company Erik Bruhn had in mind? Whether deliberately or not, its slightly awkward presence on this program foreshadowed future developments. Bruhn would maintain the classics in the National's repertoire, but he would add very little to their number and, at a time when many of the existing productions needed overhaul or replacement, would direct his energies elsewhere. The freshness and vitality of Bruhn's vision came with a cost.

Part of that cost was borne quite directly by stalwarts who had carried the company through its earlier years. One of Bruhn's first responsibilities was to conduct the housecleaning that was necessary for the company to move forward in the directions he planned for it. In order to establish his own authority, he had to dismantle and reorganize at least some of the structure that remained from Franca's days. As Franca had had to distance herself from Volkoff and Lloyd, so Bruhn had to establish his autonomy and surround himself with individuals who would share his goals. The process was swift and direct. Within a year of his arrival, George Crum, the music director, and David Scott, the principal ballet master, announced their retirements; by the end of his three-year contract,

Mary Jago had retired from dancing, and Nadia Potts and Vanessa Harwood had left the company. Transition was hard. Bruhn's judgment that the time for retirement had come didn't necessarily coincide with that of his dancers and staff. Bruhn himself shied away from the confrontations implied in restructuring; that duty often fell to Valerie Wilder.

> "Helping Erik effect some of those draconian changes was tough," she says quietly, referring to Bruhn's shake-up of principal dancers shortly after he took residence at St. Lawrence Hall. "Usually it was left to me to tell them they could no longer dance a favourite role. Or that it was time to consider retirement. It wasn't easy."[17]

In some cases, however, the necessary changes were accomplished amicably, as with Mary Jago, who came to the decision to retire independently and received from Bruhn the help and encouragement she needed to enter the next phase of her career, ten years as a ballet mistress with the company.[18]

None of the departures was easy. Those who left had made major contributions to the company over a long span of years. They became casualties in the necessary process of change, sacrifices to the youthful resurgence of the company. Nor has it become any easier. Every artistic director who followed, up to and including Karen Kain, has had to confront this unpalatable, but necessary, element of artistic administration.

Bruhn and his team also brought about a significant change in company organization: the shift to aggressive marketing and development, and the emergence of a large arm of the company devoted exclusively to these activities. Responding to the temper of the times, the company had already started moving in this direction prior to Bruhn's arrival. But in the six months of activity before he officially took over, he and Valerie Wilder played a part in the board's decision to change, for the second time in the company's history, from single-ticket to subscription sales for the Toronto season. (The first experiment in subscription sales, begun in 1967, had ended in 1971 when the massive commitment to touring for Hurok made a Toronto subscription season difficult.)[19] Effective subscription marketing implied detailed long-range planning, since subscribers wanted to know repertoire and principal casting before they would lay out their money. It also implied a more commercial focus than the company had had before,[20] and the independence of marketing as a separate activity of the company.

Although Bruhn personally disliked the public relations chores that went with aggressive fundraising, he could be extremely good at them,[21] and the team that he assembled recognized the necessity of sophisticated marketing and development practices to the survival and growth of the company. Without sacrificing his personal authority, Bruhn had surrendered the absolute control of the old-fashioned artistic director and entered the new age of corporate cooperation.

The emphasis on marketing and development put a new bureaucratic structure in place that made the company less personal than it had been and was even seen by some as representing a divergence from its primary artistic purposes. Did the company exist to dance, or to fundraise and market its product? But the new age of development and marketing brought with it two undeniable advantages. Subscription sales, whose phenomenal success came as a surprise even to their most enthusiastic proponents, brought working capital into the company's coffers twelve to eighteen months before the beginning of the season,[22] thus alleviating some of the cash-flow problems that had kept the company teetering on the verge of bankruptcy through much of its life. Instead of waiting for box office to finance expenditures after the fact, the company could now pay for many of the costs of the season out of its advance revenues, without having to go into debt. The very first campaign pre-sold 45 percent of the seats at the O'Keefe Centre and brought working capital in excess of $900,000 in to the company. Subscription sales began at 13,000 subscribers, almost double the initial goal, and rose quickly to 20,000; by the early nineties they had levelled off to about 17,500, providing a solid basis of financial and audience support for the company. In more recent years, subscriber numbers have dropped to the 10,000 mark, but because of the new pricing structure at the Four Seasons Centre have actually brought in more revenue than at the O'Keefe Centre.[23]

The second advantage could be seen in the new attitude toward budget shortfall made possible by professional, highly organized fundraising. As long as fundraising had remained a volunteer, ancillary activity, shortfalls in the annual campaign had had to be absorbed directly, by a corresponding cut in production budgets, usually at very short notice. With the advent of professional fundraising, development became an independent, revenue-generating aspect of company activities, with its own goals, its own mechanisms for assessing the likelihood of a shortfall, and its own responsibilities for compensating for one. However much some might lament the intrusion of big-business principles in the arts, those principles brought with them a level of financial security that made possible the long-range artistic planning that had been a goal of the artistic administration.

Bruhn and his team took full advantage of these new possibilities with a careful and specific plan for the company's development and re-emergence on the world stage. The company would build up a significant body of new repertoire, unique to it, over a period of four or five years, and would then concentrate on touring that repertoire internationally for a year or two.[24] As a result of Bruhn's international prestige and the inherent attractiveness of the planned repertoire, that touring would be done more on the National's own terms than ever before. After the European tour of 1985, which had been largely planned before he took over the company, Bruhn announced this part of his strategy in an internal memo.

> In particular, we must begin planning *NOW* for our appearances in the
> most important venues abroad — London, Paris, Copenhagen, Hamburg,

Spoleto — all of which have expressed a great interest in having us. So prepared, we will be able to negotiate more directly with my contacts in Europe and design tours that present us to our best advantage.[25]

Revision of the repertoire and then touring: this logical ordering of priorities revealed a strategist of the first order.

Bruhn took a three-pronged approach to the building of repertoire, reaching out to Canadian modern dance choreographers, encouraging choreographers from within the company, and developing long-term relationships with two internationally established choreographers. The process of reaching out had been clearly established at the 1984 gala. Grossman, Desrosiers, and Earle introduced the National's dancers to dance forms and approaches toward movement that few of them had encountered before. David Earle's *Realm* had been premiered just before the gala itself. Grossman returned after it to mount *Hot House: Thriving on a Riff* in the 1985–86 season, a tribute to the jazz great, Charlie (Bird) Parker. Desrosiers, who had danced with the National for one season in 1971–72

Andrew Oxenham

Bruhn commissioned work from young, radical choreographers like Robert Desrosiers. Here, artists of the ballet perform as Zebras in front of the monstrous head in his Blue Snake.

before leaving to explore more theatrical types of performance, introduced the dancers to exotic and primitive effects and handed the production department some of the most difficult challenges of its experience. *Blue Snake*, which Desrosiers created for the company's 1984–85 season, turned out to be a phantasmagoria of vaguely tropical sights and sounds, mixed with European iconography and touches of eastern mysticism. The company had rarely experienced such freedom of association, either imaginatively or professionally.[26]

In opening the company up to more recent trends in modern dance, almost overnight, Bruhn broke down long-standing barriers and fostered a sense of community in the Canadian dance scene, where, previously, uneasy rivalries and tension had been the order of the day. It was a political gesture as much as an artistic choice. The success or failure of individual works was of secondary importance to the links that this type of programming forged with other dance organizations and with a different kind of audience. Of all these works, *Blue Snake* enjoyed the greatest success in the repertoire, with thirty-two full performances and eight of excerpts on a mixed program at Ontario Place. *Hot House* achieved a respectable twenty-two, seven of them at the Metropolitan Opera House in New York, but did not remain in the repertoire beyond its second season. David Earle's *Realm*, with six performances, and Grossman's *Endangered Species*, with five, did not survive beyond their initial runs. But statistics like these told little of the real significance of this aspect of Bruhn's programming, which established him in the public mind as a friend of the avant-garde and a supporter of young Canadian talent. The introduction of such experimental programming, especially so soon after his appointment as artistic director, was one of the shrewdest moves he could have made.

Pursuing the Elusive Company Choreographer: David Allan, John Alleyne, and Constantin Patsalas

While Bruhn was reaching out to Canadian modern dance choreographers, he also took care to encourage young choreographic talent within the company. David Allan, one of the National's second soloists, had first tried his hand at choreography during the 1983 workshop. Veronica Tennant saw his ballet and liked it enough to invite Allan to create a pas de deux for her upcoming engagement at Ontario Place. *Khatchaturian Pas de Deux* impressed Bruhn so much that he took it into the company's repertoire for an engagement by a small group of its dancers in Hamilton, Bermuda, in January 1984. There followed a series of small commissions from outside the company, mostly occasional pieces, which Allan undertook with company support. Bruhn then used his influence to assist Allan and a group of eight company dancers in arranging a tour of Italy, featuring "Le Stelle e Solisti Balletto Canadese" in a program made up primarily of Allan's choreography. After the success of that tour, Bruhn took five more of Allan's short pieces into the

National's repertoire for the 1985–86 season. He then commissioned a large-scale work for the O'Keefe stage. *Masada*, a daring and controversial piece set to Rachmaninoff's *Symphonic Dances*, about the ritual self-slaughter of the Jewish zealots at Masada under Roman siege.[27] When *Masada* premiered in May 1987, it provoked outrage. Some audience members walked out on the performance, unable to accept its graphic depiction of the deaths. But it also elicited dramatic and emotional performances from the dancers, especially Veronica Tennant (always a strong supporter of Allan's work), Kim Lightheart, and Gregory Osborne. Although flawed in places, *Masada* was a striking first work for large-scale resources that promised much for the future.

But the company's perennial inability to nurture its own choreographers over the long haul struck again. After *Masada*, with no hard feelings on either side, Allan left the company to look for choreographic opportunities in his native United States. He wanted to gain a range of experience that could not be provided in the shelter of the company, but he also sensed an obstacle in the company's structure. "The way the company is structured, I don't think there's room for a resident choreographer."[28] Allan's departure, and subsequent success as a choreographer in American regional ballet, repeated a familiar pattern. As with James Kudelka, the company had nurtured a promising choreographic talent only to lose it to another company.

John Alleyne, the other budding choreographer of the eighties, received less encouragement from Bruhn. Almost immediately after graduating from the National Ballet School, Alleyne had accepted a contract to dance with the Stuttgart Ballet, under Marcia Haydée, and had worked there with the influential forces in contemporary European ballet, choreographers like John Neumeier, Maurice Béjart, William Forsythe, and Jiří Kylián. There too, he undertook his first attempts at choreography, producing ballets for the company workshop which were subsequently taken into the repertoire and resulted in his being offered a choreographer's contract by Haydée. By the time this offer came, Alleyne was already feeling the strong gravitational pull back to Toronto, where Bruhn, his former mentor and teacher at the National Ballet School, had just taken charge of the company. Unsure of the extent of his commitment to choreography, Alleyne returned to Toronto, where, ironically, Bruhn's indifference to this facet of his talents served to crystallize Alleyne's choreographic ambitions. Bruhn saw Alleyne primarily as a dancer of extraordinary power and presence, and showed little interest in promoting him as a choreographer. But neither did he attempt to hold him back. When Alleyne received commissions from Stuttgart, and later from Ballet BC, Bruhn readily gave him leave to fulfill them.[29] Alleyne's debut as a choreographer with the National, however, came later.

When Bruhn took over the artistic directorship, the company already had a resident choreographer in Constantin Patsalas, Bruhn's partner in private life, whom Bruhn supported actively in what proved to be the final period of Patsalas's career. With David Allan beginning to show considerable promise, Bruhn had to avoid placing himself in the awkward position of having too many in-house choreographers to keep busy, the problem Alexander Grant had had to face in the days of Ditchburn, Kudelka, and Patsalas. Bruhn had first met Patsalas in Europe in 1971 and had suggested that the expatriate Greek dancer, who was looking for a safe haven in troubled political times, audition for the National during its upcoming European tour.[30] Patsalas joined the company for its 1972–73 season and, soon after his arrival, demonstrated his interest in choreography at the company's workshops. Franca, Haber, and Grant all encouraged his work, which began appearing in the company's repertoire in the 1974–75 season. Meanwhile, his close personal relationship with Bruhn grew, and Bruhn also took an active interest in his development as a choreographer.[31] In 1980–81, Alexander Grant, who introduced a total of five Patsalas works into the National's repertoire, named him company choreographer, along with James Kudelka, and in 1982, after Kudelka's departure, Grant made him resident choreographer,[32] the first individual to hold that title since Grant Strate.

Peter Ottmann, Kim Lightheart and Jeremy Ransom in L'Île Inconnue.

Patsalas's regular exposure as a choreographer during Alexander Grant's administration paved the way for even greater prominence during the early years of Bruhn's. In the 1983–84 season the company premiered two large-scale Patsalas works, *L'Île Inconnue*, to Berlioz' orchestral song cycle "Les Nuits d'Été," and *Oiseaux Exotiques*, to an original score by Harry Freedman. In the following season, it presented his *Piano Concerto*, a reworking of the ballet set to Alberto Ginastera's Piano Concerto No. 1, with which he had taken first prize at the Boston Ballet choreographic competition in 1979. The work was subsequently retitled *Concerto for the Elements* and would later still become the focus for Patsalas's acrimonious and lengthy feud with the company. Appearing in two consecutive seasons, these three works established Patsalas as a vivid and popular choreographic presence. They were markedly different in character — *L'Île Inconnue* with its sustained lyricism; *Oiseaux Exotiques* in a sexy and flirtatious vein, bordering on nightclub and cabaret dancing; and *Piano Concerto* powered by an aggressive tension. Yet they defined a recognizable, coherent Patsalas style that emphasized a sinuous, long line and showed great skill in the handling of pas de deux, less confidence in manipulating larger numbers of dancers. Most important, they sprang out of a long-standing, close working relationship between choreographer and company. Patsalas had taken the measure of the National's dancers, particularly its younger generation, and had choreographed out of that knowledge. The ideal of the resident choreographer seemed finally to be fulfilling itself in a series of works, unique to the company, dependent on the company's character for their own sense of style.

The creative exertions of these two years seemed to drain Patsalas, as well they might. His *Sinfonia*, originally commissioned by the McGill Chamber Orchestra, entered the repertoire in 1985–86 for three performances at Ontario Place; the following year, *Lost in Twilight*, especially created for the company's joint appearances with the Royal Winnipeg Ballet and Les Grands Ballets Canadiens at Expo '86 in Vancouver, became Patsalas's last work for the National. He had planned a sabbatical year, for travel and gathering new ideas for forthcoming projects. A cruel and arbitrary personal fate decreed otherwise.

A STRATEGIC ALLIANCE WITH GLEN TETLEY

However much attention Bruhn paid to his company's own choreographers, he knew that the international touring and refurbished image he planned for the company would not rest on such domestic achievements. He needed choreographers of international stature to build the repertoire that would gain access to the important theatres of the world. He was not that choreographer. Bruhn had a facility for choreography, but not a real genius for it. As artistic director, he knew that the development of the repertoire could not depend on him. He needed a ready source of repertoire from a name choreographer, one who had international prestige. Bruhn had two in mind.

In one of the press stories announcing his appointment, Bruhn had been quoted as saying, "For my first year, I want to bring Jiří Kylián in to look at the company and do a work for us."[33] Kylián, the Czech-born director of the Netherlands Dance Theatre, had already earned an impressive reputation for his distinctive mix of folk dance, modern

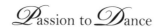

dance, and ballet vocabularies and for the strong musicality of his work. But he could not so easily be wooed away from the Netherlands for the long-term commitment of an original creation for the company. Instead, his existing work, *Transfigured Night*, entered the repertoire in the 1985–86 season, mounted by one of his assistants. Kylián himself did not visit the company until two years later, when he set another of his existing works, *Forgotten Land*.[34] The light-hearted *Dream Dances* in 1989 and the deeply moving *Soldiers' Mass* in 1995 rounded out the National's sampling of Kylián's choreography. Kylián provided valuable additions to the repertoire, but not the original work, exclusive to the company, that was essential to Bruhn's plan.

In Glen Tetley, Bruhn found the creative collaborator he needed. Alexander Grant had introduced Tetley to the company, initially hoping to persuade him to create an original work for the National, but then revising his request to ask for Tetley's existing work, *Sphinx*. Tetley's curiosity about the company had been piqued when he saw Karen Kain and Peter Ottmann dance at the Spoleto Festival; he knew, as well, that Martine van Hamel, on whom he had originally created *Sphinx* for American Ballet Theatre, was a product of the National Ballet School and the company. When Grant scaled down his request, Tetley agreed. He found the experience of working with the company fruitful and rewarding.

> Grant said, "We would like to have *Sphinx*," and that was a very concrete thing, so I agreed to come and do *Sphinx*, with Karen Kain, Frank Augustyn, Kevin Pugh, all wonderful dancers. And I had three casts, Gizella Witkowsky with David Nixon and Peter Ottmann; and Owen Montague and Sabina Allemann with Raymond Smith. They worked beautifully on it. It was a very exciting rehearsal period, and I was impressed with the way the company was set up, by the atmosphere in the studios, also the technical part of the company and the excellent way in which they constructed the set. It worked for me and it worked for the company too.

The company members had won Tetley's trust and respect, not only by the way in which they worked with him, but also by the high standards with which they maintained *Sphinx* in the repertoire during his subsequent absence. When Bruhn took over the company, he could prevail upon this strong rapport between company and choreographer, as well as on his long-standing friendship with Tetley, which went back to their days together at American Ballet Theatre.

> Erik and I were friends for many years, going back into the late fifties and sixties when Erik was a premier danseur with American Ballet Theatre. I admired Erik as one of the greatest dancers I'd ever seen, and Erik gave me a lot of confidence in my development as a dancer.

Cylla von Tiedemann

Julie Hay with artists of the ballet in Glen Tetley's Alice.

Bruhn wanted nothing less than an original Tetley work for the company, and now Tetley was happy to agree. *Alice*, a sixty-five-minute ballet set to David del Tredici's "Child Alice, Part I: In Memory of a Summer Day," explored the relationships that bound together the author of the children's classic *Alice's Adventures in Wonderland*, Lewis Carroll, the people in his life, and the characters in his work. It premiered on February 19, 1986.[35]

In *Alice*, Tetley was able to use his previous experience of the company to match his choreographic ideas unerringly to the talents and personalities of individuals. The ballet gave particular scope to the younger generation of dancers, especially Kimberly Glasco, returned to the company from American Ballet Theatre during Bruhn's second year, and Rex Harrington, in their respective roles of Child Alice and Lewis Carroll. But the mature Karen Kain played a key role as well, growing from a passionate, adult Alice Hargreaves into Alice alone in old age. Both generations of dancers within the company were thus represented, and in a fashion that took creative advantage of their generational differences. Furthermore, Tetley's personal fusion of modern dance vocabulary and techniques, particularly those of Martha Graham and Hanya Holm,[36] with classical dance synchronized perfectly with Bruhn's desire to bring the National into the twentieth century, to modify its classical schooling with movement ideas based on other traditions. The result was a work tailored to the company's personality, yet different from anything it had done before.

Tetley gave the company the precise blend of qualities it most needed in a choreographer: the international clout of a big name and the sensitivity of a resident choreographer to the dancers' individual characteristics. *Alice* opened the door of the Metropolitan Opera to the company once again, and finally on its own terms, as a company in its own right, with distinctive repertoire to offer. Since the death of Sol Hurok and the collapse of his organization, the Metropolitan itself had booked visiting attractions into the house. Jane Hermann, at that time its director of programming, saw *Alice* in Toronto and, when a last-minute cancellation created a vacancy in her upcoming summer schedule, invited the company to bring it to New York that July.[37] In what turned out to be Bruhn's final season with the company, his strategy for its development was already bearing fruit.

FOR BRUHN, REPERTOIRE PLANNING HELD THE KEY TO THE COMPANY'S DEVELOPMENT

The classical and standard sides of the repertoire interested Bruhn less than these excursions into new territory. Of the three purely classical works to enter the repertoire during his administration, two were associated in one way or another with his predecessor. Alexander Grant had arranged with Natalia Makarova that she would stage *La Bayadère: Act II — Kingdom of the Shades*,[38] to replace Valukin's *Bayaderka*, which had fared so badly at the hands of the British critics in 1979. Makarova's production, based on her recollections of the Kirov version and mounted originally for American Ballet Theatre, premiered during Bruhn's first season. Bruhn also revamped the Beriosoff *Don Quixote*, which Grant had acquired for the company, by commissioning new decor and costumes from Desmond Heeley to replace the disastrous ones purchased from the London Festival Ballet. Heeley's vivid colours and fanciful designs shored up the National's initial investment in *Don Quixote* and gave the company a durable, popular favourite for the repertoire.

As part of his own planning for the company, Bruhn invited his old friend Terry Westmoreland to produce the third act of Marius Petipa's *Raymonda* during the 1984–85 season. Bruhn had, in 1975, danced in Rudolf Nureyev's staging of the complete ballet for American Ballet Theatre,[39] but the standard practice outside Russia was usually to mount only the final act. By 1984, it was virtually the only one of the standard works in the classical canon that the company had yet to perform.

Building up the classical canon was not the primary motive behind Bruhn's choice. *Raymonda* Act III exposed the company to a teacher and coach who held a special place in Bruhn's heart. Westmoreland had been a member of Bruhn's artistic team at the Royal Swedish Ballet, where he had been appointed ballet master and principal teacher by Bruhn in 1968.[40] Bruhn took the concept of the artistic team over from his Swedish experience to his Canadian task, and had hoped to take over at least one of the team members as well. Though he was unsuccessful in his attempt to lure Westmoreland to the company on a permanent basis, as associate director,[41] Bruhn engaged him as guest ballet master for his first two seasons at the head of the National. It was exposure to Westmoreland, more than *Raymonda* itself, that Bruhn wanted to provide for the company. The classical repertoire was not the absolute ideal for Bruhn that it had been for Franca. He used it not as an end in itself, but as part of his consistent strategy to extend the range of the company by bringing it into contact with as diverse a spectrum of influences as he could attract. In this case, the personal contact was of more value than the addition to the repertoire. Westmoreland's *Raymonda*, visually heavy and unappealing, disappeared in 1987, after thirty-one performances.

Still trying to challenge his dancers with divergent influences, Bruhn also reintroduced the company to the work of Balanchine, who had died in 1983. In 1984, as a memorial, Bruhn mounted "A Tribute to George Balanchine," an evening devoted entirely to Balanchine's work, for which he revived *Serenade* and *The Four Temperaments* and added to the repertoire *Symphony in C.* The company had never before presented an exclusively Balanchine evening. Indeed, the company had never been particularly identified with the Balanchine legacy. The tribute was a generous piece of programming, because Bruhn's personal relationship with Balanchine during his brief associations with the New York City Ballet had been a troubled one. Bruhn had felt that Balanchine had misunderstood him, attributing to him the temperamental tactics of a star, when all Bruhn wanted was the chance to learn firsthand from the master.[42] The tribute to Balanchine proved to be a huge success and opened the way for further acquisitions of Balanchine's repertoire as it became more readily available in the years following his death. The company responded to the challenge and grew into the repertoire over the ensuing years, thus confirming the foresight of Bruhn's vision for it. James Kudelka would build on this foundation in his own years leading the company, with significant acquisitions of major Balanchine repertoire.

Only one of Bruhn's additions to the repertoire, *The Merry Widow*, appeared to be selected primarily for audience appeal and box-office durability. Even this choice, however, played its part in Bruhn's larger plans for the development of the company and testified to his diplomatic skills. *The Merry Widow* was the property of the Australian National Ballet, which, developing it from an idea of Sir Robert Helpmann's, had used it as a vehicle for guest appearances by Dame Margot Fonteyn.[43] According to Bruhn's correspondence, its three original creators, choreographer Ronald Hynd, designer Desmond Heeley, and orchestral arranger John Lanchbery, conceived the idea of mounting the production in Canada. Bruhn reported the idea in a letter to Helpmann, written in 1985.

> Recently Ronald Hynd, Desmond Heeley and Jack Lanchbery, at Jack's
> suggestion, approached me with the idea of doing a similar production
> for the National Ballet. Needless to say, I was thrilled and thought it

Tanya Howard, Guillaume Côté, and Rebekah Rimsay in The Merry Widow.

> would be just right for the company to present in November, 1986. While
> Ronnie, Desmond, and Jack are all ready and willing, the Australian
> Ballet seems to have certain rights and they are unwilling to release the
> work until after 1988.[44]

The copy of this letter in the National Ballet's archives, dated October 1, 1985, bears a handwritten emendation that reads: "has finally agreed to give us the rights." What persuaded the Australian Ballet to change its mind, along with mutually agreeable financial terms, was Bruhn's visit to Australia, in the fall of 1985, to stage and appear in *La Sylphide* for them. Bruhn saw his visit there in the nature of a diplomatic mission, from which he hoped to reap the reward of increased cooperation and mobility. As he wrote to the company's artistic director, Maina Gielgud, concerning *La Sylphide*: "I feel strongly that this could be a beginning of an exchange on various artistic levels for the future offering perhaps first an exchange for young dancers visiting and joining the forces between our companies for certain periods of time."[45] Bruhn had himself experienced frustration, early in his career, when he attempted to gain leave from the Royal Danish Ballet to appear elsewhere,[46] and had since then championed mobility and cooperation in the ballet world. Even the acquisition of this undisputed blockbuster, then, formed part of his overall campaign to break down barriers and open the world of ballet to its own potential as an international creative community.

The Merry Widow was one of the many ballets brought into the repertoire through the fundraising efforts of the Volunteer Committee. The origins of this committee lay in the early volunteer branches of the National Ballet Guild, local community organizations that operated in eight Ontario cities, with another three branches in Quebec and one in Buffalo, NY. As the company grew and developed a more professional structure, the branches outlived their purpose, which had been to promote the activities of the company by sponsoring its appearances in their local centres. In the early days, such sponsorship involved everything from booking the hall and selling the tickets to billeting the dancers in members' private homes. Such involvement fostered intense community identification with the company, though it didn't always result in the greatest theatrical efficiency. Before it closed, the Toronto branch had had great success with its commercial enterprise, the small shop called Paper Things, which sold fine stationery and ballet-related items and turned all of its profits back to the company. In 1972, proceeds from Paper Things sponsored the production of Antony Tudor's *Fandango*[47] and thereby established a tradition that continues today in the Volunteer Committee's Build-a-Ballet Fund.

All branches of the guild eventually closed, except the Toronto branch, which metamorphosed, in 1978,[48] into the present-day Volunteer Committee. Even before the official change, in 1976, it had sponsored *La Fille mal gardée* and since that time has raised over six million dollars for new productions.[49] With such a major contribution to the company's budget, it achieved a degree of political and economic clout within the organization, quite foreign to the old-school concept of volunteers as compliant workhorses. The Volunteer Committee now exercises the right to choose which production it wishes to sponsor and has, on one occasion, withheld its funds pending a fuller explanation of the company's proposals. This incident eventually led to a more formal understanding between the company and its Volunteer Committee. Instead of assuming the committee's support for a specific project, the company now approaches it with as full a proposal and as carefully worded an appeal as it would use for a major corporation. The company and the committee then enter into a mutually binding production donation agreement that outlines the obligations of both parties. As it has in other large arts organizations, volunteerism at the National, while maintaining its amateur status, has taken on all the trappings of big business. For the sixtieth anniversary season, the Volunteer Committee undertook to support new productions with a contribution of $250,000. The schedule included five of the forty-seven productions sponsored to that date by the Volunteer Committee.[50]

HIS VISIONARY LEADERSHIP ENABLED THE DANCERS TO TAKE NEW RISKS

Bruhn the strategist, the diplomat, the long-range planner finally had to yield to Bruhn the teacher and coach, working with his dancers. In the studio, his public demeanour at least partially forgotten, the mysteries and contradictions of his sometimes difficult personality

Erik Bruhn with Rex Harrington in the studio, 1984.

worked a wonderful alchemy on those dancers who had the initiative to accept his oblique style of guidance. Bruhn's determination to set the dancers on their own feet, to make them take charge of their own art, never wavered, no matter how frightening the process might be. Veronica Tennant described this part of his purpose.

> It took Erik Bruhn to help us make that transition — his stature and magnitude and depth as an artist and his great leadership quality. He was the one that was able to take this child and shake it out of the nest, and say, "The time has come to fly. And if you don't fly, if you fall and stumble, it's because you haven't got what it takes. You haven't dared and you have no wings. But the time has come."[51]

The "housecleaning" that Bruhn had instituted formed part of this process of establishing a company that could proceed on its own initiative. Karen Kain, one of the survivors of the housecleaning, reflected on the confidence of knowing that one's place in the company was earned, not simply left over by default. "That put everybody on edge. But we all knew it was the best thing for the company, when we saw the results and we knew that those he had there in the end were the people he really considered worthy of the positions. And he let us know that."[52] With his team members in place, and with a clear statement of his confidence in them, Bruhn proceeded to give them challenges of an order they had rarely experienced before.

Bruhn did not "produce" his dancers, in the sense of giving them detailed instructions for every movement and gesture. Instead he worked indirectly, almost mysteriously, challenging them to find their own ways to the secret knowledge he had discovered. Only by self-discovery would they make that knowledge their own. For Veronica Tennant, it was coaching as inspirational example, rather than command. When Bruhn demonstrated a movement in the studio, "it was always a demonstration which gave you a glimpse into the possibilities of what could be done, without ever telling you exactly how to do it." According to Tennant, his coaching, though difficult for some to accept, annihilated the complacency that can grow out of routine.

> He in no way told you what to do. He only made suggestions and those suggestions could change daily. Many dancers found that very difficult with Erik, because he would give you different ideas and different suggestions every single day. He would come up to you just before a performance and change something, if only to unsettle you, if only to take away any kind of automatic response that you might have ingrained in yourself, just to shake you, to force you to be spontaneous.[53]

John Alleyne recalled a similarly oblique process.

> I remember him giving me roles, and he'd say, "I'm giving this to you, John, because I think you can do something with it." And that is as much as he would say, and that meant that the way it was done was wrong and you had better find new ways to do it. And then he would come up a couple of months later, out of the blue, before a performance, and he would say, "You did it, John. Thank you." And just that was enough.[54]

Alexander Grant had defined exactly those needs in the company as the criterion necessary for its emergence as a fully professional, artistically mature organization. He had lacked the ruthless determination, however, to prune its membership and force a streamlined version of the team into this process of self-discovery. Bruhn liberated the company, but not by the simple removal of constraint. The freedom he fostered did not grant licence to perform exactly as one wished. Karen Kain commented on the powerful, though largely unspoken, control which his very presence exerted.

Somebody called him "laser eyes." He didn't miss anything from anybody. He didn't miss you if you were in the back row and you thought
nobody could see you. He would see everything you were doing, and
he let you know. He knew how to guide people without over-producing
them, without having to mould them to his way. He knew how to guide
them and pull things out of them. He made you feel like an adult, but
he also made you know that there was absolutely nothing you could get
away with that he wouldn't notice. And I think that being made to feel
like an adult was an extremely liberating thing for most of us. Because
he really did allow you to think for yourself. He didn't tell you what you
were supposed to do.[55]

Bruhn's secret touch stemmed from his ability to maintain the necessary control
without resorting to the authoritarian structures that had been ingrained in ballet organizations for centuries. Frank Augustyn felt the invigorating force of being "treated as a
human being, as an individual, as an adult. He had tremendous respect for dancers, being
a dancer himself."[56] Having faced the challenge of developing their art for themselves
under Bruhn's formidable "laser eyes," many dancers found a new sense of their own
individuality and a revaluation of their activity as central to the purpose of the company.
According to John Alleyne, this rejuvenated sense of initiative permeated other aspects of
the organization as well.

He had every single person in the corps de ballet feeling like an extremely
important member of the company. Every facet counted. He was aware
of the needs of the crews, the orchestra, and he didn't have to do much. I
guess it's because what he was aiming for was right, so we all could stand
behind him.[57]

Some degree of idealization crept into comments like these, made while Bruhn was
still fresh in the memories of many. The man had become conflated with his vision for the
company. Those who venerated him most were also the ones who discovered the most
about themselves under his direction. But the potency of his ideals cannot be overstated.
The greatest of his many gifts to the company was this courage of conviction. Believing
they were standing behind him, the dancers learned to stand on their own. The draft
notes for one of Bruhn's reports as artistic director stated these ideals in his own words.

There is more to ballet than straight lines and correct steps! I would appeal
to each of you to maintain that breadth of vision; to stay close to that
inspiration, that "something" that people talk about without analyzing. It

Andrew Oxenham

Lorraine Blouin and John Alleyne in L'Île Inconnue.

is my dream to talk less and less, and rather just show results. I am confident that our struggles are worth their work. If we were an overnight success, we would be an overnight gone. Let us go from there. Let us be outspoken in our work and in our dancing. Let us take the risks that are ultimately responsible for great art.[58]

When Bruhn finally took the helm of the company, he took it as a visionary leader with his sights set on the open waters of the future, not the confining channels of the past.

Bruhn's "temporary" assumption of the artistic directorship was initially to last for only three years, to July 1986. Toward the end of that period, he extended his contract for one further year.[59] On the evening of March 1, 1986, he appeared onstage at the farewell performance of Nadia Potts, one of the company's best-loved ballerinas. She danced the role of Lise in *La Fille mal gardée*. It was a bittersweet occasion, with Bruhn doing his best to put a diplomatic gloss on a reluctant retirement. A few days after the Potts farewell, he entered hospital for tests that indicated lung cancer.

Bruhn had always been a heavy smoker and, like many dancers, had turned a blind eye to the risks the habit presented to his health and to his performance as a professional. Shocked by the diagnosis, he drew a cloak of privacy around his hospital bed. Without fanfare or publicity, Rudolf Nureyev paid a flying visit from Paris.[60] Only one or two of his most independent dancers dared break into the inner circle to visit him. On April 1, just one month after his last public appearance, Bruhn died[61] without ever leaving the hospital, without returning to the company to put his affairs in order or bid a last farewell. For the company as a whole, and even for his close associates, there was virtually no warning.[62] Suddenly, the National had lost the leader who had set it on a new and daring path. The company was in a state of shock.

Even as he battled for his life, Bruhn showed the sense of leadership that had inspired his career with the company. From his deathbed, he wrote a letter which dancers and staff read through their tears on bulletin boards, in offices, hallways, and the dancers' lounge. It was dated March 19, 1986.

Dear Company,

From all of my irregular but honest "spies," I have heard some wonderful reports on *our* "Don Quixote" in Hamilton and London. For most of you who knew me when we began working on "Don Quixote" nearly three years ago, it was worth it all — from a production point of view and musical point of view — but it was all of your potential and talent that inspired me and overthrew the many doubts I had over the years. We have now a treasure that we can share together for many years to come.

My illness as it comes now is at the most unfortunate time, but then illnesses always are. However, I have come to realize in the last year that my nearly three years with you as a director have become the most fulfilling and rewarding experience in my entire professional life. Coming from a former first class egomaniac, this is not a small thing to admit!

I do hope that you will continue to support all that the last three years have stood for, and "you" means all of my staff. Indeed, there is no one left in the organization that I can complain of, only praise.

Let's go on from here, spirits up; with confidence, belief, and mutual respect for each other — not only go on, but go on inspiring each other. This way, you will really help me through this difficult time of mine, knowing that the outcome will be something we can share forever.

Much love to you all
as always,
Erik[63]

Visionary, martinet, and egomaniac — the letter bore testimony to the paradoxical blend of qualities that characterized Bruhn's leadership of the National. He had waited until the time was right and seized his golden opportunity. But the time was much too short.

Chapter Nine

DISCOVERING THE CENTRE

POWER STRUGGLE IN THE AFTERMATH OF BRUHN'S DEATH

Bruhn's death overtook the National with immense speed; the shockwaves it created rippled through the company at a much slower rate. While maintaining an uninterrupted, active performance schedule, the community of artists and staff had to come to terms with the abrupt removal of the man who had touched virtually each one of them in deeply personal ways. Valerie Wilder and Lynn Wallis, as Bruhn's closest associates, had to step into the breach. By Wilder's assessment, they took over a grieving company.[1] For reasons of public image and company well-being, the board and administration sought to characterize the period following Bruhn's death as one of consolidation and stability. Artistically, it was a period of transition and adjustment to a world without Bruhn, during which the company clung to the vestiges of his legacy while attempting, yet again, to redefine its destiny.

Fortunately, Bruhn's emphasis on team building had helped the company to complete the transition to an organizational structure more fully developed than the one that had prevailed in Franca's time. The company now had strong, separate divisions devoted to marketing and publicity and to fund raising and development. Most important, with the 1979 arrival of Robert Johnston as general manager (at the time, the most senior non-artistic administrative position in the organization), the company finally began to achieve a division of responsibilities between the artistic and the administrative sides of the house. It was a delicate balance, requiring goodwill on both sides, and one which Bruhn had been willing to accept. By 1986, there was a well-defined organizational structure that remained intact, even without Bruhn. In the aftermath of his death, it provided strong administrative leadership while the company grappled with its artistic future.

Wilder and Wallis, thrust without warning into the daunting role of guiding the company artistically through this emotionally difficult time, had the advantage of Bruhn's approval and of their close firsthand knowledge of his plans. But to the extent that their authority derived from their association with him, they worked at a disadvantage: they were not Erik Bruhn and could only suffer by comparison with the dead hero. Whatever their own merits, the world saw them primarily as caretakers. The brevity of their tenure as co–artistic directors was inevitable. What was remarkable was the positive contribution they were able to make to the company's development in such a short time, and the healthy state in which they passed it on to Reid Anderson. Grief could easily have torn the company apart. In the event, it played itself out during the Wallis-Wilder years, enabling Anderson to refocus the dancers' energies, unimpeded, on the challenges of artistic growth in the difficult economic climate of the nineties.

From his hospital bed, Bruhn tried to use his remaining time to put the company's affairs in order. Just one day before his farewell letter to the company, he wrote to Edmund C. Bovey, the chairman of the board, declaring his confidence that Wilder and Wallis would guide the company in the directions he had charted for it. His intentions with respect to Wilder and Wallis were clear enough: they were to provide artistic leadership for the company in fulfilling the plans already set by Bruhn and his team. His hopes for Constantin Patsalas, his lover, with whom he had lived during the final years of his life, were open to interpretation. The statement of his wishes in this respect became the centre of a troubling management controversy.

> As my first two years were marked by a certain amount of upheaval, including major staff changes, I feel that anything other than maintenance of the current direction would be damaging to the company at this point.
>
> Should I be unable to continue in my position as Artistic Director at all, it would be my wish that Constantin Patsalas join Valerie and Lynn as Artistic Advisor. Having worked closely with me for many years, Constantin is also familiar with my goals for the company and is dedicated to the National Ballet. It is not my desire, nor his, that he become Artistic Director, but as Advisor he would fill a gap left by my absence.[2]

The exact nature of Patsalas's role in this triumvirate quickly became a matter of acrimonious dispute. By specifying that an artistic adviser was *not* an artistic director, Bruhn implied a gradation of authority, but he offered no further guidance on this important subject. It was left to the board and the triumvirate of Wilder, Wallis, and Patsalas to try to work out the practical consequences of the scheme.

At a special meeting held on April 7, 1986, the board confirmed Bruhn's deathbed wishes for the artistic direction of the company, at least for an initial period, and put in

Andrew Oxenham

Karen Kain, Serge Lavoie, and Reid Anderson in Onegin.

abeyance the issue of establishing a search committee to look for a successor.[3] It named Wilder and Wallis as associate artistic directors of the company, and Patsalas, according to Bruhn's wishes, as artistic adviser. Almost as soon as it had been instituted, however, the arrangement began to unravel. As associate artistic directors (later renamed co-artistic directors), Wilder and Wallis saw themselves as the source of leadership for the National, with Patsalas providing an added creative spark. As Valerie Wilder described the situation, Patsalas saw things differently.

> Constantin's interpretation of the role of artistic adviser was, in everything except title, artistic director. He saw the team continuing really as it had. He felt that Erik had put him in that position as the artistic influence in the team, the artistic sensibility, and that we would continue helping make his artistic vision happen in the way we had with Erik. Our understanding of it was quite the reverse, that we should run the company with his assistance.[4]

It was a fundamental difference of opinion that could not be reconciled in compromise. Both parties stood their ground. Wilder and Wallis, with considerable administrative experience in their favour and with at least as great a claim to Bruhn's formal approval as Patsalas, quickly established the dominant position. In the autumn of 1986, Patsalas, denied the role he felt was his, filed suit for constructive dismissal against the National and against Wilder and Wallis as its associate artistic directors. At virtually the same time, he sought an injunction to prevent the company from performing his *Concerto for the Elements*, scheduled for the forthcoming November 1986 season.[5]

With respect to the injunction, Mr. Justice W. Gibson Gray of the Ontario Supreme Court found in favour of the company,[6] thus establishing the company's right, in law, to maintain and perform works to which it had title, without the direct presence and cooperation of the choreographer. He thereby confirmed the way in which ballet companies traditionally work, with ballet masters and mistresses taking responsibility for the faithful reproduction of a work once the choreographer has set it on the company.[7] The decision allowed the November 1986 performances of *Concerto for the Elements* to go ahead as scheduled, but did nothing to resolve the overall problem of the status of Patsalas's works in the National's repertoire. Even with a legal judgment in its favour, the company would not persist in programming his works against the choreographer's express wishes. The National had lost its resident choreographer of four years and effectively, if not legally, been cut off from the repertoire that he had created for the company over a much longer span of time. And the suit for constructive dismissal dragged on, poisoning the atmosphere as far as any resolution to the repertoire problem was concerned.

Constantin Patsalas with Amalia Schelhorn, who created roles in many of his ballets.

Constantin Patsalas left the National Ballet in the autumn of 1986. In October 1987, he presented an evening of his works at the Premiere Dance Theatre in Toronto, using independent dance artists, students from the National Ballet School, and a handful of dancers from the National Ballet. Thereafter, he went to Denmark to create a work for the Royal Danish Ballet.[8] On May 19, 1989, Patsalas died in a Toronto hospital of AIDS-related causes.[9] Before his death, the company reached an out-of-court settlement with him in the matter of his outstanding lawsuit, but despite behind-the-scenes efforts, it could not wrest from him his blessing to perform his works again in the future, as it had done so successfully in the past. Once she learned of his illness, after the board had decided to search for a new artistic director for the company, Valerie Wilder tried to resolve this issue.

> When we heard how ill he was, my main concern was a wish for him to somehow, through some intermediary, come to terms with his feeling on his repertoire and whether we could do it. So I spoke to several of his close friends and pleaded for someone to try to get through to him;

obviously it couldn't be me. I was very hopeful that before he died we would get some sort of indication from him that, yes, all is forgiven, the National Ballet can continue to do his work, especially in light of the fact that Lynn and I were not even going to be there any more, presumably his main antagonists. But that never occurred.[10]

Constantin Patsalas died embittered, his personal grievances against the company unresolved, and without the full command of his faculties that might have allowed him to respond differently to Wilder's unofficial overtures. As a consequence, the work of one of the company's resident choreographers, made for its own artists from within its own creative community, disappeared. Once again, as had been the case with Grant Strate, Ann Ditchburn, the young James Kudelka, and David Allan, the company was frustrated in its attempts to build an enduring body of repertoire by developing and supporting its own choreographers. There was no memorial tribute. When Veronica Tennant, at her farewell performance in November 1989, danced the lullaby from Patsalas's *Canciones* with Kevin Pugh, she pronounced a personal benediction on her friend and colleague. It was the last performance of a Patsalas work by dancers of the National Ballet.

Patsalas's illness materially affected the litigious nature of his concluding relationship with the company. In the final stages of AIDS, he suffered from dementia, which drove him to endless litigation and uncontrollable spending.[11] His grievances against the company unquestionably sprang from real conflicts about the nature of his role within it. The extent and bitterness of his pursuit of those grievances, however, was exaggerated by the dementia of his final days, over which he had no control and which must have crept upon him gradually, clouding his vision only slightly at first, then affecting more and more of his behaviour. At this point, the company's history mingled inextricably with private affliction. In *L'Île Inconnue*, the National had embodied for Patsalas his vision of romantic yearning for an unknown destiny. In his own life, that yearning spent itself in a bitter separation from the company that had been his home, a separation that effectively thwarted the possibility of keeping his memory alive through the performance of his work. By 2001, it was too late for rapprochement. Despite tentative overtures from Patsalas's estate, James Kudelka opted not to include any of his ballets in the company's fiftieth anniversary season celebrations.[12]

In the fall of 1986, the full significance of Patsalas's actions and departure could not be known. Clearly, however, his absence created a gap in the company's artistic administration. Bruhn had sensed the need to bring onto the team someone with artistic vision and creative daring to complement the experience and administrative skills provided by Wallis and Wilder. In Patsalas's absence, the board looked to another individual whose association with the company Bruhn had fostered. Glen Tetley, albeit hesitantly, stood ready to join the team.

After the success of *Alice*, Bruhn had suggested to Tetley some more permanent relationship with the company as a choreographer, but Tetley had shied away from any commitment that would tie him down. In the trying period after Bruhn's death and Patsalas's departure, the board turned to him for help of an even more binding nature. As Tetley recounted the events, he was sounded out about the possibility of taking on the artistic directorship. "The title that was offered me was not artistic associate, it was artistic director, to take over where Erik left off. I felt I just could not do it. I just could not take on the responsibility, because I know what that responsibility is." Having directed other major companies, including the Netherlands Dance Theatre and the Stuttgart Ballet, Tetley had firsthand experience of the trials of being an artistic director. Tetley felt a strong bond with the National, however, and was willing to accept the position of artistic associate, in which he would be relieved of administrative responsibility but would involve himself intimately in discussions of "the artistic future and policies of the company, the repertoire, the dancers, the decisions on dancers' futures."[13] Thus began a two-year period (1987–89) during which, working closely with Wilder and Wallis, he exercised a fundamental influence on the company's activities. Ironically, he thus came to fulfill precisely the role that had been envisaged for Patsalas.

The company's rift with Patsalas occurred in September 1986; Tetley's appointment was announced on January 27, 1987, to take effect on March 1 of that year.[14] Had Patsalas been displaced in order to make way for a bigger name? As Wilder later recalled the sequence of events, Tetley's availability was not the cause of Patsalas's departure. "I don't think the Tetley role had evolved far enough at that stage, so I don't think he felt edged out by Tetley."[15] Wilder acknowledged readily, however, that Patsalas's penchant for large-scale works (he had already created *Rite of Spring* and *L'Île Inconnue* and had at one point worked on a scenario for a fifty-minute ballet to a score by Olivier Messiaen)[16] conflicted with plans already in place for major new works by Tetley and the acquisition of MacMillan's *Song of the Earth*. From budget considerations alone, the company could sustain only a limited number of such initiatives. Patsalas had gambled to become the company's main creative force and lost. Fortunately for the company, Tetley was available to step into the breach.

GLEN TETLEY'S INFLUENCE ON COMPANY STYLE

Tetley brought to the company a distinctive sense of movement that blended the principles of classical ballet with the techniques of modern dance. A student of Margaret Craske (one of Cecchetti's pupils) and of Antony Tudor but also of the modern dance exponents Martha Graham and Hanya Holm,[17] Tetley forced company members to confront the second half of the twentieth century from the vantage point of their strong classical training.

Cylla von Tiedemann

Johan Persson, Rex Harrington, and Robert Tewsley (from left to right) in Glen Tetley's The Rite Of Spring.

I love the classical training because it's logical. You always can go back to the beginning plié, relevé, tendu, fondu exercises because they are what give you your strength and freedom at the same time. And there is no reason they can't be used in all of the other rediscoveries of the contemporary technique. If you know where your centre is, why can't you know where your off-centre is, and use that also, consciously?

In his original creations for the company following the success of *Alice, La Ronde* (which subsequently entered the repertoire of England's Royal Ballet), *Tagore* (which was picked up by San Francisco Ballet), and *Oracle,* Tetley placed his imprint on its style of movement. "I think that's what makes a successful company, that when you think of the company in your mind's eye you see the movement quality of the company. The movement quality of the company should be as distinctive as that of one dancer to another."[18] In addition to these works created expressly for the National, Tetley mounted significant works from his own earlier repertoire on the company. *Voluntaries* and *Daphnis and Chloë,* added in the late eighties, and *Rite of Spring,* acquired in 1992 when illness postponed the creation of *Oracle* to 1994, demonstrated just what capable exponents of Tetley's style the National's dancers had become. Under his guidance, they discovered a new centre from which their dance could flow. With a newly discovered sensuality, the dancers' stage personalities flowered under the stimulus of Tetley's rigorous demands. No single role dramatized the revolution more graphically than that of the Prostitute in *La Ronde,* whose lonely, self-absorbed preening opened and closed the ballet on an acrid note of spent desire. The role became so closely identified with Ronda Nychka, on whom it was created, that no substitute seemed possible. Yet when Nychka left the company, Tetley grafted it onto the talents of Jennifer Fournier so successfully that it seemed to have belonged to her from the beginning. In the transfer of the role, Tetley's influence could be seen, moulding the company to the new look he had defined for it.

Valerie Wilder and Lynn Wallis Maintained the Direction that Bruhn had Established

In committing themselves to Tetley, Wallis and Wilder also committed themselves to the emphasis on contemporary repertoire that Bruhn had initiated. During their leadership of the company, only one quasi-classical work, the slight *Diana and Acteon* pas de deux (staged for the company by Fernando Bujones), entered the repertoire. The existing productions of the classics were rotated through the performance schedule, but the real excitement came from the presence of major contemporary choreographers like Jiří Kylián and William Forsythe, and from the opportunities which Wallis and Wilder gave

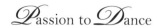

to company members David Allan and John Alleyne to develop their choreographic ambitions. As part of their strategic planning, Wallis and Wilder used the subscription program to ensure that audiences would be exposed to new and experimental works along with the more standard crowd-pleasers. According to Wilder: "We forced it, in that there has never been a series that is all classical. You cannot buy a subscription to the National Ballet and not be exposed to at least one new work. That was a principle, and I think it served what we wanted it to serve."[19]

They also successfully negotiated major works by Sir Kenneth MacMillan to add to the repertoire. The company had been trying to obtain his *Song of the Earth* since 1977;[20] in the 1987–88 season it finally arrived, accompanied by his *Concerto* and followed, two years later, by *Gloria*. These acquisitions, no longer genuinely contemporary, nevertheless rounded out the company's sampling of works by this major figure of twentieth-century dance. The National's audiences, which had hitherto known only *Élite Syncopations* and, if their memories were long enough, *Solitaire*, now saw a much more representative range of MacMillan's art. But these new works, historically significant though they were, did not make a forceful impression. Only John Alleyne's stunning performances as the Messenger of Death sustained the level of passion, commitment, and concentration that had given *Song of the Earth* such a shattering impact at its Stuttgart premiere in 1965. These additions of MacMillan repertoire did, however, signal another subtle change in the climate of the times. Wilder and Wallis were able to add these works without attracting the charge of imitating the Royal Ballet that had dogged Franca and Grant before them. The historical exercise could be assessed for what it was, an attempt to strengthen the representation of a major world choreographer in the company's repertoire, without dragging in the red herring of colonial domination.

Wallis and Wilder also revived the idea of the touring group, geared to play smaller centres with less-fully equipped stages and provided with a repertoire made up partially of works from the main company, partially of works created specifically for its needs. As Ballet Concert, such a unit had existed in the late sixties and early seventies. The new Concert Group, as it came to be known, served the needs of a particular audience and enabled the company to experiment with new choreography on a smaller scale than that required for the stages of the O'Keefe Centre or the Place des Arts. It also highlighted members of the corps. Alleyne's *Trapdance*, created for the Concert Group in the spring of 1988, revealed the dramatic talents of Nina Goldman, Sally-Ann Hickin, and Barbara Smith, all reliable members of the junior ranks, and led to his using them for roles in *Have Steps Will Travel* the following season at the O'Keefe Centre. Reid Anderson continued to use the Concert Group as a development ground for new choreography by a variety of choreographers from inside and outside the company. In May 1994, Christopher House's *Café Dances*, Jean Grand-Maître's *Frames of Mind*, John Alleyne's *Split House Geometric*, and Serge Bennathan's *The Strangeness of a Kiss*, all works originally commissioned for the Concert Group, rounded out the O'Keefe Centre mixed program in which Glen

David Street

Artists of the ballet in John Alleyne's Trapdance.

Tetley's *Oracle* received its world premiere. In later years, the Concert Group ceased to exist as a distinct entity, though small groups of dancers still did occasional run-outs to smaller centres, or when the full company could not afford to tour.

With Tetley's assistance, and relying on the structures Bruhn had put in place, Wilder and Wallis urged the company forward, using the plans Bruhn had developed as their point of departure, but giving them their own emphasis as well. Because Bruhn had encouraged real participation in his administrative team, it was impossible to tell precisely where his influence left off and their independent planning began. After several years in the job, however, it was evident that they directed the company not according to a mandate Bruhn had established, but by virtue of their own clear vision for its future. That vision included a distinctive contemporary repertoire for the company. It also called for the construction of a Ballet Opera House in Toronto and a new scale of operations appropriate to such a permanent home. Wilder and Wallis, working closely with the board, the production department, the Canadian Opera Company, and the Ballet Opera House Foundation, guided the company through years of effort, which took the project to the stage of architect selection and identification of a site, before the economic recession and change in Ontario's government put the Ballet Opera House on indefinite hold. The announcement, in June 1994,[21] that the company would move its rehearsal, wardrobe, and administrative facilities out of existing space in and around the St. Lawrence Hall to King's Landing on Queen's Quay West confirmed the abandonment of the Ballet Opera House plan, which had sought to provide all such facilities in the same building with a major new performance space. One of Wallis and Wilder's strongest initiatives, and one of Bruhn's long-standing dreams, evaporated with the demise of the project. When Toronto finally undertook the construction of an opera house, it was as the single-minded dream of the Canadian Opera Company's artistic director, Richard Bradshaw. The ballet would, in 2006, share the Four Seasons Centre with the opera, but as a tenant, not as a partner in the planning process.

With a different project, however, Wallis and Wilder fulfilled one of Bruhn's explicit wishes for the company. Bruhn had been a professional free spirit, fighting against the rigid codes of loyalty and obligation that made a dancer's movement from one company to another a difficult and emotionally trying experience. Having escaped the sheltered protection of the Royal Danish Ballet, he knew that variety of experience contributed immeasurably to the development of an individual dancer. Even as director of a company, Bruhn maintained a generosity of spirit in such matters at the cost of administrative inconvenience. Less than a year before his death, he wrote to the ballerina Sonia Arova, to whom he had been engaged during the early years of his own vagabond career, then teaching and directing a company of her own in Birmingham, Alabama.

> You express frustration over not being able to "hold onto" your best pupils and my only advice on this is "don't!" It is unreasonable to expect them to stay. Even in a company like my own, this is my experience. The need for growth and change is a constant and when a dancer leaves you cannot take it personally. You can only take pride in what you have given them and where they go when they leave.[22]

Bruhn's active attempts to encourage the interchange of dancers among companies led him to provide in his will for the establishment of an annual prize, to be awarded to the winners (one female and one male) of a competition among the four companies with which Bruhn himself had felt most closely associated: American Ballet Theatre, the National, the Royal Ballet, and the Royal Danish Ballet.[23] In the spring of 1988, Wilder and Wallis presided over the first Erik Bruhn Competition in Toronto, sponsored by the National Ballet of Canada.

The terms of the competition initially left it open to a good deal of skeptical criticism. Since participation was by invitation rather than open, and since the judges were to be the artistic directors of the four companies sending competitors, its status as a major international competition immediately came into question. Furthermore, the ambience of the first competition, determined as much by fundraising considerations as by a disinterested concern for the international standards of dance, struck some observers as antithetical to the competition's presumed purpose.

"Competition" was, as it turned out, a misnomer, Bruhn's central idea being both more radical and more useful than the institution of yet another international contest run along established lines. Between 1988 and 2011 there have been nine Erik Bruhn Prize competitions, with some broadening of the companies invited to send dancers to compete. As these versions of the competition have shown, the real value of the Erik Bruhn Prize lies in the international showcase it provides for promising young dancers and in the opportunity it creates for cooperation among major ballet companies associated in some way with the career of Erik Bruhn. Behind-the-scenes activity at the very first competition demonstrated that point clearly as, for two days, artistic staff from three different companies worked with the National's artistic and technical divisions at the O'Keefe Centre to coordinate the single performance of the event. The company took advantage of these contacts to foster the dancer exchanges so dear to Bruhn's heart. In 1990, one year after competing for the first Erik Bruhn Prize, Silja Wendrup-Schandorff and Henning Albrechtsen spent a brief period working with the National. Alexander Ritter, not a competitor, worked with their home company, the Royal Danish, in exchange. The spirit of cooperation extended beyond the terms of the competition itself when, in 1989, David McAllister of the Australian Ballet and Jeremy Ransom traded places. The real memorial to Bruhn was not the sculpture that the winners of the competition received, but the influence on their careers, and the careers of other young dancers, which the spirit of free exchange made possible.

Wallis and Wilder worked to realize this last element of Bruhn's aspirations for the company knowing that their time as its directors was drawing to a close. With less acrimony and better diplomacy on all sides than had characterized such transitions in the past, the board had, in December 1987, extended their contracts for two more years and announced that, "in response to Wilder's and Wallis's expressed wish that they not continue as Co–Artistic Directors beyond the two year period," it would institute search procedures for a new artistic director for the company to take over at the end of their contracts in 1989.[24]

The search committee, chaired once again by Lyman Henderson, discussed matters with Glen Tetley, who remained unwilling to allow his own name to stand for the position of artistic director. Tetley, a strong supporter of Wilder and Wallis, was not happy with the board's decision to institute search procedures at this point. He saw no need to change the current arrangements.[25] With no obvious in-house candidate to turn to, the committee considered a wide range of international candidates and settled eventually on the name of Reid Anderson, no stranger to the company, yet in significant ways an outsider to its traditions.

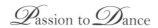

REID ANDERSON'S APPOINTMENT STRENGTHENED THE CRANKO CONNECTION

As a dancer, Anderson had been a long-standing member of John Cranko's Stuttgart Ballet and, by the time of the search in 1988, was making a reputation for himself as an interpreter and coach of his mentor's repertoire. Anderson's first direct contact with the company had come in 1984, when he staged Cranko's *Onegin* for the National. Coming just at the difficult moment of transition from Grant's régime to Bruhn's, *Onegin* was the National's contribution to the Toronto International Festival, which required new works that would then remain unperformed for a decent interval in Toronto, in order to pre-serve the festival's exclusive aura. *Onegin*, the second of the full-length story ballets with which Cranko catapulted the Stuttgart Ballet to international prominence, was to become a staple of the National's repertoire after its initial festival run, with more than one hun-dred and twenty performances to the 2010–11 season. Another lavish spectacle in the romantic tradition, it provided a dramatic challenge, in the central role of Tatiana, for the company's mature ballerinas, among them Kain and Tennant, who had been schooled in the Cranko style with his *Romeo and Juliet* twenty years earlier. Anderson himself danced two performances of the title role during the opening run opposite Marcia Haydée,[26]

Reid Anderson with Sabina Allemann as Tatiana on the set during the filming of Onegin *in 1986.*

Cranko's original Juliet and Tatiana. In subsequent years, he returned to partner Natalia Makarova in the work and to supervise some of its later performances.

With his experience and reputation almost exclusively European, Anderson's roots were in Canada. Not, however, in the National Ballet of Canada. Anderson traced his lineage from the western branch of Canadian ballet. Almost forty years after their territorial rivalries, the pioneering work of Gweneth Lloyd and Celia Franca came together in the appointment of Reid Anderson to direct the National Ballet. A native of New Westminster, BC, Anderson received his training in dance from Dolores Kirkwood, a teacher for whom he had great admiration. At an early age, he encountered both Gweneth Lloyd and Betty Farrally as adjudicators on the western festival circuit. According to Anderson, "It was actually Betty Farrally who told my father to start me into ballet lessons." With his love of performing channelled into ballet, he worked his way through the Royal Academy of Dance sequence of examinations and, as a young teenager, attended his first of four summer sessions at the Banff School of Fine Arts. There, in Betty Farrally's classes, he got his first taste of the discipline and regimen of a professional ballet company, and encountered other pillars of the Royal Winnipeg Ballet tradition, like Arnold Spohr, Brian Macdonald, and Eva von Gencsy. Anderson's closest approach to the National came when he auditioned, unsuccessfully, for admission to the National Ballet School. The refusal left no hard feelings. "Thinking back on myself at that time, I probably wasn't good enough to get into the school," he admitted. Much later, at seventeen, he went to England for a year of study at the Royal Ballet School. Following a short stint in the Royal Opera Ballet, he joined the Stuttgart Ballet on February 4, 1969. There he fell under the spell of John Cranko, who was to become the dominant artistic influence of his life.

Anderson joined the Stuttgart company on the eve of its enormously successful New York debut and stayed with it after Cranko's sudden death in 1973 to work under his successors, Glen Tetley and then Marcia Haydée. Among the choreographers active in Stuttgart during this period were Tetley, Jiří Kylián (a classmate of Anderson's at the Royal Ballet School), William Forsythe, and John Alleyne. Anderson thus absorbed the Stuttgart tradition of encouraging original choreography at the same time that he experienced the power of Cranko's personality and the intimate, family atmosphere that he created in his company. Cranko's example affected Anderson and his approach to his profession. An eye for detail, a sense of discipline and decorum, positive support for every artist, and pride in the artistic enterprise — these were some of the qualities that Anderson admired in his mentor, and which he tried to bring to the task of directing a ballet company, first, Ballet BC, during his brief association with it, and then the National.

Anderson thus came to the National as a hybrid: while he never considered himself a purely classical dancer, he had a deep-rooted respect for the classics; an exponent of Cranko's works, which had a firm place in the National's repertoire, he was also familiar with choreographers like Kylián and Forsythe, who were just beginning to enter the company's range of vision; a product of western Canadian ballet rather than the National, he nevertheless shared in some of its traditions by virtue of his association with Cranko. And through his earlier visits to the company, he already knew its dancers and was known to them. This combination of qualities made Anderson the right choice for the time. As an outsider but not a complete foreigner, he could help the company set its eyes firmly on the future without disregarding its past.[27]

It was a measure of Anderson's political astuteness that he invited Valerie Wilder to remain with the company as his associate director, and a testimony to diplomatic skills on both sides that her transition to the position was accomplished smoothly and efficiently. The team approach to administration, which Bruhn had pioneered with his own

Margaret Illmann and Raymond Smith in James Kudelka's Pastorale.

appointment, had become too deeply entrenched for Anderson to claim the autocratic control of an old-style artistic director along with his assumption of the title. Anderson chose to place himself at the head of a functioning team rather than dismantle it and start from scratch. In this way, he was able to build on the organization and momentum of the past in steering the company's future course.

The transition was not painless. Anticipating the debilitating effects of the recession, Anderson and company management made changes to both the artistic roster and the administrative staff in the early years of his appointment. Kim Lightheart and Kevin Pugh left the company; Owen Montague took a year's leave of absence to dance with the Netherlands Dance Theatre, from which he did not return. Administrative staff was reduced. Touring was curtailed. Balanchine's *Divertimento No. 15*, announced for the "Glory of Mozart" festival in 1991, had to be postponed to 1993. But by taking difficult decisions early, Anderson and his team avoided greater pain later on. By the forty-first Annual General Meeting in 1992, the company had ended its fiscal year in the black, yet Anderson could point to a successful tour of the Far East, including Hong Kong, Tokyo, Seoul, and Taipei, and the addition of major new repertoire, assisted by generous private donations and the continuing work of the Volunteer Committee, as signs of artistic health.[28] And balancing the loss of some of the well-loved principal dancers were the additions of exciting new talent like Margaret Illmann, Yseult Lendvai (whom he brought with him from Ballet BC), and Chan Hon Goh. At the 1992 Annual General Meeting, which celebrated the reduction of the deficit, the board also announced that Anderson's contract had been renewed for a further four years.[29] The renewal testified to Anderson's staying power in difficult economic times, but more than that, it acknowledged decisive artistic leadership, which took the company further into Cranko territory — as was to be expected — but also returned the company to its classical origins with significant additions to repertoire and a demanding eye for detail.

THE RETURN OF JAMES KUDELKA

Anderson concentrated a great deal of company energy on the development of new, original choreography. His first investment was in the appointment of John Alleyne as resident choreographer, a position Alleyne took on in 1990 only to surrender it in 1992 when he became artistic director of Ballet BC. Since joining the National under Bruhn's aegis in 1984, Alleyne had pursued a dual career as dancer and choreographer. Although Bruhn had seen him primarily as a dancer, Wallis and Wilder had encouraged Alleyne's interest in choreography with commissions for the Concert Group (*Trapdance*) and the main company (*Have Steps Will Travel*). They had also taken one of his outside commissions (*Blue-Eyed Trek*, for the National Ballet School) into the repertoire for the company's German tour of 1989. With his appointment as resident choreographer, Alleyne retired from dancing in order to devote himself to choreography. In 1991–92, the company premiered his *Interrogating Slam* and performed his *Split House Geometric*, a revision of a work created two years earlier for the Concert Group. In naming Alleyne resident choreographer, Anderson sought once again to place the creation of original works at the heart of the dancers' experience. Alleyne's departure for British Columbia, while a sign of personal success, interrupted yet again the continuity of choreographic collaboration that had eluded the company so often in the past.

Anderson moved quickly to try to compensate for Alleyne's loss by appointing James Kudelka to the newly created position of artist in residence. The title, deliberately more general than that of resident choreographer, was chosen by Kudelka himself, who was careful not to claim more than he could initially deliver.

> I felt that the definition of a resident choreographer at the National Ballet was an incorrect one. I find that with a company like the National Ballet of Canada, to be a choreographer who works with a core group of about twelve dancers on esoteric work on a yearly basis is not a resident choreographer.

Having thus kept expectations in check, he began producing at a rate that exceeded all expectations. *Pastorale*, which he made for the company in 1990, was followed in quick succession by *Musings* (1992), *The Miraculous Mandarin* (1993), *The Actress*, and *Spring Awakening* (1994). In Kudelka's first venture into a full-length ballet, the company's spectacular new *Nutcracker* (1995), Anderson wanted a show with production values that would compete with the lure of mega-musicals like *Sunset Boulevard* and *Beauty and the Beast*, which were threatening to cut into the company's annual *Nutcracker* sales. Two thematic interests could be traced in this body of work: the deep, sometimes tortured, never insignificant relationship between the worlds of children and of adults (*Miraculous Mandarin*, *Spring Awakening*, and *The Nutcracker*); and the enigmatic solitude of the individual in society — admired, adored, but never fully integrated (*Pastorale*, *Musings*, *The Actress*). Karen Kain emerged as the muse who inspired Kudelka's art. Of this late-blooming creative relationship, Kudelka said, "If you'd told me a year before, that it was going to start up, I would have said nonsense." The collaboration resulted in haunting tributes to a great ballerina and substantial works for the company's repertoire.

Kudelka turned his residency into an apprenticeship that brought him into contact with a wide variety of the company's operations.

> I wanted to be able to perform, to be able to teach, to coach. I haven't done all of those things, but I took the company out on concert groups and really did a strange kind of apprenticeship for about a four-year period.[30]

In all these ways, he fostered the direct rapport with the dancers that is essential to the realization of the company's mission to create original works and thus resumed the role he had abandoned so abruptly in 1981.

Anderson Charted an Aggressive Course for the Nineties

Anderson also fostered the addition of works to the National's repertoire by noted outside choreographers, including Balanchine (*Divertimento No. 15*), Glen Tetley (*Rite of Spring*), and John Neumeier (with the original creation *Now and Then*, his first collaboration with the company since *Don Juan* in 1974). Given his Stuttgart background, however, it was natural that Anderson placed a heavy emphasis on Cranko in his programming and repertoire. *Concerto for Flute and Harp*, set to Mozart's music, proved to be a pleasing exercise in Cranko classicism for ten men and two women. *Onegin* and *Romeo and Juliet* made regular appearances. But none of this was very surprising. It was a different Cranko ballet that the public anticipated, waiting to see if Anderson held it up his sleeve. Anderson indulged in a little bit of teasing. At a gala occasion early in his appointment, like Erik Bruhn before him,

Cylla von Tiedemann

In 1995, Reid Anderson commissioned new sets and costumes from Susan Benson for Romeo and Juliet, *to replace the originals by Jürgen Rose. Here, Etienne Lavigne as Tybalt, with artists of the ballet, in the entrance to the Capulet's ball.*

he signalled to the world his most significant intention with respect to the Cranko repertoire while at the same time honouring one of the company's undisputed stars.

Veronica Tennant had built a major career and impressive artistic reputation almost entirely within the National Ballet of Canada. One of the company's best-loved ballerinas, she was also a figure of national prominence on the Canadian cultural scene, an eloquent spokesperson for the importance of cultural values in the life of the nation. As such, she enjoyed a popularity and influence that went far beyond the confines of the dance world. In 1988, she caught her admirers completely off guard by announcing her retirement from the ballet stage. Her scheduled performances in Cranko's *Romeo and Juliet* in the spring season of 1988 would be her last. She was then forty-three years old, and still in full command of her expressive powers as a dancer. Her final Juliet, on February 12, 1989, was covered on nationally televised news broadcasts. Tickets to see her one last time in the role that had brought her stardom over a twenty-five-year career were impossible to come by. Those fans lucky enough to be in the theatre poured their love unstintingly across the footlights at the end of the performance with a profusion of flowers and a seemingly endless ovation. On the eve of the company's change in leadership, one of its biggest stars bowed out in a blaze of glory.

The official Tennant farewell, however, took place the following fall, just after Anderson had assumed his new position. It was a gala retrospective on November 21, 1989, with Tennant recreating some of her finest classical roles as well as excerpts of the original choreography that had been associated with her throughout her career. The new artistic director's curtain speech was gallant and unobtrusive. The evening belonged to Tennant, and to her alone. But Anderson's influence was palpable in the evening's greatest coup, the surprise appearance by Richard Cragun, star of the Stuttgart Ballet, to partner Tennant in a Cranko role she had never before performed. Her spitfire performance that evening as Katherina in the Act I pas de deux from *The Taming of the Shrew* convinced the audience that she had retired too early; it also displayed, even in the absence of any official announcement, Anderson's trump card. He would bring the complete ballet, the only one of the Cranko full-length story ballets still missing from the National, to the repertoire of his new company.

It took two and a half more years, and the extraordinary generosity of a single donor, Walter Carsen, who underwrote all the costs of the new production, but in February 1992, *Shrew* arrived on the stage of the O'Keefe Centre. It was the blockbuster ballet of Anderson's first term as artistic director, the first new full-length production for the National since *The Merry Widow* in 1986. Just as Alexander Grant's connections had brought access to some of the Ashton repertoire, Reid Anderson's connections completed for the company the Cranko trilogy of full-length story ballets and confirmed the special significance of Cranko's work in defining the character of the National for the nineties. Under Anderson's leadership, the popular appeal of the Cranko repertoire was to be one of the central supports of the company.

Veronica Tennant and Richard Cragun in the pas de deux from The Taming Of The Shrew *at Tennant's farewell performance in 1989.*

This emphasis, though hardly surprising, represented a highly significant choice for the National. In a period of increasingly constrained resources, Anderson chose to spend those resources not on a badly needed new production of *Swan Lake* or *Giselle*, the standards of the classical repertoire, but on *The Taming of the Shrew*, an entertaining comedy but hardly a work of central significance to a classically based company. In an ideal world, he could have done both. In the consumer-driven world of financial austerity, his choice confirmed a trend that dated back at least as far as Erik Bruhn: while the standard works of the classical repertoire languished in productions from the sixties and the seventies, new production money was being devoted consistently to new choreography or to lightweight crowd-pleasers like *The Merry Widow*, *The Taming of the Shrew*, and Ben Stevenson's *Cinderella* (in 1995). The company's classical emphasis was still there, but was it a high priority?

The answer was, after Cranko, yes. Anderson continued the company's long-standing practice of rotating the standard classics — *Swan Lake*, *The Sleeping Beauty*, *Coppélia*, *Giselle*, *Don Quixote* — through the performance schedule as ballast for the modern repertoire of Cranko, Ashton, and Balanchine and contemporary works by Tetley, Kylián, Forsythe, Alleyne, and Kudelka. To a cynic, this decision might represent nothing more

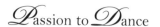

than sound business sense; the standard classics were essential to the success of the subscription campaign. But careful observers saw something more: as each of the classics appeared on its appointed round, performance standards were improving. By direct supervision and careful choice of coaches, Anderson kept a demanding eye on details, scrutinizing the corps, introducing new dancers into prominent roles, and fine-tuning the productions that were in danger of being taken for granted. If Anderson chose not to replace the old productions with new ones, he proved his ability to rejuvenate them by presenting carefully rehearsed, intelligent, and respectful readings of the old favourites.

Furthermore, he demonstrated his commitment to the Petipa heritage by the introduction into the repertoire in 1991 of *Paquita*, in Natalia Makarova's Kirov-inspired production. This single act of divertissements, all that is now produced of Petipa's two-act original, is a test-piece of technique and classical style that mercilessly exposes a company's classical character and abilities. Anderson saw it through its initial, tentative year of entry into the repertoire and brought it back the following year in a much-improved reading that revealed a stylistically cohesive and mature ensemble. Anderson's meticulous approach to the classical repertoire, while not a return to Celia Franca's single-minded vision of its centrality to the company's identity, nevertheless shifted the balance back to a recognition of its importance and thus modified the concerted emphasis on the contemporary that had characterized the company from Erik Bruhn's time onward.

Anderson's artistic directorship also spanned another significant era of change for the company, as measured by its artistic roster. A ballet company's makeup changes constantly, as dancers mature or move on and as the individual eye of different artistic directors or choreographers identifies and singles out a young new dancer in the company for prominence and recognition. Anderson's period with the company was no different in this respect. His encouragement of its women was particularly notable. Most significantly, however, with the departure of Tennant, the mature Karen Kain claimed the role of the company's undisputed senior artist, in a class by herself where once she was the first among equals. No longer simply the star who guaranteed box office, she matured into something far more interesting, the committed artist who seized every opportunity to increase her scope, unconcerned with the dire necessities of advancing a career. Her collaborations with Glen Tetley (in *Alice*) and James Kudelka (in *Musings, The Miraculous Mandarin*, and *The Actress*) revealed the depth of her commitment to her art by her willingness to sacrifice star quality to the uncompromising demands of the choreographer's vision. Her twenty-fifth anniversary season, in 1994–95, honoured the mature artist with a relinquishing of the past and a brave step into the future. Her sentimental farewell to the role of the Swan Queen in *Swan Lake* was balanced by the dramatic challenge of Natalia Petrovna in Ashton's *A Month in the Country*, in the first performances of the work by any company other than the Royal Ballet. But even Kain could not avoid the inevitable. In a final burst of energy, a seven-city Canadian farewell tour under the auspices of Garth Drabinsky's theatrical production company, Livent Inc., Kain announced her retirement

D. Brian Campbell

Karen Kain as Natalia Petrovna in Ashton's A Month in the Country.

from dancing at the end of the 1996–97 season.[31] With this change in her own status, she confirmed the more subtle change that had gradually overtaken the company under Anderson. The National had ceased trading on the star quality of its best and brightest dancers and become instead a coherent ensemble, proud of its individual dancers but prouder still of the overall look and standard of the entire company.

On the male side of the house, this change in character was occasioned as much by necessity as by conscious choice. The remarkable contingent of men brought into the company from the National Ballet School during the eighties by Grant and Bruhn had matured and begun to disperse. During his first term as artistic director, Anderson had to say goodbye to more recent recruits from the school like Alexander Ritter and Stephen Legate, on whom the company had placed great hopes, and to Owen Montague, arguably one of the most distinctive male dancers the company ever had. All went on to dance elsewhere. All had helped to account for the strengthening of the male side of the company that had made possible the new choreographic directions of the eighties and nineties. Rex Harrington, Serge Lavoie, and Raymond Smith remained to provide reliable support among the ranks of the male principals, with Jeremy Ransom and Pierre Quinn moving into new prominence. To provide new blood in the junior male ranks, Anderson began to recruit from diverse sources around the world, but without the heavy reliance on National Ballet School graduates that had characterized the company before his arrival. Subtly but decisively, the look of the company began to change.

Male dancers are always at more of a premium in the dance world than female; international competition for strong male dancers is always intense, and no company is immune to raiding. Anderson arrived just at the sunset of a golden age in male dancers within the company that could never have been expected to extend indefinitely. The extraordinary burgeoning of male talent from the National Ballet School in the late seventies and early eighties, directly influenced by Betty Oliphant and Erik Bruhn, produced a generation of men who energized the company and then became fair game in the international world of dance. Where once the company had Frank Augustyn as its male claim to fame, it suddenly had the likes of Montague, Ransom, Harrington, Lavoie, Paul Chalmer, John Alleyne, Kevin Pugh, and Anthony Randazzo. Bruhn was able to play on their loyalty toward their former teacher to keep them in the company together, but he realized that their departure was inevitable, a sign, as he had written to Arova, of their own success rather than his failure to keep them at home. In less bountiful times, Anderson had to do all he could to attract and keep a strong male contingent, and did so with the international recruitment of soloists like Aleksandar Antonijevic, Robert Conn, Johan Persson, Robert Tewsley, and Vladimir Malakhov. Of these, only Persson had received his training at the National Ballet School and all but Antonijevic moved on to international careers elsewhere. Anderson opted for the long and arduous task of maintaining a strong overall ensemble instead of relying on a star strategy, a reflection of the hard realities of supply and demand as well as a conscious strategy for the long-term artistic development of the company.

Lilian Jarvis and Earl Kraul with artists of the ballet in Michel Fokine's Les Sylphides, *in the company's early years.*

Glenn Gibson, Angela Leigh, and Ray Moller in Pas De Chance, *choreographed by David Adams (1956).*

Lawrence Adams as Agamemnon in Grant Strate's The House of Atreus *(1964)*.

David Street

Charles Kirby and Gizella Witkowsky as Lord and Lady Capulet with artists of the ballet in Romeo and Juliet, *in the 1964 designs by Jürgen Rose. Guest artist Alessandra Ferri as Juliet, in the background.*

Cylla von Tiedemann

Artists of the ballet in the ballroom scene from Romeo and Juliet *in the 1995 designs by Susan Benson.*

Four Pairs of Star-Crossed Lovers:

Karen Kain and Frank Augustyn in 1981.

Veronica Tennant and Raymond Smith in 1983.   Jaimie Tapper and Johan Persson in 1998.

Sonia Rodriguez and Aleksandar Antonijevic, with Lorna Geddes in the background, in 2006.

Erik Bruhn and Lynn Seymour as James and the Sylph in La Sylphide *(1964).*

Erik Bruhn as Prince Siegfried in Swan Lake *(1967).*

Artists of the ballet in the last act of Rudolf Nureyev's 1972 production of The Sleeping Beauty.

Backstage at The Sleeping Beauty: *Rex Harrington preparing for the role of King Florestan.*

Backstage at The Sleeping Beauty: *Rebekah Rimsay making up for the role of Carabosse.*

Artists of the ballet as the cockerel and his hens in La Fille mal gardée.

Piotr Stanczyk and Martine Lamy as Colas and Lise with artists of the ballet in La Fille mal gardée, *acquired by Alexander Grant in 1976.*

Artists of the ballet in The Merry Widow, *acquired by Erik Bruhn in 1986.*

Nina Goldman, Sally-Ann Hickin and Barbara Smith in Kim Nielsen's striking costumes for John Alleyne's Have Steps Will Travel *(1988).*

Artists of the ballet in James Kudelka's Pastorale *(1990).*

Thomas Snee and Jackson Carroll as the dancing horse with Piotr Stanczyk in James Kudelka's The Nutcracker, *choreographed in 1995.*

Artists of the ballet in the lakeside scene of James Kudelka's production of Swan Lake, *choreographed in 1998.*

Xiao Nan Yu as Odette, Jiří Jelinek as Prince Siegfried, and Patrick Lavoie as Rothbart, with artists of the ballet in James Kudelka's Swan Lake.

Lorna Geddes, Rebekah Rimsay, and Guillaume Côté with artists of the ballet in James Kudelka's The Firebird *(2000).*

Artists of the ballet in "Rubies" from George Balanchine's Jewels, *acquired by James Kudelka in 2000.*

Lorna Geddes with artists of the ballet in James Kudelka's Cinderella *(2004).*

Artists of the ballet in James Kudelka's An Italian Straw Hat, *with Heather Ogden (in white) as Hélène (2005).*

Artists of the ballet in John Cranko's Onegin, *redesigned by Santo Loquasto in 2010.*

Christopher Stalzer with artists of the ballet in Crystal Pite's Emergence *(2009).*

Above: *Jillian Vanstone and Aleksandar Antonijevic as Alice and the White Rabbit in Christopher Wheeldon's spectacular production of* Alice's Adventures in Wonderland.

Right: *Aleksandar Antonijevic as the White Rabbit in* Alice's Adventures in Wonderland.

On both the male and the female sides of the house a significant trend emerged. The new dancers of the National, as recruited by Anderson, came from all over the world, trained in many different schools. The dominant influence of the National Ballet School, and, indirectly, of Betty Oliphant, for so many years its defining force, had been significantly diminished. Anderson's training and professional experience had created in him no special allegiances to the National Ballet School. Oliphant herself retired as its director in 1989, in the first part of Anderson's tenure at the company, to be succeeded by Mavis Staines, who began to explore new directions for the school during her first years there. This period of transition at the school, and particularly the departure of Oliphant as a powerful influence on company affairs, allowed Anderson the opportunity to sever, gently but decisively, the last of the direct ties to the company's origins. The Westerner from Stuttgart asserted his independence.

A highly significant development of Anderson's first term as artistic director took place not on the stage of the O'Keefe Centre, but in the secondary schools, the community halls, and the senior citizens' homes of the province. Here, an innovative new

As part of the company's current outreach activities, company members Alejandra Perez-Gomez and Lisa Robinson work with children in the Kids Corps program at the Cinderella *movement workshop in Studio Prima at the Walter Carsen Centre.*

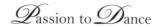

community and educational outreach program, developed by Assis Carreiro, at the time the National's manager of educational services, assembled dancers, choreographers, musicians, and scenic artists for week-long residencies in secondary schools, during which they assisted students in developing and producing their own dance creations in their schools and for their local communities. "Creating Dances in the Schools" began with a project in Toronto-area schools and was repeated in Markham; its more ambitious sibling, "Stepping Out," moved into the Niagara region and then Ottawa. While the National acted as catalyst for the project, it used artists from outside the company in addition to its own dancers or, in the case of the Ottawa stint, professional dancers from that city's companies, to carry out the work. Students had the satisfaction of seeing their completed work performed on the O'Keefe stage at one of the company's regular school matinees, but the real value of the program rested in the collaboration between professionals and students that enabled them to make the choreographic art part of their living experience.

The program was an extension of earlier and more traditional outreach efforts like Prologue to the Performing Arts (which took small-scale demonstrations of dance and theatrical craft into the schools), the Shell student matinees, pre-performance lectures and chats, and the various open houses and backstage tours that have long formed a part of the National's activities. The distinctive feature of the new program, however, was its strong community base and its attempt to preach not to the converted, but to those who had never heard the good news. By moving the participating artists into the local community, by using, as much as possible, the artistic resources available within that community, and by offering the program explicitly to students who had had no previous experience of dance, the National came to future audiences on their terms, and made genuine efforts to relate the creative principles of its art to the lives of its community. Audience building might be a happy by-product of the process, but the immediate result was the exchange of ideas that took place, eradicating the distinction between performer and spectator and replacing it with the common purpose of artistic collaboration.

In "Stepping Out," the National found one practical solution to the problem confronting all the so-called museum arts in justifying their substantial claims on the public purse, but it was only the beginning of the company's outreach initiatives. Under subsequent artistic directors, and guided by Sharon Vanderlinde, senior manager, education and archives, the company has continued its lecture demonstrations in schools through its Dance About program. And YOU Dance, under the artistic directorship of Lindsay Fischer, now gives the company's young apprentices the chance to involve school students across the province in the full spectrum of activities that go into creating and performing dance. Through programs like these, the National has demonstrated its commitment to opening the eyes of an ever-widening audience, the audience of young people, to their own creative potential through dance.

REID ANDERSON'S SURPRISE DEPARTURE

This ability to adapt to the political and social requirements of the times and to synthesize the existing elements of the National's tradition into a coherent course for future development proved to be Anderson's greatest strength as artistic director during radically changing times. The politician in him had to be as strong as the artist in order to maintain this delicate balance. And the diplomatic fundraiser had to be stronger than both. But even the adroit politician eventually got tired, while the artist and fundraiser finally grew discouraged. In the fall of 1995, the newly elected Progressive Conservative government in Ontario cut the province's support of the Ontario Arts Council by 10 percent; in turn, the council cut its direct support to several large arts organizations, including the National Ballet, by 25 percent.[32] In the National's case, this percentage decrease translated into a reduction of almost $425,000[33] to its operating budget, an overwhelmingly disheartening move coming, as it did, on top of the various freezes and gradual cuts in funding that had characterized the late eighties and nineties. Anderson had a right to be discouraged; he also had other opportunities opening to him.

On November 9, 1995, Anderson was announced as that year's recipient of the John Cranko Prize, awarded annually by the John Cranko Society of Stuttgart in recognition of excellence in interpreting or staging Cranko's legacy. In Anderson's case, the award acknowledged his success in producing Cranko's works around the world.[34] At the company's O'Keefe Centre performance the following night, Karen Kain, in a curtain speech on behalf of the entire company, shocked the capacity audience by announcing that Anderson was resigning the artistic directorship of the company, effective the following year. Visibly moved, the company members dedicated that night's performance to Anderson.

Trying to maintain and improve artistic standards in the face of constantly diminishing resources had finally become too much. Anderson had been lured away to become the artistic director at Stuttgart, the company he had long called home. In the press release announcing his departure, he took aim at the debilitating effects of government underfunding.

> My seven years at the National Ballet of Canada have been the most satisfying artistically, and personally, in my career. The continued lack of appreciation by government for art and artists and their contribution to quality of life and the economy is particularly frustrating. So is the failure of government arts agencies to give special recognition, and support, to flagship arts organizations of international stature which provide leadership through proven excellence. The recent cuts from the Ontario Arts Council have greatly discouraged me, and I feel it is time for someone else to take the challenge of running this extraordinary company.[35]

When it least expected to, the National had to look for a new leader.

A search committee was quickly constituted, once again under the leadership of Lyman Henderson. Working amid press speculation that included names like Veronica Tennant, Frank Augustyn, Karen Kain, and even the Royal Ballet's Anthony Dowell,[36] the committee produced a surprising, yet obvious, candidate — James Kudelka. For the first time in its history, the National would be led by an internationally known, practising choreographer, a product of the National Ballet School and of the company itself. The prodigal son, so recently returned, was suddenly shouldering all the responsibilities of the family head.

Heather Ogden and Guillaume Côté in The Nutcracker, *which James Kudelka mounted for the National the year before his appointment as artistic director.*

But in the years since 1981, when he left the company as a dancer, the prodigal son had hardly wasted his patrimony; he had, instead, increased his worth, first by gaining additional experience as both a choreographer and a dancer in the congenial environment of Les Grands Ballets Canadiens, then by working internationally as a choreographer with the Joffrey Ballet in New York, the San Francisco Ballet, and American Ballet Theatre. And although he stood by his earlier criticisms that the company had relied too heavily on reproduced, rather than original, works for its repertoire, he had returned to the National in 1992 as an experienced artist, no longer an angry young man. The company to which he returned had changed as well.

That was the period we were going through then and I'm not angry about any of that any more. But it was true. Erik really grabbed hold of that. I wasn't here, but you could tell, he opened it right up. And yet Erik didn't do it all. Reid had a lot to do with it too, and Valerie and Lynn. I used to hear about Reid talking to the company and saying, "You know, you just don't know how to act with a choreographer. You have to do what the choreographer says. That's what this is all about." And that was news to a lot of people.

Experience with a smaller, more innovative company away from home, international exposure, then a period of practical apprenticeship in the National — it all sounded more like a carefully rehearsed plan than a spontaneous act of rebellion. On the eve of assuming his duties, Kudelka half-jokingly acknowledged as much.

Here I am. This is probably a little bit earlier than I thought that this kind of thing might happen and yet I always knew in my master plan, in my master plan as a young man, that this was something that I would do one day. I suddenly realized that this was the time.[37]

As artistic director, Kudelka entered into an administrative structure that had changed significantly since his early days in the company. On May 1, 1996, the company announced that Robert Johnston, its general manager since 1979, would retire the following December. Valerie Wilder would become the executive director and co-chief executive officer of the company on June 1,[38] a partner to Kudelka as the artistic director. It was the team approach to artistic direction as pioneered by Erik Bruhn, but with a much smaller lineup. Whereas Bruhn had worked with Johnston, Wilder, and Wallis, Kudelka and Wilder together constituted the entire team leading the company into the new century.

*C*hapter *T*en

A CRUCIBLE FOR CREATIVITY

A Commitment to the Creative Process

Kudelka had grown up in the National Ballet. His mother had brought her children to the Royal Alex from the family farm in Newmarket to watch performances from the rush seats in the balcony. In 1965, as a child at the National Ballet School, he had danced in Franca's *Nutcracker*. In 1968, still at the school, he appeared in the film of her *Cinderella*,[1] as a grasshopper and as one o'clock on the clockface in the countdown to midnight at the ball. But in 1995 he took over the company determined to be a man, and to treat the dancers, the "boys and girls" of ballet culture, as men and women, as adults who would be partners in the exciting and sometimes disorienting process of creating new work. Furthermore, he recognized the generational gap between dancer and director, and knew which side of the divide he stood on. As he said later:

> I loved senior management. I liked working with people my own age….
> Reid wanted to do the family and I wanted to do the team. I kept saying,
> "Who needs a family? I already have a dysfunctional family. Why would
> I want to set up a dysfunctional family here?" But you can't get around it.
> Young people look up to older people. And dancers look up to directors
> in very, very infantile ways.[2]

The story of his directorship would be the story of a bold experiment — his efforts to change the culture of the company in order to transform it from a group of performers into a group of creators. The company would not be his instrument as a choreographer, but a crucible in which the molten elements of choreography fused into the final created work. Inevitably, some would be singed in the heat of the creative fires.

Not long after taking charge, Kudelka became convinced of the need to commit to writing his artistic vision for the company, so that artistic vision could drive every other aspect of the organization, including its financial planning. By around 2000, he had produced a document of a dozen pages that, with additions, revisions, and updates, guided the company through the rest of his tenure as artistic director. An artistic manifesto, it presented a capsule history of ballet in general and the company in particular, an analysis of its current context, and a statement of Kudelka's vision for its future.[3] Starting from a clear assessment of the nature of the company he had inherited, Kudelka frankly acknowledged both the strengths and weaknesses of his personal approach to artistic direction, and held up for his dancers a controversial ideal, one that elevated the ensemble at the expense of the star.

Kudelka recognized that the National's identity had been built on the acquisition of the nineteenth-century classics and the recreation of the standard works of the modern repertoire, on its preservation of the "antique, both old and new," as he characterized the company's curatorial responsibility. But too single-minded an emphasis on this responsibility had allowed the company to settle for "borrowed successes, and failures."

James Kudelka with Victoria Bertram and students of Canada's National Ballet School rehearsing The Nutcracker.

A Crucible for Creativity

What seemed to have been forgotten over the years of success and acclaim was that the National Ballet had no identity as a creative organization. The acquisition of repertoire was seen as an end in itself. The National Ballet's repertoire only put it up for comparison with all of the other companies that had the same repertoire.

His role as a choreographer was clearly to begin the creation of a new legacy, one unique to the company not just because it held the exclusive performance rights, but because it had engaged communally in its creation. An ensemble commitment to the creative process would result in works that might well be danced by others, but never with the authoritative sense of ownership that sprang from the labour of creation.

As choreographer/artistic director, Kudelka had to educate all his constituencies to this revised view of the company's mandate: to embrace the future, to dare to experiment, to challenge the old standards for success, above all, to value creative process, sometimes more than the product itself. "We are not commercial theatre," Kudelka argued, "and what you get may not be exactly what you bargained for. My life as a ballet person has always been based on the search for the underbelly of truth, and never the superficiality of beauty." His focus, he recognized, was more on advancing the art form than on curating the museum and that focus required education. "I know that I could be criticized for putting the education of the artists of the ballet ahead of the education of the public."

Given the nature of Kudelka's ideal, the re-education of the artists presented a steep learning curve in itself.

> The development of the artist comes from the development of the individual. The artists that I have total respect for tend to be extremely generous individuals whose artistry is a result of a continuing need for self-knowledge and personal growth. I encourage learning and the possibility that as much as the individual has something to learn, they also have something to teach and give toward the process of the creation of brilliant dance/ballet. I have little respect for the system which rewards ambition over passion.

In Kudelka's view, the system he inherited displayed at least some of these latter characteristics. "I remember returning to the National Ballet to revive my ballet, *Washington Square* [in 1982], and seeing a troupe of highly trained individuals who were not the least involved or implicated in their profession." Kudelka had a shock in store for those dancers whose goal was to negotiate the traditional pyramid structure of the company and progress through the ranks to principal dancer, then, perhaps, on to stardom. He believed in any case that stars were chosen by the public, not created by any company machine.

(Julia Drake, the company's veteran director of communications, would later agree with this assessment.[4]) "I am not promoting dancers one at a time but … creating an ensemble at the highest level possible … an ensemble that supports whatever the choreographic vision needs," he wrote in his vision statement. Perhaps only George Balanchine, that complete autocrat, had succeeded in running such a classless company, and many would argue that he had done it more in name than in practice. Kudelka had charted a daunting course for himself, his company, and his audience.

Taking Care of Business:
The Transition After Anderson's Departure

The 1996–97 season, Kudelka's first, had been planned well before Anderson's departure, but there were transitional headaches all the same. Margaret Illmann, Robert Tewsley, and Yseult Lendvai, three of the dancers Anderson had brought into the company, all audience favourites, all from the senior ranks, announced that they were following him to Stuttgart. Kudelka filled the gap by inviting Illmann and Tewsley to return to the National as guest artists for one more year and by promoting Robert Conn, Greta Hodgkinson, and Johan Persson within the company from first soloist to principal dancer. But even so, the senior ranks looked a little thin for Kudelka's first year. Anderson had assured the board's executive committee that he was not poaching, that he would make no overtures to company members,[5] but it was inevitable that a few dancers, especially those who had been Anderson's protegés, would jump at the chance for a European career. And that Anderson, who had a keen eye for talent, would help them make the leap. Tewsley, who was British, and Lendvai, who was French, were also moving closer to home. But observers with a long memory heard faint echoes of the rivalries of 1951, when Gweneth Lloyd accused Celia Franca of stealing dancers from Winnipeg during the cross-Canada audition tour. This more recent test of loyalties, however, was diplomatically handled. Though the press lamented these departures, there was no public name-calling.

As soon as Kudelka took over the reins, the company learned what it meant to have as its artistic director a choreographer who was active on the international scene. His appointment allowed him four weeks in the year (in addition to four weeks of vacation time) to pursue his career elsewhere.[6] In September 1996, his company made the move into its new home at the Walter Carsen Centre on Queen's Quay West without its artistic director present. Kudelka was in England, creating *Le Baiser de la Fée* for the Birmingham Royal Ballet.[7] Faxes flew back and forth between him and his assistant as he dealt, long distance, with the move and with the other minutiae of running the company, including the perennial challenge for any new artistic director, pruning the ranks of dancers to deal with personnel problems and reflect the new style he envisioned for the company. When

Bruce Zinger

Alejandra Perez-Gomez with students of Canada's National Ballet School in The Nutcracker. *Olivia Lecomte is Marie and Cesar Corrales is Misha.*

Kudelka remounted *Baiser* (under its English title, *The Fairy's Kiss*) for the National in 1999, he commented that in England *Baiser* had had "such negative press that I decided that we should do it to see if it could possibly be as bad as all that."[8]

The offhand comment illustrated two important facets of Kudelka's approach to the use of his own choreography for his own company. One was the practical principle of recycling. He couldn't possibly create new works at his old rate and run the company too. But he could put his stamp on it by remounting for the National works he had already created on other companies. Over his nine years as artistic director, the company would acquire seven Kudelka works originally mounted elsewhere, among them *Cruel World* and *Désir*.[9] The other facet was his jaunty skepticism on the subject of critical opinion. As a creator, Kudelka knew that any choreographer has more failures than successes. Furthermore, success can seldom be judged accurately on the first run. Some works must return over time before they can find an audience. As artistic director, Kudelka sometimes found himself in the awkward position of having to champion his own works against the negative reactions of public and press. But self-promotion had its limits. Two of his more controversial creations from his period as artist in residence, *The Miraculous Mandarin* and *Spring Awakening*, never received the sober second look they deserved. Kudelka felt he could not program with complete disregard for his audience's tastes. "I was unfortunately in the position that I didn't set any of my non-pointe-shoe ballets on the National Ballet for fear of the backlash I would get. So *In Paradisum* never went in, and *Fifteen Heterosexual Duets* [now widely regarded as two of his masterworks] never went in."[10]

Other important matters preoccupied the new artistic director. The financial crisis that had prompted Anderson's resignation did not go away; it only worsened. So the company, under the guidance of its executive director Valerie Wilder, entered into one of the most stringent periods of cost-cutting in its history. Every administrative expenditure was examined and pruned; all sources of revenue were reassessed; and every effort was made to keep the direct effect on the artistic side of the house to a minimum. Yet despite these efforts, dancer numbers dwindled. Kudelka had fifty-eight dancers (exclusive of guests and apprentices) when he took over in 1996–97. By the 2000–01 season, that number had shrunk to fifty-one.

The smaller company, however, had no shortage of work. Karen Kain's retirement from dancing, in 1997, turned into a national event. Garth Drabinsky, the Canadian theatre mogul whose management practices at Livent corporation had not yet come under the scrutiny of the law, decided to mount a Canadian farewell tour, covering seven cities from Montreal to Vancouver in the summer and fall of 1997. Veronica Tennant's production company would follow the tour and film it for a television documentary. The farewell's centrepiece, and the only work in which Kain herself would appear, was Kudelka's *The Actress*, created as a vehicle for her in 1994, but other repertoire was needed. The company acquired *The Red Shoes*, by American choreographer Lar Lubovitch, squeezing the preparation time into the crowded rehearsal schedule for its regular season. Lubovitch had created *The Red Shoes* as part of the choreography for a short-lived Broadway musical based on the famous 1948 movie of the same name, starring Moira Shearer. Margaret Illmann, on leave from the National, had played the lead role to very good notices in the brief 1993 Broadway run. After the show closed, Lubovitch salvaged some of the dance sequences to create an independent ballet that appeared in American Ballet Theatre's repertoire in 1994, on the same program with Kudelka's *Cruel World*.[11] With flying sequences for some of the dancers, *The Red Shoes* was a complex work to rehearse. Sonia Rodriguez, Stacey Shiori Minagawa, and Rebekah Rimsay alternated in the lead role. The pas de deux from William Forsythe's *Herman Schmerman* and George Balanchine's *Tchaikowsky pas de deux* rounded out the repertoire for the farewell tour. Sir Kenneth MacMillan's pas de deux from the 1992 British revival of Rodgers and Hammerstein's *Carousel* was announced, but never materialized.

Just before the preparations for the Livent tour got underway in earnest, Kudelka's attention had been concentrated on the creation of his first original work for the National since his appointment as artistic director. Set to Vivaldi's popular quartet of violin concertos, one for each season of the year, *The Four Seasons* showcased the talents of the company's *bona fide* matinee idol, Rex Harrington. Its four sections traced the progress of an Everyman figure (Harrington) through the stages of life, concluding with his death in a frigid, wintry landscape. The "Summer" pas de deux, a thrilling, acrobatic display, stole the show, and was performed by Harrington and Greta Hodgkinson at London's Royal Opera House in 1999.[12] *The Four Seasons* enjoyed a long life in the company's repertoire and played in New York when the National appeared at the City Center in 1998. Beneath the dazzling choreography, however, lay the strong underpinning of a gentler, more meditative Kudelka preoccupation — his desire to choreograph specifically for the maturity of the National's older generation of dancers. Anna Kisselgoff described it aptly in her review of the New York performance. "The punchline is the appearance of older character dancers in the winter section…. There is a Shakespearean tinge to this modern-dress older group, led by Victoria Bertram, the mother who cradles Mr. Harrington at the end." Lorna Geddes spoke for an entire generation of dancers — herself, Victoria Bertram, Tomas Schramek, Hazaros Surmeyan — when she described their special relationship with Kudelka. "He gave us a career. The four of us. He kept us going and he knew that we loved working with him. He fed off that too." She compared his sense of humour to Erik Bruhn's, slightly acerbic, slightly challenging, easier for an older dancer to shrug off than for the younger generation to understand. "There was a more relaxed atmosphere between us. He could say things like, 'Well I don't expect you to remember yesterday's choreography, not at your age.' That kind of thing. So there was camaraderie there. And also, wonderfully, he gave us leeway to add to our characters."[13]

There remained one bit of business to tidy up from Anderson's planning for the 1996–97 season — the acquisition of another full-length Bournonville work, *Abdallah: or Tales of the Arabian Nights*. This "lost" ballet from the Bournonville repertoire had been reconstructed by the Danes Toni Lander and Flemming Ryberg in 1985 for Bruce Marks's American company, Ballet West, in Utah. With Ryberg and Sorella Englund, both of the Royal Danish Ballet, Marks brought *Abdallah* home to the Danes in 1986 and in 1990 set it on the Boston Ballet, when he took over that company.[14] The team of Marks, Ryberg, and Englund worked with the National in preparation for *Abdallah's* company premiere in May 1997. Ryberg also taught class while he was in Toronto, helping the dancers to brush up their Bournonville technique.[15] This attention to stylistic detail paid off. A youthful sprightliness characterized the dancers' quick footwork and elegant buoyancy, and in Jeremy Ransom, one of four men to dance the title role, the company had a former student of the great Erik Bruhn himself. The National also had a long-standing Bournonville tradition of its own, stretching through *Napoli* in 1982 all the way back to *La Sylphide* in 1964. But *Abdallah* was a nostalgic curiosity, with sets and costumes rented from Boston Ballet that aimed to reproduce as accurately as possible every detail of the nineteenth-century original. As such, it had considerable charm and a limited run. It did not reappear in the repertoire after its 1997 performances.

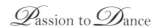

BALANCHINE REPERTOIRE AND THE BALANCHINE MYSTIQUE

Kudelka looked to the Balanchine repertoire to challenge the company's dancers and provide meaningful work for its corps de ballet. Onstage performances, not just company class, would expose the dancers and test their adaptability to a faster, more energetic style. He wanted to extend the range and flexibility of their technique for purposes of his own choreography as well. "I thought it was important to get them dancing in that exposed way, because the National always wore so much period costume. We'd never had our clothes off. And I wanted that kind of sophistication in my own work, so it was a way to get it."[16] Kudelka also wanted to ensure that, as he put it, "there was a very, very strong imprint, a very strong and direct imprint," of Balanchine the creator. So when the company premiered its new Balanchine program in the winter 1998 season, each of the works was mounted by a *répétiteur* who could demand accuracy, but also some evocation of the Balanchine mystique. *Episodes* was staged by Joysanne Sidimus, *Theme and Variations* by Patricia Neary (who had begun her career, at the age of fourteen, in the corps of the National), and *Mozartiana* by Suzanne Farrell, all of them former Balanchine ballerinas, all of them committed to perpetuating his vision of dance. They didn't just teach repertoire; they initiated the dancers into the holy mysteries.

Artists of the ballet in Theme and Variations, *taken from the wings.*

Kudelka sought out Suzanne Farrell in particular because of her intensely personal connection to the Balanchine legacy. In Farrell, the muse of Balanchine's later career, Kudelka recognized the uncompromising devotion to ballet that he himself felt. In ballet, said Kudelka, "You're either the priest or the king. Either you're serving art or you're ruling art. And I was a server." He felt that Farrell had the same selfless egotism. "We were of similar passion. We appreciated that in each other. She's a very hard person to just sit around and talk to. I sort of miss her friendship. But the only way to have her friendship is when both of us are serving. Then we were close." Kudelka's assessment of Farrell reflected something of his own personality. A server-priest, his professional relationships would always depend on mutual commitment to the highest artistic ideals. If those ideals were compromised, so was the relationship.

The acquisition of significant Balanchine repertoire continued throughout Kudelka's tenure as artistic director, with *Apollo*, staged by New York City Ballet dancer Ib Andersen, in February 1999, the first time that a male dancer had staged a Balanchine work for the company. The complete *Jewels* entered the repertoire in February 2000. Balanchine specialist Elyse Borne taught the entire work to the company in two weeks. The three individual movements were then assigned to individual Balanchine *répétiteurs* and Farrell came in to oversee the final rehearsals. *Stravinsky Violin Concerto* (November 2004) was staged by guest *répétiteur* Lindsay Fischer, a former principal with New York City Ballet who had trained at the National Ballet School. Fischer was aware of the "rumours, exaggerations and distortions" that still attached to Balanchine technique when he came to teach at the National Ballet School.

> When I came back to Canada, people took one look at how I danced and their response was, "You might as well be the devil with horns, because your heels aren't on the floor. It's wrong." And it didn't matter that I said, "I'm sorry, but there's a beautiful company, one of the best companies in the world, with 110 dancers, who all dance like this. They're not all injured. They're not all incapable of classical repertory. It's a non-issue. Can't we move on?" And now we have, which is really quite wonderful.[17]

Joysanne Sidimus, who had trained and performed with Balanchine early in her career, danced with the National in the 1960s and returned to the company in 1984. As its Balanchine *répétiteur*, she continues to work on an ongoing basis with the company whenever it performs his repertoire, bringing to this task her personal experience of working with the master in the studio and the rehearsal hall. Balanchine, she said, "demanded a kind of physicality that pushed you beyond your limits, and a geographic eating of space and a very, very particular kind of musicality, a very sophisticated approach to music. The more musical you are as a Balanchine dancer, the better the ballet will be." These

Cylla von Tiedemann

Guillaume Côté with artists of the ballet in Apollo.

memories dictate her approach to teaching his ballets. "He had a way of being in the room that infused the rehearsals and the direction of the ballets with a tremendous intention. It was crystal-clear what he wanted…. That's what I feel my responsibility is. To convey his intention as best I understood it." She recognized in Suzanne Farrell a direct link to this important tradition. "She does what Mr. B did, actually. She shows the choreography and then she sits back and watches what a dancer will do with it. And then she'll build on what they bring to it." Under influences such as these, the company's approach to Balanchine melded a respect for the steps with a fluidity that acknowledged the characteristics of new generations of dancers, in an attempt to keep the ballets, as Balanchine would have wanted them, "alive."[18]

Kudelka arranged for the acquisition of one other major Balanchine work, Suzanne Farrell's reconstruction of his full-length *Don Quixote*. Its entry into the repertoire, however, belonged to a later period in the National's history.

DEVELOPING CANADIAN CHOREOGRAPHY

He may have enjoyed a free hand to present his own work at the National, and to introduce the Balanchine repertoire he regarded as seminal for twentieth-century ballet, but as artistic director of Canada's largest dance ensemble, Kudelka also had a responsibility to mentor others on the national scene. If he did not produce Canadian work, other than his own, the watchdogs of Canadian dance would soon be snapping at his privileged heels. He needed no such coercion. His own past experience had given him sympathy for the difficult path of the emerging choreographer in Canada, and his wide experience outside of the National had given him knowledge of choreographers and trends beyond its narrow confines. Kudelka tried, from his very first season, to encourage choreographic ambitions from inside the company and to program works by important Canadian choreographers from outside.

Because of funding shortfalls, the full-scale choreographic workshops for company members, open to the public, at which Kudelka had got his start, fell into abeyance for the first four years of his artistic directorship.[19] They would resume at the Betty Oliphant Theatre of the National Ballet School in 2000 and 2002, and at the Premiere Dance Theatre in 2004. However, in June 1997, Kudelka moved to fill this temporary gap by inviting the independent choreographer Bill James to organize an in-house choreographic lab to mentor aspiring choreographers within the company. The choreographic lab removed the public performance component from the exercise, thus placing the emphasis on experimentation and innovation. Without the pressures of performance it was possible to fail, and to learn from failure.[20] Such freedom to experiment was an important part of Kudelka's vision for his dancers.

In the high-stakes world of regular performances, with its low tolerance for experimental failure, Kudelka encouraged the work of select members of the company whose

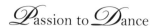

choreographic abilities had already been tested. Dominique Dumais, at the time a second soloist with the company, had attracted his attention with her work in the 1995 choreographic workshop, when Kudelka was still artist in residence, and had choreographed a pas de deux, *Tides of Mind*, for Karen Kain and Robert Conn when they appeared at the Gala des Étoiles in Israel in June 1996. Kudelka added it to the February 1997 mixed program, to flesh out the planned offerings of *The Four Seasons* and *A Month in the Country*. He went on to commission two new works from Dumais, *the weight of absence* (May 1998) and *one hundred words for snow* (in the "Inspired by Gould" mixed program, November 1999). Dumais eventually left the company to work in Germany, and in June 2009, Karen Kain brought *Skin Divers*, which she had created for the Berlin Ballett-Komische Oper, into the National's repertoire.

Matjash Mrozewski, a member of the corps when Kudelka took over as artistic director, followed a similar trajectory. A graduate of the National Ballet School, like Dumais, he had choreographed widely in workshops for both the school and the company, and independently in and around Toronto. For the full company, he created *A Delicate Battle* (May 2001), *Monument* (November 2003), and *Wolf's Court* (June 2007, after Kudelka's departure), as well as short occasional pieces for competitions and special engagements. Mrozewski danced in Europe from 1997 to 1999, when he returned and danced with the company for two more seasons before retiring from dance to pursue a career as an independent choreographer in North America and Europe.

Without doubt, Kudelka had an eye for choreographic talent. He had picked out both Dumais and Mrozewski as budding choreographers from the moment he assumed directorship of the company.[21] But he also had a lock on opportunity. As long as he directed the company, he would also be its *de facto* resident choreographer. It was no wonder Dumais and Mrozewski looked abroad to make their choreographic futures.

Among established Canadian choreographers, Kudelka extended invitations to Serge Bennathan, Édouard Lock, Jean-Pierre Perrault, and former company member John Alleyne. Both Perrault and Alleyne created original works for the company. Bennathan's *The Fall*, created for Ballet BC, was remounted for the dancers of the National on the same 1997 mixed program that included Dumais's *Tides of Mind*. Although Lock worked extensively with the dancers on an original creation for them, scheduled for May 2000, it was postponed, and eventually cancelled, when a troubling set of circumstances disrupted the creative process.[22]

INTERMISSION: LEGAL ACTIONS

Despite continuing financial crises and budgetary retrenchment, Kudelka's third season as leader of the company opened on a high note. Interrupting preparations for his full-length *Swan Lake*, he took his dancers to New York in the fall of 1998, with three different all-Canadian programs. This time they appeared, not at the Metropolitan Opera House,

Cylla von Tiedemann

Greta Hodgkinson and Rex Harrington in "Summer" from The Four Seasons.

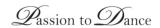

but at the New York City Center on West 55th Street in Manhattan, the original performing home of Balanchine's New York City Ballet. Given the programming, the smaller-scale venue made sense. After NYCB, City Center had been home to the Joffrey Ballet, and just the preceding year, Kevin McKenzie, the new artistic director of American Ballet Theatre, had initiated a fall season for his company at City Center to showcase shorter, more experimental repertoire, including Kudelka's own *Cruel World*.[23] The Center's ambience was good, and its audience should have been attuned to the kind of repertoire being planned — so different from the lavish spectacle with which Hurok and Nureyev had presented the company to New York at the Met. They played seven performances, from October 6 to 11, 1998, with programs made up of various combinations of Kudelka's *Désir*, *Washington Square*, *Musings*, and *The Four Seasons*, as well as John Alleyne's *Split House Geometric* and Dumais's *Tides of Mind* and *the weight of absence*.

Both critics for *The New York Times*, Jennifer Dunning and Anna Kisselgoff, reviewed the company, and both liked what they saw. "As director of the National Ballet of Canada," Dunning began her review, "Mr. Kudelka has at his disposal a troupe of vital, beautifully schooled, personable young dancers…." She lavished praise on *Désir*, but described his much earlier narrative ballet, *Washington Square*, as "threadbare" by comparison.[24] Kisselgoff, a long-time proponent of Kudelka's work, noted the change he had wrought since taking over the company.

> There is a new look. If there was any hallmark of the National Ballet style, it was the academic correctness of its training. But Mr. Kudelka has loosened the company up: the dancers, both old and new, are more daring, fluent and energetic and articulate. The high leg extensions and arrow-sharp leaps are exhilarating to watch, and yet the attention to classical ballet's body placement and line is still present.[25]

The generally positive reviews buoyed up the company's spirits, but mediocre ticket sales for the tour dragged the company even deeper into debt. As Kudelka himself put it in a letter to the choreographer William Forsythe, immediately after the tour: "We have just returned from New York, where we lost our shirts, but received good reviews."[26]

By the time the company returned from New York, Kudelka was fully engaged in creating a new version of *Swan Lake*, set to open the following May, to replace the Erik Bruhn version of 1967, which had been designed in Germanic fairy-tale style by Desmond Heeley. Kudelka chose his frequent collaborator, Santo Loquasto, as the designer, but this time he asked him to work in a style of "minimalist decadence," in contrast to the sumptuous Russian splendour of *Nutcracker*. Kudelka wanted to return to a fuller version of the Tchaikovsky score and to elements of the original libretto that Bruhn had abandoned. To that end, he included the role of Benno (the Prince's friend), a jester, and a corps of black swans (familiar from Russian versions of the ballet). But his aims were revisionist, as well as traditional. As he put it in a 1997 application to the Canada Council: "While *Swan Lake* is traditionally viewed as a showcase for the female corps de ballet, in my new staging I hope to create a male and female perspective within the ballet choreographically, to make it equally as challenging for the men."[27] The male perspective he created would account for some of *Swan Lake*'s most controversial elements.

Etienne Lavigne as Rothbart in James Kudelka's production of Swan Lake.

But other controversy dogged the production even before it opened. In a season of crippling deficits, *Swan Lake* was well into production before full funding for it had been secured. In September 1998, in a letter to Matjash Mrozewski, who was overseas at the time, Kudelka wrote: "I am still working on *Swan Lake* even though we don't have the money in place for it, and the company is barely big enough to do some things like *Manon*, and *Nutcracker* and *Taming* and *Swan Lake* (either old or new versions)."[28] But engagement in the creative process could not free Kudelka from his ongoing management responsibilities. Where the artistic director contemplated letting dancers go at the conclusion of their annual contract with the company, the union agreement in force at the time required formal notification, such notification to be given in person, in a private meeting between the dancer and the artistic director, at least six months before the expiry of the dancer's existing contract. With dancers' contracts turning over at the end of June, December was the month for this difficult ritual, and Kudelka had a number of interviews scheduled. One of them was with Kimberly Glasco, a principal with almost twenty years of service in the company. She had joined the National straight from the National Ballet School in 1979, during the Alexander Grant years. In 1981, she and Kevin Pugh had won the silver medal in their division of the Moscow International Ballet Competition. Shortly thereafter, she left the company for two years, during one of which she danced with American Ballet Theatre, then returned to the National in 1984, after Erik Bruhn had taken charge. Once back, she distinguished herself in the ballerina roles of the classical repertoire, like *Sleeping Beauty* and *La Bayadère*, created the title role in Glen Tetley's *Alice*, and appeared in many of Kudelka's ballets.[29] In their private interview, Kudelka informed Glasco that she would not be dancing with the company after the conclusion of the 1998–99 season. Whatever else may have been said is known with certainty only by the two people who were in the room at the time, and they would eventually give radically different interpretations of the conversation. On it depended a bitter dispute that involved both parties in protracted legal actions and cost the company's insurers a substantial sum of money, the exact amount of which was never disclosed. The human and creative costs, to the parties to the dispute and to the company as a whole, could not be quantified.

In 1998, Glasco was one of two elected dancers' representatives on the National's board of directors. On December 18, 1998, she issued a statement in which she said that, immediately after the December 1, 1998, board meeting: "I was called into a meeting with Mr. Kudelka and was fired from the National Ballet of Canada." Her statement continued: "I was told by Mr. Kudelka that he did not feel I supported his *Swan Lake*, and that I didn't vote for him when the Board was considering candidates for the vacant Artistic Director position in 1995/96."[30] If these were indeed Kudelka's stated reasons for not renewing Glasco's contract, his decision could be challenged under the Ontario Labour Relations Act. When asked for his side of the conversation by the press, Kudelka said that his grounds had been artistic: "I have never felt we were artistically compatible. I knew that when I took on this position. I've worked hard to sustain her career as long as I could. I've used her in my ballets and used her well."[31] Although these two sides of the question would receive myriad elaborations in the following months, the basic dispute was clear from the outset. Were the reasons for Glasco's non-renewal political (her statements and actions as a member of the board), or were they artistic (her level of performance and her compatibility as a dancer with Kudelka's vision for the company)? The company attempted some internal discussions to resolve the disagreement, but by January 29, 1999, the three major Toronto newspapers reported that Glasco had launched both a lawsuit and a human rights complaint against the National Ballet of Canada.

Essentially a dry and complex labour dispute centering on the legitimacy of the grounds for non-renewal of contract, the issue transformed itself into fodder for a hungry press, which gleefully demonized or romanticized (depending on point of view) Glasco, Kudelka, and the company as fierce antagonists in an elemental battle of good versus evil. Very quickly,

David Street

Kimberly Glasco and Rex Harrington in Glen Tetley's Alice.

media coverage took on a life of its own. By late January 1999, the Bring Back Kimberly Glasco Network had been formed by a group of supporters and friends devoted to promoting her cause, and began sending out press releases. The National's media division attempted damage control, with careful, terse statements of fact. Glasco hired a press agent of her own.[32]

Non-participants, however, felt few constraints, and public comment, almost instantly polarized as either pro-Glasco or pro-Kudelka, brought some old warhorses back from pasture. Deirdre Kelly, writing in the *Globe and Mail* in December 1998, stirred up ancient

— 311 —

rivalries by soliciting contrary opinions from Betty Oliphant (pro-Glasco — she had been one of Glasco's teachers at the National Ballet School) and Celia Franca (pro-Kudelka — she spoke as a former artistic director of the company). As matters escalated toward legal action, both women obliged a press eager to rehash their own feud of the 1970s with extended, contradictory, and surprisingly indiscreet statements of their opinions. Oliphant fired a shot across the bow in a *National Post* interview on January 4, 1999: "[Glasco] is nowhere near, as far as I'm concerned, the end of her career." With a slightly disparaging comparison to Karen Kain, who had danced five years longer than Glasco, she lamented: "To have even five years taken away from you is so cruel. It's a big loss for Canada." Franca, in a lengthy interview with Deirdre Kelly in the *Globe and Mail* on January 11, 1999, began with a series of unkind comments about former principal dancer Vanessa Harwood, who had herself retired reluctantly from the company in 1986, and who was one of the founding members of the Bring Back Kimberly Glasco Network. Franca then dismissed Glasco's claims with: "I don't think she's been using her head. I mean, what a silly thing, to publicly go against your boss." In conclusion, she invoked her old sparring partner, Rudolf Nureyev, to justify the autocratic power of the artistic director. "I can only quote Nureyev: 'Celia! Ballet must be autocrat!' There has to be one person. The artistic director is the one who has to make the choices and take the blame." Oliphant responded implicitly to Franca's comments in a letter to the *Globe* on January 18, "I am saddened by the lack of charity shown by some of my colleagues, many of whom are former pupils of mine. This issue has been a tragedy for Glasco, who has always been remarkably loyal to the company and highly respected by her peers."[33] John Fraser, who had chronicled the Franca-Oliphant feud in its glory days, broke his long silence in a piece called "Duelling Duennas," in which he chastised both women for reviving their own fight through the medium of Glasco's dispute with the company. He suggested, as well, that the flames of public interest had been fanned in this case by the cut-throat battle for circulation being waged between the *Globe* and its challenger as a national newspaper, the *National Post*, which had begun publication in 1998.

> And how typical of this captious duo to latch on to the current newspaper competition between the national dailies: Celia deploying her cantankerous fusillades in the establishment *Globe and Mail* (January 11, "Arts Argument"), and Betty happier with her rapid fire in the upstart, snappier *National Post* (January 4, front page).[34]

Though obscured by such a morass of conflicting opinions and sensational allegations, two important principles were articulated by the legal actions launched by Glasco and so vigorously defended by the company. On the one hand, Glasco and her legal team presented her case as one that hinged purely on the grounds for her non-renewal, and whether or not they were legitimate as defined by the Ontario Labour Relations Act and the Ontario Human Rights Code. The National, on the other hand, saw Glasco's claims as an assault on the autonomy and authority of the artistic director, a direct challenge to the director's ability to run the company as he saw fit, with principal regard to the artistic quality of its performances. In this view, the company was eventually joined by as many as 300 arts professionals, including artistic directors and executive directors from across the country, who signed an open letter of protest, when, in March 2000, an Ontario Superior Court judge upheld an earlier arbitrator's decision that had granted Glasco interim reinstatement in the company, pending a final decision on the actual merits of her case.[35] It was not in itself the final word, but even the interim ruling set alarm bells ringing for many artistic directors, who feared the courts would no longer allow them to choose the artists in their companies based solely on artistic criteria.

There would, in fact, be no final word. This important issue wound its way laboriously through judicial procedures for nineteen stressful months, becoming more tangled in claims and counter claims with every step. (In his book, *Max Wyman, Revealing Dance*, Max Wyman provides an excellent, step-by-step description and analysis of these events.)[36] As other company members were drawn in, professional relationships and friendships became casualties in the fray. Legal preparations and hearings ate up unbelievable hours of company time. Even its artistic activities were directly affected. "We had planned, as part of our Millennial Year programming, to premiere a new work by Édouard Lock in May 2000," wrote Kudelka in his November 2000 Artistic Statement. "This unfortunately did not happen, due to scheduling difficulties caused, in the most part, by dancers' and my involvement in a significant phase of our legal dispute."[37] Despite the public support of many members of the company, Kudelka felt the personal stress acutely.

On July 20, 2000, Toronto newspapers announced that Glasco and the National Ballet had reached an out-of-court settlement, the details of which were shrouded by a confidentiality agreement. Glasco received a substantial amount of money and an apology, and left the company for good. Whether or not the non-renewal of her contract had been a case of wrongful dismissal was never ruled upon by the courts. Like many such resolutions to disputes, it left key questions unanswered.

Did artistic directors have the authority to choose dancers for their companies as they saw fit? In practice, yes. Kudelka, and Karen Kain after him, continued to make the difficult choices regarding artistic roster that defined the look of the company on the public stage. But they did so with the knowledge that their authority, though real, was no longer arbitrary. It could be scrutinized by the public and challenged by the dancers. The company moved, through revisions to subsequent union agreements and updated employment policies and practices, to ensure that dancers received regular, documented appraisals of their work, that the requisite files were built to justify the hard personnel decisions when they came. And the artistic world as a whole took note. According to Kain, every company in North America ran differently after this highly publicized case. In her view, that was not necessarily a bad thing.

I have to meet with every single member of the company. They have to do a self-evaluation, how they think they're doing, and my staff and I do an evaluation and we compare. It's very time-consuming. It can be emotionally draining. It actually has changed everything. But I find it to be beneficial for them and for me.[38]

Such progress came at a cost. There really were no winners. A decade after the settlement, company members involved in the events had little appetite for revisiting them, and, except for a few low-profile guest appearances, Glasco never danced again.

The postscript to this agonizing process was written seven years after the settlement, at a roast for Warren Winkler, on the occasion of his appointment as Ontario Chief Justice. Speakers reminisced about Winkler's role as presiding judge in the final stages of the Glasco case.

Justice Winkler summoned the lawyers [acting for the opposing sides] after dinner one night and told them he had just written his decision. "Neither one of you is going to like this," he warned, "so I'm giving you one last chance to talk and try to reach an agreement while you still can."

They did. And they did.

Justice Winkler? He hadn't so much as set pen to paper, he later admitted. In fact, he'd gone out and enjoyed a good meal and a glass of wine in preparation for his ruse. In hunting, they call that a blind.[39]

KUDELKA'S *SWAN LAKE*: A STARTLING NEW VISION

Through all the tension and distraction caused by these legal problems, *Swan Lake* proceeded according to schedule. Funding for the $1.6 million production was eventually found from a small army of donors headed by Sandra and Jim Pitblado and Margaret and Jim Fleck.[40] In re-mounting this central document in the history of ballet, the work almost universally associated with lyricism and romance, Kudelka held true to his stated ideal of searching for "the underbelly of truth" rather than "the superficiality of beauty." The corps of swans was still there, as was much of its original Ivanov choreography, but the serenity of the lakeside had been transformed, in Santo Loquasto's ominous designs, into a marsh with proscenium-high reeds looming over it from either wing, the castle courtyard of Act One into a scruffy hunting ground, a dark and masculine domain, and the ballroom of Act Three into a barbaric baronial hall, in which the prince's selection of a bride turned into a primitive marriage market. During the transition from Act Three to Act Four (like Bruhn, Kudelka compressed

Cylla von Tiedemann

Artists of the ballet in James Kudelka's Swan Lake.

the four acts of the scenario into two theatrical acts, with only one intermission), the entire courtly civilization perished in a Wagnerian twilight of the gods. Its ruined castle, gradually sinking in the deluge, became the grim symbolic background for the final lakeside scene; and in that scene Rothbart, danced once again by a man, wrestled with Siegfried for Odette, the two men often tearing her from side to side between them in a diabolical pas de trois for control of her fate.

Kudelka's most controversial change, however, came in Act One. Here, he transformed the traditional grand waltz into an elaborately choreographed, rough-and-tumble male drinking bout, in which the knights passed around an unsuspecting wench (a new character created by Kudelka), then forced her offstage, with obviously sinister intent, while Siegfried was distracted by the haunting swan theme from the oboe in the orchestra. Bruhn's Freudian psychology had been replaced by a brutal confrontation with contemporary gender politics, viewed through the lens of fairy tale and romance. Critical response was mixed,[41] and some audience members, at least, were shocked. Kudelka explained himself in his reply to a complaint from a patron, who feared for the scene's impact on her seven-year-old daughter.

> I must point out that, thematically, I made the choice of showing the
> "Wench" being carried off by the men of the court as an important symbol,

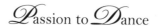

showing the decadence and evil in a world that the Prince disdains. It is meant to be a stark contrast to the beauty and spiritual peace he hopes to find among the swans. Having said that, I never intended for the scene to be graphic, and in some of our earlier performances, the male corps members were perhaps a bit more zealous than intended. This was changed in subsequent performances.[42]

There were those who loved the Bruhn version of *Swan Lake* and were inclined, out of loyalty, to see any replacement of it as an assault on tradition. Few recalled how radical Bruhn's version had been when it first appeared, how controversial his Freudian preoccupations, how unsuccessful his conception of the Black Queen. Time had hallowed it and turned it into the standard compared to which any new production was bound to fail. In this new version they did not see progress, only the wanton destruction of history — Kudelka had obliterated one of the signature works in the company's repertoire. But many more took to the new production with enthusiasm. An extra performance had to be added to the opening run of the ballet to satisfy demand,[43] and it continued to draw crowds over the years as it returned in the repertoire.

With this production, Kudelka realized his stated goal of creating both a male and female perspective within the ballet and making it, choreographically, equally as challenging for the men as for the women. Substantial choreography for Rothbart, who performed some of the lifts in the Siegfried/Odette pas de deux, a bravura part for the fool (the jester of the early Russian productions), some real dancing for Benno, Siegfried's friend, and above all, the difficult work for the male corps of knights, finally gave the men of the company the chance to exercise their technical and interpretive skills. Not, however, at the expense of the swans. Kudelka's ensemble ideals were best realized in the dramatic corps work of the swans, whose achievement he valued almost more than that of the principals. He worked intensively with the swans when he prepared the work for its run in the 2009–10 season. "It was finally *Swan* Lake, it was actually about the swans. I actually never saw a performance, but I led them through the rehearsal process and was able to say to them at a dress rehearsal, 'You have the ability to carry this whole season with it,' because they really got it."[44]

For one of Kudelka's first Odette/Odiles, the new *Swan Lake* was also a farewell. Jaimie Tapper, just recently promoted to first soloist and a rising star in the company, left at the end of the 1998–99 season to join England's Royal Ballet. A year later, she was joined by Johan Persson, a principal with the National, whom she later married. Tapper and Persson rose swiftly through the ranks at the Royal Ballet to become principal dancers there. It was a straightforward case of opportunity and fit, but nonetheless a loss for the National. Now that its dancers were competitive on the international stage, the lure of the international stage proved difficult to resist.

After *Swan Lake*, and before the fiftieth anniversary season, Kudelka created two original one-act works for the company — *A Disembodied Voice* in the fall of 1999 and *The Firebird* a year later, in 2000. *A Disembodied Voice* formed part of a single-theme mixed program, "Inspired by Gould," for which Kudelka took advantage of special funding offered through Music Canada 2000 to celebrate Canadian music in the millennial year. He used a portion of the grant to commission a striking sound collage from Canadian composer John Oswald, who had gained some notoriety with his Plunderphonics, soundscapes that borrowed freely from other composers to create a new musical entity.[45] For *A Disembodied Voice*, he ranged widely through a musical landscape important to Glenn Gould, one that included jumbled references to Bach, Mozart, Wagner, Richard Strauss, and Petula Clark's "Downtown." Kudelka, ever sensitive to the character of his musical inspiration, employed a similarly fragmented approach for the choreography. The Glenn Gould character in this loosely biographical phantasmagoria (the cast of characters also included a monkey, a rooster, and Gouldmind Woman) was played by five different dancers, Glenn 1 through Glenn 5 on the house program. The ballet's conclusion, true to its title, evoked Gould's own disembodied voice. A grand piano, its keyboard facing the audience, "performed," without a pianist, a digital transcription of the aria from Bach's *Goldberg Variations*, a work indelibly associated with Gould. The audience could see the piano keys depressing and releasing, as though controlled by a phantom, while the five Glenns performed a tender ensemble in which they eventually formed a chain of bodies, connected palm to palm, or with arms linked in a variety of combinations to suggest relationships in spirit as well as space. It was another example of Kudelka's desire to create significant, emotionally revealing choreography for men as well as women. It was a good time to be a man at the National Ballet of Canada.

The Firebird was a co-production of the National Ballet, Houston Ballet, and American Ballet Theatre. The Russian fairy-tale scenario gave the designer, Santo Loquasto once again, the chance to revisit Russia, but this time the barbaric splendours of the medieval court rather than the monied *gemütlichkeit* of *Nutcracker*'s landed gentry. He obliged with sets and costumes so monumental they dwarfed the action. A huge, mobile staircase ate up dancing space. At around fifty dancers, the company could barely muster enough forces to create the massed effect of the closing marriage tableau. Kudelka solved the problem by conscripting all the characters in the ballet, except for the bride, groom, and priestess, to conceal their previous identities and swell the anonymous throng. Robed and masked in glittering cloth of gold while Stravinsky's monumental processional music billowed out of the orchestra pit, these splendid giants seemed more ominous than celebratory. Anna Kisselgoff reviewed the first two Toronto performances for *The New York Times*. She pronounced *The Four Seasons*, which was paired with *The Firebird* on the same program, "a masterpiece for our time…. *Firebird*, however, will have to be seen as what used to be called a darn good show."[46]

Rex Harrington and Chan Hon Goh as Kastchei the Deathless and the Firebird in Kudelka's
The Firebird.

THE COMPANY AT FIFTY: MOVING FORWARD, LOOKING BACK

On Sunday November 11, 2001, the retrospective program of Balanchine's *Mozartiana*,
Kudelka's *Pastorale*, and MacMillan's *Solitaire* celebrated the company's fiftieth anniversary
with a film montage of historical footage of the company gleaned from the archives of the
CBC and of television producer Norman Campbell, who had promoted the National's television presence almost from the beginning. At the close of the performance, former members of the company, as many as could be gathered together for the event, slipped out of
their seats in the theatre and flooded the stage for an alumni curtain call. They included
former dancers, musicians, company personnel, and, of course Celia Franca. There were
many onstage reunions, and spontaneous outbursts of applause from the audience when a
special favourite from years gone by sauntered out unannounced from the wings. It was a
moment of sentiment, nostalgia, and justifiable pride, held as close to the actual anniversary
as logistics would permit. November 12, the date of the first Eaton Auditorium performance
in 1951, fell on a Monday in 2001, a night when the theatre was traditionally dark.

Celebration of this magnitude, however, could not be confined to a single event.
Kudelka had planned the entire season as a tribute to the company's history, beginning

with a tour to western Canada, followed by three Toronto seasons (dubbed the Alumni Season, the Volunteer Season, and the Conference season) with repertoire chosen to represent a wide cross-section of the company's accomplishments, and ending with appearances at the National Arts Centre in Ottawa. There were special events as well. The sixth international competition for the Erik Bruhn prize was held in May 2002. Dancers from the National had fared well in previous competitions. Stephen Legate won the male prize in 1989, Jhe Russell shared the male prize in 1999, and Jaimie Tapper and Johan Persson swept the competition in 1995. The 2002 competitors, Heather Ogden and Guillaume Côté, did not win, but went on to become principals and two of the National's most treasured dancers, nonetheless. The other special event was a Kudelka brainchild, planned for the anniversary season alone, an international conference on the past, present, and future of ballet.

PPF, as it quickly came to be known, was more retreat than academic conference, although it did have two facilitators from the university world, Penelope Reed Doob of York University and James Neufeld of Trent University. Instead of hearing papers on the subject of its title, the conference brought together, for the first time, the artistic directors of ten major international ballet companies for discussions about the practical issues confronting their art form and their profession at the beginning of the twenty-first century. Audience members at the one open forum to which the public was invited were understandably perplexed by the carefully controlled environment of the prepared statements and even the question and answer period that followed. At best, they got only a glimpse of the candid conversations at the heart of the event, which took place behind closed doors over three days of intense, confidential talks. And they saw little of the camaraderie that quickly developed within this high-powered group, united by the heavy responsibilities of running major dance organizations.

James Kudelka's personal invitation brought to Toronto Frank Andersen (the Royal Danish Ballet), Reid Anderson (the Stuttgart Ballet), Peter Martins (New York City Ballet), Monica Mason (the Royal Ballet), Kevin McKenzie (American Ballet Theatre), Mikko Nissinen (Boston Ballet), Francia Russell (Pacific Northwest Ballet), Matz Skoog (English National Ballet), and Helgi Tomasson (San Francisco Ballet). Frank Andersen had just been named to succeed Aage Thordal-Christensen as artistic director in Denmark; Monica Mason, at the time the assistant director of the Royal Ballet, would shortly follow Ross Stretton as artistic director there. All the rest were the artistic directors of their respective companies. Some had never before met face to face — none had ever been in so large a group of their peers — few had ever had the luxury of devoting three days to relaxed discussion of their professional concerns. The complexities of trying to bring together so many people with such pressing professional responsibilities were highlighted by the last-minute withdrawal, because of scheduling conflicts, of Brigitte Lefèvre (the Paris Opera Ballet), John Neumeier (the Hamburg Ballet), and Ben Stevenson (Houston Ballet). Even with these absences, Kudelka had put together a high-powered party.

In meetings that took place from May 17 to 20, 2002, the group brainstormed a succession of topics, both practical (relationships with boards, dancer-director concerns, the impact of unionization of various segments of ballet companies on overall management) and theoretical (expanding dancer training to encompass the education of the whole person; developing innovative choreographers, sometimes in the face of conservative audience tastes; the tension between curating the repertoire that constitutes a company's legacy and moving that company into new artistic territory). As the assemblage of relative strangers cohered into a group, individuals shared experiences and traded war stories. All agreed that the experience of meeting in this way would assist their future professional encounters. During meals or informal side-table conversations, plans for collaborations and future cooperation floated in the air. Given the preponderance of Scandinavians in the room, the *lingua franca* of the side-tables was as likely to be Danish as English.

Guillaume Côté as Will with artists of the ballet in The Contract (The Pied Piper).

The distinguished artistic directors assembled for PPF also became celebrity guests at the anniversary season's major premiere. Kudelka had coordinated the themes of the year-long celebrations and of the conference to lead to a grand climax, the unveiling of a large-scale new work. In *The Contract*, later renamed *The Contract (The Pied Piper)*, his first full-length original narrative ballet, Kudelka tried to work out in practical terms his own preoccupations with the role and importance of innovative new choreography for a classically based company such as the National. The libretto was by Robert Sirman, then the administrative director of the National Ballet School and now the executive director of the Canada Council for the Arts. Its story amalgamated Robert Browning's *The Pied Piper of Hamelin* with the figure of Aimee Semple McPherson, the Canadian fire-and-brimstone revival preacher and sometime faith healer, who monopolised headlines with her theatrical preaching techniques and equally theatrical disappearance in 1926, ostensibly a kidnapping, quite possibly a hoax. The dual nature of the libretto, part children's fairy tale, part exposé of religious and sexual hypocrisy, threatened to divide the audience's attention, but there was no mistaking the powerful metaphor of its final moment. The young hero, Will, both sustained and damaged by the confining traditions of his tight-knit community, ventured through a door in the front scrim, onto the lip of the stage, to confront the spectators and embrace his uncertain future. Poised between the restraints of his community and the expectations of his audience, he stood for the art form itself, nourished by the discipline of its past, searching for an identity in the twenty-first century.

At home, the ballet was well-received. Paula Citron, writing in the *Globe and Mail*, saw the choreography as a radical break for Kudelka, less complex than his previous work, pointing now to "a whole new choreographic language for story ballets, skilfully condensing movement to its bare necessities."[47] When *The Contract* played the Brooklyn Academy of Music in New York in 2005, however, John Rockwell of *The New York Times* thought the exact opposite. "The dance never stakes out all the twists and turns of the narrative," he wrote. "On a more mundane level, what are long swaths of nonmimetic dance telling us…?"[48] Audiences, both at home and in New York, failed to take *The Contract* to their hearts — an important creation, but a qualified success. Kudelka's final full-length ballets for the company would fare much better.

KUDELKA DISCOVERS A FLARE FOR COMIC WORKS

By the end of the fiftieth-anniversary season, a major change in the administrative structure of the company had already become public knowledge. Valerie Wilder, its executive director throughout Kudelka's years as artistic director, had announced her decision to leave the National in order to take up the equivalent position at Boston Ballet. (In 2008, she would move on to the Australian Ballet.) Wilder, who had danced with the company from 1970 to 1978, had returned as Erik Bruhn's artistic administrator in 1983. In a variety of positions, including that of co-artistic director, she remained a key member of the company's leadership team from then on. Like Robert Johnston before her, she had provided stability and continuity to the company through some tumultuous times.

Her successor was Kevin Garland, a woman with a passion for dance, though never a professional ballet dancer. "My original ambition when I was a kid was to be a ballet dancer and I did dance right up until my second child was three," she said of her continuing preoccupation with dance. Professionally, she made a corporate career in urban planning and commercial real estate, eventually becoming a senior vice-president of the Canadian Imperial Bank of Commerce, and then left the private sector to become the executive director of the Canadian Opera House Corporation, in charge of the planning and development of the building that would become the Four Seasons Centre for the Performing Arts in Toronto. "In that role I got to participate in the inner workings of an opera company and a major arts organization." She had also served on the ballet company's board of directors from 1993, and was frequently called on for detailed and sensitive committee work. She had, in fact, been named to the search committee to find Wilder's replacement.

> I went to probably the first two meetings of the search committee, where we outlined what the qualities of the kind of person were, and the attributes, and before we'd even started to look at a list of potential candidates I went home and thought, "Oh dear, I really want this job myself." So I called Anne Fawcett at Caldwell Partners who was conducting the search and said, "Would it be really terrible if I said that I was interested in being a candidate and stepped off the committee?" She said, "As a matter of fact, I was just about to call you and ask you if you would consider being a candidate." So at that point I stepped down from the committee and went through the normal interview process and was fortunate enough to be offered the job.

By Garland's own admission, even her work at the Opera House Corporation had not prepared her for the challenges awaiting her. "I had no idea how complex it is, how difficult to run a major arts organization. I think most people who work in the corporate world would have no clue how difficult it is."[49] But in one important respect, her past experience was essential to her new job. The company had made the decision not to join the COC as full partner in the fundraising and construction of the house much earlier, when Garland was still at the Opera House Corporation.[50] As executive director of the corporation, she had then obtained the ballet company's agreement in principle to leave the Hummingbird Centre and move into the Four Seasons Centre as a tenant of the COC. Now, as executive director of the National Ballet, one of her first jobs was to negotiate the details of the tenancy.

Throughout these last years of his tenure, although the strains of running the company exacted a mounting personal toll, Kudelka maintained the hectic creative pace he had set for himself. He had been at work for some time on a major new project, a full-length ballet version of René Clair's 1928 film farce, *Un chapeau de paille d'Italie*.

Andrew Oxenham

Rebekah Rimsay and Piotr Stanczyk in An Italian Straw Hat.

But *An Italian Straw Hat*, as it was to be called, ran into some delays. Kudelka's decision to postpone the work created an unexpected opportunity for an entirely new creation to fill the gap.

> The [musical] score was not where you wanted it to be and Santo [Loquasto] was slow with the scenery. That wasn't churning forward and I thought another year for *An Italian Straw Hat* would be really good for it. Because I had been in Celia's *Cinderella*, I knew every note of the score. I think it was brought up at a senior management meeting, if we had something like a *Cinderella*. I said, "Just give me a second." I actually went almost immediately and called Mikko [Nissinen of Boston Ballet] and Kevin [McKenzie of American Ballet Theatre] and said, "If we did a new *Cinderella*, would you get on board?" And they said yes, because they didn't want to do the one that had been out on the road so much. They actually didn't end up being partners [in the production] but they ended up buying it immediately after it was done.[51]

Thus, unexpectedly, almost casually, *Cinderella* was born, one of Kudelka's happiest, sunniest productions, and one of the National's surefire crowd pleasers. It had its world premiere on May 8, 2004.

David Boechler, an artist who had been brought to Kudelka's attention by a friend, had never designed for ballet before. His inspired sets and costumes in the art deco style of the designer and fashion illustrator Erté, evoked the louche sophistication of the 1920s and '30s for the ballroom scene. After the ball, Cinderella, missing one shoe, returned to her kitchen to perform a wistful, lopsided dance, one foot on pointe, the other barefoot, that characterized perfectly the interplay between her innocence and her dreams of romance. The kitchen, a topsy-turvy assemblage of cupboards, cabinets, and Welsh dressers, had been populated in the first act by a dipsomaniac stepmother (Victoria Bertram in one of her most vivid character creations for the company) and an ineptly wicked pair of stepsisters who broke decisively with the tradition, established by Sir Frederick Ashton and Sir Robert Helpmann, of portly, aging male dancers as pantomime dames in these roles.

Jennifer Fournier and Rebekah Rimsay, who created the roles, banished all memories of other stepsisters with their *tour de force* of comic teamwork. Fournier's was a would-be sophisticate, who aspired unsuccessfully but doggedly to the kind of genuine sexiness Fournier could otherwise create so effectively in a role like the Prostitute in Tetley's *La Ronde*. Rimsay's fluttered around this monument to self-absorption with a gregarious, loopy charm and a myopic eagerness to savour all the delights on offer that undercut completely the haughty reserve of the Prince's court. Her zany cameo, an amalgam of slapstick and human tenderness, inhabited the same comic world as Alain in Ashton's *La Fille mal gardée*, always the butt of the joke, never the life of the party.

The production fared well critically, as well as at the box office. Paula Citron, reviewing for the *Globe and Mail*, was as enthusiastic as the opening night audience. "The buzz was palpable when the cheers finally died down…. From this writer's perspective, while the new Kudelka version isn't perfect, it comes pretty damn close."[52] When *Cinderella* entered the ABT repertoire in 2006, Joan Acocella in *The New Yorker* dismissed it as a "silly" ballet, chosen by Kevin McKenzie simply to provide "a new full-evening narrative ballet, with splashy sets and a plummy old score, to please A.B.T.'s largely conservative subscribers." John Rockwell, however, in *The New York Times*, lavished on *Cinderella* the praise he had withheld from *The Contract*. "It was a choreographically enticing, visually stunning success," he wrote, and gave much of the credit to Kudelka's attention to the "plummy old score," as Acocella had described it. Rockwell continued: "In Prokofiev's score, scenes flash by in quick bursts. Mr. Kudelka manages to match mood and movement with supreme confidence; his tale unfolds as Prokofiev must have dreamed it."[53] Both Greta Hodgkinson and Rex Harrington, who had created other works for Kudelka, commented on this aspect of his choreography from the performer's perspective. Hodgkinson: "Counts and the musicality and patterns and steps, he has all those in his head. I have never seen him take a note. It's really extraordinary." Harrington: "He's innately musical.

Cylla von Tiedemann

James Kudelka, Jennifer Fournier, Sonia Rodriguez, and Rebekah Rimsay at the photo shoot for Cinderella.

When he came back for *Cinderella* in 2010, he started counting in groups of phrases: 'There's a group of ten and there's a group of nine.' I don't hear those groups. I just hear the regular beat of the music. He's unique in that sense, how he hears a phrase."[54]

Kudelka's innate musicality and creative facility came to his aid once again in preparing *An Italian Straw Hat*, which became his last work for the company, to a commissioned score by the American composer, Michael Torke, who had also done the music for *The Contract*. Peter Ottmann, who was Kudelka's assistant at the time, recalled the impossible speed with which Kudelka put the work together, and the impossible odds against which he worked. "There were other choreographers coming in who were creating new works, just short pieces, and his was a full length, and he gave them priority and left himself the dregs, what was left over, time-wise, rehearsal-wise, to do a full-length ballet." Furthermore, even with the earlier delay in the production schedule, portions of the music were still arriving piecemeal, as Kudelka choreographed. "It seemed he would get some sections of the music one day and have to choreograph to it either later that day or the next day and send back changes that needed to be made. It was all happening in the space of about three weeks. An extraordinary feat."[55]

The end result, a ballet version of French bedroom farce, depicted sexual gymnastics with a cheerful explicitness rarely seen on the ballet stage. Though fully clothed at

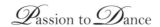

all times, the two servants, Virginia and Felix, pursued and enjoyed one another with forthright candour, more often than not with a conspiratorial wink that made the audience complicit in the shenanigans. Kudelka had planned it consciously as another move into new territory. "*An Italian Straw Hat* has interested me because I am known to have a sense of humour but to date my ballets don't. And I wondered if there was a way to use the physical nature of farce in dance."[56] But by his own assessment, it was much more than just a naughty comedy. The ballet was filled with detailed touches of character and situation, the product of a successful creative collaboration involving all the artists of the ballet. Years afterward, Kudelka mused about the genuine company creativity that contributed to *Straw Hat*'s convincing, textured, sense of detail. He would say to his dancers who were concerned about their existing repertoire, "'What's most important is what we haven't done yet … what we haven't done yet is the really, really exciting part.' And by the time we got to *Italian Straw Hat*, I looked at it and I thought, 'This community of people helped; they came up with this.' That can't be said anywhere else." A true democrat in a hierarchical art form, Kudelka valued the background that set off the main story, the corps dancers who showed the principals off to advantage. "I wanted the background. Grant Strate said it. The velvet that the diamond sits on is as important as the diamond."[57]

An Italian Straw Hat was also, in Kudelka's view, the most successful of his collaborations with Santo Loquasto. From the moment the curtain rose on preparations for an elaborate party, rendered in black and white, to the final tableau in which the romantic leads sailed off in a hot-air balloon over a breathtaking panorama of Belle Époque Paris, Loquasto created a light and airy aesthetic that showed off the dancing to advantage, and breathed an authentic Parisian air. Spectators would not soon forget the outrageously sexy horse who started the action by eating the straw hat, a male dancer in a leotard and a delicate wire construction suggesting a horse's head. But while *An Italian Straw Hat* charmed and sometimes scandalized its audiences, a far more serious drama played itself out offstage.

THINGS FALL APART

The pressures of administrative work had taken a mounting personal toll on Kudelka throughout the later years of his artistic directorship. A brief leave of absence in the spring of 2003 did little to alleviate the situation and even before his final year he was under medical care for depression. Under such circumstances, he found the trials of running the company increasingly burdensome. As he later recalled this difficult period, three factors in particular acted as catalysts to his decision to leave. The first was the company decision not to mount a new production of *Sleeping Beauty*. "*Sleeping Beauty* was a result of wanting to do *Nutcracker*, *Swan Lake* and *Sleeping Beauty* [the three Tchaikovsky landmarks of the classical repertoire]. It seemed that one would want to do all three of those. But it didn't get very far."[58] Although a Kudelka-choreographed *Sleeping Beauty* stayed on the long-range plan for some years, it was eventually cancelled for lack of funds.

The second was the move to the new theatre. Detailed negotiations for tenancy at the Four Seasons Centre necessarily involved compromise with the opera company, especially regarding the length of ballet seasons and their disposition throughout the calendar year. There were problems as well with the sight lines in the fifth ring of the house, which might serve for opera, but which provided, in Kudelka's view, far too vertical and distant a perspective for dance. These problems effectively reduced the capacity of the house for ballet by about four hundred seats, and led to increased challenges in making box office targets.[59] As Kudelka realized the full scope of the compromises required for tenancy in the new building, he began to question the wisdom of making the move at all. As he put it after the fact, "If you'd sat in a room and had what they call a blue-sky meeting for the National Ballet about everything you wanted, you would not say, 'I want to extend the season by a month, I want to have nine-week rehearsal periods with no more performances.'"[60]

The third was an unfortunate altercation that blew up between Kudelka and Santo Loquasto just four days before the premiere of *An Italian Straw Hat*. Under other circumstances, the two collaborators might have been able to survive the spat, but given the pressures under which both men were working, it ended their relationship. And coming on the other disillusionments Kudelka had been experiencing, it led him to take the final decision to resign. "I cannot work in a profession where that's how people talk to each other," was the way he put it later.[61]

An Italian Straw Hat opened on May 1, 2005. On May 18, 2005, three days after the close of the spring season, the company announced "…that after nine years as Artistic Director, James Kudelka has decided to step down from the position effective June 30, 2005. Mr. Kudelka will remain with the National Ballet as Resident Choreographer."[62] Kudelka crafted the language of the press release deliberately, "step down" rather than "resign," to signal the fact that this decision had been his alone. He had not been asked for his resignation.[63] So he went on his own terms, at his own time, but even so, the leave-taking was difficult. He had had great ambitions for the company, and had achieved much, but could only feel that his career had not played itself out quite as he had hoped.

He had thought much about legacy throughout his career — the classical legacy he had inherited, and the modern legacy he hoped to create. But that was the artistic director's legacy. Perhaps his personal legacy should be summed up by some of the dancers who worked with him. By Lorna Geddes: "I always thought he was kind of like the Gretzky of ballet, because I think he sees everything." By Rex Harrington: "I think somehow he saw a bit of himself in me. I could be just as dark as he was and I understood him, so I think it helped." By Greta Hodgkinson: "He has a wonderful sense of humour.

It can be very dark but he's very funny." By Rebekah Rimsay: "He has an extremely astute understanding of people, of character and people and how people react. A lot of my appreciation for character work comes from him and how he worked with Vicki and Lorna and Lazo and Tomas. And the respect he showed." By Jennifer Fournier: "He was like a prince in the studio. He had a very special feel for how to treat people — with such respect. He was just very respectful."[64]

Chapter Eleven

AN INTERNATIONAL STAGE

SUCCESSION

Kudelka had left his position on even shorter notice than Reid Anderson before him, but this time the board had a succession plan in place. For the preceding seven years, since the 1998–99 season, Karen Kain had been gaining experience in many aspects of senior management, as the company's artist in residence. In the fall of 2004, looking for a greater challenge for her energies and abilities, she had accepted the additional position of chair of the Canada Council for the Arts. Here, she would successfully lobby the minister of Canadian Heritage to double the council's annual budget, only to have the commitment evaporate when the Liberals lost power in the 2006 federal election. She nevertheless gained valuable experience in the political realities of arts funding in Canada, and a broad perspective on what she thought of as the "ecology of the arts," the necessity for all arts organizations, regardless of size, region, or art form, to stand together in order to improve the state of the arts nationally.[1] By 2005, she was much more than just a retired dancer, more even than her glamorous image as one of Canada's best-known artists would suggest to her many fans. She was recognized as an advocate and spokesperson for the arts on the national stage.

The ballet's board rolled out its succession plan promptly. The executive committee appointed a small subcommittee, headed by James Pitblado, who had chaired the board for seven years during the 1990s. On Pitblado's advice, it defined itself as a succession committee, not a search committee, its first task, in his words, "to assess what resources you have and whether there are resources that would lead you to say, 'We have the ideal candidate.'"[2] After a full internal needs assessment and an extensive canvass of over one hundred individuals within the company, across Canada, and internationally, the committee decided it had such a candidate in Karen Kain; it would not be necessary to proceed

Sian Richards

Karen Kain with Mandy-Jayne Richardson (left) and Tomas Schramek, and Lorna Geddes in the background, rehearsing The Sleeping Beauty *in the studio.*

to phase two of the succession plan, the possibility of a full, international search. Kain's appointment as artistic director was announced in June 2005. Notes of congratulation poured in, many of them unabashed fan letters that saw her appointment as the continuation of the country's ongoing love affair with her. Many were touchingly personal. The wardrobe department wrote: "We wish you the strength of Wonder Woman and the compassion of Mother Teresa to help you carry out your duties."[3] For possibly the first time in the company's history, the newly appointed artistic director needed no introduction, not even to strangers to ballet.

At least one voice had advocated the alternative course of action. James Kudelka argued strongly for an interim appointment, while the board conducted a full international search. He believed the same rigorous process that had selected Reid Anderson and Kudelka himself should legitimize the current decision.[4] Kain, however, made it clear that she would not consider an interim appointment[5] and, as the dissenting voice, Kudelka could not carry the day. It was a precursor to the disillusionment he would feel with the direction the company took once he was no longer in charge. That disillusionment eventually soured his position as resident choreographer, which ended after just two years. Perhaps it was inevitable. With their roles in the organization suddenly reversed, Kain could hardly be expected to acknowledge Kudelka's authority as in the past, and Kudelka would find it hard to retain a role in the senior management of the company, yet relinquish the deciding voice he had had for the past nine years. In March 2006, Kudelka oversaw final rehearsals for *An Italian Straw Hat* at the National Arts Centre in Ottawa. Though he remained the resident choreographer of the company until 2007, he did not work with the dancers again until the rehearsals for *Swan Lake*, *Cinderella*, and *The Nutcracker* in 2010.[6]

THE MOVE TO A NEW HOUSE

As one of his last major commissions for the company, Kudelka had asked Nikolaj Hübbe, the New York City Ballet principal and Bournonville specialist who had set excerpts from *Napoli* on the National in February 2003, to mount a new production of *La Sylphide*. It premiered in November 2005, a joyous reminder that the company had not lost its facility with Bournonville style. Hübbe himself (who would go on to become artistic director of the Royal Danish Ballet in 2008) danced the role of James on opening night, and Erik Aschengreen, the eminent Danish dance critic and scholar, was brought in to give the pre-performance talks.

However, as in 1965, when Nureyev had made his surprise New Year's appearance in Bruhn's production of *La Sylphide*, casting created the real sensation. On Saturday, November 26, 2005, Rebekah Rimsay, a first soloist, made her debut as the Sylph at the matinee performance; a few hours later, at the evening performance, she took on the character role of Madge, the witch, in which she had made another debut just two days earlier. In the space of a few hours she took on the two major roles in the ballet, both relatively new to her, unafraid to portray herself as the image of the ethereal Romantic ballerina at one performance, a haggard old crone at the next. As Madge, at the moment when she vanquishes the hero, she struck a note of wonder and discovery, rather than malicious evil, as though she had been testing her supernatural powers and was astounded to learn how far they extended. It was a thoughtful, subtle performance, all the more remarkable for the test of endurance she had gone through that day. Though her accomplishment didn't make any Nureyev-style headlines, it did make history. Neither Aschengreen nor Hübbe could remember any other dancer accomplishing such a ballet double play. Rimsay later recalled that she had originally been assigned to understudy the Sylph, and thought the same-day casting might have been a sheer accident of unexpected illness and combinations of partnering. She took it in her stride. "It was a lot of fun to span that kind of breadth of character in a matter of hours. I enjoy doing that. But I couldn't have done it the other way around, for the stress level."[7] All in a day's work for the experienced professional.

Kain's first year as artistic director was the company's last performing at Toronto's Hummingbird Centre (formerly the O'Keefe Centre), which would soon close for refurbishment and re-open in its third incarnation as the Sony Centre. Discussions about returning to the Sony Centre as a separate home for the ballet had never gone very far, and by the time Kain came into her position, Kevin Garland, the company's executive director, was well into negotiations for the rental agreement with the Canadian Opera Company that would make the Four Seasons Centre for the Performing Arts the ballet's new Toronto performing home. The Four Seasons Centre offered huge improvements in acoustics, technical capacity, and the audience experience of the company's productions, but it also had some drawbacks. Nothing could be done about the physical constraints of the backstage area. The size and configuration of the building site meant that most dressing rooms had had to be located on upper floors, a great distance from the stage and a long walk for dancers preparing for their entrances. Terms for sharing the existing space were up for discussion, however, and divvying up the performance year between the opera and the ballet took up much of the negotiations. Garland saw them through to the final agreement, each side having to accept some less desirable parts of the performing year in exchange for non-negotiables, like the ballet's Christmas season for *The Nutcracker*. "We traded off. They [the Canadian Opera Company] got September and October; we got November and Christmas; they got February and Valentine's day; we got March; and then they needed a long period to add an extra opera to their season and so we got June."[8] The tenancy agreement was not ideal, but given the ballet's much earlier decision not to come into the building project as a full partner with the COC, it

Kevin Garland with a bird's-eye view of the Four Seasons Centre for the Performing Arts construction site.

represented a workable compromise. Final approval for the agreement came in June 2006, just before the company's occupancy began.[9]

Everyone agreed the new house had wonderful acoustics. The National Ballet Orchestra sounded better than ever before, and not only to the audience. At the Hummingbird, before the curtain went up, dancers had had to rely on piped-in sound to hear their entrance cue from the orchestra pit, and even once the curtain rose, sound travelled so badly from the stage to the auditorium that they could mutter instructions to each other without fear of being overheard.[10] At the Four Seasons Centre they were reunited with their music once again. Moreover, they had to be warned that now their onstage whispering ("Stay in line!" "Travel, you're not travelling enough!" More *croisé*!") might be heard in the auditorium.[11]

The auditorium has a European shoebox shape as opposed to the wide fan shape of the Hummingbird. It also has a reduced seating capacity. At 2,070 seats, it is 1,130 seats smaller than the Hummingbird (3,200 seats).[12] Such a house is good for the dancers and the public in that it makes the ballet spectacle more intimate. Dancers can project better and the audience can see much more of the detail and nuance of performance. The new house also has a much higher proportion of seats with good sight lines than the Hummingbird had. But limitations on the number of performance dates available to the company had the inevitable effect of driving up ticket prices. Julia Drake, the company's director of communications, analysed the effects of the move this way:

> We moved *to* a house where more than half the seats were on the floor in the top price, *from* a place where 500 out of 3,200 seats, less than a sixth, were the top price and the rest were cheap. We suddenly had no cheap seats. We had rings 3 and 4, very small sections, but ring 5 was a challenge for our older crowd, because it's high and steep, and there are stairs involved. The average ticket price across the theatre jumped from 40 to 85 dollars. So it was a real challenge to move all our subscribers and have them happy and adjusted.[13]

The company rescaled the price structure once within the first five years of occupancy, to try to provide a better range of prices at the top end, but even so, going to the ballet in the new house, though a better experience, was more expensive than it had been in the old.

No one in the company wanted to turn back the clock. Both the dancers and the production crew quickly recognized that the new theatre's facilities allowed them to present their art to the public far better than had been possible at the Hummingbird. But memories of the Hummingbird could be tinged with nostalgia, a tribute to its significance for the company and its Toronto audience over forty-two years of National Ballet history. An older generation of dancers, like Martine van Hamel, Galina Samsova, and

Lois Smith, had loved the Royal Alex for the repertoire they had danced there. Andreea Olteanu, a corps member of a much newer generation, cherished the Hummingbird for its place in her ballet experience. "I have a sentimental attachment for it. When I first came to this country, the first show I ever saw, my Mom took me to see the ballet at the Hummingbird. She said, 'Maybe one day you'll end up there,' and I ended up there. It's the place you started."[14] The company moved on, and the Hummingbird, like the Royal Alexandra, remained bound up in its history, a nostalgic part of its past.

Nureyev's *Beauty* and Balanchine's *Don Q*

When Kain took over the direction of the National Ballet of Canada, she faced a challenge no other artistic director before her had confronted. The National had a massive investment in the choreography of her immediate predecessor. How could she put her mark on a company with his name all over it? Even after seeing through the plans he had initiated, she had to find a way to create her own administrative and artistic identity while honouring his substantial choreographic legacy. Since she had no aspirations to be a choreographer herself, she would have to make her mark by other means.

The company first appeared on the Four Seasons Centre stage on June 22, 2006, at an exclusive black-tie fundraiser so successful it set the model for the "Mad Hot" fundraising galas of the years to come. The general public, however, first saw the company in its new digs in November 2006, in Rudolf Nureyev's *Sleeping Beauty*, which Kain had restaged at the Hummingbird in February 2004. Opening night at the Four Seasons Centre struck a festive atmosphere, with souvenirs for every member of the audience and an air of celebration to welcome the company to its new home. For the move to the Four Seasons Centre, the original Georgiadis costumes and sets were (as the souvenir program put it) "gloriously refurbished." Kain, who had danced in this production throughout her career, had restaged it as a tribute to Nureyev, her mentor. Now she polished it lovingly as a gift to her new company in its new home. Her meticulous attention to the spacing of the corps revealed the sculptural symmetry of Nureyev's original conception, against which the virtuosity of the company's rising new stars could shine forth. The company may have been smaller than it was in Nureyev's day, but it had strength and depth nonetheless. The run boasted no fewer than six Princess Auroras and four Prince Florimunds, all from within company ranks, with Heather Ogden, Stacey Shiori Minagawa, and Zdenek Konvalina making debuts.

Sleeping Beauty had occupied a special place in ballet repertoire as a work with inaugural, celebratory significance, ever since the Sadler's Wells Ballet had chosen to re-open London's Royal Opera House with its landmark new production of the ballet, designed by Oliver Messel, in 1946. Nureyev's version in 1972 had marked an important coming of age for the National and been a cornerstone of its repertoire ever since. It made sense for a classically based company like the National to program it on such an important occasion.

Aleksandar Antonijevic

Bridgett Zehr and Guillaume Côté rehearsing The Sleeping Beauty.

As the word "refurbished" acknowledged, it was the return of an old friend rather than a new arrival. Earlier in the fall, the COC had captured worldwide attention with its inaugural presentation in the new house of Wagner's complete *Ring Cycle*. Coming after such operatic fanfare, the refurbished *Sleeping Beauty* attracted less general attention, but for ballet lovers it heralded a new beginning in a new house appropriately, with a graceful acknowledgement of the company's classical roots.

That first season in the new house ended in June 2007, with the completion of another project Kudelka had initiated, the company premiere of George Balanchine's *Don Quixote*, staged by Suzanne Farrell as a co-production with the Suzanne Farrell Ballet Company and the Kennedy Center in Washington, D.C. From the outset, problems bedevilled this *Don Q*. The set was delayed and went over budget. The working relationship with the Kennedy Center became strained. As Kevin Garland later described it, "It was not a happy experience all around."[15] The greatest disappointment, however, came onstage. In 1965, the year of its creation, *Don Quixote* had been an intensely personal expression of its creator's dual nature as man of the spirit and man of the flesh. It was both a spiritual statement of the sixty-one-year-old Balanchine's Russian religiosity and a secular love letter to Suzanne Farrell, his twenty-year-old muse. When Balanchine had danced the Don, with Farrell as his Dulcinea, it had idealized a personal relationship central to the development of ballet in the twentieth century. But too much time had passed. Divorced from its original context, it seemed like a curiously antiquated costume drama, and even Farrell's guiding hand could not reanimate it. After this *Don Q*, with her obligations to past commitments honoured, Kain was free to set her company's sights firmly on the future and on a new strategy for bringing the National to the world's attention.

A COMPANY OF INDIVIDUALS: "NOT YOUR COOKIE-CUTTER LOOK"

She started with basics, doing repair work within the organization necessary to help it over its period of transition and find once again the sense of confidence and pride in its dancing that would bolster performance standards and attract new talent into the ranks. That process began, as it had for almost every one of her predecessors, with the agonizing task of pruning the ranks, letting go those dancers whose work was no longer up to her standards for the company. "I've been pretty brutal I'm afraid. There have been a lot of people who have left. I've let them go … probably close to twenty dancers in five years who have gone — and not by their choice. It's the hardest part of the job, because a lot of them were people I liked. And I'm still dealing with people who were my colleagues." In approaching this difficult and ongoing part of her responsibilities, Kain drew on her wealth of experience as a dancer trying to measure up to the artistic director's standards.

Erik Bruhn taught me how to set a bar and make everyone feel you all have a fair chance of keeping your jobs if you show that you deserve to keep your jobs. How do you do that with kindness? Because they're human beings you're dealing with. Yes, I learned from every single one of them. I have drawn on my memories of Celia Franca and Alexander Grant and Erik Bruhn and Lynn Wallis and Valerie Wilder and Reid Anderson and James Kudelka [for] the ways I did not want to be and how I did want to be as a leader.

Cylla von Tiedemann

Zdenek Konvalina as Kostya in John Neumeier's The Seagull.

Next, Kain seized the opportunity to influence the look of the company through the recruitment of new dancers at all ranks. Here, she sought quality and individuality wherever she found it, rather than a uniform look or a particular school of dancing. In assessing the results of her recruitment strategies, she quoted Wayne McGregor, the contemporary dancer and resident choreographer of London's Royal Ballet, who set his ballet *Chroma* on the company in 2010.

He said, "You have so many characters in this company. It's not your cookie-cutter look." So they're all really good dancers in different ways but they're not all your typical look. And I hadn't realized that I was collecting. I just like good dancers. I don't really mind what kind of form or shape that takes, as long as when we need a cohesive whole, like when we're doing *Swan Lake* or *Sleeping Beauty*, they can fit into that too.[16]

Such a collection, of "really good dancers in different ways," needed personalized attention in order to flourish in a company environment. Here, Kain relied on the company's senior artistic staff to combine the discipline of a large, classical company with respect for the individual artist, and make freedom of expression a possibility. As a group, the coaching staff had a remarkable breadth of training, background, and experience. Magdalena Popa, principal artistic coach, had studied at the Vaganova Academy of the Kirov Ballet, and was the leading ballerina in her native Romania and a star throughout Europe during the Communist period. She had joined the company as ballet mistress in 1983. Peter Ottmann, senior ballet master, and Rex Harrington, artist in residence, were products of the National Ballet School who had come up through the ranks of the company. Kain had appointed Harrington to the artist in residence position in 2006, following his retirement from dancing in 2004. Lindsay Fischer, another National Ballet School graduate, since 2007 the artistic director of the company's youth program, YOU Dance, and ballet master, had danced with the Dutch National Ballet and as a principal with New York City Ballet. Mandy-Jayne Richardson, senior ballet mistress, trained at the Royal Ballet School in London, then danced with the Sadler's Wells Royal Ballet, the Dutch National Ballet (where she and Fischer met and married), and New York City Ballet. All members of the coaching staff had built on their initial training with their subsequent experience, observing, absorbing, and learning wherever they went. Collectively, they had a wealth of experience to pass on.

Having made the transition from performer to coach relatively recently, Rex Harrington could identify with the performer's desire for freedom.

> I think I allow the dancers, right or wrong, to have their own opinions …
> for many years even when I was dancing, there was such a cookie-cutter
> approach to putting the ballets on, I always wondered, "Why do we have
> different casts if you're not allowed to raise an eyebrow differently?" So I
> allow people to explore.[17]

Richardson, working primarily with the corps and younger dancers, emphasized the need to develop every dancer's sense of responsibility. "It's very, very important that we work together so that their curiosity is piqued and they discover something within themselves. In the end they're out there onstage and they have to understand it."[18] Popa recalled the joy of working with the young Guillaume Côté, who became a principal dancer much in demand for guest engagements around the world, when he was still new to the company. She was coaching him for the solo in *Les Sylphides*, to music by Chopin.

> When he came from the school, you could tell he was a wonderful talent, but very raw. I felt that he had so much inside that I wanted to bring it out somehow, regardless of the choreography. So I said, "Don't think about the steps at all, I don't care. Just move the way this music is inspiring you to move." By the way he started moving, I knew for sure that this is a fantastic talent.[19]

As artistic director, Kain worked directly with the dancers when she was preparing repertoire for which she was responsible, like *Sleeping Beauty* or *Élite Syncopations*, but she did not teach daily class. To supplement her own observations in the studio, she turned to her artistic staff. "I watch, I check in. I have a really good staff and I really believe in letting people feel that they're not being pushed aside by me." Working together, Kain and her staff encouraged dancers in their individual development, watched carefully for those who responded, and tried to give them performance opportunities, sometimes without regard to seniority or rank. Kain's attitude in this respect was formed by the chances she had had in her own remarkable career. As a nineteen-year-old corps member, she had approached Celia Franca about the possibility of being given a small solo and, to her great surprise, was told to learn the Swan Queen in *Swan Lake*. By coincidence, Franca had been struggling at exactly the same time with revised castings to cope with injuries and was willing to take a chance. Now that Kain had inherited Franca's role, she adapted Franca's willingness to believe in a promising beginner to the present situation. "This company is full of young people who are just delighted to explore … everybody knows that they have a chance if they are in shape and show a choreographer what they can do and something suits them…. That is how you build morale in a company. That's how I got my chance." Kain's formula was simple: give dancers individualized coaching, give them responsibility, and then give them opportunity. It was a far cry from the regimented prescription of detail with which Franca had approached the training of her first troupe, but this was a different company, as Kain knew. "I think there's a real respect for all the tradition and heritage, from me and from the dancers, but we want to be a company of today and these are young people of today. I don't think I'm re-creating anything."

Gradually, word of the opportunities at the National Ballet of Canada spread. According to Kain: "The word gets out about rep, the word gets out about how people are treated, the word gets out about how the communication is between the director and dancers and how they're looked after. So I've had a lot of people want to come."[20] People like Jiří Jelinek, trained in Europe, who joined the company as a principal in 2010.

Peter Ottmann in rehearsal with artists of the ballet.

Or like Skylar Campbell from California, spotted at the Lausanne International Ballet Competition and offered a place as an apprentice with the company in 2009. Or like the small group of expats from the Houston Ballet — Bridgett Zehr, who joined the company in 2006 and became a principal in 2009, Zdenek Konvalina, who joined as principal in 2006, and McGee Maddox, who entered the corps in 2009 and became a first soloist in 2011. In commenting on the National's attraction for dancers from outside Canada, Maddox described himself as the product of an internationalized world of dance, in which national boundaries need not hinder a professional dancer's aspirations.

> This company, San Francisco, ABT, they're becoming international companies. I think a lot of that has to do with the cultural movement of dance … especially in North America, since the North American ballet tradition is really only — 70 years old, maybe? I think it's only appropriate that there are countries from all over the world being represented in the principal ranks and in all other ranks.[21]

OPENING THE REPERTOIRE UP TO THE LATEST CHOREOGRAPHIC DEVELOPMENTS

When Kain took over the leadership of the National, it had an extensive repertoire of Canadian works, predominantly by Kudelka, but also by Alleyne, Dumais, and Mrozewski. In her view, the company needed an international perspective in order to broaden the base of its contemporary repertoire. "It's time for the company to have a taste of everything else that's happening. I want to internationalize the company, because we're still isolated [in Canada] from what's going on in the wider world of dance. Not enough comes here."[22] And if not enough of the most important recent choreography was coming to Toronto, Kain set out to bring it. She wanted her dancers to experience not just the works, but the choreographers themselves, who were making news on the international scene. And in doing so she accepted the task of transforming her audience's tastes. If she could challenge the company to pull itself up by its own bootstraps, she could encourage her audience to do the same.

She began with Christopher Wheeldon's *Polyphonia* in June 2007, followed by Christopher Bruce's *Rooster* (set to music by the Rolling Stones) in November 2007, Twyla Tharp's *In the Upper Room* (November 2008), Davide Bombana's *Carmen* (June 2009), Jorma Elo's *Pur ti Miro* (June 2010), Wayne McGregor's *Chroma* (November 2010), and Alexei Ratmansky's *Russian Seasons* (March 2011). All were one-act ballets included in mixed programs of more familiar repertoire.

Virtually all these choreographers were creating their reputations by working with companies around the world who were competing for their works, and not by their careful nurturing of a single company identified solely with them. Their international credentials reflected the status of a new breed of choreographer: their training ranged far beyond classical ballet, and they were citizens of the world, not just of one dance centre in it. Wheeldon, trained in England, resident choreographer of New York City Ballet, created works for Pennsylvania Ballet, San Francisco Ballet, London's Royal Ballet, Moscow's Bolshoi Ballet. Bruce, trained with London's Ballet Rambert, associated with Ballet Rambert, the English National Ballet, and Houston Ballet, choreographed for Sweden's Cullberg Ballet, the Geneva Ballet, and Netherlands Dance Theatre. Tharp, the popular American choreographer of modern dance, created works for Mikhail Baryshnikov, Boston Ballet, American Ballet Theatre, the Paris Opera Ballet, England's Royal Ballet, and on Broadway. Bombana, trained in Italy, danced in Italy, the United States, Great Britain, and Germany, choreographed for companies in Munich, Geneva, Moscow, and Florence. Elo, trained in Finland and Leningrad, resident choreographer of Boston Ballet, with commissions from American Ballet Theatre, New York City Ballet, Netherlands Dance Theatre, and Alberta Ballet. McGregor, the first modern dancer to be named resident choreographer of London's Royal Ballet, choreographed ballets and directed opera

Bruce Zinger

Etienne Lavigne with artists of the ballet in the finale, "Sympathy for the Devil," from Christopher Bruce's Rooster, *set to music by the Rolling Stones.*

productions for companies in England, France, the United States, the Netherlands, and Germany. Ratmansky, artistic director of the Bolshoi Ballet, then artist in residence at American Ballet Theatre, choreographed for American Ballet Theatre, New York City Ballet, Royal Danish Ballet, Royal Swedish Ballet, Dutch National Ballet, St. Petersburg's Kirov Ballet, and the Bolshoi Ballet.[23]

The company had danced the work of outside choreographers ever since Franca's days, but never such a variety over such a short period of time, and they had not always worked directly with the choreographers themselves. The list of the choreographers Kain was able to bring into the company indicated that the international world of ballet had undergone a radical change since the days of Balanchine, Ashton, and MacMillan. They had preferred, by and large, to stay put, working with their own companies, and to let their works out to others parsimoniously, often persuaded to do so by personal connections, as Ashton had been persuaded by his friend Alexander Grant to allow the National to acquire some of his works. Now, as choreographers embraced internationalization, the rules of the acquisition game had changed as well. Personal contacts were no longer as powerful as they once had been. Instead, the quality of dancers, the ability of a company to produce ambitious works with technical skill and sophistication, the degree of exposure it could provide for the choreographer's work — all these factors came into play as choreographers chose the companies, worldwide, with whom they would work. Choreographers might now be willing to travel, but they travelled on their own terms. Kain's success, the company's success, in this competitive international arena was remarkable.

Such a barrage of new works stimulated the dancers and educated their audience to the latest influences on the international dance scene. Many of these ballets challenged the tastes of conservative members of the audience, but also began to attract a more adventurous group of spectators to the theatre. Kain scheduled her new acquisitions on programs with recognized attractions. This approach to programming had been followed by others in the past, but seldom with such conspicuous success. Julia Drake, who as director of communications for the company had the responsibility of selling programs like the first performances of McGregor's *Chroma* to the public, admired what she described as Kain's "bait and switch" strategy.

> *Chroma* doesn't mean much to anybody out there, but [Crystal Pite's] *Emergence* has won four Dora awards and has a certain buzz around it. They know they're getting *Emergence*. They don't know anything about the others and they might leave talking about *Chroma* for all we know. Which is how it worked when she did [Jerome Robbins's] *West Side Story Suite*. They went away talking about [Marie Chouinard's] *24 Preludes by Chopin*. Or [Christopher Bruce's] *Rooster* and they went away talking about [Robbins's] *Glass Pieces*. Very clever.[24]

In such works, the National's audience encountered choreography that was much more physical, faster, riskier, more aggressive, decidedly less pretty than what it had been used to. For the dancers, the physical demands required more careful judgment if they were to project the excitement of the movement without doing damage to their bodies. Principal dancer Greta Hodgkinson described how she approached the new choreographic demands: "I wouldn't say more carefully, I would say smarter. But I think at the end of the day it still needs to be spontaneous and you need to throw yourself into it."[25] With physical risk came a decidedly different sense of freedom in movement. McGee Maddox, from a younger generation of dancers, described the experience of working with Wayne McGregor as "a completely different physicality. I had to apply myself non-classically. I think that I can probably use that in just about anything I do. *Chroma* was the kind of ballet where I felt if you knew it, you couldn't do a wrong step. You had to feel it, you had to get that right integrity with the movement, and then it just happened."[26]

Despite her initial emphasis on internationalization, however, Kain did not rest on the body of works by Canadian choreographers already in the company's repertoire. She took a chance on emerging Canadian voices with a program called "Innovation" (March 2009), three world premieres by Canadians Crystal Pite (*Emergence*), Peter Quanz (*IN COLOUR*),

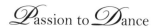

and Sabrina Matthews (*DEXTRIS*), and premiered Aszure Barton's *Watch Her* in November 2009. She invited Dominique Dumais to stage *Skin Divers* (her work for the Komische Oper Berlin) in June 2009, and brought the work of established Canadian choreographer Marie Chouinard into the company for the first time with her *24 Preludes by Chopin* in March 2008. A subsequent mixed program of Pite's *Emergence* and Chouinard's *24 Preludes by Chopin* proved enormously popular, in Toronto and also in Montreal.

Kain also acknowledged the curatorial aspect of her role. True, she exploited the popular appeal of Jerome Robbins's Broadway work with *West Side Story Suite*, but she also honoured the legacy of his career at New York City Ballet by including his much more challenging *Glass Pieces* (music by minimalist composer Philip Glass) and *In the Night* (music by Chopin), all in a single all-Robbins program in November 2007. Robbins's *A Suite of Dances*, to music from the Bach suites for unaccompanied cello, entered the repertoire in March 2010, a solo vehicle for the formidable talents of Guillaume Côté and Zdenek Konvalina, who alternated in the work.

For a special occasion in June 2008, Kain brought into the repertoire Sir Frederick Ashton's *Five Brahms Waltzes in the Manner of Isadora Duncan*, an elegiac solo he had originally created for the talents of the mature Lynn Seymour, the great Canadian star of the Royal Ballet. Seymour herself coached Jennifer Fournier, who made her farewell appearances in these performances, a solitary figure striding resolutely forward, releasing an autumnal cascade of rose petals from her outstretched hands. Fournier was grateful to Kain for this finale. "She allowed me to take control of the end of my career. I said, 'I want to retire now because I don't want anybody to make the decision for me,' and she allowed me a catharsis. I don't know if my career would have felt as complete if I hadn't had that final moment."[27]

Fournier, who had entered the company in 1986, had resigned from it in 2000 and moved to California. As the birth of her first child approached, she wrote a note to all her friends in the company, a touching mix of matters personal and professional, trivial and profound. It demonstrated how deeply, as a dancer, she felt the loss of dancing, even as she anticipated motherhood.

> Will the baby be early? Will I have a drug-free delivery? Will it be a boy? girl? share Rex's birthday? Will I ever wear clothes with a waist again? Will anyone ever hire me for the only thing I'm skilled to do in this world? No one knows and my horoscope is strangely vague on all these points.[28]

Fournier had returned to the company in 2002, happy to prove that dancers "dance better after they have kids. There's something softer but stronger, more fully formed."[29] After her memorable farewell in 2008, she enrolled as an undergraduate at the University of Toronto, and embarked on a different kind of training for life after dance.

Cylla von Tiedemann

Jennifer Fournier in her farewell performance, Five Brahms Waltzes in the Manner of Isadora Duncan.

A New Repertoire of Full-Length Ballets

According to Fournier, Kain as artistic director wanted "to make an argument for dance as an evolving art form."[30] During Kain's first five years, this aim could be seen even on the traditional side of the house, in her careful deployment of the full-length story ballets that anchored the company's box office. *Nutcracker*, of course, continued to be the annual Christmas fixture. The other major works of the historical canon from the Romantic and the Petipa eras — *Giselle, Sleeping Beauty, Swan Lake,* even the Petipa *Don Quixote* — appeared in the Toronto seasons as well, but less frequently than in the past. In the first five years of Kain's artistic directorship, *Swan Lake* played three times (twice in the 2005–06 season, once in 2010), *Sleeping Beauty* twice (in November 2006 and 2009), the other two once each (*Giselle* in May 2009, when Chan Hon Goh chose it for her farewell performance, Petipa's *Don Quixote* in March 2011). The rest of the full-lengths came from the twentieth-century and contemporary repertoire, from Cranko (*Romeo and Juliet, Onegin,* and *The Taming of the Shrew*), Kudelka (*Cinderella, An Italian Straw Hat*), Hynd (*The Merry Widow*), and Neumeier (*The Seagull*). The company's character as a classically based company thus underwent a subtle shift, from one that defined "classical" on a strictly historical basis to one that extended the meaning of the word to include modern works choreographed in a classical idiom. The shift had been initiated by Erik Bruhn, with his investment in *The Merry Widow*. Kain continued it with a succession of important initiatives.

For June 2010, Kain commissioned newly designed sets and costumes for Cranko's *Onegin* to replace the Stuttgart originals by Cranko's favoured designer, Jürgen Rose. Reid Anderson had mothballed Rose's Stuttgart designs for *Romeo and Juliet* in February 1995, and commissioned a new production designed by Susan Benson. Kain's new *Onegin* confirmed the significance of the Cranko full-lengths in the National's repertoire. Two of his three major works (*Shrew* never achieved the same popularity at the National) had been accorded the honour and the financial investment of new productions. Like the historical classical canon, these works stood on the strength of their choreography alone and could be reinterpreted by successive generations. Just as important, the imitative link to Stuttgart was broken. These works were no longer mere imitations of an original production, frozen in time. They were strong enough to live and grow with the company. The new *Onegin* paid off. It received such an enthusiastic reception in 2010 that the company rejigged its 2010–11 season on short notice, to capitalize on its success with a return engagement.[31]

Kain's choice of Santo Loquasto as designer for the new *Onegin* confirmed another evolution, one that had been taking place in the company's onstage identity over the past twenty years. Loquasto was represented in the repertoire by major productions of *Swan Lake*, *Nutcracker*, *Italian Straw Hat*, and *Onegin*, and by designs for several of Kudelka's shorter works, dating back to *Pastorale* in 1990. Though he was by no means the company's sole designer, he defined its sumptuous look in the new century, replacing the vibrant sixties palette and clean-cut lines of Jürgen Rose and the pastel shades and feathery, impressionistic brushstrokes of Desmond Heeley, the influential designer at the early Stratford Festival.

More important than these design decisions was Kain's commitment to new full-length works. In November 2008, the company acquired John Neumeier's *The Seagull*, based on Chekhov's play and set to a pastiche score by four different composers, old and new. Neumeier, the American choreographer transplanted to Germany, had worked with the National in the 1970s, when Kain had first encountered him. He created *The Seagull* for his Hamburg Ballet in 2002. Though intensely dramatic, with a stellar role for Zdenek Konvalina, who led the opening-night cast, the choreography could not completely explicate Chekhov's complicated interplay of relationships and emotions. The house program elucidated with a two-page schematic diagram of the major characters, rather like a family tree, that plotted these intricacies for the benefit of the spectators. In contrast to the complexity of the narrative, the designs (sets, costumes, and lighting by Neumeier himself) opened the stage picture with a luminous, uncluttered clarity. If the narrative was at times hard to follow, the visual picture was always striking and contemporary.

But Kain wanted the company to create new full-length work, not just reproduce it. Here, she once again built on her strategy of internationalization. Her invitations to

Aleksandar Antonijevic

Jiří Jelinek in the title role of Onegin, *newly designed by Santo Loquasto in 2010.*

choreographers to stage short existing works on the National served to familiarize them with the dancers and the company production team. On the strength of that contact, a subsequent invitation to create a new, full-length work on the company stood a much greater chance of success. Thus, Christopher Wheeldon's *Polyphonia* in June 2007 acted as prelude to his *Alice's Adventures in Wonderland* three years later. This full-length real-ization of Lewis Carroll's familiar tale, created as a co-production between the Royal Ballet and the National, premiered in London in March 2011, then in Toronto in June of the same year. As part of the co-production agreement, the National retained exclu-sive North American rights for a period of three years following the opening, with non-exclusive North American rights for another five years after that. The Royal Ballet had equivalent exclusivity in Britain and Europe. Neither company could tour the ballet in these territories without the consent of the other.[32] Nothing was left vague. Management had learned from its experience of 1964, when the informality of an agreement among friends hopelessly muddled the company's long-term rights to Cranko's *Romeo and Juliet*.

Wheeldon's new *Alice's Adventures in Wonderland* implied a decisive step forward in the evolution of the National's repertoire. A company that boasted Wheeldon's work would be unlikely to revive Glen Tetley's *Alice*, based on the same source, any time soon. Tetley's ver-sion of the Carroll classic had put the company on the July 1986 cover of *Dance Magazine* — an original creation by an international choreographer, an exclusive property that attracted international attention. Now, the coincidence of subject matter pointed up a similarity in strategy. In 1986, Erik Bruhn had recognized the need for distinctive repertoire in order to revive the National's hopes for touring. Twenty-five years later, Kain too was building a strong new repertoire, unique to the company, as part of her long-term strategy.

Kain's biggest coup in her first five years as artistic director, unquestionably, was snag-ging Alexei Ratmansky for major collaboration with the company. Ratmansky had been described by *The New York Times*, in 2009, as "the It Boy" of the ballet world and by Mikhail Baryshnikov (in the same *Times* profile) as "a Russian man with a very Western grip on movement." He had directed the Bolshoi Ballet, one of the largest ballet compa-nies on earth, before he was forty, and well before that had danced for the Royal Winnipeg. A classmate of his at the Bolshoi academy, Vladimir Malakhov, had danced for some years with the National. But since those early days of contact, direct and indirect, with Canada, Ratmansky had returned to Russia, then left it again to conquer New York with two cre-ations, *Russian Seasons* and *Concerto DSCH*, both for New York City Ballet. Both City Ballet and American Ballet Theatre had courted him on a more permanent basis, with ABT eventually the successful suitor. In part, his many commitments to other companies had scuppered a deal with NYCB.[33]

Kain had hoped to have a major new work from Ratmansky for the 2010–11 season, but circumstances forced her to settle for a remount of his *Russian Seasons* for March 2011 instead. Even that production ran into a few difficulties. Just before the company announced the 2010–11 season, it discovered that Toronto's newly reopened Sony Centre would be presenting St. Petersburg's Kirov Ballet in *Swan Lake* at precisely the same time, so *Russian Seasons* was moved to a different slot in the schedule in order to avoid the direct conflict.[34] But Kain's plans for an original creation by Ratmansky were only deferred, not shelved. In February 2011, she announced a new production of *Romeo and Juliet*, with original choreography by Alexei Ratmansky, to open the National's 2011–12, sixtieth-anniversary season.

This was more than evolution of the repertoire; this was regime change. Cranko's version had had 240 performances between its opening in 1964 and 2011. In the years since Kudelka had taken over the company, in 1996, it was the third most-programmed full-length in the repertoire, after *Nutcracker* and *Swan Lake*. Both by its historical significance, as the ballet that had inaugurated the company's move to O'Keefe Centre, and by its perennial popularity, Cranko's version of *Romeo and Juliet* had become identified with the company itself in the hearts of many of its fans. Like Kudelka when he replaced the Bruhn *Swan Lake* with his own, Kain accepted the risk of bruising a few of those hearts in order to ensure the company's development and progress.

While the company would not announce that it was abandoning such a popular favourite, it could hardly program two *Romeo and Juliet*s in close proximity to one another. For the foreseeable future at least, Ratmansky's version would supplant Cranko's. If the new version found the kind of audience favour Cranko's had enjoyed, it would, over time, change the fundamental identity of the National Ballet of Canada. With this daring choice, Kain placed her stamp on the company. The full impact of her move would not be assessed for years to come.

TOURING IN THE TWENTY-FIRST CENTURY

Kain's third major objective for the company — touring — followed logically on the first two — improving the quality of the dancing and overhauling the repertoire. The company had done some touring in the first decade of the new century, with appearances in Ottawa, in the western Canadian provinces, and in American centres, including a run of *Swan Lake* at the Kennedy Center in Washington, D.C. The National had last played eastern Canada in 2002, Montreal in 2003. Some of its touring appearances had been single-item contributions to dance festivals or celebrations, others had involved only small groups of dancers performing to piano or taped accompaniment. In recent years, the company that had started out as a touring group had been on the road less and less. Nothing dramatized the difficulty of touring a company of the National's size in a twenty-first century economic climate more starkly than Kain's decision, in 2009, to cancel a fully scheduled tour of western Canada because of the magnitude of the likely financial loss. In her own words:

I think that was the hardest decision of all. I know it was the right one because I feel I have to be responsible fiscally with this company. We always have trouble making the western tour work. If we [were to] set off in the middle of a recession out west, where they were hit harder than the rest of Canada, [could we] just expect them all to buy expensive tickets to the ballet? Everybody understood it was the right thing to do, but it was hard for our partner companies in the west, and very hard for the artists. That was at least 14 performances that they didn't get to do in a year. That was a really tough decision. I lost a lot of nights' sleep.

Artists of the ballet in Crystal Pite's Emergence.

She cushioned the blow by taking a small group of dancers to Victoria, Nanaimo, and Vancouver in September 2009, with a mixed program of easily portable works, reminiscent of the Concert Groups of years gone by. In October 2010, the full company brought its mainstage mixed program of *Emergence* and *24 Preludes by Chopin* to Montreal as part of the Place des Arts season of contemporary dance called "Danse Danse." When the National had last visited Montreal, in 2003, it appeared as part of the subscription season of Les Grands Ballets Canadiens. The company had wanted to show off some of its most recent repertoire, but Les Grands demanded Ashton's

La Fille mal gardée, seen in Montreal as far back as 1978 and clearly identified as part of the company's past. The 2010 Montreal appearance received standing ovations from an audience attuned to contemporary dance. Kain was glad of the new showcase, happy "to show Montreal that we aren't the stuffy old ballet company that they thought we were."[35]

Touring depends on many factors, financial and logistical, beyond the control of a dance company, and often unrelated to the merits of the company itself. But Kain has done as much as lies in any artistic director's power to improve her company's chances for touring, and to ensure that it is ready when opportunities present themselves. Her strategy — to groom a company of energetic, appealing individuals and provide them with a challenging, contemporary repertoire that will attract attention on an international stage. By April 2011, that strategy had begun to pay off. Kain was able to announce that the National Ballet of Canada would tour to England in the spring of 2013, appearing at the Sadler's Wells Theatre in London with a mixed program of James Kudelka's *The Four Seasons* and Crystal Pite's *Emergence*, and showcasing the new, full-length Ratmansky *Romeo and Juliet*.

THE CHANGING FACE OF BALLET IN THE TWENTY-FIRST CENTURY

A glance at touring programs from the early years reveals how much has changed in the world of ballet in the sixty years of the company's existence. The repertoire the National sold to its touring audiences then seems quaint and outdated now. More often than not, the full-length classics like *Swan Lake*, *Giselle*, and *Coppélia* were represented on tour by a single act, or cut up into various different snippets, combined with a few more snippets from *Sleeping Beauty* (of which the company did not yet have a complete version), and served up under generic titles like "Dances from the Classics." The rest of the repertoire leaned heavily on items popularized by the old Ballets Russes companies, ballets like *Les Sylphides* and *Carnaval*, and on the repertoire of short works by Tudor, Howard, Gore, and Ashton, redolent of the early days of British ballet, of the era of Marie Rambert and Ninette de Valois. Such repertoire drew audiences who wanted to be reminded of a glorious past, whose conception of ballet came second-hand, in many instances, from accounts of legendary dancers like Pavlova and Nijinsky, or from romanticized movie treatments like *The Red Shoes*. The National, created by a woman with direct links to that past, was happy to oblige, secure in the knowledge that it was part of an acknowledged tradition, that it was related to its past.

Today's tour audiences demand different fare. Conditioned to a large extent by lavish reproductions of the most recent Broadway hits, they crave spectacle, and where ballet is concerned, they want to see what is new, to feel themselves in touch with the latest developments. A public taught to demand the cutting edge has little appreciation

Ken Bell

Lilian Jarvis as Columbine, Earl Kraul as Harlequin, and Marcel Chojnacki as Pantalon in Michel Fokine's Le Carnaval, *from the company's early repertoire.*

for the past. A few pieces of canvas scenery and a scaled-down version of *Swan Lake* no longer travel well.

A larger debate, however, locates the change, not with audience tastes, but within the art form itself. A vocal group of critics argues that contemporary choreography has lost touch with the important traditions of its past, that it has become consumed with a restless search for novelty. The dance historian Jennifer Homans identifies the moment of this change sometime after the death of George Balanchine, in 1983. Homans concludes *Apollo's Angels*, her cultural history of dance, with a melancholy epilogue titled "The Masters Are Dead and Gone," in which she argues that after Balanchine, ballet "…seemed to grind to a crawl, as if the tradition itself had become clogged and exhausted."[36] She goes on to castigate the generation of choreographers now dominating the international stage for failing to find a vision of their own, for settling instead for "strident innovation."

Not everyone agrees. Perhaps contemporary ballet is simply experiencing a temporary drought, not entering the apocalypse. True, twenty-first-century choreography does have a rootless, searching quality, epitomized by its journeying choreographers, always en route to the next company hungry for their services. The older, stay-at-home generation, the generation of Balanchine and Ashton, drew boundaries within which their companies and their choreography developed distinctive characteristics and local styles. But boundaries also imposed limits. The travelling generation is open to a much wider range of ideas, eagerly absorbing influences from around the world. If it runs the risk of homogenizing the world's tastes, and causing the repertoire of every leading ballet company to resemble that of its peers, it has also gained a much greater freedom, a wider range of possibility, than was available to dance in the previous century.

At sixty, the National Ballet of Canada finds itself a child of this new age. It dances now on a world stage, in a highly competitive present, rather than in a continuum palpably linked to its classical past. For Kain, leading the company in this changed environment, the challenge is immense. How can the National compete as a modern, international organization, a company of today, and still retain a vital sense of the classical tradition that gave it birth?

The National presented the North American premiere of Christopher Wheeldon's Alice's Adventures in Wonderland, *the most complex show in the company's history, in 2011. Co-production with Britain's Royal Ballet eased the financial burden, though not the technical challenges. Jillian Vanstone as Alice and Aleksandar Antonijevic as the White Rabbit.*

OPENING EXERCISES

It is early February 2011, and Studio Prima, the company's main rehearsal and teaching studio at the Walter Carsen Centre, has been given over to visitors. Floor-to-ceiling blackout curtains obscure the large, north-facing wall of windows. Temporary bleachers opposite them provide seating space for the guests. Electronic equipment crowds the east wall of the room. All this to accommodate the press for the National Ballet's annual media conference, simultaneously live-streamed this year via webcast, to unveil the company's plans for its next season, its sixtieth-anniversary season. As Karen Kain outlines the programming for this celebration year, it is clear that she has acknowledged the need for balance in her planning. The world premiere of Ratmansky's *Romeo and Juliet* will be joined by another contemporary ballet, also based on Shakespeare, the company premiere of *Hamlet*, created by Kevin O'Day for the Stuttgart Ballet in 2008. But she has balanced these contemporary works with two that clearly acknowledge the company's own past and the continuum of classical dance itself. Her forward-looking company will present a revival of Sir Frederick Ashton's *La Fille mal gardée* and a celebratory remount of the Nureyev *Sleeping Beauty*. These are more than just nostalgic backward glances; they are carefully selected markers, touchstones of this particular company's links to its past, to its fundamental identity. "A company of today," but one "with a real respect for all the tradition and heritage." Kain's own words have enunciated the goal.

The next morning, all evidence of the media conference cleared away, Studio Prima reverts to its rightful owners as dancers drift in, singly or in small groups, for the company's daily class. The blackout curtains have been removed and light streams through the windows, which now provide a panorama of Toronto's condo skyline, bisected in the foreground by the concrete ribbon of the elevated Gardiner Expressway, with cars and trucks angling up the entry ramp in ceaseless flow. But the dancers focus their attention inwards, not on the spectacular view. Dressed in practise clothes, with leg warmers and scruffy tops, they limber up. Some, pressing themselves against a wall, stretch the kinks out of their spines. Others, assuming a modified lotus position on the floor, flex their insteps, stretch their thighs, or massage complaining muscles. At the piano in the corner, the rehearsal pianist glances through scores from a thick stack of music on the piano bench beside him. Then, with the entry of the teacher — today, one of the company's senior artistic staff, though guest teachers are not unusual — the dancers find places at the barre, ready to begin. To the casual observer, there seems to be no organization to their placement, but any newcomer to the company would know better. Apprentices and junior corps members are quick to learn which spots the principals prefer, and are careful not to usurp them. An informal hierarchy rules as the teacher begins class.

It opens, as all ballet classes open, with the fundamental exercises. Plié, a gentle bending and then straightening of the knees with the torso kept erect as the body descends and rises again; relevé, a simple rising up onto the toes; tendu, a stretching out of the leg, forward or to the side; fondu, a kind of plié executed on one leg only. The piano accompaniment establishes a supporting rhythm that keeps the dancers' execution musical, every set of exercises a finished, complete phrase. As their muscles warm up, dancers gradually shed their outer layers of clothing, tossing leg warmers and the like into the corners of the room in preparation for more energetic work to come. From the front of the studio, the teacher begins calling out more complicated steps, then combinations of those steps, using the French vocabulary of ballet terms, sometimes marking out the sequence with the curious semaphore language, hands and forearms substituting for feet and legs, with which teachers and choreographers communicate their intentions. As soon as the combination is announced, the accompanist begins playing something appropriate, choosing a score quickly from the pile, perhaps playing from memory or even improvising something in the required tempo and rhythm. The class flows seamlessly, musically, with a rhythm of its own, from combination to combination, pianist and dancers responding quickly as the teacher decides what elements are right for the demands of the upcoming day of rehearsals. It is a test of intellect and memory, as much as bodily capacity.

By now the dancers have moved away from the support of the barre, out into the centre of the floor, and the teacher moves among them, giving instructions, watching execution, adjusting an arm, a foot, or a leg here, calling out an individual correction there. Junior company members are pleased to receive attention, apprehensive of getting too much. There is, after all, a fine line between being noticed and being slow to learn. Class is one of those places where you might be spotted, perhaps kept in mind for a small solo, perhaps singled out for a warning.

As the class proceeds, bodies gradually assume the bearing that so clearly identifies them as dancers' bodies. For it is in this daily ritual that dancers condition their instruments and bring them up to the pitch required for the performance of their art — open, erect, supple, poised. The class concludes with a patter of applause and a graceful révérence, a bow to the teacher, but also to the front of the room, where, were this a theatre, the audience would be. Ballet training, based on historical principles of etiquette and courtly behaviour going all the way back to seventeenth-century France, is an education in presenting the human body to others in an outgoing, inviting, and respectful fashion. Company class repeats that education anew every day, and reinforces at the most fundamental level, in the bodies of the dancers, in their musculature and posture, the connection between ballet as a modern art form and the long tradition of movement, the ordered, courtly aesthetic, that lies behind it.

The dancers of the National Ballet of Canada, modern, urban, young people, have dedicated themselves to the rigorous training required to claim that aesthetic as their rightful inheritance. Now, their instruments conditioned, they are ready once more to go about the business of their day, which is to perpetuate the old tradition and to make it new in the modern works they present. They are vital anachronisms, grounded in the past, yet committed to the future. Custodians of a centuries-old technique, they give expression to the most radical of modern choreographic voices. Voiceless themselves, they are made eloquent by passion, the passion to speak, the passion to dance.

A NOTE ON THE APPENDICES

The National Ballet of Canada. Just what did they dance? Where did they dance it? And when? Comprehensive answers to these simple questions give the reader a vivid sense of the artistic character of the company as it has grown and changed over the first sixty years of its existence. They can be found in the statistical appendices that follow, and especially in the first, the company itinerary from 1951 to 2011.

This historical database was first created by Lynn Neufeld for the publication of *Power to Rise* in 1996. Working painstakingly from archival resources, she compiled the performance history of the company from 1951 to 1991. Every program entry was verified by at least one independent source, so that the history reflected what was actually danced, not just what had been programmed or planned.

By 1991, the company stage management department, under the guidance of Ernest Abugov and Jeff Morris, had begun to create its own ongoing electronic record of its performance statistics. After the publication of *Power to Rise*, Sharon Vanderlinde and Adrienne Nevile, who are in charge of the company's archives, took on the task of transferring the historical data from the early years into this ongoing database. The resulting database, which now combines Lynn Neufeld's historical research with the daily record keeping of the company, has become one of the most powerful and useful tools the company has for analysing its performance record. Our goal in preparing *Passion to Dance* was to update this information and make it available in print form for present readers.

To do so, it was necessary to review all the information in the complete database of some 14,000 separate records, in order to verify its accuracy and present it in readable format. Lynn Neufeld returned to this task with a passion for accuracy and a commitment to consistency that have ferreted out many lingering errors. Her efforts, combined with the work of company staff, volunteers, and interns over the years, have made possible the wealth of detailed information that follows.

In preparing the records of dancers, she had the help of Adrienne Nevile, Bridget Benn, and Brianne Price, as well as Katharine Harris of Canada's National Ballet School. Laurie Nemetz, at the National Ballet of Canada, compiled the basic information that went into the list of board membership over the years.

We want to thank all these individuals, whose commitment to archival record keeping has made such a resource possible. And I want to thank Lynn for her unwavering dedication to a task that many would find too daunting to contemplate. We hope that interested readers will find the same pleasure in these pages that can be found in browsing a good dictionary, where the search for a specific piece of information often leads to detours and byways every bit as interesting as the original quest.

James and Lynn Neufeld

$\mathcal{A}$ppendix A:

COMPANY ITINERARY

Note: This appendix lists all performances by the company from its official opening in November 1951 to June 2011. It includes performances by the Concert Group without differentiating them from the rest of the repertoire, but does not include any of the company's choreographic workshops or labs, or any of its outreach performances such as Prologue to the Performing Arts or YOU dance.

Symbols and abbreviations used:

†	=	matinee performance
‡	=	student matinee performance
Aud	=	Auditorium
FSCPA	=	Four Seasons Centre for the Performing Arts
H.S.	=	High School
Inst.	=	Institute
pdd	=	pas de deux
S.S.	=	Secondary School
U	=	University

November 1951:

12 TORONTO, ON, Eaton Aud: Polovetsian Dances; Étude; Giselle, Peasant pdd; Dance of Salomé; Les Sylphides — *repeated, November 13, 14*

December 1951:

10 TORONTO, ON, Forest Hill Collegiate Aud: Giselle, Peasant pdd; Coppélia, Act II; Étude; Les Sylphides; Don Quixote, pdd

January 1952:

14 GUELPH, ON, Guelph Collegiate Aud: Giselle, Peasant pdd; Coppélia, Act II; Étude; Les Sylphides; Don Quixote, pdd

15 KITCHENER, ON, K-W Collegiate Aud: Giselle, Peasant pdd; Coppélia, Act II; Étude; Les Sylphides; Don Quixote, pdd

28 TORONTO, ON, Eaton Aud: Casse-Noisette, Act II; Giselle, Act II; Ballet Composite — *repeated, January 29, 30*

31 MONTREAL, QC, His Majesty's Theatre: Les Sylphides; Dance of Salomé; Casse-Noisette, Act II

February 1952:

1   MONTREAL, QC, His Majesty's Theatre: Étude; Coppélia, Act II; Don Quixote, pdd; Polovetsian Dances; Ballet Composite

2† Coppélia, Act II; Casse-Noisette, Act II; Les Sylphides

2 Polovetsian Dances; Giselle, Act II; Dance of Salomé; Giselle, Peasant pdd

7 LONDON, ON, Grand Theatre: Casse-Noisette, Act II; Dance of Salomé; Les Sylphides

8 Étude; Coppélia, Act II; Les Sylphides; Don Quixote, pdd; Polovetsian Dances

9 Coppélia, Act II; Polovetsian Dances; Giselle, Act II; Giselle, Peasant pdd

26 TORONTO, ON, Maple Leaf Gardens: (Tor. Police Assoc. 33rd Ann. Concert) Don Quixote, pdd; Polovetsian Dances

April 1952:

2 ST. CATHARINES, ON, Palace Theatre: Casse-Noisette, Act II; Les Sylphides; Coppélia, Act II

21 TORONTO, ON, Eaton Aud: L'Après-midi d'un Faune; Casse-Noisette, Act II; Étude; Ballet Behind Us — *repeated, April 22, 23*

24 HAMILTON, ON, Savoy Theatre: Les Sylphides; Coppélia, Act II; Casse-Noisette, Act II

October 1952:

27 CALGARY, AB, Grand Theatre: Coppélia; Polovetsian Dances

28† Les Sylphides; Casse-Noisette, Act II; Étude; L'Après-midi d'un Faune

28 Giselle; Ballet Behind Us

29† RED DEER, AB, Red Deer Memorial Centre: Étude; L'Après-midi d'un Faune; Coppélia, Act II; Casse-Noisette, Act II

29 Les Sylphides; Ballet Behind Us; Casse-Noisette, Act II

30 EDMONTON, AB, Victoria School Aud: Les Sylphides; Le Pommier; Casse-Noisette, Act II

31 Giselle; Ballet Behind Us

November 1952:

1† EDMONTON, AB, Victoria School Aud: Coppélia, Act II; Polovetsian Dances; Les Sylphides

1 Étude; L'Après-midi d'un Faune; Coppélia

3 VANCOUVER, BC, International Cinema: Les Sylphides; Le Pommier; Casse-Noisette, Act II

4 Ballet Behind Us; Giselle

5 Étude; L'Après-midi d'un Faune; Coppélia

6 VICTORIA, BC, Royal Theatre: Coppélia, Act II; Polovetsian Dances

7 Les Sylphides; Ballet Behind Us; Casse-Noisette, Act II

10 NELSON, BC, Civic Theatre: Les Sylphides; Coppélia, Act II; Casse-Noisette, Act II

13 LETHBRIDGE, AB, Capitol Theatre: Coppélia; Polovetsian Dances

14 Casse-Noisette, Act II; Ballet Behind Us; Les Sylphides

17 SASKATOON, SK, Capitol Theatre: Les Sylphides; Le Pommier; Casse-Noisette, Act II

19 REGINA, SK, Darke Hall: L'Après-midi d'un Faune; Étude; Ballet Behind Us; Casse-Noisette, Act II

21 WINNIPEG, MB, Playhouse Theatre: Coppélia; Casse-Noisette, Act II

22 Giselle; Le Pommier

24 FORT WILLIAM, ON, Vocational School Aud: Coppélia, Act II; Les Sylphides; Casse-Noisette, Act II

January 1953:

19 TORONTO, ON, Royal Alexandra Theatre: Les Sylphides; Coppélia

20 Giselle; Ballet Behind Us

21† Étude; L'Après-midi d'un Faune; Casse-Noisette, Act II; Polovetsian Dances

21 Coppélia; Le Pommier

22 Lilac Garden; Polovetsian Dances; Les Sylphides

23 L'Après-midi d'un Faune; Lilac Garden; Casse-Noisette, Act II; Étude

24† Ballet Composite; Coppélia

24 Giselle; Le Pommier

26 LONDON, ON, Grand Theatre: Coppélia; Les Sylphides

27 Giselle; Ballet Behind Us

28 Le Pommier; Casse-Noisette, Act II; Étude; L'Après-midi d'un Faune

29 Les Sylphides; Polovetsian Dances; Lilac Garden

30 Casse-Noisette, Act II; Étude; L'Après-midi d'un Faune; Lilac Garden

31† Coppélia; Ballet Composite

31 Giselle; Le Pommier

February 1953:

3 BRANTFORD, ON, Capitol Theatre: Casse-Noisette, Act II; Coppélia

4 HAMILTON, ON, Palace Theatre: Giselle; Le Pommier

9 MONTREAL, QC, Her Majesty's Theatre: Coppélia; Les Sylphides

10 Giselle; Ballet Behind Us

11† Casse-Noisette, Act II; Polovetsian Dances; L'Après-midi d'un Faune; Étude

11 Le Pommier; Coppélia

12 Polovetsian Dances; Les Sylphides; Lilac Garden

13 Lilac Garden; Casse-Noisette, Act II; L'Après-midi d'un Faune; Étude

14† Coppélia; Ballet Composite

14 Le Pommier; Giselle

16 FREDERICTON, NB, Devon School Aud: Les Sylphides; Coppélia, Act II; Casse-Noisette, Act II

17 SAINT JOHN, NB, Saint John H.S. Aud: Giselle, Peasant pdd; Casse-Noisette, Act II; Coppélia, Act II; Coppélia, Act I Dances

18 Étude; Les Sylphides; L'Après-midi d'un Faune; Casse-Noisette, Act II

20 SYDNEY, NS, St Andrew's Hall: Casse-Noisette, Act II; Les Sylphides; Coppélia, Act II

21 Coppélia, Act I, dances from; Casse-Noisette, Act II; Giselle, Act I, dances from; Étude

23 HALIFAX, NS, Capitol Theatre: Coppélia; Polovetsian Dances

24 Giselle; Casse-Noisette, Act II

25† Coppélia; Casse-Noisette, Act II

25 Le Pommier; Ballet Behind Us; Les Sylphides

26 SACKVILLE, NB, Charles Fawcett Memorial Hall: Coppélia, Act II; Casse-Noisette, Act II; Les Sylphides

March 1953:

2 QUEBEC CITY, QC, Palais Montcalm: Casse-Noisette, Act II; Coppélia

4 OTTAWA, ON, Capitol Theatre: Casse-Noisette, Act II; Giselle

10 ST. CATHARINES, ON, Palace Theatre: Polovetsian Dances; Le Pommier; L'Après-midi d'un Faune; Étude; Giselle, Peasant pdd

11 KITCHENER, ON, K-W Collegiate Aud: Polovetsian Dances; Coppélia

12 Casse-Noisette, Act II; Giselle

13 OAKVILLE, ON, Oakville-Trafalgar H.S. Aud: Coppélia; Casse-Noisette, Act II; Les Sylphides

August 1953:

4 BECKET, MA, Jacob's Pillow: Giselle, Peasant pdd; Don Quixote, pdd; Lilac Garden; Coppélia, Act II — *repeated, August 5*

6† Casse-Noisette, Act II; Lilac Garden; Don Quixote, pdd; L'Après-midi d'un Faune

6 Lilac Garden; Don Quixote, pdd; Giselle, Peasant pdd; Coppélia, Act II

7† Casse-Noisette, Act II; L'Après-midi d'un Faune; Don Quixote, pdd; Lilac Garden

7 Lilac Garden; Don Quixote, pdd; Giselle, Peasant pdd; Coppélia, Act II

8† L'Après-midi d'un Faune; Don Quixote, pdd; Lilac Garden; Casse-Noisette, Act II

8 Don Quixote, pdd; Coppélia, Act II; Giselle, Peasant pdd; Lilac Garden

November 1953:

16 PETERBOROUGH, ON, St Peter's H.S. Aud: Coppélia, Act II; Don Quixote, pdd; L'Après-midi d'un Faune; Les Sylphides; Giselle, Peasant pdd

17 Lilac Garden; Swan Lake, Act II; Casse-Noisette, Act II

18 OTTAWA, ON, Capitol Theatre: Gala Performance; Lilac Garden; Coppélia, Act II

20 QUEBEC CITY, QC, Palais Montcalm: Gala Performance; Casse-Noisette, Act II; Swan Lake, Act II

23 FREDERICTON, NB, H.S. Aud: L'Après-midi d'un Faune; Don Quixote, pdd; Swan Lake, Act II; Giselle, Peasant pdd; Coppélia, Act II

24‡ Les Sylphides; Coppélia, Act II; Casse-Noisette, Act II

24 Les Sylphides; Casse-Noisette, Act II; Dances from the Classics

25 SAINT JOHN, NB, Capitol Theatre: Giselle; Casse-Noisette, Act II

26† Les Sylphides; Dances from the Classics; Polovetsian Dances

26 Swan Lake, Act II; Coppélia

30 HALIFAX, NS, Capitol Theatre: Gala Performance; Polovetsian Dances; Les Sylphides

December 1953:

1 HALIFAX, NS, Capitol Theatre: Swan Lake, Act II; Dark of the Moon; Gala Performance

2† Les Sylphides; Coppélia

2 Casse-Noisette, Act II; Giselle

3 SACKVILLE, NB, Charles Fawcett Mem. Hall: Swan Lake, Act II; Dances from the Classics; Coppélia

4 Casse-Noisette-Act II; Les Sylphides; Don Quixote-pdd; L'Après-midi d'un Faune; Giselle, Peasant pdd

January 1954:

19 MONTREAL, QC, Her Majesty's Theatre: Casse-Noisette, Act II; Gala Performance; Lilac Garden

20† Casse-Noisette, Act II; Lilac Garden; Les Sylphides

20 Polovetsian Dances; Dark of the Moon; Swan Lake, Act II

21 Giselle; Gala Performance

22 Don Quixote, pdd; Casse-Noisette, Act II; Dances from the Classics; Lilac Garden

23† Dances from the Classics; Swan Lake, Act II; Polovetsian Dances

23 Gala Performance; Dark of the Moon; Swan Lake, Act II

25 TORONTO, ON, Royal Alexandra Theatre: Gala Performance; Lilac Garden; Casse-Noisette, Act II

26 Coppélia; Dark of the Moon

27† Coppélia; Les Sylphides

27 Giselle; Gala Performance

28 Dark of the Moon; Swan Lake, Act II; Polovetsian Dances

29 Polovetsian Dances; Giselle

30† Swan Lake, pas de trois; Don Quixote, pdd; Casse-Noisette, Act II; Swan Lake, Act II

30 Swan Lake, Act II; Gala Performance; Lilac Garden

February 1954:

1 LONDON, ON, Grand Theatre: Gala Performance; Lilac Garden; Casse-Noisette, Act II

2 Coppélia; Dark of the Moon

3† Les Sylphides; Coppélia

3 Gala Performance; Giselle

4 Polovetsian Dances; Swan Lake, Act II; Dark of the Moon

5 Giselle; Polovetsian Dances

6† Swan Lake, Act II; Swan Lake, pas de trois; Don

Quixote, pdd; Casse-Noisette, Act II

6   Dark of the Moon; Gala Performance; Swan Lake, Act II

8   BRANTFORD, ON, Capitol Theatre: Gala Performance; Les Sylphides; Polovetsian Dances

9   ST. CATHARINES, ON, Palace Theatre: Swan Lake, Act II; Don Quixote, pdd; Dances from the Classics; Gala Performance

10   HAMILTON, ON, Palace Theatre: Casse-Noisette, Act II; Swan Lake, Act II; Lilac Garden

11   Gala Performance; Les Sylphides; Dark of the Moon

12   BUFFALO, NY, Erlanger Theatre: Giselle; Gala Performance

13†   Les Sylphides; Coppélia

13   Casse-Noisette, Act II; Dances from the Classics; Lilac Garden; Swan Lake, Act II

14   DETROIT, MI, Cass Theatre: Les Sylphides; Coppélia

15   Casse-Noisette, Act II; Lilac Garden; Don Quixote, pdd; Polovetsian Dances

16   Giselle; Gala Performance

17   Casse-Noisette, Act II; Dark of the Moon; L'Après-midi d'un Faune; Giselle, Peasant pdd

18   Swan Lake, Act II; Dark of the Moon; Swan Lake, pas de trois; Polovetsian Dances

19   Swan Lake, Act II; Lilac Garden; Dances from the Classics; Gala Performance

20†   Les Sylphides; Coppélia

20   Casse-Noisette, Act II; Giselle

22   MILWAUKEE, WI, Davidson Theatre: Swan Lake, Act II; Coppélia

23   Les Sylphides; Lilac Garden; Casse-Noisette, Act II

25   MINNEAPOLIS, MN, Lyceum Theatre: Giselle; Gala Performance

26   Program unknown

27†   Les Sylphides; Coppélia

27   Program unknown

March 1954:

4   SEATTLE, WA, Metropolitan Theatre: Gala Performance; Giselle

5   Polovetsian Dances; Giselle, Peasant pdd; Dances from the Classics; Casse-Noisette, Act II

6†   Coppélia; Les Sylphides

6   Dark of the Moon; Swan Lake, Act II; Casse-Noisette, Act II

8   VANCOUVER, BC, International Cinema: Gala Performance; Dark of the Moon; Swan Lake, Act II

9   Giselle; Polovetsian Dances

10†   Les Sylphides; Coppélia

10   Lilac Garden; Swan Lake, Act II; Casse-Noisette, Act II

11   Dark of the Moon; Coppélia

12   Lilac Garden; Gala Performance; Les Sylphides

13†   Polovetsian Dances; Casse-Noisette, Act II; Dances from the Classics

13   Giselle; Dances from the Classics

15   VICTORIA, BC, Royal Theatre: Giselle; Casse-Noisette, Act II

16   Dark of the Moon; Gala Performance; Swan Lake, Act II

17   Gala Performance; Dances from the Classics; Lilac Garden; Don Quixote, pdd

22   NELSON, BC, Civic Theatre: Swan Lake, Act II; Giselle, Peasant pdd; Don Quixote, pdd; Casse-Noisette, Act II

23   Les Sylphides; Dances from the Classics; Coppélia, Act II

25   LETHBRIDGE, AB, Capitol Theatre: Swan Lake, Act II; Casse-Noisette, Act II; Don Quixote, pdd; Giselle, Peasant pdd

26   Les Sylphides; Dances from the Classics; Coppélia, Act II

29   CALGARY, AB, Grand Theatre: Don Quixote, pdd; Giselle, Peasant pdd; Gala Performance; Swan Lake, Act II

30   Dark of the Moon; Les Sylphides; Casse-Noisette, Act II

31   Swan Lake, Act II; Dances from the Classics; Gala Performance

April 1954:

1   EDMONTON, AB, Victoria School Aud: Polovetsian Dances; Swan Lake, Act II pas de trois; Gala Performance; Swan Lake, Act II

2   Dark of the Moon; Casse-Noisette, Act II; Don Quixote, pdd; Dances from the Classics

3†   Coppélia; Casse-Noisette, Act II

3   Gala Performance; Giselle

5   WINNIPEG, MB, Playhouse Theatre: Casse-Noisette, Act II; Dark of the Moon; Les Sylphides

6   Dances from the Classics; Don Quixote, pdd; Swan Lake, Act II; Gala Performance

19   TORONTO, ON, Royal Alexandra Theatre: Swan Lake, Act II; Dark of the Moon; Gala Performance

20   Les Sylphides; Dances from the Classics; Don Quixote, pdd; Gala Performance

21†   Swan Lake, Act II; Dances from the Classics; Casse-Noisette, Act II

21   Don Quixote, pdd; Gala Performance; Swan Lake, Act II; Lilac Garden

22   Giselle; Casse-Noisette, Act II

23   Dark of the Moon; Giselle, Peasant pdd; Polovetsian Dances; Dances from the Classics

24†   Giselle, Peasant pdd; Coppélia; Polovetsian Dances

24   Les Sylphides; Lilac Garden; Casse-Noisette, Act II

January 1955:

17   ST. CATHARINES, ON, Palace Theatre: Lilac Garden; Offenbach in the Underworld; Les Sylphides

18   HAMILTON, ON, Palace Theatre: Casse-Noisette, Act II; Offenbach in the Underworld; Barbara Allen

19   Swan Lake

20   BRANTFORD, ON, Capitol Theatre: Offenbach in the Underworld; Lilac Garden; Swan Lake, Act II

21   KITCHENER, ON, Memorial Aud: Swan Lake

24   LONDON, ON, Grand Theatre: Coppélia; Offenbach in the Underworld

25   Swan Lake

26† Casse-Noisette, Act II; Les Sylphides; Offenbach in the Underworld

26   Gala Performance; Barbara Allen; Les Sylphides

27   Swan Lake

28   Casse-Noisette, Act II; Lilac Garden; Offenbach in the Underworld

29† Swan Lake — repeated, January 29

31   TORONTO, ON, Royal Alexandra Theatre: Swan Lake

February 1955:

1   TORONTO, ON, Royal Alexandra Theatre: Coppélia; Offenbach in the Underworld

2† Coppélia; Les Sylphides

2   Les Sylphides; Barbara Allen; Gala Performance

3   Lilac Garden; Gala Performance; Offenbach in the Underworld

4   Swan Lake — repeated, February 5†

5   Offenbach in the Underworld; Casse-Noisette, Act II; Barbara Allen

7   Gala Performance; Giselle

8   Swan Lake — repeated, February 9†

9   Lilac Garden; Casse-Noisette, Act II; Offenbach in the Underworld

10   Barbara Allen; Gala Performance; Les Sylphides

11   Coppélia; Offenbach in the Underworld

12† Offenbach in the Underworld; Giselle

12   Swan Lake

14   CHICAGO, IL, Great Northern Theatre: Swan Lake

15   Offenbach in the Underworld; Lilac Garden; Casse-Noisette, Act II

16† Gala Performance; Coppélia

16   Giselle; Gala Performance

17   Swan Lake

18   Les Sylphides; Barbara Allen; Offenbach in the Underworld

19† Swan Lake — repeated, February 19

21   DETROIT, MI, Shubert Theatre: Swan Lake

22† Coppélia; Offenbach in the Underworld

22   Casse-Noisette, Act II; Offenbach in the Underworld; Barbara Allen

23   Les Sylphides; Lilac Garden; Offenbach in the Underworld

24   Gala Performance; Giselle

25   Swan Lake — repeated, February 26†

26   Swan Lake, Act II; Offenbach in the Underworld; Lilac Garden

28   MONTREAL, QC, Her Majesty's Theatre: Swan Lake

March 1955:

1   MONTREAL, QC, Her Majesty's Theatre: Gala Performance; Lilac Garden; Offenbach in the Underworld

2† Les Sylphides; Casse-Noisette, Act II; Offenbach in the Underworld

2   Offenbach in the Underworld; Giselle

3   Coppélia; Gala Performance

4   Les Sylphides; Casse-Noisette, Act II; Barbara Allen

5† Swan Lake — repeated, March 5

7   OTTAWA, ON, Capitol Theatre: Swan Lake, Act II; Barbara Allen; Offenbach in the Underworld

8   KINGSTON, ON, Kingston Community Memorial Centre: Offenbach in the Underworld; Casse-Noisette, Act II; Les Sylphides

25   BROOKLYN, NY, Brooklyn Academy of Music: Swan Lake

26   Lilac Garden; Offenbach in the Underworld; Barbara Allen

June 1955:

9   WASHINGTON, DC, Carter Barron Amphitheatre: Offenbach in the Underworld; Sleeping Princess, pas de trois; Lilac Garden; Gala Performance

10   Casse-Noisette; L'Après-midi d'un Faune; Coppélia

12   Sleeping Beauty, Bluebird pdd; Offenbach in the Underworld; Giselle

13   Lady from the Sea; Giselle, Peasant pdd; Les Sylphides; Offenbach in the Underworld

14   Swan Lake

15   Offenbach in the Underworld; Barbara Allen; Lady from the Sea; Sleeping Beauty, Bluebird pdd

16   Coppélia; Barbara Allen; Gala Performance

17   Swan Lake

18   Sleeping Princess, pas de trois; Lilac Garden; Les Sylphides; Offenbach in the Underworld

November 1955:

14   BELLEVILLE, ON, Belleville Collegiate Inst.: Les Sylphides; Lilac Garden; Offenbach in the Underworld

15   KINGSTON, ON, Kingston Community Memorial Centre: Swan Lake, Act II; Dances from the Classics; Dark Elegies

17   OTTAWA, ON, Capitol Theatre: Swan Lake

19† QUEBEC CITY, QC, Capitol Theatre: Nutcracker

19   Offenbach in the Underworld; Dark Elegies; Swan Lake, Act II

21   MONTREAL, QC, Her Majesty's Theatre: Nutcracker

22   Gala Performance; Dark Elegies; Offenbach in the Underworld

23† Gala Performance; Dark Elegies; L'Après-midi d'un Faune; Sleeping Princess, pas de trois

23 Lady from the Sea; Offenbach in the Underworld; Les Sylphides

24 Swan Lake

25 Coppélia; Lady from the Sea

26† Nutcracker

26 Swan Lake

28 BRANTFORD, ON, Capitol Theatre: Offenbach in the Underworld; Lady from the Sea; Nutcracker, Snow Scene

29 HAMILTON, ON, Palace Theatre: Nutcracker

30 Dark Elegies; Offenbach in the Underworld; Lady from the Sea

December 1955:

1 KITCHENER, ON, Memorial Aud: Nutcracker

2 ST. CATHARINES, ON, Palace Theatre: Swan Lake, Act II; Lady from the Sea; Offenbach in the Underworld

January 1956:

1† TORONTO, ON, Shea's Theatre: Nutcracker

16 TORONTO, ON, Royal Alexandra Theatre: Nutcracker

17 Offenbach in the Underworld; Dark Elegies; Gala Performance

18† Offenbach in the Underworld; Lady from the Sea; Nutcracker, Snow Scene

18 Nutcracker

19 Coppélia; Les Sylphides

20 Dark Elegies; Offenbach in the Underworld; Lady from the Sea

21† Swan Lake

21 Nutcracker

23 Coppélia; Lady from the Sea

24 Pas de Deux (Franca); L'Après-midi d'un Faune; Lilac Garden; Offenbach in the Underworld; Sleeping Princess, pas de trois

25† Nutcracker

25 Swan Lake

26 Les Sylphides; Offenbach in the Underworld; Dark Elegies

27 Gala Performance; Lilac Garden; Offenbach in the Underworld

28† Nutcracker

28 Swan Lake

30 LONDON, ON, Grand Theatre: Nutcracker

31 Les Sylphides; Dark Elegies; Offenbach in the Underworld

February 1956:

1† LONDON, ON, Grand Theatre: Nutcracker, Snow Scene; Lady from the Sea; Gala Performance

1 Coppélia; Dark Elegies

2 Swan Lake

3 Lady from the Sea; Lilac Garden; Offenbach in the Underworld

4† Nutcracker

4 Swan Lake

10 ROCHESTER, NY, Eastman Theatre: Nutcracker

11 BUFFALO, NY, Erlanger Theatre: Swan Lake

12† Nutcracker

12 Offenbach in the Underworld; Les Sylphides; Lilac Garden

13† Coppélia; Offenbach in the Underworld

13 Gala Performance; Lady from the Sea; Swan Lake, Act II

14 Sleeping Princess, pas de trois; Dark Elegies; Gala Performance; L'Après-midi d'un Faune

15† Les Sylphides; Lady from the Sea; Offenbach in the Underworld

15 Nutcracker

17 BROOKLYN, NY, Brooklyn Academy of Music: Offenbach in the Underworld; Les Sylphides; Dark Elegies

18† Nutcracker

18 Swan Lake, Act II; Coppélia

20 NEWARK, NJ, Mosque Theatre: Swan Lake, Act II; Lady from the Sea; Offenbach in the Underworld

21 PHILADELPHIA, PA, Academy of Music: Dark Elegies; Offenbach in the Underworld; Les Sylphides

22 Coppélia, Act II; Gala Performance; Lilac Garden

24 BALTIMORE, MD, Lyric Theater: Swan Lake

25† Nutcracker

25 Offenbach in the Underworld; Gala Performance; Dark Elegies

27 HUNTINGTON, WV, Keith Albee Theatre: Coppélia; Offenbach in the Underworld

28 KNOXVILLE, TN, U of Tennesee Aud: Les Sylphides; Coppélia

29 GREENSBORO, NC, Aycock Aud: Les Sylphides; Lady from the Sea; Offenbach in the Underworld

March 1956:

1 COLUMBIA, SC, Columbia Township Aud: Offenbach in the Underworld; Coppélia

2 SAVANNAH, GA, Municipal Aud: Offenbach in the Underworld; Nutcracker, Act IV; Gala Performance

3 DAYTONA BEACH, FL, Peabody Aud: Offenbach in the Underworld; Nutcracker, Act IV; Gala Performance

5 MONTGOMERY, AL, Lanier Aud: Offenbach in the Underworld; Gala Performance; Nutcracker, Act IV

6 BIRMINGHAM, AL, Municipal Aud: Gala Performance; Dark Elegies; Offenbach in the Underworld

7 NASHVILLE, TN, Ryman Aud: Les Sylphides; Offenbach in the Underworld; Dark Elegies

Appendix A

8   Nutcracker

10† ATLANTA, GA, Tower Theatre: Nutcracker

10   Offenbach in the Underworld; Dark Elegies; Gala
     Performance

August 1956:

2   WASHINGTON, DC, Carter Barron Amphitheatre:
     Les Sylphides; Offenbach in the Underworld; Dark
     Elegies; Jeune Pas de Deux

3   Swan Lake

4   Nutcracker

5   Pas de Trois; Gala Performance; Coppélia

6   Swan Lake

7   Nutcracker

8   Offenbach in the Underworld; Les Sylphides; Jeune
     Pas de Deux; Lilac Garden

9   Nutcracker

10   Coppélia; Offenbach in the Underworld; Pas de Trois

11   Swan Lake

12   Nutcracker

13   Pas de Trois; Offenbach in the Underworld; Coppélia

14   Swan Lake

15   Nutcracker

November 1956:

5   HAMILTON, ON, Odeon Palace Theatre: Les
     Rendez-vous; Fisherman and His Soul; Post Script

6†   Nutcracker, Act IV; La Llamada; Post Script

6   Pas de Chance; Jeune Pas de Deux; Giselle; L'Après-
     midi d'un Faune

7   ST. CATHARINES, ON, Palace Theatre: Les Rendez-
     vous; Nutcracker, Act III; Jeune Pas de Deux; L'Après-
     midi d'un Faune; Pas de Chance

8   Post Script; La Llamada; Nutcracker, Act IV

9   KITCHENER, ON, Kitchener Memorial Aud:
     Giselle; Gala Performance

10   BELLEVILLE, ON, Belleville Collegiate Inst.: Les
     Rendez-vous; Nutcracker, Act IV; Post Script

13   OTTAWA, ON, Capitol Theatre: Fisherman and His
     Soul; Les Rendez-vous; Offenbach in the Underworld

14   La Llamada; Giselle

15   SHERBROOKE, QC, Theatre Granada: Les
     Sylphides; Pas de Chance; Jeune Pas de Deux; Post
     Script; L'Après-midi d'un Faune

17† QUEBEC CITY, QC, Capitol Theatre: Coppélia;
     Nutcracker, Act III

17   Swan Lake

19   MONTREAL, QC, Her Majesty's Theatre: Giselle; La
     Llamada

20   Post Script; Dark Elegies; Les Rendez-vous

21† Nutcracker

21   Fisherman and His Soul; Offenbach in the
     Underworld; Les Rendez-vous

22   Giselle; Offenbach in the Underworld

23   Gala Performance; Lilac Garden; Les Sylphides

24† Nutcracker

24   Post Script; Coppélia

26   Swan Lake

27   L'Après-midi d'un Faune; Pas de Chance; Fisherman
     and His Soul; La Llamada; Jeune Pas de Deux

28† Swan Lake

28   Coppélia; Fisherman and His Soul

29   Nutcracker

30   Giselle; Post Script

December 1956:

1†   MONTREAL, QC, Her Majesty's Theatre:
     Nutcracker, Act IV; L'Après-midi d'un Faune; Jeune
     Pas de Deux; Les Sylphides; Pas de Chance

1   Offenbach in the Underworld; Les Rendez-vous;
     Lilac Garden

January 1957:

7   TORONTO, ON, Royal Alexandra Theatre: Les
     Rendez-vous; Dark Elegies; Post Script

8   Les Sylphides; Fisherman and His Soul; Offenbach in
     the Underworld

9†   Nutcracker

9   La Llamada; Giselle

10   Pas de Chance; Lilac Garden; Post Script; Les
     Sylphides

11   Les Rendez-vous; Fisherman and His Soul; Gala
     Performance

12† Nutcracker

12   Giselle; Post Script

14   Swan Lake

15   Nutcracker

16† Swan Lake

16   Jeune Pas de Deux; Fisherman and His Soul; Post
     Script; Pas de Chance; L'Après-midi d'un Faune

17   Offenbach in the Underworld; Dark Elegies; Les
     Rendez-vous

18   Offenbach in the Underworld; La Llamada; Les
     Rendez-vous

19† Jeune Pas de Deux; Giselle; L'Après-midi d'un Faune;
     Pas de Chance

19   Post Script; Fisherman and His Soul; La Llamada

21   Jeune Pas de Deux; Offenbach in the Underworld;
     Lilac Garden; L'Après-midi d'un Faune; Pas de Chance

22   Les Rendez-vous; Post Script; Offenbach in the
     Underworld

23† Nutcracker — *repeated, January 23*

24† Les Rendez-vous; Nutcracker, Act III; Post Script

24   Les Rendez-vous; Fisherman and His Soul; Post Script

25   Offenbach in the Underworld; La Llamada; Dark
     Elegies

26† Post Script; Coppélia

26   Swan Lake

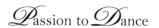

28 LONDON, ON, Grand Theatre: Les Rendez-vous; Fisherman and His Soul; Post Script

29 La Llamada; Giselle

30† Pas de Chance; Les Rendez-vous; Jeune Pas de Deux; Post Script; L'Après-midi d'un Faune

30 La Llamada; Les Rendez-vous; Offenbach in the Underworld

31 Swan Lake

February 1957:

1 LONDON, ON, Grand Theatre: Jeune Pas de Deux; Giselle; L'Après-midi d'un Faune; Pas de Chance

2† Swan Lake

2 Les Sylphides; Fisherman and His Soul; Post Script

3 WINDSOR, ON, Capitol Theatre: Post Script; Les Sylphides; Nutcracker, Act IV

6 SIOUX FALLS, SD, Sioux Falls Coliseum: Fisherman and His Soul; Les Rendez-vous; Offenbach in the Underworld

7 ALBERT LEA, MN, Albert Lea H.S. Aud: Les Sylphides; L'Après-midi d'un Faune; Pas de Chance; Post Script; Jeune Pas de Deux

8 MINNEAPOLIS, MN, Northrop Memorial Aud: Offenbach in the Underworld; Fisherman and His Soul; Les Rendez-vous

9† Nutcracker, Act IV; Coppélia

9 Post Script; Pas de Chance; L'Après-midi d'un Faune; Jeune Pas de Deux; Les Sylphides

12 EAST LANSING, MI, Michigan State U Aud: Les Sylphides; Fisherman and His Soul; Offenbach in the Underworld

13 Post Script; Les Rendez-vous; Nutcracker, Act IV

15 LAWRENCE, KS, Hoch Aud: Coppélia; Nutcracker, Act IV

16† KANSAS CITY, MO, Civic Music Hall: Swan Lake

17 OKLAHOMA CITY, OK, Civic Aud: Fisherman and His Soul; Les Rendez-vous; Offenbach in the Underworld

19 WACO, TX, Baylor Univ., Waco Hall: Fisherman and His Soul; Swan Lake, Act II; Offenbach in the Underworld

20 FORT WORTH, TX, Will Rogers Memorial Aud: Les Sylphides; Post Script; Nutcracker, Act IV

21 AUSTIN, TX, U of Texas, Gregory Gymnasium: Les Rendez-vous; Offenbach in the Underworld; Nutcracker, Act IV

22 DALLAS, TX, State Fair Music Hall: Offenbach in the Underworld; Fisherman and His Soul; Les Rendez-vous

23 Swan Lake

25 BATON ROUGE, LA, Southern U Aud-Gymnasium: Les Sylphides; Jeune Pas de Deux; L'Après-midi d'un Faune; Pas de Chance; Offenbach in the Underworld

26 GALVESTON, TX, Municipal Aud: Fisherman and His Soul; Offenbach in the Underworld; Les Rendez-vous

27 SHREVEPORT, LA, Municipal Aud: Offenbach in the Underworld; Les Rendez-vous; Pas de Chance; Jeune Pas de Deux; L'Après-midi d'un Faune

28 OXFORD, MS, U of Miss., Fulton Chapel: Les Rendez-vous; Pas de Chance; Offenbach in the Underworld; Jeune Pas de Deux; L'Après-midi d'un Faune

March 1957:

1 COLUMBUS, MS, Whitfield Hall: Post Script; Nutcracker, Act IV; Les Rendez-vous

4 TAMPA, FL, Municipal Aud: Nutcracker, Act IV; Les Rendez-vous; Post Script

5 TALLAHASSEE, FL, Westcott Aud: Offenbach in the Underworld; Fisherman and His Soul; Les Rendez-vous

6 Nutcracker, Act IV; Post Script; Les Sylphides

7 ORLANDO, FL, Municipal Aud: Post Script; Fisherman and His Soul; Les Rendez-vous

8 MIAMI, FL, Dade County Aud: Offenbach in the Underworld; Fisherman and His Soul; Les Rendez-vous

9† Coppélia; Post Script

9 Swan Lake

10† FORT LAUDERDALE, FL, War Memorial Aud: Post Script; Les Rendez-vous; Nutcracker, Act IV

12 ATLANTA, GA, Atlanta Municipal Aud: Swan Lake

13 SAVANNAH, GA, Civic Aud: Post Script; Coppélia

14 MACON, GA, Porter Family Aud: Les Rendez-vous; Les Sylphides; Post Script

19 PITTSBURGH, PA, Mount Lebanon Aud: Coppélia; Offenbach in the Underworld

20 ANN ARBOR, MI, A.W.S. Butterfield Theatre: Les Rendez-vous; Offenbach in the Underworld; Post Script

21 INDIANAPOLIS, IN, Murat Theatre: Post Script; Giselle

22 LAFAYETTE, IN, Purdue Hall of Music: Fisherman and His Soul; Offenbach in the Underworld; Les Rendez-vous

23 Coppélia; Post Script

24 LOUISVILLE, KY, Memorial Aud: Swan Lake

25 CORNING, NY, Corning Glass Center: Les Sylphides; Post Script; Pas de Chance; Jeune Pas de Deux; L'Après-midi d'un Faune

27 BINGHAMTON, NY, Capitol Theatre: Nutcracker, Act IV; Les Sylphides; Offenbach in the Underworld

29 BURLINGTON, VT, Memorial Aud: Nutcracker, Act IV; Les Sylphides; Offenbach in the Underworld

30† BROOKLYN, NY, Brooklyn Academy of Music: Fisherman and His Soul; Post Script; Les Rendez-vous

30 Casse-Noisette, Act IV pdd; L'Après-midi d'un Faune; Pas de Chance; Giselle

Appendix A

April 1957:

1 NEWARK, NJ, Mosque Theatre: Offenbach in the Underworld; Fisherman and His Soul; Les Rendez-vous

29 BARRIE, ON, Barrie Arena: Les Sylphides; Offenbach in the Underworld; Post Script

30 HUNTSVILLE, ON, Memorial Arena: Les Sylphides; Offenbach in the Underworld; Post Script

May 1957:

1 SUDBURY, ON, Sudbury Community Arena: Offenbach in the Underworld; Les Sylphides; Post Script

2 SAULT STE. MARIE, ON, Sault Ste Marie Memorial Gardens: Les Sylphides; Post Script; Offenbach in the Underworld

4 HAILEYBURY, ON, Armouries: Post Script; Offenbach in the Underworld; Les Sylphides

6 NORANDA, QC, Noranda Recreation Centre: Offenbach in the Underworld; Post Script; Les Sylphides

7 TIMMINS, ON, McIntyre Arena: Post Script; Les Sylphides; Offenbach in the Underworld

8 KAPUSKASING, ON, Kapuskasing Community Club: Post Script; Les Sylphides; Offenbach in the Underworld

10 CAMP PETAWAWA, ON, Drill Hall # 1: Les Sylphides; Post Script; Offenbach in the Underworld

11 KINGSTON, ON, Kingston Community Memorial Centre: Offenbach in the Underworld; Les Sylphides; Post Script

12 PETERBOROUGH, ON, Peterborough Memorial Centre: Les Sylphides; Offenbach in the Underworld; Post Script

July 1957:

23 BECKET, MA, Jacob's Pillow: Les Rendez-vous; Dances from The Sleeping Beauty; Dark Elegies — *repeated, July 24, 25†, 26†, 26, 27†, 27*

November 1957:

4 HAMILTON, ON, Odeon Palace Theatre: Le Carnaval; Winter Night; Offenbach in the Underworld

5† Le Carnaval; Swan Lake, Act II; Pas de Chance; Willow; La Farruca

5 Swan Lake

6 ST. CATHARINES, ON, Palace Theatre: Winter Night; Le Carnaval; Swan Lake, Act II

7 Dances from The Sleeping Beauty; La Farruca; Willow; Pas de Chance; Offenbach in the Underworld

8 KITCHENER, ON, Kitchener Memorial Aud: Offenbach in the Underworld; Les Rendez-vous; Winter Night

9† BELLEVILLE, ON, Belleville Collegiate Aud: La Farruca; Dances from The Sleeping Beauty; Swan Lake, Act II; Pas de Chance; Willow

9 Le Carnaval; Winter Night; Offenbach in the Underworld

12 OTTAWA, ON, Capitol Theatre: Swan Lake

13† Nutcracker, Acts II & IV; Willow; La Farruca; Pas de Chance

13 Winter Night; Le Carnaval; Nutcracker, Act III

14 SHERBROOKE, QC, Theatre Granada: Willow; Dances from The Sleeping Beauty; Offenbach in the Underworld, pdd; La Farruca; Nutcracker, Act III; Pas de Chance

16† QUEBEC CITY, QC, Capitol Theatre: Dances from The Sleeping Beauty; Winter Night; Le Carnaval — *repeated, November 16*

18 MONTREAL, QC, Her Majesty's Theatre: Swan Lake

19 Nutcracker

20‡ Coppélia

20 Winter Night; Le Carnaval; Dances from The Sleeping Beauty

21 Giselle; Offenbach in the Underworld

22 Swan Lake

23† Coppélia; Offenbach in the Underworld

23 Swan Lake

25 Nutcracker

26 Le Carnaval; Giselle

27† Dances from The Sleeping Beauty; Winter Night; Offenbach in the Underworld

27 Coppélia; Le Carnaval

28 Swan Lake

29 Pas de Chance; Giselle; Willow; La Farruca

30† Nutcracker

30 Le Carnaval; Winter Night; Offenbach in the Underworld

January 1958:

6 TORONTO, ON, Royal Alexandra Theatre: Swan Lake

7 Offenbach in the Underworld; Les Sylphides; Winter Night

8† Nutcracker

8 Giselle; Offenbach in the Underworld

9 Les Sylphides; Winter Night; Offenbach in the Underworld

10 Nutcracker

11† Swan Lake

11 Le Carnaval; Winter Night; Les Rendez-vous

13 Offenbach in the Underworld; Le Carnaval; Lilac Garden

14 Offenbach in the Underworld; Nutcracker, Act IV; Les Sylphides

15† Les Sylphides; Coppélia

15 Le Carnaval; Winter Night; Gala Performance

16 Swan Lake

17 Nutcracker

18† Gala Performance; Giselle

18 Offenbach in the Underworld; Fisherman and His Soul; Les Rendez-vous

20 Swan Lake

21‡ Les Sylphides; Coppélia, Act II

21 Nutcracker

22‡ Dances from The Sleeping Beauty; Willow; Pas de Chance; Offenbach in the Underworld; Nutcracker, dance from

22 Swan Lake, Act II; Lilac Garden; Le Carnaval

23 Nutcracker

24 Swan Lake

25† Les Sylphides; Nutcracker, Act III; Le Carnaval

25 Giselle; Le Carnaval

27 Nutcracker

28‡ Swan Lake, Act II; Offenbach in the Underworld

28 Swan Lake

29† Nutcracker

29 Les Rendez-vous; Winter Night; Le Carnaval

30 Offenbach in the Underworld; Le Carnaval; Fisherman and His Soul

31 Nutcracker, dance from; Pas de Chance; Willow; Giselle

February 1958:

1† TORONTO, ON, Royal Alexandra Theatre: Nutcracker

1 Swan Lake

3 LONDON, ON, Grand Theatre: Swan Lake

4 Nutcracker

5† Dances from The Sleeping Beauty; Coppélia

5 Pas de Chance; Nutcracker, dance from; Willow; Giselle

6 Swan Lake

7 Offenbach in the Underworld; Le Carnaval; Dances from The Sleeping Beauty

8† Nutcracker

8 Le Carnaval; Winter Night; Offenbach in the Underworld

9† WINDSOR, ON, Capitol Theatre: Swan Lake, Act II; Pas de Chance; Willow; La Farruca; Le Carnaval

9 Winter Night; Offenbach in the Underworld; Dances from The Sleeping Beauty

10 ANN ARBOR, MI, A.W.S. Butterfield Theatre: Dances from The Sleeping Beauty; Winter Night; Le Carnaval

11 WARREN, OH, Packard Music Hall: Offenbach in the Underworld; Dances from The Sleeping Beauty; Winter Night

12 BINGHAMTON, NY, Capitol Theatre: Le Carnaval; Pas de Chance; Swan Lake, Act II; Nutcracker, dances from; Offenbach in the Underworld, pdd

13 HARTFORD, CT, Bushnell Hall: Swan Lake, Act II; Winter Night; Le Carnaval

14 COLLEGE PARK, MD, Cole Activities Centre: Swan Lake, Act II; Nutcracker, dances from; Offenbach in the Underworld; Pas de Chance

16 PITTSBURGH, PA, Syria Mosque: Giselle; Le Carnaval

19 RALEIGH, NC, Memorial Aud: Winter Night; Offenbach in the Underworld; Le Carnaval

20 SAVANNAH, GA, City Aud: Swan Lake

21 AUGUSTA, GA, Bell Memorial Aud: Winter Night; Offenbach in the Underworld; Le Carnaval

22† ATLANTA, GA, Tower Theatre: Swan Lake, Act II; Nutcracker, dances from; Pas de Chance; Dances from The Sleeping Beauty

22 Offenbach in the Underworld; Winter Night; Le Carnaval

24 EAST LANSING, MI, Michigan State U Aud: Swan Lake

25 Le Carnaval; Winter Night; Offenbach in the Underworld

26 LAFAYETTE, IN, Elliot Hall of Music: Swan Lake

27 Le Carnaval; Winter Night; Offenbach in the Underworld

28 INDIANAPOLIS, IN, Murat Theatre: Offenbach in the Underworld; Le Carnaval; Winter Night

March 1958:

1† LOUISVILLE, KY, Memorial Aud: Offenbach in the Underworld; Le Carnaval; Winter Night

1 Swan Lake

2 MILWAUKEE, WI, Oriental Theatre: Swan Lake, Act II; Nutcracker, dances from; Dances from The Sleeping Beauty; Swan Lake, Act III Czardas; Pas de Chance; Offenbach in the Underworld, pdd

3 BLOOMINGTON, IN, Indiana U Aud: Le Carnaval; Winter Night; Offenbach in the Underworld

4 ST. LOUIS, MO, Kiel Opera House: Swan Lake, Act II; Winter Night; Le Carnaval

5 DAVENPORT, IA, Orpheum Theatre: Winter Night; Offenbach in the Underworld; Le Carnaval

6 DES MOINES, IA, K.R.N.T. Theatre: Le Carnaval; Winter Night; Offenbach in the Underworld

7 KANSAS CITY, MO, Music Hall: Giselle; Dances from The Sleeping Beauty

8† Le Carnaval; Winter Night; Nutcracker, Act IV

8 Swan Lake

9 OKLAHOMA CITY, OK, Municipal Aud: Le Carnaval; Winter Night; Offenbach in the Underworld

10 FORT WORTH, TX, Will Rogers Memorial Aud: Dances from The Sleeping Beauty; Nutcracker, dances from; Le Carnaval; Pas de Chance; Offenbach in the Underworld, pdd

11† RUSTON, LA, Howard Aud: Dances from The Sleeping Beauty; Nutcracker, dances from; Le Carnaval; Pas de Chance

11 Swan Lake, Act II; Winter Night; Offenbach in the Underworld

12 COLLEGE STATION, TX, G. Rollie White Coliseum: Le Carnaval; Winter Night; Offenbach in the Underworld

13 HARLINGEN, TX, Municipal Aud: Offenbach in the Underworld; Le Carnaval; Winter Night

14 CORPUS CHRISTI, TX, Del Mar Aud: Offenbach in the Underworld; Winter Night; Le Carnaval

15 LAREDO, TX, Martin H.S. Aud: Le Carnaval; Winter Night; Offenbach in the Underworld

17 SAN ANGELO, TX, Municipal Aud: Dances from The Sleeping Beauty; Winter Night; Offenbach in the Underworld

18 Swan Lake, Act II; Nutcracker, dances from; Le Carnaval; Pas de Chance

19 MIDLAND, TX, H.S. Aud: Le Carnaval; Winter Night; Offenbach in the Underworld

20 EL PASO, TX, Liberty Hall: Winter Night; Offenbach in the Underworld; Swan Lake, Act II

22 DENVER, CO, Denver Aud: Swan Lake

24 LOGAN, UT, Utah State U, Field House: Swan Lake, Act II; Nutcracker, dances from; Offenbach in the Underworld; Pas de Chance

25 SALT LAKE CITY, UT, Capitol Theatre: Swan Lake — *repeated, March 26†*

26 Le Carnaval; Winter Night; Offenbach in the Underworld

28 TUCSON, AZ, U of Arizona Aud: Le Carnaval; Winter Night; Offenbach in the Underworld

29† PHOENIX, AZ, West Phoenix H.S. Aud: Swan Lake, Act II; Nutcracker, dances from; Dances from The Sleeping Beauty

29 Winter Night; Offenbach in the Underworld; Le Carnaval

31 LOS ANGELES, CA, Philharmonic Aud: Swan Lake

April 1958:

1 SAN BERNARDINO, CA, California Theater of Performing Arts: Swan Lake, Act II; Le Carnaval; Offenbach in the Underworld

2 LONG BEACH, CA, Wilson H.S. Aud: Winter Night; Offenbach in the Underworld; Le Carnaval

3 PASADENA, CA, City Of Pasadena Aud: Winter Night; Offenbach in the Underworld; Le Carnaval

4 SAN DIEGO, CA, Russ Aud: Swan Lake, Act II; Le Carnaval; Offenbach in the Underworld

5† LOS ANGELES, CA, Philharmonic Aud: Swan Lake

5 Winter Night; Offenbach in the Underworld; Le Carnaval

7 BAKERSFIELD, CA, Harvey Aud: Le Carnaval; Winter Night; Offenbach in the Underworld

8 SANTA CRUZ, CA, Civic Aud: Swan Lake, Act II; Nutcracker, dances from; Offenbach in the Underworld; Pas de Chance

9 RICHMOND, CA, Memorial Aud: Swan Lake, Act II; Nutcracker, dances from; Offenbach in the Underworld; Pas de Chance

10 SAN JOSE, CA, Civic Aud: Swan Lake, Act II; Le Carnaval; Offenbach in the Underworld

11 SAN FRANCISCO, CA, War Memorial Opera House: Le Carnaval; Winter Night; Offenbach in the Underworld

12 Swan Lake

13† VISALIA, CA, Montgomery Aud: Swan Lake, Act II; Nutcracker, dances from; Offenbach in the Underworld

14 FRESNO, CA, Roosevelt H.S. Aud: Le Carnaval; Winter Night; Offenbach in the Underworld

15 SACRAMENTO, CA, Sacramento Memorial Aud: Le Carnaval; Nutcracker, dances from; Offenbach in the Underworld; La Farruca; Sleeping Princess, Aurora pdd

17 EUGENE, OR, U of Oregon, McArthur Court: Le Carnaval; Nutcracker, dances from; Offenbach in the Underworld; La Farruca; Pas de Chance

18 CORVALLIS, OR, Gill Coliseum: Swan Lake, Act II; Nutcracker, dances from; Offenbach in the Underworld; Pas de Chance

19 SEATTLE, WA, Moore Theatre: Winter Night; Offenbach in the Underworld; Dances from The Sleeping Beauty

21 WALLA WALLA, WA, Walla Walla H.S. Aud: Swan Lake, Act II; Offenbach in the Underworld

22 Le Carnaval; Nutcracker, dances from; Offenbach in the Underworld; La Farruca; Pas de Chance

25 VICTORIA, BC, Royal Theatre: Swan Lake

26† Le Carnaval; Dances from The Sleeping Beauty; Offenbach in the Underworld

26 Le Carnaval; Winter Night; Offenbach in the Underworld

28 VANCOUVER, BC, Orpheum Theatre: Le Carnaval; Offenbach in the Underworld; Winter Night

30† PENTICTON, BC, H.S. Aud: Nutcracker, dances from; Le Carnaval; Pas de Chance; Dances from The Sleeping Beauty; La Farruca

30 Swan Lake, Act II; Offenbach in the Underworld; Winter Night

May 1958:

1 TRAIL, BC, Cominco Arena: Winter Night; Offenbach in the Underworld; Swan Lake, Act II

3† LETHBRIDGE, AB, Capitol Theatre: Nutcracker, dances from; Le Carnaval; Dances from The Sleeping Beauty; Pas de Chance; La Farruca

3 Swan Lake, Act II; Winter Night; Offenbach in the Underworld

5 CALGARY, AB, Jubilee Aud: Swan Lake

6 Winter Night; Offenbach in the Underworld; Le Carnaval

7   EDMONTON, AB, Jubilee Aud: Swan Lake
8   Le Carnaval; Winter Night; Offenbach in the Underworld
10†   SASKATOON, SK, Capitol Theatre: Le Carnaval; Nutcracker, dances from; Dances from The Sleeping Beauty; Pas de Chance; La Farruca
10   Offenbach in the Underworld; Swan Lake, Act II; Winter Night
12†   REGINA, SK, Capitol Theatre: Dances from The Sleeping Beauty; Pas de Chance; Nutcracker, dances from; Le Carnaval; La Farruca
12   Swan Lake, Act II; Winter Night; Offenbach in the Underworld
14   WINNIPEG, MB, Playhouse Theatre: Winter Night; Offenbach in the Underworld; Le Carnaval
15   Swan Lake
17†   FORT WILLIAM, ON, Fort William Gardens: Pas de Chance; Dances from The Sleeping Beauty; Nutcracker, dances from; La Farruca; Le Carnaval
17   Offenbach in the Underworld; Swan Lake, Act II; Winter Night
19   SAULT STE. MARIE, ON, Sault Ste Marie Memorial Gardens: Le Carnaval; Swan Lake, Act II; Winter Night
20   SUDBURY, ON, Sudbury Arena: Swan Lake, Act II; Winter Night; Le Carnaval
31   MEXICO CITY, MEXICO, Palacio de Bellas Artes: Swan Lake

June 1958:

1   MEXICO CITY, MEXICO, Palacio de Bellas Artes: Les Rendez-vous; L'Après-midi d'un Faune; Dark Elegies; Offenbach in the Underworld
2   Offenbach in the Underworld; Dark Elegies; Les Rendez-vous
3   L'Après-midi d'un Faune; Dark Elegies; Offenbach in the Underworld; Les Rendez-vous
4   Sleeping Princess, Aurora pdd; Giselle; La Farruca; Pas de Chance
5   Swan Lake
7†   Gala Performance; Les Sylphides; Winter Night
7   Swan Lake
8†   Les Sylphides; Winter Night; Gala Performance — *repeated, June 8*
9   Offenbach in the Underworld; L'Après-midi d'un Faune; Les Sylphides; Pas de Chance; La Farruca
10   Winter Night; Les Sylphides; Gala Performance
11   Nutcracker — *repeated, June 12*
13   Coppélia; Nutcracker, Act III
14†   Le Carnaval; Les Sylphides; Fisherman and His Soul
15†   Le Carnaval; Fisherman and His Soul; Offenbach in the Underworld
15   Giselle; Le Carnaval
16   Les Rendez-vous; Coppélia
17   Le Carnaval; Giselle

18   Lilac Garden; Sleeping Princess, Aurora pdd; Offenbach in the Underworld; Les Rendez-vous
19   MEXICO CITY, MEXICO, Auditorio Nacional: Swan Lake — *repeated, June 20*
21†   Nutcracker, Acts III & IV; Les Rendez-vous
21   Giselle; Offenbach in the Underworld

October 1958:

27   PETERBOROUGH, ON, Peterborough Memorial Centre: Swan Lake, Act II; Lilac Garden; Les Rendez-vous
28   BELLEVILLE, ON, Belleville Collegiate Aud: Les Rendez-vous; Les Sylphides; Nutcracker, Act IV
29   OTTAWA, ON, Capitol Theatre: Les Rendez-vous; Ballad; Les Sylphides
30†   Coppélia — *repeated, October 30*

November 1958:

1†   SHERBROOKE, QC, Granada Theatre: Les Rendez-vous; Nutcracker, Act IV; Lilac Garden — *repeated, November 1*
3   BURLINGTON, VT, Memorial Aud: Swan Lake, Act II; Lilac Garden; Les Rendez-vous
4‡   Coppélia, Acts II and III
4   Coppélia
7   FREDERICTON, NB, Lady Beaverbrook Rink: Swan Lake, Act II; Ballad; Offenbach in the Underworld
8†   SAINT JOHN, NB, Saint John H.S. Aud: Les Sylphides; Ballad; Les Rendez-vous
8   Lilac Garden; Swan Lake, Act II; Offenbach in the Underworld
10†   HALIFAX, NS, Capitol Theatre: Coppélia
10   Les Rendez-vous; Ballad; Offenbach in the Underworld
12†   MONCTON, NB, Moncton H.S. Aud: Offenbach in the Underworld; Nutcracker, Act IV; Les Sylphides — *repeated, November 12*
13   EDMUNSTON, NB, Cormier H.S. Aud: Nutcracker, Act IV; Les Sylphides; Offenbach in the Underworld
15†   QUEBEC CITY, QC, Capitol Theatre: Coppélia
15   Les Sylphides; Offenbach in the Underworld; Ballad
17   TROIS RIVIERES, QC, Capitol Theatre: Les Sylphides; Nutcracker, Act IV; Lilac Garden
19   MONTREAL, QC, Her Majesty's Theatre: Coppélia
20   Les Rendez-vous; Giselle
21   Offenbach in the Underworld; Les Rendez-vous; Ballad
22†   Nutcracker
22   Swan Lake — *repeated, November 23‡*
24   Nutcracker
25   Ballad; Offenbach in the Underworld; Les Rendez-vous
26†   Coppélia
26   Ballad; Gala Performance; Les Sylphides

27 Lilac Garden; Les Sylphides; Gala Performance
28 Giselle; Offenbach in the Underworld
29† Coppélia — *repeated, November 29*

December 1958:
1 ST. CATHARINES, ON, Palace Theatre: Les Sylphides; Ballad; Les Rendez-vous
2 Swan Lake, Act II; Lilac Garden; Nutcracker, Act IV
3 KITCHENER, ON, Kitchener Memorial Aud: Ballad; Les Rendez-vous; Les Sylphides
4 HAMILTON, ON, Odeon Palace Theatre: Coppélia
5† Nutcracker, Acts III & IV
5 Les Sylphides; Ballad; Les Rendez-vous
6† Coppélia
6 Giselle; Gala Performance

January 1959:
2 BALTIMORE, MD, Lyric Theatre: Offenbach in the Underworld; Giselle
4† Coppélia
5 LYNCHBURG, VA, E.C. Glass H.S. Aud: Giselle; Offenbach in the Underworld
6 NORFOLK, VA, Center Theatre: Les Sylphides; Winter Night; Offenbach in the Underworld
7 RALEIGH, NC, Memorial Aud: Les Sylphides; Ballad; Coppélia, Act III
8 DURHAM, NC, Duke U, Page Aud: Les Sylphides; Winter Night; Offenbach in the Underworld
9 ASHEVILLE, NC, City Aud: Offenbach in the Underworld; Ballad; Les Sylphides
10 ATLANTA, GA, Municipal Aud: Coppélia
12 THOMASVILLE, GA, Municipal Aud: Offenbach in the Underworld; Les Sylphides; Ballad
13 PENSACOLA, FL, Municipal Aud: Offenbach in the Underworld; Winter Night; Coppélia, Act III
14 BIRMINGHAM, AL, Municipal Aud: Coppélia
15 TALLAHASSEE, FL, Westcott Aud: Coppélia
16 MIAMI, FL, Dade County Aud: Giselle; Offenbach in the Underworld
17 Coppélia
18 JACKSONVILLE, FL, National Guard Armory: Giselle; Offenbach in the Underworld
19 DAYTONA BEACH, FL, Peabody Aud: Coppélia
22 PHILADELPHIA, PA, Academy of Music: Offenbach in the Underworld; Les Sylphides; Winter Night
23 HARTFORD, CT, Bushnell Memorial Hall: Coppélia
24 ROCHESTER, NY, Eastman Theatre: Coppélia, Act III; Winter Night; Ballad
25 WINDSOR, ON, Capitol Theatre: Ballad; Les Sylphides; Les Rendez-vous
26 LONDON, ON, Grand Theatre: Giselle; Offenbach in the Underworld
27 Swan Lake — *repeated, January 28†*
28 Coppélia — *repeated, January 29‡*

29 Offenbach in the Underworld; Les Sylphides; Ballad
30 Le Carnaval; Winter Night; Gala Performance
31† Coppélia, Act III; Ballad; Le Carnaval
31 Coppélia

February 1959:
2 TORONTO, ON, Royal Alexandra Theatre: Coppélia
3 Le Carnaval; Winter Night; Gala Performance
4‡ Nutcracker, Acts III & IV
4 Coppélia — *repeated, February 5*
6 Swan Lake — *repeated, February 7†*
7 Les Rendez-vous; Winter Night; Offenbach in the Underworld
9 Les Rendez-vous; Winter Night; Gala Performance
10 Ballad; Les Sylphides; Offenbach in the Underworld
11† Ballad; Les Rendez-vous; Gala Performance
11 Le Carnaval; Offenbach in the Underworld; Winter Night
12 Offenbach in the Underworld; Lilac Garden; Le Carnaval
13 Giselle; Gala Performance
14† Coppélia — *repeated, February 14*
16 Nutcracker — *repeated, February 17*
18† Les Rendez-vous; Offenbach in the Underworld; Lilac Garden — *repeated, February 18*
19† Winter Night; Gala Performance
19 Gala Performance; Les Sylphides; Dark Elegies
20 Les Rendez-vous; Les Sylphides; Dark Elegies
21† Nutcracker — *repeated, February 21*
23 Coppélia, Act III; Giselle
24 Les Sylphides; Fisherman and His Soul; Coppélia, Act III — *repeated, February 25†*
25 Les Sylphides; Ballad; Gala Performance
26 Swan Lake — *repeated, February 27*
28† Ballad; Offenbach in the Underworld; Coppélia, Act III
28 Giselle; Les Rendez-vous

March 1959:
2 MOUNT PLEASANT, MI, Warringer Aud: Les Rendez-vous; Winter Night; Offenbach in the Underworld
3 COLUMBUS, OH, Mershon Aud: Les Rendez-vous; Offenbach in the Underworld; Winter Night
4 DAYTON, OH, National Cash Register Aud: Coppélia
5 LOUISVILLE, KY, Memorial Aud: Giselle; Coppélia, Act III
7 FORT WAYNE, IN, Scottish Rite Aud: Giselle; Offenbach in the Underworld
9 MADISON, WI, Wisconsin Union Theatre: Coppélia
10 Ballad; Offenbach in the Underworld; Les Sylphides
11 MINNEAPOLIS, MN, Northrop Aud: Offenbach in the Underworld; Giselle
12 Coppélia

13 MILWAUKEE, WI, Pabst Theatre: Ballad; Winter Night; Coppélia, Act III

14 CEDAR RAPIDS, IA, Coe College Aud: Winter Night; Les Sylphides; Offenbach in the Underworld

16 BURLINGTON, IA, Memorial Aud: Offenbach in the Underworld; Winter Night; Les Rendez-vous

17 ST. LOUIS, MO, Kiel Opera House: Coppélia

18 COLUMBIA, MO, U of Missouri, Jesse Aud: Giselle; Offenbach in the Underworld

19 TOPEKA, KS, Municipal Aud: Les Rendez-vous; Ballad; Offenbach in the Underworld

20 KANSAS CITY, MO, Music Hall: Coppélia

21‡ Coppélia, Act II

21 Ballad; Offenbach in the Underworld; Les Rendez-vous

23 LUBBOCK, TX, Lubbock Aud: Les Sylphides; Ballad; Offenbach in the Underworld

24 DALLAS, TX, State Fair Music Hall: Giselle; Offenbach in the Underworld

25 AUSTIN, TX, U of Texas, Gregory Gymnasium: Les Sylphides; Ballad; Coppélia, Act III

26 HOUSTON, TX, Music Hall: Coppélia

27 SAN ANTONIO, TX, Municipal Aud: Giselle; Offenbach in the Underworld

28 BEAUMONT, TX, City Aud: Coppélia, Act III; Ballad; Offenbach in the Underworld

30 NEW ORLEANS, LA, Municipal Aud: Coppélia

31 SHREVEPORT, LA, Municipal Aud: Coppélia

April 1959:

20 GUELPH, ON, Guelph Memorial Gardens: Les Sylphides; Offenbach in the Underworld; Nutcracker, Act IV

21 BRANTFORD, ON, Capitol Theatre: Ballad; Nutcracker, Act IV; Les Rendez-vous

22 CHATHAM, ON, Kinsmen Aud: Les Sylphides; Ballad; Nutcracker, Act IV

23 OWEN SOUND, ON, Owen Sound C.V.I. Aud: Les Rendez-vous; Ballad; Nutcracker, Act IV

25† COBOURG, ON, Cobourg Opera House: Les Sylphides; Nutcracker, Act IV; Les Rendez-vous

25 Ballad; Offenbach in the Underworld; Les Rendez-vous

27 CORNWALL, ON, Cornwall Community Arena: Offenbach in the Underworld; Les Rendez-vous; Ballad

28 MONTREAL, QC, La Comédie-Canadienne: Offenbach in the Underworld; Les Sylphides; Ballad

29† RENFREW, ON, Recreation Centre: Les Sylphides; Nutcracker, Act IV; Les Rendez-vous

29 Les Rendez-vous; Ballad; Offenbach in the Underworld

30 PEMBROKE, ON, Memorial Centre: Ballad; Offenbach in the Underworld; Les Rendez-vous

May 1959:

1 NORTH BAY, ON, Memorial Gardens: Les Rendez-vous; Ballad; Nutcracker, Act IV

2 SAULT STE. MARIE, ON, Sault Ste Marie Memorial Gardens: Les Rendez-vous; Ballad; Nutcracker, Act IV

4 NORANDA, QC, Noranda Recreation Centre: Les Rendez-vous; Ballad; Nutcracker, Act IV

5 TIMMINS, ON, McIntyre Arena: Les Rendez-vous; Ballad; Nutcracker, Act IV

6† KAPUSKASING, ON, Kapuskasing Community Club: Les Rendez-vous; Les Sylphides; Nutcracker, Act IV

6 Les Rendez-vous; Ballad; Nutcracker, Act IV

8 BRACEBRIDGE, ON, Bracebridge Memorial Community Centre: Les Rendez-vous; Ballad; Nutcracker, Act IV

November 1959:

2 HAMILTON, ON, Odeon Palace Theatre: Nutcracker

3‡ Coppélia, Acts I & II

3 Mermaid; Pineapple Poll; Le Carnaval

4‡ Coppélia, Acts II & III

4 Les Rendez-vous; Death and the Maiden; Sleeping Princess, Aurora pdd; Littlest One; Pineapple Poll

5 KITCHENER, ON, Kitchener Memorial Aud: Littlest One; Sleeping Princess, Aurora pdd; Death and the Maiden; Mermaid; Winter Night

6 ST. CATHARINES, ON, Palace Theatre: Pas de Six; Pineapple Poll; Littlest One; Mermaid; Sleeping Princess, Aurora pdd

7† Coppélia

7 Le Carnaval; Nutcracker, Act III pdd; Death and the Maiden; Offenbach in the Underworld

9 BELLEVILLE, ON, Belleville Collegiate Aud: Pas de Six; Death and the Maiden; Sleeping Princess, Aurora pdd; Le Carnaval; Swan Lake, Act II

11 MONTREAL, QC, Her Majesty's Theatre: Swan Lake

12 Les Rendez-vous; Mermaid; Offenbach in the Underworld

13 Coppélia

14† Les Rendez-vous; Mermaid; Le Carnaval

14 Gala Performance; Ballad; Littlest One; Pas de Six; Death and the Maiden

15‡ Swan Lake

17 Pas de Six; Death and the Maiden; Sleeping Princess, Aurora pdd; Dark Elegies; Pineapple Poll

18† Le Carnaval; Winter Night; Pineapple Poll

18 Coppélia

19 Swan Lake

20 Gala Performance; Ballad; Les Sylphides

21† Les Sylphides; Pas de Six; Death and the Maiden; Sleeping Princess, Aurora pdd; Offenbach in the Underworld

21 Mermaid; Dark Elegies; Pineapple Poll

22‡ Le Carnaval; Nutcracker, Acts III & IV

24 QUEBEC CITY, QC, Capitol Theatre: Swan Lake

25† Death and the Maiden; Pas de Six; Coppélia, Act III; Les Rendez-vous

25 Pineapple Poll; Le Carnaval; Mermaid

26 TROIS RIVIÈRES, QC, Capitol Theatre: Swan Lake, Act II; Littlest One; Sleeping Princess, Aurora pdd; Death and the Maiden; Le Carnaval

27 OTTAWA, ON, Capitol Theatre: Pineapple Poll; Les Rendez-vous; Mermaid

28† Littlest One; Gala Performance; Le Carnaval

28 Swan Lake, Act II; Dark Elegies; Pineapple Poll

January 1960:

6 DANVILLE, VA, George Washington H.S. Aud: Sleeping Princess, Aurora pdd; Pas de Six; Death and the Maiden; Nutcracker, Act IV; Offenbach in the Underworld

7 GREENSBORO, NC, Aycock Aud: Nutcracker, Act IV; Ballad; Pineapple Poll

8 SAVANNAH, GA, City Aud: Pas de Six; Sleeping Princess, Aurora pdd; Les Rendez-vous; Pineapple Poll; Death and the Maiden

9 COLUMBIA, SC, Columbia Township Aud: Nutcracker, Act IV; Death and the Maiden; Pas de Six; Sleeping Princess, Aurora pdd; Pineapple Poll

11 CLEMSON, SC, Clemson College Field House: Ballad; Offenbach in the Underworld; Les Rendez-vous

12 ATLANTA, GA, Municipal Aud: Death and the Maiden; Pas de Six; Sleeping Princess, Aurora pdd; Pineapple Poll; Les Rendez-vous

13 BIRMINGHAM, AL, Municipal Aud: Pineapple Poll; Les Rendez-vous; Sleeping Princess, Aurora pdd; Death and the Maiden; Pas de Six

14 KNOXVILLE, TN, Alumni Memorial Aud: Pas de Six; Death and the Maiden; Sleeping Princess, Aurora pdd; Ballad; Nutcracker, Act IV

16 JOHNSTOWN, PA, Cochran Jr. H.S. Aud: Les Rendez-vous; Death and the Maiden; Pas de Six; Sleeping Princess, Aurora pdd; Offenbach in the Underworld

17† CLEVELAND, OH, Music Hall, Public Aud: Offenbach in the Underworld; Sleeping Princess, Aurora pdd; Pas de Six; Death and the Maiden; Nutcracker, Act IV

25 LONDON, ON, Grand Theatre: Mermaid; Pineapple Poll; Les Rendez-vous

26 Swan Lake

27‡ Swan Lake, dances from Acts I & III, complete Acts II & IV

27 Death and the Maiden; Pineapple Poll; Sleeping Princess, Aurora pdd; Pas de Six; Mermaid

28 Coppélia

29 Pineapple Poll; Les Sylphides; Pas de Six; Nutcracker, Act III pdd; Death and the Maiden

30† Coppélia

30 Ballad; Les Sylphides; Gala Performance

February 1960:

1 TORONTO, ON, Royal Alexandra Theatre: Lilac Garden; Pineapple Poll; Pas de Deux Romantique; Les Rendez-vous

2 Les Rendez-vous; Mermaid; Offenbach in the Underworld

3‡ Pineapple Poll; Pas de Deux Romantique

3 Pineapple Poll; Les Sylphides; Ballad

4 Ballad; Pas de Chance; Gala Performance; Death and the Maiden; Sleeping Princess, Aurora pdd

5 Coppélia

6† Swan Lake

6 Les Sylphides; Mermaid; Pineapple Poll

8 Les Sylphides; Ballad; Pineapple Poll

9 Death and the Maiden; Offenbach in the Underworld; Sleeping Princess, Aurora pdd; Pas de Six; Fisherman and His Soul

10‡ Swan Lake, dances from Acts I, II, III, complete Act IV

10 Pas de Deux Romantique; Mermaid; Death and the Maiden; Pas de Chance; Pineapple Poll

11 Lilac Garden; Les Rendez-vous; Pineapple Poll

12 Coppélia, Act III; Fisherman and His Soul; Le Carnaval

13† Coppélia

13 Swan Lake

15 Le Carnaval; Winter Night; Coppélia, Act III

16 Swan Lake

17‡ Coppélia, excerpts Acts I and III, complete Act II

17 Pineapple Poll; Mermaid; Nutcracker, Act IV

18 Offenbach in the Underworld; Nutcracker, Act IV; Ballad

19 Mermaid; Winter Night; Le Carnaval

20† Nutcracker — *repeated, February 20*

22 Swan Lake

23 Coppélia

24† Le Carnaval; Nutcracker, Act IV; Winter Night

24 Pineapple Poll; Dark Elegies; Pas de Chance; Pas de Six; Pas de Deux Romantique

25 Fisherman and His Soul; Les Rendez-vous; Offenbach in the Underworld

26 Les Sylphides; Dark Elegies; Coppélia, Act III

27† Coppélia, Acts II and III; Les Rendez-vous

27 Pas de Six; Pas de Deux Romantique; Death and the Maiden; Mermaid; Pineapple Poll

March 1960:

1‡ RED BANK, NJ, Carlton Theatre: Nutcracker, Act IV (3 student matinees in one day)

2 HARTFORD, CT, Bushnell Memorial Hall: Swan Lake

3 RED BANK, NJ, Carlton Theatre: Les Rendez-vous; Offenbach in the Underworld; Coppélia, Act III pdd; Pas de Six; Death and the Maiden

4 BALTIMORE, MD, Lyric Theatre: Pas de Deux Romantique; Fisherman and His Soul; Death and the Maiden; Pas de Six; Pineapple Poll

5 MOUNT LEBANON, PA, Mount Lebanon H.S. Aud: Death and the Maiden; Pas de Six; Pineapple Poll; Pas de Chance; Swan Lake, Act II

8 MADISON, WI, Orpheum Theatre: Nutcracker, Act IV; Pas de Chance; Sleeping Princess, Aurora pdd; Pas de Six; Offenbach in the Underworld

9 STEVENS POINT, WI, Pacelli H.S. Aud: Pas de Chance; Offenbach in the Underworld; Sleeping Princess, Aurora pdd; Pas de Six; Nutcracker, Act IV

10 GREEN BAY, WI, Variety Theatre: Pas de Six; Offenbach in the Underworld; Nutcracker, Act IV; Pas de Chance; Sleeping Princess, Aurora pdd

13 WAUWATOSA, WI, Wauwatosa H.S. Aud: Swan Lake, Act II; Death and the Maiden; Pas de Chance; Pas de Deux Romantique; Offenbach in the Underworld

15 SAGINAW, MI, Temple Theatre: Pas de Six; Offenbach in the Underworld; Sleeping Princess, Aurora pdd; Nutcracker, Act IV; Pas de Chance

16† FLINT, MI, Capitol Theatre: Les Rendez-vous; Nutcracker, Act IV

16 Swan Lake

17 WEST LAFAYETTE, IN, Edward C. Elliott Hall of Music: Pineapple Poll; Pas de Deux Romantique; Pas de Chance; Death and the Maiden; Nutcracker, Act IV

18 Sleeping Princess, Aurora pdd; Death and the Maiden; Swan Lake, Act II; Pas de Six; Offenbach in the Underworld

19 LOUISVILLE, KY, Memorial Aud: Death and the Maiden; Sleeping Princess, Aurora pdd; Pas de Chance; Nutcracker, Act IV; Pineapple Poll

21 NEW ORLEANS, LA, Municipal Aud: Swan Lake

22 GRAMBLING, LA, Grambling State College Aud: Pas de Six; Death and the Maiden; Pas de Chance; Swan Lake, Act II; Offenbach in the Underworld

23† RUSTON, LA, Howard Aud: Pas de Chance; Les Rendez-vous; Pas de Deux Romantique; Swan Lake, Act II; Pas de Six

23 Fisherman and His Soul; Swan Lake, Act II; Les Rendez-vous

24 HOUSTON, TX, Music Hall: Pineapple Poll; Nutcracker, Act IV; Fisherman and His Soul

25 FORT WORTH, TX, Will Rogers Memorial Aud: Sleeping Princess, Aurora pdd; Offenbach in the Underworld; Pas de Six; Death and the Maiden; Les Rendez-vous

26 TULSA, OK, Municipal Aud: Nutcracker, Act IV; Fisherman and His Soul; Offenbach in the Underworld

27† WICHITA, KS, East H.S. Aud: Death and the Maiden; Pas de Deux Romantique; Les Rendez-vous; Nutcracker, Act IV; Pas de Six

28 LINCOLN, NE, Pershing Memorial Aud: Offenbach in the Underworld; Pas de Six; Les Rendez-vous; Death and the Maiden; Pas de Deux Romantique

29 OMAHA, NE, Omaha Civic Aud: Swan Lake, Act II; Pas de Chance; Death and the Maiden; Pas de Deux Romantique; Pineapple Poll

30 CEDAR FALLS, IA, Teachers College Aud: Pas de Six; Death and the Maiden; Offenbach in the Underworld; Les Rendez-vous; Sleeping Princess, Aurora pdd

31 LAWRENCE, KS, Hoch Aud: Offenbach in the Underworld; Pas de Deux Romantique; Death and the Maiden; Les Rendez-vous; Pas de Six

April 1960:

1 KANSAS CITY, MO, Music Hall: Swan Lake

2 TOPEKA, KS, Municipal Aud: Pas de Six; Les Rendez-vous; Death and the Maiden; Pas de Deux Romantique; Offenbach in the Underworld

August 1960:

23 WASHINGTON, DC, Carter Barron Amphitheatre: Les Rendez-vous; Pas de Deux Romantique; Les Sylphides; Ballad

24 Coppélia

25 Swan Lake

26 Les Rendez-vous; Les Sylphides; Ballad; Sleeping Princess, Aurora pdd

27 Swan Lake

28 Coppélia

29 Les Sylphides; Les Rendez-vous; Ballad; Pas de Deux Romantique

October 1960:

24 HAMILTON, ON, Odeon Palace Theatre: Pas de Deux Romantique; Princess Aurora; L'Après-midi d'un Faune; Antic Spring

25‡ Pineapple Poll

25 Swan Lake

26 Remarkable Rocket; Barbara Allen; Princess Aurora

27 ST. CATHARINES, ON, Palace Theatre: Princess Aurora; L'Après-midi d'un Faune; Pas de Deux Romantique; Remarkable Rocket

28 Coppélia

29† Swan Lake, Act II; Pineapple Poll; Les Rendez-vous

29 Antic Spring; Barbara Allen; Les Sylphides

November 1960:

1 KITCHENER, ON, Kitchener Memorial Aud: Coppélia

2 BELLEVILLE, ON, Belleville Collegiate Aud: Antic Spring; L'Après-midi d'un Faune; Pas de Deux

Romantique; Princess Aurora, dances from; Les Sylphides

3 OTTAWA, ON, Capitol Theatre: Antic Spring; L'Après-midi d'un Faune; Pas de Chance; Pas de Deux Romantique; Pineapple Poll

4 Barbara Allen; Remarkable Rocket; Princess Aurora

5† Pineapple Poll

5 Swan Lake

7 QUEBEC CITY, QC, Capitol Theatre: Barbara Allen; Princess Aurora; Remarkable Rocket

8† Coppélia

8 Antic Spring; Giselle

9 SHERBROOKE, QC, Theatre Granada: Coppélia, Act III; Princess Aurora, dances from; Pas de Deux Romantique; L'Après-midi d'un Faune; Antic Spring

11† BROCKVILLE, ON, Civic Aud: Swan Lake, Act II; Antic Spring; Les Rendez-vous

11 Swan Lake, Act II; Les Rendez-vous; Antic Spring

12 PETERBOROUGH, ON, Peterborough Memorial Centre: Barbara Allen; Princess Aurora; Antic Spring

15 MONTREAL, QC, Her Majesty's Theatre: Princess Aurora; Lilac Garden; Remarkable Rocket

16 Antic Spring; Giselle

17 Winter Night; Les Sylphides; Pineapple Poll

18 Princess Aurora; L'Après-midi d'un Faune; Pas de Deux Romantique; Pas de Chance; Les Rendez-vous

19† Coppélia — *repeated, November 19*

20‡ Nutcracker, Acts III & IV

21 Lilac Garden; Pas de Deux Romantique; L'Après-midi d'un Faune; Remarkable Rocket; Pas de Chance

23 Swan Lake

24 Les Rendez-vous; Pas de Chance; Pineapple Poll; Sleeping Beauty, Bluebird pdd; L'Après-midi d'un Faune

25 Antic Spring; Lilac Garden; Les Sylphides

26† Nutcracker

26 Swan Lake

27‡ Pineapple Poll

December 1960:

26† VICTORIA, BC, Royal Theatre: Princess Aurora; Coppélia, Act II; Les Sylphides

26 Pineapple Poll; Ballad; Princess Aurora

27 Coppélia

29 VANCOUVER, BC, Queen Elizabeth Theatre: Princess Aurora; Ballad; Pineapple Poll

30 Lilac Garden; Pineapple Poll; Les Sylphides

31† Coppélia — *repeated, December 31*

January 1961:

3 CALGARY, AB, Jubilee Aud: Pineapple Poll; Ballad; Princess Aurora

4† Coppélia — *repeated, January 4*

5 EDMONTON, AB, Jubilee Aud: Princess Aurora; Pineapple Poll; Ballad

6 Pineapple Poll; Les Sylphides; Lilac Garden

7† Coppélia — *repeated, January 7*

9 SASKATOON, SK, Capitol Theatre: Les Sylphides; Princess Aurora; Coppélia, Act II

11 WINNIPEG, MB, Playhouse Theatre: Les Sylphides; Coppélia, Act II; Princess Aurora

12 GRAND FORKS, ND, Central H.S. Aud: Coppélia, Act II; Princess Aurora; Les Sylphides

14 RAPID CITY, SD, H.S. Aud: Coppélia, Act II; Les Sylphides; Princess Aurora

16 VERMILLION, SD, Slagle Aud: Coppélia, Act II; Les Sylphides; Princess Aurora

17 WORTHINGTON, MN, H.S. Aud: Les Sylphides; Coppélia, Act II; Princess Aurora

18 AUSTIN, MN, Senior H.S. Aud: Les Sylphides; Coppélia, Act II; Princess Aurora

19 DES MOINES, IA, K.R.N.T. Theater: Princess Aurora; Les Sylphides; Coppélia, Act II

20 MILWAUKEE, WI, Oriental Theatre: Les Sylphides; Coppélia, Act II; Princess Aurora

21 SHEBOYGAN, WI, North H.S. Aud: Coppélia, Act II; Les Sylphides; Princess Aurora

22† APPLETON, WI, Appleton H.S. Aud: Les Sylphides; Coppélia, Act II; Princess Aurora

23 WINDSOR, ON, Cleary Aud: Swan Lake

24 Pineapple Poll; Les Sylphides; Ballad

25‡ Coppélia, Act II

25 Coppélia

26 Giselle; Antic Spring

27 Remarkable Rocket; Winter Night; Pineapple Poll

28† Death and the Maiden; Pas de Six; Princess Aurora; Nutcracker, Act IV

28 Swan Lake

30 TORONTO, ON, Royal Alexandra Theatre: Giselle; Antic Spring

31 Remarkable Rocket; Les Sylphides; Winter Night

February 1961:

1‡ TORONTO, ON, Royal Alexandra Theatre: Coppélia, Act II

1 Coppélia

2 Offenbach in the Underworld; Antic Spring; Princess Aurora

3 Giselle; Remarkable Rocket

4† Swan Lake

4 L'Après-midi d'un Faune; Death and the Maiden; Pineapple Poll; Princess Aurora

6 Coppélia

7 Offenbach in the Underworld; Remarkable Rocket; Les Rendez-vous

8‡ Swan Lake, Act II

8 Les Sylphides; Barbara Allen; Pineapple Poll

9 L'Après-midi d'un Faune; Princess Aurora; Pineapple Poll

10 Lilac Garden; Antic Spring; Offenbach in the Underworld

11† Nutcracker — *repeated, February 11*

13 Princess Aurora; Pas de Chance; Remarkable Rocket; Death and the Maiden

14 Lilac Garden; Antic Spring; Pineapple Poll

15‡ Nutcracker, Acts III & IV

15 Antic Spring; Giselle

16 Swan Lake

17 Les Sylphides; Dark Elegies; Pineapple Poll

18† Coppélia — *repeated, February 18*

20 Swan Lake

21 Barbara Allen; Antic Spring; Remarkable Rocket

22† Pas de Deux Romantique; Les Rendez-vous; Pas de Six; Pineapple Poll; Nutcracker, Act IV pdd — *repeated, February 22*

23 Le Carnaval; Princess Aurora; Barbara Allen

24 Princess Aurora; Le Carnaval; Winter Night

25† Swan Lake — *repeated, February 25*

27 Nutcracker

28 Offenbach in the Underworld; Ballad; Les Sylphides

March 1961:

1‡ TORONTO, ON, Royal Alexandra Theatre: Ballad; Les Rendez-vous

1 Offenbach in the Underworld; Dark Elegies; Les Sylphides

2† L'Après-midi d'un Faune; Nutcracker, Act IV; Sleeping Princess, dances from; Pas de Six

2 L'Après-midi d'un Faune; Pas de Six; Giselle

3 Nutcracker

4† Pas de Chance; Pas de Deux Romantique; Pas de Six; Les Rendez-vous; Pineapple Poll

4 Princess Aurora; Barbara Allen; Remarkable Rocket

6 LONDON, ON, Grand Theatre: Giselle; Offenbach in the Underworld

7 Swan Lake

8† Les Sylphides; Antic Spring

8 Antic Spring; Les Sylphides; Princess Aurora

9 Winter Night; Antic Spring; Les Rendez-vous

10 Barbara Allen; Pas de Chance; Pas de Deux Romantique; Offenbach in the Underworld; Pas de Six

11† Nutcracker — *repeated, March 11*

13† Nutcracker, Act IV; Les Rendez-vous

13 Pas de Deux Romantique; Death and the Maiden; Pas de Chance; Les Sylphides; Princess Aurora

14 Lilac Garden; Les Rendez-vous; Princess Aurora

15 Nutcracker

16 Antic Spring; Giselle

17 Nutcracker

18† Swan Lake — *repeated, March 18*

April 1961:

3 ROCHESTER, NY, Eastman Theatre: Coppélia

4 SYRACUSE, NY, Lincoln Aud: Coppélia

5‡ BUFFALO, NY, Kleinhans Music Hall: Coppélia, Act II

5 Coppélia

7 HARTFORD, CT, Bushnell Memorial Hall: Coppélia

8 BALTIMORE, MD, Lyric Theatre: Coppélia

9 STATE COLLEGE, PA, Recreation Hall: Coppélia

10 HUNTINGTON, WV, Keith Albee Theatre: Coppélia

11 CHARLESTON, WV, Municipal Aud: Coppélia

12 LYNCHBURG, VA, E.C. Glass H.S. Aud: Coppélia

13 DURHAM, NC, Duke U, Page Aud: Coppélia

14 ROCK HILL, SC, Winthrop College Aud: Coppélia

15 KNOXVILLE, TN, Alumni Memorial Aud: Coppélia

17 FLORENCE, AL, Coffee H.S. Aud: Coppélia

18 COLUMBUS, GA, Royal Theatre: Coppélia

19 TALLAHASSEE, FL, Westcott Aud: Coppélia

20 Swan Lake

22 LAFAYETTE, LA, Lafayette Municipal Aud: Swan Lake

23† Coppélia

24 BATON ROUGE, LA, Southern U Aud: Coppélia

25 HOUSTON, TX, Music Hall: Swan Lake

26 CORPUS CHRISTI, TX, Del Mar Aud: Coppélia

27 SAN ANTONIO, TX, Municipal Aud: Swan Lake

28 HOUSTON, TX, Music Hall: Coppélia

29 DALLAS, TX, State Fair Music Hall: Coppélia

May 1961:

1 BIG SPRING, TX, Municipal Aud: Coppélia

2 PAMPA, TX, Junior H.S. Aud: Coppélia

3 FORT HAYS, KS, Sheridan Coliseum State College: Coppélia

4 SALINA, KS, Fine Arts Theatre: Coppélia

5 KANSAS CITY, MO, Music Hall: Coppélia

7† CHICAGO, IL, Opera House: Coppélia

8 GRAND RAPIDS, MI, Civic Aud: Coppélia

9 EAST LANSING, MI, Michigan State U Aud: Coppélia

10 LEXINGTON, KY, Memorial Aud: Coppélia

11 LOUISVILLE, KY, Memorial Aud: Coppélia

12 CINCINNATI, OH, Music Hall: Coppélia

13 CLEVELAND, OH, Music Hall: Coppélia

14 PITTSBURGH, PA, Syria Mosque: Swan Lake

November 1961:

20 BROCKVILLE, ON, Civic Aud: Swan Lake

21 OTTAWA, ON, Capitol Theatre: Concerto Barocco; Giselle

22 Antic Spring; One in Five; Lilac Garden; Les Sylphides

23 MONTREAL, QC, Her Majesty's Theatre: Swan Lake

24 Giselle, Peasant pdd; One in Five; Les Sylphides; Dances from The Sleeping Princess, pas de trois,

Bluebird pdd; Pineapple Poll

25† Swan Lake — *repeated, November 25*

26‡ One in Five; Princess Aurora

26 Antic Spring; One in Five; Dances from The Sleeping Princess, pas de trois, Bluebird pdd; Concerto Barocco; Lilac Garden

27 QUEBEC CITY, QC, Capitol Theatre: Concerto Barocco; Pineapple Poll; Les Sylphides; One in Five

28 SHERBROOKE, QC, Granada Theatre: Dances from The Sleeping Princess; Giselle, Peasant pdd; Sleeping Princess, pas de trois; Swan Lake, Black Swan pdd; Lilac Garden; One in Five; Concerto Barroco

30‡ HAMILTON, ON, Odeon Palace Theatre: One in Five; Princess Aurora

30 Concerto Barocco; Giselle

December 1961:

1 KITCHENER, ON, Kitchener Memorial Aud: Giselle; Concerto Barocco

2 BELLEVILLE, ON, Belleville Collegiate Aud: Concerto Barocco; Princess Aurora; Giselle, Peasant pdd; Dances from The Sleeping Princess, pas de trois; One in Five

January 1962:

22 WINDSOR, ON, Cleary Aud: Giselle; One in Five

23 Concerto Barocco; Les Sylphides; Pineapple Poll

24‡ Pineapple Poll

24 Offenbach in the Underworld; Princess Aurora; Ballad

25 Giselle; Offenbach in the Underworld

26 One in Five; Pineapple Poll; Swan Lake, Act III pdd; Les Rendez-vous; Dances from The Sleeping Princess, pas de trois

27† Swan Lake — *repeated, January 27*

29 TORONTO, ON, Royal Alexandra Theatre: One in Five; Pineapple Poll; Princess Aurora

30 Les Sylphides; Concerto Barocco; Giselle, Peasant pdd; Pineapple Poll

31‡ Nutcracker

31 Offenbach in the Underworld; Les Sylphides; Concerto Barocco; One in Five

February 1962:

1 TORONTO, ON, Royal Alexandra Theatre: Giselle; Offenbach in the Underworld

2 Giselle; Antic Spring

3† Coppélia — *repeated, February 3*

5 Giselle, Acts I & II; One in Five

6 Coppélia

7† Swan Lake, Acts II, III, IV

7 Swan Lake

8 Ballad; Les Sylphides; Antic Spring

9 One in Five; Dances from The Sleeping Princess, pas de trois; Ballad; Princess Aurora

10† Swan Lake — *repeated, February 10, 12*

13 Les Rendez-vous; Concerto Barocco; Pas de Chance; Pineapple Poll

14‡ Coppélia

14 Offenbach in the Underworld; Lilac Garden; Les Rendez-vous; Dances from The Sleeping Princess, pas de trois

15 One in Five; L'Après-midi d'un Faune; Pineapple Poll; Lilac Garden

16 Nutcracker — *repeated, February 17†, 17*

19 Les Sylphides; Ballad; Princess Aurora

20 Lilac Garden; Concerto Barocco; L'Après-midi d'un Faune; Pas de Chance; Antic Spring; Dances from The Sleeping Princess, pas de trois; Giselle, Peasant pdd

21† One in Five; Giselle, Peasant pdd; Pineapple Poll

21 Concerto Barocco; Offenbach in the Underworld; Pas de Chance; One in Five; Giselle, Peasant pdd; L'Après-midi d'un Faune

22† One in Five; Offenbach in the Underworld; Concerto Barocco; L'Après-midi d'un Faune; Giselle, Peasant pdd

22 Coppélia

23 Antic Spring; Concerto Barocco; Dances from The Sleeping Princess, Bluebird pdd; Les Rendez-vous; Nutcracker, Act IV pdd; L'Après-midi d'un Faune

24† One in Five; Giselle

24 Swan Lake

March 1962:

12 LONDON, ON, Grand Theatre: Princess Aurora; Les Sylphides; One in Five; Concerto Barocco

13 Coppélia

14† Pineapple Poll; Les Sylphides; One in Five

14 Giselle; Pineapple Poll

15 Les Sylphides; Lilac Garden; Offenbach in the Underworld

16 Concerto Barocco; Lilac Garden; Offenbach in the Underworld; Dances from The Sleeping Princess, Bluebird pdd

17† Coppélia

17 Princess Aurora; Antic Spring; Concerto Barocco

19 NEWTON, MA, H.S. Aud: Lilac Garden; Princess Aurora; One in Five

21 NEW KENSINGTON, PA, New Kensington H.S. Aud: Les Sylphides; Concerto Barocco; Giselle, Peasant pdd; L'Après-midi d'un Faune; Antic Spring

22 PHILADELPHIA, PA, Academy of Music: One in Five; Concerto Barocco; Princess Aurora; Giselle, Peasant pdd; Antic Spring

23a† RED BANK, NJ, Carlton Theatre: Antic Spring; L'Après-midi d'un Faune; One in Five; Giselle, Peasant pdd — *repeated, March 23b†, 23c† (without Giselle, Peasant pdd) (three matinees on one day)*

24† BALTIMORE, MD, Lyric Theatre: Princess Aurora; One in Five; Antic Spring

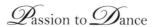

24 Princess Aurora; L'Après-midi d'un Faune; Antic Spring; Giselle, Peasant pdd; Sleeping Princess, pas de trois

26 WILMINGTON, NC, Brogden Hall: Swan Lake, Act II; One in Five; Princess Aurora

27 CLEMSON, SC, Clemson College Field House: Lilac Garden; Concerto Barocco; One in Five; Antic Spring

30 MIAMI, FL, Dade County Aud: Swan Lake, Act II; Swan Lake, Act I pas de trois; Nutcracker, Act IV pdd; Princess Aurora

31 Sleeping Princess, pas de trois; Swan Lake, Act I pas de trois; L'Après-midi d'un Faune; One in Five; Swan Lake, Act II; Concerto Barocco

April 1962:

2 ALBANY, GA, Albany Theatre: Les Sylphides; Giselle, Peasant pdd; L'Après-midi d'un Faune; Princess Aurora

3 ATLANTA, GA, Municipal Aud: One in Five; Princess Aurora; L'Après-midi d'un Faune; Lilac Garden

4 TALLAHASSEE, FL, Westcott Aud: Les Sylphides; One in Five; Giselle, Peasant pdd; L'Après-midi d'un Faune; Antic Spring

5 PANAMA CITY, FL, Municipal Aud: Les Sylphides; Giselle, Peasant pdd; Antic Spring; Sleeping Princess, pas de trois; One in Five

6 COLUMBUS, MS, Whitfield College Aud: Swan Lake, Act II; Giselle, Peasant pdd; L'Après-midi d'un Faune; Princess Aurora

7 MEMPHIS, TN, Ellis Aud: One in Five; Lilac Garden; Les Sylphides; Antic Spring

9 GRAMBLING, LA, Grambling State College Aud: Les Sylphides; One in Five; Princess Aurora

10† RUSTON, LA, Howard Aud: Les Sylphides; One in Five; Princess Aurora — *repeated, April 10*

11 FORT WORTH, TX, Will Rogers Memorial Aud: Antic Spring; Swan Lake, Act II; Sleeping Princess, pas de trois; Giselle, Peasant pdd; One in Five

12 SAN ANTONIO, TX, Municipal Aud: One in Five; Giselle, Peasant pdd; Sleeping Princess, pas de trois; Les Sylphides; Antic Spring

13 HOUSTON, TX, Music Hall: Les Sylphides; One in Five; Princess Aurora

14 Antic Spring; Concerto Barocco; Giselle, Peasant pdd; Pas de Chance; L'Après-midi d'un Faune; Sleeping Princess, pas de trois; Lilac Garden

16 WACO, TX, Waco Hall Aud: Antic Spring; One in Five; Princess Aurora

17 TYLER, TX, Municipal Aud: Antic Spring; Swan Lake, Act II; One in Five; Pas de Chance; Swan Lake, Act I pas de trois

18 AUSTIN, TX, Municipal Aud: Princess Aurora; Concerto Barocco; One in Five; L'Après-midi d'un Faune

19 WICHITA FALLS, TX, Municipal Aud: Swan Lake, Act II; One in Five; Princess Aurora

21 LAWTON, OK, McMahon Aud: One in Five; Concerto Barocco; Antic Spring; Les Sylphides

23 OMAHA, NE, Municipal Aud: Les Sylphides; Princess Aurora; Antic Spring

24 ALBERT LEA, MN, H.S. Aud: Antic Spring; Lilac Garden; One in Five; Giselle, Peasant pdd; Sleeping Princess, pas de trois; Concerto Barocco

25 MINNEAPOLIS, MN, Northrop Aud: Concerto Barocco; Princess Aurora; One in Five; Antic Spring

27 KANSAS CITY, MO, Music Hall: Princess Aurora; One in Five; Swan Lake, Act II

30 EMPORIA, KS, Civic Aud: One in Five; Princess Aurora; Les Sylphides

May 1962:

1 COLUMBIA, MO, Jesse Hall: Antic Spring; L'Après-midi d'un Faune; Giselle, Peasant pdd; One in Five; Swan Lake, Act II

2 ST. LOUIS, MO, Kiel Opera House: L'Après-midi d'un Faune; Lilac Garden; Princess Aurora; One in Five

3 CINCINNATI, OH, Music Hall: One in Five; L'Après-midi d'un Faune; Princess Aurora; Antic Spring

4 LEXINGTON, KY, Memorial Coliseum Aud: Swan Lake, Act II; Swan Lake, Act I pas de trois; Antic Spring; Nutcracker, Act IV pdd; L'Après-midi d'un Faune; One in Five

5 PITTSBURGH, PA, Syria Mosque: L'Après-midi d'un Faune; Princess Aurora; Sleeping Princess, pas de trois; Nutcracker, Act IV pdd; Swan Lake, Act II

July 1962:

13 STRATFORD, ON, Festival Theatre: Sequel; Time Cycle — *repeated, July 15*

October 1962:

15 MIDLAND, TX, Municipal Aud: Swan Lake, Act II; Concerto Barocco; Offenbach in the Underworld

16 BIG SPRING, TX, Municipal Aud: Swan Lake, Act II; Concerto Barocco; Offenbach in the Underworld

17 DENTON, TX, North Texas State U Aud: Giselle, Peasant pdd; Serenade; Judgment of Paris; One in Five; Lilac Garden

18 NATCHITOCHES, LA, Fine Arts Aud: One in Five; Giselle, Peasant pdd; Judgment of Paris; Lilac Garden; Serenade

19 SHERMAN, TX, H.S. Aud: Lilac Garden; Offenbach in the Underworld; One in Five; Le Corsaire, pdd; L'Après-midi d'un Faune

20 OKLAHOMA CITY, OK, Municipal Aud: Serenade; Swan Lake, Act II; Offenbach in the Underworld

23 CORPUS CHRISTI, TX, Del Mar Aud: Offenbach in

the Underworld; Serenade; Swan Lake, Act II

24 NACOGDOCHES, TX, Fine Arts Aud: Les Rendez-vous; Laurencia Pas de Six; L'Après-midi d'un Faune; Le Corsaire, pdd; One in Five; Judgment of Paris

25 KERRVILLE, TX, Municipal Aud: Offenbach in the Underworld; One in Five; Les Rendez-vous; Judgment of Paris

26 KINGSVILLE, TX, Jones Aud: Swan Lake, Act II; Offenbach in the Underworld; Concerto Barocco

27 HOUSTON, TX, Music Hall: Serenade; Laurencia Pas de Six; Judgment of Paris; Offenbach in the Underworld

30† GRINNEL, IA, Roberts Theatre: L'Après-midi d'un Faune; Les Rendez-vous; Judgment of Paris; Concerto Barocco; One in Five

30 Serenade; Lilac Garden; Offenbach in the Underworld

31 DES MOINES, IA, K.R.N.T. Theater: Judgment of Paris; Giselle, Peasant pdd; Les Rendez-vous; Concerto Barocco; L'Après-midi d'un Faune; One in Five

November 1962:

1 WAVERLEY, IA, Wartburg Coll. Chapel-Aud: Offenbach in the Underworld; One in Five; Giselle, Peasant pdd; L'Après-midi d'un Faune; Judgment of Paris; Le Corsaire, pdd

2 KANSAS CITY, MO, Music Hall: Serenade; Giselle, Peasant pdd; Le Corsaire, pdd; Judgment of Paris; Laurencia Pas de Six; Les Rendez-vous;

3 AMES, IA, ISU Armory: Concerto Barocco; Le Corsaire, pdd; Offenbach in the Underworld; One in Five; Giselle, Peasant pdd

5 DAYTON, OH, National Cash Register Aud: One in Five; Concerto Barocco; Giselle, Peasant pdd; L'Après-midi d'un Faune; Le Corsaire, pdd; Les Rendez-vous

6 LEXINGTON, KY, Memorial Aud: Swan Lake, Black Swan pdd; Judgment of Paris; Swan Lake, Act III, dances from; Serenade; Offenbach in the Underworld

7 LOUISVILLE, KY, Memorial Aud: Serenade; Giselle, Peasant pdd; Judgment of Paris; Laurencia Pas de Six; Lilac Garden; Les Rendez-vous;

8 COLUMBUS, OH, Mershon Aud: L'Après-midi d'un Faune; Le Corsaire, pdd; One in Five; Giselle, Peasant pdd; Laurencia Pas de Six; Serenade; Judgment of Paris

9 ANN ARBOR, MI, Hill Aud: One in Five; Concerto Barocco; Lilac Garden; Judgment of Paris; Les Rendez-vous

10 PITTSBURGH, PA, Syria Mosque: Swan Lake

December 1962:

31 HARTFORD, CT, Bushnell Memorial Hall: Les

Rendez-vous; Offenbach in the Underworld; Judgment of Paris; One in Five

January 1963:

2 CHARLOTTE, NC, Ovens Municipal Aud: Concerto Barocco; Giselle, Peasant pdd; Laurencia Pas de Six; Judgment of Paris; Les Rendez-vous; One in Five

3 ASHEVILLE, NC, Municipal Aud: Les Sylphides; Giselle, Peasant pdd; L'Après-midi d'un Faune; Offenbach in the Underworld

4 KNOXVILLE, TN, Knoxville Civic Aud: Les Sylphides; Winter Night; Les Rendez-vous

5 CHATTANOOGA, TN, Municipal Aud: Les Sylphides; Winter Night; Les Rendez-vous

7 COLUMBUS, GA, Jordan Aud: Pas de Chance; Les Rendez-vous; Pas de Deux Romantique; Serenade; Giselle, Peasant pdd

8 FLORENCE, AL, Coffee H.S. Aud: Pas de Chance; Winter Night; Death and the Maiden; One in Five; Les Rendez-vous

9 ATLANTA, GA, Municipal Aud: Judgment of Paris; Offenbach in the Underworld; Pas de Deux Romantique; Le Corsaire, pdd; Serenade; Giselle, Peasant pdd;

10 BIRMINGHAM, AL, Temple Theatre: One in Five; Concerto Barocco; Le Corsaire, pdd; Judgment of Paris; Pas de Deux Romantique; Serenade

11 MEMPHIS, TN, Municipal Aud: Le Corsaire, pdd; Death and the Maiden; Les Rendez-vous; Judgment of Paris; Pas de Chance; Serenade

12 NEW ORLEANS, LA, Municipal Aud: Serenade; Winter Night; Offenbach in the Underworld

13 LAFAYETTE, LA, Lafayette Municipal Aud: Lilac Garden; One in Five; Pas de Chance; Death and the Maiden; Offenbach in the Underworld

14 SHREVEPORT, LA, Municipal Aud: Les Sylphides; Laurencia Pas de Six; Concerto Barocco; L'Après-midi d'un Faune; Swan Lake, Black Swan pdd; Judgment of Paris

15 JACKSON, MS, Municipal Aud: Lilac Garden; One in Five; Pas de Deux Romantique; Judgment of Paris; Le Corsaire, pdd; Concerto Barocco; L'Après-midi d'un Faune

18 MIAMI, FL, Miami Beach Aud: Swan Lake

19 ST. PETERSBURG, FL, St Petersburg H.S. Aud: Judgment of Paris; Death and the Maiden; Concerto Barocco; Pas de Chance; Giselle, Peasant pdd; Les Rendez-vous

20 MIAMI, FL, Municipal Aud: One in Five; Judgment of Paris; Offenbach in the Underworld; L'Après-midi d'un Faune; Concerto Barocco; Le Corsaire, pdd

21 ORLANDO, FL, Municipal Aud: Death and the Maiden; One in Five; Les Rendez-vous; Laurencia

Pas de Six; Pas de Chance; Le Corsaire, pdd; Judgment of Paris

22 JACKSONVILLE, FL, Municipal Aud: Les Sylphides; Judgment of Paris; One in Five; Winter Night

23 COLUMBIA, SC, Township Aud: Les Sylphides; One in Five; Les Rendez-vous; Death and the Maiden; Laurencia Pas de Six

24 CHARLESTON, SC, Memminger Aud: Offenbach in the Underworld; Pas de Chance; Lilac Garden; Concerto Barocco

25 WINSTON-SALEM, NC, Reynolds Theatre: Death and the Maiden; Les Rendez-vous; Pas de Chance; L'Après-midi d'un Faune; Le Corsaire, pdd; Serenade

26 RADFORD, VA, Radford College Aud: Judgment of Paris; Les Sylphides; Les Rendez-vous; One in Five

28 RED BANK, NJ, Carlton Theatre: Pas de Chance; Le Corsaire, pdd; Les Rendez-vous; Judgment of Paris; Giselle, Peasant pdd; Concerto Barocco; Death and the Maiden

30 UTICA, NY, Stanley Theatre: Les Sylphides; Winter Night; Offenbach in the Underworld

31 ROCHESTER, NY, Eastman Theatre: Laurencia Pas de Six; Les Rendez-vous; Le Corsaire, pdd; Pas de Chance; Judgment of Paris; One in Five; L'Après-midi d'un Faune

February 1963:

1 SYRACUSE, NY, Lincoln Aud: Offenbach in the Underworld; Giselle, Peasant pdd; Death and the Maiden; One in Five; Serenade

2 BUFFALO, NY, Kleinhans Music Hall: Death and the Maiden; Judgment of Paris; Pas de Chance; Giselle, Peasant pdd; L'Après-midi d'un Faune; Le Corsaire, pdd; Les Rendez-vous; One in Five

4 WINDSOR, ON, Cleary Aud: Serenade; Winter Night; Offenbach in the Underworld

5 Judgment of Paris; Pineapple Poll; Laurencia Pas de Six; Le Corsaire, pdd; L'Après-midi d'un Faune; One in Five

6‡ Coppélia — *repeated, February 6*

7 Pas de Chance; Judgment of Paris; Giselle

8 Death and the Maiden; Les Sylphides; Nutcracker, Act IV; Concerto Barocco

9† Les Sylphides; One in Five; Nutcracker, Act IV

9 Swan Lake

13 TORONTO, ON, Royal Alexandra Theatre: Winter Night; Serenade; Judgment of Paris; One in Five

14† Swan Lake, Act II; Nutcracker, Act IV

14 Winter Night; Serenade; Offenbach in the Underworld

15 One in Five; Judgment of Paris; L'Après-midi d'un Faune; Pas de Chance; Le Corsaire, pdd; Pineapple Poll

16† Swan Lake — *repeated, February 16, 18*

19† Swan Lake, Act II; Nutcracker, Act IV

19 Don Quixote, pdd; Judgment of Paris; L'Après-midi d'un Faune; One in Five; Les Sylphides; Death and the Maiden

20 Nutcracker, Act IV; Les Rendez-vous; Death and the Maiden; Concerto Barocco; Le Corsaire, pdd — *repeated, February 21*

22 Giselle; Pas de Chance; One in Five — *repeated, February 23†, 23*

25 Pineapple Poll; Lilac Garden; Serenade — *repeated, February 26*

27‡ Coppélia — *repeated, February 27*

28 Pineapple Poll; Lilac Garden; Le Corsaire, pdd; Les Rendez-vous

March 1963:

1 TORONTO, ON, Royal Alexandra Theatre: Lilac Garden; Le Corsaire, pdd; Pineapple Poll; Les Rendez-vous

2† Coppélia — *repeated, March 2*

4 Swan Lake

5 Nutcracker, Act IV; Judgment of Paris; Le Corsaire, pdd; Pas de Chance; Les Sylphides

6† Le Corsaire, pdd; Giselle, Peasant pdd; One in Five; Les Rendez-vous

6 Offenbach in the Underworld; Winter Night; Les Sylphides

7 Giselle; Concerto Barocco; One in Five

8 Nutcracker, Act IV; Le Corsaire, pdd; L'Après-midi d'un Faune; Serenade; Giselle, Peasant pdd

9† Nutcracker, Act IV; Coppélia, Act II; Les Sylphides

9 Swan Lake

11 HAMILTON, ON, Odeon Palace Theatre: Les Rendez-vous; Judgment of Paris; Le Corsaire, pdd; One in Five; Serenade

12‡ Offenbach in the Underworld; Nutcracker, Act IV pdd; Giselle, Peasant pdd; Pas de Chance

12 Swan Lake

13 ST. CATHARINES, ON, Palace Theatre: Judgment of Paris; One in Five; Serenade; Nutcracker, Act IV

14 PORT HURON, MI, Henry G. McMorran Memorial Aud: Offenbach in the Underworld; Winter Night; Les Sylphides

15 Pas de Chance; Serenade; Giselle, Peasant pdd; Le Corsaire, pdd; Nutcracker, Act IV

16 Judgment of Paris; Le Corsaire, pdd; Concerto Barocco; Swan Lake, Act II; Les Rendez-vous

18 LONDON, ON, Grand Theatre: Les Rendez-vous; Judgment of Paris; Le Corsaire, pdd; Pas de Chance; Serenade

19 Swan Lake

20† Les Rendez-vous; Winter Night; Serenade

20 Pineapple Poll; Winter Night; Concerto Barocco

21 Swan Lake

22 Pineapple Poll; Les Sylphides; Le Corsaire, pdd; Pas de Chance
23† One in Five; Giselle
23 Les Sylphides; One in Five; Death and the Maiden; Nutcracker, Act IV; Judgment of Paris
25 OTTAWA, ON, Capitol Theatre: Nutcracker, Act IV; Judgment of Paris; Le Corsaire, pdd; Serenade; One in Five
26 Swan Lake, Act II; Winter Night; Death and the Maiden; Concerto Barocco
27 BROCKVILLE, ON, Civic Aud: Nutcracker, Act IV; Les Sylphides; Le Corsaire, pdd; L'Après-midi d'un Faune; One in Five
28 QUEBEC CITY, QC, Capitol Theatre: Le Corsaire, pdd; Winter Night; Pas de Chance; Serenade; Judgment of Paris
29 MONTREAL, QC, Her Majesty's Theatre: Winter Night; Judgment of Paris; Le Corsaire, pdd; Pas de Chance; Serenade
30† L'Après-midi d'un Faune; Giselle, Peasant pdd; Les Sylphides; Les Rendez-vous; One in Five
30 Nutcracker, Act IV; Concerto Barocco; One in Five; Les Sylphides
31† Nutcracker, Act IV; One in Five; Swan Lake, Act II
31 Giselle, Peasant pdd; Pas de Chance; Le Corsaire, pdd; Winter Night; Serenade

October 1963:
15 CONCORD, NH, Capitol Theatre: Judgment of Paris; Lilac Garden; Le Corsaire, pdd; One in Five; Les Rendez-vous
16 BOSTON, MA, Donnelly Memorial Theatre: Giselle; One in Five
17 PORTLAND, ME, State Theatre: One in Five; Les Rendez-vous; Judgment of Paris; Don Quixote, pdd; Concerto Barocco; Allégresse, pdd
18 PROVIDENCE, RI, Veterans Memorial Aud: Judgment of Paris; One in Five; Allégresse; Offenbach in the Underworld
19 BINGHAMTON, NY, Capitol Theatre: One in Five; Judgment of Paris; Allégresse; Offenbach in the Underworld
21 FLINT, MI, IMA Aud: Offenbach in the Underworld; Serenade; Don Quixote, pdd; Les Rendez-vous, pas de trois; Le Corsaire, pdd
22 PITTSBURGH, PA, Syria Mosque: Offenbach in the Underworld; Serenade; Don Quixote, pdd; Giselle, Peasant pdd; Le Corsaire, pdd
24 ST. LOUIS, MO, Kiel Opera House: Offenbach in the Underworld; Giselle
25 CARTHAGE, IL, Carthage College Aud: Concerto Barocco; Giselle, Peasant pdd; Don Quixote, pdd; Les Rendez-vous, pas de trois; Lilac Garden; Judgment of Paris; One in Five

26 MILWAUKEE, WI, Pabst Theater: One in Five; Les Rendez-vous; Le Corsaire, pdd; Serenade; Judgment of Paris
28 SALINA, KS, Fine Arts Theatre: Giselle; One in Five
29 SIOUX CITY, IA, Orpheum Theatre: Offenbach in the Underworld; Concerto Barocco; Judgment of Paris; Don Quixote, pdd; One in Five
30 RAPID CITY, SD, H.S. Aud: Le Corsaire, pdd; Les Rendez-vous; Giselle, Peasant pdd; Judgment of Paris; One in Five; Lilac Garden
31 SIOUX FALLS, SD, Sioux Falls Aud: Judgment of Paris; Concerto Barocco; Le Corsaire, pdd; Don Quixote, pdd; Allégresse; One in Five

November 1963:
2 ST. PAUL, MN, St Paul Aud Theatre: Don Quixote, pdd; Le Corsaire, pdd; Serenade; Lilac Garden; Les Rendez-vous
3 ROCHESTER, MN, Mayo Aud: Les Rendez-vous; Giselle, Peasant pdd; Lilac Garden; Serenade; Don Quixote, pdd
4 ROCKFORD, IL, Coronado Theatre: Don Quixote, pdd; Serenade; Judgment of Paris; Offenbach in the Underworld
5 MADISON, WI, Orpheum Theatre: Giselle, Peasant pdd; Offenbach in the Underworld; Lilac Garden; Les Rendez-vous
6 ISHPEMING, MI, H.S. Aud: One in Five; Le Corsaire, pdd; Concerto Barocco; Judgment of Paris; Don Quixote, pdd; Les Rendez-vous
7 FOND DU LAC, WI, Fond Du Lac Theatre: Don Quixote, pdd; One in Five; Allégresse; Offenbach in the Underworld
8 DULUTH, MN, Denfield Aud: Les Rendez-vous; Offenbach in the Underworld; Serenade
9 APPLETON, WI, Appleton H.S. Aud: One in Five; Offenbach in the Underworld; Giselle, Peasant pdd; Don Quixote, pdd; Concerto Barocco
11 EVANSVILLE, IN, Coliseum Theatre: Giselle, Peasant pdd; One in Five; Offenbach in the Underworld; Serenade

January 1964:
13 OTTAWA, ON, Capitol Theatre: Serenade; House of Atreus; Allégresse
14 One in Five; Pas de Deux Romantique; Giselle
15 QUEBEC CITY, QC, Capitol Theatre: Don Quixote, pdd; Swan Lake, Act I pas de trois; One in Five; Serenade; Allégresse; Walpurgis Night, pdd
17 HAMILTON, ON, Palace Theatre: Allégresse; Giselle
18† Swan Lake, Act II; Swan Lake, dances from; Swan Lake, Act I pas de trois
18 Serenade; House of Atreus; Les Sylphides
20 WINDSOR, ON, Cleary Aud: Concerto Barocco;

Walpurgis Night, pdd; Judgment of Paris; House of Atreus; Allégresse — *repeated, January 21*

22‡ Swan Lake, Act III, dances from; Swan Lake, Act IV

22 Swan Lake

23 Serenade; Lilac Garden; Don Quixote, pdd; Les Rendez-vous — *repeated, January 24*

25† One in Five; Le Corsaire, pdd; Swan Lake, Act II; Allégresse

25 Offenbach in the Underworld; Allégresse; House of Atreus

27 ST. CATHARINES, ON, Palace Theatre: Giselle, Peasant pdd; Les Sylphides; Don Quixote, pdd; Allégresse; Concerto Barocco

28 KITCHENER, ON, Lyric Theatre: Giselle, Peasant pdd; Concerto Barocco; Lilac Garden; Les Rendez-vous; Le Corsaire, pdd; One in Five

29 BELLEVILLE, ON, H.S. Aud: Les Rendez-vous; Allégresse; Judgment of Paris; Le Corsaire, pdd; Swan Lake, Act II pdd; Swan Lake, Act I pas de trois

30 BROCKVILLE, ON, Civic Aud: Allégresse; House of Atreus; Pineapple Poll

February 1964:

1 BROOKLYN, NY, Brooklyn Academy of Music: Concerto Barocco; Les Rendez-vous; Le Corsaire, pdd; Judgment of Paris; House of Atreus;

2† STRATFORD, CT, Stratford Theatre: Don Quixote, pdd; Giselle, Peasant pdd; Swan Lake, Act II; One in Five; Les Rendez-vous

2 Allégresse; Offenbach in the Underworld; House of Atreus

3 HARTFORD, CT, Bushnell Memorial Hall: Allégresse; House of Atreus; Serenade

4 ALBANY, NY, Palace Theatre: Serenade; Offenbach in the Underworld; Le Corsaire, pdd; One in Five

6 PHILADELPHIA, PA, Academy of Music: Serenade; Offenbach in the Underworld; Allégresse

7 CARLISLE, PA, Carlisle Senior H.S.: Giselle, Peasant pdd; Offenbach in the Underworld; Walpurgis Night, pdd; Don Quixote, pdd; One in Five; Concerto Barocco

8 BALTIMORE, MD, Lyric Theatre: One in Five; Walpurgis Night, pdd; Swan Lake, Act II; Offenbach in the Underworld

9† Swan Lake, Act I pas de trois; Les Rendez-vous; Don Quixote, pdd; One in Five; Le Corsaire, pdd; Allégresse

12 COLLEGE PARK, MD, Gymnasium: Offenbach in the Underworld; Walpurgis Night, pdd; Don Quixote, pdd; Serenade

13 HAMPTON, VA, Ogden Hall: Don Quixote, pdd; Swan Lake, Act II; Allégresse; Les Rendez-vous

14 WILLIAMSBURG, VA, Phi Beta Kappa Hall: Le Corsaire, pdd; Giselle, Peasant pdd; Swan Lake, Act

II; Offenbach in the Underworld

15 NORFOLK, VA, Center Theatre: Allégresse; Concerto Barocco; One in Five; Swan Lake, Act II

April 1964:

14 MONTREAL, QC, Place des Arts: Romeo and Juliet

15 Princess Aurora, pdd; Les Rendez-vous; House of Atreus; Serenade

16 Concerto Barocco; House of Atreus; Allégresse; Princess Aurora, pdd; Swan Lake, Act III pas de trois

17 Swan Lake

18† Swan Lake, Act II; Les Rendez-vous; Concerto Barocco; One in Five; Swan Lake, Act III pdd

18 Romeo and Juliet

21 TORONTO, ON, O'Keefe Centre: Romeo and Juliet

22 Offenbach in the Underworld; Les Sylphides; House of Atreus

23 Romeo and Juliet — *repeated, April 24*

25† One in Five; Swan Lake, Black Swan pdd; Offenbach in the Underworld; Swan Lake, Act II

25 Swan Lake

26‡ Allégresse, pdd; One in Five; Offenbach in the Underworld; Concerto Barocco; Giselle, Peasant pdd

27 Swan Lake

28 House of Atreus; Serenade; Allégresse

29† Les Rendez-vous; Pineapple Poll; Le Corsaire, pdd

29 Pineapple Poll; Le Corsaire, pdd; Allégresse, pdd; Serenade; Swan Lake, Black Swan pdd

30 Walpurgis Night, pdd; Allégresse; Concerto Barocco; Les Rendez-vous; Lilac Garden

May 1964:

1 TORONTO, ON, O'Keefe Centre: Romeo and Juliet

2† Pineapple Poll; Les Sylphides; Concerto Barocco

2 Romeo and Juliet

August 1964:

9 STRATFORD, ON, Festival Theatre: Électre

December 1964:

26† TORONTO, ON, O'Keefe Centre: Nutcracker — *repeated, 26, 27†, 28, 29†, 30†, 31†*

31 Pas de Deux (Cranko); Le Corsaire, pdd; Clair de Lune; La Sylphide; Walpurgis Night, pdd

January 1965:

1† TORONTO, ON, O'Keefe Centre: Nutcracker

1 Serenade; La Sylphide

2 Le Corsaire, pdd; Pas de Deux (Cranko); Clair de Lune; Pas de Deux (Strate); La Sylphide

4 Triptych; House of Atreus; Offenbach in the Underworld

5 Les Rendez-vous; La Sylphide

6 Serenade; La Sylphide;

7 Romeo and Juliet — *repeated, 8†, 8, 9†, 9*

11   LONDON, ON, Grand Theatre: La Sylphide; Serenade

12   Nutcracker — *repeated, January 13†*

13   One in Five; Clair de Lune; Le Corsaire, pdd; Triptych; Les Rendez-vous

14   La Sylphide; Offenbach in the Underworld

15   Pas de Deux (Strate); Les Rendez-vous; Walpurgis Night, pdd; Concerto Barocco; House of Atreus

16† Nutcracker — *repeated, January 16*

18   WINDSOR, ON, Cleary Aud: Serenade; La Sylphide

19   Nutcracker — *repeated, January 20‡, 20, 21‡*

21   Concerto Barocco; One in Five; Clair de Lune; Nutcracker, Act II pdd; House of Atreus

22   Nutcracker, Act II pdd; La Sylphide; Clair de Lune; Pas de Deux (Strate)

23† Nutcracker

23   Triptych; La Sylphide, Act II; Pas de Deux (Cranko); Les Rendez-vous;

26   MONTREAL, QC, Place des Arts: La Sylphide; Triptych

27   Romeo and Juliet

28   Nutcracker

29   House of Atreus; Le Corsaire, pdd; Pas de Deux (Cranko); Serenade; Clair de Lune

30† Clair de Lune; One in Five; Triptych; Les Rendez-vous

30   Romeo and Juliet

31† Nutcracker — *repeated, Janaury 31*

February 1965:

2†   SHERBROOKE, QC, U of Sherbrooke Aud: Nutcracker

2   La Sylphide; Triptych

3   OTTAWA, ON, Capitol Theatre: La Sylphide; Triptych

4   Nutcracker

5   QUEBEC CITY, QC, Capitol Theatre: La Sylphide; Triptych

6   BELLEVILLE, ON, H.S. Aud: Triptych; Pas de Deux (Strate); Clair de Lune; Le Corsaire, pdd; Pas de Deux (Cranko); Nutcracker, Act II

8   HAMILTON, ON, Palace Theatre: Triptych; La Sylphide

9†   Nutcracker — *repeated, February 9*

10   BRANTFORD, ON, Capitol Theatre: Serenade; Pas de Deux (Strate); Pas de Deux (Cranko); Le Corsaire, pdd; Nutcracker, Act II; Clair de Lune

11   KITCHENER, ON, Lyric Theatre: Triptych; Serenade; Nutcracker, Act II

12   ST. CATHARINES, ON, Palace Theatre: Nutcracker, Act II; Triptych; Pas de Deux (Strate); Clair de Lune; Pas de Deux (Cranko); Le Corsaire, pdd

13† STRATFORD, ON, Avon Theatre: Les Rendez-vous; Nutcracker, Act II; Serenade

13   Triptych; One in Five; Clair de Lune; Offenbach in the Underworld

17   SYRACUSE, NY, Loew's Theater: Nutcracker

19   HARTFORD, CT, Bushnell Memorial Hall: Nutcracker — *repeated, February 20†*

20   Pas de Deux (Strate); Le Corsaire, pdd; Clair de Lune; One in Five; Pas de Deux (Cranko); Triptych; Concerto Barocco

23   NASHVILLE, TN, Kean Hall: Les Rendez-vous; Pas de Deux (Cranko); Nutcracker, Act II; Serenade

24   MEMPHIS, TN, Aud Memphis: Offenbach in the Underworld; Clair de Lune; Pas de Deux (Strate); Triptych; Pas de Deux (Cranko)

25   JACKSON, MS, Municipal Aud: Offenbach in the Underworld; Triptych; Les Rendez-vous

26   BATON ROUGE, LA, Southern University Aud-Gym: Nutcracker, Act II; Clair de Lune; Triptych; One in Five

27   TYLER, TX, Tyler H.S. Aud: Triptych; Offenbach in the Underworld; Nutcracker, Act II

March 1965:

1   EL PASO, TX, Liberty Hall: Nutcracker

3   LAS VEGAS, NV, Las Vegas H.S. Aud: Offenbach in the Underworld; Nutcracker, Act II pdd; One in Five; Serenade

4   SANTA MONICA, CA, Santa Monica Civic Aud: Nutcracker

5   PASADENA, CA, Civic Aud: One in Five; Serenade; Clair de Lune; Offenbach in the Underworld

6†   Nutcracker

6   Triptych; Pas de Deux (Strate); Le Corsaire, pdd; Les Rendez-vous; Judgment of Paris; Clair de Lune

7†   SAN DIEGO, CA, San Diego Civic Theatre: Nutcracker

7   Offenbach in the Underworld; Clair de Lune; Serenade; Judgment of Paris

9   FRESNO, CA, Memorial Aud: Nutcracker

10   SANTA CRUZ, CA, Civic Aud: Nutcracker, Act II; Judgment of Paris; Triptych; One in Five

11   SAN JOSE, CA, Civic Aud: Les Rendez-vous; Le Corsaire, pdd; Clair de Lune; One in Five; Triptych

12   OAKLAND, CA, Oakland Aud Theatre: Nutcracker

13   SAN FRANCISCO, CA, War Memorial Opera House: Les Rendez-vous; Offenbach in the Underworld; Serenade

15   SACRAMENTO, CA, Memorial Aud: Serenade; Offenbach in the Underworld; Nutcracker, Act II

17   OGDEN, UT, Ogden H.S. Aud: Triptych; Les Rendez-vous; Judgment of Paris; One in Five

19   DENVER, CO, Denver Aud Theatre: Nutcracker

20   One in Five; Clair de Lune; Serenade; Offenbach in the Underworld

22   HAYS, KS, Sheridan Coliseum: Triptych; Les Rendez-vous; Concerto Barocco; One in Five

23   LAWTON, OK, McMahon Aud: Offenbach in the Underworld; Walpurgis Night, pdd; Pas de Deux

(Strate); Clair de Lune; Triptych

25 JOPLIN, MO, Memorial Aud: Nutcracker

26 KANSAS CITY, MO, Music Hall: Nutcracker

27 AMES, IA, ISU Armory: Triptych; Serenade; Clair de Lune; Judgment of Paris

28† ST. PAUL, MN, St. Paul Aud: One in Five; Clair de Lune; Triptych; Nutcracker, Act II

30 MINNEAPOLIS, MN, Northrop Aud: Nutcracker

31 ROCHESTER, MN, Mayo Civic Theatre: One in Five; Nutcracker, Act II; Triptych

April 1965:

1 WATERLOO, IA, Paramount Theatre: Nutcracker

3 ANN ARBOR, MI, Hill Aud: Offenbach in the Underworld; Nutcracker, Act II, dances from; Serenade

5 INDIANAPOLIS, IN, Clowes Memorial Hall: Triptych; Offenbach in the Underworld; Les Rendez-vous

6 LOUISVILLE, KY, Memorial Aud: Nutcracker

7 CHARLESTON, WV, Municipal Aud: Nutcracker

8 HUNTINGTON, WV, Keith Albee Theatre: Nutcracker

10 FLUSHING, NY, Charles S. Colden Aud: Nutcracker, Act II; Triptych; Serenade

August 1965:

2 WASHINGTON, DC, Carter Barron Amphitheatre: Romeo and Juliet

3 Nutcracker

4 Solitaire; Triptych

5 Solitaire; La Sylphide

6 Romeo and Juliet

7 Nutcracker

8 Romeo and Juliet

9 Triptych; One in Five; Clair de Lune; Solitaire

10 Triptych; La Sylphide

11 Nutcracker

12 Romeo and Juliet

13 Nutcracker

14 La Sylphide; Offenbach in the Underworld

15 Nutcracker

September 1965:

2 TORONTO, ON, O'Keefe Centre: Romeo and Juliet (special performance for Canadian Bar Association)

November 1965:

6 MONTREAL, QC, Place des Arts: Nutcracker, Act II; Adagio Cantabile; Rivalité; Rake's Progress

7† Nutcracker — *repeated, November 7*

9 Serenade; Rake's Progress; Solitaire

10 La Sylphide; Pulcinella;

11 Serenade; Solitaire; Pulcinella

12 Rake's Progress; Triptych; Solitaire

13† Romeo and Juliet — *repeated, November 13*

14† Solitaire; Concerto Barocco; Pulcinella; Rivalité

14 Pulcinella; La Sylphide

16 OTTAWA, ON, Capitol Theatre: Solitaire; Rake's Progress; Rivalité; Adagio Cantabile

17 Nutcracker, Act II; Pulcinella; Triptych

19† QUEBEC CITY, QC, Capitol Theatre: Adagio Cantabile; Nutcracker, Act II; Solitaire; Clair de Lune

19 Rivalité; Rake's Progress; Solitaire; Adagio Cantabile

20 SHERBROOKE, QC, U de Sherbrooke Aud: Solitaire; Concerto Barocco; Clair de Lune; Rake's Progress

21† One in Five; Pulcinella; Triptych

22 BELLEVILLE, ON, H.S. Aud: Rake's Progress; Triptych; Solitaire

23 PETERBOROUGH, ON, Peterborough Memorial Centre: Nutcracker, Act II pdd; Clair de Lune; Rivalité; Adagio Cantabile; Solitaire; One in Five

24 OSHAWA, ON, Regent Theatre: One in Five; Clair de Lune; Nutcracker, Act II; Solitaire

26 BARRIE, ON, Barrie District Central Collegiate: One in Five; Triptych; Solitaire; Clair de Lune

27† STRATFORD, ON, Avon Theatre: Solitaire; Adagio Cantabile; One in Five; Concerto Barocco; Rivalité

27 Solitaire; Rake's Progress; Triptych

29† HAMILTON, ON, Palace Theatre: Nutcracker

29 Rake's Progress; Adagio Cantabile; Rivalité; Solitaire

30† Nutcracker

30 Pulcinella; Clair de Lune; Solitaire; One in Five

December 1965:

1 KITCHENER, ON, Lyric Theatre: One in Five; Adagio Cantabile; Solitaire; Rivalité; Concerto Barocco

2 BRANTFORD, ON, Capitol Theatre: Rake's Progress; Solitaire; Rivalité; Adagio Cantabile

3 ST. CATHARINES, ON, Palace Theatre: Rake's Progress; Adagio Cantabile; Rivalité; Triptych

4† One in Five; Adagio Cantabile; Rivalité; Nutcracker, Act II

4 Concerto Barocco; Pulcinella; Solitaire

26† TORONTO, ON, O'Keefe Centre: Nutcracker — *repeated, December 27†, 27, 28†, 29†, 30†, 31a†, 31b† (two matinees in one day)*

January 1966:

1† TORONTO, ON, O'Keefe Centre: Nutcracker — *repeated, January 1*

17 LONDON, ON, Grand Theatre: La Sylphide; Solitaire

18 Adagio Cantabile; Rivalité; Rake's Progress; Triptych

19† Nutcracker — *repeated, January 19, 20*

21 La Sylphide; Pulcinella

22† One in Five; Clair de Lune; Solitaire; Pulcinella

22 One in Five; Adagio Cantabile; Rake's Progress; Solitaire

24 WINDSOR, ON, Cleary Aud: Rivalité; Solitaire; Adagio Cantabile; Rake's Progress

25 Serenade; Pulcinella; Triptych

26‡ La Sylphide

26 Solitaire; La Sylphide

27‡ La Sylphide

27 Nutcracker — *repeated, January 28*

29† Triptych; Pulcinella; Solitaire

29 Rake's Progress; One in Five; Clair de Lune; Pulcinella

April 1966:

12 TORONTO, ON, O'Keefe Centre: Rake's Progress; Solitaire; Concerto Barocco

13 Romeo and Juliet

14† La Sylphide

14 Romeo and Juliet

15 Serenade; Rivalité; Adagio Cantabile; Pulcinella

16† La Sylphide; Adagio Cantabile; One in Five

16 Solitaire; Rake's Progress; Triptych

17† Pulcinella; Offenbach in the Underworld

18 Triptych; One in Five; Clair de Lune; Pulcinella

19 Solitaire; Lilac Garden; Offenbach in the Underworld

20 Lilac Garden; Offenbach in the Underworld; Serenade

21 Solitaire; La Sylphide

22 Concerto Barocco; Rivalité; Adagio Cantabile; Lilac Garden; Rake's Progress

23† Romeo and Juliet — *repeated, April 23*

November 1966:

1† HAMILTON, ON, Palace Theatre: Solitaire; Bayaderka, Act IV

1 Mélodie; Adagio Cantabile; Bayaderka, Act IV; Solitaire

2† Solitaire; Offenbach in the Underworld

2 Serenade; Lilac Garden; Offenbach in the Underworld

3 BRANTFORD, ON, Capitol Theatre: Bayaderka, Act IV; Lilac Garden; Offenbach in the Underworld

4 WELLAND, ON, Welland Centennial S.S. Aud: Nutcracker

5† ST. CATHARINES, ON, Palace Theatre: Mélodie; Solitaire; Bayaderka, Act IV;

5 Bayaderka, Act IV; Lilac Garden; Offenbach in the Underworld

7 KINGSTON, ON, Grand Theatre: Solitaire; Bayaderka, Act IV; Lilac Garden

8 BROCKVILLE, ON, Civic Aud: Solitaire; Lilac Garden; Nutcracker, Act II

9 PETERBOROUGH, ON, Peterborough Memorial Centre: Bayaderka, Act IV; Lilac Garden; Offenbach in the Underworld

10 KITCHENER, ON, Lyric Theatre: Bayaderka, Act IV; Lilac Garden; Mélodie; Giselle, Peasant pdd; Nutcracker, Act II pdd

11 PORT CREDIT, ON, Port Credit S.S. Aud: Nutcracker, Act II; Clair de Lune; One in Five; Solitaire

12 GUELPH, ON, Ross Hall: One in Five; Mélodie; Adagio Cantabile; Lilac Garden; Solitaire

14 OTTAWA, ON, Capitol Theatre: Serenade; Lilac Garden; Offenbach in the Underworld

15 Mélodie; Giselle, Peasant pdd; Bayaderka, Act IV; Solitaire

16 NORTH BAY, ON, Capitol Theatre: Solitaire; Lilac Garden; Offenbach in the Underworld

17 BARRIE, ON, Barrie District Central Collegiate: Bayaderka, Act IV; Mélodie; Giselle, Peasant pdd; Offenbach in the Underworld

18 CHATHAM, ON, Kinsmen Aud: Lilac Garden; Adagio Cantabile; Giselle, Peasant pdd; One in Five; Solitaire

19 PORT HURON, MI, Henry G. McMorran Memorial Aud: Solitaire; Bayaderka, Act IV; Offenbach in the Underworld

20† Nutcracker

December 1966:

25† TORONTO, ON, O'Keefe Centre: Nutcracker — *repeated, December 26†, 27a†, 27b†, 28a†, 28b†, 29a†, 29b†, 30a†, 30b†, (two matinees on each day) 31†*

January 1967:

4 VANCOUVER, BC, Queen Elizabeth Theatre: Nutcracker — *repeated, January 5†, 6†, 6, 7†, 7, 8a†, 8b† (two matinees on one day)*

19 MONTREAL, QC, Place des Arts: Lilac Garden; Solitaire; Bayaderka, Act IV

20 Bayaderka, Act IV; La Sylphide

21† Nutcracker — *repeated, January 21, 22†*

24 WINDSOR, ON, Cleary Aud: Giselle, Peasant pdd; Solitaire; Mélodie; Bayaderka, Act IV

25‡ Bayaderka, Act IV; Solitaire;

25 Bayaderka, Act IV; Lilac Garden; Offenbach in the Underworld

26‡ Bayaderka, Act IV; Solitaire

26 One in Five; Rake's Progress; Offenbach in the Underworld

27 One in Five; Clair de Lune; Adagio Cantabile; Lilac Garden; Solitaire

28† Nutcracker — *repeated, January 28*

30 HALIFAX, NS, Capitol Theatre: Serenade; Lilac Garden; Solitaire

31 Nutcracker, Act II; La Sylphide

February 1967:

3 ST. JOHN'S, NL, Holy Heart of Mary Aud: Serenade; One in Five; Solitaire

4† One in Five; Bayaderka, Act IV; Nutcracker, Act II

4 La Sylphide; Nutcracker, Act II

6 SAINT JOHN, NB, Saint John H.S. Aud: Giselle, Peasant pdd; Clair de Lune; Serenade; Solitaire

7 Bayaderka, Act IV; One in Five; Mélodie; Nutcracker, Act II pdd; Solitaire

9† CHARLOTTETOWN, PEI, Confederation Centre: Nutcracker — *repeated, February 9*

10 SACKVILLE, NB, Mount Allison U Aud: Nutcracker, Act II; Lilac Garden; Solitaire

11† FREDERICTON, NB, Fredericton Playhouse: Serenade; One in Five; Solitaire

11 Bayaderka, Act IV; Nutcracker, Act II; Adagio Cantabile; One in Five

13 RIMOUSKI, QC, Centre Civique: Adagio Cantabile; Nutcracker, Act II; Solitaire; One in Five

14 QUEBEC CITY, QC, Capitol Theatre: Nutcracker, Act II; Bayaderka, Act IV; Lilac Garden

15 CHICOUTIMI, QC, Aud du Seminaire: Nutcracker, Act II; Mélodie; One in Five; Solitaire

17 SHERBROOKE, QC, U de Sherbrooke Aud: Nutcracker

18 SOREL, QC, Sorel Theatre: Solitaire; Lilac Garden; Nutcracker, Act II

March 1967:

27 TORONTO, ON, O'Keefe Centre: Swan Lake — *repeated, March 28, 29, 30, 31*

April 1967:

1† TORONTO, ON, O'Keefe Centre: Swan Lake — *repeated, April 1*

3 Solitaire; Bayaderka, Act IV; Lilac Garden — *repeated, April 4*

5 La Sylphide; Bayaderka, Act IV

6 One in Five; Mélodie; La Sylphide

7 Solitaire; La Sylphide

8† La Sylphide; One in Five

8 Bayaderka, Act IV; Rake's Progress; Offenbach in the Underworld

10 Offenbach in the Underworld; Serenade; Rake's Progress

11 Serenade; La Sylphide

12 Romeo and Juliet — *repeated, April 13, 14, 15†, 15*

18 LONDON, ON, Grand Theatre: Lilac Garden; Solitaire; Bayaderka, Act IV

19 Serenade; La Sylphide

20‡ La Sylphide

20 Bayaderka, Act IV; Rake's Progress; Solitaire

21 Swan Lake — *repeated, April 22†, 22*

May 1967:

8 OSHAWA, ON, Eastdale Collegiate Aud: EH!; Concerto Barocco; Rondo Giocoso; Death and the Maiden; One in Five; Solo (Franca)

9 ORILLIA, ON, Orillia Opera House: Rondo Giocoso; EH!; Solo (Franca); Death and the Maiden; Concerto Barocco; One in Five

10 OAKVILLE, ON, White Oaks H.S.: Concerto Barocco; Death and the Maiden; Solo (Franca); Rondo Giocoso; EH!; One in Five

11 OWEN SOUND, ON, Owen Sound Collegiate Aud: Concerto Barocco; EH!; Rondo Giocoso; Solo (Franca); One in Five; Death and the Maiden;

17 GALT, ON, Galt Collegiate Inst.: Rondo Giocoso; EH!; Solo (Franca); Death and the Maiden; Concerto Barocco; One in Five

18 SARNIA, ON, Sarnia Collegiate Institute of Technology: Concerto Barocco; Death and the Maiden; Solo (Franca); Rondo Giocoso; EH!; One in Five

19 SIMCOE, ON, Simcoe District Composite School: Rondo Giocoso; One in Five; EH!; Solo (Franca); Concerto Barocco; Death and the Maiden

23 NIAGARA FALLS, ON, Niagara Falls Coll. Vocational Institute: Rondo Giocoso; EH!; Solo (Franca); Death and the Maiden; Concerto Barocco; One in Five

26 OTTAWA, ON, Capitol Theatre: Concerto Barocco; Death and the Maiden; Solo (Franca); Rondo Giocoso; EH!; One in Five

27 PEMBROKE, ON, Champlain H.S. Aud: Concerto Barocco; Rondo Giocoso; Death and the Maiden; Solo (Franca); EH!; One in Five

August 1967:

7 WASHINGTON, DC, Carter Barron Amphitheatre: Romeo and Juliet

8 Swan Lake

9 Solitaire; Bayaderka, Act IV; Lilac Garden

10 Romeo and Juliet

11 Lilac Garden; Solitaire; Bayaderka, Act IV

12 Swan Lake

13 Romeo and Juliet

September 1967:

11 NORTH BAY, ON, Capitol Theatre: Studies In White; EH!; Rondo Giocoso; Solo (Franca); One in Five; Death and the Maiden

12† HAILEYBURY, ON, St. Mary's Academy Aud: EH!; Rondo Giocoso; Solo (Franca); Death and the Maiden; Studies in White; One in Five — *repeated, September 12*

14† KIRKLAND LAKE, ON, Strand Theatre: One in Five; Studies in White; Rondo Giocoso; EH!

14 Solo (Franca); Rondo Giocoso; EH!; Studies in White; One in Five; Death and the Maiden

15 TIMMINS, ON, Timmins H.S. Aud: Rondo Giocoso; EH!; Solo (Franca); Death and the Maiden; Studies in White; One in Five

16 KAPUSKASING, ON, Civic Centre: Studies in White; Death and the Maiden; Solo (Franca); Rondo Giocoso; EH!; One in Five

18 GERALDTON, ON, Geraldton Composite H.S.: Death and the Maiden; EH!; Solo (Franca); Studies in White; One in Five; Rondo Giocoso

19 MANITOUWADGE, ON, Manitouwadge H.S. Aud: One in Five; EH!; Rondo Giocoso; Solo (Franca); Death and the Maiden; Studies in White

20 WAWA, ON, Michipicoten H.S. Aud: Rondo Giocoso; Solo (Franca); Death and the Maiden; Studies in White; One in Five; EH!

21 SAULT STE. MARIE, ON, Sault Collegiate Aud: Studies in White; Rondo Giocoso; EH!; One in Five; Solo (Franca); Death and the Maiden — *repeated, September 22*

23 SUDBURY, ON, Sudbury H.S. Aud: Studies in White; Death and the Maiden; Solo (Franca); Rondo Giocoso; EH!; One in Five — *repeated, 24†*

October 1967:

24 MONTREAL, QC, Place des Arts: Romeo and Juliet — *repeated, October 25*

26 Bayaderka, Act IV; La Prima Ballerina

27 Swan Lake — *repeated, October 28†, 28*

30 OTTAWA, ON, Capitol Theatre: Le Corsaire, pdd; Swan Lake, dances from; La Sylphide

31 La Prima Ballerina; Don Quixote, pdd; Swan Lake, dances from

November 1967:

1 BROCKVILLE, ON, Civic Aud: Swan Lake, dances from; Don Quixote, pdd; Bayaderka, Act IV; EH!

2 KINGSTON, ON, Grand Theatre: La Prima Ballerina; Don Quixote, pdd; Le Corsaire, pdd; Swan Lake, dances from

3 BELLEVILLE, ON, Centennial S.S.: EH!; Don Quixote, pdd; Le Corsaire, pdd; One in Five; Solitaire

4 Bayaderka, Act IV; Nutcracker, pdd; Swan Lake, Black Swan pdd; Rondo Giocoso; Lilac Garden

6 PETERBOROUGH, ON, Peterborough Memorial Centre: Rondo Giocoso; Swan Lake, dances from; Death and the Maiden; Don Quixote, pdd; EH!; Studies in White

7 KITCHENER, ON, Lyric Theatre: Nutcracker, pdd; EH!; Rondo Giocoso; Death and the Maiden; Studies in White; Swan Lake, dances from

8 BARRIE, ON, Central Collegiate Aud: Lilac Garden; Le Corsaire, pdd; Death and the Maiden; EH!; Swan Lake, dances from; Nutcracker, pdd

9† BRANTFORD, ON, Capitol Theatre: Rondo Giocoso; EH!; Nutcracker, pdd; Don Quixote, pdd; One in Five

9 One in Five; EH!; Nutcracker, pdd; Swan Lake, dances from; Studies in White; Death and the Maiden

10 PORT CREDIT, ON, Port Credit S.S. Aud: Bayaderka, Act IV; Lilac Garden; Don Quixote, pdd; Nutcracker, pdd; EH!

11 GUELPH, ON, Ross Hall: Bayaderka, Act IV; Swan Lake, dances from; Nutcracker, pdd; EH!

14‡ HAMILTON, ON, Palace Theatre: Swan Lake, Act I

14 Swan Lake

15† La Prima Ballerina

15 EH!; La Prima Ballerina

16 ST. CATHARINES, ON, Palace Theatre: La Sylphide, pdd; Death and the Maiden; Swan Lake, dances from; Don Quixote, pdd; Nutcracker, pdd; Le Corsaire, pdd; EH!; Studies in White

17 WELLAND, ON, Welland Centennial S.S. Aud: Swan Lake

20 MINNEAPOLIS, MN, Northrop Aud: Swan Lake

21 La Sylphide; Solitaire

24 FORT WILLIAM, ON, Fort William Gardens: Solitaire; Lilac Garden; Bayaderka, Act IV

25 ATIKOKAN, ON, H.S. Aud: One in Five; EH!; Rondo Giocoso; Studies in White; Death and the Maiden

27 REGINA, SK, Sheldon Williams Coll. Aud: Solitaire; Nutcracker, Act II; EH!

28 Bayaderka, Act IV; Lilac Garden; Don Quixote, pdd; EH!;

29 SASKATOON, SK, Capitol Theatre: La Sylphide; Solitaire

December 1967:

1 EDMONTON, AB, Jubilee Aud: Solitaire; La Sylphide

2† Nutcracker — *repeated, December 2*

4 CALGARY, AB, Jubilee Aud: Solitaire; La Sylphide

5 Nutcracker

22a† TORONTO, ON, O'Keefe Centre: Nutcracker — *repeated, December 22b†(two matinees on one day), 23a†, 23b† (two matinees on one day), 25†, 26†, 26, 27a†, 27b† (two matinees on one day), 28, 29a†, 29b†, 30a†, 30b† (two matinees on each day)*

January 1968:

2 VANCOUVER, BC, Queen Elizabeth Theatre: Romeo and Juliet — *repeated, January 3*

4 Nutcracker — *repeated, January 5†, 5, 6†, 6,*

7 Romeo and Juliet

11† SEATTLE, WA, Seattle Opera House: Nutcracker — *repeated, January 11, 12, 13†, 13, 14†, 14*

18 EAST LANSING, MI, Michigan State U Aud: Swan Lake

19 Nutcracker

20 CLEVELAND, OH, Music Hall: Nutcracker

21 PORT HURON, MI, Henry McMorran Memorial Aud: Swan Lake

23 WINDSOR, ON, Cleary Aud: Swan Lake — *repeated, January 24†, 24, 25†, 25*

26 Concerto Barocco; Nutcracker, pdd; La Prima Ballerina

27† Nutcracker, pdd; La Prima Ballerina; Don Quixote, pdd; Le Corsaire, pdd — *repeated, January 27*

30 LONDON, ON, Grand Theatre: Swan Lake — *repeated, January 31†, 31*

February 1968:

1 LONDON, ON, Grand Theatre: Swan Lake
2 Concerto Barocco; Don Quixote, pdd; La Prima Ballerina
3† La Prima Ballerina; Le Corsaire, pdd; Nutcracker, pdd
3 La Prima Ballerina; Bayaderka, Act IV
6 MEXICO CITY, MEXICO, Palacio de Bellas Artes: Romeo and Juliet — *repeated, February 8*
9 La Sylphide; Solitaire — *repeated, February 10†*
10 Swan Lake
11 Romeo and Juliet
12 Swan Lake
13 Don Quixote, pdd; Concerto Barocco; Nutcracker, Act II; One in Five; Le Corsaire, pdd — *repeated, February 15*
16 La Sylphide; Solitaire
17† One in Five; Le Corsaire, pdd; Concerto Barocco; Don Quixote, pdd; Nutcracker, Act II
17 Swan Lake
18 La Sylphide; Solitaire
19 Romeo and Juliet
20 Swan Lake
21 JALAPA, MEXICO, Teatro del Estado: Solitaire; La Sylphide
22 Le Corsaire, pdd; Concerto Barocco; Don Quixote, pdd; Nutcracker, Act II; One in Five
25 GUADALAJARA, MEXICO, Teatro Degollado: Solitaire; La Sylphide
26† Nutcracker, Act II
26 Concerto Barocco; Le Corsaire, pdd; One in Five; Nutcracker, Act II; Don Quixote, pdd

March 1968:

1 FREEPORT, TX, Brazosport Senior H.S. Aud: Solitaire; Concerto Barocco; Swan Lake, Black Swan pdd; Nutcracker, Act II
2 HOUSTON, TX, Jones Hall: Swan Lake
3† DALLAS, TX, State Fair Music Hall: Swan Lake
4 NEW ORLEANS, LA, Municipal Aud: La Sylphide; Solitaire
7 EMPORIA, KS, Civic Aud: Nutcracker, Act II; Don Quixote, pdd; Swan Lake, Black Swan pdd; Solitaire
8 KANSAS CITY, MO, Music Hall: Swan Lake
9 ST. LOUIS, MO, Kiel Opera House: Nutcracker
11 TERRE HAUTE, IN, Tilson Music Hall: Le Corsaire, pdd; Solitaire; Swan Lake, Black Swan pdd; Don Quixote, pdd; Concerto Barocco
12 PEORIA, IL, Shrine Mosque: Nutcracker, pdd; Don Quixote, pdd; Swan Lake, Black Swan pdd; Solitaire; Concerto Barocco
13 BURLINGTON, IA, Memorial Aud: Nutcracker

April 1968:

15 TORONTO, ON, O'Keefe Centre: Cinderella

— *repeated, April 16, 17, 18, 19, 20†, 20*
22 Swan Lake — *repeated, April 23, 24, 25, 26, 27†, 27*
29 Concerto Barocco; Don Quixote, pdd; La Prima Ballerina
30 Bayaderka, Act IV; La Prima Ballerina

May 1968:

1 TORONTO, ON, O'Keefe Centre: Concerto Barocco; Le Corsaire, pdd; La Prima Ballerina
2 Bayaderka, Act IV; Solitaire; Don Quixote, pdd; Lilac Garden
3 Romeo and Juliet — *repeated, May 4†, 4*

September 1968:

23† OSHAWA, ON, Eastdale Collegiate: One in Five; Célébrations; Arena; Pas de Deux (Gordon); EH! — *repeated, September 23*
24 WEST HILL, ON, Sir Wilfrid Laurier S.S. Aud: One in Five; Célébrations; Arena; Pas de Deux (Gordon); EH!
25 VALLEYFIELD, QC, L'Auditorium du Seminaire: Célébrations; EH!; Pas de Deux (Gordon); Arena; Studies in White
26 MONTREAL, QC, Theatre Port-Royal: Célébrations; Arena; Pas de Deux (Gordon); EH!; One in Five
27 Studies in White; Arena; Pas de Deux (Gordon); EH!; Célébrations
28 CORNWALL, ON, General Varnier Aud: One in Five; Célébrations; Arena; Pas de Deux (Gordon); EH!
30 PEMBROKE, ON, Champlain H.S. Aud: Studies in White; EH!; Célébrations; Pas de Deux (Gordon); Arena

October 1968:

1 HAILEYBURY, ON, St. Mary's Academy Aud: Studies in White; Pas de Deux (Gordon); Arena; Célébrations; EH!
2 KIRKLAND LAKE, ON, Strand Theatre: EH!; One in Five; Célébrations; Arena; Pas de Deux (Gordon)
3 TIMMINS, ON, Timmins H.S. Aud: One in Five; Célébrations; Arena; Pas de Deux (Gordon); EH!
4 SUDBURY, ON, Sudbury H.S. Aud: Pas de Deux (Gordon); Arena; Célébrations; One in Five; EH!
5 PARRY SOUND, ON, Parry Sound H.S.: One in Five; Célébrations; Arena; Pas de Deux (Gordon); EH!
7 NORTH BAY, ON, Algonquin Composite Aud: Arena; Célébrations; Studies in White; EH!; Pas de Deux (Gordon)
8 LINDSAY, ON, Academy Theatre: One in Five; Célébrations; Arena; Pas de Deux (Gordon); EH!
9 KITCHENER, ON, Lyric Theatre: EH!; Studies in White; Pas de Deux (Gordon); Arena; Célébrations
10 NIAGARA FALLS, ON, Niagara Falls Coll. Voc. Inst.: EH!; Célébrations; Arena; Studies in White; Pas de Deux (Gordon)

11 STRATFORD, ON, Avon Theatre: One in Five; Célébrations; Arena; Pas de Deux (Gordon); EH!

12† OAKVILLE, ON, White Oaks H.S. Aud: Célébrations; EH!; Pas de Deux (Gordon); Arena; Studies in White

12 EAST YORK, ON, East York Coll. Aud: Pas de Deux (Gordon); Arena; Célébrations; EH!; Studies In White

29 HAMILTON, ON, Palace Theatre: Solitaire; Serenade; Cyclus

30† Nutcracker — *repeated, October 30*

31 BRANTFORD, ON, Capitol Theatre: Nutcracker, Act II; Cyclus; Solitaire

November 1968:

1† WELLAND, ON, Welland Centennial S.S. Aud: Solitaire; Nutcracker, Act II

1 Serenade; Cyclus; Solitaire

2 ST. CATHARINES, ON, Palace Theatre: Serenade; Cyclus; Solitaire

4 BELLEVILLE, ON, Belleville Centennial S.S.: Solitaire; Cyclus; Serenade

5 Studies in White; Phases; Concerto Barocco; Flower Festival in Genzano, pdd; Nutcracker, Act II

6† KINGSTON, ON, Grand Theatre: Nutcracker, Act II; Flower Festival in Genzano, pdd; One in Five

6 Serenade; Nutcracker, Act II; Cyclus

8 BROCKVILLE, ON, Civic Aud: Cyclus; Solitaire; Serenade

9† OTTAWA, ON, Capitol Theatre: Solitaire; Nutcracker, Act II

9 Solitaire; Nutcracker, pdd; Cyclus; Swan Lake, Black Swan pdd; Flower Festival in Genzano, pdd

11 SHERBROOKE, QC, U de Sherbrooke Aud: Swan Lake

12 QUEBEC CITY, QC, Capitol Theatre: Serenade; Solitaire; Cyclus

13 Swan Lake

15 FREDERICTON, NB, Fredericton Playhouse: Concerto Barocco; Flower Festival in Genzano, pdd; Cyclus; Swan Lake, Black Swan pdd; EH!

16 SACKVILLE, NB, Convocation Hall: One in Five; Serenade; Flower Festival in Genzano, pdd; Cyclus

18 HALIFAX, NS, Capitol Theatre: Swan Lake

19 One in Five; Solitaire, pdd; Cyclus; Bayaderka, Act IV

20 ANTIGONISH, NS, St. Francis Xavier U Aud: Phases; Concerto Barocco; Studies in White; EH!; One in Five

21† CHARLOTTETOWN, PEI, Playhouse Theatre: One in Five; Phases; Solitaire; EH!

21 Cyclus; Serenade; Solitaire

22 SAINT JOHN, NB, Saint John H.S. Aud: Concerto Barocco; Phases; Studies in White; Cyclus; Swan Lake, Black Swan pdd

25 FALL RIVER, MA, Durfee Theatre: Nutcracker

26 HARTFORD, CT, Bushnell Memorial Hall: Swan Lake — *repeated, November 27*

30† PITTSBURGH, PA, Syria Mosque: Nutcracker

30 Swan Lake

December 1968:

1 BALTIMORE, MD, Lyric Theatre: Swan Lake

2 HAMPTON, VA, Ogden Hall: Phases; Cyclus; Flower Festival in Genzano, pdd; One in Five; Concerto Barocco

3 WEST CHESTER, PA, Philips Memorial Aud: One in Five; Nutcracker, pdd; Concerto Barocco; Flower Festival in Genzano, pdd; Solitaire

5 CHAMPAIGN, IL, University Assembly Hall: Serenade; Cyclus; Solitaire

7† ALTON, IL, Hatheway Hall: One in Five; Phases; Flower Festival in Genzano, pdd; EH!; Serenade;

7 Bayaderka, Act IV; Cyclus; Solitaire

26† TORONTO, ON, O'Keefe Centre: Nutcracker — *repeated, December 26, 27a†, 27b†, 28a†, 28b†(two matinees on each day), 29†, 30a†, 30b† (two matinees on one day), 31†*

January 1969:

4† SEATTLE, WA, Seattle Center Opera House: Swan Lake — *repeated, January 4, 5, 6*

7 Nutcracker — *repeated, January 8, 9, 10*

11 VANCOUVER, BC, Queen Elizabeth Theatre: Swan Lake — *repeated, January 13†, 14, 15*

16† Nutcracker — *repeated, January 17†, 18†, 18*

19† VICTORIA, BC, Royal Theatre: Célébrations; Pas de Deux (Gordon); Studies in White; EH!; One in Five **(Group A)** — *repeated, January 20*

20 WEYBURN, SK, Collegiate Aud: One in Five; Rondo Giocoso; Studies in White; Célébrations **(Group B)**

21 NANAIMO, BC, Woodlands Jr. S.S. Aud: EH!; Studies in White; Pas de Deux (Gordon); One in Five; Célébrations **(Group A)**

21 MINOT, ND, McFarland Aud, Minot State College: One in Five; Studies in White; Rondo Giocoso; Célébrations **(Group B)**

22 PORT ALBERNI, BC, A.D.S.S. Aud: Célébrations; Studies in White; Pas de Deux (Gordon); EH!; One in Five **(Group A)**

22 MOOSE JAW, SK, Peacock Aud: One in Five; Rondo Giocoso; Célébrations; Studies in White **(Group B)**

23† CHILLIWACK, BC, Evergreen Hall: EH!; Studies in White; Pas de Deux (Gordon); One in Five; Célébrations **(Group A)**

23 YORKTON, SK, Yorkton Regional H.S. Theatre: Studies in White; One in Five; Rondo Giocoso; Célébrations **(Group B)**

24 KELOWNA, BC, Community Theatre: One in Five;

Célébrations; Pas de Deux (Gordon); Studies in White; EH! **(Group A)**

24   NORTH BATTLEFORD, SK, Sharp Aud: One in Five; Rondo Giocoso; Studies in White; Célébrations **(Group B)**

25   RED DEER, AB, Red Deer Memorial Centre: One in Five; Rondo Giocoso; Célébrations; Studies in White **(Group B)**

25   KIMBERLEY, BC, McKim H.S. Aud: Studies in White; EH!; Pas de Deux (Gordon); Célébrations; One in Five **(Group A)**

26   MEDICINE HAT, AB, Towne Theatre: Studies in White; One in Five; Rondo Giocoso; Célébrations **(Group B)**

28   CALGARY, AB, Jubilee Aud: Swan Lake

29   Nutcracker

30   EDMONTON, AB, Jubilee Aud: Swan Lake

31   Nutcracker

February 1969:

3   REGINA, SK, Sheldon Williams Collegiate Aud: Studies in White; Célébrations; One in Five; Rondo Giocoso **(Group B)**

4†   SASKATOON, SK, Saskatoon Centennial Aud: Swan Lake

5   Nutcracker

6   WINNIPEG, MB, Manitoba Centennial Concert Hall: Swan Lake

7†   Nutcracker — *repeated, February 7*

18   WINDSOR, ON, Cleary Aud: Studies in White; Cinderella, Act II pdd; Cyclus; Solitaire

19‡   Cinderella, Act II pdd; Nutcracker, Act II

19   Nutcracker

20‡   Nutcracker, Act II; Cinderella, Act II pdd

20   Nutcracker

21   Serenade; Cyclus; Solitaire

22†   Swan Lake — *repeated, February 22*

25   LONDON, ON, Grand Theatre: Nutcracker

26†   Cinderella, Act II pdd; Nutcracker, Act II

26   Nutcracker

27†   Solitaire, pdd; Nutcracker, Act II

27   Cyclus; Serenade; Solitaire

28   Swan Lake

March 1969:

1†   LONDON, ON, Grand Theatre: Swan Lake — *repeated, March 1*

18a†   TORONTO, ON, O'Keefe Centre: Cinderella — *repeated, March 18b†, 19a†, 19b† (two matinees each day)*

21a†   Romeo and Juliet — *repeated, 21b† (two matinees on one day), 22†, 22*

24   Four Temperaments; Nutcracker, pdd; Phases; Tchaikowsky Pas de Deux; Cyclus

25   Cyclus; Serenade; Four Temperaments

26   Concerto Barocco; Four Temperaments; Tchaikowsky Pas de Deux; Serenade

27   La Sylphide; Serenade

28   Solitaire; La Sylphide

29†   Swan Lake — *repeated, March 29*

30†   MONTREAL, QC, Place des Arts: Cinderella — *repeated, March 30*

June 1969:

2   OTTAWA, ON, National Arts Centre: Curtain Raiser; Kraanerg

3   Romeo and Juliet

4   Kraanerg; Solitaire

5   Romeo and Juliet

7†   Swan Lake — *repeated, June 7*

September 1969:

29   MILWAUKEE, WI, Uihlein Hall: Four Temperaments; Les Rendez-vous; Solitaire

30   Swan Lake

October 1969:

1   MILWAUKEE, WI, Uihlein Hall: Les Rendez-vous; Four Temperaments; Solitaire

2   Swan Lake

3   Nutcracker — *repeated, October 4†, 4*

6   OSHKOSH, WI, Civic Aud: Swan Lake

7   WAVERLEY, IA, Wartburg College, Neumann Aud: Four Temperaments; Nutcracker, Act II; Solitaire

8   ROCKFORD, IL, Coronado Theatre: Les Rendez-vous; Four Temperaments; Solitaire

9   TERRE HAUTE, IN, Tilson Music Hall: Les Rendez-vous; Four Temperaments; Nutcracker, Act II

10   KOKOMO, IN, Havens Hall: Les Rendez-vous; Bayaderka, Act IV; Solitaire

11   CLEVELAND, OH, Music Hall: Nutcracker

13   MOUNT CLEMENS, MI, Mt. Clemens H.S. Aud: Les Rendez-vous; Four Temperaments; Solitaire

14   KALAMAZOO, MI, Central H.S. Aud: Les Rendez-vous; Nutcracker, Act II; Bayaderka, Act IV

15   BATTLE CREEK, MI, W.K. Kellogg Aud: Solitaire; Les Rendez-vous; Bayaderka, Act IV

16   SAGINAW, MI, City Aud: Swan Lake

17   ANN ARBOR, MI, Hill Aud: Nutcracker, Act II; Four Temperaments; Solitaire

19   PITTSBURGH, PA, Syria Mosque: Swan Lake

20   TOLEDO, OH, Toledo Museum of Art: Les Rendez-vous; Four Temperaments; Solitaire

21   CHARLESTON, WV, Municipal Aud: Les Rendez-vous; Bayaderka, Act IV; Solitaire

22   REIDSVILLE, NC, H.S. Aud: Les Rendez-vous; Solitaire; Four Temperaments

23   CHARLESTON, SC, Civic Aud: Solitaire; Bayaderka, Act IV; Les Rendez-vous

24 ASHEVILLE, NC, Municipal Aud: Four Temperaments; Nutcracker, Act II; Les Rendez-vous

25 RICHMOND, VA, Virginia Museum Theatre: Les Rendez-vous; Bayaderka, Act IV; Solitaire

27 RALEIGH, NC, Reynolds Coliseum: Solitaire; Les Rendez-vous; Four Temperaments

28 Bayaderka, Act IV; Four Temperaments; Nutcracker, Act II

29 Les Rendez-vous; Four Temperaments; Solitaire

31 HERSHEY, PA, Community Theatre: Swan Lake

November 1969:

1 STORRS, CT, Jorgensen Aud: Solitaire; Four Temperaments; Nutcracker, Act II

2† MONTCLAIR, NJ, Montclair H.S. Aud: Solitaire; Nutcracker, Act II; Les Rendez-vous

3 RED BANK, NJ, Carlton Theatre: Les Rendez-vous; Nutcracker, Act II; Solitaire

18 TORONTO, ON, O'Keefe Centre: Kraanerg — *repeated, November 19, 20, 21, 22†, 22*

24 Swan Lake — *repeated, November 25*

26 Lesson; La Sylphide

27 Four Temperaments; Bayaderka, Act IV; Le Loup

28 Lesson; Bayaderka, Act IV; Le Loup

29† La Sylphide; Le Loup

29 Four Temperaments; Lesson; Le Loup

December 1969:

18† OTTAWA, ON, National Arts Centre: Nutcracker — *repeated, December 18, 19, 20†, 20*

26a† TORONTO, ON, O'Keefe Centre: Nutcracker — *repeated, December 26b† (two matinees on one day), 27†, 27, 28†, 29†, 30†, 31†*

January 1970:

2a† TORONTO, ON, O'Keefe Centre: Nutcracker — *repeated, January 2b†(two matinees on one day), 3†, 3*

20 KINGSTON, ON, Grand Theatre: Lesson; Nutcracker, pdd; Façade, Tango

21 BELLEVILLE, ON, Vocational School Aud: Façade, Tango; Nutcracker, pdd; Lesson

22 BURLINGTON, ON, Central H.S. Aud: Nutcracker, pdd; Façade, Tango; Lesson

February 1970:

16 HAMILTON, ON, Palace Theatre: Swan Lake

17 WINDSOR, ON, Cleary Aud: Lesson; Bayaderka, Act IV; Les Rendez-vous

18 La Sylphide; Solitaire

19† La Sylphide

19 Lesson; Solitaire; Four Temperaments

20 Bayaderka, Act IV; Le Loup; Les Rendez-vous

21† Le Loup; Solitaire; Les Rendez-vous

21 Swan Lake

24 LONDON, ON, Grand Theatre: Bayaderka, Act IV;

Four Temperaments; Les Rendez-vous

25† La Sylphide

25 Solitaire; Le Loup; Lesson

26 Lesson; Les Rendez-vous; Le Loup

27† La Sylphide

27 Les Rendez-vous; Lesson; Four Temperaments

28† Les Rendez-vous; Bayaderka, Act IV; Four Temperaments

28 Swan Lake

April 1970:

16 TORONTO, ON, O'Keefe Centre: Giselle — *repeated, April 17, 18†, 18, 19†*

21 Swan Lake

22 Concerto Barocco; Phases; Lesson; Solitaire

23 Swan Lake

24 Lesson; Concerto Barocco; Phases; Solitaire

25† Swan Lake — *repeated, April 25*

May 1970:

24 OSAKA, JAPAN, Festival Hall, Expo: Romeo and Juliet — *repeated, May 25, 26*

28 Le Loup; Solitaire; Four Temperaments — *repeated, May 29*

October 1970:

29 OTTAWA, ON, National Arts Centre: Giselle — *repeated, October 30*

31† Lesson; Le Loup; Mirror Walkers — *repeated, October 31*

November 1970:

5 OTTAWA, ON, National Arts Centre: Giselle

6 Swan Lake — *repeated, November 7†, 7*

December 1970:

16† OTTAWA, ON, National Arts Centre: Nutcracker — *repeated, December 16, 17†, 17, 18, 19†, 19*

26† TORONTO, ON, O'Keefe Centre: Nutcracker — *repeated, December 26, 27†, 28†, 29†, 29, 30†, 31†*

January 1971:

2† TORONTO, ON, O'Keefe Centre: Nutcracker — *repeated, January 2, 3†*

14 TUCSON, AZ, U of Arizona Aud: Serenade; Les Rendez-vous; Le Loup

15 Solitaire; Nutcracker, Act II; Four Temperaments

16† TEMPE, AZ, Gammage Aud: Swan Lake — *repeated, January 16*

18 LAS VEGAS, NV, Las Vegas H.S. Aud: Solitaire; Four Temperaments; Les Rendez-vous

19 SAN BERNARDINO, CA, California Theater of Performing Arts: Solitaire; Le Loup; Les Rendez-vous

20 SAN DIEGO, CA, Civic Theatre: Le Loup; Solitaire; Nutcracker, Act II

21   Kraanerg

22   LOS ANGELES, CA, Royce Hall, U.C.L.A.: Kraanerg

23†   Solitaire; Le Loup; Les Rendez-vous

23   Serenade; Le Loup; Four Temperaments

24†   Swan Lake — *repeated, January 24*

25   FRESNO, CA, Convention Centre: Serenade; Le Loup; Solitaire

27   BERKELEY, CA, Zellerbach Aud: Kraanerg — *repeated, January 28*

29   Solitaire; Le Loup; Four Temperaments

30†   Serenade; Nutcracker, Act II; Les Rendez-vous

30   Solitaire; Le Loup; Les Rendez-vous

31†   Swan Lake — *repeated, January 31*

February 1971:

1   SACRAMENTO, CA, Memorial Aud: Solitaire; Les Rendez-vous; Serenade

3   VANCOUVER, BC, Queen Elizabeth Theatre: Kraanerg

4   Solitaire; Nutcracker, Act II; Le Loup

5   PORTLAND, OR, Civic Aud: Swan Lake

6†   Nutcracker, Act II; Serenade; Les Rendez-vous

6   Swan Lake

7†   SEATTLE, WA, Seattle Opera House: Serenade; Les Rendez-vous; Nutcracker, Act II

7   Swan Lake

15   HAMILTON, ON, Palace Theatre: Giselle

16   Nutcracker

17   WINDSOR, ON, Cleary Aud: Giselle

18†   Nutcracker — *repeated, February 18*

19   Mirror Walkers; Sagar; Pas de Deux (Spain); Four Temperaments

20†   Giselle — *repeated, February 20*

23   LONDON, ON, Grand Theatre: Giselle

24†   Nutcracker — *repeated, February 24, 25†*

25   Mirror Walkers; Four Temperaments; Sagar; Pas de Deux (Spain) — *repeated, February 26*

27†   Giselle — *repeated, February 27*

April 1971:

21‡   TORONTO, ON, O'Keefe Centre: Pas de Deux Idyllic; Mirror Walkers; Sagar; Brown Earth; Journey Tree; For Internal Use As Well

21   Pas de Deux Idyllic; For Internal Use As Well; Mirror Walkers; Brown Earth; Sagar

22   Kraanerg

23   Romeo and Juliet — *repeated, April 24†*

24   Pas de Deux Idyllic; Mirror Walkers; Brown Earth; For Internal Use As Well; Sagar

28   Romeo and Juliet

29   Kraanerg

30   Giselle

May 1971:

1†   TORONTO, ON, O'Keefe Centre: Giselle — *repeated, May 1, 2†*

4   For Internal Use As Well; Pas de Deux Idyllic; Sagar; Mirror Walkers; Brown Earth

5   Mirror Walkers; Le Corsaire, pdd; Brown Earth; For Internal Use As Well; Pas de Deux Idyllic

6   Swan Lake — *repeated, May 7, 8†, 8*

June 1971:

16   TORONTO, ON, Ontario Place: Le Corsaire, pdd; Brown Earth; EH!; Swan Lake, dances from; Giselle, Peasant pdd; Nutcracker, Chinese Dance; One in Five — *repeated, June 23, 30*

July 1971:

21   TORONTO, ON, Ontario Place: Nutcracker, Chinese Dance; Brown Earth; Swan Lake, dances from; Swan Lake, Black Swan pdd; Giselle, Peasant pdd; EH!; One in Five — *repeated, July 28*

August 1971:

4   TORONTO, ON, Ontario Place: Giselle, Peasant pdd; Brown Earth; EH!; Swan Lake, dances from; Swan Lake, Black Swan pdd; Nutcracker, Chinese Dance; One in Five

11   Swan Lake, Black Swan solo; Giselle, Peasant pdd; Swan Lake, dances from; Le Corsaire, Female solo; Nutcracker, Chinese Dance; EH!; Brown Earth; One in Five

18   Giselle, Peasant pdd; EH!; Brown Earth; One in Five; Nutcracker, Chinese Dance; Swan Lake, dances from

September 1971:

8   TORONTO, ON, Ontario Place: One in Five; Giselle, Peasant pdd; Le Corsaire, pdd; Nutcracker, Chinese Dance; Swan Lake, dances from; EH!; Brown Earth

15   Nutcracker, Act II pdd; Brown Earth; EH!; Nutcracker, Chinese Dance; Giselle, Peasant pdd; One in Five; Swan Lake, dances from — *repeated, September 22*

October 1971:

1   TORONTO, ON, East York Collegiate Aud: Giselle, Peasant pdd; EH!; Autumn Song; Sleeping Beauty, dances from; Swan Lake, Black Swan pdd; Fandango

3   SUDBURY, ON, Sudbury H.S. Aud: EH!; Giselle, Peasant pdd; Sleeping Beauty, dances from; Swan Lake, Black Swan pdd; Fandango; Autumn Song

6   NORTH BAY, ON, Capitol Theatre: EH!; Autumn Song; Fandango; Swan Lake, Black Swan pdd; Giselle, Peasant pdd; Sleeping Beauty, dances from

7   KIRKLAND LAKE, ON, Northern College Aud: Fandango; Giselle, Peasant pdd; EH!; Autumn Song;

Sleeping Beauty, dances from; Swan Lake, Black Swan pdd

12 WINDSOR, ON, Centennial H.S. Aud: Giselle, Peasant pdd; Sleeping Beauty, dances from; Swan Lake, Black Swan pdd; Fandango; Autumn Song; EH!

14† LONDON, ON, Grand Theatre: EH!; Fandango; Giselle, Peasant pdd; Swan Lake, Black Swan pdd; Autumn Song; Sleeping Beauty, dances from

15 TORONTO, ON, Burton Aud, York U: Giselle, Peasant pdd; Sleeping Beauty, dances from; Swan Lake, Black Swan pdd; Fandango; Autumn Song; EH!

16† HAMILTON, ON, Mohawk College Theatre: Giselle, Peasant pdd; Autumn Song; Fandango; EH!; Sleeping Beauty, dances from; Swan Lake, Black Swan pdd — repeated, October 16

18 KINGSTON, ON, Grand Theatre: Autumn Song; Giselle, Peasant pdd; Sleeping Beauty, dances from; Fandango; EH!; Swan Lake, Black Swan pdd

19 BELLEVILLE, ON, Centennial School Aud: Fandango; Giselle, Peasant pdd; Swan Lake, Black Swan pdd; Autumn Song; EH!; Sleeping Beauty, dances from

21 PETERBOROUGH, ON, Thomas A. Stewart S.S. Aud: Giselle, Peasant pdd; Sleeping Beauty, dances from; Autumn Song; Swan Lake, Black Swan pdd; EH!; Fandango

22 ORILLIA, ON, Orillia Opera House: Swan Lake, Black Swan pdd; Autumn Song; Fandango; Giselle, Peasant pdd; EH!; Sleeping Beauty, dances from

23 DEEP RIVER, ON, C.J. Mackenzie H.S.: Autumn Song; EH!; Fandango; Swan Lake, Black Swan pdd; Sleeping Beauty, dances from; Giselle, Peasant pdd

December 1971:

15† OTTAWA, ON, National Arts Centre: Nutcracker — repeated, December 15, 16†, 16, 17, 18†, 18

26† TORONTO, ON, O'Keefe Centre: Nutcracker — repeated, December 26, 27†, 28†, 29†, 29, 30†, 31†

January 1972:

1† TORONTO, ON, O'Keefe Centre: Nutcracker — repeated, January 1, 2†

February 1972:

14 HAMILTON, ON, Palace Theatre: La Sylphide; Judgment of Paris; Fandango

15 Swan Lake

16 WINDSOR, ON, Cleary Aud: Session; La Sylphide; Judgment of Paris

17† La Sylphide

17 Session; Fandango; Evocation; Mirror Walkers

18 Intermezzo; La Sylphide

19† Swan Lake — repeated, February 19

22 LONDON, ON, Grand Theatre: Fandango; Judgment of Paris; La Sylphide

23† La Sylphide

23 Judgment of Paris; Session; Fandango; Evocation

24† La Sylphide

24 Intermezzo; Session; Judgment of Paris; Evocation

25 Swan Lake — repeated, February 26†, 26

March 1972:

24 MONTREAL, QC, Place des Arts: La Sylphide; Intermezzo

25† Evocation; La Sylphide

25 Swan Lake — repeated, March 26†

April 1972:

5† OTTAWA, ON, National Arts Centre: Kraanerg; Fandango; Session — repeated, April 5

6 Intermezzo; La Sylphide

7 Evocation; La Sylphide

8† Swan Lake — repeated, April 8

19 TORONTO, ON, O'Keefe Centre: Romeo and Juliet — repeated, April 20, 21, 22†, 22

23† La Sylphide; Fandango; Session

26 Swan Lake — repeated, April 27, 28, 29†, 29, 30†

May 1972:

2‡ TORONTO, ON, O'Keefe Centre: Swan Lake — repeated, May 3‡

3 Evocation; Fandango; Judgment of Paris; Intermezzo

4 La Sylphide; Mirror Walkers

5 Intermezzo; La Sylphide

6† Mirror Walkers; Fandango; Session; Evocation

6 Mirror Walkers; La Sylphide

17 LONDON, U.K., Coliseum: Mirror Walkers; Legende; La Sylphide

18 Intermezzo; La Sylphide

19 Mirror Walkers; La Sylphide

20† La Sylphide; Intermezzo

20 Kraanerg; Fandango; Judgment of Paris — repeated, May 22

23 Swan Lake — repeated, May 24, 25

26 Evocation; Intermezzo; Session; Fandango — repeated, May 27†, 27

30 STUTTGART, GERMANY, Württembergisches Staatstheater: La Sylphide; Intermezzo

June 1972:

5 PARIS, FRANCE, Théâtre des Champs-Elysées: Mirror Walkers; La Sylphide — repeated, June 6, 7

8 Fandango; Evocation; Session; Intermezzo — repeated, June 9, 10

11 Swan Lake — repeated, June 13

15 BRUSSELS, BELGIUM, Théâtre Royale de la Monnaie: La Sylphide; Intermezzo

16 Evocation; La Sylphide

17 Session; Kraanerg; Fandango

20 GLASGOW, U.K., King's Theatre: La Sylphide; Evocation

21 Swan Lake

22† La Sylphide; Evocation

22 Judgment of Paris; La Sylphide; Fandango

23 Fandango; Judgment of Paris; Kraanerg

24† Swan Lake — *repeated, June 24*

27 LAUSANNE, SWITZERLAND, Théâtre de Beaulieu: Intermezzo; Session; Judgment of Paris; Evocation

28 Swan Lake

July 1972:

1 MONTE CARLO, MONACO, Théâtre de Monte-Carlo, Salle Garnier: Swan Lake — *repeated, July 2*

3 Evocation; Intermezzo; Session; Judgment of Paris

September 1972:

1 OTTAWA, ON, National Arts Centre: Sleeping Beauty — *repeated, September 2†, 2, 3†, 3*

5 MONTREAL, QC, Place des Arts: Swan Lake — *repeated, September 6, 7*

8 Sleeping Beauty — *repeated, September 9, 10†, 10*

13 PHILADELPHIA, PA, Academy of Music: Sleeping Beauty — *repeated, September 14*

15 Fandango; Le Corsaire, pdd; Nutcracker, pdd; La Sylphide

16† Swan Lake — *repeated, September 16, 17†*

19 BOSTON, MA, Music Hall Theatre: La Sylphide; Nutcracker, pdd; Fandango; Le Corsaire, pdd

20 Swan Lake — *repeated, September 21, 22*

23 HARTFORD, CT, Bushnell Memorial Hall: Le Corsaire, pdd; La Sylphide; Nutcracker, pdd; Fandango

24† Swan Lake — *repeated, September 24*

26 ROCHESTER, NY, Eastman Theatre: Swan Lake — *repeated, September 27*

28 CLEVELAND, OH, Music Hall: Swan Lake

29 Nutcracker, pdd; Fandango; La Sylphide; Le Corsaire, pdd

30 COLUMBUS, OH, Veterans Memorial Aud: La Sylphide; Nutcracker, pdd; Fandango; Le Corsaire, pdd

October 1972:

1† COLUMBUS, OH, Veterans Memorial Aud: Swan Lake — *repeated, October 1*

3 BIRMINGHAM, AL, Municipal Aud: Nutcracker, pdd; Fandango; Le Corsaire, pdd; La Sylphide

4 Swan Lake

5 ATLANTA, GA, Maddox Civic Aud: Swan Lake — *repeated, October 6*

7† La Sylphide; Nutcracker, pdd; Fandango; Le Corsaire, pdd — *repeated, October 7*

8 CHARLOTTESVILLE, VA, University Hall Aud: Swan Lake

10 BALTIMORE, MD, Morris A. Mechanic Theatre: Le Corsaire, pdd; Nutcracker, pdd; La Sylphide; Fandango

11 Moor's Pavane; Fandango; La Sylphide

12 Swan Lake — *repeated, October 13, 14†, 14*

17 TORONTO, ON, O'Keefe Centre: Sleeping Beauty — *repeated, October 18, 19, 20, 21†, 21*

25 La Sylphide; Fandango; Moor's Pavane — *repeated, October 26, 27*

28† Swan Lake — *repeated, October 28, 29†, 29*

31‡ Sleeping Beauty

November 1972:

1 TORONTO, ON, O'Keefe Centre: Sleeping Beauty — *repeated, November 2, 3, 4†, 4, 5†*

December 1972:

6 WINDSOR, ON, Cleary Aud: Swan Lake

7‡ Swan Lake, Act II

7 Swan Lake

8 Nutcracker — *repeated, December 9†, 9*

13† OTTAWA, ON, National Arts Centre: Nutcracker — *repeated, December 13, 14†, 14, 15, 16†, 16*

21 TORONTO, ON, O'Keefe Centre: Nutcracker — *repeated, December 22†, 22, 23†, 23, 26†, 26, 27†, 28†, 28, 29, 30†, 30*

January 1973:

3‡ LONDON, ON, Grand Theatre: Nutcracker — *repeated, January 3, 4‡, 4*

5 Swan Lake — *repeated, January 6†, 6*

29 VANCOUVER, BC, Queen Elizabeth Theatre: Sleeping Beauty — *repeated, January 30, 31*

February 1973:

1 VANCOUVER, BC, Queen Elizabeth Theatre: La Sylphide; Fandango; Moor's Pavane

2 Swan Lake — *repeated, February 3†, 3*

5 SEATTLE, WA, Seattle Opera House: Sleeping Beauty — *repeated, February 6*

7 Fandango; Moor's Pavane; La Sylphide

8 PORTLAND, OR, Civic Aud: Swan Lake — *repeated, February 9*

10† La Sylphide; Sleeping Beauty, Act III pdd; Fandango; Nutcracker, pdd

10 Fandango; Moor's Pavane; La Sylphide

12 SAN FRANCISCO, CA, San Francisco Opera House: Sleeping Beauty — *repeated, February 13*

15 CUPERTINO, CA, Flint Centre: Moor's Pavane; Fandango; La Sylphide

16 Swan Lake

17 SAN FRANCISCO, CA, San Francisco Opera House: Sleeping Beauty — *repeated, February 18†, 18*

19 La Sylphide; Fandango; Moor's Pavane — *repeated, February 20*

22 BERKELEY, CA, Berkeley Community Theatre: Swan Lake

23 SACRAMENTO, CA, Sacramento Memorial Aud: Swan Lake

24   SAN FRANCISCO, CA, San Francisco Opera House: Swan Lake — *repeated, February 25†, 25*

27   LOS ANGELES, CA, Shrine Aud: Sleeping Beauty — *repeated, February 28*

March 1973:

1   LOS ANGELES, CA, Shrine Aud: Sleeping Beauty — *repeated, March 2*

3†   Swan Lake — *repeated, March 3, 4†*

6   HOUSTON, TX, Jones Hall: Sleeping Beauty — *repeated, March 7, 8*

9   Moor's Pavane; Fandango; La Sylphide

10†   Swan Lake — *repeated, March 10, 11†*

12   NEW ORLEANS, LA, Municipal Aud: Swan Lake

13   La Sylphide; Fandango; Moor's Pavane

15   MEMPHIS, TN, North Hall: Swan Lake

16   Fandango; La Sylphide; Moor's Pavane

17   ST. LOUIS, MO, Kiel Opera House: Swan Lake — *repeated, March 18†, 18*

20   KANSAS CITY, MO, Capri Theatre: Moor's Pavane; Fandango; La Sylphide

21   Swan Lake

22   IOWA CITY, IA, Hancher Aud: Sleeping Beauty — *repeated, March 23*

24   Fandango; La Sylphide; Moor's Pavane

25†   Swan Lake — *repeated, March 25*

27   CHAMPAIGN, IL, University Assembly Hall: Sleeping Beauty

28   Le Loup, pdd; Moor's Pavane; Fandango; La Sylphide

29   BLOOMINGTON, IN, Indiana U Aud: Sleeping Beauty

30   Swan Lake

31   INDIANAPOLIS, IN, Clowes Memorial Hall: Swan Lake

April 1973:

1   INDIANAPOLIS, IN, Clowes Memorial Hall: Swan Lake

3   GARY, IN, West Side H.S. Aud: Swan Lake

4   La Sylphide; Le Loup, pdd; Moor's Pavane; Fandango

5   CHICAGO, IL, Opera House: Sleeping Beauty — *repeated, April 6*

7   Swan Lake — *repeated, April 8†, 8*

10   GRAND RAPIDS, MI, Civic Aud: Fandango; Moor's Pavane; Le Loup, pdd; La Sylphide

11   Swan Lake

12   EAST LANSING, MI, Michigan State U Aud: Swan Lake

13   La Sylphide; Moor's Pavane; Le Loup, pdd; Fandango

14   DETROIT, MI, Masonic Aud: Swan Lake — *repeated, April 15†*

15   Moor's Pavane; La Sylphide; Fandango

24   NEW YORK, NY, Metropolitan Opera House:

Sleeping Beauty — *repeated, April 25, 26, 27, 28†, 28, 29†, 29*

May 1973:

1   NEW YORK, NY, Metropolitan Opera House: Moor's Pavane; Fandango; La Sylphide — *repeated, May 2*

3   Swan Lake — *repeated, May 4, 5†, 5, 6†, 6*

8   Sleeping Beauty — *repeated, May 9, 10, 11, 12†, 12, 13†, 13*

July 1973:

31   TORONTO, ON, Ontario Place: Swan Lake

August 1973:

2   TORONTO, ON, Ontario Place: Swan Lake — *repeated, August 7, 9, 13, 15, 17*

September 1973:

26   WINDSOR, ON, Cleary Aud: Solitaire; Le Loup; Les Sylphides

27‡   Le Loup; Les Sylphides

27   Les Sylphides; Solitaire; Le Loup

28   Giselle — *repeated, September 29†, 29*

October 1973:

1   HAMILTON, ON, Hamilton Place: Solitaire; Le Loup; Les Sylphides

2   Giselle — *repeated, October 3*

4   LONDON, ON, Grand Theatre: Solitaire; Le Loup; Les Sylphides — *repeated, October 5*

6†   Giselle — *repeated, October 6*

15   EDMONTON, AB, Jubilee Aud: Giselle — *repeated, October 16*

17   CALGARY, AB, Jubilee Aud: Swan Lake — *repeated, October 18, 19‡, 19*

23   WINNIPEG, MB, Manitoba Centennial Concert Hall: Swan Lake — *repeated, October 24, 25*

27   Giselle — *repeated, October 28†, 28*

30   REGINA, SK, Saskatchewan Centre of the Arts: Swan Lake

31‡   Swan Lake, Act II

31   Swan Lake

November 1973:

1   REGINA, SK, Saskatchewan Centre of the Arts: Giselle

5   SASKATOON, SK, Saskatoon Centennial Aud: Giselle

6   Swan Lake — *repeated, November 7‡, 7*

December 1973:

12†   OTTAWA, ON, National Arts Centre: Nutcracker — *repeated, December 12, 13†, 13, 14, 15†, 15, 16†*

19‡   TORONTO, ON, O'Keefe Centre: Nutcracker

— *repeated, December 20‡, 21, 22†, 22, 23†, 23, 26†, 26, 27†, 28†, 28, 29†, 29*

February 1974:

13 TORONTO, ON, O'Keefe Centre: Solitaire; Don Juan; Les Sylphides — *repeated, February 14, 15*

16† Les Sylphides; Moor's Pavane; Don Juan

16 Le Loup; Les Sylphides; Moor's Pavane — *repeated, February 17†, 17*

20 Sleeping Beauty — *repeated, February 21, 22, 23†, 23, 24†, 24*

26 Giselle — *repeated, February 27‡, 27, 28*

March 1974:

1 TORONTO, ON, O'Keefe Centre: Giselle — *repeated, March 2†, 2*

7 OTTAWA, ON, National Arts Centre: Solitaire; Don Juan; Les Sylphides

8‡ Le Loup; Solitaire; Les Sylphides

8 Don Juan; Les Sylphides; Moor's Pavane

9† Giselle — *repeated, March 9, 10*

12 BOSTON, MA, Boston Music Hall: Moor's Pavane; Le Loup; Flower Festival in Genzano, pdd; Les Sylphides — *repeated, March 13, 14*

15 Giselle — *repeated, March 16†, 16*

19 CHICAGO, IL, Opera House: Sleeping Beauty — *repeated, March 20, 21*

22 Giselle — *repeated, March 23†, 23, 24†*

26 SAN FRANCISCO, CA, San Francisco Opera House: Don Juan; Flower Festival in Genzano, pdd; Les Sylphides

27 CUPERTINO, CA, Flint Centre: Giselle

28 SAN FRANCISCO, CA, San Francisco Opera House: Don Juan; Flower Festival in Genzano, pdd; Les Sylphides

30† Don Juan; Le Loup; Les Sylphides — *repeated, March 30*

31† Giselle — *repeated, March 31*

April 1974:

2 LOS ANGELES, CA, Shrine Aud: Flower Festival in Genzano, pdd; Les Sylphides; Don Juan — *repeated, April 3*

4 Giselle

6† Sleeping Beauty — *repeated, April 6, 7†, 7*

9 MILWAUKEE, WI, Uihlein Hall: Les Sylphides; Don Juan; Flower Festival in Genzano, pdd

10 Giselle

11 Don Juan; Flower Festival in Genzano, pdd; Les Sylphides

12 DETROIT, MI, Masonic Aud: Giselle

13† Don Juan; Les Sylphides — *repeated, April 13*

16 HARTFORD, CT, Bushnell Memorial Theatre: Giselle

17 Les Sylphides; Don Juan — *repeated, April 18*

19 PROVIDENCE, RI, Veterans Memorial Aud: Les Sylphides; Don Juan

20† Giselle — *repeated, April 20*

23 NEW YORK, NY, Metropolitan Opera House: Sleeping Beauty — *repeated, April 24, 25*

26 Les Sylphides; Flower Festival in Genzano, pdd; Don Juan — *repeated, April 27†, 27*

28† Les Sylphides; Le Loup; Don Juan

28 Les Sylphides; Flower Festival in Genzano, pdd; Don Juan — *repeated, April 30*

May 1974:

1 NEW YORK, NY, Metropolitan Opera House: Giselle — *repeated, May 2, 3*

4† Sleeping Beauty — *repeated, May 4*

5† Les Sylphides; Flower Festival in Genzano, pdd; Don Juan — *repeated, May 5*

July 1974:

23 NEW YORK, NY, Metropolitan Opera House: Sleeping Beauty — *repeated, July 24, 25, 26, 27†, 27, 28†, 28*

30 Giselle — *repeated, July 31*

August 1974:

1 NEW YORK, NY, Metropolitan Opera House: Giselle

2 Swan Lake — *repeated, August 3†, 3, 4†, 4, 6, 7*

8 La Sylphide; Le Loup; Moor's Pavane — *repeated, August 9, 10†, 10*

14 TORONTO, ON, Ontario Place: La Sylphide — *repeated, August 15, 16, 17*

19 Swan Lake — *repeated, August 21, 23, 26, 28, 30*

October 1974:

3 QUEBEC CITY, QC, Le Grand Théâtre : Giselle

4 Inventions; Les Sylphides; Kettentanz

5 Kettentanz; Whispers of Darkness; Le Loup

8 SHERBROOKE, QC, Le Centre Culturel, U de Sherbrooke: Giselle

9 Les Sylphides; Le Loup; Kettentanz

11 FREDERICTON, NB, Fredericton Playhouse: Giselle

12 SACKVILLE, NB, Convocation Hall: Les Sylphides; Inventions; Kettentanz

16 ST. JOHN'S, NL, St. John's Arts and Culture Centre: Giselle — *repeated, October 17‡, 17*

18‡ Kettentanz; Les Sylphides; Inventions

18 Le Loup; Whispers of Darkness; Kettentanz

22 CHARLOTTETOWN, PEI, Confederation Centre of the Arts: Giselle

23 Les Sylphides; Le Loup; Kettentanz

24 ANTIGONISH, NS, St Francis Xavier U Aud: Kettentanz; Inventions; Les Sylphides

25 HALIFAX, NS, Rebecca Cohn Aud: Les Sylphides; Inventions; Kettentanz

26† Les Sylphides; Whispers of Darkness; Kettentanz — *repeated, October 26*

31‡ LONDON, ON, Grand Theatre: Les Sylphides; Kettentanz

31 Kettentanz; Whispers of Darkness; Inventions

November 1974:

1‡ LONDON, ON, Grand Theatre: Les Sylphides; Kettentanz

1 Inventions; Whispers of Darkness; Kettentanz

2 Giselle

4 WINDSOR, ON, Cleary Aud: Kettentanz; Whispers of Darkness; Inventions

5‡ Les Sylphides; Kettentanz

5 Kettentanz; Whispers of Darkness; Inventions

6 La Sylphide; Kettentanz

7 HAMILTON, ON, Hamilton Place: La Sylphide; Kettentanz

8‡ La Sylphide

8 La Sylphide; Kettentanz

9 Kettentanz; Whispers of Darkness; Inventions

December 1974:

18‡ TORONTO, ON, O'Keefe Centre: Nutcracker — *repeated, December 19‡, 19, 20, 21†, 21, 22†, 23†, 23, 26†, 26, 27, 28†, 28*

February 1975:

8 TORONTO, ON, O'Keefe Centre: Coppélia — *repeated, February 9†, 9*

12 Kettentanz; Whispers of Darkness; Inventions — *repeated, February 13*

14‡ Coppélia — *repeated, February 14, 15†, 15, 16†*

19 Kettentanz; Don Juan — *repeated, February 20, 21*

22† Giselle — *repeated, February 22, 23†, 23*

26 Sleeping Beauty — *repeated, February 27, 28*

March 1975:

1† TORONTO, ON, O'Keefe Centre: Sleeping Beauty — *repeated, March 1*

7 OTTAWA, ON, National Arts Centre: Sleeping Beauty — *repeated, March 8†, 8, 9†*

April 1975:

2 LONDON, U.K., Coliseum: Kettentanz; Flower Festival in Genzano, pdd; Don Juan

3 Giselle — *repeated, April 4*

5† Kettentanz; Don Juan — *repeated, April 5*

7 Coppélia — *repeated, April 8*

9 Giselle — *repeated, April 10*

11 Coppélia — *repeated, April 12†, 12*

15 THE HAGUE, NETHERLANDS, Nederlands Congresgebouw: Coppélia

17 EINDHOVEN, NETHERLANDS, Stadsschouwburg: Giselle

18 AMSTERDAM, NETHERLANDS, Stadsschouwburg: Giselle

19 Don Juan; Kettentanz

20† Giselle

July 1975:

22 NEW YORK, NY, Metropolitan Opera House: Sleeping Beauty — *repeated, July 23*

24 Coppélia — *repeated, July 25*

26† Sleeping Beauty — *repeated, July 26*

27† Coppélia — *repeated, July 29*

30 Swan Lake — *repeated, July 31*

August 1975:

1 NEW YORK, NY, Metropolitan Opera House: Swan Lake

2† Coppélia — *repeated, August 2*

3† Swan Lake — *repeated, August 3*

5 La Sylphide; Don Juan — *repeated, August 6*

7 Sleeping Beauty — *repeated, August 8*

9† La Sylphide; Don Juan — *repeated, August 9*

10† Sleeping Beauty — *repeated, August 10*

19 TORONTO, ON, Ontario Place: Offenbach in the Underworld; Les Sylphides — *repeated, August 20, 21†, 21, 22, 23†, 23*

September 1975:

26 MONTREAL, QC, Place des Arts: Swan Lake — *repeated, September 27*

28† La Sylphide; Kettentanz — *repeated, September 28*

October 1975:

2 VANCOUVER, BC, Queen Elizabeth Theatre: Coppélia — *repeated, October 3‡, 3*

4 Don Juan; Offenbach in the Underworld

6 EDMONTON, AB, Jubilee Aud: Kettentanz; La Sylphide

7 La Sylphide; Offenbach in the Underworld

10 BANFF, AB, Eric Harvie Theatre: Kettentanz; Kisses; Offenbach in the Underworld

11 CALGARY, AB, Jubilee Aud: La Sylphide; Kettentanz

12 La Sylphide; Offenbach in the Underworld

14 REGINA, SK, Saskatchewan Centre of the Arts: Coppélia — *repeated, October 15‡, 15*

17 SASKATOON, SK, Saskatoon Centennial Aud: Coppélia — *repeated, October 18†, 18*

20 WINNIPEG, MB, Manitoba Centennial Concert Hall: Don Juan; Kisses; Offenbach in the Underworld

21 Don Juan; Kisses; Kettentanz

22 Coppélia — *repeated, October 23, 24‡, 24*

30 HAMILTON, ON, Hamilton Place: Don Juan; Offenbach in the Underworld; Kisses

31‡ Offenbach in the Underworld; Les Sylphides

31 Les Sylphides; Kisses; Offenbach in the Underworld

November 1975:

1   HAMILTON, ON, Hamilton Place: Don Juan; Kisses; Kettentanz

3   WINDSOR, ON, Cleary Aud: Don Juan; Kisses; Offenbach in the Underworld

4‡ Kisses; Offenbach in the Underworld

4   Don Juan; Kisses; Offenbach in the Underworld

5   Les Sylphides; Kettentanz; Kisses

6   LONDON, ON, Grand Theatre: Kisses; Offenbach in the Underworld; Les Sylphides

7‡ Kisses; Offenbach in the Underworld

7   Kettentanz; Les Sylphides; Kisses

8   Offenbach in the Underworld; Don Juan; Kisses

December 1975:

2‡ OTTAWA, ON, National Arts Centre: Coppélia — *repeated, December 3, 4†, 4, 5, 6†, 6*

10 HAMILTON, ON, Hamilton Place: Nutcracker — *repeated, December 11‡, 11, 12*

23† TORONTO, ON, O'Keefe Centre: Nutcracker — *repeated, December 23, 24†, 26, 27†, 27, 29†, 29, 30, 31†, 31*

January 1976:

2   TORONTO, ON, O'Keefe Centre: Nutcracker — *repeated, January 3†, 3*

February 1976:

7   TORONTO, ON, O'Keefe Centre: Kettentanz; Monument for a Dead Boy; Offenbach in the Underworld

8† Don Juan; Kisses; Offenbach in the Underworld — *repeated, February 8*

11 Swan Lake — *repeated, February 12, 13, 14†, 14, 15*

18 Coppélia — *repeated, February 19‡, 19, 20, 21†, 21, 22†, 22*

25 Monument for a Dead Boy; La Sylphide

26 La Sylphide; Kettentanz

27 Monument for a Dead Boy; La Sylphide

28† Kettentanz; La Sylphide

28 Monument for a Dead Boy; La Sylphide

29† Offenbach in the Underworld; La Sylphide

29 Kettentanz; La Sylphide

March 1976:

3   TORONTO, ON, O'Keefe Centre: Sleeping Beauty — *repeated, March 4, 5, 6†, 6*

10 OTTAWA, ON, National Arts Centre: Swan Lake — *repeated, March 11‡, 11*

12 Kettentanz; Kisses; Offenbach in the Underworld

13† Swan Lake

13 Offenbach in the Underworld; Monument for a Dead Boy; Kettentanz

July 1976:

11 MONTREAL, QC, Place des Arts: Romeo and Juliet — *repeated, July 13, 14*

20 NEW YORK, NY, Metropolitan Opera House: Sleeping Beauty — *repeated, July 21*

22 La Sylphide; Four Schumann Pieces

23 Four Schumann Pieces; La Sylphide, Act II; Sleeping Beauty, Act III

24† Sleeping Beauty — *repeated, July 24, 25†, 27*

28 Swan Lake — *repeated, July 29*

30 Giselle

31† Swan Lake — *repeated, July 31*

August 1976:

1† NEW YORK, NY, Metropolitan Opera House: Giselle — *repeated, August 1, 3*

4   La Sylphide; Monument for a Dead Boy; Four Schumann Pieces

5   Giselle — *repeated, August 6*

7† Four Schumann Pieces; La Sylphide; Monument for a Dead Boy — *repeated, August 7*

8† Sleeping Beauty — *repeated, August 8*

16 TORONTO, ON, Ontario Place: Swan Lake — *repeated, August 17, 18†*

18 Kettentanz; Offenbach in the Underworld; Le Corsaire, pdd — *repeated, August 19, 20, 21†*

21 Swan Lake

September 1976:

22† ST. JOHN'S, NL, Newfoundland Arts and Culture Centre: Coppélia — *repeated, September 22, 23*

24‡ Offenbach in the Underworld; Four Schumann Pieces

24 Black Angels; Four Schumann Pieces; Sleeping Beauty, Act III pdd; Offenbach in the Underworld

25 Kisses; Offenbach in the Underworld; Le Corsaire, pdd; Kettentanz

29 HALIFAX, NS, Rebecca Cohn Aud: Sleeping Beauty, Act III pdd; Black Angels; Offenbach in the Underworld; Four Schumann Pieces

30‡ Kettentanz; Offenbach in the Underworld

30 Offenbach in the Underworld; Le Corsaire, pdd; Kettentanz; Kisses

October 1976:

1   HALIFAX, NS, Rebecca Cohn Aud: Four Schumann Pieces; Sleeping Beauty, Bluebird pdd; Party; Kettentanz

2   Monument for a Dead Boy; Le Corsaire, pdd; Four Schumann Pieces; Offenbach in the Underworld

5   CHARLOTTETOWN, PEI, Confederation Centre of the Arts: Coppélia

6‡ Coppélia, Act I

6   Four Schumann Pieces; Sleeping Beauty, Act III pdd; Black Angels; Offenbach in the Underworld

8   FREDERICTON, NB, Fredericton Playhouse: Coppélia

9†   Kisses; Le Corsaire, pdd; Offenbach in the
     Underworld; Kettentanz

9   Monument for a Dead Boy; Offenbach in the
     Underworld; Le Corsaire, pdd; Kettentanz

12   SHERBROOKE, QC, U de Sherbrooke: Coppélia

13   Four Schumann Pieces; Sleeping Beauty, Bluebird
     pdd; Party; Offenbach in the Underworld

November 1976:

12   TORONTO, ON, O'Keefe Centre: Romeo and Juliet
     — repeated, November 13†, 13, 14†, 14

17   La Fille mal gardée — repeated, November 18‡, 18, 19,
     20†, 20

December 1976:

8   HAMILTON, ON, Hamilton Place: Coppélia —
     repeated, December 9†, 9, 10

12   WINDSOR, ON, Cleary Aud: Coppélia — repeated,
     December 13

14‡ Coppélia, Act I

14   Coppélia

16   LONDON, ON, Grand Theatre: Coppélia — repeated,
     December 17, 18†, 18

23† TORONTO, ON, O'Keefe Centre: Nutcracker —
     repeated, December 23, 24†, 27†, 27, 28, 29†, 29, 30,
     31†, 31

February 1977:

10   TORONTO, ON, O'Keefe Centre: Romeo and Juliet
     — repeated, February 11, 12†, 12, 13

16   Party; Monotones II; Mad Shadows; Four Schumann
     Pieces

17   Four Schumann Pieces; Mad Shadows; Afternoon of
     a Faun; Black Angels

18   La Fille mal gardée — repeated, February 19†, 19, 20

23   Giselle — repeated, February 24†, 24, 25, 26†, 26

27   Kettentanz; Afternoon of a Faun; Monotones II; Four
     Schumann Pieces

March 1977:

2   TORONTO, ON, O'Keefe Centre: Swan Lake —
     repeated, March 3, 4

5†   Mad Shadows; Monotones II; Kettentanz; Party

5   Kettentanz; Afternoon of a Faun; Black Angels; Mad
     Shadows

6   Swan Lake

9   Sleeping Beauty — repeated, March 10, 11, 12†, 12

15   OTTAWA, ON, National Arts Centre: Romeo and
     Juliet — repeated, March 16, 17

18   La Fille mal gardée — repeated, March 19, 20†

June 1977:

5   TORONTO, ON, Leah Posluns Theatre: Bayaderka,
     Act IV

July 1977:

12   NEW YORK, NY, Metropolitan Opera House: La
     Fille mal gardée — repeated, July 13

14   Kettentanz; Flower Festival in Genzano, pdd;
     Monotones II; Le Corsaire, pdd; Mad Shadows

15   La Fille mal gardée

16† Le Corsaire, pdd; La Fille mal gardée

16   Collective Symphony; Kettentanz; Mad Shadows

19   Swan Lake

20   Giselle

21   Swan Lake — repeated, July 22

23† Giselle — repeated, July 23

August 1977:

17   TORONTO, ON, Ontario Place: Kettentanz,
     excerpts; Sleeping Beauty, Act III

18† Kettentanz; Sleeping Beauty, Act III — repeated,
     August 18, 20†, 21†

23   WINNIPEG, MB, Manitoba Theatre Centre:
     Monotones II (participation in 5th annual Dance in
     Canada Conference)

29   LOS ANGELES, CA, New Greek Theatre: Giselle —
     repeated, August 30, 31

September 1977:

1   LOS ANGELES, CA, New Greek Theatre: Giselle

2   Bayaderka, Act IV; Offenbach in the Underworld;
     Four Schumann Pieces — repeated, September 3, 4

6   Swan Lake — repeated, September 7, 8, 9, 10

13   CHICAGO, IL, Arie Crown Theatre: Sleeping Beauty
     — repeated, September 14, 15

16   Bayaderka, Act IV; Offenbach in the Underworld;
     Four Schumann Pieces

17   La Fille mal gardée — repeated, September 18†, 18

21   MONTREAL, QC, Place des Arts: Sleeping Beauty —
     repeated, September 22, 23, 24†, 24

25† Four Schumann Pieces; Bayaderka, Act IV; Mad
     Shadows — repeated, September 25

27   QUEBEC CITY, QC, Le Grand Théâtre: Sleeping
     Beauty — repeated, September 28, 29

October 1977:

2   WINDSOR, ON, Cleary Aud: Swan Lake — repeated,
     October 3, 4

5†   Bayaderka, Act IV; Kettentanz

5   Kettentanz; Four Schumann Pieces; Bayaderka, Act IV

6   HAMILTON, ON, Hamilton Place: Swan Lake —
     repeated, October 7†, 7

8   Kettentanz; Bayaderka, Act IV; Four Schumann Pieces

12   WINNIPEG, MB, Manitoba Centennial Concert Hall:
     Romeo and Juliet — repeated, October 13†, 13, 14

16   REGINA, SK, Saskatchewan Centre of the Arts: La
     Fille mal gardée — repeated, October 17

18‡ La Fille mal gardée, Act I

18   La Fille mal gardée

20 SASKATOON, SK, Saskatoon Centennial Aud: La Fille mal gardée — *repeated, October 21†, 21*

25 VANCOUVER, BC, Queen Elizabeth Theatre: Romeo and Juliet — *repeated, October 26†, 26, 27*

28 La Fille mal gardée — *repeated, October 29†, 29*

31 EDMONTON, AB, Jubilee Aud: Coppélia

November 1977:

1‡ EDMONTON, AB, Jubilee Aud: Coppélia, Act I

1 Coppélia

4 BANFF, AB, Eric Harvie Theatre: Coppélia

5 CALGARY, AB, Jubilee Aud: Coppélia — *repeated, November 6*

7‡ Bayaderka, Act IV; Collective Symphony

7 Bayaderka, Act IV; Afternoon of a Faun; Monotones II; Collective Symphony

17† TORONTO, ON, O'Keefe Centre: Coppélia — *repeated, November 17, 18, 19†, 19*

20 Bayaderka, Act IV; Collective Symphony; Mad Shadows — *repeated, November 23, 24*

25 Monotones II; La Sylphide; Afternoon of a Faun — *repeated, November 26†, 26*

December 1977:

13‡ OTTAWA, ON, National Arts Centre: Nutcracker — *repeated, 14, 15‡, 15, 16, 17†, 17*

20 TORONTO, ON, O'Keefe Centre: Nutcracker — *repeated, November 21†, 21, 22, 23†, 23, 24†, 27, 28†, 28, 29, 30†, 30, 31†*

February 1978:

8 TORONTO, ON, O'Keefe Centre: Sleeping Beauty — *repeated, February 9, 10, 11†, 11*

15 l'Après-midi d'un Faune; Four Schumann Pieces; Tchaikowsky Pas de Deux; Don Quixote, pdd; Dream

16 La Fille mal gardée — *repeated, February 17, 18†, 18, 19*

21 Swan Lake — *repeated, February 22, 23, 24, 25†, 25, 26*

March 1978:

1 TORONTO, ON, O'Keefe Centre: Don Juan; Dream — *repeated, March 2, 3*

4† Party; Dream; Collective Symphony — *repeated, March 4, 5*

8 Romeo and Juliet — *repeated, March 9‡, 9, 10, 11†, 11*

16 HAMILTON, ON, Hamilton Place: Sleeping Beauty — *repeated, March 17‡, 17*

20 OTTAWA, ON, National Arts Centre: Bayaderka, Act IV; Collective Symphony; Dream

21 Afternoon of a Faun; Dream; Monotones II; Mad Shadows

22 Bayaderka, Act IV; Collective Symphony; Dream

May 1978:

17 FRANKFURT/HOECHST, GERMANY,

Jahrhunderthalle: Sleeping Beauty

18 Kettentanz; Bayaderka, Act IV; Dream

20 LUDWIGSHAFEN, GERMANY, Theater im Pfalzbau: Romeo and Juliet

22 Sleeping Beauty

24 LEVERKUSEN, GERMANY, Forum: Romeo and Juliet

25 Sleeping Beauty

27 STUTTGART, GERMANY, Württembergisches Staatstheater: Sleeping Beauty

28 MULHEIM, GERMANY, Stadthalle: Dream; Bayaderka, Act IV; Kettentanz

June 1978:

1 UTRECHT, NETHERLANDS, Stadsschouwburg: Bayaderka, Act IV; Dream; Kettentanz

2 THE HAGUE, NETHERLANDS, Netherlands Congresgebouw: Bayaderka, Act IV; Kettentanz; Mad Shadows

3 Sleeping Beauty

4 AMSTERDAM, NETHERLANDS, Theater Carré: La Fille mal gardée

July 1978:

17 TORONTO, ON, Ontario Place: Bayaderka, Act IV; Sleeping Beauty, Act III — *repeated, July 19*

26 NEW YORK, NY, State Theatre: Swan Lake — *repeated, July 27*

28 Party; La Fille mal gardée — *repeated, July 29†, 29*

30† Bayaderka, Act IV; Dream; Collective Symphony — *repeated, July 30, 31*

August 1978:

4 TORONTO, ON, Ontario Place: Bayaderka, Act IV; Sleeping Beauty, Act III — *repeated, August 6†, 6, 8*

16 LEWISTON, NY, Artpark: Sleeping Beauty — *repeated, August 17†, 17*

18 La Fille mal gardée — *repeated, August 19*

20† Dream; Don Juan — *repeated, August 20*

September 1978:

20‡ ST. JOHN'S, NL, St. John's Arts and Culture Centre: La Fille mal gardée — *repeated, September 20, 21*

22† Afternoon of a Faun; Monotones II; Dream

22 Afternoon of a Faun; Monotones II; Dream; Rite of Spring

23 Bayaderka, Act IV; Sleeping Beauty, Act III; Collective Symphony

27 SACKVILLE, NB, Convocation Hall: Monotones II; Collective Symphony; La Fille mal gardée, pdd; Sleeping Beauty, Act III

28 HALIFAX, NS, Rebecca Cohn Aud: Bayaderka, Act IV; Monotones II; Rite of Spring; Don Quixote, pdd

29‡ Sleeping Beauty, Act III; Bayaderka, Act IV

29   Don Quixote, pdd; Monotones II; Bayaderka, Act IV;
      Collective Symphony
30   Sleeping Beauty, Act III; Rite of Spring; Bayaderka,
      Act IV

October 1978:

3   CHARLOTTETOWN, PEI, Confederation Centre of
      the Arts: La Fille mal gardée — *repeated, October 4‡, 4*
6   FREDERICTON, NB, Fredericton Playhouse: Rite of
      Spring; Monotones II; Dream; Afternoon of a Faun
7†   La Fille mal gardée — *repeated, October 7*
9   QUEBEC CITY, QC, Le Grand Théâtre : La Fille mal
      gardée — *repeated, October 10*
12   MONTREAL, QC, Place des Arts: La Fille mal
      gardée — *repeated, October 13, 14*
15†   Monotones II; Collective Symphony; Afternoon of a
      Faun; Dream — *repeated, October 15*
17   BROCKVILLE, ON, Civic Aud: Monotones II; Rite of
      Spring; Bayaderka, Act IV; Don Quixote, pdd
18   KINGSTON, ON, Grand Theatre: Monotones II;
      Bayaderka, Act IV; Don Quixote, pdd; Rite of Spring
20   WINDSOR, ON, Cleary Aud: Dream; Monotones
      II; Don Quixote, pdd; Sleeping Beauty, Act III —
      repeated, October 21
22†   La Fille mal gardée — *repeated, October 22, 23†*

November 1978:

8   TORONTO, ON, O'Keefe Centre: Giselle — *repeated,*
      November 9‡, 9
10   Mad Shadows; Élite Syncopations; Les Patineurs —
      repeated, November 11†, 11, 12†
15   Bayaderka, Act IV; Élite Syncopations; Don Quixote,
      pdd; Afternoon of a Faun
16   Don Quixote, pdd; Monotones II; Bayaderka, Act IV;
      Élite Syncopations
17   Giselle — *repeated, November 18†, 18*

December 1978:

6   HAMILTON, ON, Hamilton Place: Nutcracker —
      repeated, December 7†, 7, 8, 9†, 9
19   TORONTO, ON, O'Keefe Centre: Nutcracker —
      repeated, December 20, 21†, 21, 22, 23‡, 23, 24†, 27,
      28†, 28, 29, 30†, 30

February 1979:

8   TORONTO, ON, O'Keefe Centre: Romeo and Juliet
      — *repeated, February 9, 10†, 10, 11†*
14   Les Sylphides; Taming of the Shrew, pdd; Don
      Quixote, pdd; Le Corsaire, pdd; Legende; Élite
      Syncopations
16   Les Sylphides; Washington Square; Kettentanz —
      repeated, February 17†, 17, 18†, 18
22   Swan Lake — *repeated, February 23*
24   Le Loup; Rite of Spring; Les Patineurs — *repeated,*
      February 25†, 25

28   Élite Syncopations; Two Pigeons

March 1979:

1   TORONTO, ON, O'Keefe Centre: Élite Syncopations;
      Two Pigeons — *repeated, March 2, 3†, 3, 4†*
7   La Fille mal gardée — *repeated, March 8‡, 8, 9, 10†, 10*
14   OTTAWA, ON, National Arts Centre: Swan Lake —
      repeated, March 15‡, 15
16   Washington Square; Les Sylphides; Élite Syncopations
17†   Swan Lake
17   Élite Syncopations; Les Sylphides; Washington Square

June 1979:

26   CHICAGO, IL, Opera House: Swan Lake; Coppélia,
      pdd *(contributions to third international ballet festival)*
27   Swan Lake; Sleeping Beauty, Bluebird pdd; *(contribu-*
      tions to third international ballet festival)
28   Le Loup, pdd; Monotones II *(contributions to third*
      international ballet festival)
29   Swan Lake *(contributions to third international ballet*
      festival)
30   Swan Lake; Romeo and Juliet, pdd; Flower Festival
      in Genzano, pdd *(contributions to third international*
      ballet festival)

July 1979:

3   NEW YORK, NY, State Theatre: Sleeping Beauty —
      repeated, July 4, 5, 6, 7†, 7, 8†
10   Coppélia; Monotones II — *repeated, July 11, 12*
13   Giselle; Élite Syncopations
14†   Giselle; Le Loup — *repeated, July 14*
15†   Giselle; Élite Syncopations

August 1979:

6   LONDON, U.K., Royal Opera House: Swan Lake
7   Bayaderka, Act IV; Mad Shadows; Kettentanz
8   La Fille mal gardée — *repeated, August 9†, 9*
10   Swan Lake — *repeated, August 11†*
11   Kettentanz; Mad Shadows; Swan Lake, Act II, Scene I
19†   TORONTO, ON, Ontario Place: Élite Syncopations;
      Les Patineurs — *repeated, August 19*
21   LEWISTON, NY, Artpark: Giselle — *repeated,*
      August 22†, 22
23   Élite Syncopations; Les Sylphides; Washington
      Square — *repeated, August 24*
25   Coppélia — *repeated, August 26†, 26*

September 1979:

6   MONTREAL, QC, Place des Arts: Swan Lake —
      repeated, September 7, 8
9   Les Sylphides; Washington Square; Élite Syncopations
18   WINNIPEG, MB, Manitoba Centennial Concert
      Hall: Swan Lake — *repeated, September 19‡, 19*
20   Élite Syncopations; Collective Symphony; Dream —
      repeated, September 21

25 VANCOUVER, BC, Queen Elizabeth Theatre: Swan Lake — *repeated, September 26‡, 26*

27 Dream; Collective Symphony; Élite Syncopations — *repeated, September 28*

29† Élite Syncopations; Les Sylphides; Washington Square — *repeated, September 29*

30† Swan Lake

October 1979:

2 PRINCE GEORGE, BC, Prince George Opera House: Les Sylphides; Collective Symphony; Élite Syncopations

3† Les Sylphides; Élite Syncopations

3 Les Sylphides; Élite Syncopations; Collective Symphony

5 EDMONTON, AB, Jubilee Aud: Swan Lake — *repeated, October 6†, 6*

8 CALGARY, AB, Jubilee Aud: Swan Lake — *repeated, October 9‡, 9*

12 SASKATOON, SK, Saskatoon Centennial Aud: Élite Syncopations; Collective Symphony; Dream

13 Swan Lake

15 REGINA, SK, Saskatchewan Centre of the Arts: Élite Syncopations; Washington Square; Les Sylphides

16‡ Les Sylphides; Élite Syncopations

16 Les Sylphides; Élite Syncopations; Washington Square

17 Swan Lake

November 1979:

7 TORONTO, ON, O'Keefe Centre: Sleeping Beauty — *repeated, November 8, 9, 10†, 10, 11†*

14 Dream; Collective Symphony; Four Schumann Pieces — *repeated, November 15*

16 Four Schumann Pieces; Dream; Rite of Spring — *repeated, November 17†, 17*

18† Four Schumann Pieces; Dream; Collective Symphony

21 Coppélia — *repeated, November 22‡, 22, 23, 24†, 24*

December 1979:

13‡ OTTAWA, ON, National Arts Centre: Nutcracker — *repeated, December 13, 14, 15†, 15*

18 TORONTO, ON, O'Keefe Centre: Nutcracker — *repeated, December 19, 20†, 20, 21, 22†, 22, 23†, 26, 27†, 27, 28, 29†, 29*

February 1980:

6 TORONTO, ON, O'Keefe Centre: Giselle — *repeated, February 7*

8 Harlequinade Solo; Giselle; Le Corsaire, pdd; Dying Swan; Flower Festival in Genzano, pdd; Don Juan, pdd; Angali; Birds

9† Giselle — *repeated, February 9, 10†*

13 Washington Square; Monotones II; Le Spectre de la Rose; Serenade

14 Song of a Wayfarer; Washington Square; Serenade

15 Serenade; Le Spectre de la Rose; Monotones II; Washington Square — *repeated, February 16†*

16 Song of a Wayfarer; Washington Square; Serenade

17† Serenade; Le Spectre de la Rose; Monotones II; Washington Square

20 Romeo and Juliet — *repeated, February 21, 22, 23†, 23, 24†*

27 Two Pigeons; Études

28‡ Two Pigeons

28 Two Pigeons; Études — *repeated, February 29*

March 1980:

1† TORONTO, ON, O'Keefe Centre: Two Pigeons; Études — *repeated, March 1, 2†*

5 Swan Lake — *repeated, March 6, 7, 8†, 8*

11 LONDON, ON, Grand Theatre: Giselle — *repeated, March 12, 13‡, 13*

14 Washington Square; Serenade; Le Spectre de la Rose

15† Giselle

15 Washington Square; Le Spectre de la Rose; Serenade

18 HAMILTON, ON, Hamilton Place: Giselle — *repeated, March 19, 20*

21 Serenade; Le Spectre de la Rose; Washington Square — *repeated, March 22*

25‡ OTTAWA, ON, National Arts Centre: Giselle — *repeated, March 25, 26*

28 Études; Two Pigeons — *repeated, March 29†, 29*

April 1980:

27 GUANAJUATO, MEXICO, Teatro Juarez: Giselle — *repeated, April 28*

30 MEXICO CITY, MEXICO, Teatro de la Ciudad: Giselle

May 1980:

1 MEXICO CITY, MEXICO, Teatro de la Ciudad: Giselle

June 1980:

23 WASHINGTON, DC, Carter Barron Amphitheatre: Giselle

24 Rite of Spring; Serenade; Élite Syncopations

25 Giselle

26 Élite Syncopations; Rite of Spring; Serenade

27 Giselle

28 Élite Syncopations; Rite of Spring; Serenade

July 1980:

2 NERVI, ITALY, Teatro Maria Taglioni: La Fille mal gardée — *repeated, July 3, 4*

5 Serenade; Song of a Wayfarer; Le Corsaire, pdd; Élite Syncopations

August 1980:

13 TORONTO, ON, Ontario Place: Le Corsaire, pdd;

Élite Syncopations; Serenade — *repeated, August 14†, 14*

15 Le Corsaire, pdd; Rite of Spring; Serenade

16† Serenade; Le Corsaire, pdd; Élite Syncopations

16 Rite of Spring; Serenade; Le Corsaire, pdd

17† Serenade; Le Corsaire, pdd; Élite Syncopations

17 Rite of Spring; Serenade; Le Corsaire, pdd; Personal Essay

19 LEWISTON, NY, Artpark: Romeo and Juliet — *repeated, August 20†, 20*

21 Rite of Spring; Élite Syncopations; Serenade — *repeated, August 22*

23 Swan Lake — *repeated, August 24†, 24*

September 1980:

25 MONTREAL, QC, Place des Arts: Études; Two Pigeons — *repeated, September 26*

27† Giselle

27 Two Pigeons; Études

28 Giselle

30 SAINT JOHN, NB, Saint John H.S. Aud: Élite Syncopations; Serenade; Angali; Song of a Wayfarer; Dying Swan

October 1980:

1‡ SAINT JOHN, NB, Saint John H.S. Aud: Serenade; Élite Syncopations

1 Élite Syncopations; Serenade; Angali; Dying Swan; Song of a Wayfarer

3 SACKVILLE, NB, Convocation Hall: Song of a Wayfarer; Les Patineurs; Angali; Dying Swan; Élite Syncopations

6 CHARLOTTETOWN, PEI, Confederation Centre of the Arts: Swan Lake

7‡ Swan Lake, Act I, Scene II & Act II, Scene I

7 Swan Lake

9 HALIFAX, NS, Rebecca Cohn Aud: Angali; Élite Syncopations; Dying Swan; Serenade; Song of a Wayfarer

10‡ Serenade; Élite Syncopations

10 Les Patineurs; Swan Lake, Act II, Scene I; Élite Syncopations — *repeated, October 11*

15‡ ST. JOHN'S, NL, St. John's Arts and Culture Centre: Swan Lake, Act I, Scene II & Act II, Scene I

15 Swan Lake — *repeated, October 16*

17‡ Newcomers, Part I; Élite Syncopations

17 Song of a Wayfarer; Élite Syncopations; Dying Swan; Angali; Serenade

18 Playhouse; Élite Syncopations; Les Patineurs

November 1980:

12 TORONTO, ON, O'Keefe Centre: Playhouse; La Sylphide — *repeated, November 13†, 13, 14, 15†, 15, 16†*

19 Les Patineurs; Newcomers; Mad Shadows — *repeated,*

November 20†, 20, 21, 22†, 22, 23†

26 La Fille mal gardée — *repeated, November 27‡, 27, 28, 29†, 29, 30†*

December 1980:

16 HAMILTON, ON, Hamilton Place: Nutcracker — *repeated, December 17‡, 17, 18, 19, 20†, 20*

23 TORONTO, ON, O'Keefe Centre: Nutcracker — *repeated, December 24†, 26, 27†, 27, 28†, 28, 30†, 30, 31†, 31*

January 1981:

2† TORONTO, ON, O'Keefe Centre: Nutcracker — *repeated, January 2, 3†, 3*

February 1981:

11 TORONTO, ON, O'Keefe Centre: Swan Lake — *repeated, February 12†, 12, 13, 14†, 14, 15†*

18 Dream; Dark Elegies; Études

19† Études; Dream

19 Dream; Dark Elegies; Études — *repeated, February 20, 21†, 21, 22†*

25 Romeo and Juliet — *repeated, February 26†, 26, 27, 28†, 28*

March 1981:

1† TORONTO, ON, O'Keefe Centre: Romeo and Juliet

4 Song of a Wayfarer; Newcomers; Le Spectre de la Rose; Kettentanz — *repeated, March 5*

6 Belong; Le Corsaire, pdd; Diary; All Night Wonder; Plus One; Spring Dances; La Sylphide; Reflections

7† Newcomers; Kettentanz; Le Spectre de la Rose; Song of a Wayfarer — *repeated, March 7, 8†*

11 Sleeping Beauty — *repeated, March 12†, 12, 13, 14†, 14*

17 OTTAWA, ON, National Arts Centre: Sleeping Beauty

18† Kettentanz; Sleeping Beauty, Act III

18 Sleeping Beauty — *repeated, March 19*

20 Kettentanz; Newcomers; Le Spectre de la Rose; Song of a Wayfarer — *repeated, March 21*

24 KITCHENER, ON, Centre in the Square: Sleeping Beauty — *repeated, March 25*

27 WINDSOR, ON, Cleary Aud: Swan Lake — *repeated, March 28†, 28*

29† Kettentanz; Poèmes Intimes; Angali; Song of a Wayfarer; Études

29 Angali; Song of a Wayfarer; Kettentanz; Études

31 HAMILTON, ON, Hamilton Place: Sleeping Beauty

April 1981:

1† HAMILTON, ON, Hamilton Place: Sleeping Beauty — *repeated, April 1, 2†, 2*

May 1981:

3 LUXEMBOURG, LUXEMBOURG, Municipal Theatre: Swan Lake — *repeated, May 4*

6 STUTTGART, GERMANY, Würtembergisches Staatstheater: Swan Lake

7 Kettentanz; Études; Élite Syncopations

9 LUDWIGSHAFEN, GERMANY, Theater im Pfalzbau: Swan Lake

10 Élite Syncopations; Études; Monotones II; Song of a Wayfarer

12 LEVERKUSEN, GERMANY, Forum: Swan Lake — *repeated, May 13*

15 BERLIN, GERMANY, Internationales Congress Centrum Berlin: Swan Lake — *repeated, May 16*

19 FRANKFURT/HOECHST, GERMANY, Jahrhunderthalle: Swan Lake — *repeated, May 20*

22 DÜSSELDORF, GERMANY, Opernhaus Düsseldorf: Élite Syncopations; Kettentanz; Études — *repeated, May 23*

28 OTTAWA, ON, National Arts Centre: Romeo & Juliet, Ballroom Scene *(contribution to CAPDO gala)* — *repeated, May 29, 30*

August 1981:

19† TORONTO, ON, Ontario Place: Swan Lake — *repeated, August 19, 20, 21†, 21, 22†, 22*

25 LEWISTON, NY, Artpark: La Fille mal gardée — *repeated, 26†, 26*

27 Newcomers; Angali; Dying Swan; Song of a Wayfarer; Études — *repeated, August 28*

29 Sleeping Beauty — *repeated, 30†, 30*

September 1981:

1 LEWISTON, NY, Artpark: Sleeping Beauty — *repeated, September 2†, 2, 3*

10 MONTREAL, QC, Place des Arts: Sleeping Beauty — *repeated, September 11*

12† Song of a Wayfarer; Kettentanz; Le Spectre de la Rose; Newcomers; Angali — *repeated, September 12*

13 Sleeping Beauty

16 THUNDER BAY, ON, Fort William Gardens: Sleeping Beauty, Act III; Kettentanz; Sleeping Beauty, Act II, dances from; Le Corsaire, pdd (**Group A**)

16 VICTORIA, BC, University Centre: Song of a Wayfarer; Monotones II; Dying Swan; Angali; Les Sylphides, pdd; Le Corsaire, pdd; Kettentanz, selections; Sleeping Beauty, Act III pdd (**Group B**)

17‡ THUNDER BAY, ON, Fort William Gardens: Kettentanz; Sleeping Beauty, Act III (**Group A**)

17 VICTORIA, BC, University Centre: Dying Swan; Monotones II; Les Sylphides, pdd; Song of a Wayfarer; Le Corsaire, pdd; Sleeping Beauty, Act III pdd; Kettentanz, selections; Angali (**Group B**)

20 EDMONTON, AB, Jubilee Aud: Dying Swan; Song of a Wayfarer; Angali; Newcomers; Études

21 Sleeping Beauty

23 VANCOUVER, BC, Queen Elizabeth Theatre: Newcomers; Angali; Dying Swan; Song of a Wayfarer; Études

24‡ Kettentanz; Sleeping Beauty, Act III

24 Song of a Wayfarer; Angali; Dying Swan; Études; Newcomers

25 Sleeping Beauty — *repeated, September 26, 27†, 27*

30 CALGARY, AB, Jubilee Aud: Sleeping Beauty

October 1981:

1 CALGARY, AB, Jubilee Aud: Études; Newcomers; Angali; Dying Swan; Song of a Wayfarer

4 SASKATOON, SK, Saskatoon Centennial Aud: Sleeping Beauty — *repeated, October 5*

7 REGINA, SK, Saskatchewan Centre of the Arts: Sleeping Beauty

8‡ Sleeping Beauty, Act III

8 Sleeping Beauty

12 WINNIPEG, MB, Manitoba Centennial Concert Hall: Sleeping Beauty

13‡ Kettentanz; Sleeping Beauty, Act III

13 Sleeping Beauty

14 Angali; Newcomers; Dying Swan; Song of a Wayfarer; Études

November 1981:

10 TORONTO, ON, O'Keefe Centre: Napoli — *repeated, November 11, 12, 13, 14†, 14, 15†*

18 Giselle — *repeated, 19†, 19, 20, 21†, 21, 22†*

25 Les Sylphides; Los Siete Puñales; Élite Syncopations — *repeated, 26†, 26, 27, 28†, 28, 29†*

December 1981:

15 HAMILTON, ON, Hamilton Place: Nutcracker — *repeated, December 16†, 16, 17, 18, 19†, 19*

22 TORONTO, ON, O'Keefe Centre: Nutcracker — *repeated, December 23†, 23, 24†, 26, 27†, 27, 29†, 29, 30, 31†*

January 1982:

2† TORONTO, ON, O'Keefe Centre: Nutcracker — *repeated, January 2, 3†, 3*

27 HAMILTON, ON, Hamilton Place: La Fille mal gardée — *repeated, January 28‡, 28, 29*

30† Études; Élite Syncopations; Four Schumann Pieces — *repeated, January 30*

February 1982:

3 KITCHENER, ON, Centre in the Square: La Fille mal gardée — *repeated, February 4†, 4, 5*

10 TORONTO, ON, O'Keefe Centre: La Fille mal gardée — *repeated, February 11‡, 11, 12, 13†, 13, 14†*

17 Études; Four Schumann Pieces; Nataraja — *repeated, February 18†, 18, 19, 20†, 20, 21†*

24 Swan Lake — *repeated, February 25†, 25, 26, 27†, 27, 28†*

Appendix A

March 1982:

23 WEST PALM BEACH, FL, West Palm Beach Aud: Top Hat; Sleeping Beauty, Act III pdd; Don Quixote, pdd; Sylvia Pas de Deux; Dream, pdd; Le Corsaire, pdd; Sleeping Beauty, Bluebird pdd; Élite Syncopations; Don Juan, pdd

24 Monotones II; Giselle, pdd; Dying Swan; Don Quixote, pdd; La Sylphide

25 La Fille mal gardée — *repeated, March 26*

27† Angali; Swan Lake, White Swan pdd; Song of a Wayfarer; Tchaikowsky Pas de Deux; Études; Four Schumann Pieces — *repeated, March 27*

28† Monotones II; Le Corsaire, pdd; Dying Swan; Flower Festival in Genzano, pdd; Don Quixote, pdd; La Sylphide

30 HOUSTON, TX, Jesse H. Jones Hall: La Fille mal gardée

31 Swan Lake

April 1982:

1 HOUSTON, TX, Jesse H. Jones Hall: Swan Lake

2 FORT WORTH, TX, Tarrant County Convention Centre: La Sylphide; Élite Syncopations; Dying Swan; Don Quixote, pdd

3 La Sylphide; Don Quixote, pdd; Dying Swan; Études

4† La Sylphide; Dying Swan; Four Schumann Pieces; Don Quixote, pdd

May 1982:

5 TORONTO, ON, O'Keefe Centre: Napoli — *repeated, May 6†, 6, 7, 8†, 8, 9†*

12 Three Easy Tangos, excerpts from 'Late Afternoon'; Études; Manon, pdd; Le Corsaire, pdd; Kermesse in Bruges, pdd; Portrait of Love and Death; Adagio; Dream, pdd; Four Last Songs — (First Song); Monotones II

13† La Sylphide; Washington Square — *repeated, May 13, 14, 15†, 15, 16†*

19 Romeo and Juliet — *repeated, May 20†, 20, 21, 22†, 22, 23†*

26 LONDON, ON, Grand Theatre: La Fille mal gardée — *repeated, May 27‡, 27, 28*

29† Song of a Wayfarer; Études; Four Schumann Pieces; Monotones II — *repeated, May 29*

June 1982:

1 OTTAWA, ON, National Arts Centre: Napoli — *repeated, June 2, 3†, 3*

4 Nataraja; Los Siete Puñales; Four Schumann Pieces — *repeated, June 5*

August 1982:

18 TORONTO, ON, Ontario Place: La Sylphide — *repeated, August 20*

24 LEWISTON, NY, Artpark: Giselle — *repeated,*

August 25†, 25

26 Les Sylphides; Los Siete Puñales; Four Schumann Pieces — *repeated, August 27*

28 Washington Square; La Sylphide — *repeated, August 29†, 29*

September 1982:

16 MONTREAL, QC, Place des Arts: Napoli — *repeated, September 17, 18, 19*

21 FREDERICTON, NB, Fredericton Playhouse: Giselle — *repeated, September 22*

24 CHARLOTTETOWN, PEI, Confederation Centre of the Arts: Giselle — *repeated, September 25*

27 SACKVILLE, NB, Convocation Hall: Don Quixote, Act III; Rite of Spring; Kettentanz

29‡ HALIFAX, NS, Rebecca Cohn Aud: Giselle, Act I

29 Giselle — *repeated, September 30*

October 1982:

1‡ HALIFAX, NS, Rebecca Cohn Aud: Newcomers

1 Les Sylphides; Rite of Spring; Newcomers

2 Don Quixote, Act III; Kettentanz; Los Siete Puñales

6‡ ST. JOHN'S, NL, St. John's Arts and Culture Centre: Giselle — *repeated, October 6, 7, 8‡, 8*

9 Les Sylphides; Los Siete Puñales; Newcomers

10† Portrait of Love and Death; Don Quixote, Act III; Le Corsaire, pdd; Three Easy Tangos; Kettentanz — *repeated, October 10*

17 HAMILTON, ON, Hamilton Place: Rite of Spring — *repeated, October 18*

November 1982:

10 TORONTO, ON, O'Keefe Centre: Don Quixote — *repeated, November 11†, 11, 12, 13†, 13, 14†*

17 Kettentanz; Three Easy Tangos; Portrait of Love and Death; Le Corsaire, pdd; Rite of Spring

18† Rite of Spring; Los Siete Puñales; Élite Syncopations — *repeated, November 18*

19 Three Easy Tangos; Portrait of Love and Death; Le Corsaire, pdd; Rite of Spring; Newcomers

20† Newcomers; Le Spectre de la Rose; Song of a Wayfarer; Los Siete Puñales — *repeated, November 20*

21† Angali; Portrait of Love and Death; Le Corsaire, pdd; Rite of Spring; Kettentanz

24 Sleeping Beauty — *repeated, November 25†, 25, 26, 27†, 27, 28†*

December 1982:

14 OTTAWA, ON, National Arts Centre: Nutcracker — *repeated, December 15†, 15, 16, 17, 18†, 18*

21† TORONTO, ON, O'Keefe Centre: Nutcracker — *repeated, December 21, 22, 23†, 23, 24†, 27†, 27, 28, 29†, 29, 30, 31†*

January 1983:

2† TORONTO, ON, O'Keefe Centre: Nutcracker — *repeated, January 2*

25 KITCHENER, ON, Centre in the Square: Kettentanz; Le Corsaire, pdd; Napoli, dances from; Song of a Wayfarer; Dying Swan; Monotones II

26 Kettentanz; Angali; Don Juan, pdd; Portrait of Love and Death; Don Quixote, pdd; Napoli, dances from

28 WINDSOR, ON, Cleary Aud: Don Quixote, pdd; Napoli, dances from; Portrait of Love and Death; Three Easy Tangos, excerpts from 'Late Afternoon'; Les Sylphides, excerpts; Le Corsaire, pdd

29† Napoli, dances from; Les Sylphides, excerpts from; Le Corsaire, pdd; Romeo and Juliet, pdd; Portrait of Love and Death; Don Quixote, pdd

29 Three Easy Tangos, excerpts from from 'Late Afternoon'; Napoli, dances from; Don Juan, pdd; Canciones; Sleeping Beauty, Act III pdd; Le Corsaire, pdd

30† Portrait of Love and Death; Napoli, dances from; Canciones; Le Corsaire, pdd; Monotones II; Romeo and Juliet, pdd; Dying Swan

February 1983:

3† HAMILTON, ON, Hamilton Place: Le Corsaire, pdd; Napoli, dances from; Kettentanz; Angali; Song of a Wayfarer

3 Napoli, dances from; Monotones II; Le Corsaire, pdd; Song of a Wayfarer; Kettentanz

4 Nelligan; Le Corsaire, pdd; Kettentanz; Napoli, dances from; Canciones

5 Don Quixote, pdd; Nelligan; Napoli, dances from; Le Corsaire, pdd; Kettentanz; Don Juan, pdd; Angali

9 TORONTO, ON, O'Keefe Centre: Coppélia — *repeated, February 10‡, 10, 11, 12†, 12, 13†*

16 Giselle — *repeated, February 17†, 17*

18 Dream; Hedda; Offenbach in the Underworld — *repeated, February 19†, 19, 20†*

23 Canciones; Quartet; Hedda; Offenbach in the Underworld

24† Dream; Hedda; Offenbach in the Underworld

24 Canciones; Quartet; Hedda; Offenbach in the Underworld

25 Giselle — *repeated, February 26†, 26, 27†*

April 1983:

19 OTTAWA, ON, National Arts Centre: Don Quixote — *repeated, April 20, 21*

22 Dream; Hedda; Offenbach in the Underworld — *repeated, April 23*

May 1983:

4 TORONTO, ON, O'Keefe Centre: Swan Lake — *repeated, May 5†, 5, 6, 7†, 7, 8†*

11 Collective Symphony; Sphinx; Don Juan — *repeated, May 12†, 12*

13 Nataraja; Sphinx; Don Juan — *repeated, May 14†*

14 Collective Symphony; Sphinx; Don Juan

15† Nataraja; Sphinx; Don Juan

18 Napoli — *repeated, May 19†, 19, 20, 21†, 21, 22†*

August 1983:

2 TORONTO, ON, Ontario Place: Offenbach in the Underworld; Napoli, dances from; Sleeping Beauty, Act III pdd

3† Napoli, dances from; Offenbach in the Underworld — *repeated, August 3, 10†, 10*

16 LEWISTON, NY, Artpark: Don Quixote — *repeated, August 17, 18†, 18*

19 Coppélia — *repeated, August 20, 21†, 21*

September 1983:

6 QUEBEC CITY, QC, Le Grand Théâtre : Don Quixote — *repeated, September 7*

8 MONTREAL, QC, Place des Arts: Don Quixote — *repeated, September 9, 10*

14 WINNIPEG, MB, Manitoba Centennial Concert Hall: Don Quixote — *repeated, September 15*

17 REGINA, SK, Saskatchewan Centre of the Arts: Don Quixote — *repeated, September 18*

20 SASKATOON, SK, Saskatoon Centennial Aud: Don Quixote — *repeated, September 21*

23 CALGARY, AB, Jubilee Aud: Don Quixote — *repeated, September 24†, 24*

25 EDMONTON, AB, Jubilee Aud: Don Quixote — *repeated, September 26*

28 LETHBRIDGE, AB, Performing Arts Centre: Angali; Don Quixote, pdd; Romeo and Juliet, pdd; Canciones; Napoli, dances from

30 VICTORIA, BC, Royal Theatre: Canciones; Les Sylphides; Offenbach in the Underworld

October 1983:

1† VICTORIA, BC, Royal Theatre: Offenbach in the Underworld; Les Sylphides; Canciones — *repeated, October 1*

4 VANCOUVER, BC, Queen Elizabeth Theatre: Don Quixote — *repeated, October 5*

6 Les Sylphides; Canciones; Offenbach in the Underworld

7 Don Quixote — *repeated, October 8*

8 FORT MCMURRAY, AB, Keyano Theatre: Romeo and Juliet, pdd; Napoli, dances from; Angali; Canciones; Don Quixote, pdd (**Group A**)

November 1983:

9 TORONTO, ON, O'Keefe Centre: Romeo and Juliet — *repeated, November 10‡, 10, 11, 12†, 12, 13†*

16 Here We Come; Sylvia Pas de Deux; L'Île Inconnue;

Élite Syncopations — *repeated, November 17†, 17, 18, 19†, 19, 20†*

23 Don Quixote — *repeated, November 24†, 24, 25, 26†, 26, 27†*

December 1983:

13 KITCHENER, ON, Centre in the Square: Nutcracker — *repeated, December 14, 15†, 15, 16, 17†, 17*

20† TORONTO, ON, O'Keefe Centre: Nutcracker — *repeated, December 20, 21, 22†, 22, 23†, 23, 26, 27†, 27, 28, 29†, 29, 30†, 30*

January 1984:

9 HAMILTON, BERMUDA, City Hall Theatre: Coppélia, pdd; Élite Syncopations, excerpts; Don Juan, pdd; Khatchaturian Pas de Deux; Napoli, dances from — *repeated, January 10*

11 Song of a Wayfarer; Sylvia Pas de Deux; Romeo and Juliet, pdd; Sleeping Beauty, Act III pdd; Napoli, dances from — *repeated, January 12*

February 1984:

8 TORONTO, ON, O'Keefe Centre: La Fille mal gardée — *repeated, February 9†, 9, 10, 11†, 11, 12†*

15 Serenade; Endangered Species; Components; Études — *repeated, February 16†, 16, 17*

18 Curious Schools of Theatrical Dancing; In Paradisum, first movement from; L'Hôtel perdu; Master Class; Exit, Nightfall, Miserere from; Mobile; S'Agapo; Sinatra Suite; Sleeping Beauty, Act III

19† Serenade; Endangered Species; Components; Études

22 Swan Lake — *repeated, February 23†, 23, 24, 25†, 25, 26†*

29 OTTAWA, ON, National Arts Centre: Romeo and Juliet

March 1984:

1 OTTAWA, ON, National Arts Centre: Romeo and Juliet — *repeated, March 2, 3†, 3*

7 SAULT STE. MARIE, ON, White Pines Aud: Napoli, dances from; Coppélia, pdd; Don Juan, pdd; Khatchaturian Pas de Deux; Élite Syncopations

19 WEST PALM BEACH, FL, West Palm Beach Aud: Don Quixote — *repeated, March 20, 21†, 21*

22 Giselle

23 Here We Come; Sylvia Pas de Deux; L'Île Inconnue; Élite Syncopations — *repeated, March 24†*

24 Giselle

April 1984:

25 TORONTO, ON, O'Keefe Centre: Giselle — *repeated, April 26†, 26, 27, 28†, 28, 29†*

May 1984:

2 TORONTO, ON, O'Keefe Centre: Sphinx; Oiseaux

Exotiques; La Bayadère, Act II — *repeated, May 3†, 3, 4, 5†, 5, 6†*

9 Sleeping Beauty — *repeated, May 10†, 10, 11, 12†, 12, 13†*

June 1984:

14 TORONTO, ON, O'Keefe Centre: Onegin — *repeated, June 15, 16†, 16, 17†, 17*

August 1984:

2 TORONTO, ON, Ontario Place: Here We Come; Sylvia Pas de Deux; Oiseaux Exotiques — *repeated, August 3†, 3, 10†, 10, 11†, 11*

September 1984:

5 MONTREAL, QC, Place des Arts: Here We Come; Sylvia Pas de Deux; L'Île Inconnue; Élite Syncopations

6 Coppélia — *repeated, September 7, 8*

11 FREDERICTON, NB, Fredericton Playhouse: Coppélia — *repeated, September 12‡, 12*

14 CHARLOTTETOWN, PEI, Confederation Centre of the Arts: Coppélia — *repeated, September 15*

17 SACKVILLE, NB, Convocation Hall: Canciones; Oiseaux Exotiques; Mobile; Swan Lake, Black Swan pdd

19 HALIFAX, NS, Rebecca Cohn Aud: Here We Come; Sylvia Pas de Deux; L'Île Inconnue; Élite Syncopations — *repeated, September 20*

21‡ Here We Come; Sylvia Pas de Deux; Élite Syncopations

21 Oiseaux Exotiques; Le Corsaire, pdd; Canciones; Mobile

22 Oiseaux Exotiques; Swan Lake, Black Swan pdd; Mobile; Canciones

24 CORNER BROOK, NL, Arts and Culture Centre: Le Corsaire, pdd; Mobile; Canciones; Élite Syncopations, excerpts

26† ST. JOHN'S, NL, St. John's Arts and Culture Centre: Coppélia — *repeated, September 26, 27, 28‡, 28*

29 Élite Syncopations; Sylvia Pas de Deux; L'Île Inconnue; Here We Come

30† Mobile; Swan Lake, Black Swan pdd; Oiseaux Exotiques; Canciones — *repeated, September 30*

October 1984:

12 OTTAWA, ON, National Arts Centre: Here We Come; Sylvia Pas de Deux; L'Île Inconnue; Élite Syncopations — *repeated, October 13*

31 HAMILTON, ON, Hamilton Place: Coppélia

November 1984:

1 HAMILTON, ON, Hamilton Place: Coppélia — *repeated, November 2*

7 TORONTO, ON, O'Keefe Centre: Coppélia

8‡ Coppélia, Act I

8   Coppélia — *repeated, November 9, 10†, 10, 11†*

14   Serenade; Four Temperaments; Symphony in C

15‡   Symphony in C

15   Serenade; Four Temperaments; Symphony in C — *repeated, November 16, 17†, 17, 18†*

22   Components; La Sylphide — *repeated, November 23, 24†, 24, 25†*

December 1984:

11   OTTAWA, ON, National Arts Centre: Nutcracker — *repeated, December 12, 13†, 13, 14, 15†, 15*

18   HAMILTON, ON, Hamilton Place: Nutcracker — *repeated, December 19, 20‡, 20, 21, 22†, 22*

26   TORONTO, ON, O'Keefe Centre: Nutcracker — *repeated, December 27†, 27, 28, 29†, 29, 30†, 30*

January 1985:

2   TORONTO, ON, O'Keefe Centre: Nutcracker — *repeated, January 3†, 3, 4, 5†, 5, 6†, 6*

February 1985:

20   TORONTO, ON, O'Keefe Centre: Napoli

21‡   Napoli, Act III

21   Napoli — *repeated, February 22, 23†, 23, 24†*

27   Les Sylphides; Canciones; Blue Snake — *repeated, February 28*

March 1985:

1   TORONTO, ON, O'Keefe Centre: Les Sylphides; Canciones; Blue Snake — *repeated, March 2†, 2, 3†*

5   KITCHENER, ON, Centre in the Square: Don Quixote

7   WINDSOR, ON, Cleary Aud: Don Quixote — *repeated, March 8, 9†, 9*

13   OTTAWA, ON, National Arts Centre: Onegin — *repeated, March 14, 15, 16†, 16*

April 1985:

24   TORONTO, ON, O'Keefe Centre: Romeo and Juliet — *repeated, April 25, 26, 27†, 27, 28†*

May 1985:

1   TORONTO, ON, O'Keefe Centre: Piano Concerto; Realm; Raymonda, Act III — *repeated, May 2, 3, 4†, 4, 5†*

13   LUXEMBOURG, LUXEMBOURG, Nouveau Théâtre Municipal Luxembourg: Don Quixote — *repeated, May 14*

17   BERLIN, GERMANY, Internationales Congress Centrum Berlin: Don Quixote

18   L'Île Inconnue; Sphinx; Élite Syncopations

20   LUDWIGSHAFEN, GERMANY, Theater im Pfalzbau: Don Quixote

21   L'Île Inconnue; Sphinx; Élite Syncopations

22   Don Quixote

23   LEVERKUSEN, GERMANY, Forum: Don Quixote

25   WIESBADEN, GERMANY, Hessisches Staatstheater Wiesbaden: Don Quixote

26   Canciones; Coppélia, pdd; Components; Raymonda, Act III

28   ZURICH, SWITZERLAND, Opernhaus Zürich: Don Quixote — *repeated, May 29*

June 1985:

2   STUTTGART, GERMANY, Württembergisches Staatstheater: Don Quixote

3   Components; Canciones; Raymonda, Act III

6   MUNICH, GERMANY, Bayerische Staatsoper: Don Quixote

7   Canciones; Components; Raymonda, Act III

12   MILAN, ITALY, Teatro Lyrico: Don Quixote — *repeated, June 13, 14*

15   Élite Syncopations; Canciones; Components — *repeated, June 16*

17   Don Quixote — *repeated, June 18*

21   AMSTERDAM, NETHERLANDS, Theater Carré: Don Quixote

22   L'Île Inconnue; Components; Raymonda, Act III

August 1985:

7†   TORONTO, ON, Ontario Place: Blue Snake, excerpts; Raymonda, Act III; Pastel; Capriccio

7   Sinfonia; Blue Snake, excerpts; Raymonda, Act III; Pastel

8   Raymonda, Act III; Pastel; Capriccio; Blue Snake, excerpts

9†   Raymonda, Act III; Pastel; Sinfonia; Blue Snake, excerpts

9   Capriccio; Blue Snake, excerpts; Raymonda, Act III; Pastel — *repeated, August 10†*

10   Raymonda, Act III; Pastel; Sinfonia; Blue Snake, excerpts

27   LEWISTON, NY, Artpark: Onegin — *repeated, August 28*

29†   Canciones; Components; Raymonda, Act III — *repeated, August 29, 30*

31   Onegin

September 1985:

1†   LEWISTON, NY, Artpark: Onegin — *repeated, September 1*

10   OTTAWA, ON, National Arts Centre: Components; Canciones; Blue Snake — *repeated, September 11*

17   SAULT STE. MARIE, ON, White Pines Aud: Etc!; Coppélia, pdd; Canciones; Reminiscence; Le Corsaire, pdd; On Occasion

21   VICTORIA, BC, Royal Theatre: Raymonda, Act III; Le Corsaire, pdd; Villanella; Coppélia, pdd; On Occasion; Reminiscence — *repeated, September 22†, 22*

25   VANCOUVER, BC, Queen Elizabeth Theatre: Onegin — *repeated, September 26, 27, 28*

29† Coppélia, pdd; Raymonda, Act III; Villanella; Sleeping Beauty, Act III pdd; Components

October 1985:

2 CALGARY, AB, Jubilee Aud: Onegin — *repeated, October 3, 4*

6 LETHBRIDGE, AB, U of Lethbridge, University Theatre: Coppélia, pdd; Etc!; Le Corsaire, pdd; Raymonda, Act III; On Occasion; Reminiscence

7 EDMONTON, AB, Jubilee Aud: Onegin — *repeated, October 8, 9*

11 FORT MCMURRAY, AB, Keyano College Theatre: Etc!; Raymonda, Act III; On Occasion; Coppélia, pdd; Reminiscence; Le Corsaire, pdd

November 1985:

6 TORONTO, ON, O'Keefe Centre: Don Quixote

7‡ Don Quixote, Acts I & III

7 Don Quixote — *repeated, November 8, 9†, 9, 10†*

13 L'Île Inconnue; Sphinx; Élite Syncopations

14‡ L'Île Inconnue; Élite Syncopations

14 L'Île Inconnue; Sphinx; Élite Syncopations — *repeated, November 15, 16†, 16, 17†*

19 Onegin — *repeated, November 20, 21, 22, 23†, 23, 24†, 24*

December 1985:

17 HAMILTON, ON, Hamilton Place: Nutcracker — *repeated, December 18, 19†, 19, 20, 21†, 21*

24† TORONTO, ON, O'Keefe Centre: Nutcracker — *repeated, December 26†, 26, 27, 28†, 28, 29†, 29, 31†*

January 1986:

2† TORONTO, ON, O'Keefe Centre: Nutcracker — *repeated, January 2, 3, 4†, 4, 5†, 5*

8 BELLEVILLE, ON, Centennial S.S. Aud: Reminiscence; Swan Lake, Black Swan pdd; Canciones; Coppélia, pdd; On Occasion; Etc!

17 THUNDER BAY, ON, Thunder Bay Community Aud: Coppélia, pdd; Etc!; Swan Lake, Black Swan pdd; Canciones, excerpts; On Occasion, excerpts; Reminiscence, excerpts

February 1986:

19 TORONTO, ON, O'Keefe Centre: Alice; La Bayadère, Act II — *repeated, February 20, 21, 22†, 22, 23†*

26 La Fille mal gardée — *repeated, February 27‡, 27, 28*

March 1986:

1† TORONTO, ON, O'Keefe Centre: La Fille mal gardée — *repeated, March 1, 2†*

6 HAMILTON, ON, Hamilton Place: Don Quixote — *repeated, March 7, 8*

12 LONDON, ON, Grand Theatre: Don Quixote — *repeated, March 13, 14, 15†, 15*

25 OTTAWA, ON, National Arts Centre: La Fille mal gardée — *repeated, March 26‡, 26, 27*

April 1986:

30 TORONTO, ON, O'Keefe Centre: Transfigured Night; Dream; Hot House: Thriving on a Riff

May 1986:

1‡ TORONTO, ON, O'Keefe Centre: Dream; Hot House: Thriving on a Riff

1 Dream; Hot House: Thriving on a Riff; Transfigured Night — *repeated, May 2, 3†, 3, 4†*

7 Swan Lake — *repeated, May 8, 9, 10†, 10, 11†, 11*

21 Villanella, excerpt; Dying Swan; La Sylphide, excerpt; Realm, excerpt; Piano Concerto, excerpt; Blue Snake, excerpt; Oiseaux Exotiques, excerpts; Alice — excerpt; Hot House: Thriving on a Riff, excerpt; L'Île Inconnue, excerpt; Components, excerpt *(Tribute to Erik Bruhn)*

June 1986:

1† TORONTO, ON, Tanenbaum Opera Centre: Boys' Ballet Demonstration (NBSch); Angali; Oiseaux Exotiques, excerpts; Recital (NBC Workshop Rep); Bits and Pieces (NBC Workshop Rep); Kinderen Variations (NBSch); Nutcracker, Act II pdd; La Fille mal gardée, pdd; Dream, pdd *(Tribute to John Goss)*

July 1986:

22 NEW YORK, NY, Metropolitan Opera House: Hot House: Thriving on a Riff; Angali; Alice — *repeated, July 23, 24, 25, 26†*

26 Hot House: Thriving on a Riff; Angali; Villanella; Alice — *repeated, July 27†*

30† TORONTO, ON, Ontario Place: Élite Syncopations; Swan Lake, Act I, Scene II

30 Swan Lake, Act I, Scene II; Khatchaturian Pas de Deux; Hot House: Thriving on a Riff — *repeated, July 31*

August 1986:

1† TORONTO, ON, Ontario Place: Swan Lake, Act I, Scene II; Khatchaturian Pas de Deux; Hot House: Thriving on a Riff

1 Swan Lake, Act I, Scene II; Élite Syncopations — *repeated, August 2†*

2 Swan Lake, Act I, Scene II; Hot House: Thriving on a Riff; Khatchaturian Pas de Deux

4 TORONTO, ON, O'Keefe Centre: Élite Syncopations

14 VANCOUVER, BC, Queen Elizabeth Theatre: *(with Royal Winnipeg Ballet and Les Grands Ballets Canadiens)* Lost in Twilight; Collisions (Les Grands); Steps (RWB) — *repeated, August 15, 16†, 16*

22 VIENNA, VA, Wolf Trap Park: *(with Royal Winnipeg Ballet and Les Grands Ballets Canadiens)* Lost in

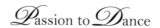

Twilight; Collisions (Les Grands); Steps (RWB) —
repeated, August 23, 24

September 1986:

12   ORILLIA, ON, Orillia Opera House: Angali;
Canciones; Don Quixote, pdd; Inner Drop; Etc!; On
Occasion

13   OSHAWA, ON, Eastdale Collegiate: Inner Drop; Don
Quixote, pdd; Etc!; Angali; On Occasion; Canciones

23   FREDERICTON, NB, Fredericton Playhouse: Don
Quixote

24† Don Quixote, Acts I & III

24   Don Quixote

26   CHARLOTTETOWN, PEI, Confederation Centre of
the Arts: Don Quixote — *repeated, September 27*

29   SACKVILLE, NB, Convocation Hall: Swan Lake, Act
I, Scene II; Transfigured Night; Khatchaturian Pas de
Deux; Hot House: Thriving on a Riff

October 1986:

1   HALIFAX, NS, Rebecca Cohn Aud: Transfigured
Night; Khatchaturian Pas de Deux; Swan Lake, Act I,
Scene II; Hot House: Thriving on a Riff

2†   Swan Lake, Act I, Scene II; Khatchaturian Pas de
Deux; Etc!

2   Khatchaturian Pas de Deux; Hot House: Thriving on
a Riff; Transfigured Night; Swan Lake, Act I, Scene II

3   Les Sylphides, pdd; Angali; Reminiscence; Don
Quixote, Act III; On Occasion — *repeated, October 4*

6   CORNER BROOK, NL, Arts and Culture Centre: On
Occasion; Angali; Transfigured Night; Don Quixote,
pdd; Reminiscence; Etc!

8‡   ST. JOHN'S, NL, St. John's Arts and Culture Centre:
Don Quixote, Acts I & III

8   Don Quixote — *repeated, October 9*

10‡ Don Quixote, Acts I & II

10   Don Quixote

11   Swan Lake, Act I, Scene II; Transfigured Night;
Angali; Hot House: Thriving on a Riff

12   GANDER, NL, Arts and Culture Centre: Angali;
Reminiscence; Etc!; Transfigured Night; On
Occasion; Don Quixote, pdd

November 1986:

7   TORONTO, ON, O'Keefe Centre: Merry Widow —
*repeated, November 8, 9†, 11, 12, 13‡, 13, 14, 15†, 15,
16†*

19   Song of a Wayfarer; Études; Concerto for the
Elements: Piano Concerto

20   Giselle — *repeated, November 21*

22† Concerto for the Elements: Piano Concerto; Song of
a Wayfarer; Études — *repeated, November 22, 23†*

25   Giselle — *repeated, November 26‡, 26*

27   Song of a Wayfarer; Études; Concerto for the
Elements: Piano Concerto — *repeated, November 28*

29† Giselle — *repeated, November 29, 30†*

December 1986:

17   TORONTO, ON, O'Keefe Centre: Nutcracker —
*repeated, December 18, 19, 20†, 20, 21†, 21, 23†, 23,
24†, 27†, 27, 28†, 28, 29, 30†, 30, 31†*

January 1987:

2†   TORONTO, ON, O'Keefe Centre: Nutcracker —
repeated, January 2

12   HAMILTON, BERMUDA, City Hall Theatre: Les
Sylphides, pdd; Transfigured Night; Inner Drop;
Swan Lake, Black Swan pdd; Etc!; On Occasion

13   Canciones; Tuwat; Don Quixote, pdd; Monotones II;
Coppélia, pdd; Reminiscence

14   On Occasion; Les Sylphides, pdd; Transfigured
Night; Inner Drop; Swan Lake, Black Swan pdd; Etc!

15   Tuwat; Canciones; Coppélia, pdd; Reminiscence;
Don Quixote, pdd; Monotones II

February 1987:

11   TORONTO, ON, O'Keefe Centre: Coppélia —
repeated, 12‡, 12, 13, 14†, 14, 15†, 15

18   Symphony in C; Four Temperaments; Serenade

19‡ Symphony in C; Four Temperaments

19   Serenade; Four Temperaments; Symphony in C —
repeated, February 20, 21†, 21, 22†

25   Overture: Dance for A Celebration; Song of a
Wayfarer; Étude; Offenbach in the Underworld, pdd;
Barbara Allen, excerpt; Pas de Deux (Spain); Don
Quixote, pdd; Impromptu; Mad Shadows, excerpt;
Polovetsian Dances, excerpt; Washington Square,
excerpt *(35th anniversary celebration)*

26   Monotones II; Transfigured Night; Raymonda, Act
III; Here We Come — *repeated, February 27, 28†, 28*

March 1987:

1†   TORONTO, ON, O'Keefe Centre: Raymonda, Act III;
Here We Come; Monotones II; Transfigured Night

13   MINNEAPOLIS, MN, Northrop Aud: Alice;
Serenade

14† Coppélia — *repeated, March 14*

16   CHICAGO, IL, Auditorium Theatre: Serenade; Swan
Lake, White Swan pdd; Alice — *repeated, March 17*

21† MIAMI, FL, Dade County Aud: Coppélia — *repeated,
March 21*

22† Serenade; Alice — *repeated, March 22*

24† CLEARWATER, FL, Ruth Eckerd Hall: Coppélia —
repeated, March 24, 25†

25   Serenade; Alice

27† WEST PALM BEACH, FL, West Palm Beach Aud:
Coppélia — *repeated, March 27*

28† Serenade; Alice — *repeated, March 28*

31   WASHINGTON, DC, Kennedy Center: Serenade;
Alice

Appendix A

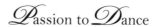

Temperaments; Voluntaries; Song of the Earth — *repeated, April 29, 30†, 30*

May 1988:

1† TORONTO, ON, O'Keefe Centre: Four Temperaments; Voluntaries; Song of the Earth

4 Onegin — *repeated, May 5‡, 5, 6, 7†, 7, 8†*

10 Four Temperaments; Voluntaries; Song of the Earth — *repeated, May 11, 12*

13 Onegin

14 Blue Snake, Balloon Head Solo (National Ballet of Canada); Don Quixote, Act III Grand pdd, (Royal Ballet, England); Four Seasons, Autumn (Royal Ballet, England); Four Seasons, Summer (Royal Ballet, England); La Sylphide, Act II pdd (Royal Danish Ballet); Leaves are Fading (Royal Danish Ballet); Rite of Spring (Tetley), The Dance of the Chosen One (National Ballet of Canada); Romeo and Juliet, Act I pdd (American Ballet Theatre); Sleeping Beauty, Act III pdd (American Ballet Theatre); Swan Lake, Black Swan pdd (National Ballet of Canada); Swan Lake, White Swan pdd (Special Appearance by Natalia Makarova); Voluntaries *(First Erik Bruhn Competition)*

15 Onegin

26 SAN DIEGO, CA, Civic Theatre: Onegin — *repeated, May 27*

28† Four Temperaments; Alice — *repeated, May 28*

30 PASADENA, CA, Pasadena Civic Aud: Onegin — *repeated, May 31*

June 1988:

1 PASADENA, CA, Pasadena Civic Aud: Onegin — *repeated, June 2*

4 Four Temperaments; Alice — *repeated, June 5†, 5*

7 COSTA MESA, CA, Orange County Perf. Arts Centre: Four Temperaments; Alice — *repeated, June 8, 9*

10 Onegin — *repeated, June 11†, 11, 12†*

July 1988:

18 NEW YORK, NY, Metropolitan Opera House: La Ronde; Blue Snake

19 Onegin — *repeated, July 20†, 20*

21 La Ronde; Blue Snake — *repeated, July 22*

23† Onegin — *repeated, July 23*

August 1988:

9 TORONTO, ON, John Bassett Theatre: Élite Syncopations

11† TORONTO, ON, Ontario Place: Concerto; La Bayadère, Act II — *repeated, August 11, 12, 13†, 13, 14†, 14*

September 1988:

11 SAINT JOHN, NB, Saint John H.S. Aud: Concerto, pdd; Death of a Lady's Man; Concerto Barocco; Etc!;

Sleeping Beauty, Act III, pdd; Trapdance

13 FREDERICTON, NB, Fredericton Playhouse: Serenade; Trapdance; Sleeping Beauty, Act III — *repeated, September 14*

16 CHARLOTTETOWN, PEI, Confederation Centre of the Arts: Serenade; Trapdance; Sleeping Beauty, Act III — *repeated, September 17*

19 SACKVILLE, NB, Convocation Hall: Serenade; Trapdance; Sleeping Beauty, Act III

21 HALIFAX, NS, Rebecca Cohn Aud: Serenade; Trapdance; Sleeping Beauty, Act III

22‡ Serenade; Sleeping Beauty, Act III

22 Serenade; Trapdance; Sleeping Beauty, Act III

23 La Bayadère, Act II; Four Temperaments; Concerto — *repeated, September 24*

26 CORNER BROOK, NL, Arts and Culture Centre: Etc!; Concerto Barocco; Concerto, pdd; Trapdance; Sleeping Beauty, Act III pdd; Death of a Lady's Man

28‡ ST. JOHN'S, NL, St. John's Arts and Culture Centre: Serenade; Sleeping Beauty, Act III

28 Serenade; Trapdance; Sleeping Beauty, Act III — *repeated, September 29*

30‡ La Bayadère, Act II; Concerto

30 La Bayadère, Act II; Four Temperaments; Concerto

October 1988:

1 ST. JOHN'S, NL, St. John's Arts and Culture Centre: La Bayadère, Act II; Four Temperaments; Concerto

6 MONTREAL, QC, Place des Arts: La Ronde; Blue Snake — *repeated, October 7, 8*

November 1988:

9 TORONTO, ON, O'Keefe Centre: Sleeping Beauty — *repeated, November 10‡, 10, 11, 12†, 12, 13†*

16 Alice; Serenade — *repeated, November 17, 18, 19†, 19, 20†*

23 Symphony in C; Blue Snake; Have Steps Will Travel

24‡ Blue Snake; Symphony in C

24 Symphony in C; Have Steps Will Travel; Blue Snake — *repeated, November 25, 26†, 26, 27†, 27*

29 Proust, pdd; Echo; Sleeping Beauty, Act III *(Kain Gala)*

30 Sleeping Beauty

December 1988:

1‡ TORONTO, ON, O'Keefe Centre: Sleeping Beauty — *repeated, December 1, 2†, 2*

13 Nutcracker — *repeated, December 14, 15‡, 15, 16, 17†, 17, 18†, 18, 20†, 20, 21, 22†, 22, 23, 24†, 27†, 27, 28*

January 1989:

20 GUELPH, ON, Ross Hall: Concerto Barocco; Etc!; Concerto, pdd; Sleeping Beauty, Act III pdd; Trapdance

21 WATERLOO, ON, U of Waterloo, Humanities

Theatre: Concerto Barocco; Etc!; Sleeping Beauty, Act III pdd; Trapdance; Concerto, pdd

February 1989:

8   TORONTO, ON, O'Keefe Centre: Romeo and Juliet — *repeated, 9‡, 9, 10, 11†, 11, 12†, 12*

15   Four Temperaments; Daphnis & Chloë — *repeated, February 16, 17, 18†, 18, 19†, 19*

22   Études; Concerto Barocco; Diana and Acteon Pas de Deux; Steptext

23‡   Steptext; Études

23   Diana and Acteon Pas de Deux; Steptext; Études; Concerto Barocco — *repeated, February 24, 25†, 25, 26†, 26*

March 1989:

15   TAMPA, FL, Festival Hall: La Ronde; Blue Snake — *repeated, March 16*

17   TAMPA FL, Festival Hall: Merry Widow — *repeated, March 18†, 18, 19†*

22   LONDON, ON, Alumni Hall: Sleeping Beauty, Act III pdd; Concerto Barocco; Trapdance; Etc!; Death of a Lady's Man; Concerto, pdd

23   ST. CATHARINES, ON, Brock Centre for the Arts, Playhouse: Etc!; Death of a Lady's Man; Sleeping Beauty, Act II pdd; Trapdance; Concerto, pdd; Concerto Barocco

31   MARKHAM, ON, Markham Theatre for Performing Arts: Envelope; Sleep Study; Song of a Wayfarer; Dream, pdd; Sleeping Beauty, Act III pdd; Giselle, Peasant pas de quatre

April 1989:

1   MARKHAM, ON, Markham Theatre for Performing Arts: Song of a Wayfarer; Giselle, Peasant pas de quatre; Sleep Study; Dream, pdd; Envelope; Sleeping Beauty, Act III pdd

19   OTTAWA, ON, National Arts Centre: Steptext; La Ronde; Études — *repeated, April 20, 21*

27   TORONTO, ON, O'Keefe Centre: Dream; Tagore — *repeated, April 28, 29†, 29, 30†*

May 1989:

2   TORONTO, ON, O'Keefe Centre: Merry Widow — *repeated, May 3, 4‡, 4, 5, 6†, 6, 7†, 7, 9†, 9, 10*

11   Dream; Tagore — *repeated, May 12*

13   Agon, pdd (Royal Danish Ballet); Allegri Diversi (Royal Ballet); Hommage à Bournonville Pas de Deux (Royal Danish Ballet); Le Corsaire, pdd (National Ballet of Canada); Le Corsaire, pdd (Royal Ballet); Sphinx, Second Movement (National Ballet of Canada); La Ronde *(Erik Bruhn Competition)*

14   Merry Widow

15   ORILLIA, ON, Orillia Opera House: Le Corsaire, pdd; Giselle, Peasant pas de quatre; Concerto, pdd;

Song of a Wayfarer; Envelope

16   KINGSTON, ON, Grand Theatre: Envelope; Le Corsaire, pdd; Concerto, pdd; Sleep Study; Song of a Wayfarer; Giselle, Peasant pas de quatre

31   LEVERKUSEN, GERMANY, Forum: Alice; Four Temperaments

June 1989:

1   LEVERKUSEN, GERMANY, Forum: Serenade; Blue Eyed Trek; La Ronde

3   BERLIN, GERMANY, Theater des Westens: Serenade; Blue Eyed Trek; La Ronde — *repeated, June 4†, 4*

6   FRIEDRICHSHAFEN, GERMANY, Graf Zeppelin Haus: Serenade; Blue Eyed Trek; La Ronde — *repeated, June 7*

10   DÜSSELDORF, GERMANY, Deutsche Oper am Rhein: Four Temperaments; Alice

11   Serenade; Blue Eyed Trek; La Ronde

13   FRANKFURT/HOECHST, GERMANY, Jahrhunderthalle: Four Temperaments; Alice

15   HAMBURG, GERMANY, Hamburgische Staatsoper: Alice; La Ronde — *repeated, June 16*

18   KIEL, GERMANY, Kiel Opernhaus: Four Temperaments; Alice

19   Serenade; Blue Eyed Trek; La Ronde

22   LUDWIGSBURG, GERMANY, Schlosspark: Serenade; Blue Eyed Trek; La Ronde

23   Four Temperaments; Alice

August 1989:

10   TORONTO, ON, Ontario Place: Giselle, Peasant pas de quatre; Etc!; Sleep Study; Serenade; Le Corsaire, pdd — *repeated, August 11†, 11, 12†, 12*

September 1989:

23   SASKATOON, SK, Saskatoon Centennial Aud: La Bayadère, Act II; La Ronde; Napoli, Act III — *repeated, September 24*

27   LETHBRIDGE, AB, U of Lethbridge, University Theatre: Concerto, pdd; Envelope; Le Corsaire, pdd; Sleep Study; Giselle, Peasant pas de quatre; Blue Eyed Trek

29   CALGARY, AB, Jubilee Aud: La Bayadère, Act II; La Ronde; Napoli, Act III — *repeated, September 30*

October 1989:

1   CALGARY, AB, Jubilee Aud: La Bayadère, Act II; La Ronde; Napoli, Act III

4   EDMONTON, AB, Jubilee Aud: La Bayadère, Act II; La Ronde; Napoli, Act III — *repeated, October 5*

6   WINNIPEG, MB, Manitoba Centennial Concert Hall: Seventh Symphony (RWB); Symphony in C (NBC & RWB); Blue Eyed Trek *(with Royal Winnipeg Ballet)* — *repeated, October 7†, 7, 8†*

10 VANCOUVER, BC, Queen Elizabeth Theatre: La Bayadère, Act II; La Ronde; Napoli, Act III — *repeated, October 11, 12, 13, 14*

16 SAULT STE. MARIE, ON, White Pines Aud: Giselle, Peasant pas de quatre; Envelope; Grand Pas Classique; Blue Eyed Trek; Concerto, pdd; Sleep Study — *repeated, October 17*

November 1989:

1 TORONTO, ON, O'Keefe Centre: Giselle — *repeated, November 2‡, 2, 3, 4†, 4, 5†*

8 Dream Dances; La Ronde; La Bayadère, Act II — *repeated, November 9, 10, 11†, 11, 12†, 12*

15 Napoli

16‡ Napoli, Acts I and III

16 Napoli — *repeated, November 17, 18†, 18, 19†*

21 Canciones, Nino Lullaby; Giselle, Act II pdd; Khatchaturian Pas de Deux; Mad Shadows, excerpts; Masada, Scene II, The Final Night, excerpts; Onegin, Act III; Taming of the Shrew, Act I pdd; Washington Square, excerpts *(Tennant farewell gala)*

22 Giselle — *repeated, November 23‡, 23, 24†, 24*

30 Blue Eyed Trek; Seventh Symphony (RWB); Symphony in C (NBC & RWB) *(with Royal Winnipeg Ballet)*

December 1989:

1‡ TORONTO, ON, O'Keefe Centre: Piano Variations (RWB); Envelope; Tarantella (RWB); Symphony in C (NBC & RWB) *(with Royal Winnipeg Ballet)*

1 Seventh Symphony (RWB); Blue Eyed Trek; Symphony in C (NBC & RWB) *(with Royal Winnipeg Ballet)* — *repeated, December 2*

19 Nutcracker — *repeated, December 20, 21‡, 21, 22, 23†, 23, 24†, 26, 27†, 27, 28, 29, 30†, 30*

31 Nutty Nutcracker

January 1990:

3† TORONTO, ON, O'Keefe Centre: Nutcracker — *repeated, January 3, 4, 5, 6†, 6, 7†, 7*

February 1990:

14 TORONTO, ON, O'Keefe Centre: La Fille mal gardée — *repeated, February 15‡, 15, 16, 17†, 17, 18†*

21 Transfigured Night; Concerto; Gloria — *repeated, February 22, 23, 24†, 24, 25†*

28 Serenade; Need; Élite Syncopations

March 1990:

1‡ TORONTO, ON, O'Keefe Centre: Serenade; Élite Syncopations

1 Serenade; Need; Élite Syncopations — *repeated, March 2, 3†, 3, 4†, 4*

29 NORTH BAY, ON, Arts Centre: Concerto, pdd; Sleep Study; Blue Eyed Trek; Le Corsaire, pdd; Envelope; Giselle, Peasant pas de quatre

30 SUDBURY, ON, Grand Theatre: Giselle, Peasant pas de quatre; Concerto, pdd; Sleep Study; Blue Eyed Trek; Le Corsaire, pdd; Envelope — *repeated, March 31*

May 1990:

2 TORONTO, ON, O'Keefe Centre: Swan Lake — *repeated, May 3‡, 3, 4, 5†, 5, 6†*

9 Les Sylphides; Pastorale; Voluntaries — *repeated, May 10, 11, 12†, 12, 13†*

15‡ Swan Lake — *repeated, May 15, 16, 17, 18†, 18, 19*

23 OTTAWA, ON, National Arts Centre: Swan Lake — *repeated, May 24, 25, 26*

31 LONDON, ON, Grand Theatre: Split House Geometric; Envelope; Le Corsaire, pdd; Transfigured Night; Sleep Study; Flower Festival in Genzano, pdd

June 1990:

1 LONDON, ON, Grand Theatre: Split House Geometric; Sleep Study; Transfigured Night; Le Corsaire, pdd; Envelope; Flower Festival in Genzano, pdd

2 HAMILTON, ON, Sir John A. MacDonald S.S.: Transfigured Night; Le Corsaire, pdd; Envelope; Split House Geometric; Sleep Study; Flower Festival in Genzano, pdd

3† LEWISTON, NY, Artpark: Split House Geometric; Sleep Study; Transfigured Night; Le Corsaire, pdd; Envelope; Flower Festival in Genzano, pdd

August 1990:

9 TORONTO, ON, Ontario Place: Dream Dances; Don Quixote, pdd; Swan Lake, White Swan pdd; Troy Game — *repeated, August 10†, 10, 11†, 11*

21 LEWISTON, NY, Artpark: Don Quixote — *repeated, August 22, 23†, 23*

24 Dream Dances; Steptext; Études — *repeated, August 25, 26†*

September 1990:

21 FREDERICTON, NB, Fredericton Playhouse: Don Quixote, pdd; Dream Dances; Steptext; Concerto for Flute and Harp — *repeated, September 22*

23 SACKVILLE, NB, Convocation Hall: Don Quixote, pdd; Dream Dances; Steptext; Concerto for Flute and Harp

25 HALIFAX, NS, Rebecca Cohn Aud: Don Quixote, pdd; Dream Dances; Steptext; Concerto for Flute and Harp, — *repeated, September 26*

October 1990:

1 OTTAWA, ON, National Arts Centre: Concerto for Flute and Harp; Need; Dream Dances — *repeated, October 2, 3*

6 QUEBEC CITY, QC, Le Grand Théâtre : Concerto for Flute and Harp; Need; Dream Dances

11 MONTREAL, QC, Place des Arts: Onegin — *repeated, October 12, 13*

15 NEPEAN, ON, Centrepointe Theatre: Concerto for Flute and Harp; Steptext; Troy Game

31 TORONTO, ON, O'Keefe Centre: Onegin

November 1990:

1‡ TORONTO, ON, O'Keefe Centre: Onegin — *repeated, November 1, 2, 3†, 3, 4†, 4*

7 Don Quixote — *repeated, November 8‡, 8, 9, 10†, 10, 11†, 11*

14 Leaves are Fading; Steptext; Études — *repeated, November 15, 16, 17†, 17, 18†*

20 Onegin — *repeated, November 21, 22‡, 22, 23†, 23*

December 1990:

11 OTTAWA, ON, National Arts Centre: Nutcracker — *repeated, December 12, 13, 14, 15†, 15*

18‡ TORONTO, ON, O'Keefe Centre: Nutcracker — *repeated, December 18, 19, 20†, 20, 21, 22†, 22, 23†, 23, 26, 27†, 27, 28, 29†, 29, 30†, 30*

January 1991:

2 TORONTO, ON, O'Keefe Centre: Nutcracker — *repeated, January 3†, 3, 4, 5†, 5, 6†, 6*

17 GUELPH, ON, E.L. Fox Auditorium: Concerto for Flute and Harp; Steptext; Concerto, pdd; Troy Game

19 OAKVILLE, ON, Oakville Centre: Troy Game; Concerto for Flute and Harp; Steptext; Concerto, pdd

February 1991:

13 TORONTO, ON, O'Keefe Centre: Coppélia — *repeated, February 14‡, 14, 15, 16†, 16, 17†*

20 Concerto Barocco; Sphinx; second detail — *repeated, February 21, 22, 23†, 23, 24†, 24*

27 Paquita; Song of the Earth — *repeated, February 28*

March 1991:

1 TORONTO, ON, O'Keefe Centre: Paquita; Song of the Earth — *repeated, March 2†, 2, 3†, 3*

5 Hommage au Bolshoi; Top Hat; In the Middle, Somewhat Elevated, pdd; Giselle, Act II pdd; Greek Dances; Paquita; Romeo and Juliet, pdd; Défilé *(40th anniversary gala)*

6 Coppélia — *repeated, March 7‡*

May 1991:

1 TORONTO, ON, O'Keefe Centre: Time Out With Lola; Daphnis & Chloë

2‡ Daphnis & Chloë

2 Time Out With Lola; Daphnis & Chloë — *repeated, May 3, 4†, 4, 5†*

9 Sleeping Beauty — *repeated, May 10, 11†, 11, 12†, 14†, 14, 15*

16‡ Sleeping Beauty, Prologue, Act I, Awakening, & Act III

16 Sleeping Beauty — *repeated, May 17, 18, 19†*

22 LONDON, ON, Grand Theatre: Concerto Barocco; Troy Game; Sleeping Beauty, dances from — *repeated, May 23*

August 1991:

6 TORONTO, ON, Ontario Place: second detail, dances from; Swan Lake, Black Swan pdd; Swan Lake, Act I, Scene II — *repeated, August 7†, 7, 8†, 8*

20 LEWISTON, NY, Artpark: Concerto for Flute and Harp; Musings; second detail — *repeated, August 21*

22 Swan Lake — *repeated, August 23†, 23, 24, 25†*

September 1991:

18 OTTAWA, ON, National Arts Centre: Merry Widow — *repeated, September 19, 20*

23 WINNIPEG, MB, Manitoba Centennial Concert Hall: Merry Widow — *repeated, September 24, 25*

27 SASKATOON, SK, Saskatoon Centennial Aud: Merry Widow

29 EDMONTON, AB, Jubilee Aud: Merry Widow — *repeated, September 30*

October 1991:

2 CALGARY, AB, Jubilee Aud: Merry Widow — *repeated, October 3*

8 COSTA MESA, CA, Orange County Perf. Arts Centre: Concerto for Flute and Harp; Musings; second detail — *repeated, October 9*

10 Merry Widow — *repeated, October 11, 12†, 12, 13†*

24 ST. CATHARINES, ON, Brock Centre for the Arts, Playhouse: Concerto for Flute and Harp; Café Dances; Swan Lake, White Swan pdd; Troy Game

25 NIAGARA FALLS, ON, Niagara Falls S.S.: Concerto for Flute and Harp; Café Dances; Swan Lake, White Swan pdd; Troy Game

26 WELLAND, ON, Centennial Collegiate: Swan Lake, White Swan pdd; Troy Game; Café Dances; Concerto for Flute and Harp

November 1991:

6 TORONTO, ON, O'Keefe Centre: Swan Lake — *repeated, November 7‡, 7, 8, 9†, 9, 10†*

13 Concerto for Flute and Harp; Interrogating Slam; Pastorale — *repeated, November 14, 15, 16†, 16, 17†*

19 Swan Lake — *repeated, November 20, 21†, 21, 22‡, 22*

December 1991:

12† KITCHENER, ON, Centre in the Square: Nutcracker — *repeated, December 12, 13, 14†, 14, 15†*

17† TORONTO, ON, O'Keefe Centre: Nutcracker — *repeated, December 17, 18, 19†, 19, 20, 21†, 21, 22†, 22, 23†, 26, 27, 28†, 28, 29†, 29, 30†*

January 1992:

2† TORONTO, ON, O'Keefe Centre: Nutcracker — *repeated, January 2, 3, 4†, 4, 5†, 5*

February 1992:

13 TORONTO, ON, O'Keefe Centre: Taming of the Shrew — *repeated, February 14, 15†, 15, 16†*

19 Four Temperaments; Alice — *repeated, February 20, 21, 22†, 22, 23†, 23*

25 Taming of the Shrew — *repeated, February 26, 27‡, 27, 28, 29†, 29*

March 1992:

1† TORONTO, ON, O'Keefe Centre: Taming of the Shrew

4 Forgotten Land; Symphony in C; Troy Game

5† Symphony in C; Troy Game

5 Forgotten Land; Symphony in C; Troy Game — *repeated, March 6, 7†, 7, 8†*

April 1992:

3 BRANTFORD, ON, Sanderson Centre for the Performing Arts: Troy Game; Concerto for Flute and Harp; Split House Geometric; Swan Lake, White Swan pdd

29 TORONTO, ON, O'Keefe Centre: Merry Widow — *repeated, April 30‡, 30*

May 1992:

1 TORONTO, ON, O'Keefe Centre: Merry Widow — *repeated, May 2†, 2, 3†*

6 Paquita; Split House Geometric; Sylvia Pas de Deux; Rite of Spring

7† Paquita; Class-trophobia; Rite of Spring

7 Paquita; Split House Geometric; Sylvia Pas de Deux; Rite of Spring — *repeated, May 8, 9†, 9, 10†, 10*

12 Merry Widow — *repeated, May 13, 14†, 14, 15†, 15*

27 HONG KONG, HONG KONG, Hong Kong Cultural Centre, Grand Theatre: Paquita; Concerto for Flute and Harp; Split House Geometric; Swan Lake, White Swan pdd; Sylvia Pas de Deux — *repeated, May 28*

29† Taming of the Shrew — *repeated, May 29, 30, 31†, 31*

June 1992:

6 YOKOHAMA, JAPAN, Kanagawa Kenmin Hall: Swan Lake

7† Nutcracker

8 MATSUDO, JAPAN, Seitoku Gakuen Kawanami Memorial Hall: Concerto for Flute and Harp; Troy Game; Sylvia Pas de Deux; Split House Geometric; Swan Lake, White Swan pdd

9† YOKOHAMA, JAPAN, Toin Memorial Hall: Concerto for Flute and Harp; Split House Geometric; Swan Lake, White Swan pdd; Don Quixote, pdd; Troy Game

12 TOKYO, JAPAN, Tokyo Bunka Kaikan: Nutcracker — *repeated, June 13†, 13, 14†*

15 TOKYO, JAPAN, Bunkamura Orchard Hall: Swan Lake — *repeated, June 16†, 16, 17*

19 OSAKA, JAPAN, Festival Hall: Swan Lake — *repeated, June 20*

21 TAKAMATSU, JAPAN, Kagawaken Kenmin Hall: Nutcracker

24 TOKYO, JAPAN, Bunkamura Orchard Hall: Sylvia Pas de Deux; Nuages; Don Quixote, pdd; Taming of the Shrew, pdd; Musings, Movement II; Love Songs; Le Corsaire, pdd; Romeo and Juliet, pdd; Paquita; Split House Geometric; Sleeping Beauty, pdd

26 SEOUL, KOREA, Sejong Cultural Centre: Swan Lake — *repeated, June 27†, 27*

30 TAIPEI, TAIWAN, National Theatre: Nutcracker, Act II; Sylvia Pas de Deux; Split House Geometric; Concerto for Flute and Harp; Swan Lake, White Swan pdd

July 1992:

1 TAIPEI, TAIWAN, National Theatre: Concerto for Flute and Harp; Split House Geometric; Swan Lake, White Swan pdd; Sylvia Pas de Deux; Nutcracker, Act II — *repeated, July 2*

4† Taming of the Shrew — *repeated, July 4, 5†, 5*

August 1992:

25 LEWISTON, NY, Artpark: Les Sylphides; Café Dances; Élite Syncopations — *repeated, August 26*

27 Taming of the Shrew — *repeated, August 28, 29†, 29, 30†*

September 1992:

29 WASHINGTON, DC, Kennedy Center: Musings; second detail; Études — *repeated, September 30*

October 1992:

1 WASHINGTON, DC, Kennedy Center: Études; Musings; second detail

2 Taming of the Shrew — *repeated, October 3†, 3, 4†*

6 MONTREAL, QC, Place des Arts: Interrogating Slam; second detail — *repeated, October 7*

15 SAULT STE. MARIE, ON, White Pines Aud: Musings; Café Dances; Swan Lake, White Swan pdd; Troy Game

21 OTTAWA, ON, National Arts Centre: Giselle — *repeated, October 22, 23‡, 23, 24*

November 1992:

4 TORONTO, ON, O'Keefe Centre: Giselle — *repeated, November 5†, 5, 6, 7†, 7, 8†*

11 La Fille mal gardée — *repeated, November 12†, 12, 13, 14†, 14, 15†*

18 Les Sylphides; Musings; Élite Syncopations

19‡ Les Sylphides; Élite Syncopations
19 Les Sylphides; Musings; Élite Syncopations —
 repeated, November 20, 21†, 21, 22†
24 Giselle — *repeated, November 25, 26, 27†, 27*

December 1992:
15 TORONTO, ON, O'Keefe Centre: Nutcracker —
 repeated, December 16, 17‡, 17, 18, 19†, 19, 20†, 20,
 22†, 22, 23†, 23, 26†, 26, 27†, 27, 29†, 29, 30†, 30

January 1993:
2† TORONTO, ON, O'Keefe Centre: Nutcracker —
 repeated, January 2, 3†, 3

February 1993:
10 TORONTO, ON, O'Keefe Centre: Don Quixote —
 repeated, February 11†, 11, 12, 13†, 13, 14†
17 second detail; La Ronde; Divertimento No. 15 —
 repeated, February 18, 19, 20†, 20, 21†
24 Dream Dances; Now and Then; Études
25‡ Dream Dances; Études
25 Dream Dances; Now and Then; Études — *repeated,*
 February 26, 27†, 27, 28†

March 1993:
2 TORONTO, ON, O'Keefe Centre: Dream Dances;
 Now and Then; Études
3 Don Quixote — *repeated, March 4‡, 4, 5*
6 5 Tangos Solo (Royal Ballet); Flower Festival in
 Genzano, pdd (Royal Danish Ballet); Giselle, Act II
 pdd (American Ballet Theatre); Grand Pas Classique
 (National Ballet of Canada); La Somnambula,
 Harlequin solo (Royal Danish Ballet); Polacca (Royal
 Danish Ballet); Romeo and Juliet, Balcony pdd
 (American Ballet Theatre); Sleeping Beauty, Act III
 Grand pdd (Royal Ballet); Soiree Musicale, Bolero
 (Royal Ballet); Vittoria Pas de Deux (National Ballet
 of Canada); second detail *(Erik Bruhn Competition)*

April 1993:
1 MONTREAL, QC, Place des Arts: Don Quixote —
 repeated, April 2, 3
7 MARKHAM, ON, Markham Theatre: Troy Game;
 Swan Lake, White Swan pdd; Musings; Strangeness
 of a Kiss
28 TORONTO, ON, O'Keefe Centre: Romeo and Juliet
 — *repeated, April 29‡, 29, 30*

May 1993:
1† TORONTO, ON, O'Keefe Centre: Romeo and Juliet
 — *repeated, May 1, 2†*
5 Miraculous Mandarin; Voluntaries; Serenade —
 repeated, May 6, 7, 8†, 8, 9†, 9
11 Romeo and Juliet — *repeated, May 12, 13‡, 13, 14†,*
 14

20 NORWICH, ON, Civic Centre: Sleeping Beauty,
 pdd; Strangeness of a Kiss; Musings; Troy Game

August 1993:
17 TORONTO, ON, Earl Bales Amphitheatre: Romeo
 and Juliet, Balcony pdd; Troy Game; Swan Lake, White
 Swan pdd; Le Corsaire, pdd; Strangeness of a Kiss

September 1993:
14 OTTAWA, ON, National Arts Centre: Taming of the
 Shrew — *repeated, September 15, 16*
20 SASKATOON, SK, Saskatoon Centennial Aud:
 Taming of the Shrew — *repeated, September 21*
23 REGINA, SK, Saskatchewan Centre of the Arts:
 Taming of the Shrew — *repeated, September 24*
27 WINNIPEG, MB, Manitoba Centennial Concert Hall:
 Taming of the Shrew — *repeated, September 28, 29*

October 1993:
2 CALGARY, AB, Jubilee Aud: Taming of the Shrew —
 repeated, October 3
5 EDMONTON, AB, Jubilee Aud: Taming of the
 Shrew — *repeated, October 6*
9 VICTORIA, BC, Royal Theatre: Strangeness of a
 Kiss; Romeo and Juliet, Balcony pdd; La Sylphide,
 Act II; Musings — *repeated, October 10*
13 VANCOUVER, BC, Queen Elizabeth Theatre:
 Taming of the Shrew — *repeated, October 14, 15, 16*

November 1993:
3 TORONTO, ON, O'Keefe Centre: Taming of the
 Shrew — *repeated, November 4†, 4, 5, 6†, 6, 7†, 7*
10 Pastorale; Herman Schmerman; Rite of Spring
11‡ Herman Schmerman; Rite of Spring
11 Pastorale; Herman Schmerman; Rite of Spring —
 repeated, November 12, 13†, 13, 14†
17 Four Temperaments; La Sylphide
18‡ La Sylphide
18 Four Temperaments; La Sylphide — *repeated,*
 November 19, 20†, 20, 21†, 23, 24

December 1993:
8 OTTAWA, ON, National Arts Centre: Nutcracker —
 repeated, December 9, 10, 11†, 11, 12†
14 TORONTO, ON, O'Keefe Centre: Nutcracker —
 repeated, December 15, 16†, 16, 17, 18†, 18, 19†, 19, 21†,
 21, 22, 23†, 23, 24†, 27, 28†, 28, 29, 30†, 30, 31†

January 1994:
2† TORONTO, ON, O'Keefe Centre: Nutcracker —
 repeated, January 2

February 1994:
9 TORONTO, ON, O'Keefe Centre: Coppélia —
 repeated, February 10†, 10, 11, 12†, 12, 13†, 13

16   Actress; Paquita; Forgotten Land

17‡   Paquita; Actress

17   Actress; Paquita; Forgotten Land — *repeated,*
February 18, 19†, 19, 20†, 20

23   Onegin — *repeated, February 24†, 24, 25, 26†, 26, 27†*

March 1994:

24   WINDSOR, ON, Chrysler Theatre: Frames of Mind;
Now and Then; Strangeness of a Kiss; Sleeping
Beauty, Act III Aurora's Wedding

27   BRANTFORD, ON, Sanderson Centre for the
Performing Arts: Sleeping Beauty, Act III Aurora's
Wedding; Strangeness of a Kiss; Now and Then

April 1994:

27‡   TORONTO, ON, O'Keefe Centre: Sleeping Beauty —
repeated, April 27, 28, 29, 30†, 30

May 1994:

1†   TORONTO, ON, O'Keefe Centre: Sleeping Beauty

4   Split House Geometric; Strangeness of a Kiss; Frames
of Mind; Oracle; Café Dances

5   Café Dances; Frames of Mind; Strangeness of a Kiss;
Oracle

6   Split House Geometric; Strangeness of a Kiss; Frames
of Mind; Oracle; Café Dances — *repeated, May 7†, 7,
8†, 8*

10   Sleeping Beauty — *repeated, May 11, 12, 13, 14†, 14,
15†*

20   MUNICH, GERMANY, Bayerische Staatsoper:
Coppélia — *repeated, May 21*

22   second detail; Now and Then; Pastorale

25   CAESAREA, ISRAEL, Roman Amphitheatre:
Sleeping Beauty — *repeated, May 26, 28, 29*

31   LUXEMBOURG, LUXEMBOURG, Municipal
Theatre: Coppélia

June 1994:

1   LUXEMBOURG, LUXEMBOURG, Municipal
Theatre: Coppélia — *repeated, June 2*

4   THE HAGUE, NETHERLANDS, AT&T Dance
Theatre: Coppélia — *repeated, June 5*

8   FRANKFURT/HOECHST, GERMANY,
Jahrhunderthalle: Coppélia

10   LUDWIGSBURG, GERMANY, Schlosspark:
Pastorale; second detail; Now and Then — *repeated,*
June 11

15   HAMBURG, GERMANY, Hamburgische Staatsoper:
second detail; Frames of Mind; Split House
Geometric; Pastorale — *repeated, June 16*

August 1994:

16   TORONTO, ON, Earl Bales Amphitheatre: Sleeping
Beauty, pdd; Etc!; Élite Syncopations, excerpts;
Frames of Mind — *repeated, August 17*

26   LEWISTON, NY, Artpark: Merry Widow — *repeated,*
August 27, 28†

30   TORONTO, ON, O'Keefe Centre: Merry Widow, Act
III; Élite Syncopations

September 1994:

22   OTTAWA, ON, National Arts Centre: Swan Lake —
repeated, September 23, 24

30   WICHITA, KS, Century II Convention Centre: Élite
Syncopations; Divertimento No. 15; Frames of Mind;
Strangeness of a Kiss

October 1994:

2†   WICHITA, KS, Century II Convention Centre: Swan
Lake — *repeated, October 2*

4   MINNEAPOLIS, MN, Northrop Aud: Swan Lake —
repeated, October 5

7   IOWA CITY, IA, Hancher Aud: Swan Lake —
repeated, 9†

20   LINDSAY, ON, Lindsay Recreation Complex:
Frames of Mind; Strangeness of a Kiss; Swan Lake,
White Swan pdd; Élite Syncopations, excerpts; Etc!

22   SAULT STE. MARIE, ON, White Pines Aud: Élite
Syncopations, excerpts; Frames of Mind; Gluck Pas
de Deux; Strangeness of a Kiss; Sleeping Beauty, pdd
— *repeated, October 23*

November 1994:

2   TORONTO, ON, O'Keefe Centre: Divertimento
No. 15; Spring Awakening; Concert — *repeated,*
November 3

5†   Swan Lake — *repeated, 5, 6†, 8, 9, 10‡, 10*

11   Divertimento No. 15; Spring Awakening; Concert —
repeated, November 12, 13†

16   Merry Widow — *repeated, November 17‡, 17, 18, 19†,*
19, 20†

22   Divertimento No. 15; Spring Awakening; Concert —
repeated, November 23

24   Swan Lake — *repeated, November 25‡, 25*

December 1994:

14   TORONTO, ON, O'Keefe Centre: Nutcracker —
repeated, December 15†, 15, 16, 17†, 17, 18†, 18, 20,
21†, 21, 22, 23†, 23, 27†, 27, 28, 29†, 29, 30†, 30

January 1995:

13   HAMILTON, BERMUDA, Hamilton City Hall
and Arts Center: Split House Geometric; Swan
Lake, White Swan pdd; Frames of Mind; Élite
Syncopations, excerpts; Romeo and Juliet, Balcony
pdd — *repeated, January 14, 15, 16*

February 1995:

8   TORONTO, ON, O'Keefe Centre: Romeo and Juliet
— *repeated, February 9†, 9, 10, 11†, 11, 12†*

15 Now and Then; Soldiers' Mass; La Bayadère, Act II

16‡ La Bayadère, Act II; Now and Then

16 Now and Then; Soldiers' Mass; La Bayadère, Act II — *repeated, February 17, 18†, 18, 19†*

21 Romeo and Juliet — *repeated, February 22†, 22*

24 Swan Lake — *repeated, February 25†, 25, 26†*

28 Aureole Movement IV (Royal Danish Ballet); Danses Concertantes, Fourth Variation (Royal Ballet); Façade, Polka (Royal Ballet); Kermesse at Bruges, Act I pdd (Royal Danish Ballet); La Bayadère, Act I variations (American Ballet Theatre); Le Corsaire, pdd (National Ballet of Canada); Manon, Act II Solo (American Ballet Theatre); Romeo and Juliet, Balcony pdd (National Ballet of Canada); Romeo and Juliet, Ballroom Variation (American Ballet Theatre); Sleeping Beauty, Act III Bluebird pdd (Royal Ballet); Élite Syncopations, selections from *(Erik Bruhn Competition)*

March 1995:

3 LONDON, ON, Grand Theatre: Élite Syncopations, excerpts; Three French Words; Gluck Pas de Deux; Strangeness of a Kiss — *repeated, March 4†, 4*

9 MONTREAL, QC, Place des Arts: Romeo and Juliet — *repeated, March 10, 11†, 11*

May 1995:

3 TORONTO, ON, O'Keefe Centre: Month in the Country; Monotones I; Monotones II; Dream — *repeated, May 4, 5, 6†, 6, 7†*

11 Cinderella — *repeated, May 12, 13†, 13, 14†, 14, 16, 17†, 17*

19 Romeo and Juliet — *repeated, May 20†, 20*

August 1995:

9 TORONTO, ON, Earl Bales Amphitheatre: Soldiers' Mass; Holberg Pas de Deux; Pompadour; Monotones II; Don Quixote, pdd

18 TORONTO, ON, Harbourfront, Molson Place: Don Quixote, pdd; Romeo and Juliet, Balcony pdd; Holberg Pas de Deux; Élite Syncopations

19a Monotones II; Don Quixote, pdd; Romeo and Juliet, Balcony pdd; Élite Syncopations

19b Monotones II; Holberg Pas de Deux; Romeo and Juliet, Balcony pdd; Élite Syncopations *(two performances in one evening)*

25 LEWISTON, NY, Artpark: Romeo and Juliet— *repeated, August 26, 27†*

September 1995:

25 WINNIPEG, MB, Manitoba Centennial Concert Hall: Giselle — *repeated, September 26, 27*

29 REGINA, SK, Saskatchewan Centre of the Arts: Giselle — *repeated, September 30*

October 1995:

3 SASKATOON, SK, Saskatoon Centennial Aud: Giselle — *repeated, 4‡, 4*

9 VICTORIA, BC, Royal Theatre: Giselle — *repeated, October 10*

12 VANCOUVER, BC, Queen Elizabeth Theatre: Giselle — *repeated, October 13†, 13, 14*

20 OTTAWA, ON, National Arts Centre: Romeo and Juliet — *repeated, October 21, 22*

November 1995:

1 TORONTO, ON, O'Keefe Centre: Echo; Tchaikowsky Pas de Deux; Leaves are Fading; Company B

2‡ Leaves are Fading; Company B

2 Echo; Tchaikowsky Pas de Deux; Leaves are Fading; Company B

4† Giselle — *repeated, November 4, 5†, 7, 8, 9‡, 9*

10 Echo; Tchaikowsky Pas de Deux; Leaves are Fading; Company B — *repeated, November 11†, 11, 12†*

14 Holberg Pas de Deux; Tchaikowsky Pas de Deux; Company B; Leaves are Fading — *repeated, November 15*

16 Giselle — *repeated, November 17†, 17*

December 1995:

21 TORONTO, ON, O'Keefe Centre: Nutcracker — *repeated, December 22, 23†, 23, 24†, 26†, 26, 27, 28†, 28, 29, 30†, 30, 31†*

January 1996:

2 TORONTO, ON, O'Keefe Centre: Nutcracker — *repeated, January 3, 4†, 4, 5, 6†, 6, 7†, 7*

February 1996:

14 TORONTO, ON, O'Keefe Centre: Don Quixote — *repeated, February 15‡, 15, 16, 17†, 17, 18†*

21 Washington Square; Musings; second detail — *repeated, February 22, 23, 24†, 24, 25†*

27‡ Don Quixote — *repeated, February 27, 28†, 28*

March 1996:

1 TORONTO, ON, O'Keefe Centre: Giselle — *repeated, March 2†, 2*

April 1996:

10 GUELPH, ON, Ross Hall: Monotones II; Musings; Company B; Swan Lake, White Swan pdd; Holberg Pas de Deux

11 BRANTFORD, ON, Sanderson Centre for the Performing Arts: Holberg Pas de Deux; Musings; Monotones II; Swan Lake, White Swan pdd; Company B

12 LONDON, ON, Grand Theatre: Musings; Holberg Pas de Deux; Swan Lake, White Swan pdd; Company B; Monotones II — *repeated, April 13*

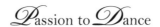

May 1996:

2   TORONTO, ON, O'Keefe Centre: Manon — *repeated, May 3, 4†, 4, 5†*

8   Symphonic Variations; La Ronde; Serenade — *repeated, May 9†, 9, 10, 11†*

11   Sphinx; Serenade; Symphonic Variations

12† Symphonic Variations; La Ronde; Serenade — *repeated, May 12*

14   Manon — *repeated, May 15‡, 15, 16†, 16*

18   Don Quixote — *repeated, May 19†*

30   OTTAWA, ON, National Arts Centre: Manon — *repeated, May 31*

June 1996:

1   OTTAWA, ON, National Arts Centre: Manon

15   Cruel World *(contribution to Canada Dance Festival)*

September 1996:

26   LONDON, ON, Grand Theatre: Giselle — *repeated, September 27†, 27, 28†28*

October 1996:

1   KITCHENER, ON, Centre in the Square: Giselle — *repeated, October 2*

4   WINDSOR, ON, Cleary Aud: Giselle — *repeated, October 5†, 5*

11   HAMILTON, ON, Hamilton Place: Giselle — *repeated, October 12*

November 1996:

13   TORONTO, ON, O'Keefe Centre: Onegin — *repeated, November 14†, 14, 15, 16†, 16, 17†*

20   Paquita; Voluntaries; Cruel World — *repeated, November 21, 22, 23†, 23, 24†, 26*

27   Onegin — *repeated, November 28†, 28*

30   TORONTO, ON, Hummingbird Centre: Piece for Walter; Grand Tarantelle; Cry

December 1996:

12   TORONTO, ON, Hummingbird Centre: Nutcracker — *repeated, December 13, 14†, 14, 15†, 16, 18, 19†, 19, 20, 21†, 21, 22†, 22, 23†, 23, 26†, 27†, 28†, 28, 29†, 29, 30†, 30*

January 1997:

2† TORONTO, ON, Hummingbird Centre: Nutcracker — *repeated, January 2, 3†, 4, 5†*

February 1997:

12   TORONTO, ON, Hummingbird Centre: Four Seasons; Tides of Mind; Fall; Month in the Country — *repeated, February 13†, 13, 14, 15†, 15, 16†, 16*

19   Sleeping Beauty — *repeated, February 20, 21, 22†, 22, 23†, 25‡, 25, 26, 27‡, 27*

April 1997:

4   OTTAWA, ON, National Arts Centre: Month in the Country; Four Seasons; Fall; Tides of Mind — *repeated, April 5*

10   MONTREAL, QC, Place des Arts: Sleeping Beauty — *repeated, April 11, 12†, 12*

30   TORONTO, ON, Hummingbird Centre: Abdallah: Tales of the Arabian Nights

May 1997:

1   TORONTO, ON, Hummingbird Centre: Abdallah: Tales of the Arabian Nights — *repeated, May 2, 3†, 3, 4†*

7   Four Temperaments; Les Sylphides; Élite Syncopations — *repeated, May 8, 9, 10†, 10, 11†*

13   Abdallah: Tales of the Arabian Nights — *repeated, May 14†, 14, 15‡, 16, 17†, 17*

24   Herman Schmerman, pdd; Red Shoes; Tchaikowsky Pas de Deux; Actress — *repeated, May 25, 27, 28, 30, 31*

June 1997:

1† TORONTO, ON, Hummingbird Centre: Herman Schmerman, pdd; Red Shoes; Tchaikowsky Pas de Deux; Actress — *repeated, June 3, 4, 6, 7, 8†*

11   OTTAWA, ON, National Arts Centre, Opera: Actress; Herman Schmerman; Red Shoes — *repeated, June 12, 13, 14*

18   MONTREAL, QC, Place des Arts: Red Shoes; Actress; Tchaikowsky Pas de Deux; Herman Schmerman, pdd — *repeated, June 19*

20   Red Shoes; Herman Schmerman; Actress — *repeated, June 21*

September 1997:

15   EDMONTON, AB, Jubilee Aud: Red Shoes; Herman Schmerman; Actress — *repeated, September 16*

19   CALGARY, AB, Jubilee Aud: Red Shoes; Herman Schmerman; Actress — *repeated, September 20, 21†*

24   VANCOUVER, BC, Queen Elizabeth Theatre: Red Shoes; Herman Schmerman; Actress — *repeated, September 25, 26, 27*

October 1997:

1   WINNIPEG, MB, Manitoba Centennial Concert Hall: Red Shoes; Herman Schmerman; Actress — *repeated, October 2, 3, 4*

November 1997:

5   TORONTO, ON, Hummingbird Centre: Merry Widow — *repeated, November 6†, 6, 7, 8†, 8, 9†*

12   Forgotten Land; Sphinx; Terra Firma — *repeated, November 13†, 13, 14, 15†, 15, 16†*

Appendix A

December 1997:

13† TORONTO, ON, Hummingbird Centre: Nutcracker — *repeated, December 13, 14†, 16, 17†, 17, 18, 19, 20†, 20, 21†, 23†, 23, 24†, 26†, 27†, 27, 28†, 30†, 30, 31†*

January 1998:

2† TORONTO, ON, Hummingbird Centre: Nutcracker — *repeated, January 2*

21 OTTAWA, ON, National Arts Centre: Merry Widow — *repeated, January 22, 23*

February 1998:

13 TORONTO, ON, Hummingbird Centre: Romeo and Juliet — *repeated, February 14†, 14, 15†*

18 Mozartiana; Episodes; Theme and Variations — *repeated, February 19†, 19, 20, 21†, 21, 22†*

24‡ Romeo and Juliet — *repeated, February 24, 25, 26†, 26, 27, 28†*

March 1998:

5 MONTREAL, QC, Place des Arts: Merry Widow — *repeated, March 6, 7†, 7*

12† COLUMBUS, OH, Ohio Theatre: Sphinx *(contribution to Ballet Met 20th anniversary gala)* — *repeated, March 13, 14†, 14*

April 1998:

14 IOWA CITY, IA, Hancher Aud: Musings; Sphinx; Désir

17 ST. LOUIS, MO, Fox Theatre: Musings; Sphinx; Désir — *repeated, April 18*

29 TORONTO, ON, Hummingbird Centre: Coppélia — *repeated, April 30†, 30*

May 1998:

1 TORONTO, ON, Hummingbird Centre: Coppélia — *repeated, 2†, 2, 3†*

6 Washington Square; Désir; weight of absence — *repeated, May 7†, 7, 8, 9†, 9, 10†*

June 1998:

13 OTTAWA, ON, National Arts Centre: Terra Firma, pdd; Désir; weight of absence *(contribution to 1998 Canada Dance Festival)*

October 1998:

6 NEW YORK, NY, City Center: Tides of Mind; Four Seasons; Musings; Split House Geometric

7 Washington Square; weight of absence; Désir

8 Musings; Split House Geometric; Tides of Mind; Four Seasons

9 Washington Square; weight of absence; Désir

10† Musings; Split House Geometric; Tides of Mind; Four Seasons — *repeated, October 10*

11† Four Seasons; Washington Square

November 1998:

18 TORONTO, ON, Hummingbird Centre: Manon — *repeated, November 19†, 19, 20, 21†, 21, 22†*

25 Four Seasons; Split House Geometric; La Bayadère, Act II — *repeated, November 26, 27, 28†, 28, 29†*

December 1998:

10† TORONTO, ON, Hummingbird Centre: Nutcracker — *repeated, December 10, 11, 12†, 12, 13†, 15, 16, 17, 18, 19†, 19, 20†, 22†, 22, 23†, 23, 27†, 28†, 29†, 29*

February 1999:

10 TORONTO, ON, Hummingbird Centre: Taming of the Shrew — *repeated, February 11‡, 11, 12, 13†, 13, 14†*

18 Apollo; Fairy's Kiss; Septet — *repeated, February 19, 20†, 20, 21†*

23 Amusing Mozart (Royal Danish Ballet); Apollo, Variations & pdd (Royal Danish Ballet, Bruhn Competition Alumni); Don Quixote, Act III Grand pdd (National Ballet of Canada); End, solo (National Ballet of Canada); La Sylphide, Act II pdd (Royal Danish Ballet); Nutcracker, Act II Grand pdd (San Francisco Ballet) Post No Scriptum (American Ballet Theatre); Romeo and Juliet, Balcony pdd (National Ballet of Canada, Bruhn Competition Alumni); Swan Lake, Act III Grand pdd (American Ballet Theatre); Swan Lake, Russian Princess Solo (National Ballet of Canada); Two Bits (San Francisco Ballet) *(Erik Bruhn Competition)*

24† Apollo; Fairy's Kiss; Septet — *repeated, February 24*

April 1999:

8 LONDON, ON, Grand Theatre: Washington Square; Four Seasons — *repeated, April 9, 10†, 10*

15 MONTREAL, QC, Place des Arts: Manon — *repeated, April 16, 17†, 17*

May 1999

5 TORONTO, ON, Hummingbird Centre: Swan Lake — *repeated, May 6, 7, 8†, 8, 9†, 11‡, 11, 12, 13†, 13, 14, 15†*

19 OTTAWA, ON, National Arts Centre: Swan Lake — *repeated, May 20, 21, 22*

September 1999:

24 SASKATOON, SK, Saskatoon Centennial Aud: Swan Lake — *repeated, September 25*

28 EDMONTON, AB, Jubilee Aud: Swan Lake — *repeated, September 29*

October 1999:

1 CALGARY, AB, Jubilee Aud: Swan Lake — *repeated, October 2†, 2*

6 VANCOUVER, BC, Queen Elizabeth Theatre: Swan Lake

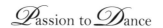

7†   Swan Lake, Act II

7   Swan Lake — *repeated, October 8, 9*

November 1999:

20   TORONTO, ON, Hummingbird Centre: one hundred words for snow; Disembodied Voice — *repeated, November 21†, 24, 25, 26, 27†, 27*

December 1999:

11†   TORONTO, ON, Hummingbird Centre: Nutcracker — *repeated, December 11, 12†, 15†, 15, 16, 17, 18†, 18, 19†, 19, 21†, 21, 22, 23†, 23, 26†, 27†, 28†, 29†, 29, 30†*

February 2000:

11   TORONTO, ON, Hummingbird Centre: Jewels — *repeated, February 12, 13†*

16   Onegin — *repeated, February 17†, 17, 18, 19†, 19, 20†, 22*

23   Jewels — *repeated, February 24†, 24, 25, 26†*

March 2000:

9   OTTAWA, ON, National Arts Centre: Jewels — *repeated, February 10, 11*

May 2000:

5   TORONTO, ON, Hummingbird Centre: Cinderella — *repeated, May 6†*

10   Tides of Mind; Manon, pdd; Désir; Les Sylphides

11†   Nuages; Les Sylphides; Tides of Mind; Désir

11   Les Sylphides; Désir; Manon, pdd; Tides of Mind — *repeated, May 12, 13†*

13   Manon, pdd; Désir; Les Sylphides; Nuages

14†   Les Sylphides; Nuages; Tides of Mind; Désir

17   Cinderella — *repeated, May 18†, 18, 19, 20†, 20, 21†*

24   Giselle — *repeated, May 25†, 25, 26, 27†, 27, 28†*

June 2000:

17   OTTAWA, ON, National Arts Centre: Septet; one hundred words for snow; Disembodied Voice *(contribution to Canada Dance Festival)*

August 2000:

18   TORONTO, ON, Harbourfront, Concert Stage: Désir; Swan Lake, Act IV pdd; Four Seasons, Summer pdd; Les Sylphides; Tides of Mind

19   Les Sylphides

November 2000:

10   TORONTO, ON, Hummingbird Centre: Four Seasons; Firebird — *repeated, November 11†, 11, 12†*

15   Don Quixote — *repeated, November 16†, 16, 17, 18†, 18, 19†*

21   Four Seasons; Firebird — *repeated, November 22, 23†, 23*

December 2000:

9†   TORONTO, ON, Hummingbird Centre: Nutcracker — *repeated, December 9, 10†, 13†, 14†, 14, 15, 16†, 16, 17†, 17, 20, 21, 22, 23†, 23, 27†, 27, 28†, 29†, 29, 30†*

February 2001:

10†   TORONTO, ON, Hummingbird Centre: Swan Lake — *repeated, February 10, 11†*

14   Dream; Comforts of Solitude — *repeated, February 15, 16, 17†, 17, 18†*

20‡   Swan Lake — *repeated, February 21, 22†, 22, 23, 24, 25†*

March 2001:

8   OTTAWA, ON, National Arts Centre, Southam Hall: Don Quixote — *repeated, March 9, 10*

April 2001:

28   TORONTO, ON, Hummingbird Centre: Madame Butterfly; Serenade — *repeated, April 29†*

May 2001:

2   TORONTO, ON, Hummingbird Centre: Theme and Variations; Septet; Delicate Battle — *repeated, May 3, 4, 5†, 5, 6†*

8   Serenade; Madame Butterfly — *repeated, May 9, 10†, 10, 11, 12†, 12*

August 2001:

21   TORONTO, ON, Harbourfront, Norigen Stage: Romeo and Juliet, Balcony pdd; Delicate Battle, Movement I; Paquita, dances from; Pastorale, Movement II; Romeo and Juliet, dances from; Theme and Variations — *repeated, August 22, 23*

September 2001:

18   EDMONTON, AB, Jubilee Aud: Romeo and Juliet — *repeated, September 19*

21   CALGARY, AB, Jubilee Aud: Romeo and Juliet — *repeated, September 22†, 22*

25   VICTORIA, BC, Royal Theatre: Romeo and Juliet, Balcony pdd; Theme and Variations; Delicate Battle; Romeo and Juliet, dances from

27   VANCOUVER, BC, Queen Elizabeth Theatre: Romeo and Juliet — *repeated, September 28†, 28, 29*

October 2001:

31   TORONTO, ON, Hummingbird Centre: Merry Widow

November 2001:

1†   TORONTO, ON, Hummingbird Centre: Merry Widow — *repeated, November 1, 2, 3†, 3, 4†*

7   Pastorale; Mozartiana; Solitaire — *repeated, November 8, 9, 10†, 10, 11†*

30   OTTAWA, ON, National Arts Centre, Southam Hall:
       Nutcracker

December 2001:

1†   OTTAWA, ON, National Arts Centre, Southam Hall:
       Nutcracker — *repeated, December 1, 2†, 2, 4, 5, 6, 7,*
       8†, 8

16†   TORONTO, ON, Hummingbird Centre: Nutcracker
       — *repeated, 16, 18, 19, 20, 21, 22†, 22, 23†, 23, 26†,*
       27†, 27, 28†, 29†, 29, 30†, 30

February 2002:

8   TORONTO, ON, Hummingbird Centre: Romeo and
       Juliet — *repeated, February 9, 10†, 12‡, 13, 14†, 14,*
       15, 16†, 16, 17†

20   Sleeping Beauty, Act III; Paquita; Monotones II;
       Monotones I — *repeated, February 21†, 21, 22, 23†,*
       23, 24†

May 2002:

4   TORONTO, ON, Hummingbird Centre: Contract —
       repeated, May 5†

8   Apollo; Voluntaries; Intermezzo — *repeated, May 9†,*
       9, 10, 11†, 11, 12†

14   Contract — *repeated, May 15, 16, 17, 18†, 18*

20   5th Symphony of Gustav Mahler, Adagietto (Royal
       Danish Ballet); CollectiveSonataforTwo (National
       Ballet of Canada); Continuum (San Francisco
       Ballet); Giselle, Act II pdd (Stuttgart Ballet); Grand
       Pas Classique (American Ballet Theatre); In the
       Middle Somewhat Elevated, pdd (Stuttgart Ballet);
       Manon, Act II Bedroom pdd (American Ballet
       Theatre); Paquita, pdd (San Francisco Ballet);
       Swan Lake, Black Swan pdd (National Ballet of
       Canada); Swan Lake, Black Swan pdd (Royal
       Danish Ballet) *(Erik Bruhn Competition)*

23   OTTAWA, ON, National Arts Centre, Southam Hall:
       Contract — *repeated, May 24, 25*

June 2002:

3   HALIFAX, NS, Rebecca Cohn Aud: Intermezzo;
       Apollo; Monotones II; Sleeping Beauty, Act III pdd —
       repeated, June 4

6   SAINT JOHN, NB, Imperial Theatre: Intermezzo;
       Apollo; Monotones II; Sleeping Beauty, Act III pdd

8   FREDERICTON, NB, Playhouse: Intermezzo;
       Apollo; Monotones II; Sleeping Beauty, Act III pdd

15   OTTAWA, ON, National Arts Centre, Southam
       Hall: Delicate Battle *(contribution to Canada Dance
       Festival)*

October 2002:

5   SAULT STE. MARIE, ON, Kiwanis Community
       Theatre: Désir, 1st pdd; Nutcracker, Snow Trio;
       Intermezzo; Sleeping Beauty, Bluebird pdd

November 2002:

16   TORONTO, ON, Hummingbird Centre: Firebird;
       Delicate Battle; La Bayadère, Act II — *repeated,*
       November 17†

20   La Fille mal gardée — *repeated, November 21†, 21, 22,*
       23†, 23, 24†, 26†

27   Firebird; Delicate Battle; La Bayadère, Act II —
       repeated, November 28, 29, 30†, 30

December 2002:

1†   TORONTO, ON, Hummingbird Centre: Firebird;
       Delicate Battle; La Bayadère, Act II

14†   Nutcracker — *repeated, December 14, 15†, 15, 18‡,*
       19‡, 19, 20, 21†, 21, 22a†, 22b† (two matinees on one
       day), 26†, 27†, 28†, 28, 29a†, 29b† (two matinees on
       one day), 31†

January 2003:

2†   TORONTO, ON, Hummingbird Centre: Nutcracker
       — *repeated, January 2*

February 2003:

14   TORONTO, ON, Hummingbird Centre: Swan Lake
       — *repeated, February 15†, 15, 16†*

19   Napoli, dances from; Le Spectre de la Rose;
       Judgment of Paris; Élite Syncopations — *repeated,*
       February 20†, 20, 21, 22†, 22, 23†

26   Swan Lake — *repeated, February 27†, 27, 28*

March 2003:

1   TORONTO, ON, Hummingbird Centre: Swan Lake
       — *repeated, March 2†*

13   OTTAWA, ON, National Arts Centre, Southam Hall:
       Swan Lake — *repeated, March 14, 15*

April 2003:

10   MONTREAL, QC, Place des Arts: La Fille mal gardée
       — *repeated, April 11, 12†, 12*

May 2003:

2   TORONTO, ON, Hummingbird Centre: Tristan and
       Isolde — *repeated, May 3†, 3, 4†*

7   Jewels — *repeated, May 8†, 8, 9, 10†, 10, 11†, 13*

14   Tristan and Isolde — *repeated, May 15*

24   CHARLESTON, SC, Gaillard Aud: Four Seasons;
       Apollo; Delicate Battle — *repeated, May 25†, 25*
       (Spoleto Festival)

August 2003:

19   TORONTO, ON, Harbourfront, CIBC Stage:
       Intermezzo; Judgment of Paris; Apollo; Napoli,
       dances from — *repeated, August 20, 21*

September 2003:

12   SASKATOON, SK, Saskatoon Centennial Aud: Four

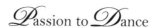

Seasons; Firebird — *repeated, September 13*

16 EDMONTON, AB, Jubilee Aud: Four Seasons; Firebird — *repeated, September 17*

19 CALGARY, AB, Jubilee Aud: Four Seasons; Firebird — *repeated, September 20*

23 VICTORIA, BC, Royal Theatre: Apollo; Judgment of Paris; Four Seasons; Napoli, dances from

25 VANCOUVER, BC, Queen Elizabeth Theatre: Four Seasons; Firebird — *repeated, September 26†, 26, 27*

November 2003:

13 TORONTO, ON, Hummingbird Centre: End, excerpt; Monument; Gazebo Dances, excerpt; There, below; one hundred words for snow — *repeated, November 14, 15†, 15, 16†, 19*

22 Onegin — *repeated, November 26, 27†, 27, 28, 29†, 29, 30*

December 2003:

13† TORONTO, ON, Hummingbird Centre: Nutcracker — *repeated, December 13, 14†, 17†, 18†, 18, 19, 20†, 20, 21†, 21, 23†, 23, 24†, 27†, 27, 28†, 28, 30†, 30*

February 2004:

14 TORONTO, ON, Hummingbird Centre: Sleeping Beauty — *repeated, February 15†*

18 Serenade; Alice — *repeated, February 19†, 20, 21†, 21, 22†*

24‡ Sleeping Beauty — *repeated, February 25, 26†, 26, 27, 28†, 28, 29†*

March 2004:

18 OTTAWA, ON, National Arts Centre, Southam Hall: Onegin — *repeated, March 19, 20*

May 2004:

8 TORONTO, ON, Hummingbird Centre: Cinderella — *repeated, May 9†, 12, 13†, 13, 14, 15†, 15, 16†*

19 Four Seasons; Cruel World; Theme and Variations — *repeated, May 20, 21, 22†, 22, 23†*

August 2004:

24 TORONTO, ON, Harbourfront, CIBC Stage: Dances from The Sleeping Beauty; There, below; Musings, Movements I, II, & IV — *repeated, August 25, 26*

September 2004:

30 BERKELEY, CA, Zellerbach Hall: Chacony; There, below; Four Seasons; Apollo

October 2004:

1 BERKELEY, CA, Zellerbach Hall: Chacony; There, below; Four Seasons; Apollo — *repeated, October 2, 3†*

7 DETROIT, MI, Detroit Opera House: Four Seasons; Firebird — *repeated, 8, 9, 10†*

November 2004:

17 TORONTO, ON, Hummingbird Centre: Stravinsky Violin Concerto; Giselle — *repeated, November 18†, 18, 19, 20†, 20, 21†*

24 Contract (The Pied Piper) — *repeated, November 25†, 25, 26, 27†, 27, 28†*

December 2004:

11† TORONTO, ON, Hummingbird Centre: Nutcracker — *repeated, December 11, 12a†, 12b† (two matinees on one day), 14†, 15†, 16, 17, 18†, 18, 19†, 19, 21†, 21, 22, 23†, 23, 28†, 28, 29†*

February 2005:

23 TORONTO, ON, Hummingbird Centre: Madame Butterfly; Désir — *repeated, February 24†, 24, 25, 26†, 26, 27†*

March 2005:

2 TORONTO, ON, Hummingbird Centre: La Ronde; Opus 19/The Dreamer; Les Sylphides — *repeated, March 3, 4, 5†, 5, 6†*

17 OTTAWA, ON, National Arts Centre, Southam Hall: Cinderella — *repeated, March 18, 19*

April 2005:

5 BROOKLYN, NY, Howard Gilman Opera House, BAM: Contract (The Pied Piper) — *repeated, April 7, 8, 9†, 9*

23† TORONTO, ON, Hummingbird Centre: Cinderella — *repeated, April 23, 24†, 24*

May 2005:

1† TORONTO, ON, Hummingbird Centre: Italian Straw Hat

4 Études; Jewels, Rubies; Musings — *repeated, May 5, 6, 7†, 7, 8†*

10‡ Italian Straw Hat — *repeated, May 11, 12†, 12, 13, 14†, 14, 15†*

August 2005:

23 TORONTO, ON, Harbourfront, CIBC Stage: Full Circles; La Sylphide, Act II excerpt; Romeo and Juliet before parting; Theme and Variations — *repeated, August 24, 25*

September 2005:

12 SASKATOON, SK, Saskatoon Centennial Aud: Swan Lake — *repeated, September 13*

16 CALGARY, AB, Jubilee Aud: Swan Lake — *repeated, September 17*

20 EDMONTON, AB, Jubilee Aud: Swan Lake — *repeated, September 21*

23 VICTORIA, BC, Royal Theatre: Romeo and Juliet before parting; Swan Lake, Act II; Theme and

Variations; Swan Lake, Black Swan pdd; Full Circles — *repeated, September 24*

26 NANAIMO, BC, Port Theatre: Theme and Variations; Swan Lake, Act II; Full Circles; Romeo and Juliet before parting; Swan Lake, Black Swan pdd

28 VANCOUVER, BC, Centre for the Arts: Swan Lake — *repeated, September 29, 30*

October 2005:

1† VANCOUVER, BC, Centre for the Arts: Swan Lake — *repeated, September 1*

November 2005:

16 TORONTO, ON, Hummingbird Centre: Swan Lake — *repeated, November 17†, 17, 18, 19†, 19, 20†*

23 Intermezzo; La Sylphide — *repeated, November 24†, 24, 25, 26†, 26, 27†*

December 2005:

10† TORONTO, ON, Hummingbird Centre: Nutcracker — *repeated, December 10, 11a†, 11b† (two matinees on one day), 14‡, 15‡, 15, 16, 17†, 17, 18a†, 18b† (two matinees on one day), 21, 22, 23, 28a†, 28b† (two matinees on one day), 29a†, 29b† (two matinees on one day)*

January 2006:

17 WASHINGTON, DC, Kennedy Center: Swan Lake — *repeated, January 18, 19, 20, 21†, 21, 22†*

27 CLEVELAND, OH, Playhouse Square Center State Theatre: Firebird; Four Seasons — *repeated, January 28, 29†*

February 2006:

17 TORONTO, ON, Hummingbird Centre: Swan Lake — *repeated, February 18, 19†*

22 Jewels — *repeated, February 23, 24, 25†, 25, 26†*

March 2006:

1 TORONTO, ON, Hummingbird Centre: Four Temperaments; Apollo; Theme and Variations — *repeated, March 2, 3, 4†, 4, 5†*

23 OTTAWA, ON, National Arts Centre, Southam Hall: Italian Straw Hat— *repeated, March 24, 25*

April 2006:

29 TORONTO, ON, Hummingbird Centre: Romeo and Juliet — *repeated, April 30†*

May 2006:

2‡ TORONTO, ON, Hummingbird Centre: Romeo and Juliet — *repeated, May 3, 4†, 4, 5, 6†, 6, 7†*

10 Grand Pas Classique; Petrouchka; There, below; Delicate Battle — *repeated, May 11†, 11, 12*

13† There, below; Delicate Battle; C.V.; Petrouchka

13 There, below; Grand Pas Classique; Petrouchka; Delicate Battle

14† There, below; Delicate Battle; C.V.; Petrouchka

19 LONDON, U.K., Royal Opera House, Linbury Studio: C.V. — *repeated, May 20†, 20, 21† (contribution to Royal Opera House Two celebrations for Royal Ballet's 75th anniversary)*

June 2006:

22 TORONTO, ON, FSCPA: Herman Schmerman, pdd; Romeo and Juliet before parting; Grand Pas Classique; Sleeping Beauty, Bluebird pdd; Don Quixote, pdd; Tchaikowsky Pas de Deux; Désir, Movement IV *(Illuminata gala)*

August 2006:

11 SAINT-SAUVEUR, QC, Le Grand Chapiteau: Apollo; Intermezzo; There, below

November 2006:

9 TORONTO, ON, FSCPA: Sleeping Beauty — *repeated, November 10, 11†, 11, 12†, 14, 15, 16†, 16, 17, 18†, 18, 19†, 19*

22 Symphony in C; Song of the Earth — *repeated, November 23, 24, 25†, 25, 26†*

December 2006:

9† TORONTO, ON, FSCPA: Nutcracker — *repeated, December 9, 10†, 10, 12†, 13, 14, 15, 16†, 16, 17†, 19, 20, 21, 22, 23†, 23, 27†, 27, 28, 29†, 29, 30†, 30*

March 2007:

3 TORONTO, ON, FSCPA: Flower Festival in Genzano, pdd (Royal Danish Ballet); Le Corsaire, pdd (National Ballet of Canada); opus (Royal Danish Ballet); Petite Mort, excerpt (American Ballet Theatre); Romeo and Juliet (Cranko), Balcony pdd (National Ballet of Canada); Romeo and Juliet (MacMillan), Balcony pdd (Royal Ballet); Sleeping Beauty, Bluebird pdd (Royal Ballet); Sleeping Beauty, Grand pdd (American Ballet Theatre); Voluntaries (National Ballet of Canada) *(Erik Bruhn Competition)*

10 Taming of the Shrew — *repeated, March 11†, 13, 14, 15†, 15, 16, 17†, 17, 18†*

21 Footstep of Air; Opus 19/The Dreamer; Voluntaries — *repeated, March 22, 23, 24†, 24, 25†*

April 2007:

12 OTTAWA, ON, National Arts Centre, Southam Hall: Footstep of Air; Opus 19/The Dreamer; Voluntaries — *repeated, April 13, 14*

June 2007:

2 TORONTO, ON, FSCPA: Four Seasons; Polyphonia;

Wolf's Court — *repeated, June 3†, 5†, 6, 7†, 7, 8, 9†, 9*

15 Don Quixote (Balanchine) — *repeated, June 16†, 16, 17†, 20, 21†, 21, 22, 23, 24†*

28 Élite Syncopations, excerpts; Seven Greek Dances, excerpts; Four Seasons, Summer pdd; Didj "U" Know?; clearing; Symphony in C, Finale *(Mad Hot Gala)*

September 2007:

10 SASKATOON, SK, TCU Place, Sid Buckwold Theatre: Polyphonia; Giselle — *repeated, September 11*

13 CALGARY, AB, Jubilee Aud: Polyphonia; Giselle — *repeated, September 14, 15*

18 EDMONTON, AB, Jubilee Aud: Polyphonia; Giselle — *repeated, September 19*

21 VICTORIA, BC, Royal Theatre: Polyphonia; Giselle — *repeated, September 22*

24 NANAIMO, BC, Port Theatre: Polyphonia; Giselle

26 VANCOUVER, BC, Centre for the Arts: Polyphonia; Giselle — *repeated, September 27, 28, 29†, 29*

November 2007:

8 TORONTO, ON, FSCPA: Glass Pieces; In The Night; West Side Story Suite — *repeated, November 9, 10†, 10, 11†, 13‡, 14, 15†, 15, 16, 17, 18†*

21 Merry Widow — *repeated, November 22†, 22, 23, 24†, 24, 25†*

December 2007:

8† TORONTO, ON, FSCPA: Nutcracker — *repeated, December 8, 9†, 9, 11†, 12, 13, 14, 15†, 15, 16†, 16, 18, 19, 20, 21, 22†, 22, 23†, 23, 27†, 27, 28†, 29†, 29, 30†*

February 2008:

27 TORONTO, ON, FSCPA: Italian Straw Hat — *repeated, February 28, 29*

March 2008:

1† TORONTO, ON, FSCPA: Italian Straw Hat — *repeated, March 1, 2†*

8 24 Preludes by Chopin; Soldiers' Mass; Rooster — *repeated, March 9†, 11, 12, 13, 14, 15†, 15, 16†*

21 HOUSTON, TX, Cullen Theater: Polyphonia — *repeated, March 22 (contribution Dance Salad Festival)*

April 2008:

1 SAN FRANCISCO, CA, War Memorial & Performing Arts Center: Delicate Battle — *repeated, April 2, 3, 4, 5†, 5, 6† (contribution to International Salute to the San Francisco Ballet)*

24 OTTAWA, ON, National Arts Centre, Southam Hall: Merry Widow — *repeated, April 25, 26*

May 2008:

28 TORONTO, ON, FSCPA: Cinderella — *repeated, May 29†, 29, 30, 31†, 31*

June 2008:

1† TORONTO, ON, FSCPA: Cinderella — *repeated, June 3‡, 4‡, 5, 6, 7, 8†*

13 Études; second detail; Five Brahms Waltzes in the Manner of Isadora Duncan — *repeated, June 14†, 14, 15†*

17 Études, excerpts; Jewels, Rubies; Tchaikowsky Pas de Deux; veer *(Mad Hot II)*

18 Études; second detail; Five Brahms Waltzes in the Manner of Isadora Duncan — *repeated, June 19†, 19, 20, 21, 22†*

September 2008:

17 NEW YORK, NY, City Center: Soldiers' Mass — *repeated, September 18 (contribution to Fall for Dance, 2008)*

October 2008:

2 COSTA MESA, CA, Orange County Perf. Arts Centre: Soldiers' Mass — *repeated, October 3*

November 2008:

5 TORONTO, ON, FSCPA: In the Upper Room; Polyphonia; Symphony in C — *repeated, November 6†, 6, 7, 8†, 8, 9†*

14 Seagull — *repeated, November 15†, 15, 16†, 18†, 19, 20†, 20, 21, 22, 23†*

December 2008:

6† TORONTO, ON, FSCPA: Nutcracker — *repeated, December 6, 7†, 9†, 10, 11, 12, 13†, 13, 14†, 14, 16, 17, 18, 19, 20†, 20, 21†, 21, 23†, 23, 24†, 27†, 27, 28†, 28*

March 2009:

4 TORONTO, ON, FSCPA: DEXTRIS; Emergence; IN COLOUR — *repeated, March 5, 6, 7†, 7, 8†*

11 Romeo and Juliet — *repeated, March 12†, 12, 13, 14†, 14, 15†*

18 Dénouement (National Ballet of Canada); Ebony Concerto (San Francisco Ballet); Elegy for Us (Royal Danish Ballet); End (Gomes) (American Ballet Theatre); Giselle, Act II pdd (San Francisco Ballet); La Grande Parade du Funk (Stuggart Ballet); La Sylphide, Act II pdd (Royal Danish Ballet); Le Corsaire, pdd (National Ballet of Canada); Swan Lake, Act III, Black Swan pdd (American Ballet Theatre); Swan Lake, Act III, Black Swan pdd (Stuggart Ballet); DEXTRIS, excerpts *(Erik Bruhn Competition)*

19 Romeo and Juliet — *repeated, March 20, 21†, 21, 22†*

April 2009:

16 OTTAWA, ON, National Arts Centre, Southam Hall: Romeo and Juliet — *repeated, April 17, 18*

Appendix A

May 2009:

27   TORONTO, ON, FSCPA: Giselle — *repeated, May 28†, 28, 29, 30†, 30, 31†*

June 2009:

6†   TORONTO, ON, FSCPA: Skin Divers; Carmen — *repeated, June 6, 7†, 10, 11, 12, 13†, 13, 14†*

18   Prokofiev Pas de Deux; Dénouement; Lady of the Camellias, Act I pdd; Le Corsaire, pdd; Valse Triste; Seven Greek Dances — excerpts *(White Hot Gala)*

September 2009:

16   TORONTO, ON, Dundas Square: Watch her — excerpts *(contribution to Toronto International Film Festival)*

26   VICTORIA, BC, Royal Theatre: Musings; Sleeping Beauty, Act III pdd; Apollo; Lady of the Camellias, Act I pdd

28   NANAIMO, BC, Port Theatre: Musings; Sleeping Beauty, Act III pdd; Apollo; Lady of the Camellias, Act I pdd

30   VANCOUVER, BC, Vancouver Playhouse: Lady of the Camellias, Act I pdd; Apollo; Sleeping Beauty, Act III pdd *(contributions to Ballet BC Gala)*

November 2009:

5   OTTAWA, ON, National Arts Centre, Southam Hall: Sleeping Beauty — *repeated, November 6, 7*

13   TORONTO, ON, FSCPA: Sleeping Beauty — *repeated, November 14†, 14, 15†, 18, 19†, 19, 20, 21†, 21, 22†*

25   Glass Pieces; Watch her; Four Temperaments — *repeated, November 26, 27, 28†, 28, 29†*

December 2009:

12†   TORONTO, ON, FSCPA: Nutcracker — *repeated, December 12, 13†, 13, 16, 17, 18, 19†, 19, 20†, 20, 22†, 22, 23†, 23, 27†, 27, 28†, 29†, 29, 30†, 30*

January 2010:

2†   TORONTO, ON, FSCPA: Nutcracker — *repeated, January 2, 3†*

February 2010:

13   VANCOUVER, BC, Queen Elizabeth Theatre: 24 Preludes by Chopin — *repeated, February 14 (contribution to Vancouver 2010 Cultural Olympiad)*

March 2010:

3   TORONTO, ON, FSCPA: Four Seasons; Suite of Dances; 24 Preludes by Chopin — *repeated, March 4, 5, 6†, 6, 7†*

11   Swan Lake — *repeated, March 12, 13†, 13, 14†, 16, 17, 18†, 18, 19, 20†, 20, 21†*

June 2010:

4   TORONTO, ON, FSCPA: Pur ti Miro; Opus 19/The Dreamer; West Side Story Suite — *repeated, June 5†, 5, 6†*

8   Jewels, Diamonds pdd; Onegin, Mirror pdd; As Above, So Below; Musings; Polyphonia, Eyes Wide Shut *(Gala 2010)*

9   Pur ti Miro; Opus 19/The Dreamer; West Side Story Suite — *repeated, June 10†, 10, 11, 12, 13†*

19†   Onegin — *repeated, June 19, 20†, 22, 23, 24†, 24, 25*

October 2010:

13   QUEBEC CITY, QC, Grand Théâtre de Québec: Emergence; 24 Preludes by Chopin

15   MONTREAL, QC, Place des Arts, Salle Wilfrid-Pelletier: Emergence; 24 Preludes by Chopin — *repeated, October 16*

21   OTTAWA, ON, National Arts Centre, Southam Hall: 24 Preludes by Chopin; Emergence; Serenade — *repeated, October 22, 23*

November 2010:

11   TORONTO, ON, FSCPA: Cinderella — *repeated, November 12, 13†, 13, 14†, 17, 18†, 18, 19, 20†, 20*

24   Emergence, Chroma, Serenade — *repeated, November 25, 26, 27†, 27, 28†*

December 2010:

11†   TORONTO, ON, FSCPA: Nutcracker — *repeated, December 11, 12†, 12, 15, 16, 17, 18†, 18, 19†, 19, 21†, 21, 22†, 22, 23†, 23, 24†, 28†, 28, 29†, 29, 30†, 30*

January 2011:

2†   TORONTO, ON, FSCPA: Nutcracker — *repeated, January 2*

March 2011:

5   TORONTO, ON, FSCPA: Passacaglia (National Ballet of Canada); Sleeping Beauty, Bluebird pdd (National Ballet of Canada); La Sylphide, Act II pdd (American Ballet Theatre); Divergent Connectivity (American Ballet Theatre); Giselle, Act II pdd (Hamburg Ballet); Chopin Dialogue (Hamburg Ballet); Flower Festival in Genzano, pdd (Royal Danish Ballet); Meron Nign (Royal Danish Ballet); Don Quixote, Act III pdd (Stuttgart Ballet); Little Monsters (Stuttgart Ballet); Theme and Variations *(Erik Bruhn Competition)*

9   Don Quixote — *repeated, March 10†, 10, 11, 12†, 12, 13†*

17   Onegin — *repeated, March 18, 19†, 19, 20†*

23   Russian Seasons; Apollo; Theme and Variations — *repeated, March 24, 25, 26†, 26, 27†*

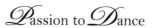

June 2011:

4   TORONTO, ON, FSCPA: Alice's Adventures in
Wonderland — *repeated, June 5†, 8, 9†, 9, 10, 11†,*
11, 12

15   In the Upper Room; Mozartiana; Other Dances —
repeated, June 16†, 16, 17, 18†, 18, 19†

21   *(Mad Hot Wonderland)*

23   Alice's Adventures in Wonderland — *repeated, June*
24, 25†, 25

Appendix B:

COMPANY REPERTOIRE

1951/52
L'Après-midi d'un Faune (Celia Franca)
Ballet Behind Us (David Adams)
Ballet Composite (David Adams)
Casse-Noisette: Act II (Lev Ivanov)
Coppélia: Act II (Arthur Saint-Léon)
The Dance of Salomé (Celia Franca)
Étude (Kay Armstrong)
Giselle: Act II (Jean Coralli/Jules Perrot)
Pas de Deux from Don Quixote (Marius Petipa)
Pas de Deux from The Nutcracker (Lev Ivanov)
Peasant pas de deux from Giselle (Jean Coralli/Jules Perrot)
Polovetsian Dances from Prince Igor (Michel Fokine)
Les Sylphides (Michel Fokine)

1952/53
Coppélia (Two Acts) (Arthur Saint-Léon)
Giselle (Jean Coralli/Jules Perrot)
Lilac Garden (Antony Tudor)
Le Pommier (Celia Franca)

1953/54
Dances from the Classics (Marius Petipa/Lev Ivanov)
Dark of the Moon (Joey Harris) [name changed to Barbara Allen, January to June, 1955]
Gala Performance (Antony Tudor)
Swan Lake: Act II (Marius Petipa/Lev Ivanov)

1954/55
Dances from The Sleeping Princess (Petipa)
The Lady from the Sea (Elizabeth Leese)
Offenbach in the Underworld (Antony Tudor)
Swan Lake (Marius Petipa/Lev Ivanov)

1955/56
Dark Elegies (Antony Tudor)
The Nutcracker (Celia Franca, after Lev Ivanov)

1956/57
The Fisherman and His Soul (Grant Strate)
Giselle (Jean Coralli/Jules Perrot)
Jeune Pas de Deux (Grant Strate)
La Llamada (Ray Moller)
Pas de Chance (David Adams)
Post Script (Brian Macdonald)
Les Rendez-vous (Frederick Ashton)

1957/58
Le Carnaval (Michel Fokine)
Dances from The Sleeping Beauty (after Marius Petipa)
La Farucca (Ray Moller)
The Willow (Grant Strate)
Winter Night (after Walter Gore)

1958/59
Ballad (Grant Strate)
Coppélia (new production) (after Arthur Saint-Léon)

1959/60
Death and the Maiden (Andrée Howard)
The Littlest One (David Adams)
The Mermaid (Andrée Howard)
Pas de Deux Romantique (David Adams)
Pas de Six (David Adams)
Pineapple Poll (John Cranko)

1960/61
Antic Spring (Grant Strate)

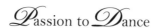

Barbara Allen (David Adams)
Princess Aurora (Marius Petipa, additional choreography
    by Celia Franca)
The Remarkable Rocket (Don Gillies)

1961/62
Concerto Barocco (George Balanchine)
One in Five (Ray Powell)

1962/63
Le Corsaire, pas de deux from (Robert Klavin)
The Judgment of Paris (Antony Tudor)
Laurencia Pas de Six (Vakhtang Chabukiane, staged by
    Galina Samsova)
Sequel (Grant Strate)
Serenade (George Balanchine)
Time Cycle (Grant Strate)

1963/64
Allégresse (Zachary Solov)
Don Quixote, pas de deux (from Marius Petipa, staged by
    Eugen Valukin)
Don Quixote, pas de deux (from Marius Petipa, staged by
    Svetlana Beriosova)
House of Atreus (Grant Strate)
Romeo and Juliet (John Cranko)
Walpurgis Night, pas de deux (from L. Lavrovsky)

1964/65
Clair de Lune (Eugen Valukin)
Électre (Grant Strate)
The Nutcracker (new production) (Celia Franca, after
    Marius Petipa)
Pas de Deux (Grant Strate)
Pas de Deux (John Cranko)
La Sylphide (Erik Bruhn, after August Bournonville)
Triptych (Grant Strate)

1965/66
Adagio Cantabile (Heinz Poll)
Lilac Garden (revival) (Antony Tudor)
Pulcinella (Grant Strate)
The Rake's Progress (Dame Ninette de Valois)
Rivalité (Daniel Seillier)
Solitaire (Kenneth MacMillan)

1966/67
La Bayaderka: Act IV (Marius Petipa)
Eh! (Celia Franca)
Mélodie (Eugen Valukin)
Rondo Giocoso (Heinz Poll)
Swan Lake (new production) (Erik Bruhn, after Marius
    Petipa and Lev Ivanov)

1967/68
Cinderella (Celia Franca)
La Prima Ballerina (Heino Heiden)
Studies in White (Grant Strate)

1968/69
The Arena (Grant Strate)
Célébrations (Heinz Poll)
Cyclus (Grant Strate)
Flower Festival in Genzano, pas de deux (from August
    Bournonville)
The Four Temperaments (George Balanchine)
Kraanerg (Roland Petit)
Pas de Deux (David Gordon)
Phases (Grant Strate)

1969/70
Giselle (new production) (produced by Peter Wright, after
    Coralli/Perrot/Petipa)
The Lesson (Fleming Flindt, after Ionesco)
Le Loup (Roland Petit)

1970/71
Brown Earth (Ann Ditchburn)
For Internal Use As Well (Tim Spain)
The Mirror Walkers (Peter Wright)
Sagar (Tim Spain)

1971/72
Evocation (staged by Daniel Seillier)
Fandango (Antony Tudor)
Intermezzo (Eliot Feld)
Session (Robert Iscove)

1972/73
The Moor's Pavane (José Limòn)
The Sleeping Beauty (Rudolf Nureyev, after Marius Petipa)

1973/74
Don Juan (John Neumeier)
Flower Festival in Genzano, pas de deux (new production)
    (from August Bournonville)
Les Sylphides (new production) (Michel Fokine, produced
    by Celia Franca and Erik Bruhn)

1974/75
Coppélia (new production) (Erik Bruhn)
Inventions (Constantin Patsalas)
Kettentanz (Gerald Arpino)
Whispers of Darkness (Norbert Vesak)

1975/76
Kisses (Ann Ditchburn)
Monument for a Dead Boy (Rudi van Dantzig)

Offenbach in the Underworld (revival) (Antony Tudor)

1976/77

Afternoon of a Faun (Jerome Robbins)

Black Angels (Constantin Patsalas)

La Fille mal gardée (Frederick Ashton)

Four Schumann Pieces (Hans van Manen)

Mad Shadows (Ann Ditchburn)

Monotones II (Frederick Ashton)

A Party (James Kudelka)

Romeo and Juliet (revival) (John Cranko)

1977/78

La Bayaderka: Act IV (revival) (Marius Petipa)

Collective Symphony (Hans van Manen/Toer van Schayk/
    Rudi van Dantzig)

The Dream (Frederick Ashton)

1978/79

Élite Syncopations (Kenneth MacMillan)

Les Patineurs (Frederick Ashton)

The Rite of Spring (Constantin Patsalas)

The Two Pigeons (Frederick Ashton)

Washington Square (James Kudelka)

1979/80

Études (Harald Lander)

Serenade (revival) (George Balanchine)

Song of a Wayfarer (Maurice Béjart)

Le Spectre de la Rose (Michel Fokine)

Swan Lake (new production) (Erik Bruhn, after Marius
    Petipa)

1980/81

Angali (Constantin Patsalas)

Dark Elegies (revival) (Antony Tudor)

The Dying Swan (Michel Fokine, staged by Nicholas
    Beriozoff)

Newcomers (Brian Macdonald)

Playhouse (James Kudelka)

1981/82

Napoli (Peter Schaufuss, after August Bournonville)

Nataraja (Constantin Patsalas)

Portrait of Love and Death (Vicente Nebrada)

Los Siete Puñales/The Seven Daggers (Susana)

Three Easy Tangos (Luk de Layress)

1982/83

Canciones (Constantin Patsalas)

Don Juan (revival) (John Neumeier)

Don Quixote (Nicolas Beriozoff, after Marius Petipa and
    Alexander Gorsky)

Hedda (James Kudelka)

Offenbach in the Underworld (revival) (Antony Tudor)

Quartet (Michael Peters)

Sphinx (Glen Tetley)

1983/84

La Bayadère: Act II, Kingdom of the Shades (new
    production) (Marius Petipa, staged by Natalia
    Makarova)

Components (John McFall)

Endangered Species (Danny Grossman)

Here We Come (Erik Bruhn)

L'Île Inconnue (Constantin Patsalas)

Khatchaturian Pas de Deux (David Allan)

Mobile (Tomm Ruud)

Oiseaux Exotiques (Constantin Patsalas)

Onegin (John Cranko)

Sylvia Pas de Deux (staged by Michael Lland, after
    George Balanchine and André Eglevsky)

1984/85

Blue Snake (Robert Desrosiers)

Concerto for the Elements: Piano Concerto (Constantin
    Patsalas)

The Four Temperaments (revival) (George Balanchine)

Raymonda: Act III (Terry Westmoreland, after Marius
    Petipa)

Realm (David Earle)

Symphony in C (George Balanchine)

1985/86

Alice (Glen Tetley)

Capriccio (David Allan)

Don Quixote (new production) (Nicolas Beriozoff, after
    Marius Petipa and Alexander Gorsky)

Etc! (David Allan)

Hot House: Thriving on a Riff (Danny Grossman)

On Occasion (David Allan)

Pastel (David Allan)

Reminiscence (Luc Amyôt)

Sinfonia (Constantin Patsalas)

Transfigured Night (Jiří Kylián)

Villanella (David Allan)

1986/87

Lost in Twilight (Constantin Patsalas)

Masada (David Allan)

The Merry Widow (Ronald Hynd, scenario by Robert
    Helpmann)

1987/88

Concerto (Kenneth MacMillan)

Concerto Barocco (revival) (George Balanchine)

Death of a Lady's Man (David Allan)

Forgotten Land (Jiří Kylián)

Inner Drop (Donald Dawson)
La Ronde (Glen Tetley)
Song of the Earth (Kenneth MacMillan)
Trapdance (John Alleyne)
Tuwat (Bengt Jörgen)
Voluntaries (Glen Tetley)

1988/89
Blue-Eyed Trek (John Alleyne)
Daphnis and Chloë (Glen Tetley)
Diana and Acteon Pas de Deux (Agrippina Vaganova)
The Envelope (David Parsons)
Have Steps Will Travel (John Alleyne)
Sleep Study (David Parsons)
Steptext (William Forsythe)
Tagore (Glen Tetley)

1989/90
Dream Dances (Jiří Kylián)
Gloria (Kenneth MacMillan)
The Need (David Parsons)
Pastorale (James Kudelka)
Split House Geometric (John Alleyne)

1990/91
Concerto for Flute and Harp (John Cranko)
The Leaves Are Fading (Antony Tudor)
Paquita (Natalia Makarova, after Marius Petipa)
the second detail (William Forsythe)
Time Out With Lola (John Alleyne)
Troy Game (Robert North)

1991/92
Café Dances (Christopher House)
Interrogating Slam (John Alleyne)
Musings (James Kudelka)
The Rite of Spring (new production) (Glen Tetley)
The Taming of the Shrew (John Cranko)

1992/93
Divertimento No. 15 (George Balanchine)
The Miraculous Mandarin (James Kudelka)
Now and Then (John Neumeier)
The Strangeness of a Kiss (Serge Bennathan)
Les Sylphides (revival) (Michel Fokine)

1993/94
The Actress (James Kudelka)
Frames of Mind (Jean Grand-Maître)
Herman Schmerman (William Forsythe)
Oracle (Glen Tetley)
La Sylphide (new production) (Erik Bruhn, after August
    Bournonville)

1994/95
Cinderella (new production) (Ben Stevenson)
The Concert (Jerome Robbins)
Gluck Pas de Deux (James Kudelka)
Monotones I (Frederick Ashton)
A Month in the Country (Frederick Ashton)
Romeo and Juliet (new production) (John Cranko)
Soldiers' Mass (Jiří Kylián)
Spring Awakening (James Kudelka)
Three French Words (Matjash Mrozewski)

1995/96
Company B (Paul Taylor)
Echo (Eliot Feld)
Manon (Kenneth MacMillan)
The Nutcracker (new production) (James Kudelka)
Symphonic Variations (Frederick Ashton)
Tchaikowsky Pas de Deux (George Balanchine)

1996/97
Cruel World (James Kudelka)
The Fall (Serge Bennathan)
The Four Seasons (James Kudelka)
Tales of the Arabian Nights: The Story of Abdallah
    (August Bournonville)
Tides of Mind (Dominique Dumais)

1997/98
Désir (James Kudelka)
Episodes (George Balanchine)
Mozartiana (George Balanchine)
Terra Firma (James Kudelka)
Theme and Variations (George Balanchine)
the weight of absence (Dominique Dumais)

1998/99
Apollo (George Balanchine)
The Fairy's Kiss (James Kudelka)
Septet (John Alleyne)
Swan Lake (new production) (James Kudelka)

1999/00
A Disembodied Voice (James Kudelka)
Jewels (George Balanchine)
one hundred words for snow (Dominique Dumais)

2000/01
The Comforts of Solitude (Jean-Pierre Perreault)
A Delicate Battle (Matjash Mrozewski)
The Firebird (James Kudelka)
Madame Butterfly (Stanton Welch)

2001/02
The Contract (The Pied Piper) (James Kudelka)

Appendix B

Intermezzo (revival) (Eliot Feld)
Solitaire (revival) (Kenneth MacMillan)

2002/03
Tristan and Isolde (John Alleyne)

2003/04
Cinderella (new production) (James Kudelka)
The End (solo) (James Kudelka)
Gazebo Dances (excerpt) (James Kudelka)
Monument (Matjash Mrozewski)
There, below (James Kudelka)

2004/05
Chacony (James Kudelka)
Études (revival) (Harald Lander)
An Italian Straw Hat (James Kudelka)
Opus 19/The Dreamer (Jerome Robbins)
Stravinsky Violin Concerto (George Balanchine)

2005/06
C.V. (Matjash Mrozewski)
Full Circles (James Kudelka)
Grand Pas Classique (after Victor Gsovsky)
Petrouchka (Michel Fokine)
Romeo and Juliet before parting (James Kudelka)
La Sylphide (revival) (Nikolaj Hübbe)

2006/07
Don Quixote (George Balanchine)
A Footstep of Air (Eliot Feld)
Polyphonia (Christopher Wheeldon)
Wolf's Court (Matjash Mrozewski)

2007/08
24 Preludes by Chopin (Marie Chouinard)
Five Brahms Waltzes in the Manner of Isadora Duncan
    (Frederick Ashton)
Glass Pieces (Jerome Robbins)
In the Night (Jerome Robbins)
Rooster (Christopher Bruce)
West Side Story Suite (Jerome Robbins, co-choreographer:
    Peter Gennaro)

2008/09
Carmen (Davide Bombana)
DEXTRIS (Sabrina Matthews)
Emergence (Crystal Pite)
IN COLOUR (Peter Quanz)
In the Upper Room (Twyla Tharp)
The Seagull (John Neumeier)
Skin Divers (Dominique Dumais)

2009/10
Onegin (new production) (John Cranko)
Pur ti Miro (Jorma Elo)
A Suite of Dances (Jerome Robbins)
Watch her (Aszure Barton)

2010/11
Alice's Adventures in Wonderland (Christopher Wheeldon)
Chroma (Wayne McGregor)
Russian Seasons (Alexei Ratmansky)

Appendix C:

DANCERS

Note: Dancers' names are followed by their continuous seasons with the company and the highest rank attained in their final seasons. Until the 1977–78 souvenir program, the company's practice was to indicate differences in rank not with titles, but simply by different sizes of typeface. No consistency was observed from year to year as to the number of ranks in the company. For the seasons until 1977–78, therefore, rank is indicated by two roman numerals, the first indicating the level achieved in the final season of employment and the second the number of levels into which the company was divided for that season. For example, "55–60 (II/III); 63–69 (I/III)" following a dancer's name indicates someone who served continuously from the 1955–56 to the 1959–60 seasons, finally attaining the second ranking in a year in which three rankings were used. The same dancer returned to the company for the 1963–64 to the 1968–69 seasons, finally attaining the first rank in a year in which three rankings were used.

An end date of 2011 following a dancer's name indicates that the dancer was listed on the company roster when *Passion to Dance* went to press.

From 1977–78 on, abbreviations for the various company ranks are used, as explained below.

Abbreviations:

c	=	corps
fs	=	first soloist
p	=	principal dancer
pca	=	principal character artist
ss	=	second soloist
nbs	=	training received at Canada's National Ballet School

A

Aaron, Myrna   51–55 (III/III); 59–61 (III/III)

Abbey, Susan   59–61 (III/III)

Acevedo, Donald[nbs]   80–82 (c)

Adam, Julie[nbs]   84–88 (c)

Adam, Mark[nbs]   88–90 (c)

Adams, David   51–64 (I/II)

Adams, Lawrence   55–60 (II/III); 63–69 (I/III)

Alexander, Joseph   95–96 (c)

Alexander, Ronald   74–76 (IV/IV)

Allan, David[nbs]   74–78 (ss)

Allemann, Sabina[nbs]   80–89 (p)

Alleyne, John[nbs]   84–90 (fs)

Amos, Ian   71–73 (III/III)

Amyôt, Luc[nbs]   75–79; (p); 83–85 (fs)

Androse, Edward   64–65 (II/II)

Antonijevic, Aleksandar   91–11 (p)

Apiné, Irene   51–55 (I/III)

Armstrong, Amber[nbs]   86–97 (c)
Armstrong, Brian   71–75 (III/III)
Arnett, Charles   57–58 (III/III)
Arnold, Stephana[nbs]   92–95 (c)
Ash, Taryn   88–92 (c)
Ashworth, Corrine   55–58 (III/III)
Aubrey, John   73–80 (c)
Auger, Yolande[nbs]   72–88 (c)
Augustyn, Frank[nbs]   70–89 (p)
Auld, Alexandra[nbs]   77–85 (ss)

B

Bain, Joy[nbs]   79–80 (c); 81–82 (c)
Banfield, Beverly   56–60 (III/III)
Banks, Joanna   68–69 (III/III)
Bannerman, Christopher   69–72 (III/III)
Barrios, Maria   72–74 (III/III)
Bates, Julius[nbs]   94–98 (c)
Bauer, Ellen   84–86 (c)
Baurac, Josephine   73–74 (III/III); 77–79 (c)
Bayer, Marijan   69–70 (I/III)
Becker, Douglas   79–80 (c)
Beesmyer, Karla   77–79 (c)
Beevers, Lawrence   67–71 (III/III)
Beliveau, Bernadette   57–59 (III/III)
Bertram, Victoria[nbs]   63–10 (pca)
Bezerra, Danyla   10–11 (c)
Blagg, Dallas   05–07 (c)
Blanton, Jeremy   62–71 (I/III)
Blouin, Lorraine[nbs]   81–88 (ss)
Bodie, Susan   75–85 (c)
Body, Christopher[nbs]   94–01 (fs); 05–09 (fs)
Bolton, Laura[nbs]   01–07 (c)
Bomers, Carina[nbs]   73–76 (IV/IV)
Bonnell, Gloria   56–59 (III/III)
Boorne, Ryan[nbs]   92–07 (p)
Booth, Ryan   09–11 (c)
Bornhausen, Angelica   69–71 (I/III)
Boutilier, Sean[nbs]   76–83 (ss)
Bowen, Richard   73–75 (III/III)
Bowes, Karen[nbs]   66–72 (I/III)
Bowles, Kevin D.   02–11 (pca)
Brandt, Edelayne   54–57 (III/III)
Brayley, Sally   56–62 (IV/IV)
Brown, Suzanne[nbs]   80–84 (c)
Brownlow, Audrey   81–84 (c)
Bryan, Rebecca   62–66 (I/II)
Burgess, Walter   53–55 (III/III)
Burk, Susan   80–88 (c)
Burke, Charles   64–68 (III/III)
Burne, Gary   67–68 (I/III)
Burridge, Andrea   93–01 (c)
Butko, Natalia   51–54 (II/II)
Byrnes, Anne   75–76 (IV/IV)

C

Cadrin, Thérèse   65–67 (II/II)
Cahill, Tom   58–59 (III/III)
Campanella, Roberto   93–96 (ss)
Campbell, Connie   51–52 (II/II)
Capouch, Daniel   71–76 (III/IV); 77–79 (ss)
Caref, Benjamin   72–73 (III/III)
Carhart, Glenda   75–76 (IV/IV)
Carman, Philip   72–73 (III/III)
Carr, Catherine   56–59 (III/III); 61–64 (II/II)
Carrell, John (*see* Aubrey, John)
Carter, Todd[nbs]   79–89 (c)
Cassels, Jeanette   57–62 (IV/IV)
Castellan, Deborah[nbs]   72–75 (III/III)
Causey, Maurice   88–91 (c)
Chalmer, Paul[nbs]   79–81 (c)
Chen, Wei   08–10 (c)
Childerhose, Diane   51–55 (III/III)
Chojnacki, Marcel   55–59 (III/III)
Christie, Robert   54–55 (III/III)
Cimino, Gerre   69–75 (III/III)
Cissoko, Adji   10–11 (c)
Colau, Jean-Sébastien   02–05 (ss)
Cole, Robert   79–83 (c)
Collingwood, Katherine   73–74 (III/III)
Collins, Brendan[nbs]   86–88 (c); 89–90 (c)
Collins, Susan (*see* Bodie, Susan)
Colpman, Judie   51–62 (III/IV)
Conn, Robert   93–97 (p)
Consolati, Maureen (*see* Webster, Maureen)
Cool, Colleen[nbs]   67–73 (II/III); 74–83 (fs)
Corey, Winthrop   72–75 (I/III)
Côté, Guillaume[nbs]   99–11 (p)
Cousineau, Yves   54–62 (III/IV); 63–72 (I/III)
Crawford, Elaine[nbs]   61–70 (II/III)
Crawford, Susan   55–57 (III/III)
Cui, Chen   10–11 (c)
Cumberland, Christy[nbs]   68–75 (III/III)
Cyopik, Ainslie   82–83 (c)
Czyzewski, Christopher   70–71 (III/III)

D

da Silva, Harold   55–59 (II/III)
Dabin, Joël   76–80 (fs)
Darling, Christopher   64–66 (II/II)
Daumec, Jordana[nbs]   04–11 (ss)
Davidson, Andrea[nbs]   71–75 (II/III)
Davis, Robert   63–64 (I/II)
Dawson, Donald   79–88 (ss); 90–92 (fs)
de Lichtenberg, Maryann   59–63 (IV/IV)
De Luca, Norma   72–73 (III/III)
Deininger, Eric   82–83 (c)
Dennis, Kristen[nbs]   95–98 (c)
Denvers, Robert   73–74 (II/III)

Houle, Julie[nbs]   83–87 (c)
Howard, David   63–64 (I/II)
Howard, Tanya[nbs]   99–11 (fs)
Hunter, Fergus   51–54 (II/II)
Hurde, Patrick   59–63 (III/III)
Hutchison, Stephanie[nbs]   97–11 (fs)
Hutter, Victoria   78–79 (c)

I

Ichino, Yoko   82–90 (p)
Iles, Valerie   75–77 (IV/IV)
Illmann, Margaret   89–97 (p)
Intini, Vanda   54–57 (III/III)
Ireland, Dianne   55–59 (III/III)
Ito, Robert   51–55 (III/III); 57–58 (III/III)
Ivey, Joanna   92–00 (c)
Ivings, Jacqueline   53–61 (II/III); 62–67 (I/II)

J

Jago, Mary   66–84 (p)
Jago, Paul   75–79 (c)
Jarvis, Lilian   51–60 (I/III); 61–63 (II/IV)
Jarvis, Lillian (*see* Jarvis, Lilian)
Jeanes, Rosemary   68–72 (III/III)
Jeffries, Stephen   76–77 (I/IV)
Jelinek, Jiří   10–11 (p)
Johnson, Jill[nbs]   88–91 (c); 96–98 (ss)
Jones, Lisa[nbs]   91–94 (c)
Jones, Tamara[nbs]   03–11 (c)
Jörgen, Bengt   82–85(c)
Jourdain, Lise-Marie   02–11 (c)
Joyner, Kathryn[nbs]   72–75 (III/III)
Just, Ole   88–89 (c)

K

Kabayama, Maki[nbs]   70–73 (III/III)
Kain, Karen[nbs]   69–97 (p)
Kaiser, Gregory   76–77 (IV/IV)
Kaloczy, Anton   74–81 (c)
Kash, Shirley   54–55 (III/III)
Katz, Ruth   84–85 (c)
Keeble, Elizabeth[nbs]   64–68 (II/III)
Keen, Susan[nbs]   75–80 (c)
Keiss, Vera   51–53 (II/II)
Kenney, Colleen   51–57 (II/III)
Kent, Louise   67–69 (III/III)
Kerval, David   55–58 (III/III)
Khan, Nicholas[nbs]   89–97 (fs)
Kilgour, Murray   67–71 (II/III)
Killoran, Joan   61–66 (II/II)
King, Gregory (*see* Kaiser, Gregory)
Kirby, Charles   65–71 (III/III); 72–98 (pca)
Kish, Nehemiah[nbs]   01–09 (p)
Kiss, Christopher[nbs]   91–97 (c)

Klampfer, John[nbs]   64–68 (II/III)
Kniazeff, Youra   71–72 (I/III)
Knight, Tiffany[nbs]   95–03 (ss)
Knobbs, Christopher   66–70 (III/III)
Koff, Gillian   80–83 (c)
Kolzova, Mimi   52–54 (II/II)
Konvalina, Zdenek   2006–11 (p)
Kovacs, Liza[nbs]   85–89 (c)
Kozlow, Nathaniel[nbs]   04–06 (c)
Kraul, Earl   51–70 (I/III)
Kropac, Jennifer   91–97 (c)
Kudelka, James[nbs]   72–81 (fs)
Kurt, Erkan   08–08 (fs)

L

Laerkesen, Anna   67–68 (I/III)
Laidlaw, Susan   67–69 (III/III)
Laing, Simon   79–80 (c)
Laird, Jennifer[nbs]   73–77 (IV/IV)
Lambros, Annette[nbs]   77–80 (c)
Lamy, Martine[nbs]   83–05 (p)
Landry, Richard[nbs]   92–10 (fs)
Landry, Stephanie[nbs]   76–91 (c)
Larson, Kenneth   81–85 (c)
Lau, Philip[nbs]   91–04 (c)
Laurence, James   68–69 (III/III)
Lavigne, Etienne   97–11 (fs)
Lavoie, Patrick   97–11 (fs)
Lavoie, Serge[nbs]   81–86 (ss); 87–97 (p)
Law, Kevin[nbs]   96–01 (c)
Lay, Deanne[nbs]   76–77 (IV/IV)
Leahy, Leonie   60–61 (III/III)
Legate, Stephen   86–91 (ss)
Leigh, Angela   51–63 (II/IV); 64–66 (I/II)
Leigh, Stephanie[nbs]   69–72 (III/III)
Leigh, Victoria   70–71 (II/III)
Leja, James   03–11 (c)
Lendvai, Yseult   89–96 (fs)
Léonard, Stéphane   93–95 (c)
Letendre, Sophie[nbs]   91–98 (c); 02–06 (c)
Lewis, Maria   60–63 (IV/IV)
Lightheart, Kim[nbs]   80–91 (p)
Lindinger, Martin   07–09 (c)
Lipitz, Kenneth   71–73 (II/III)
Little, Brenda[nbs]   92–01 (ss)
Lobsanova, Elena[nbs]   05–11 (ss)
Logvinova, Mimi   54–56 (II/II)
Long, Noah[nbs]   06–11 (ss)
Loomis, Daphne[nbs]   73–79 (c)
Lucas, Cynthia   73–89 (fs)
Luckett, Clinton   87–92 (ss)
Luoma, Gloria[nbs]   72–83 (fs)
Lyon, Valerie   57–61 (III/III)

M

MacCarthy, Jerome   72–73 (III/III)
MacDonald, Alexandra   08–11 (c)
Macdonald, Brian   51–53 (II/II)
Macdonald, Diane   60–63 (IV/IV)
Macedo, Cynthia[nbs]   82–92 (ss); 92–95 (ss)
MacGillivray, David   90–91 (ss)
Mackintosh, Laird   90–92 (c)
Maddox, McGee   09–11 (ss)
Madonia, Valerie[nbs]   79–81 (c)
Maggs, Caitlan   76–80 (c)
Mahler, Donald   56–61 (II/III)
Maitland, Catherine[nbs]   07–10 (c)
Malakhov, Vladimir   94–97 (p)
Malan, Angela   89–94 (c)
Malinowski, Barbara[nbs]   69–71 (III/III)
Mann, Teresa   56–61 (III/III)
Mantei, Daniel   07–07 (ss)
Marcus, Howard   64–69 (II/III); 71–72 (II/III)
Marks, Dianna   71–73 (III/III)
Marks, Sarah[nbs]   93–99 (c)
Markus, Tibor   95–98 (c)
Marni, Guido   85–86 (c)
Marrable, Elizabeth[nbs]   08–11 (c)
Marrié, William   90–98 (fs); 00–02 (p)
Martin, Nicholas (*see* Hilferink, Nicolas)
Martinelli, Antonella[nbs]   08–10 (c)
Mason, Sylvia   53–63 (III/IV)
Matinzi, Michael   73–75 (III/III)
Matthews, Brenda   82–95 (c)
Mawson, Karin[nbs]   75–85 (ss)
Maybarduk, Linda[nbs]   69–84 (fs)
McCarthy, JoAnn   79–81 (ss)
McCormack, Moira   77–78 (c)
McCullagh, Pauline   55–56 (II/II)
McElligott, Jane   81–85 (c)
McKay, Suzanne   88–91 (c)
McKim, Michael[nbs]   73–74 (III/III)
McKim, Ross   67–68 (III/III); 70–71 (III/III)
McLean, Laura   78–80 (c)
McNamara, Joseph   88–89 (c)
Meadows, Howard   51–64 (II/II)
Meadows, William   73–75 (III/III)
Mears, Graeme[nbs]   90–95 (ss)
Meinke, David   85–90 (c)
Meiss, Chelsy   08–11 (c)
Meister, Hans   57–62 (III/IV)
Meister, Ronald   71–72 (III/III)
Mejia, Mark   72–73 (III/III)
Meloche, Katherine   73–74 (III/III)
Melville, Kenneth   60–63 (III/IV)
Melvin, Sheila   62–63 (III/IV)
Meng, Martin   85–86 (c)
Meunier, Francesca   62–64 (II/II)

Miles, Maralyn   62–66 (II/II)
Miles, Rosemary   66–67 (II/II)
Milton, Anthony   66–68 (III/III)
Minagawa, Stacey Shiori   95–11 (fs)
Mitchell, Gregory   72–73 (III/III)
Moller, Ray   53–58 (II/III)
Molnar, Emily[nbs]   90–94 (c)
Montague, Owen[nbs]   82–90 (p)
Monty, Barbara   55–56 (III/III)
Moore, Claudia[nbs]   71–72 (III/III)
Morgan, Anthea   86–92 (c)
Mori, Shino[nbs]   09–11 (c)
Morrissey, Melissa[nbs]   95–98 (c)
Moses, Samuel   64–66 (II/II)
Mosher, Tiffany[nbs]   00–11 (c)
Mrozewski, Matjash[nbs]   94–97 (c); 99–01 (ss)
Munro, Alastair   64–70 (III/III)
Munro, Amber[nbs]   07–10 (c)
Murillo, Esther[nbs]   73–81 (fs)
Murphy, Gwendolyn   66–69 (III/III)

N

Nasmith, Jeremy   96–01 (ss)
Neary, Patricia   57–60 (III/III)
Needhammer, Andrew   84–91 (c)
Nelson, Daniel   85–88 (c)
Neville, Anne   59–61 (III/III)
Newburger, Gretchen   80–85 (ss)
Ng, Yuri[nbs]   83–90 (c)
Nichols, Edward   59–62 (IV/IV); 66–67 (II/II)
Nicholson, Dido   79–80 (c)
Nicholson, Thomas   73–77 (IV/IV)
Niedzwiecki, Jacob[nbs]   05–07 (c)
Nisbet, Joanne   59–61 (III/III)
Nixon, David[nbs]   78–84 (fs); 88–90 (p)
Noelle, Allynne   10–11 (c)
Norman, Bardi[nbs]   64–67 (II/II); 68–70 (III/III)
Norman, Gary   75–76 (I/IV)
Nussbaumer, Cathy   81–82 (c)
Nychka, Ronda[nbs]   84–89 (ss)
Nyland, Diane   61–62 (IV/IV)

O

O'Connor, James   90–00 (ss)
O'Rourke, Kevyn   68–70 (III/III)
Oakley, Jaclyn   99–10 (c)
Ogden, Heather   99–11 (p)
Ohno, Daisuke[nbs]   00–06 (c)
Olteanu, Andreea[nbs]   99–11 (c)
Oney, Patricia[nbs]   68–83 (ss)
Orlando, Simone[nbs]   90–94 (c)
Orr, Jennifer[nbs]   74–77 (IV/IV)
Osborne, Gregory   83–89 (p)
Otter, Elizabeth   88–90 (c)

Ottmann, Peter[nbs]   76–93 (fs)
Oxenham, Andrew[nbs]   64–70 (II/III); 73–75 (II/III)

P

Padvorac, Theresa   76–78 (c)
Page, Frances   61–63 (IV/IV)
Paige, Cecily   57–59 (III/III)
Paige, Frances (*see* Page, Frances)
Palmer, Sylvia   60–66 (II/II)
Parsons, Ian[nbs]   07–09 (c)
Parzei, Marissa[nbs]   06–11 (c)
Patsalas, Constantin   72–84 (fs)
Paulk, Terrell   72–73 (III/III)
Pauzé, Alain[nbs]   70–72 (III/III)
Peden, David   87–90 (fs)
Pegliasco, René   67–69 (III/III)
Pereira, Tina[nbs]   02–04 (c); 06–11 (fs)
Perez-Gomez, Alejandra   98–11 (ss)
Perry, Sabra[nbs]   92–93 (ss)
Persson, Johan[nbs]   90–00 (p)
Pérusse, Sonia[nbs]   72–76 (II/IV); 77–78 (fs)
Pick, Gunter   66–67 (II/II)
Pierin, Marco   83–84 (p)
Place, Pamela[nbs]   84–92 (ss)
Poole, Robert   81–82 (c)
Pope, Betty   54–59 (II/III)
Popescu, Luminita[nbs]   96–98 (c)
Potts, Nadia[nbs]   64–65 (II/II); 66–86 (p)
Powers, Patricia   61–66 (II/II); 67–68 (III/III)
Proulx, Michelle[nbs]   78–79 (c)
Puente, Blair[nbs]   01–02 (c)
Pugh, Kevin[nbs]   78–91 (p)

Q

Quinn, Pierre[nbs]   83–94 (p)

R

Raab, Mark   81–90 (c)
Rachedi, Louisa[nbs]   04–07 (c)
Raimondi, Letizia   67–69 (III/III)
Randazzo, Anthony[nbs]   81–87 (c)
Randolph, Craig[nbs]   78–84 (ss)
Ransom, Jeremy[nbs]   80–86 (fs); 87–01 (p)
Rathbun, Catherine[nbs]   61–62 (IV/IV)
Rea, Kathleen[nbs]   92–95 (c)
Reiser, Wendy[nbs]   71–78 (fs)
Renna, Jonathan[nbs]   98–11 (fs)
Rhatigan, Summer Lee   86–88 (ss)
Richardson, Caroline[nbs]   85–95 (fs)
Richardson, Courtney[nbs]   01–03 (c)
Richardson, Erin[nbs]   00–06 (c)
Rimsay, Rebekah[nbs]   90–11 (fs)
Ritter, Alexander[nbs]   88–91 (c)
Roberts, Chester   74–76 (IV/IV)

Robertson, Eva[nbs]   84–85 (c)
Robertson, Ian   58–61 (III/III)
Robinson, Lisa   99–10 (ss)
Rochman, Linda   73–74 (III/III)
Rodriguez, Sonia   90–11 (p)
Rodwell, Frank   52–56 (II/II)
Rollo, Marilyn   51–56 (II/II)
Romanova, Natalia   00–02 (c)
Rome, Gilbert   63–66 (II/II)
Ronald, Heather[nbs]   74–81 (c)
Ronaldson, James   53–56 (II/II)
Rooney, Sarah[nbs]   99–00 (c)
Roselli, Maria   89–90 (c)
Rothwell, Clinton   67–71 (I/III); 75–81 (p)
Rothwell, Maureen   67–68 (III/III); 69–71 (II/III)
Rousseau, Hélène[nbs]   79–87 (c)
Roxander, David   72–88 (fs)
Roy, Danielle   66–69 (III/III)
Rubin, Donna   84–88 (c)
Rudnick, Lesley   86–87 (c)
Rudnick, Lia   68–69 (III/III)
Russell, Jhe[nbs]   95–02 (ss)

S

Sacklen, Per   87–88 (c)
Sakamoto, Kanako   02–06 (c)
Salas, Je-an[nbs]   94–08 (ss)
Samsova, Galina   61–64 (I/II)
Samtsova, Galina (*see* Samsova, Galina)
Sandonato, Barbara   72–73 (I/III)
Saunders, Gillian   85–90 (c)
Saunders, Jane[nbs]   71–72 (III/III)
Savella, Jenna[nbs]   05–11 (ss)
Saye, Brendan[nbs]   09–11 (c)
Schaufuss, Peter   67–69 (II/III); 77–84 (p)
Scheidegger, Katherine   74–78 (c)
Schelhorn, Amalia[nbs]   78–86 (fs)
Schmidt, Hans   61–63 (IV/IV)
Schramek, Tomas   69–11 (pca)
Schroeter, Leslie   02–07 (c)
Schwenker, Nancy   61–62 (IV/IV); 63–64 (II/II)
Scott, Brian   61–70 (III/III)
Scott, Bryan (*see* Scott, Brian)
Scott, David   59–63 (III/IV)
Sealander, Kristina   66–68 (II/III)
Segarra, Ramón   64–65 (II/II)
Semeniuk, Garry[nbs]   70–72 (III/III)
Seo, Dong Hyun[nbs]   01–07 (ss)
Sewell, Marilyn   52–54 (II/II)
Shee, James   08–10 (c)
Sheng, Bei-Di[nbs]   95–00 (c)
Sherval, Barbara   66–70 (III/III)
Sidimus, Joysanne   63–68 (I/III)
Silberg, Sheri   80–82 (c)

Appendix C

Y

Yamamoto, Hansuke   99–01 (c)
Yeigh, Elizabeth   72–73 (III/III)
Yokose, Misa   94–99 (c)
Yu, Xiao Nan[nbs]   98–11 (p)
Yudenich, Alexei   72–73 (I/III)

Z

Zanne, Eugénie   66–69 (III/III)
Zehr, Bridgett   06–11 (p)
Zeichner, Aino   91–94 (fs)
Zorina, Leila   57–61 (III/III)
Zurowski, Diane   90–94 (c)

Appendix D:

COMPANY LEADERSHIP AND BOARD MEMBERSHIP

Artistic Directors

Celia Franca 1951–1973
Celia Franca and David Haber 1973–1974
David Haber 1974–1975
Alexander Grant 1976–1983
Erik Bruhn 1983–1986
Lynn Wallis, Valerie Wilder (co–artistic directors) 1986–1989
Reid Anderson 1989–1996
James Kudelka 1996–2005
Karen Kain 2005–

General Managers/Executive Directors

Walter Homburger 1951–1955
Carman Guild 1955–1964
Anthony B. Lawless 1964–1966
John H. Wilson 1966–1967
Wallace A. Russell 1967–1972
Gerry Eldred 1972–1981
Robert H. Johnston 1981–1997
Valerie Wilder 1997–2002
Kevin Garland 2002–

Members of the Board of Directors

An end date of 2011 following a board member's name indicates that the board member was listed on the board roster when *Passion to Dance* went to press.

Appendix D

A

Abel, Thomas P. 1961–67
Agnew, Mrs. Herbert (Elsie) 1957–61
Aitken, Donald C. 1965–69
Alexander, Michael O. 1986–92
Alexander, Deborah M. 1994–95
Allen, J.C.L. 1951–55
Allen, John M. 1974–77
Allen, Susan 2003–06
Allen, Jane 2007–11
Anderson, Lt. Gen. William A. B. 1978–84
Anderson, Reid 1989–96
Anderson, William D. 1998–02
Andras, Kenneth B. 1961–66
Angus, Mrs. Brook 1969–70
Antonijevic, Aleksandar 2010–11
Armstrong, Mrs. G. 1971–72
Aspinall, Philip 1966–68
Aspinall, Judith 1987–96
Atkins, David 1986–88
Augimeri, Maria 1988–94
AvRutick, Julian 1961–64

B

Bachand, André 1952–61
Bailey, John 2006–11
Baker, Rose 2000–06
Baldwin, Martin 1951–58
Balfour Jr., Mrs. St. Clair (Helen) 1961–69
Band, Charles S. 1952–54
Bandeen, Mona 1985–91
BANKS, DAVID 2001–08; Chair 2004–08
Barber, Mrs. D.C. 1957–58
Barnard, William S. 1985–89
Barnett, R.V. 1951–65
Barrett, J. Flavelle 1968–77
Barrett, June 1976–79
Bassett, Douglas G. 1978–85
Bata, Thomas J. 1963–74
Batshaw, Hon. Justice Harry 1955–57
Beattie, Peter G. 1976–88
Beattie, W. Geoffrey 1994–00
Beatty, David M. 1991–97, 2001–03
Beaulieu, Roger L. 1966–74
Beck, Howard 1996–98
Bedard, Mrs. Paul 1962–63
Bell, G. Maxwell 1969–71
Bell, Mary Grace 1979–81
Bennett, J.W. 1957–59
Bennett, James E. 1978–82
Bennett, Avie J. 1984–94
Bethune, Mrs. Donald S. 1970–72
Binet, David 2008–11
Birkett, John C. 1998–00

Bishop, Arthur 1965–66
Bisset, Susan 1986–91
Blackburn, Mrs. Walter 1961–63
Bladen, Dr. Vincent 1969–72
Blythe, J.D.W. 1961–63
Body, Christopher 2006–09
Boggs, William B. 1979–82
Bongard, Jr., D. Strachan 1964–71
Booth, Ronald 2004–07
Botterell, Dr. E. H. 1956–57
Boudrias, M. Gerard 1952–54
Bourk, T. Larry 1988–90
BOVEY, EDMUND C. 1981–90; President 1985–87
Bowen, Walter M. 1967–70
Brand, Mrs. Ronald G. 1970–72
Break, Paul D. 1974–80
Brennan, Joseph 2004–10
Bronfman, Marsha 2000–02
Bronskill, Dr. Joan 1960–62
Brophy, Peter 1986–87
Brown, David G. R. 1963–64
Brown, Shelley 2001–03
Bruhn, Erik 1983–86
Bunting, Pierce 1965–66
Burrow, Dr. Gerard N. 1983–88
Burrows, Thomas B. 1975–79

C

Callaghan, Michael B. 1966–70
Campbell, John D. 1962–68
Campbell, Elaine 1971–89
Campbell, Pat 1975–76
Canavan, Joseph 2000–07
Cantor, Lynn 1990–92
Carder, Paul 1983–89
Carradine, William J. 1979–84
Carter, Mrs. Owen 1959–60
Cassels, Mrs. Patrick (Betty) 1959–61
CASSELS, JR., HAMILTON 1960–72; President 1965–67; Chairman 1967–68
Cassels, Jr., Mrs. Hamilton 1955–60
Chambers, Tom 2000–04
Chant, Diana 1987–00
Chasty, Mrs. J. K. 1966–68
Cheesman, William J. 1969–72
Chisholm, Mrs. Robert F. 1966–71
Chiu, Yvonne 1990–96
Chiu, John 2001–06
Church, Minette 1981–83
Clark, Gavin C. 1963–72
Clark, Mrs. A.G. 1970–71
Clark, W. Edmund 1987–92
Cohen, Irena 1977–80
COHEN, JUDITH LOEB 1985–92; President 1987–90

Coleman, J. Gordon 1982–87

Collier, Russell 1965–66

Collins–Williams, Mrs. Cecil 1966–67

Comfort, Charles F. 1960–64

Conacher, Judi 2002–10

Conn, Robert 1996–97

Conway, Dr. John J. 1968–71

Corber, Marvin 1977–79

Corcoran, Thomas F. 1990–92

Corey, C.R. 1963–68

Corrigan, J.S. 1962–66

Corrigan, Harold 1977–83

Coutts, James. E. 1974–75

Cowperthwaite, John 1985–86

Cox, Norman A. 1962–66

Craig, G.H. 1951–53

Cran, James 1966–70

Cranston, Cathryn E. 2001–11

Crawford, Mrs. L. G. 1963–68

Cristall, Mrs. T 1951–58

Crosbie, Missy 2002–09

D

Dalley, Mrs. S.G. 1962–64

Dalley, Mrs. D.N. 1966–68

Darlington, Earl 1998–00

Davidson, Nancy-Anne 1986–87

Davis, Jeanie 1980–89, 1998–09

Davis, Mark 2004–10

De Brabant, Jean 1972–85

Dea, Joan 1997–08

DEACON, PAUL S. 1969–90; President 1975–78

Decter, Michael 2003–08

Dehni, Jason 2009–11

DelZotto, Marlene 2001–11

Delaney, Catherine A. 1995–98

Delorme, Jean–Claude 1979–82

Dennis, David L. 1972–73, 1989–92

DePencier, John D. 1965–72

Dewis, Joan 1972–77

Disero, Betty 1998–00

Dodds, Richard W. 1978–90

Douglas, Mrs. C.R. (Betty) 1965–71

Dover, Mrs. M.G. 1951–53

Drouin, Mrs. Paulette 1964–67

Dunlap, Nancy 1984–87

Dupuis, Mrs. Gilles 1963–64

E

Earle, Dr. Arthur 1982–85

Eaton, M.G. 1975–78

Eaton, Sherry Taylor 1986–92

Eaton, Nicole 2003–11

Eldred, Gerry 1972–79

Ellis, John F. 1964–68

Elwood, Mrs. E.C. 1958–61

Erickson, Arthur 1972–75

Esposto, Ed 2001–05

F

Faire, Sandra 2004–11

Ferchat, Robert A. 1989–92

Firestone, D. Morgan 1970–74

Fiset, Mrs. Edouard 1960–61

Fleck, Dr. James D. 1966–74, 1975–86

Flexer, Bernard 1962–63

Fotinos, Dennis 1991–92

Fountain, David Glenn 1987–93

Fournier, Jennifer 1999–00

Fowler, Robert M. 1952–53

Fox–Revett, Mrs. C. Stephen (Joan) 1968–79

Franca, Celia 1952–74

Frum, Dr. Murray 1985–91

Fuller, Dorinda 1977–79

G

Gage, Ronald G. 1993–99

Gagliano, Lina 2002–11

Gagnon, Charles 1972–73

GALIPEAULT, ANDRÉ J. 1976–92; President 1980–82

Galloway, Bruce 1986–92

Gardner, Kay 1985–89

Garland, Kevin 1993–11

Gaston, S. James 1976–87

GELBER, ARTHUR E. 1951–69, 1985–91; President 1961–63; Chairman 1963–65

Gelber, Judith 2007–11

Gibbings, Brian R. 1994–98

Gibson, Gordon 1958–64

Gibson, R.C. 1962–63

Gibson, J. Douglas 1971–73

Givens, Philip G. 1967–71

Glasco, Kimberly 1996–98

Glass, Ogden 1961–65

Glista, Ted A. 1972–73

GODFREY, JOHN M. 1961–70; President 1967–69

Godfrey, John F. 1987–88

GOODMAN, EDWIN A. 1951–65, 1969–73; President 1958–60

Gopie, Kamala–Jean 1990–96

Gorrissen, Jacques 1975–81, 1982–83

Grant, Alexander 1975–83

Grant, Peter 1980–82

Gravel, Louis J.M. 1961–62

GRIFFIN, A.G.S. 1953–61, 1969–72; President, 1954–57

Griffin, Mrs. Eric 1956–57

Griffin, Peter 1958–62

Guglielmin, Alfred A. 1979–82

H

Haas, Mrs. Max 1953–55, 1958–60
Haas, Max 1954–59
Haber, David 1973–75
Haeberlin, Janice 1976–77
Hall, Mrs. O. 1972–73
Hamilton, John W. 1961–63
Hamilton, Lynda 2007–09
Harding, Col. C.M. 1963–65
Harris, Peter D. 1962–66
Harris, Susan 2009–11
Harris, Mrs. P. 1968–69
Harris, William B. 1978–90, 1992–94
Hawkins, M.C. 1954–55
Hawthorne, Neville 1961–65
Hay, Frank 1958–64
HEES, MRS. GEORGE 1951–57; President 1953–54
Heidt, W. Daniel 1991–93
Heilig, Mrs. Daniel 1965–66
Heintzman Jr., Bradford 1951–53
Heisey, W. Lawrence 1988–99
Hellyer, The Hon. Paul 1970–75
HENDERSON, LYMAN G. 1963–78; President 1969–72
Henderson, Ann 1982–88
Herridge, William R. 1970–73, 1985–94
Hetherington, A.E. 1966–73
Heyland, E. Bruce 1985–92
Higginbotham, D.C. 1956–59, 1970–71
Hirsch, John 1975–78
Hodgkinson, Greta 2000–02
Hogarth, Ann 2009–11
Holland, H. Peter 1971–72
Holton, Mrs. Mark 1953–55, 1956–62
Holton, Mrs. Luther 1960–74
Hope, Ying 1982–86
Houghton, Tony E. 1990–92
HOULDING, JOHN D. 1976–88; President 1982–85
Hughes, The Hon. Samuel H. 1960–64
Hulton, W.S. 1961–72
Hunnakko, Tuija 1972–87
Hutchison, Mrs. Keith 1952–54, 1964–71

I

Iannuzzi Jr., Dan 1972–73
Irwin, Peter 1995–98
Ivory, Joan 1989–96

J

Jaffary, Karl 1972–74
Jago, Mary 1973–76, 1980–83
Jarvis, Alan 1960–64
Jarvis, Thomas E. 1967–74
Johnson, Donald K. 1993–99
Johnston, Robert D. 1979–96

Jones, Prof. E.M. 1951–55
Jones, M.F. 1962–63
Jörgen, Bengt 1983–85
JOSEPH, LUCILLE 2003–11; Chair 2008–11
Joyner, Dr. Robert C. 1971–72
Jurist, Paul 1986–92

K

Kain, Karen 1979–80, 1983–85, 1989–96, 2005–11
Kassie, David 1996–98
Keefe, Dennis 2001–04
Kellam, F.G. 1961–62
Kelly, Helen 1974–77
Kershaw, Derrick F. 1977–86
King, G. Edmond 1978–86
Knowlton, Leo 1958–61
Koerner, Michael 1962–74
Kofman, Joyce 1979–88
Kraszewski, Mrs. R.J. 1973–74
Kudelka, James 1996–05

L

Labatt, Mrs. Hugh F. 1951–58
Labatt, Sonia 1995–97
Landry, Stephanie 1985–89
Landry, Richard 2001–07
Lang, The Hon. Daniel 1969–75
Lang, John E. 1979–81, 1984–85
LASH, Z.R.B. 1951–53; President 1952–53
Lavigne, Etienne 2009–11
Lawrie, Robert 2004–11
Leahy, Mrs. Jean 1961–62, 1964–70
Leahy, Jean 1961–65
Leather, Harold 1956–57
Leggett, Karen 2009–11
Lennard, Gordon H. 1963–70
Lettner, Pearce 1963–70
Levitt, Rosabel 1974–79
Li, Chris 1995–98
Lieberman, Philip 2006–11
Lindsay, Janet 1992–95
Lloyd, Samantha 1996–02
Lortie, Dr. Léon 1957–61
Lortie, Pierre 1987–90
Lougheed, Jeanne. E. 1976–85
Lounsbery, Phillips 1970–72
Lowrie, Joliann 1984–88
Lowy, Dr. Frederick 1989–95
Lozinski, Jerry 2001–11

M

Macdonald, His Hon. Judge Bruce J. 1965–68
Macdonald, Mrs. C.D. 1974–75
Macdonald Jr., Mrs. W.B. 1955–56

Macdonald, W.L. 1955–57

MacDonald, Carol–Ann 1992–94

MacDonald, David C.W. 1994–01, 2006–11

MacDonald, Timothy 1997–03

MacDougall, Eve 1985–91

MacGowan, Mrs. Bruce 1967–68

MacKenzie, J.P.S 1971–73

MacKillop, Malcolm 2000–05

MacKinnon, Mrs. D.I. 1962–66, 1967–72

MacLachlan, Peter 1967–72

MacTavish, Duncan K. 1957–58

Makin, Murray J. 1993–99

Manderville, Kathleen 1969–70, 1977–79

Marcil, André 1958–69

MARPLE, ALLEN C. 1989–96, 1997–99; Chairman 1997–99

Marshall, Carol 1988–94

Martin, R.K. 1960–62

Matthews, Bryn C. 1963–68

MATTHEWS, SUE 1994–05; Chair 2001–04

Maudsley, Mrs. J.H. 1965–69

Maybarduk, Linda 1978–79

Maxwell, Troy 2010–11

McBean, Mrs. W. Stanley 1972–74

McBirnie, Mrs. S.K. 1956–57

McCabe, Mrs. P.C. 1959–61

McCain, Eleanor 1996–99

McCain, Margaret Norrie 1998–02

McCarthy, Leighton 1969–72

McCarthy, Brenda 1984–90

McDiarmid, Barbara 1985–86

McDonald, H.J. 1964–67

McDonald, Mrs. Ross F. 1968–70

McGavin, Robert J. 1986–92

McGee, The Hon. Frank C. 1965–68

McGough, George V. 1987–90

McGovern, James L. 1997–08

MCLEOD, IAN H. 1970–79, 1985–87; President 1972–75

McMenemy, D. Miles 1986–91

McTavish, Duncan 1956–58

Medland, Julie 1989–98

Meen, David 1982–90

Meighen, The Hon. Michael A. 1986–92

Menendez, Mrs. C.J. 1963–65

Menkes, Murray 1988–92

Meredith, E.A. 1975–76

Merrick, William B. 1971–73

Minden, Arthur 1958–59

Mingie, Mary 1978–82

Minto, Clive 1990–96

Mitchell, William T. 1982–93

Molson, P.T. 1964–66

Moore–Ede, Mrs. W.O. 1952–53

Morgan, Mrs. R.T. (Marg) 1963–69

Morison, D.W. 1963–68, 1970–73

Morton, Paul 2005–07

Mrozewski, Matjash 2000–01

Mulqueen, Mrs. F.J. 1951–55

Murray, Susan A. 1990–93

N

NAPIER, MARK 1955–62; President 1958

Nash, Knowlton 1988–90

Nederpelt, J.H.B. 1986–91

Nesker, Carol 1988–92

Ness, R. George 1969–73

Newell, E.W. 1963–69

Nixon, Gordon 1996–99

Noftall, Bob 1999–01

Norman, Henry G. 1956–58

Norman, M.R. 1965–68

Norman, Mrs. Douglas 1973–74

Nunziata, Frances 1997–99

O

O'Connor, James 1997–00

O'Donoghue, Paul H. 1984–90

Ogden, June 1975–77

O'Hagan, Wanda 1989–92

O'Leary, Linda 2007–11

Oliphant, Betty 1969–89

Oliphant, Peter 1963–70

O'Loughlin, Gwen 1958–61

Ondaatje, Christopher 1987–90

Osler, The Hon. Mr. Justice John H. 1957–66, 1969–71

Overbury, Nina 1971–72, 1975–78, 1983–86

Owen, David S. 1969–70

P

Padulo, Richard 1995–00

PANKRATZ, HENRY J. 1999–01; Chairman 1999–01

Pape, William M. 1970–72, 1979–81

Paton, Lynne 1980–82

Patten di Giacomo, Rose 1992–98

Payne, P. David 1981–84, 1989–90

Peel, Robert E. 1961–70

Peene, Miss Vida H. 1954–58

Pelletier, Maria 2003–11

Pencer, Nancy 2003–11

Penny, P. Wayne 1968–72

Pepler, Mrs. H.E.E. (Clare) 1972–74

Pepler, H.E.E. (Ted) 1974–77

Perlin, John C. 1972–90

Perry, Mrs. Richard 1968–69

Peterson, James 1975–80, 1986–89

PITBLADO, JAMES B. 1988–97; President 1990–93; Chairman 1994–97

Pitman, Walter G. 1991–94

Pollack, I.C. 1957–62
Pollock, C.A. 1959–64
Pollock, Jack 1972–73
Porter Jr., R.F. 1953–55
Pouliot, Mme Omer 1957–59
Powis, Shirley 1975–78
Prince, Lynda 1999–11
Protter, Bernard 1968–73
Protter, Mrs. Bernard (Patsy) 1971–73

R
Randall, S.J. 1959–60
Rechnitzer, E.V. 1962–64
Reed, Greg A. 1992–98
Regent, Aaron 1998–07
Reid, Mrs. J. K. 1954–55, 1956–59
Reisman, Heather 1993–96
Reynolds, Dr. J. Keith 1981–89
Rice, Victor 1983–86
Richards, Charles 2006–08
Riggin, Margaret 2002–04
Riggs, Leona 1958–60
Rimsay, Rebekah 2002–06
Roberts, Marion 1983–85
Robertson, Mrs. John 1962–65
Robertson, Russel C. 1994–00
Rogers, E. Jane 1978–81
Rolland, Lucien 1961–70
Romanchuk, Judi 1986–92
Rose, Barrie D. 1966–80
Rosen, Andrea S. 1996–99
Ross, William C. 1993–98
Ross, Gretchen 2003–11
Rotman, Sandra 1987–93
Rounding, Marie 2002–05
Royce, Victor 2010–11
Rozovsky, Lorne Elkin 1991–93
Rubin, Alex J. 1964–70
Rudge, Chris 1999–06
Russell, Wallace A. 1969–72
Ryan, Peter K. 1966–68

S
Saffer, David 2007–10
Salmon, Bev 1993–97
SAMPLES, R. MCCARTNEY 1971–89; President 1978–80
Sauvage, Suzanne 2006–11
Savard, Jean Paul 1965–66
Scace, Susan 1992–98
Schaeffer, Irene 2006–08
Schipper, Norman H. 1962–66
Schramek, Tomas 1981–82, 1985–96
Scobell, S.C. 1954–62
Scott, Eric 1956–57

Scott, Mrs. Douglas 1966–70
Scott, Clayton 1993–95
Scott, Penelope 2000–01
Seagram Jr., Norman O. 1951–56
Sefton, Lawrence F. 1962–68
Sharwood, Gordon 1965–69
Shaw, Sir Neil 2004–07
Sheard, Mrs. Terence 1961–62
Shoniker, E.J. 1959–63
Sicotte, Guy 1965–66
Sifton, Heather 1987–93
Silva, Mario 2002–03
SIMONDS, LT. GEN. GUY G. 1960–67, 1968–69;
　　　President 1963–65; Chairman 1965–67
Sinclair, Bruce 1981–82
Sissons, Henry J. 1962–66
Sjogren, Dorothy 1996–98
Skinner, Dr. H. Alan 1951–66
Slater, James 1977–80
Small, Mrs. Gordon 1955–63
Smith, Mrs. Bruce 1958–59
Smith, Mrs. Gerald E. 1968–70
Smith, Ronald S. 1988–93
Solway, Elaine 2005–06
Southam, D. Cargill 1953–54
Southam, Audrey 1977–80
Sparks, Karen 2008–11
Sparrow, Mrs. G.R. 1961–62
Speke, Nicholas 1972–73
Spotton, Beverley 1999–00
Spragge, Mrs. J.G. 1953–54
Squibb, G. Wayne 1994–00
St. Laurent, Renault 1957–70
Staiger, John G. 1970–73
Staines, Mavis 1989–11
Starita, Paul F. 1986–92
Stearns, Marshal 1955–56
Steiner, Mrs. Robert N. 1968–70
Stevens, Linda 1994–95
Stewart, Timothy 1976–88
Stikeman, H. Heward 1954–57
Stintz, Karen 2003–07
Stuart, Mary Alice 1979–86
Style, Humphrey B. 1958–59
Sullivan, Daniel F. 2006–11
Sutton, W.J. 1967–70
Svensson, Sten G. 1972–74
Sweeney, Terrance A. 1972–74
Sweeney, Thecla 1972–73, 1982–86
Switzer, John H. 1990–93

T
Tait, Mrs. Burton (Judith) 1970–71, 1974–79
Tait, Burton 1971–80

Tanner, Mrs. Robert 1956–58
Tatrallyay, Geza 1996–97
Taylor, Noreen 2010–11
Taylor, Mrs. Paul D. 1972–75
Tennant, Veronica 1970–73, 1984–85
Thibault, Claude 1966–70
Thomas, Mrs. J.K. 1963–70
Thompson, David 1996–02
Timbrell, David Y. 1959–65, 1970–72
Tizzard, Raymond 1997–99
Torno, Philip 1961–64
Tory, David 2002–06
Townsend, F.G. 1962–69
Trimmer, Joyce 1977–79
Tsiofas, John 2000–05
Tsubouchi, David 2004–05
Turnbull, Robert L. 1968–71
Turner, Murray 1965–67
Turner, John N. 1990–91
Tyityan, Edward S. 1988–91

U
Underwood, Mrs. P.L. (Jan) 1963–68
Urquhart, Phyllis 2000–02

V
Vaile, Robin 1988–94
Van Beurden, Harry A.C. 1965–71
Van Gelder, Peter 1951–54
Vanaselja, Siim 2003–04
Vanstone, Jillian 2006 –10
Vineberg, Stanley 1952–55
Vorster, A. Hans 1972–73

W
Wait, Mrs. A.H. 1959–69
Wait, A.H. 1964–65
Walker, Hugh P. 1958–74
**WALKER, W.P. 1959–68; President 1960–63; Chairman
      1961–63**
Wallis, Lynn 1986–89
Walters, Mrs. Michael 1962–65

Walters, Lenore 1986–90
Walton, Alexander 1952–55, 1964–79
Walwyn, J.P. 1952–53
Weatherill, J.F.W 1966–73
Webster, Donald C. 1966–69
Weinstein, Leon E. 1966–67
Weldon, Col. Douglas B. 1965–70
Weldon, William 1989–96
Whitaker, Denis 1962–64
Whitaker, Mrs. W.D. 1964–66
White, Peter G. 1978–84
Whitehead, Mrs. R.B. 1951–58
Whiteside, Mrs. John 1961–66
Whitley, Mrs. T.F. (Mollie) 1951–53
WHITLEY, T.F. 1951–52, 1956–64; President 1957–58
Whitmore, Joseph A. 1951–54, 1961–62
Whittall, Fred 1960–61
Wickson, Miss Mildred 1954–61
Wilder, W.P. 1958–61
Wilder, Valerie 1976–78, 1986–89, 1996–02
Williams, Patricia 2004–06
Wilson, Beth 2007–11
Wilson, Mrs. C.I. 1966–68, 1972–73
Wilson, Graham 1986–88
Wilson, Gordon F. 1988–94
Wilson, W. David 1992–97
Wilson, Lynne 1994–96
Wimbs, John 1979–81
Wolfe, Ray D. 1964–65, 1971–72
Wolfe, Mrs. R.D. 1972–74
Wolfe, Jonathan A. 1990–93
Woodard, Carolyn I. 1988–90
Woods, Mrs. J.D. 1951–58
Wright, Michael E. 1972–73

Y
Young, Mrs. David 1958–60
Young, Robert G. 1971–73

Z
Zandmer, Mrs. Myron 1956–59
Zufelt, Veronica 2008–09

Notes

The essential facts of the company's history come primarily from three sources: the company's archives; Library and Archives Canada in Ottawa, which house Celia Franca's personal papers and the records of the Canada Council; and interviews with dancers and others associated with the company throughout its development. The notes to the text try to document clearly all sources for statements about the company, indicating the locations of those sources, so that readers may examine them for themselves, as necessary. I wish to acknowledge here, with thanks, the National Ballet of Canada, for permission to quote from documents in its archives, and Celia Franca, for permission to quote from her papers in Library and Archives Canada.

Those whose names are listed below consented to speak with me about their involvement with the company. Conversations with them are cited in the individual notes, along with the date on which the conversation took place.

For *Power to Rise*:

Lawrence Adams, David Adams, Miriam Adams, David Allan, Jocelyn Allen, John Alleyne, Reid Anderson, Frank Augustyn, James Austin, Larry Beevers, Carol Beevers, Victoria Bertram, Natalia Butko, Assis Carreiro, Lou Ann Cassels, Stephen Chadwick, Judie Colpman, George Crum, Dame Ninette de Valois, John de Pencier, Ann Ditchburn, Walter Foster, Celia Franca, Lorna Geddes, Arthur Gelber, Alexander Grant, Tony Griffin, David Haber, Lyman Henderson, Mary Jago, Robert Johnston, Karen Kain, Charles Kirby, Earl Kraul, James Kudelka, Charles Lester, Marquita Lester, Beth Lockhart, Linda Maybarduk, Mary McDonald, Howard Meadows, Joanne Nisbet, Rudolf Nureyev, Betty Oliphant, Dieter Penzhorn, Magdalena Popa, Timothy Porteous, Kevin Pugh, Wendy Reid, Galina Samsova, Peter Schaufuss, Georg Schlögl, Tomas Schramek, Patricia Scott, David Scott, Lois Smith, Grant Strate, Veronica Tennant, Glen Tetley, Martine van Hamel, David Walker, Lynn Wallis, Valerie Wilder, Gizella Witkowsky.

For *Passion to Dance*:

Skylar Campbell, Julia Drake, Lindsay Fischer, Jennifer Fournier, Kevin Garland, Lorna Geddes, Kimberly Glasco, Rex Harrington, Greta Hodgkinson, Lucille Joseph, Karen Kain, James Kudelka, McGee Maddox, Andreea Olteanu, Peter Ottmann, James Pitblado, Magdalena Popa, Diana Reitberger, Mandy-Jayne Richardson, Rebekah Rimsay, Joysanne Sidimus, Valerie Wilder.

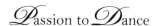

Chapter 1

1. For a contemporary expression of this point of view, see Harry Warlaw, "Ballet in Canada Is Here to Stay," *Saturday Night*, Vol. 64, No. 20 (February 22, 1949), and *Mayfair*, December 1951, p. 112.

2. David Adams in conversation with the author, April 11, 1988.

3. Lois Smith in conversation with the author, May 24, 1988.

4. Rasa Gustaitis, *Melissa Hayden, Ballerina* (London, New York: Nelson, 1967), pp. 27, 28–9, and 41; Ken Bell and Celia Franca, *The National Ballet of Canada: A Celebration* (Toronto: University of Toronto Press, 1978), p. 221.

5. Guy Glover, "Reflections on Canadian Ballet, 1950," *Canadian Art*, VIII, 3 (Spring, 1951), p. 127. Glover's article provides a detailed description of the Third Annual Canadian Ballet Festival.

6. Kathrine Sorley Walker, *De Basil's Ballets Russes* (London: Hutchinson, 1982), p. 190. See also Leland Windreich, "Vancouver Dancers in the Ballet Russe: Three 'Canadian Exotics,'" *Vandance*, May 1978.

7. Lois Smith in conversation with the author, May 24, 1988.

8. Lillian Leonora Mitchell, *Boris Volkoff: Dancer, Teacher, Choreographer* (Ann Arbor, MI: University Microfilms International, 1982), pp. 22–40.

9. Max Wyman, *The Royal Winnipeg Ballet, the First Forty Years* (Toronto: Doubleday Canada, 1978), p. 17.

10. Betty Oliphant in conversation with the author, August 17, 1988. See also "Brief to the Royal Commission, Submitted on Behalf of the Canadian Ballet Festival Association," November 4, 1949, p. 9, Dance Collection Danse.

11. "Exile-Inspired Ballet: Halifax Group Organized by Latvians," *Toronto Telegram*, October 13, 1950; Herbert Whittaker, "Latvian Dancers Highlight Ballet Panorama at Eaton Auditorium, Saturday," *Globe and Mail*, October 16, 1950.

12. Wyman, *The Royal Winnipeg Ballet*, pp. 76, 79, 265.

13. NBOC Archives, notes from Boris Volkoff to Aileen Woods, April 28, 1964, Aileen Woods File. See also Herbert Whittaker, *Canada's National Ballet* (Toronto: McClelland and Stewart, 1967), p. 8; Mitchell, *Boris Volkoff*, pp. 71–85; and Agnes De Mille, *Martha: The Life and Work of Martha Graham* (New York: Random House, 1956, 1991), pp. 223–4.

14. Mitchell, *Boris Volkoff*, p. 215; Natalia Butko in conversation with the author, July 7, 1988.

15. For fuller descriptions of these festivals, see Wyman, *The Royal Winnipeg Ballet*, pp. 58–63, 66–7, 73, 76, and 230; see also Max Wyman, *Dance Canada: An Illustrated History* (Vancouver: Douglas & McIntyre, 1989), pp. 38–41.

16. Wyman, *The Royal Winnipeg Ballet*, p. 76. Celia Franca acknowledged as well that Gweneth Lloyd had been involved in the consultation process (conversation with the author, October 14, 1987).

17. Metropolitan Toronto Reference Library, Boris Volkoff Papers, Scrapbook #11.

18. NBOC Archives, notes from Boris Volkoff to Aileen Woods, April 28, 1964, Aileen Woods File.

19. Metropolitan Toronto Reference Library, Volkoff to James, January 5, 1949, Boris Volkoff Papers, Box #1, Envelope #3.

20. Whittaker, *Canada's National Ballet*, p. 15.

21. Stewart James to the *Globe and Mail*, June 18, 1977; Library and Archives Canada, "Ballet — Guy Glover," Franca Papers (21-12).

22. Natalia Butko in conversation with the author, July 7, 1988. See also Carol Bishop Gwyn, *The Pursuit of Perfection: A Life of Celia Franca*, consulted in ms.

23. Dame Ninette de Valois in conversation with the author, March 16, 1988.

24. Celia Franca in conversation with the author, October 14, 1987.

25. NBOC Archives, Aileen Woods File.

26. NBOC Archives, Woods to Franca, October 19, 1950, "Founding of Nat. Ballet — 1950–52" File.

27. Brian Macdonald, "The Impact of British Ballet on the Canadian Dance Scene," *Dancing Times*, April 1963, p. 419.

28. Wyman, *The Royal Winnipeg Ballet*, pp. 74–6. Natalia Butko, in conversation with the author, July 7, 1988, believed that both Lloyd and Volkoff may have had their eyes on the artistic directorship and that some form of compromise was necessary to avoid offending one or the other of them.

29. Celia Franca in conversation with the author, October 14, 1987.

30. NBOC Archives, Aileen Woods File.

31. NBOC Archives, notes from Boris Volkoff to Aileen Woods, April 28, 1964, Aileen Woods File.

32. Celia Franca in conversation with the author, October 14, 1987.

33. NBOC Archives, handwritten notes dated October 27, Aileen Woods File.

34. NBOC Archives, "Founding of Nat. Ballet — 1950–52" File.

35. Library and Archives Canada, notes by Sydney Mulqueen, May 15, 1963, Franca Papers (20-2).

36. NBOC Archives, Bernadette Carpenter to Aileen Woods, March 29, [1964?], Aileen Woods File.

37. David Adams in conversation with the author, April 11, 1988; Celia Franca in conversation with the author, October 14, 1987. See also notes by Celia Franca for a lecture to the Ballet Circle, April 24, 1949, p. 6, which give an account of David Adams's

dancing with the Metropolitan Ballet, Library and Archives Canada, Franca Papers (9-1).

38. Celia Franca in conversation with the author, August 19, 1988.

39. Dame Ninette de Valois in conversation with the author, March 16, 1988.

40. Whittaker, *Canada's National Ballet*, p. 16, enshrines the comment, which can be found in numerous early press releases and publicity biographies.

41. Celia Franca in conversation with the author, August 19, 1988.

42. Ballet Rambert Archives, notes by Patricia Clogstoun on preparation of *Dark Elegies*; opening night program. Although the opening night program is dated February 15, 1937, Clogstoun's notes indicate that the first performance had to be postponed to February19.

43. Bell and Franca, *The National Ballet: A Celebration*, p. 8. See also Gwyn, *The Pursuit of Perfection*.

44. Alexander Grant in conversation with the author, March 22, 1988.

45. David Adams in conversation with the author, April 11, 1988.

46. Alexander Bland, *The Royal Ballet: The First Fifty Years* (Garden City, NY: Doubleday, 1981), p. 296.

47. Celia Franca in conversation with the author, October 14, 1987.

48. See John Percival in *The London Times*, May 16, 1972.

49. Library and Archives Canada, notes for a lecture to the Ballet Circle, April 24, 1949, Franca Papers (9-1).

50. John Gruen, *Erik Bruhn: Danseur Noble* (New York: Viking Press, 1979), p. 38.

51. In addition to the works and individuals already cited in notes to this paragraph, I have consulted the following sources in reconstructing the London period of Celia Franca's career: NBOC Archives, draft listing for *Creative Canada: A Biographical Dictionary of Twentieth-Century Canadians in Literature and the Arts*, dated 1967, Franca Files, Box #1; Ferdinand Reyna, *Concise Encyclopedia of Ballet* (London and Glasgow: Collins, 1974), entries under "Franca" and "Metropolitan Ballet"; Mary Clarke and David Vaughan, eds, *The Encyclopedia of Dance and Ballet* (London: Peerage Books, 1977), entries under "Franca" and "Metropolitan Ballet"; Martha Bremser, *International Dictionary of Ballet* (Detroit: St. James Press, 1993), entry under "Franca."

52. Wyman, *The Royal Winnipeg Ballet*, pp. 11–5.

53. Reyna, *Concise Encyclopedia of Ballet*, entry under "Volkov." See also Mitchell, *Boris Volkoff*, pp. 20–7.

54. Celia Franca in conversation with the author, October 14, 1987.

55. Mitchell, *Boris Volkoff*, p. 333.

56. Betty Oliphant in conversation with the author, August 17, 1988.

57. Celia Franca in conversation with the author, August 19, 1988.

58. NBOC Archives, Board Minutes for May 21, 1952. See also Whittaker, *Canada's National Ballet*, p. 40.

59. NBOC Archives, Board Minutes for October 31, 1951, Aileen Woods File.

60. Lois Smith in conversation with the author, May 24, 1988; Galina Samsova in conversation with the author, March 14,1988; Lawrence Adams in conversation with the author, November 17, 1989.

61. Mitchell, *Boris Volkoff*, pp. 291–2; a program for Toronto Theatre Ballet's appearance at a Promenade Concert on July 17, 1952, is in the Boris Volkoff Papers, Box #1, Envelope #7B, in the Metropolitan Toronto Reference Library.

62. Celia Franca in conversation with the author, October 14, 1987; see also Whittaker, *Canada's National Ballet*, pp. 20–1.

63. Betty Oliphant in conversation with the author, August 17, 1988; Celia Franca in conversation with the author, October 14, 1987. See also Bell and Franca, *The National Ballet of Canada*, p. 14.

64. Celia Franca in conversation with the author, October 14, 1987.

65. Celia Franca in conversation with the author, August 19, 1988; Betty Oliphant in conversation with the author, August 17, 1988.

66. Betty Oliphant in conversation with the author, August 17, 1988.

67. Betty Oliphant in conversation with the author, August 17, 1988.

68. Betty Oliphant in conversation with the author, August 17, 1988.

69. Whittaker, *Canada's National Ballet*, pp. 28–9; Betty Oliphant in conversation with the author, August 17, 1988.

70. Celia Franca in conversation with the author, October 14, 1987; see also Whittaker, *Canada's National Ballet*, p. 20.

71. Natalia Butko in conversation with the author, July 7, 1988.

72. Whittaker, *Canada's National Ballet*, p. 27; NBOC Archives, Aileen Woods File; Betty Oliphant in conversation with the author, August 17, 1988.

73. Library and Archives Canada, publicity pamphlet for first summer session, Franca Papers (19-11).

74. Whittaker, *Canada's National Ballet*, p. 28, places the date at 1965. See also Norma Sue Fisher-Stitt, *The Ballet Class: Canada's National Ballet School, 1959–2009* (Toronto: Canada's National Ballet School, 2010), pp. 13–8 and 69–71, which provide greater detail and suggest that either 1960, the year in which

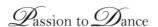

the summer school moved to the premises of the National Ballet School, or 1964, the summer after the National Ballet School attained charitable organization status distinct from the National Ballet Guild, may be more accurate dates.

75. Celia Franca in conversation with the author, October 14, 1987.

76. Celia Franca in conversation with the author, August 19, 1988.

77. Betty Oliphant in conversation with the author, August 17, 1988.

78. Betty Oliphant in conversation with the author, August 17, 1988.

79. Bernard Taper, *Balanchine: A Biography* (New York: Times Books, 1984), p. 151.

80. Celia Franca in conversation with the author, August 19, 1988.

81. Betty Oliphant in conversation with the author, August 17, 1988.

82. Judie Colpman in conversation with the author, January 20, 1988.

83. Howard Meadows in conversation with the author, May 3, 1988.

84. David Adams in conversation with the author, April 11, 1988.

85. Lois Smith in conversation with the author, May 24, 1988; Celia Franca in conversation with the author, October 14, 1987.

86. For accounts of these performances, see Bell and Franca, *The National Ballet of Canada*, p. 18, and Whittaker, *Canada's National Ballet*, pp. 23–6.

87. Metropolitan Toronto Reference Library, Boris Volkoff Papers, Programmes 1940–53, Box #1, Envelope #7B.

88. Betty Oliphant in conversation with the author, August 17, 1988.

89. Bell and Franca, *The National Ballet of Canada*, p. 20; see also NBOC Archives, "Pearl's Condensed Minutes II," Minutes for 14th Meeting (August 22, [1951?]), Aileen Woods File, thanking Franca for financing audition tour with proceeds of summer school.

90. NBOC Archives, Board Minutes for September 19, 1951, Aileen Woods File.

91. NBOC Archives, Board Minutes for September 5, 1951, Aileen Woods File; for a sample of editorial reaction in the Winnipeg press of the time, see Wyman, *The Royal Winnipeg Ballet*, p. 77.

92. *Winnipeg Free Press*, August 30, 1951.

93. See "Artistic Director's Address to New Directors," January 20, 1972, NBOC Archives, Ballet Production Files, "Miscellaneous."

94. Whittaker, *Canada's National Ballet*, p. 29.

95. Wyman, *The Royal Winnipeg Ballet*, pp. 79, 93.

96. Celia Franca in conversation with the author, August 19, 1988.

97. Wyman, *The Royal Winnipeg Ballet*, p. 79.

98. Grant Strate in conversation with the author, April 15, 1988.

99. Betty Oliphant in conversation with the author, August 17, 1988.

100. Earl Kraul in conversation with the author, April 15, 1988.

101. Judie Colpman in conversation with the author, January 20, 1988.

102. Natalia Butko in conversation with the author, July 7, 1988.

103. David Adams in conversation with the author, April 11, 1988.

104. Natalia Butko in conversation with the author, 7 July 1988.

Chapter 2

1. For detailed information on *Les Sylphides* and Michel Fokine, consult Selma Jeanne Cohen, editor, *International Encyclopedia of Dance* (New York: Oxford University Press, 1998) under the appropriate entries.

2. Celia Franca in conversation with the author, October 14, 1987.

3. Judie Colpman in conversation with the author, January 20, 1988.

4. Celia Franca in conversation with the author, October 14, 1987.

5. Natalia Butko in conversation with the author, July 7, 1988.

6. Celia Franca in conversation with the author, October 14, 1987.

7. Celia Franca in conversation with the author, October 14, 1987.

8. Betty Oliphant in conversation with the author, August 17, 1988.

9. Earl Kraul in conversation with the author, April 15, 1988.

10. *Royal Academy of Dancing Gazette*, [1951?], p. 49, Dance Collection Danse.

11. Betty Oliphant in conversation with the author, August 17, 1988.

12. NBOC Archives, Artistic Director's Report to the Fifth Annual Meeting of the Guild, June 14, 1956.

13. Celia Franca in conversation with the author, October 14, 1987.

14. Lois Smith in conversation with the author, May 24, 1988.

15. NBOC Archives, Board Minutes for January 16, 1952, Aileen Woods File.

16. See Franca's report on the Canadian Ballet Festival,

1950, in the *Royal Academy of Dancing Gazette*, [1951?], p. 49, Dance Collection Danse, and Anatole Chujoy's review of the Festival in the *Globe and Mail*, November 22, 1950.

17. See review and display advertisement in the *Globe and Mail*, February 13, 1941. See also Mitchell, *Boris Volkoff*, pp. 108–9, 127, and programs for the period 1940–53 in the Boris Volkoff Papers, Metropolitan Toronto Reference Library, Box #1, Envelope #7B.

18. Howard Meadows in conversation with the author, May 3, 1988.

19. Earl Kraul in conversation with the author, April 15, 1988.

20. "Franca's Perfect Ballet Art Lifts Company to Stardom," *Toronto Telegram*, November 13, 1951.

21. "National Ballet Opens with Rousing Program," *Globe and Mail*, November 13, 1951.

22. Betty Oliphant in conversation with the author, August 17, 1988.

23. Mitchell, *Boris Volkoff*, p. 285.

24. NBOC Archives, Board Minutes for March 19, 1952.

25. NBOC Archives, Notes dated October 27, Aileen Woods File.

26. Library and Archives Canada, Board Minutes for October 17, 1951, Franca Papers (13-7); George Crum in conversation with the author, December 13, 1989; NBOC Archives, Board Minutes for April 5, 1984.

27. NBOC Archives, Souvenir Program, 1958–59.

28. NBOC Archives, notes by David Haber for Board Meeting, November 21, 1974, David Haber Correspondence.

29. NBOC Archives, Bob Osborne to NBOC, January 1963, Administration Files 1962–63; see also Veronica Tenant, *Celia Franca: Tour de Force* (Sound Venture, 2006), Bonus CD, for McDonald's own account of her Louisiana adventure.

30. Joanne Nisbet and David Scott in conversation with the author, May 13, 1988.

31. NBOC Archives, Board Minutes for May 21, 1952, and March 1, 1956.

32. Bell and Franca, *The National Ballet of Canada*, p. 55. For resignation date, see NBOC Archives, Board Minutes for April 6, 1955.

33. NBOC Archives, Board Minutes for September 9, 1952.

34. Betty Oliphant in conversation with the author, August 17, 1988.

35. NBOC Archives, Artistic Director's Report to the Fifth Annual Meeting of the Guild, June 14, 1956.

36. Celia Franca in conversation with the author, October 14, 1987, and August 19, 1988.

37. Celia Franca in conversation with the author, October 14, 1987.

38. Celia Franca in conversation with the author, October 14, 1987.

39. Library and Archives Canada, "Report of the National Ballet Company's Visit to Vancouver," Franca Papers (8-17).

40. Howard Meadows in conversation with the author, May 3, 1988; Judie Colpman in conversation with the author, January 20, 1988.

41. Library and Archives Canada, "Report of the National Ballet Company's Visit to Vancouver," Franca Papers (8-17).

42. Judie Colpman in conversation with the author, January 20, 1988; Howard Meadows in conversation with the author, May 3, 1988.

43. Celia Franca in conversation with the author, October 14, 1987.

44. Judie Colpman in conversation with the author, January 20, 1988; Howard Meadows in conversation with the author, May 3, 1988.

45. Celia Franca in conversation with the author, October 14, 1987.

46. Celia Franca in conversation with the author, October 14, 1988.

47. Celia Franca in conversation with the author, October 14, 1988; Judie Colpman in conversation with the author, January 20, 1988.

48. Betty Oliphant in conversation with the author, August 17, 1988.

49. NBOC Archives, Board Minutes for September 9, 1952.

50. Celia Franca in conversation with the author, October 14, 1987.

51. Judie Colpman in conversation with the author, January 20, 1988.

52. Rubin, Don, "Celia Franca: Tartar in a Tutu," *Chatelaine*, March 1974.

53. Celia Franca in conversation with the author, October 14, 1987.

54. NBOC Archives, Board Minutes for March 23, 1962.

55. NBOC Archives, Franca Files.

56. Grant Strate in conversation with the author, April 15, 1988.

57. NBOC Archives, President's Report to the Twelfth Annual Meeting of the Guild, 1963.

58. Grant Strate in conversation with the author, April 15, 1988. Strate himself placed the number of his works choreographed for the National at sixteen, not including the curtain-raiser he choreographed for the opening of the National Arts Centre in 1969.

59. Grant Strate in conversation with the author, April 15, 1988.

60. Victoria Bertram in conversation with the author, May 10, 1988; Grant Strate in conversation with the author, April 15, 1988.

61. NBOC Archives, Grant Strate to John Paterson, [n.d.], Personal Files, Strate.

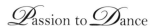

62. Grant Strate in conversation with the author, April 15, 1988.

Chapter 3

1. Bell and Franca, *The National Ballet of Canada*, p. 22.
2. Lois Smith in conversation with the author, May 24, 1988.
3. NBOC Archives, Executive Committee Minutes for May 20, 1959; suggest that the city contemplated a year-round lease as early as 1959; a letter from Hamilton Cassels, Jr., to George H. Bates, September 9, 1966, Hamilton Cassels, Jr., Correspondence, indicates that the company was still using the Orange Lodge as late as that date.
4. NBOC Archives, Board Minutes for October 1, 1952.
5. NBOC Archives, Hamilton Cassels, Jr., to George H. Bates, September 9, 1966, Hamilton Cassels, Jr., Correspondence.
6. Library and Archives Canada, "Notes on the Canadian Tour of November 1969," by André Dufresne, Franca Papers (19-7).
7. Lois Smith in conversation with the author, May 24, 1988.
8. NBOC Archives, Artistic Director's Report to the Annual Meeting (October 15, 1959), p. 1.
9. NBOC Archives, submission to the Canada Council, May 3, 1963, p. 8, Canada Council Files.
10. Library and Archives Canada, Celia Franca to Alan Skinner, March 28, 1953, p. 5, Franca Papers (14-22).
11. NBOC Archives, Antony Tudor to Carman Guild, June 5, 1962, Ballet Production Files, *Judgment of Paris*.
12. NBOC Archives, handwritten notes, "Organization to Date," [n.d.], Aileen Woods File.
13. NBOC Archives, Board Minutes for April 7, 1952.
14. NBOC Archives, Aileen Woods File.
15. NBOC Archives, "Artistic Director's Address to New Directors," January 20, 1972, Ballet Production Files, "Miscellaneous."
16. Library and Archives Canada, lecture by Celia Franca to the Ballet Circle on Sunday, April 24, 1949, p. 8, Franca Papers (9-1).
17. NBOC Archives, Board Minutes for April 3, 1951, Aileen Woods File.
18. Library and Archives Canada, Celia Franca to Alan Skinner, January 21, 1954, Franca Papers (15-11).
19. *Toronto Evening Telegram*, January 25, 1954. See also Wyman, *The Royal Winnipeg Ballet*, p. 87.
20. Walter O'Hearn, "Ballet Squabbles Fast Becoming a Headache," *Montreal Star*, January 30, 1954.
21. NBOC Archives, Board Minutes for March 18, 1954; Executive Committee Minutes for February 1, 1954; Artistic Files for 1995–96, Audience Response Letters for November, 1995.
22. Library and Archives Canada, notes to Draft Policy Report, [n.d.], p. 7, #4, Franca Papers (18-7).
23. Celia Franca in conversation with the author, October 14, 1987.
24. See entry under "Sergeyev, Nicholas" in Bremser, *International Dictionary of Ballet*.
25. Celia Franca in conversation with the author, August 19, 1988.
26. See also Erik Bruhn's analysis of the Sergeyev influence with respect to *Giselle* in his essay "Restaging the Classics," in Charles Payne, *American Ballet Theatre* (New York: Knopf, 1979), p. 327.
27. Celia Franca in conversation with the author, October 14, 1987.
28. Library and Archives Canada, summary of press comments, [n.d.], Franca Papers (15-9). (trans. J.N.)
29. Karen Kain in conversation with the author, May 18, 1988.
30. Lois Smith in conversation with the author, May 24, 1988.
31. Library and Archives Canada, Celia Franca to Alan Skinner, November 21, 1951, Franca Papers (14-22).
32. Celia Franca in conversation with the author, October 14, 1987.
33. Howard Meadows in conversation with Lynn Neufeld, 1989.
34. Janice Ross and Stephen Corbett Steinberg, *Why a Swan? Essays, Interviews, & Conversations on "Swan Lake"* (San Francisco: San Francisco Performing Arts Library and Museum, 1989), p. 65.
35. Jack Anderson, *The Nutcracker Ballet* (London: Bison Books, 1979), p. 108. The Ottawa Ballet Company's 1947 production was thus not the first North American *Nutcracker*, as its program claimed. See Wyman, *Dance Canada*, p. 41.
36. Payne, *American Ballet Theatre*, pp. 360, 362.
37. Leslie George Katz, Nancy Lasalle, and Harvey Simmonds, eds., *Choreography by George Balanchine: A Catalogue of Works* (New York: Viking Penguin, 1984), pp. 210–1.
38. Ross and Steinberg, *Why a Swan?*, pp. 65–6, 70.
39. Katz, *Choreography by George Balanchine*, pp. 202–3.
40. Celia Franca in conversation with the author, October 14, 1987.
41. Sydney Johnson, "*Giselle* Illuminated," *Montreal Star*, January 22, 1954.
42. John Martin, "Young Canadian Ballet Pays a Brief Visit," *The New York Times*, April 3, 1955.
43. NBOC Archives, Board Minutes for December 3, 1952.
44. Celia Franca in conversation with the author, October 14, 1987. NBOC Archives, Ballet Production Files, *Offenbach in the Underworld*.
45. The National performed *Offenbach in the Underworld* at the Brooklyn Academy of Music on

March 26, 1955; ABT premiered its production at the Metropolitan Opera House on April 18, 1956 (Payne, *American Ballet Theatre*, p. 364).

46. Grant Strate in conversation with the author, April 15, 1988.

47. Celia Franca in conversation with the author, October 14, 1987.

48. See reviews in *Dance and Dancers* for July 1950 and March 1962.

49. Marie Rambert, "Andrée Howard: An Appreciation," *Dancing Times*, March 1943.

50. NBOC Archives, Franca to Cyril Frankel, February 8, 1959, Ballet Production Files, *The Mermaid*.

51. NBOC Archives, Howard to Franca, February 3, 1959, Ballet Production Files, *The Mermaid*.

52. Celia Franca in conversation with the author, October 14, 1987.

53. NBOC Archives, Lenore Crawford, *London Free Press*, [exact date unknown] 1959, Personal Files, Kraul.

54. Celia Franca in conversation with the author, October 14, 1987.

55. Celia Franca in conversation with the author, August 19, 1988.

56. John Percival, *Theatre in My Blood: A Biography of John Cranko* (London: Herbert Press, 1983), pp. 107, 124, and 126.

57. Percival, *Theatre in My Blood*, p. 125.

58. Grant Strate in conversation with the author, April 15, 1988. See also Bell and Franca, *The National Ballet of Canada*, p. 192.

59. NBOC Archives, Franca to Michael Wood, Royal Opera House, Covent Garden, September 5, 1963, Franca Files, Box #1.

60. Library and Archives Canada, Franca to Ashton, January 11, 1967, Franca Papers (3-8).

61. NBOC Archives, Artistic Director's Report to the Fifth Annual Meeting of the Guild, June 14, 1956, #109-A.

62. NBOC Archives, Franca to Michael Wood, Royal Opera House, Covent Garden, September 5, 1963, Franca Files, Box #1.

63. Dame Ninette de Valois in conversation with the author, March 16, 1988.

64. Wyman, *The Royal Winnipeg Ballet*, p. 255.

65. David Adams in conversation with the author, April 11, 1988.

66. Lois Smith in conversation with the author, May 24, 1988.

67. David Adams in conversation with the author, April 11, 1988.

68. Library and Archives Canada, Walter Homburger to Alan Skinner, January 8, 1955, Franca Papers (15-14); NBOC Archives, Ballet Production Files, *Dark of the Moon*; Celia Franca in conversation with the

author, October 14, 1987.

69. David Adams in conversation with the author, April 11, 1988.

70. Celia Franca in conversation with the author, October 14, 1987.

71. David Adams in conversation with the author, April 11, 1988.

72. Library and Archives Canada, Franca to Cranko, March 2, 1964, Franca Papers (6-3).

73. Grant Strate in conversation with the author, April 15, 1988.

74. NBOC Archives, Address by Grant Strate to the Toronto Committee of the National Ballet Guild, February 20, 1964, Aileen Woods File.

75. Grant Strate in conversation with the author, April 15, 1988.

76. NBOC Archives, as quoted by Don Rubin in an unidentified clipping, Personal Files, Strate.

77. Grant Strate in conversation with the author, April 15, 1988.

78. NBOC Archives, Address by Grant Strate to the Toronto Committee of the National Ballet Guild, February 20, 1964, Aileen Woods File; Grant Strate in conversation with the author, April 15, 1988.

79. NBOC Archives, Board Minutes for June 29, 1966.

80. Grant Strate in conversation with the author, April 15, 1988.

81. NBOC Archives, report by Grant Strate to the Canada Council on Senior Arts Fellowship Grant, March 7, 1963, Canada Council Files.

82. NBOC Archives, Strate to John Paterson, November 25, 1962, Personal Files, Strate.

83. NBOC Archives, report by Grant Strate to the Canada Council on Senior Arts Fellowship Grant, March 7, 1963, Canada Council Files.

84. Allen Hughes, *The New York Times*, February 3, 1964.

85. Grant Strate in conversation with the author, April 15, 1988.

86. Celia Franca in conversation with the author, October 14, 1987.

87. Paul Roussel, *Le Canada*, February 14, 1953. "A few lively variations, some good solos, and the elimination of its folklore inspiration would convert *Le Pommier* into a pretty divertissement." (Trans. J.N.) For Franca's account of *Le Pommier* and its Montreal reception, see *The National Ballet of Canada*, p. 85. See also Gwyn, *The Pursuit of Perfection*.

88. David Adams in conversation with the author, April 11, 1988; see also Wyman, *Dance Canada*, p. 73.

89. Celia Franca in conversation with the author, August 19, 1988.

90. Celia Franca in conversation with the author, October 14, 1987.

91. Nathan Cohen, *Toronto Star*, January 31, 1961.

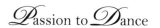
92. Lois Smith in conversation with the author, May 24, 1988.

93. Galina Samsova in conversation with the author, March 14, 1988.

94. Martine van Hamel in conversation with the author, December 15, 1989.

Chapter 4

1. Library and Archives Canada, Draft Report by Celia Franca to the Annual General Meeting, October 1961, Franca Papers (11-9).

2. Natalia Butko in conversation with the author, July 7, 1988; Lorna Geddes in conversation with the author, October 19, 2010.

3. P. B. Waite, *Lord of Point Grey* (Vancouver: University of British Columbia Press, 1987), p. 180.

4. Wyman, *Dance Canada*, p. 79; see also Cohen, *International Encyclopedia of Dance*, entry under "Chiriaeff."

5. NBOC Archives, Board Minutes for February 2,1956, p. 3; President's Report to the Fifth Annual Meeting of the Guild, June 14, 1956, p. 3. Library and Archives Canada, Peter Dwyer to E.P. Taylor, August 28, 1959, Canada Council Files (RG 63 Vol. 224).

6. Grant Strate in conversation with the author, April 15, 1988.

7. Miss Kai's position in the company as indicated in NYCB program for 1966, in the author's private collection. NBOC Archives, correspondence between Franca and Una Kai, April and May 1961, and letter from Joseph Martinson to Franca, May 17, 1961, Ballet Production Files, *Concerto Barocco*.

8. Bell and Franca, *The National Ballet of Canada*, p. 221; Lorna Geddes in conversation with the author, July 15, 1988.

9. NBOC Archives, Betty Cage to Carman Guild, July 12, 1962, Ballet Production Files, *Serenade*.

10. Library and Archives Canada, Notice of Award, January 29, 1963, Canada Council Files (RG 63 Vol. 225).

11. Galina Samsova in conversation with the author, March 14, 1988; Jocelyn Allen, in email correspondence with the author (February 18, 2011), confirmed Samsova's early gymnastic training.

12. The National premiered the work on October 24, 1962. The Royal Ballet gave its first performance on November 3, 1962 (Bland, *The Royal Ballet*, p. 287).

13. See John Kraglund, "Younger, Handsomer Bolshoi Is All Stars," *Globe and Mail*, December 11, 1962. For detail on the Bolshoi's first North American tour, see Harold Robinson, *The Last Impresario: The Life, Times, and Legacy of Sol Hurok* (New York: Viking, 1994), pp. 373–7.

14. See photo in the *Globe and Mail*, December 6, 1962.

15. Betty Oliphant in conversation with the author, August 17, 1988; NBOC Archives, Carman Guild to A.C. Smith, Department of External Affairs, December 29, 1962, Administration Files, 1962–63.

16. Herbert Whittaker, "Ulanova at the National Ballet," *Globe and Mail*, December 15, 1962.

17. Figures for the Royal Alexandra Theatre from *The Canadian Encyclopedia*; for the O'Keefe Centre from Joan Parkhill Baillie, *Look at the Record: An Album of Toronto's Lyric Theatres, 1825–1984* (Oakville, New York: Mosaic Press; Flatiron Book Distributors, 1985).

18. NBOC Archives, Board Minutes for February 4, 1959.

19. NBOC Archives, Board Minutes for April 17, 1963.

20. NBOC Archives, Board Minutes for April 17, 1963.

21. Bland, *The Royal Ballet*, p. 272.

22. NBOC Archives, Celia Franca to Michael Wood, Royal Opera House, September 5, 1963, Franca Files, Box #1.

23. Bell and Franca, *The National Ballet of Canada*, pp. 192–3.

24. Grant Strate in conversation with the author, April 15, 1988.

25. Library and Archives Canada, Peter Dwyer to Guy Glover, April 7, 1964, Canada Council Files (RG 63 Vol. 715).

26. Grant Strate in conversation with the author, April 15, 1988.

27. NBOC Archives, Carman Guild to John Cranko, April 21, 1964, Ballet Production Files, *Romeo and Juliet*.

28. NBOC Archives, Wallace A. Russell to Hamilton Southam, September 1, 1967, Hamilton Cassels, Jr., Correspondence; Celia Franca in conversation with the author, August 19, 1988.

29. Grant Strate in conversation with the author, April 15, 1988.

30. Grant Strate in conversation with the author, April 15, 1988; NBOC Archives, report by Grant Strate to the Artistic Council, June 28, 1969, Personal Files, Strate.

31. NBOC Archives, Dieter Gräfe to Wallace Russell, April 28, 1970, Ballet Production Files, *Romeo and Juliet*.

32. Library and Archives Canada, Celia Franca to John Cranko, May 8, 1970, Franca Papers (6-3).

33. Library and Archives Canada, John Cranko to National Ballet Guild, [n.d.], Franca Papers (6-3).

34. NBOC Archives, Jürgen Rose to Celia Franca, September 1, 1965, Personal Files, Rose and Franca. "Hat sich viel in Eurer Kompanie verändert? — Irgendwie hänge ich sehr an all den Kindern. Es ist schon ein sehr lieber Haufen. Ärger gibt es überall einmal, aber bei Euch kommt man schnell darüber hinweg, weil alle so begeistert bei der Sache sind, jeder gibt sein Bestes, und das ist ein sehr schönes Gefühl!" (Trans. J.N.)

35. Earl Kraul in conversation with the author, April 15, 1988.

36. Galina Samsova in conversation with the author, March 14, 1988.

37. David Adams in conversation with the author, April 11, 1988.

38. Library and Archives Canada, [Celia Franca] to John Cranko, March 2, 1964, Franca Papers (6-3).

39. Lois Smith in conversation with the author, May 24, 1988.

40. Veronica Tennant in conversation with the author, May 9, 1988.

41. Celia Franca in conversation with the author, August 19, 1988.

42. *Ballet Notes*, "Romeo and Juliet," compiled by Assis Carriero for the National Ballet of Canada, author's private collection.

43. Joanne Nisbet in conversation with the author, May 13, 1988.

44. Galina Samsova in conversation with the author, March 14, 1988.

45. NBOC Archives, Lilian [Jarvis] to John [Paterson], December 5, [1963], Personal Files, Samsova.

46. Galina Samsova in conversation with the author, March 14, 1988.

47. Martine van Hamel in conversation with the author, December 15, 1989.

48. Galina Samsova in conversation with the author, March 14, 1988; Martine van Hamel in conversation with the author, December 15, 1989.

49. Library and Archives Canada, Artistic Director's Report to the Eighth Annual Meeting, September 1959, Franca Papers (13-4).

50. NBOC Archives, Minutes of the Annual General Meeting, September 25, 1958.

51. NBOC Archives, Celia Franca to Niels Bjørn Larsen, August 27, 1962, Franca Files, Box #1.

52. Rudolf Nureyev in conversation with the author, August 30, 1989.

53. See, for example, Ralph Hicklin, "Toronto Thanks Bruhn for Gift with 25 Cheering Curtain Calls," *Globe and Mail*, January 7, 1965.

54. Earl Kraul in conversation with the author, April 15, 1988.

55. Rudolf Nureyev in conversation with the author, August 30, 1989.

56. Lois Smith in conversation with the author, May 24, 1988.

57. Nathan Cohen, "Honorable, but Unsuccessful," *Toronto Daily Star*, January 6, 1965; Ralph Hicklin, "Toronto Thanks Bruhn for Gift with 25 Cheering Curtain Calls," *Globe and Mail*, January 7, 1965; Nathan Cohen, "25 Curtain Calls for Bruhn — All Earned," *Toronto Daily Star*, January 7, 1965.

58. Nathan Cohen, "25 Curtain Calls for Bruhn — All Earned," *Toronto Daily Star*, January 7, 1965. For Cohen's review of *Romeo and Juliet*, see "Opulent — but Spiritless," *Toronto Daily Star*, January 8, 1965.

59. Peter Schaufuss in conversation with the author, November 17, 1989.

60. Payne, *American Ballet Theatre*, p. 367.

61. See display ads in the *Globe and Mail* for October 23, 1961, September 29, 1964 (the Kirov); June 6, 1959, December 8, 1962 (the Bolshoi). For the Royal Ballet, see Herbert Whittaker, "Royal Ballet Reaches but Misses Its Lofty Perch," *Globe and Mail*, January 13, 1961; announcement in *Globe and Mail*, June 1, 1963; display ad in *Globe and Mail*, June 1, 1965.

62. Gruen, *Erik Bruhn*, pp. 150–1.

63. Earl Kraul in conversation with the author, April 15, 1988.

64. Bland, *The Royal Ballet*, p. 285; Rudolf Nureyev in conversation with the author, August 30, 1989.

65. Rudolf Nureyev in conversation with the author, August 30, 1989.

66. NBOC Archives, Notes by Grant Strate, "Discussion with Erik Bruhn — Montreal — October 15, 1965," Ballet Production Files, *Swan Lake*.

67. Rudolf Nureyev in conversation with the author, August 30, 1989.

68. Martin Bernheimer, "Nureyev at the Crossroads," *Los Angeles Times*, September 4, 1977.

69. NBOC Archives, George Crum, Notes on Music, [n.d.], Ballet Production Files, *Swan Lake*; Celia Franca to Erik Bruhn, [n.d.] (in response to his letter of January 13, 1966), Franca Files, Box #1.

70. Rudolf Nureyev in conversation with the author, August 30, 1989.

71. Grant Strate in conversation with the author, April 15, 1988.

72. Celia Franca in conversation with the author, August 19, 1988.

73. Grant Strate in conversation with the author, April 15, 1988.

74. Celia Franca in conversation with the author, August 19, 1988.

75. Victoria Bertram in conversation with the author, May 10, 1988.

76. Lois Smith in conversation with the author, May 24, 1988.

77. Victoria Bertram in conversation with the author, May 10, 1988.

78. William Littler, "Celia: First Lady of Canadian Ballet," *Toronto Star*, April 6, 1968.

79. Library and Archives Canada, Gerry Eldred to Celia Franca, December 29, 1976, Franca Papers (11-4).

80. NBOC Archives, Executive Committee Minutes for January 19, 1968, and March 19, 1968.

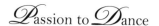
81. NBOC Archives, Board Minutes for June 21, 1967.

82. NBOC Archives, Executive Committee Minutes for February 27, 1968.

83. Clive Barnes, "Canada's National Ballet Stages 'Cinderella,'" *The New York Times*, April 22, 1968.

84. Ralph Hicklin, "A Decorous Cinderella," *Toronto Telegram*, April 16, 1968.

85. Clive Barnes, "Canada's National Ballet Stages 'Cinderella,'" *The New York Times*, April 22, 1968.

86. Wendy Michener, "Celia's Cinderella Suggests Embalmer's Loving Care," *Globe and Mail*, April 16, 1968.

87. NBOC Archives, Celia Franca to Gerald Arpino, November 6, 1973 and November 20, 1973, Ballet Production Files, *Kettentanz*.

88. For her own account of the *Cinderella* taping, see Bell and Franca, *The National Ballet of Canada*, pp. 148, 152.

89. NBOC Archives, Erik Bruhn to Celia Franca, January 13, 1969, Bruhn Files.

90. Ralph Hicklin, "Small Group Best of Strate Night in Performance Lacking Subtlety," *Globe and Mail*, January 5, 1965.

91. Lois Smith in conversation with the author, May 24, 1988.

92. NBOC Archives, André Fortier to John Godfrey, February 21, 1968, Hamilton Cassels, Jr., Correspondence.

93. As quoted by Nathan Cohen, "Celia Franca Says She Isn't Wanted and Quits the National Ballet," *Toronto Star*, November 16, 1968.

Chapter 5

1. As quoted by Nathan Cohen, "Celia Franca Says She Isn't Wanted and Quits the National Ballet," *Toronto Star*, November 16, 1968.

2. NBOC Archives, notes by Hamilton Cassels, Jr., November 22, 1968, Hamilton Cassels, Jr., Correspondence.

3. Lawrence Adams in conversation with the author, November 17, 1989.

4. Dancers' Council to John Godfrey, November 25, 1968, Dance Collection Danse.

5. Dancers' Council to John Godfrey, November 25, 1968, Dance Collection Danse.

6. Lawrence Adams in conversation with the author, November 17, 1989.

7. Library and Archives Canada, Memo to File from Peter Dwyer, November 18, 1968, Canada Council Files (RG 63 Vol. 788).

8. NBOC Archives, Notes by Hamilton Cassels, Jr., November 15, November 16, November 17, November 24, December 3, December 12, 1968,

Hamilton Cassels, Jr., Correspondence.

9. NBOC Archives, Executive Committee Minutes for December 15, 1966, and for December 16, 1968.

10. NBOC Archives, Board Minutes for December 3, 1968.

11. NBOC Archives, Press Release, December 20, 1968, Franca Files, Box #1.

12. Dieter Penzhorn in conversation with the author, May 2, 1988.

13. NBOC Archives, Board Minutes for December 20, 1968.

14. NBOC Archives, Celia Franca to Aileen Woods, November 18, 1968, Franca Files, Box #1.

15. NBOC Archives, Board Minutes for October 9, 1968.

16. NBOC Archives, Board Minutes for October 9, 1968.

17. *Debates of the Senate of Canada* (Hansard), November 16, 1976, p.147.

18. NBOC Archives, Petit-Franca correspondence, June 11 and 19, 1968, Ballet Production Files, Petit Administrative Correspondence; W.A. Russell to Roland Petit, May 31, 1968 and April 4, 1968; Ballet Production Files, *Kraanerg*.

19. NBOC Archives, Executive Committee Minutes for July 31, 1967.

20. David Haber in conversation with the author, December 14, 1989.

21. NBOC Archives, Peter Dwyer to Lyman Henderson, October 30, 1969, Canada Council Files. See also NBOC Archives, "Special Dress Rehearsal (*Kraanerg*) 1969," Canada Council Files.

22. Sid Adilman, "National Ballet Won't Perform *Kraanerg* in Paris," *Toronto Star*, June 2, 1972; NBOC Archives, Artistic Management Committee Minutes, November 23, 1971, Franca Files, Box #2.

23. NBOC Archives, notes by Grant Strate and Louis Applebaum, Ballet Production Files (Curtain-Raiser File).

24. David Haber in conversation with the author, December 14, 1989.

25. Grant Strate in conversation with the author, April 15, 1988.

26. Victoria Bertram in conversation with the author, May 10, 1988.

27. NBOC Archives, Artistic Director's Report to the Annual General Meeting, November 12, 1971.

28. NBOC Archives, Artistic Director's Report to the Annual General Meeting, November 12, 1971.

29. Victoria Bertram in conversation with the author, May 10, 1988.

30. NBOC Archives, presentation by Franca to the Board Meeting of August 7, 1969, National Ballet Guild of Canada — Season 1969–70.

31. NBOC Archives, Artistic Management Committee Minutes, November 11, 1969, Administration Files 1969–70.

32. John Percival, "Promising Canadians," *The London Times*, April 4, 1975.

33. Richard Buckle, "Worthy of a Prince," *The London Sunday Times*, April 13, 1975.

34. For details of Hart's biography, see Max Wyman, *Evelyn Hart, an Intimate Portrait* (Toronto: McClelland & Stewart, 1991).

35. Library and Archives Canada, Klaus Kolmar to Carman Guild, December 2, 1955, Franca Papers (18-6).

36. NBOC Archives, Artistic Director's Report to the Annual General Meeting, November 12, 1971.

37. NBOC Archives, W.P. Walker to Arthur Gelber, June 3, 1964, Administration Files 1964–65.

38. Wyman, *The Royal Winnipeg Ballet*, pp. 124–5; NBOC Archives, Executive Committee Minutes, October 20, 1965.

39. David Haber in conversation with the author, December 14, 1989.

40. NBOC Archives, Board Minutes for December 10, 1969.

41. NBOC Archives, Wallace Russell to Christopher Allan (for Erik Bruhn), December 6, 1971, Bruhn Files.

42. Gruen, *Erik Bruhn*, pp. 169–75.

43. NBOC Archives, Christopher Allan (for Erik Bruhn) to Celia Franca, January 4, 1972, Bruhn Files.

44. David Haber in conversation with the author, December 14, 1989.

45. Ann Ditchburn in conversation with the author, March 19, 1990.

46. Veronica Tennant in conversation with the author, May 9, 1988.

47. *Dance and Dancers*, Vol. 23, No. 7, Issue 271 (July 1972).

48. James Monahan, "The National Ballet of Canada," *Dancing Times*, July 1972, p. 519.

49. Karen Kain in conversation with the author, September 14, 2010.

50. Dieter Penzhorn in conversation with the author, May 2, 1988.

51. Celia Franca in conversation with the author, August 19, 1988.

52. Celia Franca in conversation with the author, August 19, 1988.

53. Lyman Henderson in conversation with the author, July 13, 1988.

54. Veronica Tennant in conversation with the author, May 9, 1988.

55. Celia Franca in conversation with the author, August 19, 1988. See also NBOC Archives, "National Ballet Guild March 4, 1972," Hamilton Cassels, Jr., Correspondence.

56. Betty Oliphant in conversation with the author, August 17, 1988.

57. NBOC Archives, Executive Committee Minutes for January 19, 1972, and for March 15, 1972.

58. Celia Franca in conversation with the author, August 19, 1988.

59. David Haber in conversation with the author, December 14, 1989.

60. Celia Franca in conversation with the author, August 19, 1988.

61. Betty Oliphant in conversation with the author, August 17, 1988.

62. Betty Oliphant in conversation with the author, August 17, 1988.

63. NBOC Archives, David Haber to Betty Oliphant, August 14, 1972, David Haber Correspondence.

64. David Haber in conversation with the author, December 14, 1989.

65. Celia Franca in conversation with the author, August 19, 1988.

Chapter 6

1. Library and Archives Canada, Celia Franca, Appointment Book for 1972–73, Franca Papers (12-12).

2. Rudolf Nureyev in conversation with the author, August 30, 1989.

3. NBOC Archives, Artistic Director's report to the Annual General Meeting, September 11, 1973. For Franca's further account of the production, see *The National Ballet of Canada*, pp. 244–52.

4. Rudolf Nureyev in conversation with the author, August 30, 1989.

5. Mary Jago in conversation with the author, July 14, 1988.

6. Karen Kain in conversation with the author, May 18, 1988.

7. Veronica Tennant in conversation with the author, May 9, 1988.

8. Tomas Schramek in conversation with the author, May 20, 1988.

9. Victoria Bertram in conversation with the author, May 10, 1988.

10. Celia Franca in conversation with the author, August 19, 1988.

11. Rudolf Nureyev in conversation with the author, August 30, 1989.

12. See Bremser, *International Dictionary of Ballet*, entry under "Franca."

13. Celia Franca in conversation with the author, August 19, 1988.

14. Dieter Penzhorn in conversation with the author, May 2, 1988; Larry Beevers in conversation with the author, April 21, 1988.

15. Larry Beevers in conversation with the author, April 21, 1988.

16. Dieter Penzhorn in conversation with the author, May 2, 1988.

17. Dieter Penzhorn in conversation with the author, May 2, 1988.

18. Veronica Tennant in conversation with the author, May 9, 1988.

19. Clive Barnes, "To Play the Met, Get Nureyev," *The New York Times*, May 6, 1973.

20. Robert J. Landry, "Canada Comes On Strong in Met Debut; Well-Staged, New *Sleeping Beauty*," *Variety*, May 2, 1973.

21. Veronica Tennant in conversation with the author, May 9, 1988.

22. NBOC Archives, Board Minutes for June 19, 1973; Board Minutes for November 22, 1995.

23. NBOC Archives, Brief accompanying the 1975–76 submission to the Canada Council, Canada Council Files, "Submissions 1975–76."

24. NBOC Archives, draft Brief to the Canada Council, January 5, 1972, Canada Council Files, "Briefs 1972."

25. Celia Franca in conversation with the author, August 19, 1988.

26. Dieter Penzhorn in conversation with the author, May 2, 1988.

27. Betty Oliphant in conversation with the author, August 17, 1988.

28. Karen Kain in conversation with the author, May 18, 1988.

29. Bell and Franca, *The National Ballet of Canada*, p. 248.

30. Karen Kain in conversation with the author, May 18, 1988.

31. Library and Archives Canada, Celia Franca, Report on Varna Competition, 1970, Franca Papers (10-10).

32. Karen Kain in conversation with the author, May 18, 1988.

33. NBOC Archives, transcript of press conference held November 30, 1972, David Haber Correspondence.

34. NBOC Archives, Celia Franca to John Neumeier, July 4, 1973, Ballet Production Files, *Don Juan*.

35. NBOC Archives, *Coppélia* contract, Ballet Production Files, *Coppélia*.

36. Angela Warnick, "It's Hard to Argue with Her Record," *Hamilton Spectator*, November 15, 1973.

37. Library and Archives Canada, Lawrence Schafer to Celia Franca, December 2, 1972, Franca Papers (1-14).

38. Gruen, *Erik Bruhn*, pp. 187–8.

39. NBOC Archives, Celia Franca to Erik Bruhn, January 30, 1974, Ballet Production Files, *Coppélia*.

40. NBOC Archives, Ian H. McLeod to Robert A. Laidlaw, October 15, 1974, Administration Files 1973.

41. David Haber in conversation with the author, December 14, 1989.

42. Gruen, *Erik Bruhn*, pp. 189–90.

43. Michael Iachetta, "Rudi Makes Bruhn's Role His Own," *New York Daily News*, August 9, 1974.

44. NBOC Archives, Johnson Ashley to Gerry Eldred, February 21, 1975, Bruhn Files.

45. Notes by David Haber for Board Meeting of October 7, 1974, David Haber Correspondence.

46. Gruen, *Erik Bruhn*, p. 190.

47. NBOC Archives, Ian H. McLeod to Board of Directors, January 11, 1974. Press Release, January 11, 1974, Franca Files, Box #1.

48. Bland, *The Royal Ballet*, pp. 137–8.

49. NBOC Archives, Minutes of the Annual General Meeting, September 9, 1974.

50. Celia Franca in conversation with the author, August 19, 1988.

51. John Fraser, "Oliphant Resigns from National Ballet," *Globe and Mail*, March 4, 1975.

52. Celia Franca in conversation with the author, August 19, 1988.

53. David Haber in conversation with the author, December 14, 1989.

54. David Haber in conversation with the author, December 14, 1989.

55. Details regarding the production of *Mad Shadows* provided by David Haber in conversation with the author, December 14, 1989, and by Ann Ditchburn in conversation with the author, March 19, 1990.

56. David Haber in conversation with the author, December 14, 1989.

57. David Haber in conversation with the author, December 14, 1989; see also NBOC Archives, David Haber to Monique Michaud, March 4, 1975, Canada Council Files, "Meetings 1975."

58. NBOC Archives, David Haber to John Neumeier, January 27, 1975, Ballet Production Files, *Don Juan* Lighting Plot.

59. NBOC Archives, Ballet Production Files, *Le Coq d'Or, passim*.

60. David Haber in conversation with the author, December 14, 1989.

61. NBOC Archives, Nicholas Beriosoff to Celia Franca, January 14, 1974, Ballet Production Files, *Le Coq d'Or*; David Haber in conversation with the author, December 14, 1989.

62. David Haber in conversation with the author, December 14, 1989.

63. NBOC Archives, Nicholas Beriosoff to Gerry Eldred, August 18, 1975, Ballet Production Files, *Le Coq d'Or*.

64. John Fraser, "Oliphant Resigns from National Ballet," *Globe and Mail*, March 4, 1975.

65. NBOC Archives, David Haber to the Board, March 26, 1975, Haber Correspondence.

66. Lyman Henderson in conversation with the author, July 13, 1988.

67. NBOC Archives, Haber to Beriosoff, May 20, 1975, Ballet Production Files, *Le Coq d'Or*.

68. NBOC Archives, Executive Committee Minutes for October 7, 1975.

69. Library and Archives Canada, notation in Appointment Book for June 3, 1975, Franca Papers (12-14).

70. NBOC Archives, Press Release, June 7, 1975, Administration Files 1975–76.

71. Lyman Henderson in conversation with the author, July 13, 1988.

72. NBOC Archives, Press Release, June 7, 1975, Administration Files 1975–76.

73. See Sid Adilman's column, *Toronto Star*, September 26, 1975.

74. Library and Archives Canada, Celia Franca to Jock McLeod, September 18, 1975, Franca Papers (21-9).

Chapter 7

1. Library and Archives Canada, Erik Bruhn to Celia Franca, October 1, 1964, Franca Papers (20-2).

2. David Haber in conversation with the author, December 14, 1989.

3. NBOC Archives, Gerry Eldred to Erik Bruhn, June 20, 1975, Bruhn Files.

4. Rudolf Nureyev in conversation with the author, August 30, 1989.

5. Veronica Tennant in conversation with the author, May 9, 1988.

6. Rudolf Nureyev in conversation with the author, August 30, 1989.

7. NBOC Archives, Gerry Eldred to David Haber, November 25, 1974, Ballet Production Files, *Coppélia*.

8. Gruen, *Erik Bruhn*, pp. 73–6, 157–8, 193–5.

9. John Fraser, "Nureyev, Leave Canadian Ballet Alone," *The New York Times*, July 27, 1975.

10. Clive Barnes, "Nureyev – The Canadians' Passport," *The New York Times*, August 17, 1975.

11. "Letters," *The New York Times*, August 3, 1975.

12. NBOC Archives, Artistic Director's Report to the Annual General Meeting, September 11, 1973.

13. NBOC Archives, I.H. McLeod to Gerry Eldred, March 14, 1973, Administration Files 1972–73.

14. Payne, *American Ballet Theatre*, pp. 129ff.

15. Edward Thorpe, *Kenneth MacMillan: The Man and His Ballets* (London: Hamish Hamilton, 1985), p. 84; Richard Austin, *Lynn Seymour: An Authorised Biography* (London: Angus and Robertson, 1980), p. 132.

16. NBOC Archives, Board Minutes for July 18, 1972; Executive Committee Minutes for April 25, 1974.

17. Alexander Grant in conversation with the author, March 22, 1988. For the rights to *Fille*, see Alexander

18. Alexander Grant in conversation with the author, March 22, 1988.

19. Bland, *The Royal Ballet*, p. 248.

20. Alexander Grant in conversation with the author, March 22, 1988.

21. Alexander Grant in conversation with the author, March 22, 1988.

22. Lauretta Thistle, "Appointment Raises Questions," *Ottawa Citizen*, November 1, 1975.

23. Alexander Grant in conversation with the author, March 22, 1988.

24. NBOC Archives, Erik Bruhn to Gerry Eldred, June 29, 1976, Bruhn Files.

25. Alexander Grant in conversation with the author, March 22, 1988.

26. NBOC Archives, David Allport (for Erik Bruhn) to Gerry Eldred, July 12, 1976, Bruhn Files. By January 4, 1977, Bruhn had once again granted permission for his name to appear on the credits of *Swan Lake*. See NBOC Archives, Gerry Eldred to Mary Jolliffe, January 4, 1977, Ballet Production Files, *Swan Lake*.

27. NBOC Archives, Board Minutes for October 7, 1975; see also *Toronto Star*, November 29, 1975.

28. NBOC Archives, Celia Franca to Michael M. Koerner, June 25, 1971, Administration Files 1971–72; Gerry Eldred to Peter Sever, July 14, 1976, Administration Files 1975–76, 1976–77.

29. Alexander Grant in conversation with the author, March 22, 1988.

30. David Vaughan, *Frederick Ashton and His Ballets* (London: A&C Black, 1977), pp. 493–4.

31. Lawrence O'Toole, "Did Franca slight Oliphant?" *Globe and Mail*, November 18, 1976.

32. Alexander Grant, note to the author, November 1994.

33. Vaughan, *Frederick Ashton*, p. 322.

34. NBOC Archives, Board Minutes for April 25, 1978.

35. Alexander Grant in conversation with the author, March 22, 1988.

36. Details regarding Ballet Revue from Ann Ditchburn in conversation with the author, March 19, 1990, and Tomas Schramek in conversation with the author, May 20, 1988. Statistics regarding ticket sales courtesy Mr. Schramek, who functioned as business manager for the group.

37. Doug Hughes, "National's Grant Takes Sour Milk with Ice Cream," *Vancouver Province*, October 1979.

38. Ann Ditchburn in conversation with the author, March 19, 1990. NBOC Archives, Ann Ditchburn to Erik Bruhn, November 1, 1985, Bruhn Files.

39. William Littler, "Ballet Takes On a Life of Its Own," *Toronto Star*, April 12, 1977; Gina Mallet, "No Sign

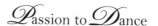

of Skimping in New Ballet," *Toronto Sunday Star*, February 18, 1979.

40. As quoted by Paula Citron in "James Kudelka: Profile of an Enigma," *Dance in Canada*, Spring 1985, p. 14.

41. NBOC Archives, Souvenir Programs for 1980–81 and 1981–82.

42. Gruen, *Erik Bruhn*, p. 156; Wyman, *Dance Canada*, p. 145.

43. NBOC Archives, Board Minutes for January 18, 1979; Letter of Agreement between Imperial Oil and the National Ballet of Canada, Ballet Production Files, *Newcomers*.

44. Walter Terry, "Making It to Ballet's 'Big Time,'" *Saturday Review*, September 3, 1977, p. 41.

45. Alexander Grant in conversation with the author, March 22, 1988.

46. Peter Schaufuss in conversation with the author, November 17, 1989.

47. NBOC Archives, Executive Committee Minutes for April 16, 1973.

48. NBOC Archives, Board Minutes for June 20, 1978.

49. Alexander Grant in conversation with the author, March 22, 1988.

50. Galina Samsova in conversation with the author, March 14, 1988.

51. Alexander Grant in conversation with the author, March 22, 1988.

52. Alexander Bland, "A Case of Taking Colas to Newcastle," *Observer*, August 12, 1979.

53. Mary Clarke, "Triple Bill," *Guardian*, August 8, 1979.

54. Clement Crisp, "Swan Lake," *Financial Times*, August 7, 1979.

55. Fernau Hall, "Brave Try with a Masterpiece," *Daily Telegraph*, August 7, 1979.

56. Alexander Bland, "A Case of Taking Colas to Newcastle," *Observer*, August 12, 1979.

57. Mary Clarke, "Triple Bill," *Guardian*, August 8, 1979.

58. Clement Crisp, "Jago and Schaufuss," *Financial Times*, August 8, 1979.

59. Fernau Hall, *Daily Telegraph*, August 8, 1979.

60. Clement Crisp, "La Fille Mal Gardée," *Financial Times*, August 9, 1979.

61. Alexander Grant, note to the author, November 1994.

62. Nicholas Dromgoole, "Born to Dance," *Sunday Telegraph*, August 12, 1979.

63. John Percival, "Something Old, Something New, Something Borrowed…," *Dance and Dancers*, September 1979, pp. 28–41.

64. Both Grant and Oliphant as quoted in "Grant's Remarks Anger Oliphant," *Globe and Mail*, August 17, 1979.

65. See *Performing Arts Magazine*, August 1982.

66. Alexander Grant in conversation with the author, March 22, 1988; Michael Crabb, "Alexander Grant's

Dismissal from the Complex National Ballet: An Artistic Director's Lot," *Performing Arts*, Winter/Spring 1983, p. 37.

67. NBOC Archives, Board Minutes for April 19, 1979.

68. Karen Kain in conversation with the author, May 18, 1988; Frank Augustyn in conversation with the author, July 15, 1988.

69. Stephen Godfrey, "Karen Kain Strikes Back at the National Ballet," *Globe and Mail*, May 26, 1982; "National 'Needs New Ballets,'" *Globe and Mail*, May 29, 1982. For Kain's own account of these events see Karen Kain, *Movement Never Lies: An Autobiography* (Toronto: McClelland & Stewart, 1994), pp. 147–51.

70. Betty Oliphant in conversation with the author, August 17, 1988.

71. Helen Bullock, "National Ballet Drops Grant," *Toronto Star*, June 30, 1982.

72. Karen Kain in conversation with the author, May 18, 1988.

73. NBOC Archives, Board Minutes for June 17, 1970.

74. Karen Kain in conversation with the author, May 18, 1988.

75. Helen Bullock, "National Ballet Drops Grant," *Toronto Star*, June 30, 1982.

76. Robert Johnston in conversation with the author, May 2, 1988.

77. Peter Schaufuss in conversation with the author, November 17, 1989.

78. NBOC Archives, photocopy of playbill for the Scottish Ballet, 1978, Ballet Production Files, *Napoli*.

79. NBOC Archives, Board Minutes for 26 November 1981.

80. NBOC Archives, Monique Michaud to R. McCartney Samples, May 29, 1980, Canada Council Files 1980–81.

81. See Karen Kain in Stephen Godfrey, "Karen Kain Strikes Back at the National Ballet," *Globe and Mail*, May 26, 1982, and Frank Augustyn in Stephen Godfrey, "National 'Needs New Ballets,'" *Globe and Mail*, May 29, 1982.

82. NBOC Archives, Board Minutes for June 25, 1980.

83. NBOC Archives, Board Minutes for September 18, 1980.

84. Peter Schaufuss in conversation with the author, November 17, 1989.

85. Alexander Grant in conversation with the author, March 22, 1988.

86. Alexander Grant in conversation with the author, March 22, 1988.

87. Lois Smith in conversation with the author, May 24, 1988.

88. Alexander Grant in conversation with the author, March 22, 1988.

Notes

Chapter 8

1. Lina Fattah, interview with Erik Bruhn, *Dance and Dancers*, December 1983; Celia Franca in conversation with the author, August 19, 1988. The invitation could have been issued during the run of American Ballet Theatre at the Royal Alexandra Theatre in 1952. The program for February 4, 1952 (Metropolitan Toronto Reference Library, Boris Volkoff Papers, Scrapbook #11) lists Bruhn among the dancers for that engagement. That date falls between the National's tour engagements in Montreal (February 2) and London (February 7).

2. Helen Bullock, "National Ballet Drops Grant," *Toronto Star*, June 30, 1982.

3. Robert Johnston in conversation with the author, May 2, 1988.

4. NBOC Archives, Board Minutes for September 29, 1982.

5. Lyman Henderson in conversation with the author, July 13, 1988.

6. Valerie Wilder in conversation with the author, August 17, 1988.

7. Betty Oliphant in conversation with the author, August 17, 1988.

8. Lina Fattah, interview with Erik Bruhn, *Dance and Dancers*, December 1983.

9. David Adams in conversation with the author, April 11, 1988.

10. Details regarding search procedures with respect to immigration regulations from Lyman Henderson in conversation with the author, July 13, 1988.

11. Erik Bruhn, as quoted in the program notes for *Here We Come*, National Ballet of Canada house program, O'Keefe Centre, for November 16 to 20, 1983.

12. Lynn Wallis in conversation with the author, August 17, 1988.

13. Valerie Wilder in conversation with the author, August 17, 1988.

14. NBOC Archives, "Observations and Thoughts on Our First Completed Tour of Europe '85," Copenhagen, June 1985, Bruhn Files.

15. Veronica Tennant in conversation with the author, May 9, 1988.

16. Lina Fattah, interview with Erik Bruhn, *Dance and Dancers*, December 1983.

17. Gary Smith, "Custodians or Creators?," *Hamilton Spectator*, October 10, 1987.

18. Mary Jago in conversation with the author, July 14, 1988.

19. NBOC Archives, Executive Minutes for December 15, 1966; Board Minutes for January 13, 1971.

20. Valerie Wilder in conversation with the author, August 17, 1988.

21. Frank Augustyn in conversation with the author, July 15, 1988; Robert Johnston in conversation with the author, May 2, 1988.

22. Robert Johnston in conversation with the author, May 2, 1988.

23. NBOC Archives, Board Minutes for September 25, 1984; Wendy Reid in conversation with the author, May 6, 1988; current subscription statistics provided by Julia Drake in email to the author, October 20, 2010.

24. NBOC Archives, Erik Bruhn to Pierre Wyss, December 8, 1985, and Valerie Wilder to Robert Trinchero, August 26, 1985, Bruhn Files.

25. NBOC Archives, Erik Bruhn to Artistic Staff, July 23, 1985, Bruhn Files.

26. Valerie Wilder in conversation with the author, August 17, 1988.

27. Details regarding Allan's repertoire and the development of *Masada* from David Allan in conversation with the author, May 9, 1988.

28. David Allan in conversation with the author, May 9, 1988.

29. Details concerning Alleyne's Stuttgart background and choreographic ambitions from John Alleyne in conversation with the author, May 13, 1988.

30. Paula Citron, "Patsalas Comes Back to Ballet," *Toronto Star*, October 23, 1987.

31. Gruen, *Erik Bruhn*, p. 212; NBOC Archives, Board Minutes for March 26, 1975.

32. NBOC Archives, Souvenir Programs, 1980–81 and 1982–83.

33. William Littler, "World Veteran Bruhn Takes Helm of National," *Toronto Star*, December 9, 1982.

34. Valerie Wilder in conversation with the author, August 17, 1988.

35. Details on Tetley's views of the company and background to the acquisition of *Sphinx* and *Alice* from Glen Tetley in conversation with the author, July 14, 1988.

36. Glen Tetley in conversation with the author, July 14, 1988.

37. NBOC Archives, Board Minutes for March 18, 1986; Valerie Wilder in conversation with the author, August 17, 1988.

38. NBOC Archives, Alexander Grant–Natalia Makarova correspondence, October 30, 1981 to November 18, 1981, Ballet Production Files, *La Bayadère*.

39. Payne, *American Ballet Theatre*, p. 365.

40. NBOC Archives, Program Note, O'Keefe Centre House Program of May 1–5, 1985.

41. NBOC Archives, ms, by Erik Bruhn, of tribute to Terry Westmoreland, [n.d.], Bruhn Files.

42. Gruen, *Erik Bruhn*, pp. 86–91, 138–40.

43. NBOC Archives, Sir Robert Helpmann to Robert Johnston, April 16, 1986, Bruhn Files.

44. NBOC Archives, Erik Bruhn to Sir Robert Helpmann, October 1, 1985, Bruhn Files.

45. NBOC Archives, Erik Bruhn to Maina [Gielgud], [n.d.], Bruhn Files.

46. Gruen, *Erik Bruhn*, pp. 36, 44.

47. NBOC Archives, Board Minutes for April 12, 1972; Press Release for Annual General Meeting (2010), October 6, 2010 (#2010-08).

48. NBOC Archives, Board Minutes for September 12, 1978.

49. NBOC Fact Sheet, "The Volunteer Committee of The National Ballet of Canada," distributed at media announcement for the sixtieth-anniversary season, February 7, 2011.

50. Wendy Reid in conversation with the author, May 6, 1988; see also Board Minutes for April 22, 1985, and Board Minutes for February 18, 2010, and June 23, 2010. See also NBOC archives, Report from Volunteer Committee, November 21, 2001, File Folder 2001-2002 Artistic General.

51. Veronica Tennant in conversation with the author, May 9, 1988.

52. Karen Kain in conversation with the author, May 18, 1988.

53. Veronica Tennant in conversation with the author, May 9, 1988.

54. John Alleyne in conversation with the author, May 13, 1988.

55. Karen Kain in conversation with the author, May 18, 1988.

56. Frank Augustyn in conversation with the author, July 15, 1988.

57. John Alleyne in conversation with the author, May 13, 1988.

58. NBOC Archives, draft ms, by Erik Bruhn, of Artistic Director's Report on 1984–85 season, Bruhn Files.

59. Robert Johnston in conversation with the author, May 2, 1988.

60. Diane Solway, *Nureyev, His Life* (New York: William Morrow, 1998), p. 480.

61. Veronica Tennant in conversation with the author, May 9, 1988; Donn Downey, "Danish Dancer Fostered New Canadian Ballets," *Globe and Mail*, April 2, 1986; William Littler, "Erik Bruhn Helped Ballet Soar," *Toronto Star*, April 2, 1986.

62. Lynn Wallis in conversation with the author, August 17, 1988.

63. NBOC Archives, Erik Bruhn to all the National Ballet of Canada, March 19, 1986, Bruhn Files.

Chapter 9

1. Valerie Wilder in conversation with the author, June 7, 1990.

2. NBOC Archives, Erik Bruhn to Edmund C. Bovey, March 18, 1986, Personal Files, Patsalas. See also Deirdre Kelly, "National Ballet Appoints Team to Carry on Bruhn's Work," *Globe and Mail*, April 9, 1986.

3. NBOC Archives, Board Minutes for April 7, 1986.

4. Valerie Wilder in conversation with the author, June 7, 1990.

5. Constantin Patsalas, letter to the editor of the *Globe and Mail*, November 21, 1986; Donn Downey, "Concerto Goes to Court," *Globe and Mail*, November 6, 1986.

6. Thomas Claridge and Deirdre Kelly, "Patsalas Fails in Bid to Bar Ballet," *Globe and Mail*, November 8, 1986.

7. Valerie Wilder in conversation with the author, August 17, 1988.

8. Program Notes for "A Program of Dance Works by Constantin Patsalas," October 27–31, 1987, author's private collection.

9. Death notice, *Globe and Mail*, May 22, 1989.

10. Valerie Wilder in conversation with the author, June 7, 1990.

11. Paul Taylor, "Legal, Medical, Social Work Advice Available at Innovative AIDS Clinic," *Globe and Mail*, July 20, 1989.

12. NBOC Archives, letter from Valerie Wilder to Amalia Schelhorn, April 4, 2001 (2000-2001/Artistic/ Dancers/James Kudelka Files); James Kudelka in conversation with the author, October 14, 2010.

13. Glen Tetley in conversation with the author, July 14, 1988.

14. NBOC Archives, Press Release #27/36.

15. Valerie Wilder in conversation with the author, June 7, 1990.

16. NBOC Archives, Submission to the Canada Council for 1976–77, Canada Council Files 1976.

17. Bremser, *International Dictionary of Ballet*, entry under "Tetley."

18. Glen Tetley in conversation with the author, July 14, 1988.

19. Valerie Wilder in conversation with the author, August 17, 1988.

20. NBOC Archives, Board Minutes for December 20, 1977.

21. NBOC Archives, Press Release #48/43.

22. NBOC Archives, Erik Bruhn to Sonia Arova, September 12, 1985, Bruhn Files; Gruen, *Erik Bruhn*, pp. 38–40ff.

23. NBOC Archives, Program Note to Program for First Annual Erik Bruhn Prize, May 14, 1988.

24. NBOC Archives, Press Release #24/37.

25. Lyman Henderson in telephone conversation with the author, July 15, 1993.

26. NBOC Archives, O'Keefe Centre Program for June 14–17, 1984.

27. Details on Anderson's background and career from Reid Anderson in conversation with the author, June 8, 1990.

28. NBOC Archives, Press Release #5/42.

29. NBOC Archives, Press Release #7/42.

30. James Kudelka in conversation with the author, May 10, 1996.

31. NBOC Archives, Media Release #27/45.

32. Sid Adilman, "Harris Says Sorry for Kain Snub," *Toronto Star*, January 16, 1996.

33. Deirdre Kelly, "Anderson Quits National, Blames Government Cutbacks," *Globe and Mail*, November 11, 1995.

34. NBOC Media Release, #15/45.

35. NBOC Media Release, #16/45.

36. "Augustyn or Tennant May Follow Anderson," *Globe and Mail*, January 9, 1996.

37. James Kudelka in conversation with the author, May 10, 1996.

38. NBOC Media Release, #38/45.

Chapter 10

1. NBOC Archives, James Kudelka to Paul Mack, July 19, 1993, 1995–96 Artistic Files Reid Anderson; James Kudelka in conversation with the author, October 14, 2010.

2. James Kudelka in conversation with the author, October 14, 2010.

3. James Kudelka in conversation with the author, October 14, 2010. A draft version of the document, probably dating from around 2000, can be found in NBOC Archives, 2000–2001 Artistic General Files (2). All subsequent quotations from Kudelka's planning document are from this version.

4. Julia Drake in conversation with the author, October 19, 2010.

5. NBOC Archives, Executive Committee Minutes, November 20, 1995.

6. NBOC Archives, Board Minutes, February 29, 1996.

7. NBOC Archives, Artistic 1996–97, Correspondence Files.

8. NBOC Archives, James Kudelka to Brian Macdonald, April 27, 1998, 1997–98 Artistic Files Artistic Collaborators Correspondence.

9. *Cruel World* (fall 1996; American Ballet Theatre, 1994), *Terra Firma* (fall 1997; San Francisco Ballet, 1995), *Désir* (spring 1998; Les Grands Ballets Canadiens, 1991), *The Fairy's Kiss* (winter 1999; Birmingham Royal Ballet, 1996), *The End* [excerpt] (fall 2003; San Francisco Ballet, 1992), *There Below* (fall 2003; Ballet Met, 1989), *Gazebo Dances* [excerpt] (fall 2003; Ballet Met, 2003).

10. James Kudelka in conversation with the author, October 14, 2010.

11. See Tobi Tobias, "The Bad and the Beautiful," *New York*, January 3, 1994, and Tobi Tobias, "Found Objects," *New York*, May 30, 1994; see also correspondence regarding *The Red Shoes* in NBOC Archives, 1996–1997 Artistic General Files.

12. NBOC Archives, contract between James Kudelka and the Royal Ballet, London, in 1999–2000 Artistic Season, James Kudelka Files, Dancers.

13. Anna Kisselgoff, "Classical Yet Looser, A Troupe Renewed," *The New York Times*, October 8, 1998; Lorna Geddes in conversation with the author, October 19, 2010.

14. Anna Kisselgoff, "Bournonville 'Abdallah' Re-created," *The New York Times*, June 19, 1988.

15. NBOC Archives, correspondence between James Kudelka and Flemming Ryberg, June, 1996, in 1996–1997 Artistic Files General.

16. James Kudelka in conversation with the author, October 14, 2010.

17. Lindsay Fischer in conversation with the author, October 19, 2010.

18. Joysanne Sidiumus in conversation with the author, December 16, 2010.

19. NBOC Archives, Canada Council Application Materials for three-year block grant, 2001–02 to 2003–04 seasons, in 2000–2001 Artistic General Files (2).

20. NBOC Archives, correspondence, Wendy McDowell to Nathan Gilbert, Laidlaw Foundation, June 13, 1997, in 1996–1997 Artistic Files General; James Kudelka to Nathan Gilbert, January 24, 1997, in 1996–97 Artistic Files Departments Dancers; James Kudelka to Nathan Gilbert, April 8, 1996, in 1996–1997 Artistic Files General.

21. James Kudelka in conversation with the author, May 10, 1996.

22. Postponement announced in NBOC media release #30/49, May 1, 2000.

23. Paul Ben-Itzak, "The Resurrection of ABT," *Dance Magazine*, May 1997.

24. Jennifer Dunning, "Earthbound or Skyborne in a Dance of Playfulness," *The New York Times*, October 14, 1998.

25. Anna Kisselgoff, "Classical Yet Looser, A Troupe Renewed," *The New York Times*, October 8, 1998.

26. NBOC Archives, James Kudelka to William Forsythe, October 14, 1998, in 1999–2000 Artistic Season, James Kudelka Files, Dancers.

27. NBOC Archives, submission to the Laidlaw Foundation, June 20, 1997, in 1996–97 Artistic Files General; Canada Council application materials, December 15, 1997, in 1997–98 Artistic Files General.

28. NBOC Archives, James Kudelka to Matjash Mrozewski, September 20, 1998, in 2000–01 Artistic Files Dancers James Kudelka.

29. Kimberly Glasco in conversation with the author, October 27, 2010; "Silver medals for National duo," *Globe and Mail*, June 25, 1981.

30. NBOC Archives, press release from Kimberly Glasco, December 18, 1998, in 2000–01 Artistic Files Dancers James Kudelka.

31. Quoted in Susan Walker, "Curtain Comes Down on Veteran Ballerina," *Toronto Star*, December 19, 1998.

32. Susan Walker, "Dancer Gets $1.5 Million, Sources Say," *Toronto Star*, July 21, 2000.

33. Deirdre Kelly, "Is Glasco Really Too Old to Dance?" *Globe and Mail*, December 24, 1998; Stewart Bell, "Senior Ballet Teacher Defends Axed Dancer," *National Post*, January 4, 1999; Deirdre Kelly, "Putting Primas In Their Place," *Globe and Mail*, January 11, 1999; Betty Oliphant, in "Arts and Argument" section, *Globe and Mail*, January 18, 1999.

34. John Fraser, "Duelling Duennas," *National Post*, January 15, 1999.

35. "Directors Attack Judge Over Ruling on Glasco," *Globe and Mail*, April 14, 2000.

36. Max Wyman, "Kimberly Glasco Versus the National Ballet," in *Max Wyman, Revealing Dance: Selected Writings 1970's–2001* (Toronto: Dance Collection Danse Press/es, 2001), pp.267–312.

37. NBOC Archives, James Kudelka Artistic Statement, November, 2000, in 2000–01 Artistic Files General (1).

38. Karen Kain in conversation with the author, September 14, 2010.

39. Sandra Rubin, "Saluting the Man from Pincher Creek," *National Post*, May 16, 2007.

40. The final cost of the production was reported in various newspaper reviews of the opening, including Anna Kisselgoff, "Canadians' New 'Swan Lake,' Full of Passion and Perversity," *The New York Times*, May 18, 1999, and Deirdre Kelly, "Emotion Frozen Out of Kudelka's Swan Lake," *Globe and Mail*, May 6, 1999; the full list of donors appeared in the opening night house programs. For costing of the ballet, see also NBOC Archives, 2001–02 Operating Plan, in 2001–02 Artistic Files General.

41. See, for example, Kisselgoff and Kelly reviews, above.

42. NBOC Archives, James Kudelka to a ballet patron, June 14, 1999, in 1998–99 Artistic Files Dancers Correspondence.

43. NBOC display ad for *Swan Lake* in *Globe and Mail*, May 8, 1999.

44. James Kudelka in conversation with the author, October 14, 2010.

45. Oswald biography in NBOC house program, Hummingbird Centre, November 20–27, 1999.

46. Anna Kisselgoff, "A Wizard, Cute Lizards and a Prince with a Feather," *The New York Times*, November 14, 2000.

47. Paula Citron, "Pointing the Way Forward," *Globe and Mail*, May 6, 2002.

48. John Rockwell, "Both Evangelist and Pied Piper," *The New York Times*, April 7, 2005.

49. Kevin Garland in conversation with the author, September 14, 2010.

50. Kevin Garland in conversation with the author, September 14, 2010.

51. James Kudelka in conversation with the author, October 14, 2010.

52. Paula Citron, "Cinderella Nearly Reaches Nirvana," *Globe and Mail*, May 10, 2004.

53. Joan Acocella, "Secrets: American Ballet Theatre at the Met," *The New Yorker*, July 10, 2006; John Rockwell, "This Cinderella Finds Jazz, New Toe Shoes and Happiness," *The New York Times*, June 5, 2006.

54. Greta Hodgkinson in conversation with the author, December 16, 2010; Rex Harrington in conversation with the author, October 10, 2010.

55. Peter Ottmann in conversation with the author, December 16, 2010.

56. NBOC Archives, James Kudelka, Artistic Statement on Canada Council funding application, November 15, 2003, in 2004–05 File General New Productions.

57. James Kudelka in conversation with the author, October 14, 2010.

58. James Kudelka in conversation with the author, October 14, 2010.

59. Kevin Garland in conversation with the author, September 14, 2010.

60. James Kudelka in conversation with the author, October 14, 2010.

61. James Kudelka in conversation with the author, October 14, 2010.

62. NBOC media release #42/55, May 18, 2005.

63. James Kudelka in conversation with the author, October 14, 2010.

64. Lorna Geddes and Rex Harrington in conversation with the author, October 19, 2010; Greta Hodgkinson, Rebekah Rimsay, and Jennifer Fournier in conversation with the author, December 16, 2010.

Chapter 11

1. Karen Kain in conversation with the author, September 14, 2010.

2. James Pitblado in conversation with the author, October 19, 2010.

3. See correspondence in NBOC Archives, 2005–06 General File, New AD Well Wishes.

Notes

4. James Kudelka in conversation with the author, October 14, 2010.

5. Karen Kain in conversation with the author, September 14, 2010.

6. James Kudelka, telephone conversation with the author, February 2, 2011.

7. Rebekah Rimsay in conversation with the author, December 16, 2010.

8. Kevin Garland in conversation with the author, September 14, 2010.

9. NBOC Board minutes for June 22, 2006.

10. Lorna Geddes in conversation with the author, October 19, 2010.

11. Andreea Olteanu in conversation with the author, December 16, 2010.

12. Capacity for the Hummingbird Centre from Baillie, *Look at the Record*; for the Four Seasons Centre for the Performing Arts from the Canadian Opera Company official website, *www.coc.ca/AboutTheCOC/FourSeasonsCentre/AbouttheFSC/FactSheet.aspx*, accessed on January 14, 2011.

13. Julia Drake in conversation with the author, October 19, 2010.

14. Andreea Olteanu in conversation with the author, December 16, 2010.

15. Kevin Garland in conversation with the author, September 14, 2010.

16. Karen Kain in conversation with the author, September 14, 2010.

17. Rex Harrington in conversation with the author, October 19, 2010.

18. Mandy-Jayne Richardson in conversation with the author, January 11, 2011.

19. Magdalena Popa in conversation with the author, December 16, 2010.

20. Karen Kain in conversation with the author, September 14, 2010.

21. McGee Maddox in conversation with the author, January 11, 2011.

22. Karen Kain in conversation with the author, September 14, 2010.

23. Biographical material on choreographers from the relevant performance programs and from Cohen, *International Encyclopedia of Dance*.

24. Julia Drake in conversation with the author, October 19, 2010.

25. Greta Hodgkinson in conversation with the author, December 16, 2010.

26. McGee Maddox in conversation with the author, January 11, 2011.

27. Jennifer Fournier in conversation with the author, December 16, 2010.

28. Letter from Jennifer Fournier to National Ballet, October 28, 2000, in NBOC archives, 2000–01 Artistic Files, Departments, Season, Correspondence.

29. Jennifer Fournier in conversation with the author, December 16, 2010.

30. Jennifer Fournier in conversation with the author, December 16, 2010.

31. Julia Drake in conversation with the author, October 19, 2010.

32. Kevin Garland, in email correspondence with the author, January 24, 2011.

33. Roslyn Sulcas, "Alexei Ratmansky," *The New York Times*, May 28, 2009.

34. Karen Kain in conversation with the author, September 14, 2010.

35. Karen Kain in conversation with the author, September 14, 2010.

36. Jennifer Homans, *Apollo's Angels: A History of Ballet* (New York: Random House, 2010), pp. 540–1.

$\mathcal{S}$elected $\mathcal{B}$ibliography

Ambrose, Kay. *The Ballet-Lover's Companion: Aesthetics Without Tears for the Ballet-Lover.* London: Adam and Charles Black, 1949.

___. *The Ballet-Lover's Pocket-Book: Technique without Tears for the Ballet-Lover.* New York: Knopf, 1947.

___. *Beginners, Please!* London: Adam and Charles Black, 1953.

Anderson, Jack. *The Nutcracker Ballet.* London: Bison Books, 1979.

Austin, Richard. *Lynn Seymour: An Authorised Biography.* London: Angus and Robertson, 1980.

Baillie, Joan Parkhill. *Look at the Record: An Album of Toronto's Lyric Theatres, 1825–1984.* Oakville, New York: Mosaic Press; Flatiron Book Distributors, 1985.

Bell, Ken, and Celia Franca. *The National Ballet of Canada: A Celebration.* Toronto: University of Toronto Press, 1978.

Bland, Alexander. *The Royal Ballet: The First Fifty Years.* Garden City, NY: Doubleday, 1981.

Bremser, Martha, and Larraine Nicholas, eds. *International Dictionary of Ballet.* Detroit: St. James Press, 1993.

Bruhn, Erik, and Lillian Moore. *Bournonville and Ballet Technique: Studies and Comments on August Bournonville's Études Chorégraphiques.* London: A&C Black, 1961.

Clarke, Mary, and David Vaughan, eds. *The Encyclopedia of Dance and Ballet.* London: Peerage Books, 1977.

Cohen, Selma Jeanne, and Dance Perspectives Foundation. *International Encyclopedia of Dance: A Project of Dance Perspectives Foundation, Inc.* New York: Oxford University Press, 1998.

Crabb, Michael, and National Ballet of Canada. *Visions, Ballet and its Future: Essays from the International Dance Conference to Commemorate the 25th Anniversary of the National Ballet of Canada.* Toronto: Simon & Pierre, 1978.

Fisher-Stitt, Norma Sue. *The Ballet Class: Canada's National Ballet School, 1959–2009.* Toronto: Canada's National Ballet School, 2010.

Getz, Leslie. *Dancers and Choreographers: A Selected Bibliography.* Wakefield, R.I.: Asphodel Press, 1995.

Goodman, Edwin A. *Life of the Party: Memoirs of Eddie Goodman.* Toronto: Key Porter Books, 1988.

Granatstein, J. L. *Canada 1957–1967: The Years of Uncertainty and Innovation.* Vol. 19. Toronto: McClelland and Stewart, 1986.

Gruen, John. *Erik Bruhn: Danseur Noble.* New York: Viking Press, 1979.

Gustaitis, Rasa. *Melissa Hayden, Ballerina.* London, New York: Nelson, 1967.

Gwyn, Carol Bishop. *The Pursuit of Perfection: A Life of Celia Franca.* In manuscript at press time.

Homans, Jennifer. *Apollo's Angels: A History of Ballet.* New York: Random House, 2010.

Jennings, Sarah. *Art and Politics: The History of the National Arts Centre.* Toronto: Dundurn, 2009.

Kain, Karen, Stephen Godfrey, and Penelope Reed Doob. *Karen Kain: Movement Never Lies: An Autobiography.* Toronto: McClelland & Stewart, 1994.

Katz, Leslie George, Nancy Lasalle, and Harvey Simmonds, eds. *Choreography by George Balanchine: A Catalogue of Works.* New York: Viking Penguin, 1984.

Kavanagh, Julie. *Nureyev: The Life.* New York: Pantheon Books, 2007.

___. *Secret Muses: The Life of Frederick Ashton.* London: Faber & Faber, 1996.

Selected Bibliography

Marsh, James H. *The Canadian Encyclopedia*. 2nd ed. Edmonton: Hurtig Publishers, 1988.

McKinsey and Company, Management Consultants. *Directions for the Dance in Canada: A Study on the Future Development, Management and Funding of Canada's Dance Companies and Dance Schools*. Ottawa: Canada Council Information Services, 1973.

Mitchell, Lillian Leonora. *Boris Volkoff: Dancer, Teacher, Choreographer*. Ann Arbor, MI: University Microfilms International, 1982.

Neufeld, James. *Power to Rise: The Story of the National Ballet of Canada*. Toronto: University of Toronto Press, 1996.

Oxenham, Andrew, and Michael Crabb. *Dance Today in Canada*. Toronto: Simon & Pierre Pub. Co., 1977.

Payne, Charles. *American Ballet Theatre*. New York: Knopf, 1979.

Percival, John. *Theatre in My Blood: A Biography of John Cranko*. London: Herbert Press, 1983.

Perlmutter, Donna. *Shadowplay: The Life of Antony Tudor*. New York: Viking, 1991.

Pettigrew, John, and Jamie Portman. *Stratford: The First Thirty Years*. Toronto: Macmillan of Canada, 1985.

Reyna, Ferdinand, ed. *Concise Encyclopedia of Ballet*. London and Glasgow: Collins, 1974.

Ross, Janice, and Stephen Cobbett Steinberg. *Why a Swan?: Essays, Interviews, & Conversations on "Swan Lake."* Vol. 1. San Francisco: San Francisco Performing Arts Library and Museum, 1989.

Solway, Diane. *Nureyev, His Life*. New York: William Morrow, 1998.

Sparshott, Francis Edward. *A Measured Pace: Towards a Philosophical Understanding of the Arts of Dance*. Toronto: University of Toronto Press, 1995.

___. *Off the Ground: First Steps to a Philosophical Consideration of the Dance*. Princeton, NJ: Princeton University Press, 1988.

Stuart, Otis. *Perpetual Motion: The Public and Private Lives of Rudolf Nureyev*. New York: Simon & Schuster, 1995.

Taper, Bernard. *Balanchine: A Biography*. New York: Times Books, 1984.

Tennant, Veronica, director, and Sound Venture Productions. *Celia Franca, Tour De Force*. Sound Venture, 2006.

Thorpe, Edward. *Kenneth MacMillan: The Man and the Ballets*. London: Hamish Hamilton, 1985.

Trueman, Albert W. *A Second View of Things: A Memoir*. Toronto: McClelland and Stewart, 1982.

Vaughan, David. *Frederick Ashton and His Ballets*. London: A&C Black, 1977.

Waite, P. B. *Lord of Point Grey*. Vancouver: University of British Columbia Press, 1987.

Walker, Hugh. *The O'Keefe Centre*. Toronto: Key Porter Books, 1991.

Walker, Kathrine Sorley. *De Basil's Ballets Russes*. London: Hutchinson, 1982.

Watson, Peter. *Nureyev: A Biography*. London: Hodder & Stoughton, 1994.

Whittaker, Herbert. *Canada's National Ballet*. Toronto: McClelland and Stewart, 1967.

Wyman, Max. *Dance Canada: An Illustrated History*. Vancouver: Douglas & McIntyre, 1989.

___. *Evelyn Hart, an Intimate Portrait*. Toronto: McClelland & Stewart, 1991.

___. *Max Wyman, Revealing Dance: Selected Writings, 1970's–2001*. Toronto: Dance Collection Danse Press/es, 2001.

___. *The Royal Winnipeg Ballet, the First Forty Years*. Toronto: Doubleday Canada, 1978.

Index

Information in **bold italics** at the end of the entries indicates references in photo captions, either in the text or in the colour insert.

Index

Index

Index

Index